Humanistic Studies in the Communication Arts

GEORGE N. GORDON, General Editor

DRAMA IN LIFE

The Uses of Communication in Society

Humanistic Studies in the Communication Arts

GEORGE N. GORDON, General Editor

A TAXONOMY OF
CONCEPTS IN COMMUNICATION
by Reed H. Blake and Edwin O. Haroldsen

COMMUNICATIONS AND MEDIA
Constructing a Cross Discipline
by George N. Gordon

ETHICS AND THE PRESS
Readings in Mass Media Morality
Edited by John C. Merrill and Ralph D. Barney

DRAMA IN LIFE
The Uses of Communication in Society
Edited by James E. Combs and Michael W. Mansfield

INTERNATIONAL AND
INTERCULTURAL COMMUNICATION
Edited by Heinz-Dietrich Fischer and John C. Merrill

H|S
C|A *Humanistic Studies in the Communication Arts*

DRAMA IN LIFE

The Uses of Communication in Society

Edited by

JAMES E. COMBS
Valparaiso University

and

MICHAEL W. MANSFIELD
Baylor University

COMMUNICATION ARTS BOOKS

HASTINGS HOUSE · PUBLISHERS

New York 10016

To Beth and Dan

LIBRARY OF CONGRESS CATALOGING IN PUBLICATION DATA

Main entry under title:
Drama in life.

    (Humanistic studies in the communication arts)
(Communication arts books)
    Includes bibliographies and index.
    1. Communication—Psychological aspects—Addresses,
essays, lectures. 2. Mass media—Social aspects—Ad-
dresses, essays, lectures. 3. Interpersonal relations—
Addresses, essays, lectures. I. Combs, James E.
II. Mansfield, Michael W.
HM258.D7 1976   301.14   75-33835
ISBN 0-8038-1555-7
ISBN 0-8038-1556-5 pbk.

Published simultaneously in Canada by
Saunders of Toronto, Ltd., Don Mills, Ontario

Printed in the United States of America
Designed by Al Lichtenberg

CONTENTS

Part Two | SOCIAL INTERACTION AS DRAMA

Part Three | MASS COMMUNICATION AS DRAMA

Part Four | PUBLIC DRAMAS

Part Five | ORGANIZATIONAL DRAMATURGY

Part Six | CULTURE AND HISTORY AS DRAMA

A CONCLUDING REMARK:

Existence, Communications, and the Dramaturgial Perspective 429

ACKNOWLEDGMENTS

One cannot be involved in a work such as this without owing much to many people. Our former professor and colleague, Dan Nimmo, led us to the study of this aspect of human behavior and communication. He has provided us with many personal and intellectual insights for which we will always be grateful. We are indebted to Kenneth Burke who shared his inspired approach to the dramaturgical perspective with us through his writings and on a visit to the University of Missouri in 1972. A special expression of thanks is due George N. Gordon. He was willing to give unselfishly of his time and advice whenever asked. His interest, enthusiasm, and encouragement has made possible the completion of this volume. Dean L. Yarwood provided valuable assistance in the early stages of this project. We are also grateful to Russell Neale, who has been present at the beginning and end of this joint effort, for his support and patience. Our gratitude goes to Dorothy Hitt, Sherri Riddle and Teresa Collazo for their pains in helping prepare this manuscript. Finally, we thank all the authors who have contributed their works to this reader.

INTRODUCTION

I am delighted to introduce for this series, *Humanistic Studies in the Communication Arts, Drama in Life,* a comprehensive anthology concerning the dramaturgical aspects of both interpersonal and public communications. I think that it will make a contribution to the literature of two topics: drama and communication studies, and should be of equal value to students of both.

Call it an accident of training or sentimental bias, but I have long nurtured the notion that the anthropological (and therefore social) roots of the drama and origins of the wide range of other activities we call today "communication" share a common cradle in the history of our race. Both probably followed similar (or the same) lines of development, cleaving one from the other as recently, possibly, as ten thousand years ago.

In my youth, as a theatrical aspirant, I had been deeply impressed by the capacity of the drama on stage to represent, in John Gassner's words, "humanity in moments of maximum tension, conflict, and crisis . . . ," not so much holding that well-known mirror up to life, but by exacerbating life and alchemizing the telling of lies and the pretense of masquerade in ritualized Reality, to me, at any rate, *realer* than life.

My personal theatrical aspirations died for many reasons. But the curiosity I had observed as a playhouse habitué lived on. As years passed, however, I also became aware of the mirror image of this sorcery, and came eventually to regard much in both my personal life and in society at large in the many of the ways that Drs. Combs and Mansfield discuss in their introductory comments that follow. *All* the world is decidedly not a stage, of course, except in metaphor, but the matrices of human and social interaction are provided with form, structure and, most important, *meaning* because of formal rituals of civilization that follow in various ways the rhetoric of drama and, sometimes, the conventions of theatre. I cannot avoid the conclusion that many of the activities we apparently blunder through in our lives, and within the institutions of society, are, in fact, defined by the human intellect *as* real mainly *because* they are dramatic.

The hyper-reality of theatre wherever it occurs—on stage, in films, on television—is no accident, nor is it merely a refraction of aspects of life. And what we call "life," on the other hand, is imbued, I think, in all its manifestation with value and meaning, because it depends upon the same imitative intelligence (put there by God knows what!) that illuminates the rituals of theatrical representation.

How brilliant I thought I was—until time passed and I began to read some of the writers included in this anthology (with one exception): Kenneth Burke, Erving Goffman, William Stephenson, Lloyd Warner, Georg Simmel and Hugh Duncan, to name a few. I discovered, naturally, that my genius-stroke had been merely the late and feeble personal discovery of a tired long-distance runner who was not even entitled to feel lonely. Better minds than mine had also noticed the obvious and had found better ways of expressing it—and noticed more subtle considerations more colorfully and clearly than I had.

A fertile and important subject, however, invariably demands a multiplicity of viewpoints and a wide range of perspectives. For this reason, I consider *Drama in Life* a seminal book that should not only evoke academic interest but also the attention of readers who, like me, love the theatre in spite of its sins and/or are looking for novel insights into the ways that people communicate with one another, with and without technological intervention, individually and in masses. This single volume provides for us a wide and, to some degree, startling range of speculation, theory and case studies concerning how the drama, when all is said and done, defines the roles we play in life and the institutions with which we grapple. Some of it is serious and, by implication, close to the heartbeat of modern culture. Some is funny, and, in *its* way, deadly serious too—as most funny things are. From the aesthetics of our daily "role playing" in culture to the use of "fiddles" in the game of life to the ritual pretenses of medical interviews, *Drama in Life* winds its way through a clever maze of modern social, cultural and political affairs, ending with the ultimate dramatic event to which all life leads: one's own death. (How interesting that this latter concept is beautifully articulated in the final chapter of Irwin Shaw's recent novel, *Evening in Byzantium!*)

I hesitate to call any book "definitive," but I think *Drama in Life* hits somewhere near the mark, considering the present state of inquiry into this aspect of communication today. Mostly, I hope that this collection stimulates further investigation into the reciprocal refractions of drama *into* life and vice-versa by means of the stimuli to thought that it provokes. Such intellectual adventures will, I hope, eventually lead us back to the primeval roots of meaning in the experience of man as a communicating animal and also possibly stimulate the birth of a catholic theory of communication as art and as science that will have power to unify the grab-bag of hypotheses that are presently scattered across disciplines and into mysticism, as they attempt to explain or describe communication processes and systems. Not only do I hope it will; I bet it will; although many of us who now pollute the environment may not survive to see it.

Of all mankind's activities, one of the most persistently humane has been, for at least two thousand years, the drama—although I must admit that, like all humanistic endeavors, it has indeed had its cruel and barbarous moments. *Humanistic Studies in the Communication Arts* is therefore aiming right at dead center of its main concern, the human animal as a secular being and as an active agent, using the techniques and technologies he has invented to communicate with others. While all the books in this series may not hit this bullseye of intention as squarely as *Drama in Life,* I anticipate that this contribution of Drs. Combs and Mansfield will stimulate other writers and editors to emulate the excitement of the readings they have selected on the pages after this all too pedantic prologue.

So, curtain up!

GEORGE N. GORDON PH.D.
Professor; Chairman
Communications Department
Hofstra University

Preface

The Perspective of Life as Theatre

The language of the theatre has long been used to characterize social events. Man is said to be an "actor"; one has a "role" in an event; one observes the social "scene"; politicians have a "dramatic" confrontation; an event is said to be "staged"; a drunk at a party puts on a real "performance." Journalists, for example, thrive on dramatic metaphors; they give tempo, interest, and in a word, "drama" to events. The Watergate story was characterized in precisely this way, by both journalists and the *dramatis personae* in the story. The Dean testimony, we were told, was "high drama"; the Ervin committee was accused of putting on a "show"; Hunt and Liddy were described as "James Bond characters"; Kalmbach conducted the pay-offs according to "scenarios." The idea that "all the world's a stage" has been a recurrent speculation of past thinkers, including Aristotle, Goethe and Carlyle. But it is only in recent years that systematic work has emerged in the social sciences utilizing dramatic ideas (such as "role") and, more exclusively, the "dramaturgical perspective" to describe or explain social actions or events. The literature using this perspective is loose and varied, but it is beginning to take shape with common interests, subject matter, and theoretical perspective. The dramatic idea, in short, is an idea whose time has come.

In light of this burgeoning literature, it seemed to us that a selective sample of the better efforts in this area was needed. It is the purpose of this work to present a range of edited efforts that will introduce the interested reader to the scope, depth and perhaps even the insight of the dramaturgical perspective on social action. The selections reprinted here all stem from the notion that many "real-life" actions and events can most adequately be understood in terms of drama. For instance, the mass of actions subsumed under the rubric "Watergate" might best be envisioned as a dramatic unity, with at least some of the more important actions therein possessing qualities that may best be called "dramatic." For this perspective, then, the real effect of "Watergate" would not be any specific piece of legislation, but rather what it dramatized: our concern with standards of public morality, the dangers of a monarchical Presidency, the power of Congress and the integrity of the courts.

Politics is only one example. The range of applicability of the dramaturgical perspective is wide, involving scholarship in many academic disciplines. In the present volume, there are selections concerned with social theory, social interactions, roles, social psychology, social movements, ritual and ceremony, leadership, mass communications, as well as politics, history and culture understood as drama. For this reason, the collection here is not confined to one discipline, but may be of interest to scholars in a wide assortment of fields: social sciences, communications and journalism research, as well as "applied" fields such as advertising and campaign management. We feel that the volume is also of considerable interest to scholars in the humanities, most obviously to those in the dramatic arts. The dramaturgical perspective is a bridge between these two areas of inquiry, since it is based on the assumption that not only does art imitate life, but also that life imitates art.

There is one central concept, however, that informs both the social sciences and humanities and to which the idea of dramaturgy ultimately refers: communication. This collection is included in a series concerned with humanism in the "communication arts." Communication, indeed, is an art, an art for both the stage and the social actor. If the idea of social drama has merit, it stems from the basic human resources of communications. The first section of this book includes various conceptualizations of human life as a drama of communications, where the "symbol-using animal" adds art to life, becoming a communicating "actor." It is suggested here that communications research is one of the most important innovations in social (and humanistic) inquiry in recent years, and we hope this collection is a contribution to that effort.

Images of Man

In a fundamental sense, then, this book is about an important contemporary image of man. The dramatic image is a fresh and exciting perspective in social inquiry, and one which is worth serious consideration by social inquirers in various fields. The study of man—whether literary, philosophical or sociological—is at root an effort to define an image of man that "locates" him in the world. Intellectual history is rich in the variability of actual or potential human images, of what man is or what he may be. Indeed, present-day inquiry is characterized by the competition of a stock of images, with the inevitable consequences of both healthy pluralism and interdisciplinary confusion. Are Skinnerian psychologists, phenomenologists and poets all talking about the same being? It is clear that the gap appears to be greatest between the humanities and the sciences, including the social sciences. It may well be that the "objectification" of man is ultimately futile, with elusive man always breaking out of the net and away; but no one can deny the importance of the quest of a "synoptic vision" of man-in-the-universe, or the convenience that emerges from interdisciplinary agreement on the "nature" of the subject-matter.

The seismic fault that exists between Snow's "two cultures"—the sciences and the humanities—is even more acute in light of the almost total dependence of the social sciences on "root metaphors" derived mainly from the physical sciences. However, the quest for a synoptic image of man is the province of the humanities as well as the social sciences. Surely Oedipus and Ahab and Holden Caulfield tell us as much about the human condition as the automata of the psychology laboratory. But the point is that communication between the sciences and the humanities at their most crucial link—the social sciences—is not informed by cross-disciplinary agreement on the image of man, which heightens the gap. It would seem to be useful for the two sets of enterprises to be linked by an encompassing image of man that would transcend the specialized images peculiar to a given discipline, that Professor Skinner meet Captain Ahab.

The contemporary confusion over the most proper and incisive image of man is perhaps best exemplified by the social sciences. The images of economic man (the rational consumer), political man (the rational citizen), and social man (the institutionalized man), have been shattered in recent inquiry by the discovery of irrational drives which may be manipulated by propaganda, of alienation and the like. But for many observers the alteration in the social-scientific image of man does not involve the abandonment of a root metaphor drawn from the social sciences. It is rather a shift from the Newtonian to the Einsteinian model. The former envisioned human behavior in terms of atomistic and mechanistic causal patterns. Society, for example, is governed by natural laws; men are interactional atoms in causal interdependence one to another. The latter, more recent physicalistic image posits a field of human behavior in "transactional" process. Here social life is a complex matrix of reciprocal relations, or "conditions," not reducible to causal chains or structural laws. Human behavior may therefore be most elegantly explained in terms of the full set of social and individual conditions, and, even then, is not easily subject to mere causal explanations in such a processural world.

No one will deny the simple power of the Newtonian model or the recognition of complexity of the Einsteinian model. What is disturbing to many is the dependence on a few models of social life derived from models of physical processes (physics, astronomy, chemistry, biology). The objection is made that, for all the heuristic value of such physicalistic models, they are also misleading—in the sense that they were originally conceived as images of physical processes, not of human life. It is not that there is something fundamentally "wrong" about these images, but rather that they exclude from inquiry those aspects of human life known to the humanities: Man as "subject" as well as "object," Ahab *as well as* automaton.

The problem of the image of man is still salient, comparable to the search described by Thomas Kuhn in his provocative work, *The Structure of Scientific Revolutions*. Scientific enterprises, he claims, are guided by a "paradigm," a set of assumptions or *Gestalt* which defines the parameters and concerns of a field of inquiry. When anomalies begin to appear in the "paradigm," it may be abandoned for a new image of the field that is more psychologically satisfying. Science can be understood, then, in the relativistic terms of intellectual history just as any other enterprise; the succession of images of the universe are "as if" assumptions that do not necessarily approximate closely the "real" structure of the Cosmos. This is a controversial thesis, but it serves to illustrate our problem here.

The social sciences are, in Kuhn's terms, in a "preparadigmatic" stage of development, where there is a healthy competition of paradigms, or images, of human life. The physical paradigms we have already described. Their fruits may be seen in a perusal of contemporary social and political theory (structural-functional, systems, game, exchange, group and field theories for example, all derive from physical metaphors). This book, of course, is about quite a different kind of paradigm, one that attempts to bridge the gap between the social sciences and the humanities by deriving its root metaphor from the one of the most characteristic of all human enterprises, the theatre.

It might be objected that the search for a metaphor is unnecessary, that one should stick to the "facts." But the position here is that an image of human life is necessary as a guide to what the "facts" mean, as to what men are and what they are about. The recounting of a sequence of events is not history, nor is the collection of statistics a social science. A paradigm of human life places unrelated facts into an ordered schemata, a framework, which reveals the "meaning" of the facts. Such a creative process has been termed by Arthur Koestler a "bisociation," involving the juxtaposition of unrelated sets of facts, or placing facts in a new framework, whereby the "matrices" add a new level of knowledge, or at least place facts in such an association that new insight results. Thus Hobbes placed human behavior in the framework of the physical laws of motions; Spencer placed society in the new evolutionary image; and more recent scholars have utilized innovations in systems theory, cybernetics and market behavior as images of social life.

The present collection gathers works by contemporary scholars who place human behavior in the bisociative framework of the theatre. They tend to find physical metaphors of social life unsatisfying, and have turned to the ancient and intuitive, and yet refreshingly new idea that life is theatre. It is a root metaphor that stems from a specifically human creation, an activity that represents the qualities of human life itself, and not the behavior of non-human things. Hence, it may be argued that the dramatic image of man emphasizes the "human" qualities of man, while physical metaphors emphasize the "physical" qualities. But that may be too simple. It will be seen in the following readings that the dramatic image has both considerable power and complexity and offers a degree of insight, and even verisimilitude, denied to physical metaphors. Indeed, the steady application of the bisociation of drama and life may contribute to the quest for cross-disciplinary agreement on an image of man that facilitates communication again between the social sciences and humanities.

Kenneth Burke

One seminal lawgiver of the dramaturgical perspective on social life is Kenneth Burke. Through a long and distinguished career, Burke has developed the central idea of "dramatism," a "philosophical" terminology which he claims is the most appropriate for the consideration of man in general. Burke calls "terministic screens" what we have called "paradigms" or "images," and insists that the "dramatistic screen" refers to human action. He makes a key distinction between action and motion. Men are "symbol-using animals" who have an essential capacity for symbolic activity, and therefore are not explainable in purely physicalistic terms. Actions is the province of conscious men, not reducible to motion. *Things* move, *men* act.

For Burke, the implications of these ideas lead to the dramatistic paradigm. Men build symbolic structures on nature, adding art to life. Language gives our species a "moral sense," wherein meaning is attributed to the world, to self and to others. Burke argues that man is the only animal able to conceive (and act upon) negatives and can control and structure his "actions" upon the basis of symbolic meanings that are not reducible to "natural" motives. Humans do not simply mate, they marry; they do not simply kill for food, but for gods and countries; territory is not simply defended, it is named. Men are, then, separated from their "natural condition" by their own creation of a symbolic world which "overlays" the natural one. Men inhabit a symbolic universe as well as a physical one. Human life cannot be "contained" in a physical metaphor as a kind of behavior that is simply more complex than that of rats. It is qualitatively different, requiring imagery drawn from activities which are homologous to it.

For Burke, the inference is clear: life *is* drama. Action means structured behavior in terms of symbols, which implies choice, conflict and cooperation, which men communicate to each other. Society is a drama in which actions, in terms of social symbols, are the crucial events. The difference between "staged" drama and the drama of real life is the difference between human obstacles imagined by an artist and those actually experienced. The realms are homologous: life and art both deal with the fundamental problems of human existence, and both aim at the symbolic resolution of conflict through communication. Hence the vocabulary of social inquiry should be drawn from the activity that "represents" the realm of action (drama) rather than from disciplines that study the realm of motion.

Action is conceptualized in a dramatic paradigm. The paradigm "fills out" the dimensions or "moments" of action in a formal sense: Scene, Act, Agent, Agency, Purpose (Burke later adds "attitude" as incipient act). These dimensions are what the inquirer needs to understand action, whether it be in the context of a drama or in real life. Actions occur within the framework of a social scene or milieu; the action is conducted by an agent with a conception, or "attitude," about what is "appropriate" to the scene; the actor uses the means at his disposal to accomplish the action; and the action is done for some purpose.

This rather Aristotelian paradigm coordinates the classical questions: when and where was something done, what was done, who did it, how was it done, and why was it done? (Hugh Duncan, Burke's major sociological disciple, restates the paradigm as: stage or social situation, kind of act, social role, means of expression, and ends, goals or values.) Burke claims that many philosophies emphasize only one dimension of this action paradigm. Marxism, for example, reduces explanation to scene (environmental determinism); idealists have overemphasized the agent in "Great Man" theories; and communications theorists (like McLuhan) have stressed the means of communication too much. In each situation, a different "ratio" may obtain (e.g., scene-act, agent-purpose, etc.) based on what is "emphasized" or develops in a particular situation. Hence Burke's paradigm is not only a formal structure of action (an "ontology") but also a variable description of what inheres in situations. Hitler, for example, defined the German national purpose with himself in an "agent-purpose" ratio. The other moments of action must be there, but symbolically, dramatically, the actor defined the situation as one where the Leader infallibly guided the community to its rightful ends.

We cannot discuss in detail Burke's provocative social theory, partially dealt with in the selection by Duncan below. Our point here is that Burke's influence is not being widely felt. Most of the writers collected in this book are directly or indirectly influenced by his work. Many contemporary social scientists have abandoned physical metaphors as inadequate, and find that the dramaturgical perspective developed by Burke has a depth and explanatory power denied to other paradigms. Many social scientists have also noted the almost independent development of concepts or perspectives in recent inquiry that relate directly to social dramaturgy: role theory, symbolic interactionism, transactional psychology, communications theory. Although all such inquiry cannot be said to be a footnote to Burke, his impact is clear and growing.

Related Perspectives in Contemporary Social Inquiry

We cannot claim to ascertain whether these new notions constitute an emerging paradigm in social inquiry, but certainly they all seem to point to a similar conception of human action. We feel it useful here to mention some of the essential elements of these related perspectives, especially their relationship to the dramaturgical perspective we present here. Many of the works in this text are derived from these related fields.

The most general perspective in social inquiry relevant to these viewpoints is symbolic interactionism. This perspective is derived from such figures as Simmel, Mead, and Cooley, and several of the works herein are drawn from this tradition (Goffman, Lyman and Scott, Edelman). The symbolic interactionists view the social world as one of process, as something actively problematic and constructed rather than settled. Men create and manipulate a "symbolic environment," wherein they construct their interactions. In any cultural context, then, order is "negotiated" in an ongoing "definition of the situation." Hence, men are voluntary, conscious actors who enter problematic situations with a certain self-concept and communicative purposes. Men are patently social: the self is a socially constructed "thing," presented in ongoing situations, where communications is controlled in accord with the definition of the situation. In a sense, the symbolic interactionist's world is almost a world of existential absurdity with which the actor attempts to cope. He would no doubt agree with Camus' statement: "The actor taught us this: there is no difference between appearing and being."

That the symbolic interactionist vision of the world is implicitly dramatic may be further illuminated by looking at its central concept, *role*. Role is, of course, directly borrowed from drama, and refers to that structured behavior the individual constructs and presents in a particular social context. Role is the aspect of society *in* man; society provides the script, the man plays the role variously—with verve, mechanically or however. The *homo sociologus* of the symbolic interactionists, then, is a role-player in an ongoing social drama where one presents self in everyday scenes on the basis of a definition of the situation. For Burke and his followers, if the symbolic interactionists filled out the implications of their argument, they would come to the same conclusion he did: life is theatre. Role is simply the "agent" dimension of the full vision of society as drama.

Perhaps the most explicitly dramaturgical corpus of work that has emerged from the symbolic interactionist and role theory traditions is that of Erving Goffman. (See below for selections from both Goffman and his students.) He is basically interested in delineating what is going on in social interaction, where individuals mutually present themselves to one another. He argues that the most appropriate "analogy" to use is precisely the theatrical one: human interaction can best be studied as theatrical performance, where actors present impressions to other actors in order to further some definition of themselves in the situation. All social relationships are drama, involving the delicate balance between the social demands on an individual and the individual's need to maintain self-esteem in the face of these demands. People are *persona,* masks, in their relations with each other. They attempt, through performance, to control the impressions they communicate to others. The process may be witnessed in, at least, various crucial points in marriage, group life or politics. The key aspect of social life, then, is role performance, the actual conduct of one's communications in the ongoing social drama.

An example may be useful: Goffman is surely not describing *every* interaction, but is describing those interactions which involve a high level of "performance," where the individual is under scrutiny. The soldier who goes into combat is under pressure to conform, to display the virtues valued by the organization: to be brave, aggressive, even heroic. For most soldiers, fear is something to be suppressed from one's peers and one's superiors. To avoid degradation (or a firing squad) the soldier must act as if those virtues were an essential part of his self. The "mask" or role taken on by the soldier is that of brave soldier, and he advances and fights with the rest of his unit. If he loses control of his "face," he may be subject to humiliation and punishment. But if he is successful, he is socially acceptable and "takes on" the attributes that he had so much difficulty displaying with his inner fear. In other words, he has become the mask that he wore; his being, his identity, is what he appears to be.

This does not necessarily mean, as some of Goffman's critics have asserted, that social man is a "phony," that "life is a con game" in which one deceives others and oneself, or that men of many roles have no essential character (e.g., modern "other-directed" men). Goffman and other dramaturgical theorists argue that role-playing is ubiquitous and not something peculiar to modern consumer societies. It may be that there are multiple roles to play in a pluralistic society like ours with a high degree of "psychological mobility," but roles seem to be a universal socially derived structure imposed on behavior by "socialization" processes. Further, they do not deny that man can play their roles in "bad faith," or at what Goffman calls "role distance." The young corporation executive on the way up the ladder of success, the high school "make-out artist," indeed the confidence man, are all "phonies,'' but most people appear to believe implicitly in the sincerity and ''oughtness'' of their own identity. Most people are what they communicate, and believe in those communications. Men are ''actors'' in the sense that they usually attempt to adopt a line of action which is appropriate to the situation, to convey what the event calls for: the preacher conducting a funeral, for instance, does not tell jokes or scurrilous stories about the deceased. Human interaction, then, is a process of negotiation between conscious actors: a drama.

Goffman and the symbolic interactionists have tended to limit themselves to the conduct of small-scale social interactions, but that is not to depreciate their importance. This book will consider such phenomena as the occurrence of ''stage fright'' in everyday life, the phenomenon of dramaturgy in organizations, the dramatic handling of ''first time'' events such as marriage, rites of passage and death. Only in recent years has the dramaturgical perspective begun to be applied to some of the larger processes of social life: ritual and pageant, leadership, mass media and politics. Scholars have recently begun to move closer to consideration of Burke and Duncan's inclusive claim of analyzing the social process *in toto* as theatre. Other selections included below speak to this bold application of the dramaturgical perspective.

A major concern of this text (and the series in which it is published) is the development of new facets and articulations of communications theory. Duncan and the symbolic interactionists have recognized that interpersonal and social dramatics *are* communications, and have suggested the necessity of theoretical linkage. To date, communications theory has been dominated by physicalistic metaphors in model-building, especially those of a cybernetics system or a radio schematic. This is all well and good, but the quality of these metaphors may ultimately have to be challenged. It is the argument of the dramaturgical theorists that human communication is qualitatively different from that of computers and radios; precisely, it is dramatic in form and social in content. Human communication is dramatic because it involves symbols, imagined conceptions (mainly metaphors themselves) which structure the behavior of the organism. Hence the formal moments of ''field,'' ''source,'' ''message,'' ''medium'' and ''receiver,'' become Scene, Agent, Act, Agency and Purpose by the ''humanization'' of the process. Human beings add ''art'' to the process, Ahab, at last, as well as automaton.

Happily, the humanistic elements of communications are today coming to the fore. The symbolic interactionists mentioned above are now exploring the subtleties of human ''communications nets'' in an almost existential sense. Transactional psychologists (such as Berne; see below) are investigating the patterns and pathologies of interpersonal ''games'' and the dramatic ''scripting'' of children by parents. Other work is being done on the role of elite-mass ''transactions'' through the mass media, especially the possibility of economic or political manipulation through the dramatic manipulation of images. It is now recognized that communication is not simply ''information,'' but also what George Herbert Mead called ''significant symbols,'' complex, often group-sanctioned images, the ''art'' that man adds to nature. They are the ''terms in which interpersonal and social drama are enacted, the White Whale that spurs Ahab on,'' in his words.

Hence communications theorists increasingly regard communication as a social as well as a natural event. To be sure, physical activity such as the shaping of breath is involved, but the ability to communicate symbols enriches the process. The creation of a symbolic environment gives the world, and hence our actions in it, *meaning*. The world we imagine, act in and value is a world animated by something more than our "natural condition." Indeed, the features of symbolic communication are what make drama possible. Communication occurs in a process universe where a "system" or meaningful structure (a marriage, company or nation) persists by the existence of an agreement on the definition of the situation. However, communication is an irreversible process. The ambiguous and artificial nature of symbols permits an element of "openness"—of the possibility of redefinition—into the system, requiring reaffirmation, acceptance of a new definition or abandonment. Hence communication involves a degree of "play" or indeterminacy.

For Burke and the dramaturgical perspective, positing such an existential world lends to the conclusion that life is, in all constructions, dramatic. Since human relationships are meaningful and indeterminate, their success or failure is dependent upon the quality of our performances, how well we "play" our roles. Man is the only animal with a sense of the "aesthetics" of life, that the *how*, the form, of our communications structures *what* is communicated, that is, the content. Sexual communication for example, usually involves a physical attraction between members of the opposite sex, but it is also more than this. It acquires an aesthetic, indeed a dramatic quality, by the development of subtle and sophisticated communications: sex is common to all animals, but man is the only one who seems to construct "romantic love." The enactment of symbolic relationships gives life a dramatic quality peculiar to our curious species. The implication is, of course, that man possesses a "dramatic sense" (what Francis Fergusson has called a "histrionic sensibility"). With such a sense, we are able to plan our actions before a perceived audience and then attempt to "manage impressions" by the successful conduct of our performances.

Messinger and associates (see below) refer to this awareness of dramatic performance as being "on." In other words, the actor is at times acutely aware of the scrutiny of others, and therefore of his own conduct. His success in controlling the definition of these situations, in conveying what he wants, varies according to the quality of his performance. Ordinarily, individuals are "off-stage"; but under such circumstances, they may also be said to be "on-stage," performing for an audience. Lovers perform in private for one another, reaffirming the relationship by dramatic communications ("sweet nothings," etc.). The confidence man must get his audience to take seriously his "pitch," so that they will entrust him with their money. In both cases, the communications are "dramatic" in the sense of performance, but the former is in "good faith," while the latter is in "bad faith." The "on" social actor is not necessarily a "phony," but he *may* be: Don Juan may have been as much a con artist as Professor Harold Hill.

This conception of social action analytically separates many mundane, routine "non-dramatic" actions from the more explicitly dramatic, but it does not destroy the concept. Nor does it destroy the notion that people are not "insincere" or "inauthentic" when they are acting in-role. The "charismatic" leader (a Jesus, Gandhi, Hitler) is usually convinced of his own rectitude. But he is also usually aware of the potential drama of his own public actions and structures them accordingly. This distinction helps us delineate precisely those actions which are dramatic because they are planned and executed as drama. In other words, we can establish criteria by which we can separate the dramatic from the nondramatic. These criteria might include: the awareness of a symbolic relationship that is valued; forethought, or projection of the action before it occurs; a perceived audience before which the action is to be taken; the "dramatic sense" or awareness of the appropriateness of dramatic control; and actual performance, the controlled communication of the symbolic relationship.

Goffman and his students have dealt with many such dramatic events in everyday life. Lyman and Scott (see below) treat the coping strategies people use to overcome "stage fright" in those crucial performances common to our lives. For example, we "rehearse" such encounters (a speech, a proposal of marriage, strategy in court), attempting to give dramatic force to our anticipated communications. We are aware of the importance of our performance in a variety of social contexts, especially those where we are under scrutiny by an audience whose opinion we value or fear. The new soldier may enter combat wrung with fear, but he also fears both the censure of his peers and the sanction of the organization. Indeed, as Glaser and Strauss point out, there is one existential performance difficult to rehearse—death. Individuals aware of their impending death do not only become concerned with what death entails, but also of the quality of their final performance. Many express fear of breaking down, of upsetting relatives, of not showing courage and resolution in the face of the ultimately uncontrollable situation. In short, there is an awareness of the drama of the situation, of the value of "cool" and decorum of controlled action. No doubt, many rehearse how they will handle their relatives, and even what their last lines will be. Historically, condemned criminals have been praised for their noble bearing on the scaffold, and prisoners have worried about breaking down or losing bowel control during the proceedings (e.g., Perry White in Capote's *In Cold Blood*). Many other examples will be discussed in the articles that follow, but the point is that many episodes in ordinary life are perceived as, and acted within, as dramatic.

Other articles printed here go beyond the traditional symbolic interactionist focus on "everyday life" and attempt to treat more inclusive aspects of social life as theatre. As Burke and Duncan insist, societies are not only "functional" structures, nor are groups only instrumental; they are also symbolic organizations and evoke dramatic meaning and action. Hence, the collective actions of groups, of leadership, the evocation of collective symbols in ritual and ceremony, the condensation of events through the "dramatizing" filter of the mass media, indeed, the history of a particular culture or society are all dramatic. We have attempted here to capture the spirit of such sociological conceptions, and to give the range and vision of the idea.

The Dimensions of Social Drama

Let us attempt to indicate to the reader the general thrust of these widely diverse views of social drama. Many social scientists have found that structural-functional and conflict theories do not offer a wholly credible image of modern social and political processes, and have turned to symbolic-interactionist and communications theories for assistance. For instance, Gusfield argues that the Prohibition movement cannot easily be explained in terms of the class position or bourgeois values of the movement, nor as the rational "input" of an autonomous subsystem in the world of the systems theorists and structural-functionalists. He came to believe that group activity is not always strictly "rational" or "instrumental" but rather is symbolic— that a group may become concerned with the status of certain symbols, and through dramatic activity communicate these values both to themselves and to the outside world.

Since societies are symbolic as well as functional-systematic organizations, it seems that the leadership must recurrently demonstrate the validity and continuity of social symbols. In other words, social organization not only performs tasks, controls behavior and maintains peace, but does it so in a certain way: in terms of certain consensually valued symbols. Men conceive and extol the symbolic meaning of Christian marriage, capitalism, democracy and so on. Indeed, people appear to feel universally the necessity for public demonstration of the validity of these symbols, and to control access to them. Mass media publicity sanctifies the symbols themselves, and the marriage ceremony controls access to a sanctified relationship "within" the symbolic umbrella of the Church. Periodically, the validity of the symbols themselves must be demonstrated through the dramatic activity of ritual and ceremony. Access or sanction within them is usually ritualized also: the marriage ceremony dramatizes the relationship, but within the symbolic framework of the institution.

The role of ritual and ceremony in social life is a sadly neglected subject in the social sciences. We may merely note the ubiquity of such activity, both formally and informally. The "rite of passage," for example, ranges from the highly formalized ritual of the Bar Mitzvah to the awarding of the key to the executive washroom to the young upward-mobile executive in the corporation. Such ceremonies give the individual new status and privileges, and not incidentally, control his behavior by defining what is correct role behavior in terms of the institution. Young people married in a church not only acquire physical access to each other, but also a conception of what "good" behavior in the relationship is for the religious institution. Role conceptions are often institutional, and are dramatized and sanctified by the institution in ritual and ceremony. These processes appear to apply to many groups, from street gangs to college fraternities to Presidential inaugurations. However, as Garfinkel points out, many ceremonies lower or destroy one's status also, in "degradation ceremonies." The identity of the individual is often symbolically denied, especially in terms of his access to symbolic "grace" within the institution. The admission to Eucharist and Confessional admits the public identity of the communicant, while excommunication denies his existence and his access to good standing. The military "drumming out" ceremony, the diplomatic declaration of *persona non grata,* the English labor union practice of "sending to Coventry" (not speaking to) recalcitrant workers all dramatically degrade the individual by the institution.

Similarly, the role of ritual for the political order has not been subjected to any depth of analysis, apart from some of the articles reprinted here (Shils and Young, for instance). But certainly, such collective acts of "communion" are important, and at least almost universal. The coronation of kings, the inauguration of Presidents, the Soviet May Day parade, the Nazi Nuremberg rally are all dramatic "pseudo-events" that apparently function to reaffirm or "remind" everyone of the validity and power of political symbols. Indeed, if there is a major social disruption, such a ritual may serve as an occasional reminder of social continuity. The funeral of the slain President Kennedy, for example, provided a dramatic framework for the demonstration of social meaning and a vehicle of collective solace in the wake of a sudden political shock. Studies have indicated the increase in anxiety (people drank more, slept poorly, etc., in the days after the assassination), and undoubtedly the televised and highly emotional ceremonies (the military funeral parade with the riderless horse, the entourage of world leaders, the High Mass, the burial at Arlington, etc.) served as a dramatic reassurance of the survival of political symbols beyond the individual fallen leader. It was, in Duncan's words, a "moment of mystification" that not only served to honor the dead leader, but also reasserted the continuity of political symbols themselves—that the ship would sail on.

Another area of social inquiry kept alive by the dramaturgical perspective is the study of leadership. It is curious that inquiry into the psychology, the functions, relation to followers and actions of leaders has fallen on hard times. Several articles are nevertheless presented here that indicate the concern of the perspective in question for leadership processes (e.g., Klapp, Brown, Warner, etc.). The general feeling appears to be that a leader comes to "personify" something for the group he represents, or more generally, the audience that he performs for. Often a public actor becomes a "symbolic leader," in that the audience identifies him with certain symbols or interpretations of symbols. Hence Huey Long became the embodiment of Depression populism; Joe McCarthy the symbolic representation of militant anti-communism or Neanderthal boorishness (depending on your point of view); and the aforementioned John Kennedy, in death, became a nostalgic symbol of the lost Camelot.

Social drama is, of course, usually conducted by leaders. Since much social conflict in "open societies" is public, leaders come to be seen by followers as the personification of some symbol with which they can identify and as someone who provides them with vicarious entertainment. In an institutional setting such as the United States, a leader may emerge by his performance in "dramatic encounters." A leader stands out from an institution (such as the Senate) by his conduct in dramatic events that are communicated to the masses, and through which he comes to have an "image" with this audience. Public roles may be enacted routinely, wherein the actor is perceived as competent or non-controversial (many House members, for instance); but the actor who wishes to stand out from the institution and develop a following, or at least an audience, larger than the usual electoral coalition in his own district or state must "test" himself in the crucible of dramatic encounters. George Wallace, for example, came to be a "symbolic leader" with a clientele more inclusive than Alabama Democrats by his famous "stand in the doorway" in 1963. Joe McCarthy and Richard Nixon became nationally famous via dramatic revelations. The masses, who do not directly, but only vicariously, participate in this elite "entertainment," come to identify elite actors as "heroes, villains or fools" based on the image communicated to them by elite actors.

As Boorstin, Warner and others point out, the conduct of dramaturgy by elite actors is made possible by the development of mass media in modern societies. Elite figures, both political and non-political, are aware of the importance of the "image" they project to the mass audience, and also of the opportunities for manipulation. The proliferation of propaganda—public relations, advertising, cosmetics—in modern society is well-known. The works relevant to this development offered here attempt to explain aspects of the process. Boorstin deals with the modern phenomenon of the "pseudo-event," a carefully constructed and entertaining "happening," a dramatic performance that controls the presentation of individual or group image to a mass public. The development of movie stars by the film organization is a long-standing practice. Surely no one would suggest that the Democratic convention of 1964 or the Republican convention of 1972 were "real" events. Television has contributed to this process, from the early development of the "laugh track" and the staged quiz shows to the "planned spontaneity" of the talk programs. Increasingly, public events are scripted to eliminate as many unforeseen or discordant elements in the presentation as possible. Further, the media themselves appear to give a "dramatic unity" to elite actors and events that they do not actually possess. As Stephenson points out, the mass media permit the audience to "play," to be entertained and participate vicariously without direct involvement. As Horton and Wohl indicate, television can make the communications "parasocial," an intimate, dramatic relationship between the media-contrived *persona* and the individual viewer. The lower-class Irish of Warner's study could identify with the *persona* of Biggy Muldoon in the political "play" they witnessed through the mass media. Muldoon became a hero, villain or fool to the mass audience through the condensation of his public character in the media.

The power of the mass media to structure events is one of the primary social forces (and hence dangers) of open societies. Campaigns to promote a product, both human and non-human, use advanced knowledge about human psychology and media impact to sell their product, from soap to presidents. As Gordon stresses, communication from elite to mass usually involves persuasion. Advertising constructs dramatic "pseudo-events" that associate the product with myths, values or fantasies (e.g., the lonely housewife suddenly confronted with a muscular and virile god, armed with oven-cleaner, entreating her to "try it"!). This persuasive process is fraught with dangers, from the economic structuring of wants to the political "engineering of consent." Perhaps the ultimate use of mass media for such a purpose is projected in Orwell's *1984,* where a political elite conducts an endless "pseudo-event" of propaganda about a remote war and mysterious internal conspiracy that binds men forever to the paternal protection of Big Brother.

Other articles in this volume utilize many of these notions to discuss politics as drama (see Merelman, Nimmo and others). Politics appears to be one of those "symbolic environments" where men—usually leaders—struggle over the definition of symbols, and over control of the institutions that embody those symbols.

Much political life is therefore dramatic. The political campaign is only one instance of the crucial role of dramatic action by elites to court mass. The aforementioned manipulation of the mass media has been most evident in the USA in the development of the "image" campaign and professional campaign-management firms, but the presence of campaign dramatics long predates these recent innovations. Anyone familiar with southern American politics knows that rhetorical and behavioral flamboyance has long been a crucial factor in many state primaries and was a key to the rise of some of the more colorful of the Dixie demagogues (e.g., Long, Talmadge, Bilbo, Folsom, etc.). But political life in general is replete with leaders and events that achieve dramatic status. Political arenas (e.g., courts, legislatures, convention halls, committee rooms, parade sites, and sadly, battle-fields) may be transformed in a dramatic event either by careful control of the event or by the development of conflict by actors in the setting. The Watergate hearings were in this respect "dramatic" in two senses: first, in general, they dramatized the power of Congress, and, second, specific acts within the setting were dramatic (e.g., the Stans plea, the Erlichmann-Weicker exchange, the committee vote to subpoena the tapes, etc.). Many of the ideas in this volume speak to the analysis of politics as drama, and it is to be hoped that they will stimulate further and similar research into this aspect of political science.

The notion of politics as a dramatic struggle over symbols is extended in the final, and perhaps most ambitious, section of the text, dealing with the conduct of history and culture *in toto* as drama. For Kinser and Klineman and Warner, the basic fabric of social order is symbolic and must be celebrated and enacted, especially when the symbolic meaning of the order is threatened or confused. To extend Berne's idea mentioned earlier, we might speculate that cultures, like individuals, have "scripts" which they enact to reaffirm or fulfill their "OK-ness." Such dramatic visions of the meaning and purpose of a culture and its historical mission are usually called "myths." Myths are the "primitive beliefs" of a community, the persistent cultural symbols that explain the origin, structure and meaning of the culture. Myths provide the symbolic umbrella for cultural institutions and action, sustaining (for instance) the family as an institution and role behavior in it. Myths are therefore the dramatic "public dreams" of the society they sustain and imbue that society with dramatic identity and purpose. The validity and power of the myth must be constantly reaffirmed by ritual, rhetoric and action. Warner's Yankee City collectively states its own identity by ritualizing the past in a pageant; political and religious rhetoric reaffirms our faith in the symbol; and action is taken on the basis of a socially validated role concept (e.g., a husband, a teacher, a President). With threat or confusion, the cultural impulse is to reaffirm the symbols. (Recall the extolling of American virtues and achievements during the post-war periods of both the late 1940's and 1960's.) Kinser and Klineman argue that the Nazi movement overwhelmed Germany in the wake of post-war confusion and disillusionment because Hitler did not treat politics as workaday stuff, but as theatre. The Nazis came to represent for many the embodiment of the myth, the group that believed most in what many people wanted desperately to believe in again ("the old German values"). Hitler became the Hero of the drama, the heroic feudal king struggling against the foreign dwarf (the Jews) and his allies who were sieging the feudal king-dom. Kinser and Klineman quote Thomas Mann's famous statement, "National so-cialism means: I do not care for the social issue at all. What I want is the folk tale." The Nuremberg rallies, the Beyreuth Wagnerian cycle, the revival of feudal forms of architecture, the celebration of the blond Nordic Siegfried and Brunhilde, the quest for *Lebensraum* all appealed to deeply held and long persistent elements in the German mythic structure. The dramatization of these "folk tales" played a key role in the triumph of National socialism. Indeed, if there was a script to the German drama, we may fairly say that the folk tale had an end, an end almost inevitable in terms of its own myth: in the *Götterdammerung* of World War II. This finale was inherent in the "socio-logic" of Nazi mythology, an unconscious but scripted part of the play, the *Thanatos* within the myth. All of these notions are of course quite speculative, but they constitute a major application of the dramaturgical perspective and indicate examples of what may be done with it.

The Unanswered Questions

It is hoped that the foregoing discussion has provided the reader with a glimpse of the range and possibilities of the dramaturgical perspective. But the reader should be aware of some of the tough questions about this perspective that will be raised, but not decisively answered, by the authors gathered herein. A first difficulty that will be raised by Messinger, Goffman and others is the so-called "ontological sta-tus" of the idea of life as theatre. The basic problem is whether the dramaturgical perspective is an organization of social conduct, and therefore *imposed* on reality, or whether it is a description of actual conduct, and therefore *inheres* in reality. In other words, the question is whether the image of human life we have drawn is a simile, where dissimilar structures or characteristics are likened (e.g., "a heart as big as a whale"), or a homology, where the structures match as isomorphic ("God is love"). Is it simply useful to say that life is *like* theatre, or more ambitiously, that life *is* theatre? If the former is the case, then the image may be only a convenient metaphor of considerable heurism; if the latter, then the bisociation of theatre and social life may add a new level of insight to social inquiry.

Another criticism expressed about the dramaturgical perspective is the claim that it is specific to the structure of modern post-industrial societies and reflects the "inauthenticity" of such societies. The shift from producing to consuming social organization is manifest in the change in emphasis on man *doing* to man *being*. Modern social structure has changed social behavior from an inner-direct autonomy to an other-directed flexibility. Hence modern men are said to be rootless, inauthen-tic role-players, the "phonies" identified by Holden Caufield in *The Catcher in the Rye*. All of us become little Machiavellian princes, concerned with our own image, not our products; using others, never losing our "cool," getting ahead, replacing essentials with the artificial. These critics do not appear to deny that men are actors, only that this "theatrical" condition is peculiar to one type of social structure, and that it raises difficult moral questions. In response, let us point out that the "phony" as a social type is not peculiar to modern societies alone, but may be found in a variety of cultures. Deception did not begin with the rise of the post-industrial world. It can be found in the Greek Sophists, the medieval troubadour in the Renaissance *Book of the Courtier*, Melville's *The Confidence Man*, as well as in Salinger and Sartre. The history of Western thought contains both the quest for authenticity as well as inauthenticity. The question unanswered, however, is this: Is the authentic actor any less an actor-in-role than the inauthentic one? Indeed, is it possible for men to be completely "authentic," or are we *all* in some sense phonies? This is not only a socio-historical question but basically an existential one.

These questions underscore the necessity, noted above, to place the dramaturgical perspective in a larger sociological and philosophical framework. It is easy enough to indicate many social contexts that appear to be "dramatic." What is crucial is to elucidate the existential grounds of human life. Such an inquiry is beyond the scope both of this essay and book, and not treated in any real depth by the writers collected here. But if the Burkean perspective, or for that matter any view of human action, is to have universal applicability, the "onto-logic" of that image must be subjected to philosophical analysis. Further, it would seem useful to place the idea of dramaturgy in the larger context of social theory. At present, there is little unity for such an enterprise. The most promising tack, combining the humanistic concerns of the dramatists and symbolic interactionists with the rigor of behavioral models, may be communications theory. Possibly, the desparate concerns of the many social sciences may discover some threads of unity, and some acceptance by the humanities, in the development of new and fertile communications theories (or hypotheses) that recognize the complexity of human behavior as manifest in symbols.

We feel that the dramaturgical perspective is exciting and illuminating enough to inspire further research in this area, and more importantly, research collaboration between the "two cultures." Many of the questions raised here might be fruitfully approached by dramatic theorists, philosophers and social scientists in conjoint. Such dialogue might move us closer to an image of man that transcends the two cultures, a not unworthy intellectual goal.

The Structure of the Book

The selections are organized into sections designed to represent the major concerns of the dramaturgical perspective in social inquiry. The first section, entitled "The Variation of Perspectives," focuses on the ontological aspects of the image, i.e., in what sense we may meaningfully talk about drama occurring in life. The second section, "Social Interaction as Drama," deals with the occurrence of social drama at the microcosmic level, the interpersonal symbolic interactions of everyday life. The section on "Mass Communications" concerns the projection of drama through the mass media, and how this contributes to the social life of modern societies. The fourth section treats the wide variety of literature dealing with "Public Dramas," ranging from the dramatic aspects of group life, leadership, and ritual and ceremony to the dimensions of politics that are dramatic. The fifth section collects some perspectives on organizational life as drama, or the occurrence of drama in an institutional setting. Finally, we include a brief section on ''Culture and History as Drama,'' where the script of a community or a society are enacted, either symbolically or realistically. We hope that the selections chosen and the divisions of the book will give the reader the sense of this perspective, and we will reveal to him a refreshing and potentially powerful insight into social life.

A Final Word

Long ago the Greeks invented a technique of communication that has persisted through the ages—theatre. It soon took on the familiar features we know so well: auditorium, proscenium, orchestra. The actors wore masks, or *personae,* which represented the role they enacted. They soon began to interpret their parts through histrionics, or the art of acting or affectation. Greek drama became so sophisticated and powerful that it was transmitted throughout the civilized world at the time. Philosophers began to write about what it meant. Aristotle saw a ''mimetic'' quality to drama, where human experience was represented, or ''imitated,'' in the context of the play, and the auditor could vicariously participate through imagination and identification, thereby ''purging'' emotions. Since then, theatre has taken many forms, but it has retained that essential quality of a place where people act in plays.

One may readily see how theatre pervades our language, indeed our perceptions. The question of this book is provocative: does the dramatic metaphor and structure apply to social life? If so, where and how? Have Burke and the others come across something fundamental concerning the human situation? It is said that in Shakespeare's day there was an inscription above the entrance to the Globe theatre in London: *Totus Mundus Agit Histrionem*—All the world's a theatre. The reader of this book may better judge that statement: the old idea that society is a place where people act in plays.

Part One

The Variation

of Perspectives

THE FIRST SECTION of the book contains a variety of formulations of what the "dramaturgical perspective" amounts to. The authors presented here proceed with various assumptions and purposes, but all in one way or another speak to a fundamental question about the perspective: does it make sense to use it, and why? This difficult problem has invited attempts to place the idea of "life as theater" in philosophical and sociological context, or more specifically, to investigate what we may call the "ontological" roots of the perspective. Our concern here is not with the application of dramaturgical concepts to a particular social or historical context, but rather with the exploration of the meaning, implications and limits of the perspective. We hope that these selections will expose the reader to a range of views and insights useful later in subsequent sections of the book.

The selection by drama theorist Bernard Beckerman provides a good short definition of "theater" itself, especially for the application of dramatic concepts to real life and not simply to formal drama. The argument that theatre is occurring when people, isolated in time and/or space, "present" themselves to others gives us a general framework for analysis. This view suggests that drama may happen in a variety of contexts, involving many kinds of presented activity, and it is a task of inquiry to delineate the elements of such communication.

The convergence of dramatic and social categories has been a central interest of one of America's most eminent men of letters in this century, Kenneth Burke. Burke has sought to pin down the implications of man's basic symbolic capability in the various forms of human action, and his work provides the theoretical base for much of the subsequent analysis of "human relations" reprinted here. His article (from the *International Encyclopedia of the Social Sciences*) is a brief recent statement of Burke's position, with a succinct passage on the sociological aspects of "dramatistic" analysis. Burke's work invites scholars to investigate the grounds of his entire system of "dramatism" in the study of the role of symbols in human life and the ontology of human action.

Burke has stimulated one such treatment by communications theorist George Gordon, in his study of the plural "languages" of communications. Following the Burkean definition of man as a "symbol-using animal," Gordon attempts to trace the implications of such "symbolicity" for human communications. Gordon's analysis provides a grounding in the centrality of symbolism for human life and is also a necessary preface for the writers that follow.

The role of "significant symbols" in the conduct of social life is stressed by social theorist Hugh Duncan. Duncan has attempted one of the most systematic statements of the Burkean perspective on social order yet attempted. Further, he links the conduct of "sociodrama" to the process of social communication; indeed, the communications of symbols *is* dramatic. Because society itself is based on symbols, we can say that society *is* drama. This selection from Duncan's most concise work explores the ramifications of a set of "axiomatic" and "theoretical" propositions. More than anyone else, Duncan has brought Burke to social inquiry and has tried to apply Burkean concepts and categories to social life, especially in relation to social structure.

Another noted social theorist, Peter Berger, treats society as drama in a slightly different sense. For Berger, drama is one of a number of alternative "pictures" of society—or rather one of the plural dimensions of social life. Like Duncan, he is trying to link social drama to other contemporary social theorists, such as Simmel and Mead. However, Berger paints a phenomenological picture, linking the dramaturgy of life to the subjective problems of "fictions," inauthenticity, "bad faith" and the like. Life is drama because of its problematic, "as if" nature; the drama continues because the symbols they evoke shield us from negatives, assuring us that the lights will never go out, that the music will always play, that the show will go on.

Maurice Natanson is another eminent scholar who has been influenced by European phenomenology (e.g., Alfred Schutz). In his article, however, his discussion is more directly ontological than that of Berger. He is concerned with the perceptual problems involved in the apprehension of action, both on the stage and in society. Man is an "actor" in both contexts, and the condensed aesthetic life of the theatrical role provides an analogue for his mundane roles of everyday life. Stage acting simply organizes, condenses and presents "hermeneutic" interpretation of the problems of human life, problems which, in a messier way, are experienced by the social actor.

The article by George Simmel complements more eloquently, what Natanson is getting at. It is an aesthetic statement, but reflects the idea that the "attitude of dramatic acting" is part of man's mode of being. Dramatic art—the aesthetics of performance—stems from human "life processes" and gives symbolic unity to the "creative expression of life." The implication here, too, is that the aesthetics of acting extend into "act-ual" human performance.

The subtlety and range of dramatics in mundane "everyday life" has been brilliantly explored in a series of works by Erving Goffman. The selection reprinted here is a short discussion of the dramaturgical framework, the "analogy" in terms of which social interaction can be understood. Goffman's world is one of "impression management," occuring in a fragile, open, problematic world that is constantly amenable to breakdown. Life is a series of dramatic performances that maintain the tissue of human personality relationships and social structure *in toto*. Goffman takes contemporary role theory to the logical conclusion one draws from that dramatic concept: men play social roles *as if* they were in a drama, because, to a large extent, they are.

The final work in this section is a critique of Goffman, and raises most of the difficult questions that remain about the dramaturgical perspective. Messinger and associates argue that the social actor does not himself experience "life as theater," and that the perspective is a useful simile but not a homology, i.e., it does not inhere in actual behavior. This raises again the fundamental ontological questions about the perspective: What criteria do one use to determine if, and when, an action is dramaturgical? Several authors (including Goffman) will refer to dramatism as an "analogy," but will then discuss action as if it possessed dramatic qualities. We have suggested that the dramatic image of human life is a most useful one, but the extent of its utility is yet unclear: Is it just an intellectual "image" that organizes human activity as a convenient unity, or does the persistence and appeal of the image mean that, in some sense, it substantively corresponds with actual behavior "out there?"

1.

DEFINITIONS—THEATER

Bernard Beckerman

. . . Definitions are hazardous enterprises. Like sands in the desert they may shift when they seem most firm. Yet we cannot do without them. They are the referents by which we gauge our understanding. They are also tools with which we do our work. To comprehend the relation of drama to theater, consequently, we need to agree on what is meant by theater.

DEFINITION: Theater . . . What shall the verb be? Shall we write "Theater is . . ."? But theater is not a thing. Theater is not an object to be manipulated. It does not have the solidity of a physical form which one can touch, like sculpture, or the permanence of a printed form to which one can return, like poetry. We cannot write, "Theater is . . ." Instead we might write, "Theater occurs . . ." Theater does not exist except when it is occurring. The building may exist. The performers may exist individually. The script may exist as well as the scenery. A poem is a thing made. Theater is not. It is something happening.

Thus, theater *occurs when one or more human beings* . . . The occurrence of theater is dependent upon human presence. Eliminate the actuality of man and eliminate theater. Such a definition excludes cinema from the boundaries of theater. Immediately, there will be objections. Cinema, it will be asserted, is clearly a form of theater. Is it not shown in theaters? Does not the cinema present dramatizations of events through the medium of characters? No, it does not. Cinema presents a sequence of visual images which can be used to tell a story or describe a place or record an event. It makes use of actors, but they are subordinate to the images. It is the work of the man who arranges the images not the work of the actors themselves that reaches us, the viewers.

The unbridgeable gap between the film and theater arises from the fact that the medium of film is celluloid and of theater, man. One can argue that this difference is not essential to the meaning of life that can be conveyed by these media. But meaning is not the end of art; experience and impact of experience are. And the experience of seeing human beings battling time and space cannot be the same as seeing visual images upon a screen. Without the living presence of beings assuring us that what is offered is not a thing made, but an event occurring, we do not have theater.

Is puppetry a theater art? After all, the puppets or marionettes are not human. They are media, but no more alive than the film image. Yet puppetry belongs in the theater. Like every subdivision of the theater, it involves human presence, though that presence may very well be screened. In the Bunraku doll theater the human performers who sing or manage the dolls are visible as well as audible. In the typical

Reprinted by permission from *Dynamics of Drama*, Alfred A. Knopf, 1970.

Punch and Judy show the human performer is seen through the effects he produces and is heard through his characterizing of the puppets. In both, the puppet play occurs, and therefore allows room for communal interplay. Though partially veiled, the human presence is felt throughout the presentation.

Theater occurs when one or more human beings present themselves . . . People make theater occur. What are they doing? Not pursuing tasks or activities oblivious of others. They are consciously displaying themselves. Man is not only the creator but also the means. This, then, is perhaps the most unique aspect of theater. The performers manipulate the media for expressive purposes, while they themselves are the media being manipulated. Through their skills, personalities, sensibilities, they make an offering. What is the nature of the offering? When we think of theater, we assume that the offering is a fictitious story, which we call drama. But that assumption divorces one part of theater from its close ties with other parts. Theater includes men performing a story. It also includes men performing tricks (gymnastic or illusionary), dances, songs, demonstrations, even rites under certain conditions. The lecturer, too, as *Our Town* has so affectionately shown, may operate within a theatrical context.

The act of conscious self-presentation distinguishes theater-as-a-socio-aesthetic experience from games or madness. Imagine a game of cops and robbers. When played by children, it is an imaginative form of play; when played by adults who believe their roles, it becomes a form of delusion. Presented by children or adults to others, it is a form of theater. As game its purpose is to provide pleasure for the participants. As theater its purpose is to affect spectators.

The act of presentation implies another or others to whom the presentation is being offered. In primitive cultures there are instances where an entire social unit presents itself to the gods thus giving us the archetypal form of theater. The spectator is a god or becomes god-endowed. Witnessing is an act of godhood though the temptation does arise in every age for the spectator to abandon his godhood and descend, whether to the dancing circle or to the stage, in order to participate in the presentation.

Our definition then becomes: *Theater occurs when one or more human beings present themselves to another or others.* But does not such a definition include too much? It includes the circus, dancing, and may even include sporting events. Exactly. Theater is potpourri. It can contain anything that man offers to others in his person. Its vital image might be most truly reflected by those omnibus vaudeville programs which toured the United States fifty years ago. On a single bill were included singers, dancers, dog acts, and comic sketches, notorious or celebrated figures as well as world famous actors or actresses appearing in scenes from Shakespeare. In microcosm, such bills sum up the authority and province of theater.

One observation must be made about sporting events. Although Brecht found theatrical possibilities in prizefighting, sporting events are not strictly theatrical events or, at the very least, are on the outer fringes of theater. In a sporting event one or more individuals engage one or more opponents in a contest of some sort. The basic act is challenge, not presentation. The validity of the contest is not certified by the spectators, but is inherent in the contest itself. It may be uneconomic, but not unusual, for sporting events to be held without the presence of spectators. Their absence in no way invalidates the occurrence but does remove sporting events from the province of theater.

By definition I state that the presentation can be to one person as well as to others. Presentation to a single person is rare though not completely unknown. In recent years performances have been given at the White House before the President with dignitaries of various rank also attending. Yet, it is the Presidential presence that is crucial and, in this respect, faintly reminiscent of the Court performances of the Renaissance, when the monarch, seated in state, served as *the* essential spectator. Primitive communities, as we have already seen, presented themselves to the gods. The more advanced civilization of Athens preserved this relationship by placing the statue of Dionysos as a symbolic spectator in the theater named for this god. Later ages brought other gods to life. Elizabeth I and Louis XIV were terrestrial deities who viewed from their seats of state the theater, which existed by their sufferance and for their glory.

The definition is almost complete. Only one final qualification need be added. Theater occurs when one or more human beings *isolated in time and space* present themselves to another or others. The performers and spectators must be separated from each other so that the spectators can observe what is happening. But this isolation is not merely utilitarian; it is both physical and psychological. A sacred grove may be selected, a dancing circle may be circumscribed, a platform may be erected. Somehow, an area is defined, which then becomes the servant of the performer. It is manipulable, both as actual and imaginative space; it is the place where presentations can be made. Recently, in drama, we have had instances, in productions such as *The Connection* and *The Blacks,* in the work of Jerzy Grotowski, and in novelties such as Happenings, where a breakdown of isolation is sought. Frequently, roles are reversed, and the spectator, instead of being god, becomes scapegoat. Such attempts to erase the line between presenter and presentee only define it more sharply. The auditor becomes acutely aware not only of the performers but of himself, thereby sensing that he has been cast in the role of a particular kind of spectator. Isolation is not eliminated, merely recharacterized. Demarcation is crucial in theater if the oscillation of stimulus and response between presenter and presentee is to occur.

The degree of isolation varies considerably from one kind of theater to another. During the same historical period, for example, the Elizabethan theater observed three different degrees of audience intimacy. In the public playhouse, the separation between stage and audience was sharply marked. In the private theaters, there were constant encroachments upon the stage by cavaliers eager to share the glory of the performers. Despite the efforts of the actors, the gallants would thrust their stools upon the platform, even to the very rushes, or reeds, upon which the actors played. Not the performers but the spectators sought to break down the separation of presentation space from viewing space. In the Court theaters, during the performance of the masque, the presentation space remained isolated during the first part of the presentation, the anti-masque. But then, as the dance began, the performers invited certain of the spectators to enter the dancing circle, become participants and, in effect, performers. Nonetheless, in this theater as in the private theaters, the principle of isolated performer persisted. In fact, only the special aura of the playing area lent piquancy to the spectators' incursions.

Just as space is defined for presentation, so is time. Ritual drama observed set days for performance. The five days of the Greek tragic contests and the nine days of the Hopi Snake dance were equally sacred periods of presentation. Only through the knowledge and the power to conclude a showing do the performers have the capacity to begin one. They divorce themselves from actual life and enter into imaginative existence. Without isolation and temporal control presentation is merely life.

Theater, then, occurs when one or more human beings, isolated in time and/or space, present themselves to another or others. Such a definition is not an attempt to limit the nature of theater, but to distinguish the quintessential conditions that govern its character. The breadth of the definition should remind us that the ease with which one type of performance, the circus, for example, can slip into another, such as the burlesque, arises from the common bond linking these diverse forms. Dancing and singing readily become dramatic, because, although they are not necessarily theatrical, they can be easily utilized in the theater. Theater is a glutton. It will swallow any kind of material and experience that can be turned into performance.

2.

DRAMATISM

Kenneth Burke

Dramatism is a method of analysis and a corresponding critique of teminology designed to show that the most direct route to the study of human relations and human motives is via a methodical inquiry into cycles or clusters of terms and their functions.

The dramatistic approach is implicit in the key term "act." "Act" is thus a terministic center from which many related considerations can be shown to "radiate," as though it were a "god-term" from which a whole universe of terms is derived. The dramatistic study of language comes to a focus in a philosophy of language (and of "symbolicity" in general); the latter provides the basis for a general conception of man and of human relations. The present article will consider primarily the dramatistic concern with the resources, limitations, and paradoxes of terminology, particularly in connection with the imputing of motives.

The Dramatistic Approach to Action

Dramatism centers in observations of this sort: for there to be an *act,* there must be an *agent.* Similarly, there must be a *scene* in which the agent acts. To act in a scene, the agent must employ some means, or *agency.* And it can be called an act in the full sense of the term only if it involves a *purpose* (that is, if a support happens to give way and one falls, such motion on the agent's part is not an act, but an accident). These five terms (act, scene, agent, agency, purpose) have been labeled the dramatistic pentad; the aim of calling attention to them in this way is to show how the functions which they designate operate in the imputing of motives (Burke [1945–1950] 1962, Introduction). The pattern is incipiently a hexad when viewed in connection with the different but complementary analysis of *attitude* (as an ambiguous term for *incipient* action) undertaken by George Herbert Mead (1938) and by I. A. Richards (1959).

Later we shall consider the question whether the key terms of dramatism are literal or metaphorical. In the meantime, other important things about the terms themselves should be noted.

Obviously, for instance, the concept of scene can be widened or narrowed (conceived of in terms of varying "scope" or circumference). Thus, an agent's behavior ("act") might be thought of as taking place against a polytheistic background; or the over-all scene may be thought of as grounded in one god; or the circumference of the situation can be narrowed to naturalistic limits, as in Darwinism; or it can be localized in such terms as "Western civilization," "Elizabethanism," "capitalism," "D day," "10 Downing Street," "on this train ride," and so on, endlessly. Any change of the circumference in terms of which an act is viewed implies a corresponding change in one's view of the quality of the act's motivation. Such a loose yet compelling correspondence between act and scene is called a "scene-act ratio" (Burke [1945–1950] 1962, pp. 1–7).

All the terms are capable of similar relationships. A "purpose-agency ratio," for instance, would concern the logic of "means selecting," the relation of means to ends (as the Supereme Court might decide that an emergency measure is constitutional because it was taken in an emergency situation). An "agent-act ratio" would reflect the correspondence between a man's character and the character of his behavior (as, in a drama, the principles of formal consistency require that each member of the dramatis personae act in character, though such correspondences in art can have a perfection not often found in life). In actual practice, such ratios are used sometimes to explain an act and sometimes to *justify* it (*ibid.,* pp. 15–20). Such correlations are not strict, but analogical. Thus, by "scene–act ratio" is meant a proposition such as: Though agent and act are necessarily different in many of their attributes, some notable element of one is implicitly or analogously present in the other.

David Hume's *An Inquiry Concerning Human Understanding* (first published in 1748) throws a serviceable light upon the dramatistic "ratios." His treatise begins with the observation that "moral philosophy, or the science of human nature, may be treated after two different manners." One of these "considers man chiefly as born for action." The other would "consider man in the light of a reasonable rather than an active being, and endeavor to form his understanding more than cultivate his manners" ([1748] 1952, p. 451). Here, in essence, is the distinction between a dramatistic approach in terms of *action* and an approach in terms of *knowledge*. For, as a "reasonable being," Hume says, man "receives from science" his proper food and nourishment. But man "is a sociable, no less than a reasonable being. . . . Man is also an active being; and from that disposition, as well as from the various necessities of human life, must submit to business and occupation" (*ibid.*, p. 452).

Insofar as men's actions are to be interpreted in terms of the circumstances in which they are acting, their behavior would fall under the heading of a "scene–act ratio." But insofar as their acts reveal their different characters, their behavior would fall under the heading of an "agent–act ratio." For instance, in a time of great crisis, such as a shipwreck, the conduct of all persons involved in that crisis could be expected to manifest in some way the motivating influence of the crisis. Yet, within such a "scene–act ratio" there would be a range of "agent–act ratios," insofar as one man was "proved" to be cowardly, another bold, another resourceful, and so on.

Talcott Parsons, in one of his earlier works, has analytically unfolded, for sociological purposes, much the same set of terministic functions that is here being called dramatistic (owing to their nature as implied in the idea of an "act"). Thus, in dealing with "the unit of action systems," Parsons writes:

> An "act" involves logically the following: (1) It implies an agent, an "actor." (2) For purposes of definition the act must have an "end," a future state of affairs toward which the process of action is oriented. (3) It must be initiated in a "situation" of which the trends of development differ in one or more important respects from the state of affairs to which the action is oriented, the end. This situation is in turn analyzable into two elements: those over which the actor has no control, that is which he cannot alter, or prevent from being altered, in conformity with his end, and those over which he has such control. The former may be termed the "conditions" of action, the latter the "means." Finally (4) there is inherent in the conception of this unit, in its analytical uses, a certain mode of relationship between these elements. That is, in the choice of alternative means to the end, in so far as the situation allows alternatives, there is a "normative orientation" of actions. (1937, p. 44)

Aristotle, from whom Aquinas got his definition of God as "pure act," gives us much the same lineup when enumerating the circumstances about which we may be ignorant, with corresponding inability to act voluntarily:

> A man may be ignorant, then, of who he is, what he is doing, what or whom he is acting on, and sometimes also what (e.g. what instrument) he is doing it with, and to what end (e.g. he may think his act will conduce to some one's safety), and how he is doing it (e.g. whether gently or violently). (*Nichomachean Ethics* 1111a5)

This pattern became fixed in the medieval questions: *quis* (agent), *quid* (act), *ubi* (scene defined as place), *quibus auxiliis* (agency), *cur* (purpose), *quo modo* (manner, "attitude"), *quando* (scene defined temporarily).

The Nature of Symbolic Action

Within the practically limitless range of scenes (or motivating situations) in terms of which human action can be defined and studied, there is one over-all dramatistic distinction as regards the widening or narrowing of circumference. This is the distinction between "action" and "sheer motion." "Action," is a term for the kind of behavior possible to a typically symbol-using animal (such as man) in contrast with the extrasymbolic or nonsymbolic operations of nature.

Whatever terministic paradoxes we may encounter en route (and the dramatistic view of terminology leads one to expect them on the grounds that language is primarily a species of action, or expression of attitudes, rather than an instrument of definition), there is the self-evident distinction between symbol and *symbolized* (in the sense that the *word* "tree" is categorically distinguishable from the *thing* tree). Whatever may be the ultimate confusions that result from man's intrinsic involvement with "symbolicity" as a necessary part of his nature, one can at least *begin* with this sufficiently clear distinction between a "thing" and its name.

The distinction is generalized in dramatism as one between "sheer motion" and "action." It involves an empirical shift of circumference in the sense that although man's ability to speak depends upon the existence of speechless nature, the existence of speechless nature does not depend upon man's ability to speak. The relation between these two distinct terministic realms can be summed up in three propositions:

(1) There can be no action without motion—that is, even the "symbolic action" of pure thought requires corresponding motions of the brain.

(2) There can be motion without action. (For instance, the motions of the tides, of sunlight, of growth and decay.)

(3) Action is not reducible to terms of motion. For instance, the "essence" or "meaning" of a sentence is not reducible to its sheer physical existence as sounds in the air or marks on the page, although material motions of some sort are necessary for the production, transmission, and reception of the sentence. As has been said by Talcott Parsons:

> Certainly the situation of action includes parts of what is called in common-sense terms the physical environment and the biological organism . . . these elements of the situation of action are capable of analysis in terms of the physical and biological sciences, and the phenomena in question are subject to analysis in terms of the units in use in those sciences. Thus a bridge may, with perfect truth, be said to consist of atoms of iron, a small amount of carbon, etc., and their constituent electrons, protons, neutrons and the like. Must the sudent of action, then, become a physicist, chemist, biologist in order to understand his subject? In a sense this is true, but for purposes of the theory of action it is not necessary or desirable to carry such analyses as far as science in general is capable of doing. A limit is set by the frame of reference with which the student of action is working. That is, he is interested in phenomena with an aspect not reducible to action terms only in so far as they impinge on the schema of action in a relevant way—in the role of conditions or means. . . . For the purposes of the theory of action the smallest conceivable concrete unit is the unit act, and while it is in turn analyzable into the elements to which reference has been made—end, means, conditions and guiding norms—further analysis of the phenomena of which these are in turn aspects is

relevant to the theory of action only in so far as the units arrived at can be referred to as constituting such elements of a unit act or a system of them. (1937, pp. 47–48)

Is dramatism merely metaphorical? Although such prototypically dramatistic usages as "all the world's a stage" are clearly metaphors, the situation looks quite otherwise when approached from another point of view. For instance, a physical scientist's relation to the materials involved in the study of motion differs in quality from his relation to his colleagues. He would never think of "petitioning" the objects of his experiment or "arguing with them," as he would with persons whom he asks to collaborate with him or to judge the results of his experiment. Implicit in these two relations is the distinction between the sheer motion of things and the actions of persons.

In this sense, man is defined literally as an animal characterized by his special aptitude for "symbolic action," which is itself a literal term. And from there on, drama is employed, not as a metaphor but as a fixed form that helps us discover what the implications of the terms "act" and "person" *really are*. Once we choose a generalized term for what people do, it is certainly as literal to say that "people act" as it is to say that they "but move like mere things."

Dramatism and the social system. Strictly speaking, then, dramatism is a theory of terminology. In this respect a nomenclature could be called dramatistic only if it were specifically designed to talk, at one remove, about the cycle of terms implicit in the idea of an act. But in a wider sense any study of human relations in terms of "action" could to that extent be called dramatistic. A major difficulty in delimiting the field of reference derives from the fact that common-sense vocabularies of motives are spontaneously personalistic, hence innately given to drama-laden terms. And the turn from the naïve to the speculative is marked by such "action words" as *tao, karma, dike, hodos, islām* (to designate a submissive *attitude*), all of which are clearly dramatistic when contrasted with the terminological ideals proper to the natural sciences (Burke [1945–1950] 1962, p. 15).

The dramatistic nature of the Bible is proclaimed in the verb (*bara*) of the opening sentence that designates God's creative act; and the series of fiats that follows identifies such action with the principle of symbolicity ("the Word"). Both Plato's philosophy of the Good as ultimate motive and Aristotle's potentiality-actuality pair would obviously belong here, as would the strategic accountancy of active and passive in Spinoza's *Ethics* (Burke [1945–1950] 1962, pp. 146–152). The modern sociological concern with "values" as motives does not differ in principle from Aristotle's list of persuasive "topics" in his *Rhetoric*. One need not look very closely at Lucretius' atomism to discern the personality of those willful particles. Contemporary theories of role-taking would obviously fall within this looser usage, as indicated or, its face by the term itself. Rhetorical studies of political exhortation meet the same test, as do typical news reports of people's actions, predicaments, and expressions. Most historiography would be similarly classed, insofar as its modes of systematization and generalization can be called a scientifically documented species of storytelling. And humanistic criticism (of either ethical or aesthetic sorts) usually embodies, in the broad sense, a dramatistic attitude toward questions of personality. Shifts in the locus and scope of a terminology's circumference allow for countless subdivisions, ranging from words like "transaction," "exchange," "competition," and "cooperation," or the maneuvers studied in the obviously dramalike situations of game theories, down to the endless individual verbs designed to narrate specifically what some one person did, or said, or thought at some one time. Thus Duncan (1962) has explicitly applied a dramatistic nomenclature to hierarchy and the sociology of comedy. Similarly, Goffman (1956) has characterized his study of "impression management" as "dramaturgical."

Does dramatism have a scientific use? If the dramatistic nature of terms for human motives is made obvious in Burke's pentad (act, scene, agent, agency, purpose), is this element radically eliminated if we but introduce a *synonym* for each of those terms? Have we, for instance, effectively dodged the dramatistic "logic" if instead of "act" we say "response," instead of "scene" we say "situation" or "stimulus," instead of "agent" we say "subject" or "the specimen under observation in this case," instead of "agency" we say "implementation," and instead of "purpose" we use some term like "target"? Or to what extent has reduction *wholly* taken place when the dramatistic grammar of "active," "passive," and "reflexive" gets for its analogues, in the realm of sheer motion, "effectors," "receptors" (output, input), and "feedback," respectively? Might we have here but a *truncated* terminology of action, rather than a terminology intrinsically nondramatistic? Such issues are not resolved by a dramatistic perspective; but they are systematically brought up for consideration.

A dramatistic analysis of nomenclature can make clear the paradoxical ways in which even systematically generated "theories of action" can culminate in kinds of observation best described by analogy with mechanistic models. The resultant of many disparate acts cannot itself be considered an act in the same purposive sense that characterizes each one of such acts (just as the movement of the stock market in its totality is not "personal" in the sense of the myriad decisions made by each of the variously minded traders). Thus, a systematic analysis of interactions among a society of agents whose individual acts variously reinforce and counter one another may best be carried out in terms of concepts of "equilibrium" and "disequilibrium" borrowed from the terminology of mechanics.

In this regard it should also be noted that although equilibrium theories are usually interpreted as intrinsically adapted only to an upholding of the *status quo,* according to the dramatistic perspective this need not be the case. A work such as Albert Mathiez's *The French Revolution* (1922–1927) could be viewed as the expression of an *anima naturaliter dramatistica* in that it traces step by step an ironic development whereby a succession of unintentionally wrong moves led to unwanted results. If one viewed this whole disorderly sequence as itself a species of order, then each of the stages in its advance could be interpreted as if "designed" to stabilize, in constantly changing circumstances, the underlying pattern of conditions favorable to the eventual outcome (namely, the kind of equilibrium that could be maintained only by a series of progressive developments leading into, through, and beyond the Terror).

Though a drama is a mode of symbolic action so designed that an audience might be induced to "act symbolically" in sympathy with it, insofar as the drama serves this function it may be studied as a "perfect mechanism" composed of parts moving in mutual adjustment to one another like clockwork. The paradox is not unlike that which happened in metaphysics when a mystical view of the world as a manifestation of God's purposes prepared the way for mechanistic views, since the perfect representation of such a "design" seemed to be a machine in perfect order.

This brings up the further consideration that mechanical models might best be analyzed, not as downright antidramatistic, but as fragments of the dramatistic. For whatever humanist critics might say about the "dehumanizing" effects of the machine, it is a characteristically *human* invention, conceived by the perfecting of some human aptitudes and the elimination of others (thus in effect being not inhuman, but man's powerful "caricature" of himself—a kind of mighty homunculus).

If, on the other hand, it is held that a dramatistic nomenclature is to be avoided in any form as categorically inappropriate to a science of social relations, then a systematic study of symbolic action could at least be of use in helping to reveal any hitherto undetected traces of dramatistic thinking that might still survive. For otherwise the old Adam of human symbolicity, whereby man still persists in thinking of himself as a *personal agent capable of acting,* may lurk in a symbol system undetected (a tendency revealed in the fact that the distinction between "action" and "sheer motion" so readily gets lost, as with a term like *kinesis* in Aristotle or the shift between the mechanistic connotations of "equilibrium" and the histrionic connotations of "equilibrist"). Similarly, since pragmatist terminologies lay great stress upon "agencies" (means) and since all machines have a kind of built-in purpose, any nomenclature conceived along the lines of pragmatist instrumentalism offers a halfway house between teleology and sheer aimless motion.

At one point dramatism as a critique of terminology is necessarily at odds with dramatism as applied for specifically scientific purposes. This has been made clear in an article by Wrong (1961), who charges that although "modern sociology after all originated as a protest against the partial views of man contained in such doctrines as utilitarianism, classical economics, social Darwinism, and vulgar Marxism," it risks contributing to "the creation of yet another reified abstraction in socialized man, the status-seeker of our contemporary sociologists" (p. 190). He grants that "such an image of man is . . . valuable for limited purposes," but only "so long as it is not taken for the whole truth" (p. 190). He offers various corrections, among them a stress upon "role-playing," and upon "forces in man that are resistant to socialization," such as certain "biological" and "psychological" factors—even though some sociologists might promptly see "the specter of 'biological determinism' " (p. 191) and others might complain that already there is "too much 'psychologism' in contemporary sociology" (p. 192).

Viewed from the standpoint of dramatism as a critique of terminology, Wrong's article suggests two notable problems. Insofar as any science has a nomenclature especially adapted to its particular field of study, the extension of its *special* terms to provide a definition of man *in general* would necessarily oversociologize, overbiologize, overpsychologize, or overphysicize, etc., its subject; or the definition would have to be corrected by the addition of elements from other specialized nomenclatures (thereby producing a kind of amalgam that would lie outside the strict methodic confines of any specialized scientific discipline). A dramatistic view of this situation suggests that an over-all definition of man would be not strictly "scientific," but philosophical.

Similarly, the dramatistic concept of a scene–act ratio aims to admonish against an overly positivistic view of descriptive terms, or "empirical data," as regards an account of the conditions that men are thought to confront at a given time in history. For insofar as such a grammatical function does figure in our thoughts about motives and purpose, in the choice and scope of the terms that are used for characterizing a given situation dramatism would discern implicit corresponding attitudes and programs of action. If the principle of the scene–act ratio always figures in some form, it follows that one could not possibly select descriptive terms in which policies of some sort are not more or less clearly inherent. In the selection of terms for describing a scene, one automatically prescribes the range of acts that will seem reasonable, implicit, or necessary in that situation.

Dramatistic Analyses of Order

Following a lead from Bergson (1907, especially chapter 4), dramatism is devoted to a stress upon the all-importance of the negative as a specifically linguistic invention. But whereas Bergson's fertile chapter on "the idea of nothing" centers in the propositional negative ("It is not"), the dramatistic emphasis focuses attention upon the "moralistic" or "hortatory" negative ("Thou shalt not"). Burke (1961, pp. 183–196) has applied this principle of negativity to a cycle of terms implicit in the idea of "order," in keeping with the fact that "order," being a polar term, implies a corresponding idea of "disorder," while these terms in turn involve ideas of "obedience" or "disobedience" to the "authority" implicit in "order" (with further terministic radiations, such as the attitude of "humility" that leads to the act of obedience or the attitude of "pride" that leads to the act of disobedience, these in turn involving ideas of guidance or temptation, reward or punishment, and so on).

On the side of order, or control, there are the variants of faith and reason (faith to the extent that one accepts a given command, proscription, or statement as authoritative; reason to the extent that one's acceptance is contingent upon such proofs as are established by a methodic weighing of doubts and rebuttals). On the side of disorder there are the temptations of the senses and the imagination. The senses can function as temptations to the extent that the prescribed order does not wholly gratify our impulses (whether they are natural or a by-product of the very order that requires their control). Similarly, the imagination falls on the side of disorder insofar as it encourages interests inimical to the given order, though it is serviceable to order if used as a deterrent by picturing the risks of disorder—or, in other words, if it is kept "under the control of reason."

Midway between the two slopes of order and disorder (technically the realm where one can say yes or no to a thou-shalt-not) there is an area of indeterminacy often called the will. Ontologically, action is treated as a function of the will. But logologically the situation is reversed: the idea of the will is viewed as derivable from the idea of an act.

From ideas of the will there follow in turn ideas of grace, or an intrinsic ability to make proper choices (though such an aptitude can be impaired by various factors), and sacrifice (insofar as any choices involve the "mortification" of some desires). The dramatistic perspective thus rounds out the pattern in accordance with the notion that insofar as a given order involves sacrifices of some sort, the sacrificial principle is intrinsic to the nature of order. Hence, since substitution is a prime resource available to symbol systems, the sacrificial principle comes to ultimate fulfillment in vicarious sacrifice, which is variously rationalized, and can be viewed accordingly as a way to some kind of ultimate rewards.

By tracing and analyzing such terms, a dramatistic analysis shows how the negativistic principle of guilt implicit in the nature of order combines with the principles of thoroughness (or "perfection") and substitution that are characteristic of symbol systems in such a way that the sacrificial principle of victimage (the "scapegoat") is intrinsic to human congregation. The intricate line of exposition might be summed up thus: If order, then guilt; if guilt, then need for redemption; but any such "payment" is victimage. Or: If action, then drama; if drama, then conflict; if conflict, then victimage.

Adapting theology ("words about God") to secular, empirical purposes ("words about words"), dramatistic analysis stresses the perennial vitality of the scapegoat principle, explaining why it fits so disastrously well into the "logologic" of man's symbolic resources. It aims to show why, just as the two primary and sometimes conflicting functions of religion (solace and control) worked together in the doctrines of Christianity, we should expect to find their analogues in any society. Dramatism, as so conceived, asks not how the sacrificial motives revealed in the institutions of magic and religion might be eliminated in a scientific culture, but what new forms they take (Burke [1945–1950] 1962, pp. 406–408).

This view of vicarious victimage extends the range of those manifestations far beyond the areas ordinarily so labeled. Besides extreme instances like Hitlerite genocide, or the symbolic "cleansings" sought in wars, uprisings, and heated political campaigns, victimage would include psychogenic illness, social exclusiveness (the malaise of the "hierarchal psychosis"), "beatnik" art, rabid partisanship in sports, the excessive pollution of air and streams, the "bulldozer mentality" that rips into natural conditions without qualms, the many enterprises that keep men busy destroying in the name of progress or profit the ecological balance on which, in the last analysis, our eventual well-being depends, and so on.

The strongly terministic, or logological, emphasis of dramatism would view the scapegoat principle not primarily as a survival from earlier eras, but as a device natural to language here and now. Aristotle, in the third book of his *Rhetoric* (chapter 10), particularly stresses the stylistic importance of antithesis as a means of persuasion (as when a policy is recommended in terms of what it is *against*). In this spirit dramatism would look upon the scapegoat (or the principle of vicarious victimage) as but a special case of antithesis, combined with another major resource of symbol systems, namely, substitution.

In the polemics of politics, the use of the scapegoat to establish identification in terms of an enemy shared in common is also said to have the notable rhetorical advantage that the candidate who presents himself as a spokesman for "us" can prod his audience to consider local ills primarily in terms of alien figures viewed as the outstanding causes of those ills. In accord with this emphasis, when analyzing the rhetorical tactics of *Mein Kampf,* Burke (1922–1961) lays particular stress upon Hitler's use of such deflections to provide a "noneconomic interpretation of economic ills."

While recognizing the amenities of property and holding that "mine-ownness" or "our-ownness" in some form or other is an inevitable aspect of human congregation, dramatistic analysis also contends that property in any form sets the conditions for conflict (and hence culminates in some sort of victimage). It is pointed out that the recent great advances in the development of technological power require a corresponding extension in the realm of negativity (the "thou-shalt-nots" of control). Thus, the strikingly "positive" nature of such resources (as described in terms of "sheer motion") is viewed dramatistically as deceptive; for they may seem too simply like "promises," whereas in being *powers* they are *properties,* and all properties are *problems,* since powers are bones of contention (Burke 1960).

A dramatistic view of human motives thus culminates in the ironic admonition that perversions of the sacrificial principle (purgation by scapegoat, congregation by segregation) are the constant temptation of human societies, whose orders are built by a kind of animal exceptionally adept in the ways of symbolic action (Burke [1941] 1957, pp. 87–113).

BIBLIOGRAPHY

Benne, Kenneth D. 1964 From Polarization to Paradox. Pages 216–247 in Leland P. Bradford, Jack R. Gibb, and Kenneth D. Benne (editors), *T-Group Theory and Laboratory Method: Innovation in Reeducation.* New York: Wiley.

Bergson, Henri (1907) 1944 *Creative Evolution.* New York: Modern Library. → First published in French.

Burke, Kenneth (1922–1961) 1964 *Perspectives by Incongruity* and *Terms for Order.* Edited by Stanley Edgar Hyman. Bloomington: Indiana Univ. Press. → Two representative collections of readings from Burke's works. Each collection is also available separately in paperback from the same publisher.

Burke, Kenneth (1937) 1959 *Attitudes Toward History.* 2d ed., rev. Los Altos, Calif.: Hermes.

Burke, Kenneth (1941) 1957 *The Philosophy of Literary Form: Studies in Symbolic Action.* Rev. ed., abridged by the author. New York: Vintage. → The Louisiana State University Press reprinted the unabridged edition in 1967.

Burke, Kenneth (1945–1950) 1962 *A Grammar of Motives* and *A Rhetoric of Motives.* Cleveland: World.

Burke, Kenneth 1955 Linguistic Approach to Problems of Education. Pages 259–303 in National Society for the Study of Education. Committee on Modern Philosophies and Education. *Modern Philosophies and Education.* Edited by Nelson B. Henry. National Society for the Study of Education Yearbook 54, Part 1. Univ. of Chicago Press.

Burke, Kenneth 1960 Motion, Action, Words. *Teachers College Record* 62:244–249.

Burke, Kenneth 1961 *The Rhetoric of Religion: Studies in Logology.* Boston: Beacon.
Burke, Kenneth 1966 *Language as Symbolic Action: Essays on Life, Literature, and Method.* Berkeley: Univ. of California Press.
Duncan, Hugh D. 1962 *Communication and Social Order.* Totowa, N.J.: Bedminster Press.
Goffman, Erving (1956) 1959 *The Presentation of Self in Everyday Life.* Garden City, N.Y.: Doubleday.
Hume, David, (1748) 1952 An Inquiry Concerning Human Understanding. Pages 451–509 in *Great Books of the Western World.* Volume 35: Locke, Berkeley, Hume. Chicago: Penton.
Mathiez, Albert (1922–1927) 1962 *The French Revolution.* New York: Russell. → First published in French in three volumes. A paperback edition was published in 1964 by Grosset and Dunlap.
Mead, George Herbert 1938 *The Philosophy of the Act.* Univ. of Chicago Press. → Consists almost entirely of unpublished papers which Mead left at his death in 1931.
Parsons, Talcott 1937 *The Structure of Social Action: A Study in Social Theory With Special Reference to a Group of Recent European Writers.* New York: McGraw-Hill.
Richards, Ivor A. (1959) 1961 *Principles of Literary Criticism.* New York: Harcourt.
Rueckert, William H. 1963 *Kenneth Burke and the Drama of Human Relations.* Minneapolis: Univ. of Minnesota Press.
Wrong, Dennis H. 1961 The Oversocialized Conception of Man in Modern Sociology. *American Sociological Review* 26:183–193.

3.

SYMBOLS AND MEN

George N. Gordon

In a recent book, Kenneth Burke has described the human being as follows:

Man is
the symbol using (symbol-making, symbol-misusing) animal
inventor of the negative (or moralized by the negative)
separated from his natural condition by instruments of his own making
goaded by the spirit of hierarchy (or moved by a sense of order)
and rotten with perfection [1]

Burke subsequently defends each of these propositions in a brilliant discourse.[2] The characteristics stem one from the other in proper order and delineate the concept "man" as Burke sees him. If we recognize him as a psychologically determined beast, impelled to a limited degree of harshly determined logical behavior (but aware of his own limits and perversities), we are probably talking about the same type of creature Burke is.

Note that Burke places man's symbol using and abusing characteristics *second* on the list; that is, immediately after he has affirmed man's *essence.* Most contem-

---

Reprinted by permission from *Languages of Communication,* Hastings House, 1969.

porary observers agree with him, because modern perspectives of man literally force us to consider the symbol as basic to our fundamental processes of awareness.

In the words of von Bertalanffy, "Man's unique position is based on the dominance of symbols in his life. Except in the immediate satisfaction of biological needs, man lives in a world not of things but of symbols. . . . Symbols can be defined as signs that are freely created, represent some content and are transmitted by tradition. It appears that the characteristics indicated are necessary and sufficient to distinguish symbolism . . . from subhuman forms of behavior." [3]

A. N. Whitehead has demonstrated [4] tersely that knowledge is mediated to the human being either directly (as when one is slapped in the face) or through a symbolic screen (as when one understands the *meaning* of a slap on the face). Whitehead writes: "There is one great difference between symbolism and direct knowledge. Direct experience is infallible. What you have experienced, you have experienced. But symbolism is very fallible, in the sense that it may induce actions, feelings, emotions, and beliefs and things which are mere notions without that exemplification in the world which the symbolism leads us to presuppose." [5]

Human beings in every culture of which man has known have been dependent upon that "world which symbolism leads us to presuppose" for hundreds of thousands of years, but the symbolic world itself has been taken for granted for most of this time; that is, seen as an *extension* of the world of direct experience. A poignant illustration of this fact may be found at the end of the Ingmar Bergman film, *The Virgin Spring*. A father (skilfully played by Max von Sydow) having avenged the rape and brutal murder of his daughter by killing her assassins, raises high his hands, their fingers just touching, to God. We are then told that at the place where he stands a spring began to flow and a great cathedral was built. As the film ends, we see von Sydow from the back, on his toes, head to the heavens, his arms arched, transformed in a human replica of a church. For an instant, a perceptive film maker has given us a glimpse of the architecture of a house of worship *as a symbolic extension of the physical figure of man himself, in excelsis,* praying to his God. He has also illustrated the simplicity (and perhaps inevitability) of the generation of such symbols, and, incidentally, the source of their power.

Symbolic insights of this sort were probably generally taken for granted for thousands of years. Certainly, traditional wisdom did not impel men, before the middle of the last century, to examine their symbol structure in the ways writers like Burke, von Bertalanffy and Whitehead have done in recent times. Many poets and philosophers for centuries, on the other hand, seemed frequently impressed by the symbolic "truths" with which they dealt, but they dared not conjecture that any symbol system—much less language itself—was likely to be less than an infallible guide to "truth" when opposed to experience. One hundred years ago—even three generations ago—the following paragraph by Burke would probably have been considered the work of a deranged mind. Yet, to our senses it is hardly revolutionary, merely descriptive of what most of us already know. Burke says:

> Can we bring ourselves to realize . . . just how overwhelmingly much of what we mean by "reality" has been built up for us through nothing but our symbol systems? Take away our books, and what do we know about history, biography, even some

things so "down to earth" as the positive position of seas and continents? What is our reality for today (beyond the paper-thin line of our own particular lives) but all this clutter of symbols about the past combined with whatever things we know mainly through maps, magazines, newspapers and the like about the present? In school, as they go from class to class, students turn from one idiom to another. The various courses in the curriculum are in effect but so many different terminologies. And however important to us is the tiny sliver of reality each of us has experienced firsthand, the whole overall "picture" is but a construct of our symbol systems. To meditate on this fact until one sees its full implications is much like peering over the edge of things into an ultimate abyss. And doubtless that's one reason why, though man is typically the symbol-using animal, he clings to a kind of naïve verbal realism that refuses to realize the full extent of the role played by symbolicity in his notions of reality.[6]

Recognition of Symbols

Burke's observation, above, however, *in no way* frees man from the symbol system in which his own writing and thinking are enmeshed. Nor are we freed on these pages themselves from the symbolic environment of the society in which these words are written merely because we are discussing symbols.[7] Knowledge of a symbol system gives one little but psychological power over it. The holiness of a church is not reduced by Bergman's insight of the extenuation of a religious symbol from the human form. For the religiously inclined, the derivation of such a symbol even enhances its value—should an individual question the "human" purpose for the construction of cathedrals (to God's glory) while men live in hovels. *The Virgin Spring* provides *an answer,* satisfactory to some of us and unsatisfactory to others, but a clear and irrefutable answer. . . .

Some communications analysts go to great pains to differentiate between *symbols* and *signs,* conscious of the oddity that signs are understood by non-human animals, while symbols are almost entirely bound to human perceptions. The difference is misleading, primarily because a sign to one individual in one culture may be a symbol to another. Different signs, also, may vary in symbolic value through the history of a single culture. Ashley Montagu has, however, recorded the difference quite succinctly. "A sign is a concrete denoter: it signals 'This is it. Do something about it,' " he writes. "A symbol, on the other hand, is abstract, connotative, contemplative, knowing, knowledgeable. A sign is eternal. A symbol is internal. Signs relate mostly to the world of things, symbols to the world of ideas. A symbol is an abstract meaning of value conferred by those who use it upon anything, tangible or intangible. A sign, on the other hand, is a physical thing which is apprehended as standing for something else." [8]

Can a symbol be more specifically defined? If it can, we are on our way to specifying the symbolic base of the various languages of communication. If it cannot, we are hurled into a mystical discourse where, unfortunately, much current discussion of symbolism (particularly as it applies to the arts) is held. Of many attempts at definition one of the clearest is Susanne K. Langer's short statement, "A symbol is any device where we are enabled to make an abstraction." [9]

Let us examine this deceptively simple sentence. First, "A symbol is a device. . . ." Symbolism is therefore not a medium of communication *but a way in which ideas are transmitted by means of mediums.* Neither is a symbol a unit of language. There exists no "language of symbols" or discourse solely by means of symbols, unless certain specific ideas are lined up (or somehow arranged) and thereafter symbolized in turn.[10] By means of this parade of symbols we are neither creating a symbolic sentence nor constructing a meaningful vocabulary of them, but merely arranging a number of simple symbols into one long, complex symbol. We may analyze the components of this complex symbol, but it will lack, *sui generis,* a grammar, a syntax and probably even a clear aesthetic.

The definition continues ". . . whereby we are enabled to make an abstraction." The nature and burden of symbolism are therefore subsumed under considerations of the psychologics of communication. While the logics may be drawn upon in inducing the *history* of a symbol (or a symbol system) and its social function, and it may be amenable to description in the logical mode, the process of symbolism itself is psychological. The fabrication of abstractions stems from our psychological rather than logical proclivities. The activity of symbolism does not, however, preclude logic in communication. Arithmetic, for instance, a highly abstract method of manipulating the environment, is quite logical. The process by which concrete elements are first, translated into abstractions, and second, translated back into concrete entities (arithmetic included) is more likely to involve the psychologics of communication than their logics. The words ". . . we are enabled" in Langer's definition clearly indicates that the process is one of *mind.*

Modern psychological theory deals, therefore, both fully and profitably with the symbolic aspect of man's mind-life. Freud is mainly given both credit and blame for the development of modern schools of symbology and for their influences on so much of our cultural life. Philosophers were, of course, investigating the role of symbols in the lives of men well before Freud, although the focus of their interest was less upon symbolic influences upon neuroses and other behavior disorders than upon letters and art, particularly graphic arts and the theater.

Mordecai Gorelik, noted scene designer and theatrical historian, speculated some years ago that the currents of thought which led to the analysis of symbolism in modern terms began in the period between 1849 and 1869 in the grand visions of Richard Wagner.[11]

First, Wagner was raised in the Germanic theatrical tradition, which had been strongly influenced by Duke Georg of Saxe-Meiningen's non-naturalistic "director's theatre." The Duke had broken with tradition by treating the stage not as a vehicle for individual virtuoso actors or as a platform for well made plots, but as an orchestrated, abstracted *event,* analogous to the musical symphony.

Wagner's imagination was fired by this first *self-consciously symbolic art form* that had been conceived in the West, an art form in which the stage setting, lighting, music and lyrics all were intentionally contrived to "stand for" a totality greater than the sum of the parts. In this self-conscious conceptual arena, Wagner attempted to capture the Teutonic spirit of "folk, blood and soil." [12]

The myths upon which Wagner's operas were based (including the Faust play), were (and remain) some of the most highly charged symbolic material in the folklore of Europe, the result of cultural mysticism centuries old.

What emerged was a theatre of symbolism, "suggestion, vagueness of outline, posteresque light and shadow and, most of all, an impenetrable blending, 'a complex and rhythmic fusion of setting, lights, actors and play.' " [13] Its symbols implied what it did not state directly about Germanic nobility, the perfection of primitivism, and the evils of effete civilization. The theatre, for Wagner, was a vehicle for the expression of those specific symbols which could manipulate his special audience's thoughts and feelings appropriately. [14]

Against this artistic and nationalistic background began the scientific period of "great doubting" during the last half of the past century. Another genius, schooled in Germanic traditions, grasped at the newly enfranchised symbol. Freud discovered an emancipated symbology in middle-European thought, freed from its place in the world of objective reality and located in the basic psychological, universal, human system of perceptions.

Here was Freud's response to the fundamental question posed to him by philosophers of his day: How could he know anything about the workings of the unconscious if the unconscious was, by definition, closed to perception? The most convincing answer was the *symbol*, that by-product of an unconscious human process which had been secretly fueling human consciousness for hundreds of thousands of years without man being aware of it. Wagner had located it in the theatre and had developed a near-religious theory of symbolism to justify the enormity of his dramatic undertakings. Freud's concept was no less heroic. He enshrined the symbol as the *lingua franca* of man's instinctual processes, speaking in its own strangely potent vocabulary to his patients from the polite middle-class world of old Vienna.

When the American psychologist Clark Hull later attempted to articulate what he hoped would be a valedictory general theory of human behavior "communicational symbolism . . . the use of symbolism in individual problem solution involving thought and reasoning; . . . : social or ritualistic symbolism," [15] headed his list of concerns. The time was now the 1940's. Hull even promised his colleagues a veritable model of symbolism, a "mathematico-deductive" theory which would apply to—and crack the riddles of—virtually every problem known to social science.

Hull himself was an outstanding experimentalist with a bias towards analogies which employed mechanistic explanations in explaining behavior. [16] His strict determinism took for granted a full-blown, clearly articulated concept of symbolism, which had emerged tentatively little more than two generations before from hypotheses of artists, philosophers and psychologists who were trying desperately to interconnect history, mythology and religion with the new sciences of biology and psychology.

The intervening years had seen the growth and spread of the concept of the universality and power of symbols. At the same time, many of the basic religious, mythological (and even nationalistic) objects for which the symbols stood were examined and rejected. Men of the stature of William James [17] and Sir James Frazer [18] were to search the corners of the earth for primitive cultures in order to study the rites of antique religions and their yield of specific symbols and symbol systems which hopefully might appear in similar manifestations in widely different cultures. By implication, they attempted to demonstrate for all time that the Western

Judeo-Christian tradition was not exempted by virtue of recency from the same kind of symbolic behaviors in which our ancestors had indulged thousands of years ago. . . .

The Ubiquity of Symbols

From a logical frame of reference, George Herbert Mead explains the ubiquity of symbols:

> Thinking always implies a symbol which will call out the same response in another that it calls out in the thinker. Such a symbol is a universal of discourse; it is universal in its character. We always assume the symbol we use is the one which will call out in the other person the same response, provided it is a part of his mechanism of conduct. A person who is saying something is saying *to himself* what he is saying to others; otherwise he does not know what he is thinking about. . . .[19]
>
> The isolation of the symbol, as such, enables one to hold on to . . . given characteristics and to isolate them in their relationship to the object, and consequently in their relationship to the response. It is that, I think, which characterizes our human intelligence to a peculiar degree. We have a set of symbols by means of which we indicate certain characters, and in indicating those characters hold them apart from their immediate environment, and keep simply one relationship clear.[20]

Mead provides us with a clear description of *how* a symbol is formed; *what* it accomplishes everywhere; and *why* observers as logically dissimilar as Hull and Burke place symbols first in importance as an artifact of human endeavor, ahead of fire, the axe or the tribe.

Mead's points apply to the *single* symbol. What about *symbolism,* the *total* process by which symbols are somehow combined into complex and sophisticated formalities and preserved as events called "rites" or as "rituals" or "ceremonies"?

Our explanation must necessarily move from the lucid and relatively simple form of logical analysis to the operation of psychologics. From the psychological reference point, there is no diminution in the sweep, scope or pervasiveness of symbolic activity in the lives of men. What emerges is the degree of the individual's immersion in the universe of symbols, insofar as the *emotional* or *feeling* side of his nature is concerned. We discover amazing elaborations and combinations of symbols which, while rarely satisfying the logics of language, often appear, nevertheless, to satisfy deep human cravings.

Symbols, first and most strikingly, attempt to define, clarify or manage the fundamental enigmas of existence: matters relating to birth, reproduction and death. They appear to unite the role of man with the processes of nature. The ubiquity of symbolism in this context indicates that the psychologics of symbolism go far beyond Mead's explanation of symbolic intercourse, based on sheer (or mere) utility and facility of social communications.

S. Gideon describes these psychological processes thus, comparing them functionally as modern manifestations to their roles in primitive societies:

> Today's symbols are anonymous; they seem to exist for themselves alone, without any direct significance. Yet they are imbued with an inexplicable attraction: the magic

of their forms. In a sense, they represent a regenerative or healing process, a flight from technological frenzy. Beside these anonymous symbols or forms without direct significance, age-old symbols from the remote past have been revived and integrated into new contexts . . .[21]

The essential nature of the symbol has always consisted in an urge to express the inherently inexpressible, but in primitive times the crystallization of a concept in the form of a symbol portrayed reality before that reality came to pass. The symbol itself was reality, for it was believed to possess the power of working magic, and thus of directly affecting the course of events: the wish, the prayer or the spell to be fulfilled.[22]

Sometimes symbols are conceived of, however, in so general a psychological sense, that they may refer to *any* so-called "sign" which is a substitute for another "sign," as they are, for instance, by Charles Morris.[23] Under these circumstances, symbolic ideation transcends Burke's poetic definition of man, although Burke does not say that man is the *only* animal that is a symbol user. "Sign" substitution may be seen in the behaviors of apes, hooded rats (trained in laboratories) and other mammals. One may discover it in the colorful habits of hundreds of thousands of species of invertebrates.

Konrad Lorenz clearly differentiates between the kind of symbol evident in the animal kingdom carried on by sign substitution and the kind that man employs in communication. "No means of communication, no learned rituals are ever handed down by tradition in animals. In other words, animals have no culture." [24] Symbols, in Morris' semantic sense, are far more ubiquitous than symbols in the tradition-cultural sense, but they lack utterly an historic or cultural function and their psychological ramifications for the explanation of human communications appear to be nil.

The difference between the use of symbols individually to enhance meaning and the employment of rites, rituals and ceremonies to perform far more elaborate psychological tasks is small. Because symbolism in any form is *not* itself a medium of communication, it does not lend itself to the kind of distinctive logical and psychological analysis that the mediums permit. Instead, a symbol's pschological power is derived from relationship with specific culture traits. Without them as references, it is meaningless. For instance, the pine tree may be the discrete symbol of winter in the Christmas ceremony performed in the United States. But the celebration of Christ's birth, with all its religious and materialistic manifestations, is a nearly *total societal* obeisance in our culture, not necessarily confined to religious Christians, but observed by Jews, atheists and others. The American Christmas ceremony entails a complicated set of rituals, the mixture of many individual symbols, psychologically best described by an enumeration of its logics. These logical events appear to contain considerable psychological power in our culture, particularly for children.[25]

Burke differentiates the *symbol* from *symbolism* by treating the former as "scientistic" (or amenable to atomistic and frequently logical analysis). The latter he calls "dramatist" (or totalities more psychologically oriented), which are captured and communicated in "stories, plays, poems, the rhetoric of oratory and advertising, mythologies, theologies and philosophies after the classic model." [26]

The former may yield to semantic analysis. The latter demands a cultural perspective to be understood. It is developed in "the tribe's way of living (the practical role of symbolism in what anthropologist Malenowski has called 'context of situation'). Such considerations are involved in . . . the 'dramatistic,' stressing language as an aspect of 'action,' that is as 'symbolic action.' " [27] Symbolism, the elaboration of symbols, is therefore primarily an anthropological matter, while discrete symbols, behavioral, logical and/or psychological are perhaps semantic manifestations of the kind discussed previously in the work of Mead, Hull and others.

Because one must employ them in different contexts, however, does not isolate the notion of symbol from symbolism or demand totally exclusive categories for the study of each. It appears merely that the psychologically elaborate process of ceremony is located at one end of a continuum on which the single symbol in its logical phase (as shown by Mead) is located at the other.

Burke's "dramatistic approach" must represent the accumulation and interplay of numerous isolated "scientistically" derived atomistic symbols. Experience demonstrates the ease with which we may untangle almost any aspect of "dramatistic" life into its individual symbolic elements, even in a culture with as many complex ceremonies, rites and rituals as ours. Indeed, "symbol-hunting" of many kinds has become an appropriate (and not unprofitable) activity for countless people. "Symbolic criticism" of drama and literature is presently much in vogue. That such criticism is often brought cleverly to bear upon the classics as well as modern works demonstrates the ease with which the complex "dramatistic" symbolic structures may be broken down into their "scientistic" elements. [28]

The Function of Symbols

To ascribe, therefore, discrete psychological and logical functions to symbols and symbolisms is to stumble into an easy but well-worn trap which permits one to "explain" symbols without understanding the role they play in communication. [29] Having differentiated between symbol and symbolism in matters of *kind* rather than complexity and/or *degree,* we are likely to indulge in the kind of "interpretation" and hair-splitting one finds so frequently in the present literature of semantics and in numerous types of language study. . . .

Burke offers our first problem, namely the *difference* between *symbolic* reality and *real* reality. Is there any? Burke responds: "Our presence in a room is immediate, but the room's relation to our country as a nation, and beyond that, to international relations and cosmic relations, dissolves into a web of ideas and images through our senses only insofar as the symbol system, that report on them are heard and seen. To mistake this vast tangle of ideas for immediate experience is much more fallacious than to accept a dream as immediate experience." [30]

Burke has identified a concept discussed also by Daniel J. Boorstein,[31] that of the *pseudo-environment* which is made up largely (or entirely) of symbols. This pseudo-environment so influences our patterns of life and thought that we seem to have lost the ability to distinguish between a real environment and the artificial, symbolic one. While Boorstein extrapolates this idea into the speculative territory of mass culture, he considers this psychological problem a sickness endemic to our entire culture. Perhaps he has exaggerated the symptoms as extravagantly as he has diagnosed the disease, but it *is* difficult to gainsay the hard truth that, when we deal with individuals who cannot recognize the nature of genuine experiences, we are dealing with people who manifest psychoses. It is also as difficult to deny that an uncomfortable amount of such behavior is easily visible in our culture, even in highly exalted circles. . . .

There appears to be little either startling or upsetting about a certain degree of confusion manifest in *individuals* between symbols and reality. Our nervous systems and brains probably have been conditioned to allow for this peculiarity of perception. One is not aware as he writes that he is using a symbol system. Occasionally one confuses the process of composition with a live discourse and responds accordingly with a vocalized expletive, for instance. But the confusion is momentary, and one exercises a large measure of control over the symbols used in written language.

Is someone who cherishes a religious icon blessed by a spiritual leader unrealistic because he ascribes power to that particular symbol? Consider the many psychoanalsts who keep a framed picture of Freud (or Jung or Reik) in their offices. Note also the tendency to preserve the personal possessions and original documents of men like these and other great scientists. Let us not forget the General Semanticists' reverence for trivia surrounding the life and times of Count Korzybski, or our reactions to a man in a police uniform or a laboratory robe, and our recent passion for naming objects after dead martyrs.

Is, therefore, the confusion between the real and symbolic environment a symptom of individual psychological disturbance, or is it an inevitable manifestation of symbol usage? May it be both?

In severely disturbed people, of course, confusion between symbols and reality reaches bizarre dimensions. That this confusion is less one of *kind* than degree indicates an uncomfortable probability that so-called mental illness is frequently a variant of "normal" behavior in an incompatible environment. Fenichel notes that "schizophrenics, for example, show an intuitive understanding of symbolism. Interpretations of symbols, which neurotics find so difficult to accept in analysis, are made spontaneously and as a matter of course by schizophrenics. Symbolic thinking for them *is not merely a method of distortion but actually their archaic type of thinking.*" [32]

Symbolic confusions in severely disturbed individuals have stimulated close investigations of the pathological aspect of symbol usage. These studies have sired "disciplines" which attempt, vainly many believe, to create a cognitive, logical type of discourse in which continual differentiation between the symbolic environment and reality is demanded. One such system asks us continually to bear in mind, for instance, slogans like "A word is not a thing," or "A map is not a territory," in order to insure the relevance of language to cognition. The "school" of General Semantics [33] is motivated (undoubtedly sincerely) to utilize language precisely and to minimize entropy in communication.

What Semanticists do not take into account—and obscure from their mechanistic perspectives—is that symbols *themselves* are as formidable a part of man's psychological reality as the "things" and "territories," his logical realities, to which discourse is reduced in their system. Meaning is rarely clarified by the compulsion to "define" symbols, be they words, pictures or objects. The subtle potentiality for sophisticated thought and the elaboration of emotion of which man is capable is thereby lost. Language—and communication—is reduced by General Semantics to a relatively crude instrument. It has cleared the "semantic mist", but it has been sterilized also of *nearly the entire spectrum of communications in the psychological mode which our symbol-making capacity permits*.

The value of this spectrum to human communications depends upon the relevant analysis of what symbols stand for and how they function. Perhaps such analysis is impossible to accomplish at present for the major symbols in our culture. It may be a task beyond the capacities of human intellect. It would necessarily start with the assumption that *all symbols are analogues* and that all symbolism is a method of making metaphors of different kinds. These analogues and metaphors are psychologically—but *not* necessarily logically—more *convenient* for most people to handle conceptually than whatever they stood for. Or they make possible—again by analogue—a type of conviction or thought or feeling which would otherwise be impossible to generate without a particular symbol or certain symbol system.

The analogous quality of language is self-evident. Our dictionaries and concepts of "definition" attempt, in complicated ways, to untwine the analogues of words. Critics and teachers battle with the more analogues of words. Critics and teachers battle with the more complicated metaphors enclosed in the symbolism of the elaborations of language. Some kinds of symbols—those identified by Freud, for instance—are believed to allow us to formulate benign analogies and metaphors for repressed or unconscious material which would, according to theory, threaten us too dangerously in raw form. A mystical or religious symbol is an analogue of an historical event, a subjective feeling, or a rite or ritual. An icon is a metaphor that stands for a complex array of events, spiritual inclinations, objects, and other matters of relevance to one particular aspect of psychological life.

The analogous function of *all* symbolism does not diminish either the power or the importance either of that which is symbolized or the symbol itself. In other words, one cannot disparage a symbol (or its power) merely *because* it is a symbol and therefore *only* an analogue of something else. Here we have the "genetic fallacy" which, according to Langer "arises from the historical method in philosophy and criticism: the error of confusing the *origin* of a thing with its *import*. . . ." Langer specifically notes that *"all elementary symbolic forms have their origin in something else than symbolic interest."* [34] One might quarrel with the word *"elementary"; complex* symbols also have their origins in elementary symbols, which have their origin in an analogue in the world of reality. The statue of Abraham Lincoln, for instance, in the Lincoln Memorial, is a fairly complex symbol of many qualities that it is believed Lincoln himself *today* stands for. They, in turn, are metaphors of the Lincoln who has been symbolized in the process we call "history." This process is an analogy system based upon reality: the things that really happened to President Lincoln during his lifetime. The part of reality which relates to this analogy system is, in fact, very small—a fraction of what actually occurred to the real Lincoln: president, man, Republican, politician, father, writer, sage and so forth. But it is, as Langer would say, this part which yields the *important* analogues of the symbol structure related to the statue in Washington, D. C., as perceived by most of us.

Much the same (but far more complex) types of analogues and metaphors systems are involved also in artistic and religious symbols. The vision of life which they provide our apprehensions modifies reality (*crude* reality in most cases) into a refined series of metaphors which are at once pleasurable and logically and psychologically valuable experiences.

Will we ever ascertain for certain the "reality" which provided Cervantes the metaphor he created in the person of *Don Quixote?* Of course not; but we may safely conjecture that the Knight of the Woeful Countenance had some (or many) sorts of equivalent in reality that were economically drawn together into Cervante's metaphorical hero.

All artists (and all saints) speak to us by metaphor. Their symbol systems act as analogues of life, "mirrors of nature," not so much *reflecting* reality as *translating* it into suitable and digestible metaphors.

The mirror facilitates communication in even so abtract an art as music, where the *particular* analogues of musical sounds are usually far less precisely articulated than in other arts. Music has traveled the route from program music to high abstraction. Modern composers, tired of the tenuous analogies in their "art form," began introducing taxicab horns, boat and factory whistles into their compositions to orient them to reality in the same manner that program music once had done. The compass point of musical symbolism then swung to its origin: back to nature that had provided the first chance variations of sounds which a primitive musician, ages ago, had first translated into a musical symbol.

Conclusion

Analogy and metaphor are found in the heart of the communication process. From them, we create symbols that are the instruments by which the languages of communication become possible, and through which we transmit an enormous range of logical and psychological data. Symbols are the keystones of the words used in language, and are therefore fundamental to human thought itself. They are, as many observers have recorded, distinctively human when they arrive at certain degrees of complexity, logically, psychologically or both.

The present era has seen human enquiry into the ubiquity of symbols manifest in both primitive and sophisticated cultures, as they are employed in both to serve many of the same ends. In the process, we have achieved some *degree of control* over the use of symbols in Western culture by the speculations associated with certain modern schools of psychology and philosophy. Many old and some ancient symbol systems, having found their way to us through the maze of history, retain their power, usefulness and relevance to contemporary society. Among them, one finds numerous forms of art and religion—both of which appear to employ profound and differential varieties of communication from men to men. That they have persisted into this era of symbol dissection indicates how indispensable the role of the analogue is to the process of human communication, even in a computer technology. The essence of symbolism is merely the deceptively simple ability to create the appropriate analogue (thence symbol) of the appropriate object at the appropriate time.

NOTES

[1] Kenneth Burke, *Language as Symbolic Action* (Berkeley and Los Angeles: University of California Press, 1966), p. 16. This is a recent collection of essays, poems, papers, criticism and other odds and ends, and comprises a hearteningly lucid collection of Burke's ideas. Since it may be examined almost at random and deals with the entire range of the author's interests, it is especially recommended for readers who may have become discouraged by the density of Burke's more formal books.

[2] *Ibid.,* pp. 3–22.

[3] Ludwig von Bertalanffy, "The Tree of Knowledge" in Gyorgy Kepes, *op. cit.,* p. 274.

[4] Alfred North Whitehead, *Symbolism* (New York: The Macmillan Company, 1958), pp. 1–6. Whitehead's concept of symbolism will form the matrix for the discussion of symbolism in society in Chapter V, and therefore will be discussed only briefly here. The author wishes, however, at this point to record his indebtedness to Dr. Joe R. Burnett of the University of Illinois for his patient instruction in Whitehead's thinking while they were colleagues at New York University.

[5] *Ibid.,* p. 6.

[6] Burke, *op. cit.,* p. 5.

[7] Psychological reasons for this phenomenon may elicit considerable speculation. Plato's allegory of the cave gives us one clue: that men born and raised in an environment of darkness cannot conceive of sunlight. Carried further, a prisoner is not free to roam at will, whether or not he is ignorant of the fact that he is imprisoned. His logical condition (of incarceration) is the reality through which he is forced to live, and what he knows (or does not know) is irrelevant to his condition. It is difficult to say that we are "imprisoned" by our symbol systems, but in many ways this is how it appears. When we reach beyond them, our behavior is apt to be regarded as deviant, and we may even run into trouble with that great symbol of societal order: the law. We are thus impelled by ongoing pressures to continue symbolic cooperations which our society demands from us.

[8] Ashley Montagu, "Communication, Evolution, Education," in Matson and Montagu, *op. cit.,* p. 446.

[9] Langer, *Feeling and Form,* p. 11.

[10] Certain kinds of surrealistic paintings deal with symbols in this manner, but they *never* articulate a symbolic sentence with linguistic rigor. Each painting, so "loaded" with symbolic material becomes a new *inter*-symbol of new interest in its own right.

[11] Mordecai Gorelick, *New Theatres for Old* (New York: Samuel French, 1947), pp. 189–190.

[12] This was the same mystique one finds in the work of Nietzsche. Hitler utilized it as a propaganda tool years later in his deliberate grasp at potent symbols to capture the loyalty of the German people.

[13] *Ibid.,* p. 190.

[14] Wagner's operas continue to move the vulnerable and to provide podiums for the virtuosity of certain kinds of singers. To some they are as repellant as they are attractive to others, largely, one suspects, because of the relevance of the symbolic manipulation they involve to the value and peculiar (sic) symbol sensivities of the auditor's. What is curious is not that Germanic symbolism had such power in the theatre, but that the construct of the "Wagnerian type" symbol clings so consistently at present to Middle European-style of thought, even at the hands of so Americanized a thinker as Langer. Her debt to the Germanic fashion of symbolic analysis—especially that of Rudolph Carnap and Ernst Cassirer—is obvious. Note her agreement with Cassirer's basic psychological observation about symbolism: that to the naïve mind it "is not sharply divided into symbol and object, but both tend to unite in a perfectly undif-

ferentiated fusion," as quoted in Susanne K. Langer, *Philosophy in a New Key* (New York: The New American Library, 1948), p. 199. The statement appears to include the conceptual springboard for her own discussion of symbolism, but it might satisfy the most avid Wagnerian.

[15] Clark L. Hull, *Principles of Behavior* (New Haven: Yale University Press, 1952), p. 399.

[16] See Clark L. Hull *et al., Mathematico-Deductive Theory of Rote Learning* (New Haven: Yale University Press, 1940), for, at least, statements of the promises offered by Hull's psychological system.

[17] See William James, *Varieties of Religious Experience* (New York: The New American Library, 1958). This classic work was originally published in 1902.

[18] See James G. Frazer, *The Golden Bough* (New York: The Macmillan Company, 1923). The one volume abridged edition is sufficient for readers whose intention is to acquaint themselves with the general range of this remarkable study.

[19] Anselm Strauss, *The Social Psychology of George Herbert Mead* (Chicago: The University of Chicago Press, 1956), p. 224 (italics added). Mead notes that dissemblers and actors may be exceptions here, who, in a sense, know *more* than their audience does. An actor, says Mead, is "able to respond to his own gesture in same sense as his audience does."

[20] *Ibid.,* p. 198.

[21] S. Gideon, "Symbolic Expression in Prehistory and in the First High Civilizations," in Kepes, *op. cit.,* p. 79.

[22] *Ibid.,* p. 87.

[23] See Charles Morris, *Signs, Language and Behavior* (New York: George Braziller Inc. 1955), pp. 23–27. Morris is concerned almost entirely with the semantic restrictions upon the use of the word "symbol" and apparently with their function in facilitating psychologically man's control of his environment.

[24] From ON AGGRESSION by Konrad Lorenz., copyright © 1963, by Dr. Borotha-Schoeler Verlag, Wien, Austria; English translation, copyright © 1966 by Konrad Lorenz. All quotes reprinted by permission of Harcourt, Brace & World, Inc.

[25] The same observation may be made, of course, of the totally religious Christmas. The *symbol* of Christ the messiah has been elaborated into a complex ceremony accenting birth, love, peace and benevolence. This ceremony (formulated in an exciting era of intellectual revolt and philosophical activity) appears to offer the masses less psychological satisfaction than the religious-materialist Christmas in America and some parts of Western Europe. In the U.S.S.R. the virtual abolition of the religious Christmas and the preservation of the pagan one appears to have solved contradictions between the two. Possibly the Soviet ceremony absolves the participants of a sense of hypocrisy on the one hand and satisfies yearnings for "old fashioned" religion on the other.

[26] Burke, *op. cit., pp.* 44–45.

[27] *Ibid.,* p. 44.

[28] Note particularly of the abundance of Marxist symbolic criticism which was brought to much literature, contemporoary and classic, during the nineteen-thirties, as well as the psychoanalytic-oriented middle-class criticism, now so prevalent in fashionable magazines.

[29] See Chapters 7, 8, 9 and 10.

[30] Burke, *op. cit.,* p. 49.

[31] Daniel J. Boorstein, *The Image* (New York: Harper and Row, 1964).

[32] Otto Fenichel, *The Pschoanalytic Theory of Neurosis* (New York: W. W. Norton and Company, Inc., 1945), p. 422. (italics added.) Fenichel, like most Freudians of his period, tends to regard symbol-making as ego regressive, distortive and pre-logical—a magical antithesis to the "reality principle" and logic. The particular symbols of most interest to therapists are those which neurotic patients frequently employ to deny some aspects of reality and which seem to be generated spontaneously in patient after patient. See *Ibid., pp.* 48–51.

[33] See the classic, S. I. Hayakawa's *Language in Thought and Action (New York: Harcourt, Brace and Company, 1949), for a well written, simple and frequently amusing explanation in layman's terms of the General Semanticist's position. The nä*iveté of the movement is immediately apparent in Hayakawa's discourse, particularly in regard to the treatment of symbols in culture. The book contains, however, numerous valuable common sense observations about language.

[34] Langer, *Philosophy in a New Key,* p. 201. (Italics are Langer's.)

4.

AXIOMATIC PROPOSITIONS

HUGH DUNCAN

AXIOMATIC PROPOSITION 1
**Society arises in, and continues to exist through, the communication of
significant symbols.**

. . . By "significant symbol" we mean a symbol which not only "signals" to
or "stimulates" another, but also arouses in the self the same meaning it does in
others. Like Mead, we say that the significant symbol, like all spoken symbols, is
an expression experienced as a form of address to the self when it is addressed to
another. Communication thus determines social relationships because language
gives us the capacity to indicate to ourselves what other persons are going to do, and
then to assume their attitudes on the basis of that indication.

No theoretical social system can be constructed without *some* category of communication. Even Parsons, whose equilibrium model of sociation is mechanistic,
says that his social system could not be constructed without taking language into account, and in his discussion of his action frame of reference he tells us that the
elaboration of human action systems would be impossible without relatively stable
symbolic systems. For without such systems the "situations" of two actors could
never be identical, and if we could not abstract meanings from particular situations,
communication would be impossible. The stability of a symbol system, in turn, extends between individuals and over time because it occurs in a connection process
determined by the interaction of a plurality of actors. In saying this, Parsons
expresses a traditional sociological view: that it is impossible to think about society
without thinking about symbols.

. . . Now if symbols do what they are said to do by philosophers, anthropologists, sociologists, psychologists, educators, and then communication must be a
constituent category of experience. And if we refuse to believe that symbols, like
Jung's engrams or Freud's memory-traces, are "derived" from some kind of archaic heritage or archetypes which are passed on through the "collective unconscious," then we must show how symbols do affect social relationships. If we say
that we cannot act toward objects and persons until they are named, and that the process of naming is a symbolic process, and, finally, that this process is subject to
laws, we must state the grounds for this assertion. The search then for an understanding of how society and communication are related must *begin* with questions
on *how* symbolic laws operate in social communication, not with statements, however elaborate, that there are such laws, or that because we use certain techniques to

Reprinted by permission from *Symbols in Society,* Oxford University Press, 1968.

study communication, that this is the way communication "works" in social relationships.

Man creates the significant symbols he uses in communication.

Machines signal through built-in message tracks, animals communicate through gesture and sound, but man, and man alone, *creates* the symbols he uses in communication. He is able not only to communicate, but to communicate about communication. No matter how "fixed" a meaning may be in ritual, magic, or tradition, it must always pass the test of relevance; that is, it must help men to deal with problems which arise as men act together. Action is always tested in the symbolic phase of the act by exploring in imagination of the past and future the ways in which ends and means can be related to action in the present. All symbolic phases of action are hypothetical. We act "as if" the way we are acting will reach an imagined end, and the end imagined determines the means we select to reach this end. Thus, while action may be fixed in tradition, it is fixed only so long as traditional forms of expression help us to organize activity in a present, just as utopian forms of expression are fixed as permanent goals only so long as they help to solve problems in the present. The present, in which man communicates with other men, is the locus of social interaction.

Emotions, as well as thought and will, are learned in communication.

A feeling is a somatic charge, not an emotion. I feel hungry, but I satisfy my hunger through the conventions of eating proper to those with whom I eat. I feel sexual desire, but I can find a "proper" sexual partner only through observing the proprieties of courtship. We "need" a woman as a "sexual outlet" but we demand a certain kind of woman, not any woman. I want to rule others, but I must rule according to proper canons of ruling. Emotions thus depend on formal expression. There is no unexpressed emotion, for there can be no emotion until the feelings, which are the biological base of an emotion, are expressed. *How* an emotion is expressed, the *form* in which it is expressed, determines its effect just as thought in mathematics is determined by the kind of mathematical symbols available for use in such thought. Emotions arise *in* communication. At birth we do not know shame, envy, pride, disgust, remorse, and the thousand and one emotional nuances we "feel" as we act together. We learn these "social feelings" in communication with others whose response teaches us what our acts mean to them, and thus to ourselves, as we play out roles in the community.

AXIOMATIC PROPOSITION 4

Symbols affect social motives by determining the forms in which the contents of relationships can be expressed.

All social relations are born in appeals to others to respond to us in ways which satisfy social, as well as physical, personal, supernatural, and linguistic needs. The child cries and reaches for the breast of the mother, men and women court each other to relate sexually and to create families, superiors parade before inferiors to convince them (and themselves) of their majesty and sublimity. *How* they express needs, the *forms* of expression, determine satisfaction. Without form there can be no content, just as without content form becomes meaningless in social experience. And in purely social relations, as Simmel points out, we play society through social forms called manners, whose meaning (in purely social moments, at least) can be explained only by our pleasure in the formal play itself. Manners determine status, but they also are forms of sociation which bind us together in moments of pure sociability simply by their power *as* forms.

Images, visions, and all imaginings of the future are symbolic forms, for when the future becomes the present, and thus becomes "real," new features are created to guide our search for solutions to problems in the present which emerge as we try to create order in our relationships. Every act contains a past, present, and a future, but the temporal structure and function of symbolic actions is determined by our need to act in a present. We turn to the past, as well as to the future, to create forms in which we can act. The recapture of the past is really a reconstruction, just as the vision of the future is not "real" as action in a present where our relations are both "real" and "symbolic." But even the simplest motor act can be directed to its end only through the organization of attitudes that direct this act to an imagined goal. Attitudes are formed in communication, because only in communication can we envision the end we hope to reach in acting together. So, unless we assume that action is "patterned" by some extrasymbolic "force," or is "determined" by a past, or a future, or is simply a random activity, we must assume that action is determined by the forms in which men communicate as they act together, and that the creation of such forms is, therefore, the creation of the ways in which we relate in society.

AXIOMATIC PROPOSITION 5

From a sociological view motives must be understood as man's need for order in his social relationships.

Some kind of structure must exist in social relationships if we are to act at all. Such structures range from the loose informal ties of a small group sauntering down a street, to the highly formal "sacred" order of a religious body. Man in society, we are told by social theorists, is determined variously by nature, family, economics, politics, or God. And so he is. All we can stress as sociologists is the irreducible *social* element, the need for forms of relationships with others, which is the basis of human society.

. . . Social forms, the *ways* in which we satisfy needs, determine the satisfaction of the needs. Needs are always satisfied in relationships; relationships, in turn, are possible only because we understand what people mean by the forms in which they play their roles. Role-playing is the enactment of a part in some kind of social drama which, from a purely sociological view, is a drama of order. Social drama is a drama of legitimation, the attempt to legitimize authority by persuading those involved that such order is "necessary" to the survival of the community. In personal relations, manners, customs, tradition, mores, and style are used to legitimize our right to purely social status. It is *how* we court, *how* we eat, *how* we rule and are ruled, *how* we worship, and even *how* we die, in short, the forms in which we act, that determine our feelings of propriety regarding our own actions and the actions of others. For it is through such forms that we interpret the meaning of actions performed by others, just as they interpret the meaning of our performance. Such forms, then, *are* the relationships between us.

AXIOMATIC PROPOSITION 6
Symbols are directly observable data of meaning in social relationships.

. . . All we know about the meaning of what happened, or is happening, in a social relationship is what someone says about its meaning. "Saying" involves many kinds of expression. A diplomat *participates* in foreign negotiations. Historians *describe* a battle. An Australian savage *dances* the history of his tribe. The Indian *paints* his myths of tribal origin in sand. Witnesses verify what "really happened" through creating expressive forms in which they depict the event. Ascriptions of meaning to forces, processes, energy, or cathexis, are based on analogies, not on direct observations of concrete human acts. Like all analogies, such ascriptions are interpretations, *not* observations. If we follow the canon of parsimony in science, we must, in our study of society, turn to the most directly observable of all social data, namely, the symbols we use in social relationships.

AXIOMATIC PROPOSITION 7
Social order is expressed through hierarchies which differentiate men into ranks, classes, and status groups, and, at the same time, resolve differentiation through appeals to principles of order which transcend those upon which differentiation is based.

. . . Social order is always expressed in some kind of hierarchy. This differentiates men and women in ranks determined by age, sex, family lineage, skill, ownership, or authority, which are scaled in some kind of social ladder. Such differentiation is always resolved through appeals to some universal "higher" principle superior to local principles in which ultimate principles are "latent," or struggling to perfection. Men and women differ greatly in their masculinity and femininity, and make every attempt to express this difference in dress, manners, bearing, and behavior, but this difference must be subordinated to a "higher" social principle of marriage, love, or parenthood. Social classes and status groups struggle to differentiate from each other, but they can do so only because their differentiation is understood as a "way" to some kind of order which transcends their differences.

Authorities seek to invest local symbols, the symbols of their institutions, class, or status groups, with universal symbols which are "above" local concern. This is done by persuading us that local symbols will guarantee social order because in using them we pass from a "lower" to a "higher" meaning. In language we move from the particular to the general, in religion from man to God, in science from description to analyses, in law from anarchy to order, in nature from the animal to the human. Sexual love is justified only because through such love we create a family, and through learning to love our family we learn to love our community, until finally we learn to love God. Thus, we justify each level as a step toward a higher level, and every level is invested with belief in some "final" or "universal" kind of order which justifies hierarchal differentiation because the immanence of a final end (the moment of transcendence) makes each a step toward the absolute where all steps end—as they begin.

AXIOMATIC PROPOSITION 8
Hierarchy is expressed through the symbolization of superiority, inferiority, and equality, and of passage from one to the other.

In hierarchal relations we are superiors, inferiors, or equals, and we must be prepared to pass one position to another as we are born, marry, age, and die. Positions of superiority, inferiority, and equality must be be signified clearly, and we must be taught, as we must teach others, how to play roles as inferiors, superiors, and equals. This is true of all societies. Even the most powerful father must meet as an equal with other powerful fathers to decide issues which cannot be decided within the family alone. The proud aristocrat must meet with other aristocrats in courts of honor where all are equal in the honor of rank, if not in wealth, power, and skill. In times of war democratic communities give their war leaders absolute power.

Positions of superiority, inferiority, and equality are fixed, but only through passage from one to the other. Fixed social positions can be opened to new members, and can be filled with those who possess skills required for community survival. There is a time, in intimate familial relations as in the community, to rule, but there is a time to be ruled, and, finally, there is a time to die. There is a time to wage war and a time to seek peace. If we are to live in peace, leadership of the community must pass from men of war to men of peace. Passage always involves desanctifying the old, providing bridges from the old to the new, and entering—or, more rarely, creating—a new role. These moments of passage are a constituent element in hierarchy and must never be subordinated in theory to "changeless" sacred moments of fixed positions of social order. A social order is an order *in,* as well as *beyond,* change. A social structure exists *in passage from old to new, as well as in fixed principles of order.*

AXIOMATIC PROPOSITION 9
Hierarchy functions through persuasion, which takes the form of courtship in social relationships.

Superiors must *persuade* inferiors to accept their rule. This is done through the glorification of symbols of majesty and power as symbols of social order in many kinds of social dramas wherein the power and the glory of the ruler as a "representative" of some transcendent principle of social order is dramatized. Such dramatization is intended to create and uphold the dignity of the office as a representation of a principle of social order, not the man himself. Hitler did not rule as a man, but as a "savior" of the German people. His life was an allegory of every German life. His mandate, so he taught and so his followers believed, came from some supernatural "historic" source. He was an agent of a "higher power," whose mystery could be penetrated only by semidivine heroes who did what they "had to do" because they were moved by a divine historic will. Yet no one in modern times was more careful than Hitler to stage great community dramas in which the German people were persuaded to believe in laws of destiny which were immutable and "beyond" reason.

Inferiors must persuade superiors to accept them as loyal followers, but in doing so they must subordinate themselves to principles of order, as well as to the personal will of their superiors. The ideal subordinate (from the superior as well as the inferior point of view) must believe in the "right" of his superior to rule because he rules in the name of a "sacred" principle of order. Max Weber calls such beliefs "legitimations," and distinguishes tradition, charisma, law, and usage as grounds for such rights. We ask inferiors to obey us because what we ask them to do has always been done in a certain way (as when we teach children table manners).

. . . The greatest analogue for courtship (in contemporary discussion) is sexual courtship, but the forms of sexual courtship are really derived from historical forms of social courtship. We do not seek "sexual outlets," but "sexual partners," and in our society we seek partners in a drama of romantic love called courtship. In this "feudalization of love," it is the social, as well as the sexual, expression which determines success in erotic love. In our tradition of courtship, we must be humble, courteous (that is, be a "gentleman"), and convey the conviction (if only for a few months) that "love is all that matters." As lovers, we must be humble and abject in our devotion to our "beloved." We must obey our lady's slightest wish, indulge her whims, and acquiesce in her rebukes (however unjust). Love is a "service" (in our society a service of money), a vassalage of an inferior to a superior. But for the superior it is also a service in which he pays homage to the spirit of love. The beloved, too, is bound by the conventions of her court. She must be a "lady," which in our society means she must know how to spend money "graciously" (as we see in the "Christmas madonna," the giver of gifts money will buy).

There is equality, as well as superiority and inferiority, in social relations, and if we are to live successfully in society (authoritarian and democratic alike) we must learn to live in agreement with peers, as well as to command inferiors and to obey superiors. Peer relationships are public in committee relationships, comradeship in arms, membership on a team, and in all forms of play; they are private in friendship. We learn to relate as equals by acting together under rules, for only through rules which are subject to change by those who made them (and thus represent the will of equals) is democratic community possible—just as only through open, free, and intimate talk is equality among individuals possible. We court friends because a friend is another self, the most important self to our development as an individual. In talk as friends we explore the meaning of social experience, our role playing, on a very personal basis. The burdens of rank fall away in all equal relationships; we know as equals that agreement under rules binds us together, and while we recognize the compelling nature of bonds forged under rules (as in concepts of honor), we know that we can change them through common agreement.

AXIOMATIC PROPOSITION 10
The expression of hierarchy is best conceived through forms of drama which are both comic and tragic.

The social drama of hierarchy is both comic and tragic. Those in power present themselves as heroes struggling against villainous powers who seek to destroy sacred principles of social order. When we suffer deep guilt, or live in fear of defeat, we turn to tragedy, which is based on a principle of victimage. Tragic victims range from the public scapegoat on whom we project our evil to a guilty inner self whose punishment expiates our sin. In the eyes of authority, sin is simply disobedience, "the breaking of the commandments," and guilt is fear of being excommunicated by authorities with whom we must communicate if we are to have order in our relationships, and thus to be saved from the stress of disorder and the chaos of revolt.

Since the social appeal of tragedy is based on guilt and fear, and offers us vicarious atonement through the suffering and death of the sacrificial victim, its power is very great. We cannot live long in fear, any more than we can long endure a heavy burden of guilt. Public punishment of others, like public and private punishment of the self, is a kind of purgation. As we revile, torture, and kill the villain, either on the stage or in the streets (as when we torture and kill a Negro, execute a criminal, or hunt down Jews to ship them off as victims for ritual cleansing of German blood in torture and death), we personify our fear and guilt. Because of such personification, we are able to act, as well as to feel, and to think, "about" our guilt. In social, political, and art dramas, we enact a drama of purgation, a drama in which dark fears are given forms, and thus brought into consciousness, so we can express attitudes and take part in actions necessary to the riddance of fear and guilt. Tragedy thrives on mystery; it makes its final appeal to ultimate and supernatural powers through invoking mysterious and dark powers with whom we seek to communicate even though we may believe that such powers are "beyond" communication.

The social appeal of comedy is based on belief in reason in society. Comedy is sanctioned doubt, a permitted and honored way of expressing doubt over the majesty and wisdom of our superiors, the loyalty and devotion of our inferiors, and the trust of our friends. Comedy, like tragedy, punishes the "sin of pride," but of pride against men, not the gods. Comedy teaches us that only so long as reason can function openly in society can men confront and correct their evil as men, not as cowering slaves or as worshipers of gods who "reveal" but do not communicate their truths to men. Comedy teaches that whatever separates men from men, not from the gods as in tragedy, is evil. The ultimate good in comedy is a social good which can be reached only so long as men can communicate freely as men. Comedy is never simply an "escape valve" or a way of "blowing off steam," but a form in which we bring into consciousness the many incongruities between ends and the means employed to achieve them. Tyrannies and democracies alike use comedy for this purpose. *Krokodil,* which circulates widely through the Soviet Union, is the *official* Soviet humor magazine.

AXIOMATIC PROPOSITION 11

Social order is created and sustained in social dramas through intensive and frequent communal presentations of tragic and comic roles whose proper enactment is believed necessary to community survival.

The community is kept alive only by intense and frequent reenactments of the roles believed necessary to social order. Savages dancing before the evening fire, college students cheering and snakedancing at a pre-game rally, political parties parading down main street, women thronging to a fashion show, salesmen gathering for a rally before the opening of the "Big Sale," are creating or recreating the meaning and purpose of their roles. In dancing, cheering, singing, talking, or marching together, we develop a deep sense of community because we are acting out in the presence of each other the roles we believe necessary to life in the community. Social euphoria, born of laughter, deepens our social bonds; simply being together in euphoric moments becomes a kind of communion. Comedy allows us to face problems in community life which we cannot face in any other way. To blaspheme against God brings swift and terrible punishment, but in jokes about gods, parents, and all authority, we are permitted to say things which do not threaten the majesty and mystery of our gods, even though their mystery is opened to doubt and inquiry.

Social groups must stage themselves before audiences whose approval legitimizes their power. Audiences, in turn, must see the problems of the community acted out in some kind of dramatic presentation, for it is only through the forms created in such action that community problems become comprehensible as *actions.* We learn to act, not simply by preparing to act, or by thinking "about" action, but by playing roles in various kinds of dramas. These roles begin in simple play, then pass to games, festivals, and ceremonies, and the formal dramas of art, until finally we end in rites which fix community values. The artist struggles to achieve a "pure" form of art in his dramatic presentations, but whatever his intention, his community turns to him to learn how to stage dramas of community life, just as the individual turns to art to discover forms which he can use in playing his own role in society. The staging of roles in dramatic structures is, then, a staging, or presentation, of our selves to public and private audiences whose approval gives us a sense of identity or belonging.

AXIOMATIC PROPOSITION 12

Social order is always a resolution of acceptance, doubt, or rejection of the principles that are believed to guarantee such order.

Order in society comes from resolving conflicting claims to power. There are three basic modes of adjustment to those who seek to legitimize their power over us in the name of some principle of social order. We may accept their commandments as our duty; we may doubt their commandments, in the hope that in doubt and inquiry we can overcome incongruity; or we may reject them. Doubt is not simply the absence of belief, but a method of inquiry which society institutionalizes as much as it does acceptance and rejection of principles of order in religion and politics. Our schools teach us to question how we know what we know, and thus institutionalizes critical intelligence; our comedy clarifies incongruities between ideals and practices; our parties in power (in democracies, at least) honor their "loyal" opposition; our businessmen use commercial magicians to make customers doubtful and discontented with what they have. Criticism (in its various social forms) exists when a lack of congruity between means and ends is recognized, and when there is hope that such incongruities, once recognized, can be overcome. In democratic society the expression of difference in debate, discussion, and argument is not a way to discord but to a superior truth, because opposition, in competition and rivalry, makes us think harder about the rights of others and leads us to act in more humane ways. It is our *duty* to disagree, if only to *help* our opponent, as we in turn expect him to disagree with us, for in doing so he tests our thought. Thus, in our society, the ability to tolerate disagreement, and in turn, to develop skill in argument and disputation, is considered strength, not weakness.

5.

SOCIETY AS DRAMA

Peter Berger

We arrive at a third picture of society, after those of the prison and the puppet theater, namely that of society as a stage populated with living actors. This third picture does not obliterate the previous two, but it is more adequate in terms of the additional social phenomena we have considered. That is, the dramatic model of society at which we have arrived now does not deny that the actors on the stage are

From *Invitation to Sociology*, copyright © 1963 by Peter L. Berger. Reprinted by permission of Doubleday & Company, Inc.

constrained by all the external controls set up by the impresario and the internal ones of the role itself. All the same, they have options—of playing their parts enthusiastically or sullenly, of playing with inner conviction or with "distance," and, sometimes, of refusing to play at all. Looking at society through the medium of this dramatic model greatly changes our general sociological perspective. Social reality now seems to be precariously perched on the cooperation of many individual actors—or perhaps a better simile would be that of acrobats engaged in perilous balancing acts, holding up between them the swaying structure of the social world.

Stage, theater, circus and even carnival—here we have the imagery of our dramatic model, with a conception of society as precarious, uncertain, often unpredictable. The institutions of society, while they do in fact constrain and coerce us, appear at the same time as dramatic conventions, even fictions. They have been invented by past impresarios, and future ones may cast them back into the nothingness whence they emerged. Acting out the social drama we keep pretending that these precarious conventions are eternal verities. We act *as if* there were no other way of being a man, a political subject, a religious devotee or one who exercises a certain profession—yet at times the thought passes through the minds of even the dimmest among us that we could do very, very different things. If social reality is dramatically created, it must also be dramatically malleable. In this way, the dramatic model opens up a passage out of the rigid determinism into which sociological thought originally led us.

Before we leave behind us our narrower sociological argument who would like to point to a classical contribution that is very relevant to the points just made—the theory of sociability of the German sociologist Georg Simmel, a contemporary of Weber's whose approach to sociology differed considerably from the latter's. Simmel argued that sociability (in the usual meaning of this word) is the play-form of social interaction. At a party people "play society," that is, they engage in many forms of social interaction, but without their usual sting of seriousness. Sociability changes serious communication to noncommittal conversation, *eros* to coquetry, ethics to manners, aesthetics to taste. As Simmel shows, the world of sociability is a precarious and artificial creation that can be shattered at any moment by someone who refuses to play the game. The man who engages in passionate debate at a party spoils the game, as does the one who carries flirtation to the point of open seduction (a party is *not* an orgy) or the one who openly promotes business interests under the guise of harmless chitchat (party conversation must at least pretend to be disinterested). Those who participate in a situation of pure sociability temporarily leave behind their "serious" identities and move into transitory world of make-believe, which consists among other things of the playful pretense that those concerned have been freed from the weights of position, property and passions normally attached to them. Anyone who brings in the gravity (in both senses of the word) of "serious" outside interests immediately shatters this fragile artifice of make-believe. This, incidentally, is why pure sociability is rarely possible except among social equals, since otherwise the pretense is too strenuous to maintain—as every office party shows painfully.

We are not particularly interested in the phenomenon of sociability for its own sake, but we can now relate what Simmel maintains about it to our earlier consideration of Mead's notion that social roles are learned through play. We contend that sociability could not exist at all as the artifice it is if society at large did not have a similarly artificial character. In other words, sociability is a special case of "playing society," more consciously fictitious, less tied up with the urgent ambitions of one's career—but yet of one piece with a much larger social fabric that one can also play with. It is precisely through such play, as we have seen, that the child learns to take on his "serious" roles. In sociability we return for some moments to the masquerading of childhood—hence perhaps the pleasure of it.

But it is assuming too much to think that the masks of the "serious" world are terribly different from those of this world of play. One plays the masterful *raconteur* at the party and the man of firm will at the office. Party tact has a way of being translated into political finesse, shrewdness in business into the adroit handling of etiquette for purposes of sociability. Or, if you like, there is a nexus between "social graces" and social skills in general. In this fact lies the sociological justification of the "social" training of diplomats as well as of debutantes. By "playing society" one learns how to be a social actor anywhere. And this is possible only because society as a whole has the character of a play. As the Dutch historian Johan Huizinga has brilliantly shown in his book *Homo ludens,* it is impossible to grasp human culture at all unless we look at it *sub specie ludi*—under the aspect of play and playfulness.

With these thoughts we have come to the very limits of what it is still possible to say within a social-scientific frame of reference. Within the latter, we cannot go any further in lifting from the reader the deterministic burden of our earlier argumentation. Compared with this argumentation, what has been said in the present chapter so far may appear rather weak and less than conclusive. This is unavoidable. To repeat ourselves, it is impossible *a priori* to come upon freedom in its full sense by scientific means or within a scientific universe of discourse. The closest we have been able to come is to show, in certain situations, a certain freedom *from* social controls. We cannot possibly discover freedom *to* act socially by scientific means. Even if we should find holes in the order of causality that can be established sociologically, the psychologist, the biologist or some other dealer in causations will step in and stuff up our hole with materials spun from *his* cloth of determinism. But since we have made no promises in this book to limit ourselves ascetically to scientific logic, we are now ready to approach social existence from a very different direction. We have not been able to get at freedom sociologically, and we realize that we never can. So be it. Let us see now how we can look at our sociological model itself from a different vantage point.

As we remarked before, only an intellectual barbarian is likely to maintain that reality is only that which can be grasped by scientific methods. Since, hopefully, we have tried to stay out of this category, our sociologizing has been carried on in the foreground of another view of human existence that is not itself sociological or even scientific. Nor is this view particularly eccentric, but rather the common (if very differently elaborated) anthropology of those who credit man with the capacity for freedom. Obviously a philosophical discussion of such an anthropology would utterly break the framework of this book and would, for that matter, lie beyond the competence of its writer. But while no attempt will be made here to provide a philosophical introduction to the question of human freedom, it is necessary to our argument that at least some indications be given of how it is possible to think sociologically without abandoning this notion of freedom, and, more than that, in what way a view of man that includes the idea of freedom may take cognizance of the social dimension. We contend that here is an important area of dialogue between philosophy and the social sciences that still contains vast tracts of virgin territory. We point to the work of Alfred Schuetz and to the contemporary efforts of Maurice Natanson as indicating the direction in which this dialogue could move. Our own remarks in the following pages will, of necessity, be exceedingly sketchy. But it is hoped that they will suffice to indicate to the reader that sociological thought need not necessarily end in a positivistic swamp.

We shall now begin with the postulate that men are free and from this new starting point return to the same problem of social existence. In doing this, we shall find helpful some concepts developed by existentialist philosophers (though we shall use these without any doctrinaire intentions). Herewith the reader is invited to undertake an epistemological *salto mortale*—and this behind him, to return to the matter at hand.

Let us retrace our steps to the point where we looked at Gehlen's theory of institutions. The latter, we will recall, are interpreted in this theory as channeling human conduct very much along the lines that instincts channel the behavior of animals. When we considered this theory, we made the remark that there is, however, one crucial difference between the two kinds of channeling: The animal, if it reflected on the matter of following its instincts, would say, "I have no choice." Men, explaining why they obey their institutional imperatives, say the same. The difference is that the animal would be saying the truth; the men are deceiving themselves. Why? Because, in fact, they *can* say "no" to society, and often have done so. There may be very unpleasant consequences if they take this course. They may not even think about it as a possibility, because they take their own obedience for granted. Their institutional character may be the only identity they can imagine having, with the alternative seeming to them as a jump into madness. This does not change the fact that the statement "I must" is a deceptive one in almost every social situation.

From our new vantage point, within an anthropological frame of reference that recognizes man as free, we can usefully apply to this problem what Jean-Paul Sartre has called "bad faith." To put it very simply, "bad faith" is to pretend something is necessary that in fact is voluntary. "Bad faith" is thus a flight from freedom, a dishonest evasion of the "agony of choice." "Bad faith" expresses itself in innumerable human situations from the most commonplace to the most catastrophic. The waiter shuffling through his appointed rounds in a café is in "bad faith" insofar as he pretends to himself that the waiter role constitutes his real existence, that, if only for the hours he is hired, he *is* the waiter. The woman who lets her body be seduced step by step while continuing to carry on an innocent conversation is in "bad faith," insofar as she pretends that what is happening to her body is not under her control. The terrorist who kills excuses himself by saying that he had no choice because the party ordered him to kill is in "bad faith," because he pretends that his existence is necessarily linked with the party, while in fact this linkage is the consequence of his own choice. It can easily be seen that "bad faith" covers society like a film of lies. The very possibility of "bad faith," however, shows us the reality of freedom. Man can be in "bad faith" only because he is free and does not wish to face his freedom. "Bad faith" is the shadow of human liberty. Its attempt to escape that liberty is doomed to defeat. For, as Sartre has famously put it, we are "condemned to freedom."

If we apply this concept to our sociological perspective, we will suddenly be faced with a startling conclusion. The complex of roles within which we exist in society now appears to us as an immense apparatus of "bad faith." Each role carries with it the possibility of "bad faith." Every man who says "I have no choice" in referring to what his social role demands of him is engaged in "bad faith." Now, we can easily imgine circumstances in which this confession will be true to the extent that there is no choice *within that particular role*. Nevertheless, the individual has the choice of stepping outside the role. It is true that, given certain circumstances, a businessman has "no choice" but brutally to destroy a competitor, unless he is to go bankrupt himself, but it is he who chooses brutality over bankruptcy. It is true that a man has "no choice" but to betray a homosexual attachment if he is to retain his position in respectable society, but he is the one making the choice between respectability and loyalty to that attachment. It is true that in some cases a judge has "no choice" but to sentence a man to death, but in doing so he chooses to remain a judge, an occupation chosen by him in the knowledge that it might lead to this, and he chooses not to resign instead when faced with the prospect of this duty. Men are responsible for their actions. They are in "bad faith" when they attribute to iron necessity what they themselves are choosing to do. Even the law itself, that master fortress of "bad faith," has begun to take cognizance of that fact in its dealings with Nazi war criminals.

Sartre has given us a masterful vista of the operation of "bad faith" at its most malevolent in his portrayal of the anti-Semite as a human type. The anti-Semite is the man who frantically identifies himself with mythological entities ("nation," "race," *"Volk"*) and in doing so seeks to divest himself of the knowledge of his own freedom. Anti-Semitism (or, we might add, any other form of racism or fanatical nationalism) is "bad faith" *par excellence* because it identifies men in their human totality with their social character. Humanity itself becomes a facticity devoid of freedom. One then loves, hates and kills within a mythological world in which all men *are* their social designations, as the SS man *is* what his insignia say and the Jew *is* the symbol of despicability sewn on his concentration-camp uniform.

"Bad faith" in this form of ultimate malignancy, however, is not limited to the Kafkaesque world of Nazism and its totalitarian analogies. It exists in our own society in identical patterns of self-deception. It is only as one long series of acts of "bad faith" that capital punishment continues to exist in allegedly humane societies. Our torturers, just like Nazi ones, present themselves as conscientious public servants, with an impeccable if mediocre private morality, who reluctantly overcome their weakness in order to do their duty.

We will not at this point go into the ethical implications of such "bad faith." We shall do so briefly in the excursus that follows this chapter. We would rather return here to the startling view of society that we have reached as a result of these considerations. Since society exists as a network of social roles, each one of which can become a chronic or a momentary alibi from taking responsibility for its bearer, we can say that deception and self-deception are at the very heart of social reality. Nor is this an accidental quality that could somehow be eradicated by some moral reformation or other. The deception inherent in social structures is a functional imperative. Society can maintain itself only if its fictions (its "as if" character, to use Hans Vaihinger's term) are accorded ontological status by at least some of its members some of the time—or, let us say, society as we have so far known it in human history.

Society provides for the individual a gigantic mechanism by which he can hide from himself his own freedom. Yet this character of society as an immense conspiracy in "bad faith" is, just as in the case of the individual, but an expression of the possibility of freedom that exists by virtue of society. We are social beings and our existence is bound to specific social locations. The same social situations that can become traps of "bad faith" can also be occasions for freedom. Every social role can be played knowingly or blindly. And insofar as it is played knowingly, it can become a vehicle of our own decisions. Every social institution can be an alibi, an instrument of alienation from our freedom. But at least some institutions can become protective shields for the actions of free men. In this way, an understanding of "bad faith" does not necessarily lead us to a view of society as the universal realm of illusion, but rather illuminates more clearly the paradoxical and infinitely precarious character of social existence.

Another concept of existentialist philosophy useful for our argument is what Martin Heidegger has called *das Man*. The German word is untranslatable literally into English. It is used in German in the same way that "one" is used in English in such a sentence as "One does not do that" (*"Man tut das nicht"*). The French word *on* conveys the same meaning, and José Ortega y Gasset has caught Heidegger's intention well in Spanish with his concept of *lo que se hace*. In other words, *Man* refers to a deliberately vague generality of human beings. It is not this man who will not do this, nor that man, nor you nor I—it is, in some way, all men, but so generally that it may just as well be nobody. It is in this vague sense that a child is told "one does not pick one's nose in public." The concrete child, with his concretely irritating nose, is subsumed under an anonymous generality that has no face—and yet bears down powerfully on the child's conduct. In fact (and this ought to give us a long pause), Heidegger's *Man* bears an uncanny resemblance to what Mead has called the "generalized other."

In Heidegger's system of thought the concept of the *Man* is related to his discussion of authenticity and inauthenticity. To exist authentically is to live in full awareness of the unique, irreplaceable and incomparable quality of one's individuality.

By contrast, inauthentic existence is to lose oneself in the anonymity of the *Man,* surrendering one's uniqueness to the socially constituted abstractions. This is especially important in the way one faces death. The truth of the matter is that it is always one single, solitary individual who dies. But society comforts the bereaved and those who are to die themselves by subsuming each death under general categories that appear to assuage its horror. A man dies, and we say "Well, we all have to go someday." This "we all" is an exact rendition of the *Man*—it is everybody and thus nobody, and by putting ourselves under its generality we hide from ourselves the inevitable fact that we too shall die, singly and solitarily. Heidegger himself has referred to Tolstoi's story *The Death of Ivan Ilyitch* as the best literary expression of inauthenticity in the facing of death. As an illustration of authenticity to the point of torment we would submit Federico García Lorca's unforgettable poem about the death of a bullfighter, *Lament for Ignacio Sánchez Mejías.*

Heidegger's concept of *Man* is relevant for our view of society not so much in its normative as in its cognitive aspects. Under the aspect of "bad faith" we have seen society as a mechanism to provide alibis from freedom. Under the aspect of the *Man* we see society as a defense against terror. Society provides us with taken-for-granted structures (we could also speak here of the "okay world") within which, as long as we follow the rules, we are shielded from the naked terrors of our condition. The "okay world" provides routines and rituals through which these terrors are organized in such a way that we can face them with a measure of calm.

All rites of passage illustrate this function. The miracle of birth, the mystery of desire, the horror of death—all these are carefully camouflaged as we are led gently over one threshold after another, apparently in a natural and self-evident sequence; we all are born, lust and must die, and thus every one of us can be protected against the unthinkable wonder of these events. The *Man* enables us to live inauthentically by sealing up the metaphysical questions that our existence poses. We are surrounded by darkness on all sides as we rush through our brief span of life toward inevitable death. The agonized question "Why?" that almost every man feels at some moment or other as he becomes conscious of his condition is quickly stifled by the cliché answers that society has available. Society provides us with religious systems and social rituals, ready-made, that relieve us of such questioning. The "world-taken-for-granted," the social world that tells us that everything is quite okay, is the location of our inauthenticity.

Let us take a man who wakes up at night from one of those nightmares in which one loses all sense of identity and location. Even in the moment of waking, the reality of one's own being and of one's world appears as a dreamlike phantasmagorion that could vanish or be metamorphosed in the twinkling of an eye. One lies in bed in a sort of metaphysical paralysis, feeling oneself but one step removed from that annihilation that had loomed over one in the nightmare just passed. For a few moments of painfully clear consciousness one is at the point of almost smelling the slow approach of death and, with it, of nothingness. And then one gropes for a cigarette and, as the saying goes, "comes back to reality." One reminds oneself of one's name, address and occupation, of one's plans for the next day. One walks about one's house, full of proofs of past and present identity. One listens to the noises of the city. Perhaps one wakes up wife or children and is reassured by their annoyed protests. Soon one can laughingly dismiss the foolishness of what has just transpired, raid the refrigerator for a bite or the liquor closet for a nightcap, and go to sleep with the determination to dream of one's next promotion.

So far, so good. But what exactly is the "reality" to which one has just returned? It is the "reality" of one's socially constructed world, that "okay world" in which metaphysical questions are always laughable unless they have been captured and castrated in taken-for-granted religious ritualism. The truth is that this "reality" is a very precarious one indeed. Names, addresses, occupations and wives have a way of disappearing. All plans end in extinction. All houses eventually become empty. And even if we live all our lives without having to face the agonizing contingency of all we are and do, in the end we must return to that nightmare moment when we feel ourselves stripped of all names and all identities. What is more, we know this— which makes for the inauthenticity of our scurrying for shelter. Society gives us names to shield us from nothingness. It builds a world for us to live in and thus protects us from the chaos that surrounds us on all sides. It provides us with a language and with meanings that make this world believable. And it supplies a steady chorus of voices that confirm our belief and still our dormant doubts.

Again we would repeat in this slightly altered context what we have said before about "bad faith." It is correct that society, in its aspect of *Man*, is a conspiracy to bring about inauthentic existence. The walls of society are a Potemkin village erected in front of the abyss of being. They function to protect us from terror, to organize for us a cosmos of meaning within which our lives make sense. But it is also true that authentic existence can take place only within society. All meanings are transmitted in social processes. One cannot be human, authentically *or* inauthentically, except in society. And the very avenues that lead to a wondering contemplation of being, be they religious or philosophical or aesthetic, have social locations. Just as society can be a flight from freedom or an occasion for it, society can bury our metaphysical quest or provide forms in which it can be pursued. We come up once more on the persistently Janus-faced paradox of our social existence. All the same, there can be but little doubt that society functions as alibi and as Potemkin village for more people than it functions for as an avenue of liberation. If we maintain that authenticity in society is possible, we are not thereby maintaining that most men are indeed making use of this possibility. Wherever we ourselves may be socially located, one look around us will tell us otherwise.

With these observations we have come once more to the edge of ethical considerations that we want to postpone for another moment. We would stress at this point, however, that "ecstasy," as we have defined it, has metaphysical as well as sociological significance. Only by stepping out of the taken-for-granted routines of society is it possible for us to confront the human condition without comforting mystifications. This does not mean that only the marginal man or the rebel can be authentic. It does mean that freedom presupposes a certain liberation of consciousness. Whatever possibilities of freedom we may have, they cannot be realized if we continue to assume that the "okay world" of society is the only world there is. Society provides us with warm, reasonably comfortable caves, in which we can huddle with our fellows, beating on the drums that drown out the howling hyenas of the surrounding darkness. "Ecstasy" is the act of stepping outside the caves, alone, to face the night.

———————

6.

MAN AS AN ACTOR

Maurice Natanson

There is an evident ambiguity in the title of this paper, for man is both an agent performing acts in the social world and an actor performing in a theatrical play. At least he may be an actor in one sense or the other. Am I going to talk about social reality or the stage? The point is that the two are connected in interesting ways, and I propose to explore the ambiguity—in fact, to capitalize on it. Every actor on the stage is also an actor in ordinary life; every actor in ordinary life is capable of grasping the bare fact, the sheer quality of an actor taking a role in a play. And since mundane existence includes the taking of multiple social roles by all of us, the peculiarity of the problem is marked by its extent: there seems to be social action of a sort in all acting whether ordinary or staged; perhaps there is also a theatrical dimension in all social action. But this is not to tinkle an antique bell, for we already know that "all the world's a stage"; what we don't understand is what a "stage" is, let alone a "world." And most certainly we are unclear as to what "playing a part" means. The metaphor has lost its force for our purposes precisely because its initial power yielded a sense of the mundane which has since come to be incorporated into the mundane: Shakespeare's lines are part of the "world" he originally assaulted with those lines. So too, we might say, contemporary theory of social roles and role-playing are quickly becoming part of the casual order of existence which they were meant to illuminate. What is needed is a fresh viewing of the form and character of action in life and on stage.

What is it like for a member of the audience to see a performance of a stage play? How does stage-action appear to the perceiver who is not part of the play? The paradoxes are striking: the concrete individuals who are the actors in the play are present on the stage only as incidental though necessary accidents; they are and are not there. The audience that comes to see Richard Burton and not Hamlet is either transformed by the performance into seeing Hamlet or else is present at the play in an abortive sense. Burton's father is not Hamlet's father; Burton's life is not Hamlet's life; and Burton survives Hamlet's death at each performance. Nor is it merely a

Reprinted by permission from *Philosophy and Phenomenological Research*, Vol. XXVI, 1966.

matter of seeing Burton *as* Hamlet. It is seeing Hamlet to begin with that is puzzling. Each time I look at the stage when Hamlet is there I see a man of a certain age, weight, height, complexion, etc. The body-fact in terms of credit as the program lists it is that of Burton; the body-acting, the body theatrically incarnate on the stage belongs to Hamlet, *is* Hamlet. Nor will the usual dodges satisfy us. I don't make-believe see, nor willfully suspend my disbelief, nor project the characters and their action in some imaginative mode. I do see Hamlet; I see him through the aesthetics of the play, by which I mean the play-character of all sound, gesture, movement, action. And seeing the play as play is possible through the *epoché* of aesthetic attitude. Here is a mode of seeing, just as seeing the painting as an aesthetic unity is seeing the presentation as that unique being it is, that tableau I see but cannot enter, which I can never change or destroy even if I black over or cut up the canvas. It is the canvas I change, not the aesthetic object. So with the stage play. I see the action as an on-going unity I can only appreciate in its qualitative peculiarity. I am free to leave the theater; I can never leave the play because I never entered it. At best, I can walk out on the particular performance. But then I have severed the aesthetic bond which made the play possible for me. The decision may affect the performers, it cannot affect the characters. Similarly, a coughing, hacking, sneezing, rasping audience may unsettle Richard Burton; it can never disturb Hamlet. It is Hamlet who disturbs Hamlet.

There is, then, a certain insularity to the play as an aesthetic unity. As a member of the audience I cannot affect it. I am bound to my place even if I am free to leave my seat. Though I can disrupt the proceedings by unseemly or even fantastic behavior, I cannot transcend the aesthetic limits of the play. Thus, the paratroopers who caused a scandal at the French production of *The Deputy* by dropping on to the stage from low overhanging balconies in the midst of a performance, shouting *"Á bas les juifs!"* were able to interrupt the performance, not the play. During their demonstration, the play, we suggest, went out of being, retreated into a kind of latency. Aesthetic unity is inviolable from the standpoint of the audience. From the vantage point of the artist, the creator, different questions arise; I will not attempt to deal with them here. The emphasis, by design, is on action in the stage play in terms of the audience and, as we shall see presently, in terms of the stage actors. The aesthetic dynamic under consideration is purposely limited to this range. Within it, though, the problems are real enough. The paradoxes dramatize them.

The stage-actor's realm is equally charged with ambiguity, for a certain deceitfulness pervades his scene. Burton knows what will happen to Hamlet throughout the play, but Hamlet doesn't know. We in the audience know that Burton knows, and Burton knows that we his audience already acquainted with the play know, but Hamlet has no audience. The last point may, of course, be argued. Let us say minimally that at least one way of understanding the play is to take it as unfolding in rooms whose four walls are intact but which have been magically removed in part so that the audience spies on the events which transpire. Even if the play includes instructions to director and actors with regard to the audience, even if part of the play consists in addressing the audience, appealing to the audience, or even entering the audience and mixing with them (as in some *avant-garde* plays), still the actual audience of men and women present at any given performance remains outside the aesthetic order of the play. Just as the member of the audience cannot enter the play, so the actor in the play cannot enter the audience. The deceitfulness in question offers some curious features. What I know about a stage actor's knowledge of the play must be set aside to permit that actor to appear as part of the play. Similarly, the stage actor must set aside his own knowledge of the play in order to participate in its action. Burton knows the story of *Hamlet,* the drama, but he lives the deceit of not permitting that knowledge to penetrate the world of Hamlet, the Prince of Denmark. Burton is Hamlet when the deceit is fulfilled; Hamlet is unachieved when the deceit falters. Obviously I am not interested here in the career of Richard Burton, nor the psychology of the actor, nor the evident variances in the actual playing of parts. The line of attack is eidetic, not empiric.

Seeing the action of a stage play, then, is something like seeing persons in painted portraits: there is a strangeness and a fragility to their mode of being, for they are unreal in their physical reality and real in their fictive unreality. What is happening on the stage is happening within the play but not *really* happening in mundane life. The puzzling thing is, though, that if the play is not part of ordinary life it makes no sense to say that it is or is not happening in mundane existence. What is meant is more complex: the paradox of stage action and life action is that both are *seen* as real yet are *known* to be disjunctive in their ontological status. The difficulty might be probed further through another question: What is it like for a man in daily life to see an act performed in the mundane realm? What is ordinary seeing? An example may help. In walking from one car to another in a train, I advance down the aisle and see a leg draped across the side of the chair. I see only a leg. Let us consider a rather minimal appendage: trousered, hosed, shod. A man's leg. The initial seeing, though, includes in its focus only the leg, not the man. I see nothing originally of the man, his head, his hair, his shoulders, any part of his suit jacket. Only the leg. Now I want to say that I see the leg initially as belonging to a body. That I take it to be a man's body is of secondary interest. The leg is seen as "bodied." This is not to say that first I see the leg, that I *know* that legs are parts of bodies, therefore that the leg belongs to a body. There is no reasoning from a general principle to some concrete application. I see the leg as bodied. To say this, however, is not to argue that I must be right with regard to the factual status of a claim that then might be made on the basis of my seeing: that what I see is the leg of man, that a man is indeed seated or sprawled out in the immediate vicinity of that leg. It is quite possible that I'm wrong: some drummer for display dummies may be unpacking his traveling case; a futuristic, trans-beatified pilgrim may be escorting an isolated model of a limb to some undisclosed destination for undisclosable reasons. But I'm not making claims about the leg, merely reporting what is immediately perceived. The interesting point is that perception of an object yields the region or situation in which that object has its life.

Now the way in which the mundane object is seen is partly the way in which the theatrical object is seen. But to advance the argument at this stage it is necessary to complicate it. Instead of continuing with the paradigm of the member of the audience viewing the stage production, let's consider the case of the actor in the stage play viewing a fellow actor, viewing him *within* the performance of the play. The personal identities of the actors are, of course, known to each other along with more or less intimate or far-reaching knowledge of personal traits, life-history, etc. And though one actor sees his fellow actor on stage, talks to him, acts with him, it is with Hamlet, with Horatio, with Gertrude or Ophelia that the play-action occurs. Is personal knowledge then bracketed in some sense when one actor addresses another on stage? Or is stage-speech directed both to the individual playing the part and the role-part being enacted? Here we may turn for help to what one actor has said about his own acting experience. In an interview Morris Carnovsky remarks:

> . . . I remember once sitting on the stage before a performance of *Awake and Sing* many years ago in Cleveland. It was a matinée, and I came on stage, as I sometimes do, to kind of think a little bit about the part, and I said to myself, "Today I'm going to relate to Stella Adler (who was playing my daughter in the play) not as my daughter, Bessie Berger, but as Stella Adler. I know it's Stella. She knows it's me. It's Morris. She knows. She doesn't have to be told that. I know it's Stella. I don't have to say that's Bessie Berger. I don't have to do her creation for her. All I know is, that is Stella." So I said to myself, "I'm going to relate to her today, Morris to Stella." It did an extraordinary thing for me. It was my own hunch, you know, that I was following. And Stella herself commented on it afterward. And as a matter of fact I related that way to all the people in the play—to Sandy, Art, to Joe, to Phoebe, and so on. And Stella said, "What happened today? There was a — a —" I said, "What was it? What did you see?' She said, 'Well, there was a certain exciting actuality about it. It was true, very true, beyond what it had been. It excited me. It made me wonder what was going on." Well, I made a discovery for myself in exploring this particular facet of craft. It has to do again with the sense of self, one self relating to another.

The interviewer asks: "Wouldn't that take away from this thing called the intent? If you accept Stella Adler on the basis of being Stella Adler—which may bring a whole host of associations to you, about Stella Adler, having nothing to do with her role, about the vacation she's taking in two weeks or that she had told you about how her feet hurt—wouldn't these take away from the whole image you were building?"

And Carnovsky answers:

> No, because those associations are not the important things about the Stella Adler which I encounter within the image of the part. Bessie Berger. You see, I'm not interested in Bessie Berger's vacation or her feet; I'm only interested in Bessie Berger, the character that Stella is playing. And within that particular image there is an essential Stella whom I know and to whom I relate with my eyes, with my ears, with my senses, with my attitude. She at the same time is doing so to me in the same way—I hope. And this is what makes a scene. This is what makes it pulse.[1]

To the penetrating claim that it is the "essential Stella" who is at issue on the stage it may be claimed also—and Carnovsky is suggesting this as well—that there is an essential Bessie Berger, that each person and each character possess an interior form, an essential structure which the presenting self merely hints at or points toward. Thus, whether the actor starts with his theatrical alter ego as character or as actual person, his task and challenge is to transcend the manifest self for the essential self. It is the inner form of Stella Adler that Carnovsky plays to; it is the inner form of the character Bessie Berger that he seeks. The converse is no less forceful, we may suggest. The very sense of the character may have a certain resonance for the inner form of the person playing that part. To say this is to admit to the reality of theatrical failure, for the search may not yield the prize sought for; an actor may find himself with neither the essential form of the person nor that of the character. And there is a still further dimension which intensifies the situation, for the actor may be said to be playing to his audience, to other actors in the play, and also to and for himself. There is an essential Carnovsky no less than an essential Stella Adler, and Carnovsky is in search of himself continuously in his career as an actor. He comments:

> Suppose you were to ask an artist, a painter, what it is he is trying fundamentally to say. He will have to answer, I am trying to say "myself." I am trying to say myself in relation to the world I live in. Now this is fundamental. I want to say it in a certain way. A Van Gogh found himself expressing himself in these sharp, passionate daubs on canvas, which have since become so recognizable and so famous and so necessary for the understanding of his art. I don't care who the artist is, or whether he's a composer or a pianist or a writer—I feel what he wants to do is find out how to say himself. I as an actor want to find out how to say myself through O'Neill, through Shakespeare, through Chekhov, through whoever. It is not a matter of soul-searching; it can be everything. We are not sacrosanct material, you see; it happens that the actor is the material of his own making. He presents himself in various aspects. That is to say, he does use his soul as well as his body. And you cannot draw any distinction between them. Technique . . . is not a matter of simply knowing how to cavort and how to dispose of yourself in pleasing ways, or in moving ways around the stage. Behind every movement of the actor, whether it be a movement of his hands, of his body, of his voice, of his eyes, of his face, of anything—is an inner movement which I regret to have to call his soul.[2]

One is tempted to say that the object of acting is the uncovering of the soul. However, just as Carnovsky is careful not to confuse the actor's pursuit of himself with "soul-searching," so we must also guard against translating all of this into the claim that the actor is concerned with "self-expression." Rather, it is the inner self which is so elusive here, and which, oddly enough, comes to clarity when the actor discovers the inner self of his alter ego. The individual locates himself through his fellow man.

Here now is the similarity between seeing the object naively within the mundane world—seeing that leg as "bodied"—and seeing Hamlet on the stage. I see both selectively, penetratingly, discriminatingly. My worldly seeing is selective insofar as I attend, perceptually, to the presentational unity given and not to perceptual asides or minutiae. It is the leg as leg I see, not this or that bit of the leg. And to say that I see the leg as "bodied" means that the leg is taken as part of someone's body. Seeing, in this sense, is much more than visual perception; it is a mode of comprehending. So it is with the audience seeing the actor on stage in the play. Seeing Hamlet is seeing him as "bodied" in the anatomy of the play. His way of being on stage is grasped, *seen,* selectively, penetratingly, discriminatingly. The differences are equally important. When I see the leg I perceive it as touchable. Its manipulable aspect is appresented along with its purely visual features. In seeing that leg I am, in a way, also touching it, though the touch is internalized and the experience truncated. When I see Hamlet, however, I see him as untouchable by me, though as touchable by his fellows within the play. My perception does not hold, condensed within it, a subjunctive manipulation. Hamlet's associates within the play are taken as proxy for my touch. To see Hamlet from my seat in the theatre is precisely not to be able to touch him. But I know that this state of affairs cannot be changed by changing my seat, for I cannot, as pointed out earlier, enter the play even if I force my way on the stage. There is an ontological distance, a zone of isolation, which separates me forever from the players within the play. My seeing the play is contingent on that recognition, and recognition manifests itself through the selectivity of perception. I see the leg as touchable; I do not infer that it can be touched. I see Hamlet as untouchable; I do not infer that he can't be touched without breaking the rules of the game. Perception holds in condensed form the fuller range of awareness. In the striking formulation of George H. Mead, "the percept is a collapsed act." [3]

How then does this line of approach apply to the perception of stage actors of each other within the play? It is not enough to answer with the suggestion that how Hamlet sees Claudius can be discerned by reading the text of the play. We are talking about the play as performed on stage and of the actors as performers, human beings bearing, in some difficult sense, the action which constitutes the play. Carnovsky has already given a clue to the interpretation of the problem. As Morris Carnovsky he is of course aware of the actress playing opposite him as his daughter. He is well aware of the actress Stella Adler. But the person in question in the performance is the "essential Stella," the actress insofar as she is at issue in playing the daughter, Bessie Berger, in the play by Clifford Odets. Carnovsky says that he decided to play his part by relating to Stella, not Bessie. This meant that a dimension, a selective aspect of Stella would enable him, if it worked, to make theatrical contact with Bessie Berger. Carnovsky's seeing the person on stage as Stella, the "essential Stella," is a selective reversal, a purposeful mode of refusal of an ordinary seeing of that person as simply Stella, the non-essential, already known, already interpreted Stella of everyday life. This may be understood as a mode of condensation by way of theatrical conversion. It is rendered possible through the form of the play, though approximate analogues can be found in ranges of experience which are not theatrical. Before we turn to an illustrative analogue, the notions of condensation and conversion must be clarified.

In mundane perception I see a part of the human body as "bodied." As a member of an audience I see the stage actor as "bodied" within the aesthetics of the play. As an actor within the play I see my fellow actors on stage as dramatically living and developing in the ontological zone of the action of the play. I am part of that action and live within that zone on stage. Continually, in principle if not in fact, I see the gesture, the movement, the speech, the total action of my fellow actors as that present but momentary realization of the formal possibilities of the play. Although the person playing Polonius knows that character is destined to be killed in the course of the drama, he cannot act upon his extra-theatrical knowledge. Throughout the play, so long as he lives, Polonius acts as a man whose death is not imminent, and he is treated by the other characters in the same way. The death of Polonius, then, is set aside by the actors, until that death occurs. Polonius is taken as a man who is expected, in the ordinary sense, to continue to live. The blunder of his death takes all participants by surprise, and that can be only because the way in which they interpreted his life depended upon and was constituted out of a building up, from scene to scene, of a theatrical reality which necessitated that death. Paradoxically, if his fellow actors did not know Polonius was to die in the way he did, they would be surprised or shocked out of the play. Their stage surprise is made possible by taking all of Polonius' action as pointing toward his death and then setting aside that knowledge in the context and form of their roles. As actors, they must convert their knowledge of the character in such a way as to make possible seeing him as both a character and an actor. Perhaps this is realized when, in Carnovsky's phrase, the actor sees the "essential" actor playing opposite him and so discovers the essential character. It must be emphasized, though, that such theatrical seeing is not achieved in one perceptual decision. It is built up in the course of a temporal unfolding of character and actor within the enactment of the play. It depends on what I have called condensation and conversion, seeing the full range of an event in a perceptual unit and then setting aside what is known in favor of the immediate givenness of that unit. It is like recognizing a marginal or extreme quality in a person through comprehending the implications of a limited act and then purposely refusing to see that act apart from its immediate quality. As an actor playing Hamlet, I know that I am going to murder Polonius, yet I appropriate that knowledge in the negative reversal which makes it possible, even necessary, for me to act toward Polonius as though I did not know he was to die in this way. The character of Hamlet in the play gives me the form through which I can achieve this strange translation of experience. And since the building of a character in the course of an actor's performance necessarily involves a temporal progression each of whose parts must be mastered, the problem of condensation and conversion is a permanent feature of the actor's craft. Carnovsky makes the point in this way:

> You see, a part is built up moment by moment. The actor . . . knows that in the third act he is going to have to justify what he does in the first act. The sense of form leads him into a development . . . so that he knows "By the time I get there I must justify what I begin here." So if the animosity which is pursued in terms of action in the first act is correctly developed by the time he gets to the third act, the climax comes in terms of the very same action, and it will be justified. It is unified.[4]

To appreciate the condensation of perceptual experience as exemplified in the stage play is also to have some intimation of analogues of the same mode of awareness in mundane existence. I am not interested in establishing genetic or epistemological priorities here. In certain instances I see some facet of ordinary life as though it were a fiction; at times, as a theatre-goer, I see fictive events as though they were real. And they *are* real, in a way; and the flesh and blood event in real life taken as fictive *is* unreal, in a way. It is time for an illustration of an analogue, within ordinary, mundane experience, of the ontological bivouac we have been reconnoitering. The notion of "zones" has already been mentioned. A zone separates stage actors from their audience; a zone separates strangers and familiars in ordinary life. Taking a fragment of perceptual experience *as* a unit of its own places it in a zone. To violate the zone in aesthetic experience may be to force the object out of its region. Of course, it is certainly not the case that zoning is automatic and its results fixed and right. Zones are transspatial regions ontologically activated when individuals become aware of some alteration between the simple, mundane existence of an object or event and its function in some different, some secondary mode of experience. Zones are thus separators and dividers; yet they are structurally part of the integral world of the individual's experience. In some instances we can cross them; in others, crossing is tantamount to losing or destroying the aesthetic experience altogether. We have already turned to the kind of zone which cannot in principle be crossed—the theatre. Now we may consider a contrary case, that of the traveller who enters a zonal domain when he boards his train. He agrees implicitly to accepting an in-betweenness in his journeying, and he agrees to set aside his alliances and commitments to the world outside his moving train. Even if he has made the same trip dozens of times, or even if it is a part of his daily routine, the already known features of what he will pass through and pass by take on a zonal quality. In a perceptive essay, Walker Percy describes the texture of zonal experience as realized by the commuter:

> Beyond all doubt he is in Metuchen, New Jersey during the few seconds the train stops there, yet in what a strange sense is he there—he passes through without so much as leaving his breath behind. Even if this is the one-thousandth time he has stopped there, even if he knows a certain concrete pillar better than anything else in the world, yet he remains as total a stranger to Metuchen as if he had never been there.[5]

The life of the commuter is indeed one of crossing areas he knows and yet does not enter, for the railroad car insulates him in a peculiar way: it permits him to see what lies and transpires "out there" beyond his window, but to observe it as hermetically sealed—the way in which the mercury is clearly visible through the glass of the thermometer. But the glass can be shattered and the commuter can be shocked out of his sealed train. Percy writes:

> . . . Suppose the eight-fifteen breaks down between Mount Vernon and New Rochelle, breaks down beside a yellow cottage with a certain lobular stain on the wall which the commuter knows as well as he knows the face of his wife. Suppose he takes a stroll along the right-of-way while the crew is at work. To his astonishment he hears someone speak to him; it is a man standing on the porch of the yellow house. They talk and the man offers to take him the rest of way in his car. The commuter steps into the man's back yard and enters the house. This trivial event, which is of no significance objectively-empirically, is of considerable significance aesthetically-existentially. A zone-crossing has taken place.[6]

The illustration is instructive for our purposes to the extent that it functions as an analogue in mundane existence of the kind of condensation which occurs in theatrical existence. The commuter originally sees that yellow house as that which is, objectively, enterable but which he will never enter. And so he sees it as never-to-be-entered by him. Such seeing is not a matter of a predication attached to the seeing; it is rather the guts of the seeing, the ontological mode in which seeing is realized. Once again: I am saying that a member of the audience seeing a stage play sees it as unenterable, or, more properly, to see the play as a play, to witness the aesthetics of the play, is to see it as permanently insulated. And for the actor on stage to see his fellow actor in character in the midst of a scene is for the actor to seize what is essential in both person and role; it is to practice condensation and conversion as privileged instruments of the actor's craft.

I am suggesting that condensation and conversion are aspects of all acting, off-stage as well as on stage, that mundane seeing is selective, that seeing is encapsulated touching, as Mead indicates, but that daily "in the world" living action is partly the consequence of acting in the theatrical sense. More is at issue and much more is involved than role-taking. The life-actor controls his own course of action, decides on limits, finds thematic points of shifting or yielding, compromising or excluding or demanding. As the stage actor constitutes his part in the building up of his character from first act to third act, so, in a similar way, the life-actor handles and translates his on-going possibilities along loosely defined yet differentiated and controlled lines.

Life-action, then, is a condensed rehearsal in on-going imagination of limits and possibilities. The actor in life is probing, feeling out, thrusting himself toward decisions he knows he can and will make. The irruption of anger, of violence, of emotive disobedience is traced out projectively on an inner horizon. In this sense we choose the point at which we no longer can choose but merely irrupt. And having crossed that point in choice we look back with weariness and pity of the lost possibilities. We pity ourselves for what we had to do and knew all along we were about to do. The analogue in life for what occurs on the stage points to the power as well as the omnipresence of condensation. And with the analogue goes a revealing or at least a suggestion of a massive realm of experience which underlies mundane life, which is available to reflection and theoretical scrutiny, but which is not fully self-conscious or immediately present to mind. This is the marginal or fringe dimension of perception. It is from this domain that the materials for checks and guides to explicit, overt action are drawn. And it is such materials which are utilized by the actor on stage for the interpretation of his role. The ultimate analogue is this: stage acting is a kind of transliteration of the marginal language of proto-reflective life. Part of what excites the theatre goer is that he discerns in the performance the original nuances of his mundane existence, which otherwise have not been given structure and voice. Seeing from the audience seat is following the form of an inner life of gesture and speech which the aesthetics of the play liberates and illuminates. In attending to the stage play I see what I sense I can remember. Rimbaud said this for the total range of art in a line which haunts the poem that contains it:

"Sometimes I've seen what men believe they can recall." [7]

We are now at a considerable distance from our original point of departure: the puzzlement about seeing Hamlet. Our conclusion will consist of a final appraisal of the puzzle. Actually we have been pursuing the limits and possibilities of a perceptual metaphor: aesthetic seeing is a mode of condensation. Since condensation is a feature of mundane seeing as well, the question of more precise criteria of distinction between action on stage and in life must be faced. The general contrast is not too difficult to outline. Actors on stage have prepared lines, prescribed limits for their action. Hamlet is not free to make his peace with Claudius or to marry Ophelia. Actors in life are free to improvise, to choose, to change. Lines are not assigned them, roles are not defined by a playwright or director. Further, there is a fundamental priority given to the actor as a human being as distinguished from the same actor as a character in a play. Not too long ago, a performance of *The Caucasian Chalk Circle* in London had to be interrupted to save one of the stars from literal death on the gallows. Hugh Griffith had, in a scene involving a character almost hanged, almost succeeded in getting himself actually hanged. Presumably his fellow actors saved him in order to preserve the integrity of the play. Griffith had almost managed to cross a zone Brecht never projected. What happens to the individual is more important than what happens to the character. Finally, the living person has a past and a future that do involve others, others who can be encountered or who once were encountered. With respect to them, action is volatile and consequential. In the case of the stage play, those who are in a character's past, his relations, friends, acquaintances who are not part of the play, are fictions in the mind of a fiction; they are fictions of the second degree.

Unfortunately, these outlined distinctions are unsatisfactory for our purposes. They hardly get at the puzzlement originally in question, for they take for granted much of what we are trying to examine as epistemically problematic. To be sure, Hamlet is not free to marry Ophelia if "not free" means that the play as written does not include their marriage. But Hamlet is free to marry Ophelia while the action of the play is on-going. Hamlet's possibilities and Ophelia's possibilities are real in the reality of the drama. That, even so, either character is *really* free to marry tells us something about Hamlet and about Ophelia. Part of the puzzlement I experience in seeing Hamlet is precisely that, knowing the play, I see him as free to transcend the action of the play at the same time that the action of the play is possible only through being formally set and so, in principle, incapable of transcension. Similarly, the priority of the individual actor over the character he plays hinges on the difference between the performance and the play. An actor who goes blank in the middle of a speech and who can't pick up his lines from the prompter may simply have to stop the performance and then start again. Granting the preciousness of the life of Hugh Griffith, it is nevertheless necessary to say that his fellow actors on stage helped him out of the noose; they couldn't help the character he was playing. Is Richard Burton more important than Hamlet? The question is clearly misposed. What choice do we have between them? Lastly, the present, past, and future of characters in a play is as ontologically strange as the equivalent dimensions of temporality in the mundane creature. We can only assume that Hamlet's past, his early childhood let us say, is qualitatively different from the past of a concrete historical man if we take it for granted that we are quite clear about the nature of the past in the human scene. Things are not that simple, and, interestingly enough, the stage play teaches us that. The puzzlement remains. After all of the mention of aesthetics, condensation, conversion, zones, and ontology, the mystery remains. If anything, the situation is worse, for we are left not only with the strangeness on stage but with the strangeness in the audience. Theatre and life are, it would seem, sides of the same dubious coin. What exit is there from these perilous entrances?

To see Hamlet is to see him "bodied" within the aesthetics of the play. To see him is to recognize, imminently, the zone of his theatrical being as different from the ways in which men *are* in ordinary life. To see Hamlet is to perceive him as though he were independent of the actor who portrays him, and then to convert that perception into an acceptance of what transpires as irreal. Such seeing may be termed the appropriation of the subjunctive. Its realization occurs in and through the process of the play's enactment. It is that which the audience senses in watching creatively, understandingly, compassionately. I am able to grasp Hamlet's being because I am resonant with the actor's way of seeing. He, too, is confronted with a distance between his personal vision and his character's sight. Hamlet within the unity of his action nevertheless must give himself perceptual ballast. As Jean-Louis Barrault has pointed out, when Hamlet hears Polonius behind the arras and draws his sword and cries "A rat?" that moment gives him what he otherwise might not be capable of translating into action, for as Barrault says, "he is able to draw his sword to kill a rat, but he would not perhaps be capable of drawing his sword to kill a man." [8] Barrault is speaking of the essential Hamlet.

What then of the actor in life, the player of mundane roles, the man simply *there?* What, at last, shall we say of him? At least this: as a theatre-goer he may see something of the presence of his perceptual life as it is understood, most subtly, by the continual imagery of schematic meaning. To see the action on stage is to make available, in an indirect and fragmentary manner, the larger range of elements condensed in the course of action. Seeing Hamlet, in a way, is like seeing, across the zone of possibilities, the stranger you will never meet or know, the conversation you will never enter, the home finally beyond your access. Nor is this a kind of "soul-searching." it is rather a location of the soul, a victory of essence over accidence. For though it is possible to cross zones in real life and enter yellow cottages we had subjunctively abandoned, it is still the case that there are interior limits to possibility and decision. The ambiguity with which we began remains. Man as an actor is both social agent and theatrical artificer, both self and character. All acting is a search for the essential in both person and role, and the essential self, whether in life or on the stage, is the soul. Acting is the hermeneutics of the soul.

NOTES

[1] Lewis Funke and John E. Booth, *Actors Talk About Acting: Fourteen Interviews with Stars of the Theatre,* New York: Random House, 1961, pp. 282–284.

[2] *Ibid.,* pp. 263–264.

[3] George H. Mead, *The Philosophy of the Act,* edited by Charles W. Morris in collaboration with John M. Brewster, Albert M. Dunham, David L. Miller, Chicago: University of Chicago Press, 1938, p. 128.

[4] *Op. cit.,* p. 282.

[5] Walker Percy, "The Man on the Train: Three Existential Modes," *Partisan Review,* Vol. XIII, 1956, p. 482.

[6] *Ibid.,* pp. 482–483.

[7] Arthur Rimbaud, "Bateau Ivre": "Et j'ai vu quelquefois ce que l'homme a cru voir," translated by Norman Cameron in *The Limits of Art,* edited by Huntington Cairns, New York: Pantheon Books, 1948.

[8] Jean-Louis Barrault, *Le Phénomène Théâtral:* The Zaharoff Lecture for 1961, Oxford: Clarendon Press, 1961, p. 31 (my translation).

7.

THE DRAMATIC ACTOR AND REALITY

Georg Simmel

As uncertain and critical as one may be of "public opinion," that is, the *vox populi,* generally there is a core of relevant and reliable content in the dark premonitions, instincts, and evaluations of the masses. Obviously this core is surrounded by a thick shell of superficial trivialities and biased information. Nevertheless, its fundamental accuracy will usually become apparent in the realms of religion and politics, or in intellectual and ethical matters. Only in one area, the field of the art, which appears to be even more accessible than others, is the judgment of the masses hopelessly misguided and completely inadequate, especially with respect to fundamental issues. An abyss without bridges cuts off the majority from insight into the essence of art forms. Therein rests the deep social tragedy of art.

In the dramatic arts, which appeal more directly to a public audience than any other, genuine artistic values seem to be sprung not from the intentions of the artist, but from the immediate impression he makes on the audience. Because of this democratized mass appeal, dramatic art would seem to be more profoundly naturalistic than any other art form. Thus public opinion sees the essence of dramatic art not in the written drama, but in the dramatic actor.

A dramatic play exists as a self-contained work of art. Does the contribution of the actor now elevate this play into an art form of greater magnitude? If this question seems inappropriate, we might rephrase it. Does the actor transform the work of art to a more convincing level through his physical, live appearance? But, if this is true, why do we demand that this performance should somehow bear the imprint of art, and not simply that of mere realistic naturalism? All the problems dealing with the philosophy of the dramatic art converge on these questions.

The role of the actor, as it is expressed in written drama, is not a total person. The role is not a man, but a complex of things which can be said about a person through literary devices. The poet cannot give the actor unambiguous instructions concerning the inflection of language, the tone of voice, or the pace of delivery. He can only project the fate, the appearance, and the soul of a person through the one-dimensional process of poetic imagery. The actor then translates this image into a three-dimensional character accessible to all the senses.

The actor's essential mistake is to identify the sensual interpretation of an artistic content with its full realization. For the ultimate realization of drama is a metaphysical idea which cannot be embodied through sensuous impressions. The content which the poet molds into a dramatic script reveals completely different connota-

Reprinted by permission of the publisher from K. Peter Etzkorn, translator, *Georg Simmel: The Conflict in Modern Culture and Other Essays.* (New York: Teachers College Press, copyright 1968 by Teachers College, Columbia University), pp. 91–97.

tions whan transformed into sensuous expression. The actor gives meaning to the script, but he does not transform its content into reality. This is why his acting can become art, which, by definition, reality could never be. Thus, if painting appears as the art of visual sensuality and music as the art of acoustic sensuality, dramatic art appears as the art form of total sensuality.

In the realm of reality every single element and event is placed in an infinitely expanding series of spatial, conceptual, and dynamic relationships. For this reason every identifiable element of reality is only a fragment and not a totality. It is the nature of art, on the other hand, to mold the contents of existence into self-contained unity. The actor raises *all* the visual and acoustical elements of reality into a perfectly framed unity. This is accomplished through the balance of style, the logic of rhythm, the movement of moods, the recognizable relationship between character and action, and through the subordination of all details under the apex of the whole. The actor thus stylizes all sensual phenomena into a unity.

As this point reality seems again to penetrate the realm of the arts in order to bridge a void. How does the actor acquire the mode of conduct appropriate to his role when, as we have seen, this mode is not explicit in the script and cannot be made so? It seems to me that the actor cannot know how to perform Hamlet except through his own experience. He will rely on external and (more important) inner experience to realize how a human being who talks like Hamlet and has encountered Hamlet's fate generally behaves. Thus the actor submerges himself in the foundations of reality from which Shakespeare originally had derived the role. From this he recreates the dramatic work of art, in the form of Hamlet. The dramatic composition guides the actor by providing a system of realistic coordinates corresponding to the individual's inner and outer experiences, reactions, rates, events, and their environmental surroundings. However, regardless of how much guidance he might get from the play, he could not understand its clues unless he had been empirically acquainted with them or similar ones already. At this point the contribution of naturalism ends. Besides the written words of Shakespeare concerning Hamlet, the actor only has empirical reality with which to reconstruct everything Shakespeare did not say. Thus, he has to behave like a real Hamlet who has been restricted by the words and events prescribed for him by Shakespeare.

But this argument is quite erroneous. The activity of giving artistic form and constructing the artistic imprint transcends that reality on which the actor leans under the guidance of the script. The actor does not content himself with empirical reality. The coordinates of reality must become reallocated: accents become toned down, measures of time become subjected to rhythm, and from all the alternatives offered by reality, only those that can be uniformly stylized are selected. In short, the actor does not transform the dramatic work of art into reality; on the contrary, he makes use of reality, and transforms the reality which has been assigned to him into a work of art.

There are many sophisticated people today who explain their aversion towards the theater by saying that it portrays too many artificial pretenses. This opinion may be justified, not because of a shortage of reality, but because of a surfeit of it. The dramatic actor can be convincing to us only if he stays within artistic logic, and eschews additional elements of realism obeying a completely different logic.

It is wrong to consider it a "falsification" if the actor is different in reality from the role he assumes on stage. After all, no one charges a locomotive engineer with falsifying himself if he fails to run locomotives around his family table. It is not a deception when the penniless actor assumes the role of a king on stage. For he is a king in his function as an artist, an *ideal* king, but perhaps for this very reason, not a *real* king. This impression of falsehood is generated only by a poor actor, who either permits traces of his role in reality as a poor individual to enter into his stage role of a king, or else acts so very realistically that he carries us into the sphere of realism. In the latter case he creates a painful competition between two realistic images which contradict one another. This contradiction would never occur if the dramatic presentation kept the audience in the sphere of art, which is essentially estranged from reality.

We now see the total error in the idea that the actor must realize the poetic creation. In the dramatic presentation the actor exercises a special and unified form of art which is as far removed from reality as the poetic work of art itself. Thus we can immediately understand why a good imitator is not a good actor. The gift of being able to imitate other people has nothing to do with the artistically creative talent of an actor. This is true because the subject matter of the imitator is reality, and thus he strives to be received as a form of reality. The actor, however, like the painter of a portrait, is not the imitator of the real world, but the creator of a new one. This artistic world, of course, is related to the phenomenon of reality, since both the real and artistic worlds are built on the accumulated content of all being. Reality, however, represents the first impression received of these contents. This stimulates the illusion, as though reality was the true subject of art.

In order to obtain the most refined method of keeping the dramatic arts in the sphere of reality, the dramatic writer derives his material from his psychological integration of previous experience. The words of the poet demand a reconstruction based on psychological experience. The task of the actor should make us conceive of the prescribed words and events as inevitable. Thus, his art should be applied or *practical* psychology. According to this view, the task of the actor is fulfilled by placing before our eyes convincingly and emphatically the essence of a human soul with its inner determination, its reaction to fate, its drives, and its emotional anguish.

The proper artistic contribution of the dramatic actor cannot be found in the apparent depth of his interpretation. Certainly it is only through his own spiritual experiences that an actor can understand the role of Hamlet. Moreover, the actor would only be a puppet or a phonograph if he were not able to represent this spiritual reality to the viewer for a chance to experience it, too. However, true art transcends this experience of a reproduced psychic reality. It flows from an ideal fountain, from the beginning, never towards a finished reality, but towards new demands.

We see here a revival, new in aesthetics, of the old error overcome long ago in philosophy—the idea that mental reality is something transcendent, ideal, superior to physical reality. Art, however, demands that the mere causality of factual processes should explicate meanings, that all the threads which extend into infinity of time and place should be laced together into a self-satisfactory whole, and that the confusion of reality should be rhythmically ordered. These demands do not correspond to the reality that flows from the dark fountain of being, inaccessible to our consciousness, even if this reality were of a psychic variety.

There is no doubt that these postulates concerning art originate in the minds of real human beings, as do ideas about the appropriate relation between the form and the content of reality. However, the content and meaning of the artistic work is juxtaposed in one's mind with the reality which the mind reconstructs from experience. The dramatic actor must make us understand the role of Hamlet and portray the turmoils of his fate. Through his gestures and the pitch and rhythm of his voice, he must also provide us with psychological insight, so that we all draw the conclusion that a given character *must* speak these words under the given circumstances. The genuine artistic process, however, only begins after all this has happened—after the role of Hamlet is made into more than a series of resounding words and exterior events, and has been resolved through the contribution of the actor into a spiritual reality which contrasts with the immediacy of excitement and empathy. Here the spiritually recreated process of reality crystallizes into an image. This is analogous to the sensually perceived impressions of the world of physical bodies which are transformed by the painter into a painting. This spiritual reality has thus become a picture for the dramatic writer.

We can now formulate these ideas into an axiom: *The dramatic arts as such transcend both poetry and reality*. The dramatic actor is neither what popular naturalism demands, an imitator of a man who finds himself in a given situation, nor what literary idealism demands, a marionette of his role with no artistic task besides what is already prescribed in the lines of the poetic work.

This literary point of view is particularly seductive to naturalism. If one does not permit the dramatic actor an individual contribution, produced according to autonomous artistic principles based on the final foundations of all art, then the actor becomes only the *realization* of a written role. A work of art, however, cannot be the material subject for another work of art. On the contrary, a dramatic play is a channel through which a stream, flowing from the very fundamentals of being, is directed towards the specifically individual artistic contribution of the dramatic actor. If it were otherwise, there would be no other final principles then those of drama and reality. On such a basis, then, the actor's task could only be considered dangerously close to naturalism, namely, to provide the appearance of reality for the dramatic play.

The attractive notion that the dramatic actor only infuses the dramatic play with life, and presents the life realization of a poetic work, leads to the disappearance of the genuine and incomparable dramatic art which lives in the realm between the written play and reality. It is just as distinctively *original* to represent elements of life through the medium of dramatic acting as to represent them through painting or poetry, or to recreate them through epistemology or religion. And the art form of the dramatic actor is something which is genuinely rooted in unity, despite the great variety of sensuous impressions and emotional reactions that it produces. It is not a composite of independent optical stimuli, acoustic rhythms, emotional shocks, or states of empathy. On the contrary, dramatic acting represents an inner unity produced from the diversity of all those great elements of which the dramatic impressions seem to be composed. In reality, they are only developments from a single root, just as the multitude of different words in a sentence represents a single pattern of thought. There simply seems to exist an *attitude of dramatic acting* which man brings into this world as part of his manner of being and which makes him creative in this unique way.

The decisive point is the fact that the dramatic actor creates within himself a complete unity with its unique laws. His art, just as that of the poet, has its roots in the same fundamentals as do all other art forms. This is true even though it demands another art form, the poetic work, for its medium. Only the autonomous status of the dramatic art explains the strange fact that a poetic role, although conceived as an unambiguous one, can be presented by a variety of dramatic actors with completely different interpretations, each of which may be fully adequate, and none of which would be more correct or more erroneous than any other. This would be completely incomprehensible if the dramatic actor lived entirely within the dualism between the poetic work and reality. Within the frameworks of both the poetic role and reality (which might be thought of as the poetic counter-image), there exists only *one* Don Carlos or *one* Gregers Werle. Without a third, genuine, independent foundation, this separation of the various branches of the dramatic arts would lead to the destruction of the unities existing both within poetic works and within reality.

Thus dramatic acting is not, as is commonly thought, the reconciliation between the realism of poetry and reality. Nor is it the servant of those two lords. The accuracy with which the dramatic actor follows the poetic role, and the truth of the given world, are not mechanical copies of each other. Rather, the dramatic actor's personality interweaves those two roles as organic elements in this creative expression of life. He was born as a personality and not with a predetermined dependence on written dramatic works, or with a reality which he is expected to redraft.

Here we find one more example of an important historic task which confronts the present age: to replace mechanism with life processes. We have come to see how each individual's reality contains in itself a condensation of life, which determines its essence and includes in its development all those living realizations which surround it in organic interdependence. The mechanical principle, on the other hand, de-individualizes all these phenomena and reconstructs them, more or less externally, as mere combinations of others. If we understand the dramatic art as an expression of the primary artistic energy of the human soul, which assimilates both the poetic art and reality into one living process, instead of being composed of these elements in a mechanical fashion, then our interpretation of this art coincides with our distinctively modern way of understanding the modern world.

8.

THE PRESENTATION OF SELF IN EVERYDAY LIFE

Erving Goffman

CONCLUSION

The Framework

A social establishment is any place surrounded by fixed barriers to perception in which a particular kind of activity regularly takes place. I have suggested that any social establishment may be studied profitably from the point of view of impression management. Within the walls of a social establishment we find a team of performers who cooperate to present to an audience a given definition of the situation. This will include the conception of own team and of audience and assumptions concerning the ethos that is to be maintained by rules of politeness and decorum. We often find a division into back region, where the performance of a routine is prepared, and front region, where the performance is presented. Access to these regions is controlled in order to prevent the audience from seeing backstage and to prevent outsiders from coming into a performance that is not addressed to them. Among members of the team we find that familiarity prevails, solidarity is likely to develop, and that secrets that could give the show away are shared and kept. A tacit agreement is maintained between performers and audience to act as if a given degree of opposition and of accord existed between them. Typically, but not always, agreement is stressed and opposition is underplayed. The resulting working consensus tends to be contradicted by the attitude toward the audience which the performers express in the absence of the audience and by carefully controlled communication out of character conveyed by the performers while the audience is present. We find that discrepant roles develop: some of the individuals who are apparently teammates, or audience, or outsiders acquire information about the performance and relations to the team which are not apparent and which complicate the problem of putting on a show. Sometimes disruptions occur through unmeant gestures, faux pas, and scenes, thus discrediting or contradicting the definition of the situation that is being maintained. The mythology of the team will dwell upon these disruptive events. We find that performers, audience, and outsiders all utilize techniques for saving the show, whether by avoiding likely disruptions or by correcting for unavoided ones, or by making it possible for others to do so. To ensure that these techniques will be employed, the team will tend to select members who are loyal, disciplined, and circumspect, and to select an audience that is tactful.

These features and elements, then, comprise the framework I claim to be characteristic of much social interaction as it occurs in natural settings in our Anglo-American society. This framework is formal and abstract in the sense that it can be applied to any social establishment; it is not, however, merely a static classification. The framework bears upon dynamic issues created by the motivation to sustain a definition of the situation that has been projected before others.

The Analytical Context

This report has been chiefly concerned with social establishments as relatively closed systems. It has been assumed that the relation of one establishment to others is itself an intelligible area of study and ought to be treated analytically as part of a different order of fact—the order of institutional integration. It might be well here to try to place the perspective taken in this report in the context of other perspectives which seem to be the ones currently employed, implicitly or explicitly, in the study of social establishments as closed systems. Four such perspectives may be tentatively suggested.

An establishment may be viewed "technically," in terms of its efficiency and inefficiency as an intentionally organized system of activity for the achievement of predefined objectives. An establishment may be viewed "politically," in terms of the actions which each participant (or class of participants) can demand of other participants, the kinds of deprivations and indulgences which can be meted out in order to enforce these demands, and the kinds of social controls which guide this exercise of command and use of sanctions. An establishment may be viewed "structurally," in terms of the horizontal and vertical status divisions and the kinds of social relations which relate these several groupings to one another. Finally, an establishment may be viewed "culturally," in terms of the moral values which influence activity in the establishment—values pertaining to fashions, customs, and matters of taste, to politeness and decorum, to ultimate ends and normative restrictions on means, etc. It is to be noted that all the facts that can be discovered about an establishment are relevant to each of the four perspectives but that each perspective gives its own priority and order to these facts.

It seems to me that the dramaturgical approach may constitute a fifth perspective, to be added to the technical, political, structural, and cultural perspectives.[1] The dramaturgical perspective, like each of the other four, can be employed as the endpoint of analysis, as a final way of ordering facts. This would lead us to describe the techniques of impression management employed in a given establishment, the principal problems of impression management in the establishment, and the identity and interrelationships of the several performance teams which operate in the establishment. But, as with the facts utilized in each of the other perspectives, the facts specifically pertaining to impression management also play a part in the matters that are a concern in all the other perspectives. It may be useful to illustrate this briefly.

The technical and dramaturgical perspectives intersect most clearly, perhaps, in regard to standards of work. Important for both perspectives is the fact that one set of individuals will be concerned with testing the unapparent characteristics and qualities of the work-accomplishments of another set of individuals, and this other set will be concerned with giving the impression that their work embodies these hidden attributes. The political and dramaturgical perspectives intersect clearly in regard to the capacities of one individual to direct the activity of another. For one thing, if an individual is to direct others, he will often find it useful to keep strategic secrets from them. Further, if one individual attempts to direct the activity of others by means of example, enlightenment, persuasion, exchange, manipulation, authority, threat, punishment, or coercion, it will be necessary, regardless of his power position, to convey effectively what he wants done, what he is prepared to do to get it done and what he will do if it is not done. Power of any kind must be clothed in effective means of displaying it, and will have different effects depending upon how it is dramatized. (Of course, the capacity to convey effectively a definition of the situation may be of little use if one is not in a position to give example, exchange, punishment, etc.) Thus the most objective form of naked power, i.e., physical coercion, is often neither objective nor naked but rather functions as a display for persuading the audience; it is often a means of communication, not merely a means of action. The structural and dramaturgical perspectives seem to intersect most clearly in regard to social distance. The image that one status grouping is able to maintain in the eyes of an audience of other status groupings will depend upon the performers' capacity to restrict communicative contact with the audience. The cultural and dramaturgical perspectives intersect most clearly in regard to the maintenance of moral standards. The cultural values of an establishment will determine in detail how the participants are to feel about many matters and at the same time establish a framework of appearances that must be maintained, whether or not there is feeling behind the appearances.

Personality-Interaction-Society

In recent years there have been elaborate attempts to bring into one framework the concepts and findings derived from three different areas of inquiry: the individual personality, social interaction, and society. I would like to suggest here a simple addition to these inter-disciplinary attempts.

When an individual appears before others, he knowingly and unwittingly projects a definition of the situation, of which a conception of himself is an important part. When an event occurs which is expressively incompatible with this fostered impression, significant consequences are simultaneously felt in three levels of social reality, each of which involves a different point of reference and a different order of fact.

First, the social interaction, treated here as a dialogue between two teams, may come to an embarrassed and confused halt; the situation may cease to be defined, previous positions may become no longer tenable, and participants may find themselves without a charted course of action. The participants typically sense a false note in the situation and come to feel awkward, flustered, and, literally, out of countenance. In other words, the minute social system created and sustained by orderly social interaction becomes disorganized. These are the consequences that the disruption has from the point of view of social interaction.

Secondly, in addition to these disorganizing consequences for action at the moment, performance disruptions may have consequences of a more far-reaching kind. Audiences tend to accept the self projected by the individual performer during any current performance as a responsible representative of his colleague-grouping, of his team, and of his social establishment. Audiences also accept the individual's particular performance as evidence of his capacity to perform the routine and even as evidence of his capacity to perform any routine. In a sense these larger social units—teams, establishments, etc.—become committed every time the individual performs his routine; with each performance the legitimacy of these units will tend to be tested anew and their permanent reputation put at stake. This kind of commitment is especially strong during some performances. Thus, when a surgeon and his nurse both turn from the operating table and the anesthetized patient accidentally rolls off the table to his death, not only is the operation disrupted in an embarrassing way, but the reputation of the doctor, as a doctor and as a man, and also the reputation of the hospital may be weakened. These are the consequences that disruptions may have from the point of view of social structure.

Finally, we often find that the individual may deeply involve his ego in his identification with a particular part, establishment, and group, and in his self-conception as someone who does not disrupt social interaction or let down the social units which depend upon that interaction. When a disruption occurs, then, we may find that the self-conceptions around which his personality has been built may become discredited. These are consequences that disruptions may have from the point of view of individual personality.

Performance disruptions, then, have consequences at three levels of abstraction: personality, interaction, and social structure. While the likelihood of disruption will vary widely from interaction to interaction, and while the social importance of likely disruptions will vary from interaction to interaction, still it seems that there is no interaction in which the participants do not take an appreciable chance of being slightly embarrassed or a slight chance of being deeply humiliated. Life may not be much of a gamble, but interaction is. Further, in so far as individuals make efforts to avoid disruptions or to correct for ones not avoided, these efforts, too, will have simultaneous consequences at the three levels. Here, then, we have one simple way of articulating three levels of abstraction and three perspectives from which social life has been studied.

Comparisons and Study

In this report, use has been made of illustrations from societies other than our Anglo-American one. In doing this I did not mean to imply that the framework presented here is culture-free or applicable in the same areas of social life in non-Western societies as in our own. We lead an indoor social life. We specialize in fixed settings, in keeping strangers out, and in giving the performer some privacy in which to prepare himself for the show. Once we begin a performance, we are inclined to finish it, and we are sensitive to jarring notes which may occur during it. If we are caught out in a misrepresentation we feel deeply humiliated. Given our general dramaturgical rules and inclinations for conducting action, we must not overlook areas of life in other societies in which other rules are apparently followed. Reports by Western travelers are filled with instances in which their dramaturgical sense was offended or surprised, and if we are to generalize to other cultures we must consider these instances as well as more favorable ones. We must be ready to see in China that while actions and décor may be wonderfully harmonious and coherent in a private tearoom, extremely elaborate meals may be served in extremely plain restaurants, and shops that look like hovels staffed with surly, familiar clerks may contain within their recesses, wrapped in old brown paper, wonderfully delicate bolts of silk.[2] And among a people said to be careful to save each other's face, we must be prepared to read that:

> Fortunately the Chinese do not believe in the privacy of a home as we do. They do not mind having the whole details of their daily experience seen by everyone that cares to look. How they live, what they eat, and even the family jars that we try to hush up from the public are things that seem to be common property, and not to belong exclusively to this particular family who are most concerned.[3]

And we must be prepared to see that in societies with settled inequalitarian status systems and strong religious orientations, individuals are sometimes less earnest about the whole civic drama than we are, and will cross social barriers with brief gestures that give more recognition to the man behind the mask than we might find permissible.

Furthermore, we must be very cautious in any effort to characterize our own society as a whole with respect to dramaturgical practices. For example, in current management-labor relations, we know that a team may enter joint consultation meetings with the opposition with the knowledge that it may be necessary to give the appearance of stalking out of the meeting in a huff. Diplomatic teams are sometimes required to stage a similar show. In other words, while teams in our society are usually obliged to suppress their rage behind a working consensus, there are times when teams are obliged to suppress the appearance of sober opposition behind a demonstration of outraged feelings. Similarly, there are occasions when individuals, whether they wish to or not, will feel obliged to destroy an interaction in order to save their honor and their face. It would be more prudent, then, to begin with smaller units, with social establishments or classes of establishments, or with particular statuses, and document comparisons and changes in a modest way by means of the case-history method. For example, we have the following kind of information about the shows that businessmen are legally allowed to put on:

> The last half-century has seen a marked change in the attitude of the courts toward the question of justifiable reliance. Earlier decisions, under the influence of the prevalent doctrine of "caveat emptor," laid great stress upon the plaintiff's "duty" to protect himself and distrust his antagonist, and held that he was not entitled to rely even upon positive assertions of fact made by one with whom he was dealing at arm's length. It was assumed that anyone may be expected to overreach another in a bargain if he can, and that only a fool will expect common honesty. Therefore the plaintiff must make a reasonable investigation, and form his own judgment. The recognition of a new standard of business ethics, demanding that statements of fact be at least

honestly and carefully made, and in many cases that they be warranted to be true, has led to an almost complete shift in this point of view.

It is now held that assertions of fact as to the quantity or quality of land or goods sold, the financial status of the corporations, and similar matters inducing commercial transactions, may justifiably be relied on without investigation, not only where such investigation would be burdensome and difficult, as where land which is sold lies at a distance, but likewise where the falsity of the representation might be discovered with little effort by means easily at hand.[4]

And while frankness may be increasing in business relations, we have some evidence that marriage counselors are increasingly agreed that an individual ought not to feel obliged to tell his or her spouse about previous "affairs," as this might only lead to needless strain. Other examples may be cited. We know, for example, that up to about 1830 pubs in Britain provided a backstage setting for workmen, little distinguishable from their own kitchens, and that after that date the gin palace suddenly burst upon the scene to provide much the same clientele with a fancier front region than they could dream of.[5] We have records of the social history of particular American towns, telling us of the recent decline in the elaborateness of domestic and avocational fronts of the local upper classes. In contrast, some material is available which describes the recent increase in elaborateness of the setting that union organizations employ,[6] and the increasing tendency to "stock" the setting with academically-trained experts who provide an aura of thought and respectability.[7] We can trace changes in the plant layout of specific industrial and commercial organizations and show an increase in front, both as regards the exterior of the head-office building and as regards the conference rooms, main halls, and waiting rooms of these buildings. We can trace in a particular crofting community how the barn for animals, once backstage to the kitchen and accessible by a small door next the stove, has lately been removed a distance from the house, and how the house itself, once set down in an unprotected way in the midst of garden, croft equipment, garbage, and grazing stock, is becoming, in a sense, public-relations oriented, with a front yard fenced off and kept somewhat clean, presenting a dressed-up side to the community while debris is strewn at random in the unfenced back regions. And as the connected byre disappears, and the scullery itself starts to become less frequent, we can observe the up-grading of domestic establishments, wherein the kitchen, which once possessed its own back regions, is now coming to be the least presentable region of the house while at the same time becoming more and more presentable. We can also trace that peculiar social movement which led some factories, ships, restaurants, and households to clean up their backstages to such an extent that, like monks, Communists, or German aldermen, their guards are always up and there is no place where their front is down, while at the same time members of the audience become sufficiently entranced with the society's id to explore the places that had been cleaned up for them. Paid attendance at symphony orchestra rehearsals is only one of the latest examples. We can observe what Everett Hughes calls collective mobility, through which the occupants of a status attempt to alter the bundle of tasks performed by them so that no act will be required which is expressively inconsistent with the image of self that these incumbents are attempting to establish for themselves. And we can observe a parallel process, which might be called "role enterprise," within a particular social establishment, whereby a particular member attempts not so much to move into a higher position already established as to create a new position for himself, a position involving duties which suitably express attributes that are congenial to him. We can examine the process of specialization, whereby many performers come to make brief communal use of very elaborate social settings, being content to sleep alone in a cubicle of no pretension. We can follow the diffusion of crucial fronts—such as the laboratory complex of glass, stainless steel, rubber gloves, white tile, and lab coat—which allow an increasing number of persons connected with unseemly tasks a way of self-purification. Starting with the tendency in highly authoritarian organizations for one team to be required to spend its time infusing a rigorously ordered cleanliness in the setting the other team will perform in, we can trace, in establishments such as hospitals, air force bases, and large households, a current decline in the hypertrophic strictness of such settings. And finally, we can follow the rise and diffusion of the jazz and "West Coast" cultural patterns, in which terms such as bit, goof, scene, drag, dig, are given currency, allowing individuals to maintain something of a professional stage performer's relation to the technical aspects of daily performances.

The Role of Expression Is Conveying Impressions of Self

Perhaps a moral note can be permitted at the end. In this report the expressive component of social life has been treated as a source of impressions given to or taken by others. Impression, in turn, has been treated as a source of information about unapparent facts and as a means by which the recipients can guide their response to the informant without having to wait for the full consequences of the informant's actions to be felt. Expression, then, has been treated in terms of the communicative role it plays during social interaction and not, for example, in terms of consummatory or tension-release function it might have for the expresser.[8]

Underlying all social interaction there seems to be a fundamental dialectic. When one individual enters the presence of others, he will want to discover the facts of the situation. Were he to possess this information, he could know, and make allowances for, what will come to happen and he could give the others present as much of their due as is consistent with his enlightened self-interest. To uncover fully the factual nature of the situation, it would be necessary for the individual to know all the relevant social data about the others. It would also be necessary for the individual to know the actual outcome or end product of the activity of the others during the interaction, as well as their innermost feelings concerning him. Full information of this order is rarely available; in its absence, the individual tends to employ substitutes—cues, tests, hints, expressive gestures, status symbols, etc.—as predictive devices. In short, since the reality that the individual is concerned with is unperceivable at the moment, appearances must be relied upon in its stead. And, paradoxically, the more the individual is concerned with the reality that is not available to perception, the more must he concentrate his attention on appearances.

The individual tends to treat the others present on the basis of the impression they give now about the past and the future. It is here that communicative acts are translated into moral ones. The impressions that the others give tend to be treated as claims and promises they have implicitly made, and claims and promises tend to have a moral character. In his mind the individual says: "I am using these impressions of you as a way of checking up on you and your activity, and you ought not to lead me astray." The peculiar thing about this is that the individual tends to take this stand even though he expects the others to be unconscious of many of their expressive behaviors and even though he may expect to exploit the others on the basis of the information he gleans about them. Since the sources of impression used by the observing individual involve a multitude of standards pertaining to politeness and decorum, pertaining both to social intercourse and task-performance, we can appreciate afresh how daily life is enmeshed in moral lines of discrimination.

Let us shift now to the point of view of the others. If they are to be gentlemanly, and play the individual's game, they will give little conscious heed to the fact that impressions are being formed about them but rather act without guile or contrivance, enabling the individual to receive valid impressions about them and their efforts. And if they happen to give thought to the fact that they are being observed, they will not allow this to influence them unduly, content in the belief that the individual will obtain a correct impression and give them their due because of it. Should they be concerned with influencing the treatment that the individual gives them, and this is properly to be expected, then a gentlemanly means will be available to them. They need only guide their action in the present so that its future consequences will be the kind that would lead a just individual to treat them now in a way they want to be treated; once this is done, they have only to rely on the perceptiveness and justness of the individual who observes them.

Sometimes those who are observed do, of course, employ these proper means of influencing the way in which the observer treats them. But there is another way, a shorter and more efficient way, in which the observed can influence the observer. Instead of allowing an impression of their activity to arise as an incidental by-product of their activity, they can reorient their frame of reference and devote their efforts to the creation of desired impressions. Instead of attempting to achieve certain ends by acceptable means, they can attempt to achieve the impression that they are achieving certain ends by acceptable means. It is always possible to manipulate the impression the observer uses as a substitute for reality because a sign for the presence of a thing, not being that thing, can be employed in the absence of it. The observer's need to rely on representations of things itself creates the possibility of misrepresentation.

There are many sets of persons who feel they could not stay in business, whatever their business, if they limited themselves to the gentlemanly means of influencing the individual who observes them. At some point or other in the round of their activity they feel it is necessary to band together and directly manipulate the impression that they give. The observed become a performing team and the observers become the audience. Actions which appear to be done on objects become gestures addressed to the audience. The round of activity becomes dramatized.

We come now to the basic dialectic. In their capacity as performers, individuals will be concerned with maintaining the impression that they are living up to the many standards by which they and their products are judged. Because these standards are so numerous and so pervasive, the individuals who are performers dwell more than we might think in a moral world. But, *qua* performers, individuals are concerned not with the moral issue of realizing these standards, but with the amoral issue of engineering a convincing impression that these standards are being realized. Our activity, then, is largely concerned with moral matters, but as performers we do not have a moral concern with them. As performers we are merchants of morality. Our day is given over to intimate contact with the goods we display and our minds are filled with intimate understandings of them; but it may well be that the more attention we give to these goods, then the more distant we feel from them and from those who are believing enough to buy them. To use a different imagery, the very obligation and profitability of appearing always in a steady moral light, of being a socialized character, forces one to be the sort of person who is practiced in the ways of the stage.

Staging and the Self

The general notion that we make a presentation of ourselves to others is hardly novel; what ought to be stressed in conclusion is that the very structure of the self can be seen in terms of how we arrange for such performances in our Anglo-American society.

In this report, the individual was divided by implication into two basic parts: he was viewed as a *performer,* a harried fabricator of impressions involved in the all-too-human task of staging a performance; he was viewed as a *character,* a figure, typically a fine one, whose spirit, strength, and other sterling qualities the performance was designed to evoke. The attributes of a performer and the attributes of a character are of a different order, quite basically so, yet both sets have their meaning in terms of the show that must go on.

First, character. In our society the character one performs and one's self are somewhat equated, and this self-as-character is usually seen as something housed within the body of its possessor, especially the upper parts thereof, being a nodule, somehow, in the psychobiology of personality. I suggest that this view is an implied part of what we are all trying to present, but provides, just because of this, a bad analysis of the presentation. In this report the performed self was seen as some kind of image, usually creditable, which the individual on stage and in character effectively attempts to induce others of hold in regard to him. While this image is entertained *concerning* the individual, so that a self is imputed to him, this self itself does not derive from its possessor, but from the whole scene of his action, being generated by that attribute of local events which renders them interpretable by witnesses. A correctly staged and performed scene leads the audience to impute a self to a performed character, but this imputation—this self—is a *product* of a scene that comes off, and is not a *cause* of it. The self, then, as a performed character, is not an organic thing that has a specific location, whose fundamental fate is to be born, to mature, and to die; it is a dramatic effect arising diffusely from a scene that is presented, and the characteristic issue, the crucial concern, is whether it will be credited or discredited.

In analyzing the self then we are drawn from its possessor, from the person who will profit or lose most by it, for he and his body merely provide the peg on which something of collaborative manufacture will be hung for a time. And the means for producing and maintaining selves do not reside inside the peg; in fact these means are often bolted down in social establishments. There will be a back region with its tools for shaping the body, and a front region with its fixed props. There will be a team of persons whose activity on stage in conjunction with available props will constitute the scene from which the performed character's self will emerge, and another team, the audience, whose interpretive activity will be necessary for this emergence. The self is a product of all of these arrangements, and in all of its parts bears the marks of this genesis.

The whole machinery of self-production is cumbersome, of course, and sometimes breaks down, exposing its separate components: back region control; team collusion; audience tact; and so forth. But, well oiled, impressions will flow from it fast enough to put us in the grips of one of our types of reality—the performance will come off and the firm self accorded each performed character will appear to emanate intrinsically from its performer.

Let us turn now from the individual as character performed to the individual as performer. He has a capacity to learn, this being exercised in the task of training for a part. He is given to having fantasies and dreams, some that pleasurably unfold a triumphant performance, others full of anxiety and dread that nervously deal with vital discreditings in a public front region. He often manifests a gregarious desire for teammates and audiences, a tactful considerateness for their concerns; and he has a capacity for deeply felt shame, leading him to minimize the chances he takes of exposure.

These attributes of the individual *qua* performer are not merely a depicted effect of particular performances; they are psychobiological in nature, and yet they seem to arise out of intimate interaction with the contingencies of staging performances.

And now a final comment. In developing the conceptual framework employed in this report, some language of the stage was used. I spoke of performers and audiences; of routines and parts; of performances coming off or falling flat; of cues, stage settings and backstage; of dramaturgical needs, dramaturgical skills, and dramaturgical strategies. Now it should be admitted that this attempt to press a mere analogy so far was in part a rhetoric and a maneuver.

The claim that all the world's a stage is sufficiently commonplace for readers to be familiar with its limitations and tolerant of its presentation, knowing that at any time they will easily be able to demonstrate to themselves that it is not to be taken too seriously. An action staged in a theater is a relatively contrived illusion and an admitted one; unlike ordinary life, nothing real or actual can happen to the performed characters—although at another level of course something real and actual can happen to the reputation of performers *qua* professionals whose everyday job is to put on theatrical performances.

And so here the language and mask of the stage will be dropped. Scaffolds, after all, are to build other things with, and should be erected with an eye to taking them down. This report is not concerned with aspects of theater that creep into everyday life. It is concerned with the structure of social encounters—the structure of those entities in social life that come into being whenever persons enter one another's immediate physical presence. The key factor in this structure is the maintenance of a single definition of the situation, this definition having to be expressed, and this expression sustained in the face of a multitude of potential disruptions.

A character staged in a theater is not in some ways real, nor does it have the same kind of real consequences as does the thoroughly contrived character performed by a confidence man; but the *successful* staging of either of these types of false figures involves use of *real* techniques—the same techniques by which everyday persons sustain their real social situations. Those who conduct face to face interaction on a theater's stage must meet the key requirement of real situations; they must expressively sustain a definition of the situation: but this they do in circumstances that have facilitated their developing an apt terminology for the interactional tasks that all of us share.

NOTES

[1] Compare the position taken by Oswald Hall in regard to possible perspectives for the study of closed systems in his "Methods and Techniques of Research in Human Relations" (April, 1952), reported in E. C. Hughes *et al.*, *Cases on Field Work* (forthcoming).

[2] Macgowan, op. cit., pp. 178–79.

[3] *Ibid.*, pp. 180–81.

[4] Prosser, *op. cit.*, pp. 749–50.

[5] M. Gorham and H. Dunnett, *Inside the Pub* (London: The Architectural Press, 1950), pp. 23–24.

[6] See, for example, Hunter, *op. cit.*, p. 19.

[7] See Wilensky, *op. cit.*, chap. iv, for a discussion of the "window-dressing" function of staff experts. For reference to the business counterpart of this movement see Riesman, *op. cit.*, pp. 138–39.

[8] A recent treatment of this kind may be found in Talcott Parsons, Robert F. Bales, and Edward A. Shils, *Working Papers in the Theory of Action* (Glencoe, Ill.: The Free Press, 1953), Chap. II, "The Theory of Symbolism in Relation to Action."

9.

LIFE AS THEATER: Some Notes on the Dramaturgic Approach to Social Reality

Sheldon L. Messinger

with Harold Sampson and Robert D. Towne

The aim of this paper is to raise some questions about the uses of the "dramaturgic approach" [1] to social experience, a mode of analysis finding increasing use in social-psychological circles. In particular, we wish to inquire into and comment upon the nature of the actor's [2] perspective in everyday life, as this is sometimes assumed to appear to the dramaturgic analyst.

To this end, we shall describe a perspective on the world and the self within it, a perspective that renders life a kind of "theater" in which a "show" is "staged." Someone viewing self and world from within this perpective will be said to be "on." In order to show the incompatibility of this perspective with the view that persons in everyday life seem to consider "natural," we shall present some observations by and about mental patients taken from a recently completed study.[3] Finally, we shall suggest that the perspective of persons who are "on" is akin or identical to the view seemingly attributed by the dramaturgic analyst to his subjects, that is, to persons plying their routine rounds of daily activities. We shall hold that this seeming attribution is a misreading of dramaturgic analysis, if a misreading against which the dramaturgic analyst has not sufficiently guarded.

I

A reported comment by Sammy Davis, Jr. first suggested our usage of the term "to be on." Remarking on the hazards of fame, he said, "As soon as I go out the front door of my house in the morning, I'm on, Daddy, I'm on." [4] And further, "But when I'm with the group I can relax. We trust each other" (12). Drawing on his experience in the theater, Davis seems to be saying that there are times when, although "off-stage," he feels "on-stage." He contrasts this perspective on self and other with another associated with "relaxation" and "trust."

Seeing that someone who has been "on-stage" may find the same experience in everyday life, we can appreciate that those who have never crossed the boards may attain the same perspective, even though they may have no consistent name for it. Thus Bernard Wolfe tells us that, seldom out of sight of a white audience, "Negroes in our culture spend most of their lives 'on' . . . . Every Negro is to some extent a performer." At other times, "relaxing among themselves," Negroes will "mock the 'type' personalities they are obliged to assume when they're 'on' " (11, p. 202).

Reprinted by permission from *Sociometry,* Vol. XXV, 1962.

We may expect, perhaps, that the members of any oppressed group will have similar experiences.

But there seems no reason to confine these experiences to the oppressed. It would seem that adolescents at graduation ceremonies, as well as buying drinks at bars, and clerks taken for store owners, as well as those mistaken for customers, share with Norman Mailer's "hip" the need to "come on strong" (8). And we can see that a person may be rendered "on" when he has no prior reason to believe that this will be his fate. Thus, the plight of one "put on" by joking if sadistic friends, and the person suddenly made aware of a *gaffe* by another's inability to be tactful (3, 5).

All of these situations point up the fact that under some circumstances in everyday life the actor becomes, is, or is made *aware* of an actual or potential discrepancy between his "real" and his "projected" selves, between his "self" and his "character." [5] He may greet this sensed discrepancy with joy or anxiety; presumably he usually finds himself somewhere between these affective poles. However this may be, insofar as he *consciously* orients himself to narrow, sustain, or widen this discrepancy and thereby achieves a sense of "playing a role" or "managing a character," he is "on" in the sense intended here. It may be inferred that it is during such periods, if his projection is a joint enterprise, that the actor *experiences* the constraints of "dramaturgic loyalty," "discipline," and "circumspection" (6, pp. 212–228); although, as we shall try to make clear later, it may *not* be inferred that when the actor fails to experience these constraints they have ceased to operate. It is at these other times, however when the actor is not "on," that we shall refer to his perspective as "natural." At these other times persons tell us that their conduct appears to them as "spontaneous."

II

We may be better able to appreciate the difference between being "on" and being "natural"—and the difference this difference makes—if we turn to the experiences of a class of persons who must cope with it for a relatively long period of time. Entertainers would seem to be such a class, as Davis' statement suggests. Davis' statement also suggests, however, that a relatively well supported hiatus exists for entertainers between occasions of being "on" and "natural." There are those before whom one is "on," like the "public," and those with whom one is "natural," like the "group." These worlds may on occasion touch or even overlap, but presumably the boundaries usually remain clear. [6] What we seek is a class of persons who have difficulty creating or sustaining such a hiatus. For them, presumably, the incompatibilities of being "on" and being "natural," should such incompatibilities exist, will be magnified. Mental patients are such a class of persons.

There can be little doubt but that mental patients are in a situation productive of being "on." Bereft of membership in the group of reasonable men, they are forced to address the task of restoring their "character," of becoming "sane persons" again. It does not take mental patients long to discover that, as they lost their "sanity" in the eyes of others through what they did and said, so may they regain it. Under these conditions, we might expect mental patients to be "on" without reserve, that for them, truly, life becomes a theater.[7] There is some truth in this: mental patients are "on" at times and feel under pressure to be "on" even more often. But, given their motives to be "on" and the pressure they are under, it is perhaps more remarkable that mental patients cannot sustain this perspective without experiencing severe anxiety and discomfort. From this, as from other experiences of mental patients, we may learn something of importance about everyday life.[8]

We can get at this experience by considering more closely some aspects of the perspective of being "on." Let us consider that, when one is "on," activities come to be regarded as "performances," other persons as an "audience," and the world around as a series of "scenes" and "props." Let us also consider how this view conflicts with what mental patients consider "natural."

Like others who are "on," the mental patient comes to regard his own activities as potential "performances," as potential means of creating and sustaining a "character" for the benefit of others. At times, he uses them this way. Unlike some who are "on," however, the mental patient faces a dilemma. The "show" he experiences himself as "staging" concerns a fundamental matter, a matter that, as he sees it, should not and should not need to be "staged"; namely, his "normality." This is not only an aspect of self that he wants others to again take for granted. This he might indeed accomplish through a judicious "performance." More important, "normality" is an aspect of self the mental patient *himself* profoundly desires to take for granted again. And regarding his activities as "performances" interferes with this crucial aim.

Thus, a patient may enact a "normal character," succeed in "taking in" the audience, and retrospectively discover that he has, in the process, left himself more unconvinced than ever about the "reality" of his "normality."

> Mr. Yale [9] told the interviewer that a nurse had remarked to him that his wife was much "improved." As a mark of "improvement" the nurse cited the fact that Mrs. Yale was playing "Scrabble" (a word game) a great deal. The next day, after some hesitance about confidentiality, Mrs. Yale confided to the interviewer that she and her friends had recently taken to playing "Scrabble" as a means of impressing the staff with their ability to think clearly and be sociable. During the balance of the interview, Mrs. Yale expressed a great deal of concern over whether she was "really" better or had merely misled personnel.

Or, anticipating this sort of conflict, a patient may pointedly avoid "performing."

> Mrs. White said that, if she decided to, she could easily get out of the hospital: she realized that she had come to learn what one was "supposed to say and do" to accomplish this. However, she added, *to* do these things was to deny one's "own self" and what "one felt."

Finally, what the patient has been saying and doing may be defined by an authoritative other *as* "performing," thereby provoking conflict.

> Mrs. Quinn said that when Dr. X suggested that she was "painting the picture too rosy," she realized that she had been trying to impress hospital staff just to get out of the hospital, and this frightened her.

We are led to see, then, that the mental patient is not satisfied to *appear* "normal," he strives to *be* "normal." Paradoxically, this means, in part, that he wants to "appear normal" to *himself*. Striving to "appear normal" for others—"putting on a show of normality"—interferes with this objective.

It may also be noted that the mental patient addresses others as a potential "audience." The hospital, self-defined as a place of "observation," is obviously conducive to this effect. Others, the patient learns, are "witnesses" of as well as "participants" in his activities. With this a matter of awareness—and, moreover, assumed by the patient to be a matter of awareness for the other—it becomes difficult for a patient to have a relationship in which the impression the other receives of his "illness" or lack of it is not relevant.

During hospitalization patients tend to construe all situations as, potentially, "test" situations in which their "sanity" is being assessed. Thus, many patients make a particular point of knowing the day, month, year, and season, anticipating that "requests for information" will in fact be "orientation examinations." And others, not appreciating how seldom hospital personnel have a chance to become familiar with "the record," consider what are in fact requests for information (like, "how many children do you have?") as further tests. The perspective, in a few cases, tends to become omnipresent: thus, Mrs. Karr believed throughout her hospitalization that several of the "patients" were "spies" who collected information for the hospital and were only feigning illness. And, of course, there is little reason to believe that regarding others as an "audience" ends with release from the hospital. So for a time during the post-hospital period several patients responded to the greeting "How are you?" by launching a description of their mental health or by inquiring into the interviewers' motives for asking such a "question." Information received from patients' relatives suggests that this kind of response was not confined to the interview situation.

These kinds of responses suggest that, within his perspective, the patient consciously follows a kind of "script" in which his primary appearance is that of a "suspect person." In part, it is the others who have these "suspicions" and the patient must disabuse them of these. This is to be accomplished by "watching" one's own "reactions" and by fitting them to the model of a "normal person," also included in the "script." As well, the patient attempts to restrict the actions of others toward him to those which may appropriately be directed to a "normal person."

But, again, the patient's appearance before others is only part of a weighty problem. Not only must he fashion a "normal character" for others and attempt to induce them to provide the social conditions under which he can carry this off, he must do these things while remaining the most critical "audience" of his own "show." Viewing his own activities from "inside," the mental patient finds that he must work with "reactions" which *he* perceives as contrived and controlled. And for him, as for his other "audiences," a critical aspect of "normality" is that "reactions" are just that: they appear "spontaneous." More is at stake, then, than "putting on" a creditable "performance" for an "audience"; indeed, doing so would seem to undermine the most important "show" of all.

Finally, let us note that the mental patient tends to view things as potential "props." That is, "things," including persons and places ("scenes"), tend to be appreciated directly for the information they potentially and actually convey about the self, for their communicative value in creating, sustaining, or disrupting a "character."

Thus some patients, as well as some sociologists, recognize that the limited expressive materials afforded by the hospital insure that many activities will almost certainly "look crazy." And patients feel under constant pressure to remain aware of the communicative value of their own affective expressions.

> Mrs. Vick said, "Life is a pretense. I have to pretend every day that I'm here. That I'm gay and happy in order to stay out of the isolation ward. So I laugh and pretend to be gay."

Other persons, too, may be regarded as "props" to be maneuvered in the interests of the "show" at hand. Thus patients frequently demand that relatives visibly express affection and need for them on the ward. Such expressions were correctly perceived by patients as important to personnel in establishing the patients' "return to normality."

The problem with this view of "things" is that the patient reinforces his own uncertainty as to what is "real" and what is "mere appearance." Thus, the effort to appear "gay" seems to make patients wonder if all "gayness" isn't "mere appearance"; and prearrangements with relatives seem to make patients more uncertain about just what their relatives "really" feel toward them, as well as how they "really" feel toward their relatives. Indeed, this seems to be the core problem with being "on" in regard to fundamental matters: not only can the patient no longer trust others but, most devastating of all, he can no longer trust himself. He is, for a while, anxiously uncertain as to whether the "normal character" he projects *is* his "self." And the more he appears to himself as "acting"—the more singlemindedly he strives for "effect"—the more uncertain he seems to become.

The foregoing may be summarized in this way. The mental patient is under pressure to experience the world, with his self at its center, in a "technical" way. Like the stage actor contemplating the cloak-over-self he will don for his audience, so the mental patient comes to address his own character. Instead of a "natural" phenomenon, flowing from and reflecting the self, the mental patient's character comes to appear to him as a "constructed object," [10] as a "function" of manipulated activities and contrived scenes, of the assessments of an audience and the standards they invoke, and of the nature and availability of props.[11] The connection between self and character becomes a questionable, undependable matter. Or, to use another figure, this connection becomes a matter of wit and stagecraft, of the contingencies of "staging a show." An intrinsic link is shattered.

III

We have said that, for a while, the mental patient is "on." It remains to note that this perspective bears a remarkable resemblance to the perspective that the dramaturgic analyst seems to attribute to the individual in everyday life, whatever the mental status of the latter. Thus, the dramaturgic analyst conceives the individual as a "performer" whose activities function to create the "appearance" of a "self"—a "character"—for an "audience." In the process of maintaining or changing his "character" for others, the individual manipulates things as "props." Others are related to the individual in terms of their "parts" in putting a "show" together, of witnessing it, of sustaining it, or of disrupting it. Places become "scenes" which are fitted or unfitted for the creation of "character" at hand. The outcome of interest to the analyst is the "effective" creation of a "character" which, by "taking in" the "audience" or failing to do so, will permit the individual to continue a rewarding line of activity or to avoid an unrewarding one, or which will result in his being "discredited." Finally, the dramaturgic analyst seems to make mental patients of us all, for he conceives the individual as "staging" *fundamental* qualities: aspects of self taken for granted *with* intimate others.[12]

This vision of the world is for a time, as we have tried to show, a core aspect of the mental patient's perspective. Finding himself in the eyes of others either a doubtful person or a thoroughly discredited one, he may consciously undertake to fashion an image of "normality." Insofar as this is the case, he will "act" with full awareness; he will see himself as "acting"; he will be "on."

Now we must ask, is the dramaturgic analyst asserting that individuals are "on" in everyday life, routinely and as a matter of course? Is he suggesting that ordinarily, say among family and friends, the individual views "life as theater"? If so, what shall we make of the fact that the mental patient experiences being "on" as an *interruption* of his "normal" perspective and as a source of anxiety and alienation? How shall we account for the patient's intense desire to get "off"?

We wish to suggest that no paradox is involved. In viewing "life as theater," the dramaturgic analyst does not present us with a model of the actor's consciousness; *he is not suggesting that this is the way his subjects understand the world.* Instead, the dramaturgic analyst invokes the theatrical model as a device, a tool, to permit *him* to focus attention on the consequences of the actor's activities for others' perceptions of the actor. The dramaturgic analyst finds this important because, according to *his* theory of social stability and change, others' "impressions" determine the ways they will act toward the actor. Thus, whether the actor self-consciously takes account of these "impressions" or not, whether or not he is even aware that he is creating an "impression," such "impressions" are demonstrably relevant to the fate of such interaction as the actor enters.

In one sense, then, the actor's "perspective," that is, the actor's view of what he is doing, is not relevant to the dramaturgic analyst. For whatever the actor believes he is doing, so long as he is engaged in interaction, the analyst finds and focusses on the "impression" the actor is making on others. The analyst's "frame of reference," his rules for converting the actor's motions into conduct (1), are given by the theatrical simile. This frame of reference, these rules, may be quite different than those used by the actor to understand his own behavior.[13] This feature of dramaturgic analysis seems to be frequently misunderstood, even by its appreciators.[14] At least in part, this seems to be due to a lack of explicitness, if not a lack of clarity,[15] on the part of those using the dramaturgic framework.

In another sense, however, the actor's perspective is quite relevant to the dramaturgic analyst. As a social-psychologist, the dramaturgic analyst is little interested in documenting what "everybody knows." Instead he wants to get at *how* everybody knows what they know, at "hidden" effects or *latent* functions of interaction. The theatrical simile, like any of the similes invoked by the dramaturgic analyst, is revealing precisely insofar as it clarifies a latent function. Moreover, it seems to do so only when the actor is "unconscious" of the "impressive" effects of his activities, that is, only insofar as the actor "takes for granted" or "takes notice of without seeing" these effects. This may be appreciated by considering what a dramaturgic analysis of a theatrical performance might be.

A dramaturgic analysis of a theatrical performance would presumably *not* focus on how stage actors manage to bring a play "to life" for an audience. An analysis in these terms would be merely a technical analysis of the business at hand as the principles and the audience define this business. It would produce a manual of stage directions. In order to produce an account of interest to the dramaturgic analyst, what would have to be considered is how stage actors manage to keep the audience continually convinced that the play they are witnessing *is a play*. Such an analysis might point out, for example, that, by altering the segments of time within which events can "really" be accomplished, actors provide the audience with a sense of "play" as distinguished from "reality." It might document the gestures actors employ on stage which *interrupt* the audience member's sense of emerging character, which remind the audience that "character" and actor are not the same. It might note that returning for bows after the curtain has fallen not only services actors' egos, but also functions to remind the audience that there *is* someone "behind" the "appearance" they have been attending, for example, that the "appearance" of the dead man was "merely an appearance." Such an analysis might inquire as to which members of the audience, children under certain ages, for example, cannot retain the sense of the play *as* a play. And more. In general, a dramaturgic analysis of a theatrical performance would ask, what are the relations between the world in which the attitude of "play acting" prevails and that in which the attitude of "daily life" or "fundamental reality" obtains? What are the social devices whereby these worlds are kept distinct, and under what circumstances does this distinction collapse?

It should be noted that, insofar as the above is correct, the dramaturgic analyst seeks to describe the ways in which "impressions" are created, sustained, and ruptured under the condition that the actor is "unconscious" or only dimly "conscious" that this is a part of the business he is in. The other "models" used by the dramaturgic analyst reveal the same feature. Thus, the "con man" instructs us how, in everyday life, without being explicitly aware of it, those who do not conceive themselves as "con men" may sustain another's conception of themselves as "trustworthy" in the face of events which might lead him to conceive them quite differently. And persons who attach television aerials to their houses but do not own sets, those who put exotic travel labels on luggage that gets no further than the front door, in brief, those who *intentionally* misrepresent their qualities, thereby taking on a "character" for the audience to which they feel they have no "real" claim, are interesting to the dramaturgic analyst, not in themselves, but as persons who furnish "clear-cut evidence of the impressive function of presumably instrumental objects" and acts (6, p. 67).

Indeed, it does not seem too much to say that the power of dramaturgic analysis lies *in* the discrepancy between the perspective of the actor and that of the analyst. It is through this discrepancy that the analyst is able to elucidate matters that are beyond the immediate awareness of his subjects. It is when this discrepancy exists, when, for example, the actor provides "impressions" without being aware that he is doing so, that the theatrical simile is most revealing. What it reveals is this: the ways in which interactants *manage,* that is, *produce through their own activities,* that which they "take for granted" is "out there, really." Since the dramaturgic analyst aims to explore the conditions of constancy and change in others' impressions of actors as "being" what they claim, the theatrical simile seems exquisitely suited to his purpose. It focusses attention on that *aspect* of interaction of central interest to the analyst; affecting others' perceptions is the principal business of those in the theater. In the theater, creating appearances is regarded as a *task;* thus the analyst can more easily consider what individuals in everyday life *do* to create and sustain the realities they honor, even though they are not entirely aware of their doings. In the theater, the "expressive" and "impressive" functions of activity are *separated;* therefore the analyst can consider in isolation that function of interaction so central to his theory of social stability and change.

All this adds up to pointing out some of the ways in which the theatrical simile is a simile, not a homology. It is a simile, a frame of reference, invoked by the analyst to segregate and permit him to analyze *one* of the multiple functions of interaction: its "'impressive" function. The purpose is facilitated *because* this function is segregated in the theater; in daily life, this function is a concretely inextricable part of a larger complex.

It is also worth noting that this frame of reference enables the analyst to himself abandon, if only for a while, the perspective of everyday life; it enables or forces him to *stop* taking for granted what his subjects *do* take for granted, thereby permitting him to talk *about* these matters. In this way, the perspective stands ready, as does the anthropologist's "tribe," to furnish a lens through which "what everybody knows" can be rendered problematic. We may then ask what we do that stabilizes Grand Central Station as a place for people with destinations, and not a place to live, subway cars as objects for travel, not for sleeping, a hotel lounge as a place to meet people in, a library for reading, a fire escape for survival, and more (7, p. 182).

But, as with any model, so the theatrical one has limits which, if not observed, pose dangers to analysis. The analyst and his readers run the risk of considering the dramaturgic framework to represent his subjects' model of the world. Because "impression management" is critical in the *analyst's* scheme of things, because in any situation it is this dimension that *he* attends to, he may leave the impression that this is the way things "are" as his subjects see things—or at least that, if they could be brought to be honest for a bit, they would see and admit that this is the case. There is, of course, no justification for this. Indeed, within the dramaturgic framework one must address in all seriousness the subjects' view of self and world; this is, after all, the topic of analysis. On the other hand, there is no justification for overlooking the impressive function of daily activities in an analysis of human conduct. Adding the dramaturgic perspective to the social-psychological tool kit should go some way toward preventing this.

Second, if we are correct in asserting that the dramaturgic analyst does not present "life as theater" as his subjects' view of the world, then we must ask after the relation between his subjects' view and "life as theater." The dramaturgic analyst does not claim that the actor is aware of the impressive functions of his activities; indeed, he seems to claim that, to the extent that the actor is aware of these functions, he becomes alienated from interaction and, moreover, from himself (5). We concur with this view and have presented some observations by and about mental patients to help warrant it. But, although in the dramaturgic vision the actor does not attend to the impressive effects of his activities *as* impressive effects, he nonetheless exhibits a remarkable ability to produce the right effect at just the right time, or, short, of this, to correct for the errors he and his teammates may make. How is this accomplished? More pointedly, what is the relation between the *actor's* model of the world and the *dramaturgic analyst's* model? Is the actor merely the outcome of a dynamicized set of "organizational principles" which shove and haul him about without his awareness? Anyone committed to an understanding of everyday life and of the "actor's world" must cope with such a question. The dramaturgic analyst is self-admittedly so committed.

Finally, the theatrical simile may encourage the analyst to forget another important aspect of any everyday actor's communications: the actor is communicating *about* himself, and this constrains the attitude he may take toward the qualities he projects.

The stage actor's obligations do not ordinarily include a belief that the character he projects be a "presentation of self." It is an "Anybody" that the stage actor presents, if a particular one: an other-than-himself. His task, as usually defined, is to employ whatever means will facilitate the "coming alive" of the character for the audience. This leaves the actor free, or relatively so, to select an attitude toward the character he plays. He may, for example, conceive that getting "inside" the character will aid the accomplishment of his task; he may conceive that this is not necessary, taking a "classical" stance rather than a "method" one. So long as he convinces the audience that the character he portrays is a plausible one, his obligations are fulfilled. It is presumably only "method" actors, however, who succeed in experiencing the characters they are projecting as their selves, however temporarily.

The everyday actor's obligations, at least so far as fundamental qualities are concerned, do not leave him free to select an attitude toward the character he communicates. He does not, finally, experience life as theater. He does not expect the curtain to ring down, returning what came before to the realm of make-believe. He is constrained to *be* what he claims, and mental patients suggest that these constraints operate "inside" the individual as well as "on" him. Indeed, his need to believe in himself seems even stronger than his need to be certain that others entertain a particular view of him. He is in the grip of an ethic, and he violates this ethic so long as he is "on."

The basic task joined by mental patients would seem to be the locating and fixing of the reality of themselves. In this, they differ from stage actors; they cannot remain "on" with impunity. And in this, mental patients represent us all.

NOTES

[1] This phrase is used by Erving Goffman in (4). Reference (6) is a revised and enlarged edition of the same work. Our criticism, as well as appreciation, of the "dramaturgic approach" are directed primarily at Goffman's work as its foremost exponent.

[2] When used in an unqualified way, we intend the term "actor" to refer to that "Anybody" whose "action" is the subject of the dramaturgic analyst's analytic efforts. "Anybody" need not be a stage actor.

[3] The study was carried out by the California Department of Mental Hygiene and partially supported by Grant 3M-9124 from the National Institute of Mental Health. The study, carried out by the authors and others, consisted in observing and frequently interviewing the members of 17 families in which the wife was hospitalized for "schizophrenia." A description of the study group and of study procedures may be found in (10).

[4] The context of his remarks is Davis' discussion of a group of intimates of which he is a member—known as the "Clan" by some, the "Rat Pack" by others—and the relations between this group and the "public."

[5] Perhaps the best description of the variety of these situations is found in Goffman (5).

[6] Jonathan Winters, an entertainer, provides us with an example of the breakdown of these boundaries. Of a period in his life when he experienced a "crack-up" he says, "I was 'on' all the time, always playing the part—in parks, restaurants, whenever [sic] I went—and I couldn't get 'off.' Well, I got 'off.' I look around now and think how much I have to be thankful for. And there's no use throwing myself on the floor because once in a while something bugs me" (13, p. 32). Stories about stage actors who carry their "parts" home, as well as audience members who take "character" for "reality," are common, if the events they point to infrequent.

[7] Goffman has something like this in mind when he remarks that the mental patient "can learn, at least for a time, to practice before all groups the amoral arts of shamelessness" (7, "The Moral Career of the Mental Patient," p. 169).

[8] The whole remarkable series of papers by Goffman on mental patients and their keepers provides an example of what we may learn about everyday life from them (7).

[9] This, as the other patients' and relatives' names we have used, is fictitious. We have, however, consistently used the same names for identical patients and relatives throughout the several papers we have published or are publishing.

[10] Harold Garfinkel has used this term—and "assembled object"—in a similar way, but in another connection, in his unpublished work.

[11] Compare Goffman's view of the "self" in (6), especially pp. 252–253, in (2), "The Moral Career . . . ," pp. 168–169, and in (3), p. 271.

[12] Consider Goffman's statement to the effect that "when we observe a young American middle-class girl playing dumb for the benefit of her boy friend, we are ready to point to items of guile and contrivance in her behavior. But like herself and her boy friend, we accept as an unperformed fact that this performer *is* a young American middle-class girl. But surely here we neglect the greater part of the performance. . . . The unthinking ease with which performers consistently carry off such standard-maintaining routines does not deny that a performance has occurred, merely that the participants have been aware of it" (6, pp. 74–75).

[13] In this respect, if in no other, the dramaturgic analyst's approach resembles that of the psychoanalytic psychiatrist. The psychoanalyst, too, is professionally engaged in attributing meanings to the behavior of individuals which are variant from the individuals' understandings of their own behavior.

[14] For example, Don Martindale (9, pp. 61–72) discusses Goffman's work as if it were a representation of the growing amorality of urban individuals. We are explicitly disagreeing with this interpretation and would hold that the dramaturgic approach is applicable to the analysis of moral conduct in any age. We agree with Martindale, however, that the growing amorality of urban individuals may help account for the emergence of the dramaturgic perspective.

[15] Surely it does little to clarify matters to suggest that "the *object* of a performer is to sustain a particular definition of the situation, this representing, as it were, his claim as to what reality is" (6, p. 85, italics added). "Performer" here refers to a person in everyday life carrying out his routine projects of action, *not* to someone who is "on."

BIBLIOGRAPHY

1. Burke, K., *A Grammar of Motives,* New York: Prentice-Hall, 1952.
2. Goffman, E., "Cooling the Mark Out: Some Aspects of Adaptation to Failure," *Psychiatry,* 1952, 25, 451–463.
3. Goffman, E., "Embarrassment and Social Organization," *The American Journal of Sociology,* 1956, 62, 264–271.
4. Goffman, E., *The Presentation of Self in Everyday Life.* Edinburgh: University of Edinburgh Social Sciences Research Centre, 1956.
5. Goffman, E., "Alienation from Interaction," *Human Relations,* 1957, 10, 47–60.
6. Goffman, E., *The Presentation of Self in Everyday Life,* Garden City, New York: Doubleday, 1959.
7. Goffman, E., *Asylums,* New York: Doubleday, 1961.
8. Mailer, N., *Advertisements for Myself,* New York: The New American Libarary of World Literature, 1960.
9. Martindale, D., *American Society,* New York: D. Van Nostrand, 1960.
10. Sampson, H., S. L. Messinger, and R. D. Towne, "The Mental Hospital and Marital Family Ties," *Social Problems,* 1961, 9, 141–155.
11. Wolfe, B., "Ecstatic in Blackface: The Negro as a Song-and-Dance Man," *Modern Review,* 1950, 111, 196–208.
12. *Life Magazine,* December 22, 1958, 45, p. 116.
13. *San Francisco Chronicle,* January 24, 1961, p. 32.

Part Two

Social Interaction as Drama

Drama occurs in life at various levels of complexity, but most obviously at the microcosmic level, with individuals in social interaction. Here we encounter both ourselves and others in the drama of internal and interpersonal relations. We identify both our internal conflicts and our relations with others (at least the most important ones) as "dramatic." Mental conflict over an important decision, a proposal of marriage, killing or being killed in combat, becoming a parent, awareness of having a terminal disease—all at least *seem* to us dramatic, and we act in these contexts as if they were dramatic. The dramaturgy of social encounters has been a major concern of recent social science inquiry, and this section contains some representative pieces in this area.

The first selection is drawn from transactional psychologist Eric Berne's posthumous book. Berne's insight reveals that people live out "scripts" in the dramatic sense. These life dramas are "written" in childhood under parental influence and guide one throughout his life towards his "destiny." Actors are scripted as "O.K." or "not-O.K." For Berne, the "life-script" determines our important decisions, and indeed our fates: whether we marry happily, if our career is the one we "really" want, whether it succeeds or not, how we face death. The question, of course, is the extent to which we are *aware* of such a script, and how much we *consciously* act upon it. Certainly, self-consciousness alters the script and therefore the enactment. There are, however, limits that Berne rightly stresses: we cannot escape the previous acts or, more inclusively, the "circumference" of the whole play; nor can we escape the convergence of the "patterns" of archetypical dramas and the universal problems of people. But do we see our own lives, and the major events in those lives, as drama? Does this have its origins "from our sires"? What are the universal themes of human drama?

In any event, we do not come into social interactions cold, but with complicated backgrounds derived from socialization and experience. We are trained as social performers to act within the status and role systems of our society. But, as Ernest Becker understands, people "present" themselves to each other with their own "self" at stake; one's own self-esteem can be attacked and even destroyed in a social encounter. We learn how to present a "face," or *persona,* to the world, and fully expect others to do the same. Social interaction proceeds on the basis of such conventions, permitting communications and joint action, but at the same time protecting one's vital self-esteem. Society provides the buffer for many situations *in role,* which tells us how to act "onstage" as doctor, lawyer, Indian chief. In sum, our most mundane of social interactions are dramatic. One can well understand such a characterization, given the "gamble" always involved in social intercourse. But does such a broad use of the dramatic metaphor leave us with no way to distinguish between those interactions which are clearly dramatic to us and those which seem to be routine?

As Becker points out, one of the great modern observers of the subtlety and intricateness of ordinary social interaction is Erving Goffman. In the tradition of Simmel, Goffman dissects the little theatrical dramas at the interactional base of society for which we have all been so laboriously trained by culture. "Interaction ritual" involves this fundamental dramaturgical training through which the self can engage in social intercourse while retaining one's esteem or distance from others. One cannot refuse to play, but one can expect the social game to be played by certain rules: deference and demeanor, "face-saving," handling embarrassment and so on. Social actors make claims on each other, but they only can do so with proper observance of certain "moral" norms. Goffman claims that such dramaturgy is fundamental to the way society works; the ritual organization of mundane life provides the subtle framework within which social encounters are made for the actors. They are the "stage directions" for the social play.

Lyman and Scott draw upon aspects of the theatre to illuminate certain phenomena of everyday social life. "Stage fright" is experienced by social actors in situations where they must achieve a measure of "role perfection" before an audience. One's social "identity" may well be at stake. Anxiety results from fears about the quality of one's performance. They wish to restrict "theater in life" to certain specific encounters in which a high quality of performance or stringent requirements are involved. The soldier first going into combat, the virgin bride on her wedding night, the prisoner being executed, the politician making a televised campaign speech, all are *aware* of the drama of the situation and of their own high requirements in the situation. Indeed, the authors argue that modern societies constantly make demands that individuals "perform," and that this is a major reason for the high level of anxiety in such societies: We are all beset by "stage fright."

The final article, by Robert R. Smith and the late Robert W. Hawles, is at the same time serious and tongue-in-cheek. Like Lyman and Scott, they see anxiety present in many kinds of social interactions. To reduce anxiety and to facilitate communication, people, they say, introduce "fiddles" into the interaction. In Goffmanesque fashion, fiddles are subtle activities—dramatic devices, one might add—

that aid the common communicative task at hand. "Fidget fiddles," for example, relieve anxiety by a simple activity unrelated to the purpose of the interaction. Much cigarette smoking is simply "fiddling" to reduce tension. (Readers of J. D. Salinger will recall the extent to which cigarettes are used as fiddles.) Fiddles are a familiar dramatic strategy which facilitate not only communications among the actors, but with the audience as well. The teacher who cracks a joke the first day of school is fiddling to break down the tension among the new students.

The study of social interaction has long been a major concern of both the social sciences and humanities. The dramatic vision of life appears to offer insight into the conduct of social life denied to other perspectives. However, the question must remain: To what extent is the dramaturgical framework the most adequate description of social interaction?

10.

HUMAN DESTINY

Eric Berne

A. Life Plans

The destiny of every human being is decided by what goes on inside his skull when he is confronted with what goes on outside his skull. Each person designs his own life. Freedom gives him the power to carry out his own designs, and power gives him the freedom to interfere with the designs of others. Even if the outcome is decided by men he has never met or germs he will never see, his last words and the words on his gravestone will cry out his striving. If by great misfortune he dies in dust and silence, only those who know him best will get the slogan right, and all outside the private chambers of friendship, marriage, and medicine will see him wrong. In most cases he has spent his life deceiving the world, and usually himself as well. We will hear more about these illusions later.

Each person decides in early childhood how he will live and how he will die, and that plan, which he carries in his head wherever he goes, is called his script. His trivial behavior may be decided by reason, but his important decisions are already made: what kind of person he will marry, how many children he will have, what kind of bed he will die in, and who will be there when he does. It may not be what he wants, but it is what he wants it to be.

Magda

Magda was a devoted wife and mother, but when her youngest boy got very sick, she realized to her horror that in the back of her mind was an idea, a picture, or perhaps even a wish that the much-loved son would die. It reminded her of the time when her husband was overseas with the army and the same thing had happened. She was haunted by an eerie wish that he would get killed. In both cases she pictured herself in terrible grief and affliction. This would be her cross to bear, and everyone would admire the way she bore it.

Q. What would happen after that?

A. I never got that far. I'd be free, and then I could do what I wanted to. Start over.

When Magda was in grade school she had had many sexual adventures with her classmates, and the guilt of that had been with her ever since. The death of her son or husband would be a punishment or an expiation for this, and would free her from her mother's curse. She would no longer feel like an outcast. People would exclaim:

Reprinted by permission from *What Do You Say After You Say Hello?*, Grove Press, 1972.

"Isn't she courageous!" and acknowledge her as a fullfledged member of the human race.

Throughout most of her life she had had this tragic cinema planned out and pictured in her mind. It was the third act of her life drama, or script, as written in her childhood. Act I: Sexual Guilt and Confusion. Act II: Mother's Curse. Act III: Expiation. Act IV: Release, and a New Life. But in reality she was leading a very conventional life, in accordance with the teachings of her parents, and doing what she could to keep her loved ones healthy and happy. This was counter to the plot of her script—a counterscript—and was certainly not as dramatic or exciting.

A script is an ongoing life plan formed in early childhood under parental pressure. It is the psychological force which propels the person toward his destiny, regardless of whether he fights it or says it is his own free will.

It is not our intention in this book to reduce all human behavior or all human life to a formula. Quite the contrary. A real person may be defined as one who acts spontaneously in a rational and trustworthy way with decent consideration for others. One who follows a formula is a not-real, or unreal, person. But since these seem to constitute the bulk of humanity, it is necessary to try to learn something about them.

Della

Della was a neighbor of Magda's, in her late twenties, and led much the same kind of domestic life. But her husband, a salesman, traveled a lot. Sometimes when he was away Della would start out drinking and end up far away from home. She "blacked out" these episodes, and as is common in such cases, she knew what happened only because she would find herself in strange places with the names and telephone numbers of strange men in her purse when she came to. This not only horrified her, but terrified her, since it meant that she could ruin her life some day by picking up an indiscreet or evil man.

Scripts are planned early in childhood, so if this was a script, it must have had its origins there. Della's mother died when she was little and her father was away all day, working. Della didn't get along very well with the other kids in school. She felt inferior, and led a lonely life. But late in childhood she discovered a way to be popular. Like Magda, she offered herself for sexy play to a gang of little boys. She had never thought of the connection between those school days in the hayloft and her current behavior. But all along in her head she was carrying the outline of her life drama. Act I: The setup. Fun and Guilt in a Hayloft. Act II: An outbreak of script. Fun and Guilt While Drunk and Irresponsible. Act III: The payoff. Denunciation and Ruin. She loses everything—husband, children, and position. Act IV: The final release. Suicide. Then everybody feels sorry and forgives her.

Both Magda and Della lived in their peaceful counterscripts with a feeling of impending doom. The script was a tragic drama which would bring them release and reconciliation. The difference was that Magda was waiting patiently for an act of God to fulfill her destiny—salvation; while Della, propelled by the compulsion of an inner demon, was hurrying impatiently toward hers—damnation, death, and forgiveness. Thus, from the same beginnings ("sexual delinquency") these two women were moving by diverse means to different ends.

The psychotherapist is sitting in his office like a wise man and is getting paid to do something about all this. Both Magda and Della will be free if somebody dies, but his job is to find a better way to free them. He leaves his office and walks down the street past the stockbroker's, the taxi stand, and the saloon. Nearly everybody he sees is waiting for a Big Killing. In the grocery store a woman is shouting at her daughter: "How many times have I got to tell you not to touch that?" while somebody admires her little boy: "Isn't he cute!" When he gets to the hospital, a paranoid says: "How do I get out of here, doctor?" A depressive says: "What am I living for?" and a schizophrenic answers: "Don't diet, liveit. I'm not really that stupid." That's what they all said yesterday. They're stuck, while the ones on the outside are still hoping. "Shall we increase his dose of medication?" asks a medical student. Dr. Q turns to the schizophrenic and looks him in the eye. The schizophrenic looks back at him. "Shall we increase your medication?" asks Dr. Q. The boy thinks a while and then replies. "No." Dr. Q puts out his hand and says: "Hello." The schizophrenic shakes hands with him and says: "Hello." Then they both turn to the medical student, and Dr. Q says: "Hello." The medical student looks flustered, but five years later, at a psychiatric meeting, he walks up to Dr. Q and says: "Hi, Dr. Q. Hello."

Mary

"Some day I'm going to open a nursery school, get married four times, make a lot of money on the stock market, and become a famous surgeon," said drunken Mary.

This is *not* a script. First, she didn't get any of these ideas from her parents. They hated children, didn't believe in divorce, thought the stock market was too speculative, and that surgeons charged too much. Second, her personality was not suited to any of these things. She was up tight with children, frigidly cool with men, scared of the market, and her hands shook from drinking. Thirdly, she had long ago decided to be a realtor during the day, and an alcoholic evenings and weekends. Fourthly, none of those projects really turned her on. They were more expressions of what she couldn't do rather than of what she could. And fifthly, it was obvious to anyone who heard her that she wasn't ever going to do any of them.

A script requires (1) Parental directives. (2) A suitable personality development. (3) A childhood decision. (4) A real turn-on to a particular method of success or failure, and (5) A convincing attitude (or a credible stance, as they say nowadays).

In this book we will consider what is known so far about the script apparatus, and what can be done to change it.

B. On Stage and Off Stage

Theatrical scripts are intuitively derived from life scripts, and a good way to start is to consider the connections and similarities between them.[1]

1. Both are based on a limited number of themes, the best known of which is the Oedipal tragedy. The others can likewise be found in Greek drama and Greek mythology. Other people had the rude dithyrambs and lewd orgies of the ancient priestly dramas, but the Greeks and Hebrews were the first to distill out and record the more homely and recognizable patterns of human living. Human life, it is true, is full of epic Agon, Pathos, Threnos, and Theophany, as in the Primal Rituals, but these are much easier to understand and contemplate if they are played out in ordinary language, Bam! and Wow! with a man and a maid in the moonlight under the laurel tree when along comes Bigmouth, whoever he or she may be. Reduced to this level by the Greek poets, the life of every human being is already charted in Bulfinch or Graves. If the gods smile on him, he will be a going concern. But if they frown he becomes something else, and if he wants to remove the curse or live more comfortably with it, he becomes a patient.

For the transactional script analyst, as for the play analyst, this means that if you know the plot and the character, you know what his outcome will be, unless some changes can be made. For example, it is clear to the psychotherapist, as to the drama critic, that Medea had her mind made up to kill her children, unless someone could talk her out of it; and it should be equally clear to both of them that if she had gone to her treatment group that week, the whole thing would never have happened.

2. Not only do certain life courses have predictable outcomes if they are allowed to go on as they are, but a certain dialogue of specific words spoken a certain way is necessary to establish the proper motivation for the outcome. In both the theater and in real life, the cues have to be memorized and spoken just right so that the other people will respond in a way that justifies and advances the action. If the hero changes his lines and his ego state, the other people respond differently. This throws the whole script off, and that is the aim of therapeutic script analysis. If Hamlet begins to use lines from *Abie's Irish Rose,* Ophelia has to change her lines, too, in order to make sense of it, and the whole performance will proceed differently. The two of them might then take off together instead of skulking around the castle— a bad play, but probably a better life.[2]

3. A script has to be rehearsed and rewritten before it is ready for the most dramatic performance. In the theater there are readings, rewrites, rehearsals, and tryouts before the big time. A life script starts off in childhood in a primitive form called the *protocol.* Here the other players are limited to parents and brothers and sisters; or in an institution or foster home, to tablemates and those in charge. These all play their roles rather rigidly because every family is an institution, and the child does not learn much flexibility from them. As he moves into adolescence, he begins to meet more people. He seeks out those who will play the roles his script requires (they will do it because he plays some role their scripts require). At this time, he rewrites his script to take account of his new environment. The basic plot remains the same, but the action is a little different. In most cases (except for adolescent suicide or murder), this is rehearsal—something like a small-town tryout. Through several such adaptations, he gets it into final form for the biggest production of all— the farewell performance, the final payoff on the script. If it is a "good" one, it takes place at a farewell dinner. If it is a "bad" one, he says good-by from a hospi-

tal bed, the door of a prison cell or psychiatric ward, the gallows, or the morgue.

4. Almost every script has roles for "good guys" and "bad guys," and for "winners" and "losers." What is considered good or bad,[3] and what is a winner or a loser, is something peculiar to each script, but it is very clear that every script has these four characters, sometimes combined in two roles. In a cowboy script, for example, the good guy is a winner and the bad guy is a loser. Good means brave, quick on the draw, honest, and pure; bad may mean cowardly, slow on the draw, crooked, and interested in girls. A winner is someone who survives; a loser is someone who is hanged or gets shot. In a soap opera, a winner is a girl who gets a man; a loser is a girl who loses a man. In a paper-shuffle opera, the winner is the man who gets the best contract or the most proxies; a loser is a man who doesn't know how to shuffle papers.

In script analysis, winners are called "princes" or "princesses," and losers are called "frogs." The object of script analysis is to turn frogs into princes and princesses. In order to do this, the therapist has to find out who the good guys and the bad guys are in the patient's script, and also what kind of a winner he can be. The patient fights being a winner because he is not in treatment for that purpose, but only to be made into a braver loser. This is natural enough, since if he becomes a braver loser, he can follow his script more comfortably, whereas if he becomes a winner he has to throw away all or most of his script and start over, which most people are reluctant to do.

5. All scripts, whether in the theater or in real life, are essentially answers to the basic question of human encounter: "What do you say after you say Hello?" The Oedipal drama and the Oedipal life, for example, both hinge entirely on this question. Whenever Oedipus meets an older man, he first says Hello. The next thing he has to say, driven by his script, is: "Wanna fight?" If the older man says "No," Oedipus has nothing further to say to him, and can only stand dumbly wondering whether to talk about the weather, the conduct of the current war, or who is going to win in the Olympic games. The easiest way out is to mumble "Pleased to meetcha," *"Si vales bene est, ego valeo,"* or "Everything in moderation," and go on his way. But if the older one says "Yes," Oedipus answers: "Groovy!" because now he has found his man and he knows what to say next.

6. Life-script scenes have to be set up and motivated ahead of time, just like theatrical scenes. A simple example is running out of gas. This is nearly always set up two or three days in advance by looking at the gauge, "planning" to get gas "sometime soon," and then not doing it. In fact it is impossible to run out of gas "right now" except in a strange car with a broken gauge. It is nearly always an impending event, a preplanned scene in a loser's script. Many winners go through a whole lifetime without ever running dry.

Life scripts are based on parental programing, which the child seeks out for three reasons. (1) It gives a purpose to life where it might otherwise be wanting. A child does most things for the sake of people, usually his parents. (2) It gives him an acceptable way to structure his time (acceptable, that is, to his parents). (3) People have to be told how to do things. Learning for oneself may be inspiring, but it is not very practical. A man does not become a good pilot by wrecking a few airplanes and learning by his errors. He has to learn through other people's failures, not his own. A surgeon has to have a teacher, rather than taking out appendixes one after the other to find out all the things that can go wrong. So parents program their children by passing on to them what they have learned, or what they think they have learned. If they are losers, they will pass on to them their loser's programing, and if they are winners, then they will pass on that kind of program. The long-term pattern always has a story line. While the outcome is determined for better or for worse by parental programing, the child is often free to select his own plot.

C. Myths and Fairy Tales

The first and most archaic version of the script, the primal protocol, is conceived in the mind of the child at an age when few people outside his immediate family are real to him. We assume that his parents appear to him as huge figures endowed with magic powers, like the giants and giantesses, ogres and gorgons of mythology, if only because they are three times as tall and ten times as big as he is.

As he grows older and becomes more sophisticated, he moves from this classical universe into a more romantic world. He devises the first palimpsest, or rewrite, of his script, to make it correspond with his new view of his surroundings. If conditions are right, he is helped here by fairy tales and animal stories at first read to him by his mother, and later read by himself in his leisure hours when he is free to let his imagination roam. There is magic in these, too, but less earthshaking. They give him a whole new set of characters to play their roles in his fancies: all the personalities in the animal kingdom, which are familiar to him either as warm-blooded playmates and companions, or as fleeting figures of fear or fascination seen or heard in the distance, or as semi-imaginary creatures of unknown capabilities that he has only heard or read about. Or perhaps this comes to him from the television screen, where at that age even the commercials have a halo. Even in the worst case, without book or screen, or even mother, somewhere he knows there is a cow, or can imagine his own distorted beasts.

In the first stage he is dealing with magical people who can perhaps on occasion turn themselves into animals. In this second stage he is merely attributing to animals certain human characteristics, a tendency which persists in adult life to some degree in people associated with stables, kennels, and dolphin tanks.

In the third stage, in adolescence, he reviews his script once more to adapt it to the current reality as he hopes it will be, still romanticized and still golden, or sometimes gilded with the aid of drugs. Gradually, as the years go by, he moves closer to reality, which is the actual likelihood that the people and things around him will give the desired responses. In this way, through the decades, he prepares himself for his farewell performance. It is this farewell performance which, above all, it is the therapist's business to change. . . .

D. Waiting for *Rigor Mortis*

One object of script analysis is to fit the patient's life plan into the grand historical psychology of the whole human race, a psychology which apparently has changed but little from cave days, through the early farming and ranching settlements and the great totalitarian governments of the Middle East, up to the present time. Joseph Campbell, in *The Hero With A Thousand Faces,* which is the best textbook for script analysts, summarizes this as follows:

"Freud, Jung, and their followers have demonstrated irrefutably that the logic, the heroes, and the deeds of myth survive into modern times. . . . The latest incarnation of Oedipus, the continued romance of Beauty and the Beast, stand this afternoon on the corner of Forty-Second Street and Fifth Avenue, waiting for the traffic light to change." He points out that while the hero of myth achieves a world-historical triumph, the hero of the fairy tale achieves merely a small domestic victory. And patients are patients, we may add, because they cannot achieve the victories they aim for and still survive. Hence they come to the doctor, "the knower of all the secret ways and words of potency. His role is precisely that of the Wise Old Man of the myths and fairy tales whose words assist the hero through the trials and terrors of the weird adventure."

That, at any rate, is the way the Child in the patient sees it, no matter how his Adult tells the story, and it is quite evident that all children, since the beginning of humanity, have had to cope with the same problems, and have had about the same weapons at their disposal. When it comes to the cutting, life is the same old wine in new bottles: coconut and bamboo bottles gave way to goatskins, goatskins to pottery, pottery to glass, and glass to plastic, but the grapes have hardly changed at all, and there is the same old intoxication on top and the same old dregs at the bottom. So, as Campbell says, there will be found little variation in the shapes of the adventures and the characters involved. Hence, if we know some of the elements of the patient's script, we can predict with some confidence where he is heading, and head him off before he meets with misfortune or disaster. That is called preventive psychiatry, or "making progress." Even better, we can get him to change his script or give it up altogether, which is curative psychiatry, or "getting well."

Thus, it is not a matter of doctrine or necessity to find precisely the myth or fairy tale which the patient is following; but the closer we can come, the better. Without such a historical foundation, errors are frequent. A mere episode in the patient's life, or his favorite game, may be mistaken for the whole script; or the occurrence of a single animal symbol, such as a wolf, may lead the therapist to bark up the wrong tree. Relating the patient's life or his Child's life plan to a coherent story which has survived for hundreds or thousands of years because of its universal appeal to the primitive layers of the human mind, at least gives a feeling of working from a solid foundation, and at best may give very precise clues as to what needs to be done to avert or change a bad ending.

The Waiting for Rigor Mortis Script

For example, a fairy tale may reveal elements of a script which are otherwise hard to dig up, such as the "script illusion." The transactional analyst believes that psychiatric symptoms result from some form of self-deception. But patients can be cured just because their lives and their disabilities are based on a figment of the imagination.

In the script known as "Frigid Woman," or "Waiting for *Rigor Mortis*" (WRM), the mother keeps telling her daughter that men are beasts, but it is a wife's duty to submit to their bestiality. If the mother pushes hard enough, the girl may even get the idea that she will die if she has an orgasm. Usually such mothers are great snobs, and they offer a release or an "antiscript" that will lift the curse. It is all right for the daughter to have sex if she marries a very important person, such as the Prince with the Golden Apples. But failing that, she tells her erroneously, "all your troubles will be over when you reach your menopause, because then you won't be in danger of feeling sexy any more."

Now it already appears as though we have three illusions: Orgathanatos, or the fatal orgasm; the Prince with the Golden Apples; and Blessed Relief, or the purifying menopause. But none of these is the real script illusion. The girl has tested Orgathanatos by masturbation, and knows it is not fatal. The Prince with the Golden Apples is not an illusion, because it is just possible that she might find such a man, just as she might win the Irish Sweepstakes or get four aces in a poker game; both of these things are unlikely, but not mythical; they do happen. And Blessed Relief is not something her Child really wants. In order to find the script illusion, we need the fairy tale which corresponds to WRM.

The Story of Sleeping Beauty

An angry fairy says that Briar Rose will prick her finger with a spindle and fall down dead. Another fairy commutes this to a hundred years of sleep. When she is fifteen Briar Rose does prick her finger, and immediately falls asleep. At the same moment everybody and everything else in the castle also fall asleep. During the hundred years, many princes try to get to her through the briars which have grown up around her, but none succeeds. At last, after the time is up, a prince arrives who manages to get through because the briars let him. When he finds the princess and kisses her, she wakes up and they fall in love. At the same moment, everybody and everything else in the castle take up exactly where they left off, as though nothing had happened and no time had passed since they fell asleep. The princess herself is still only fifteen years old, not 115. She and the prince get married, and in one version, they live happily ever after; in another, this is only the beginning of their troubles.[4]

There are many magic sleeps in mythology. Perhaps the best known is that of Brunhilde, who is left sleeping on the mountain with a ring of fire around her which only a hero can penetrate, and that is accomplished by Siegfriede.[5]

In one way or another, with slight alterations, almost everything in the story of Sleeping Beauty could actually happen. Girls do prick their fingers and faint, and they do fall asleep in their towers, and princes do wander around in the forest and look for fair maidens. The one thing that cannot happen is for everything and everybody to be unchanged and unaged after the lapse of so many years. This is a real illusion because it is not only improbable, it is impossible. And this is just the illusion on which WRM scripts are based: that when the Prince does come, Rose will be fifteen years old again instead of thirty, forty, or fifty, and they will have a whole lifetime ahead of them. This is the illusion of sustained youth, a modest daughter of the illusion of immortality. It is hard to tell Rose in real life that princes are younger men, and that by the time they reach her age they have become kings, and are much less interesting. That is the most distressing part of the script analyst's job: to break up the illusion, to inform the patient's Child that there is no Santa Claus, and make it stick. It is much easier for both of them if there is the patient's favorite fairy tale to work with.

One of the practical problems of WRM is that if Rose does find the Prince with the Golden Apples, she often feels outclassed and has to find fault and play "Blemish" to bring him down to her level, so that he ends up wishing she would go back in the briars and fall asleep again. On the other hand, if she settles for less—the Prince with the Silver Apples, or even ordinary McIntoshes from the grocery store—she will feel cheated and take it out on him, meanwhile always keeping an eye out for the Golden One. Thus, neither the frigid script nor the magic antiscript offers much chance for fulfillment. Also, as in the fairy tale, there is his mother to contend with as well as her witch.

This script is important because a great many people in the world, in one way or another, spend their lives waiting for *rigor mortis*.

E. The Family Drama

Another good way to uncover the plot and some of the most important lines in a person's script is to ask: "If your family life were put on the stage, what kind of play would it be?" Such family dramas are usually named after the Greek Oedipus and Electra plays, in which the boy competes with father for his mommy and the girl wants daddy for her own.[6] But the script analyst has to know what the parents called for convenience Supideo and Artcele, are up to meanwhile. Supideo is the other side of the Oedipus drama, and expresses the frank or disguised sexual feelings of the mother for her son, while Artcele is the other side of Electra and shows father's feelings for the girl. A close inquiry will nearly always reveal rather obvious transactions which demonstrate that these feelings are not imaginary, even though the parent tries to conceal them, usually by playing "Uproar" with the child. That is, the disturbed parent tries to cover up his Child sexual feelings for his offspring by coming on Parental and ordering the offspring about in a quarrelsome way. But on certain occasions they leak out, despite all efforts to disguise them by "Uproar" and other devices. Actually, the happiest parents are often those who openly admire the attractiveness of their children.

The Supideo and Artcele dramas, like Oedipus and Electra, have many variations. As the children grow older, they may be played out as mother sleeping with son's boyfriend or father sleeping with his daughter's chum. Farther out and even more "gamy" versions are mother sleeping with daughter's boyfriend or father sleeping with son's girl.* This compliment may be returned by the young Oedipus sleeping with father's mistress, or Electra with mother's lover. Sometimes the family script calls for one or several members to be homosexual, with corresponding variations in child sex play, incest between siblings, and later seductions of each other's partners. Any deviations from the standard Oedipus (son wondering or dreaming about sex with mother) or Electra (daughter wondering or dreaming about father) roles will undoubtedly influence the whole life course of the person.

In addition to, or beyond, the sexual aspects of the family drama, there are even more poignant ones. A jilted homosexual girl attacked her lover, held a knife to her throat, and cried: "You'll let me give you these wounds, but you won't let me heal them." This perhaps is the motto of all family dramas, the origin of all parental anguish, the basis for youthful rebellion, and the cry of couples not yet ready for divorce. The wounded flee, and the cry above is the Martian translation of the ad: "Mary, come home. All is forgiven." And that is why children stick with even the most miserable parents. It hurts to be wounded, but it feels so good to be healed.

F. Human Destiny

It is incredible to think, at first, that man's fate, all his nobility and all his degradation, is decided by a child no more than six years old, and usually three, but that is what script theory claims. It is a little easier to believe after talking to a child of six, or maybe three. And it is very easy to believe by looking around at what is happening in the world today, and what happened yesterday, and seeing what will probably happen tomorrow. The history of human scripts can be found on ancient monuments, in courtrooms and morgues, in gambling houses and letters to the editor, and in political debates, where whole nations are talked down the righteous road by somebody trying to prove that what his parents told him in the nursery will work for the whole world. But fortunately, some people have good scripts, and some even succeed in freeing themselves to do things their own way.

Human destiny shows that, by diverse means, men come to the same ends, and by the same means they come to diverse ends. They carry their scripts and their counterscripts around in their heads in the form of Parental voices telling them what to do and not do, and their aspirations in the form of Child pictures of how they would like it to be, and among the three of them they put their shows on the road. There they find themselves entangled in a web of other people's scripts: first their parents, then their spouses, and over all of them, the scripts of those who govern the places where they live. There are also chemical hazards like infectious diseases, and physical ones, such as hard objects that the human body is not constructed to withstand.

The script is what the person planned to do in early childhood, and the life course is what actually happens. The life course is determined by genes, by parental background, and by external circumstances. An individual whose genes cause men-

---

* This may occur when mother has no son of her own to play Jocasta with, and similarly if father has no daughter of his own.

tal retardation, physical deformity, or early death from cancer or diabetes, will have little opportunity to make his own life decisions or to carry them through to completion. The course of his life will be determined by inheritance (or perhaps birth injury). If the parents themselves suffered from severe physical or emotional deprivation as infants, that may destroy their children's chances of carrying out a script, or perhaps even of forming one. They may kill their offspring by neglect or abuse, or condemn them to life in an institution from an early age. Diseases, accidents, oppression, and war may terminate even the most carefully thought out and best supported life plan. So can a walk or a drive through the script of an unknown person: an assassin, thug, or car-crasher. A combination of these—genes plus oppression, for example—may close so many avenues to members of a certain line that they have few choices in planning their scripts, and it may make a tragic life course almost inevitable.

But even with strict limitations, there are nearly always some alternatives open. An aerial bomb, an epidemic, or a massacre may leave no choice at all, but at the next level, the person may be able to choose between killing, being killed, or killing himself, and there his choice will depend on his script, that is, the kind of decision he made in early childhood.

. . . Although men are not laboratory animals, they often behave as though they are. Sometimes they are put in cages and treated like rats, manipulated and sacrificed at the will of their masters. But many times the cage has an open door, and a man has only to walk out if he wishes. If he does not, it is usually his script which keeps him there. That is familiar and reassuring, and after looking out at the great world of freedom with all its joys and dangers, he turns back to the cage with its buttons and levers, knowing that if he keeps busy pushing them, and pushes the right one at the right time, he will be assured of food, drink, and an occasional thrill. But always, such a caged person hopes or fears that some force greater than himself, the Great Experimenter or the Great Computer, will change or end it all.

The forces of human destiny are foursome and fearsome: demonic parental programing, abetted by the inner voice the ancients called the *Daemon;* constructive parental programing, aided by the thrust of life called *Phusis* long ago; external forces, still called Fate; and independent aspirations, for which the ancients had no human name, since for them such were the privileges mainly of gods and kings. And as a resultant of these forces there are four kinds of life courses, which may be mixed, and lead to one or another kind of final destiny: scripty, counterscripty, forced, and independent.

G. Historical

As a clinician, the psychiatrist or the clinical psychologist is interested in *everything* that may affect the patient's behavior. In the following chapters no attempt is made to discuss all the factors which might affect the life *course* of the individual, but only those which are known at present to have a strong influence on the life *plan.*

But before we go on to consider how scripts are chosen, reinforced, and put into operation, and to dissect out the elements which make them up, we should state that the idea is not entirely new. There are many allusions in classical and modern literature to the fact that all the world's a stage and all the people in it merely players, but allusions are different from a sustained and informed investigation into the matter. Such investigations have been carried on by many psychiatrists and their pupils, but they have been unable to go very far in a systematic way because they did not have at their disposal the powerful weapons of structural analysis (diagraming and classifying transactions), game analysis (uncovering the con, the gimmick, the switch, and the payoff), and script analysis (the script matrix with the dreams, sweat shirts, trading stamps, and other elements derived from it).

The general idea that human lives follow the patterns found in myths, legends, and fairy tales, is most elegantly elaborated in Joseph Campbell's book, previously referred to. He bases his psychological thinking mainly on Jung and Freud. Jung's best-known ideas in this connection are the Archetypes (corresponding to the magic figures in a script) and the Persona (which is the style the script is played in).[7] The rest of Jung's ideas are not easy to understand or to relate to real people without very special training, and even then they are subject to different interpretations. In general, Jung is in favor of thinking about myths and fairy tales, and that is an important part of his influence.

Freud directly relates many aspects of human living to a single drama, the Oedipus myth. In psychoanalytic language, the patient is Oedipus, a "character" who exhibits "reactions." Oedipus is something going on in the patient's head. In script analysis, Oedipus is an ongoing drama that is actually taking place right now, divided into scenes and acts, with a build-up, a climax, and an ending. It is essential for others to play their parts, and the patient sees that they do. He only knows what to say to people whose scripts match or dovetail with his own. If his script calls for him to kill a king and marry a queen, he has to find a king whose script calls for him to be killed, and a queen whose script calls for her to be stupid enough to marry him. Some of Freud's followers, such as Glover, are beginning to recognize that Oedipus is a drama rather than merely a set of "reactions," while Rank, Campbell's chief predecessor, showed that most important myths and fairy tales come from a single basic plot, and that this plot appears in the dreams and lives of large numbers of people all over the world.

Freud speaks of the repetition compulsion and the destiny compulsion,[7] but his followers have not pursued these ideas very far to apply them to the entire life courses of their patients. Erikson is the most active psychoanalyst in making systematic studies of the human life-cycle from birth to death, and naturally, many of his findings are corroborated by script analysis. In general, it may be said that script analysis is Freudian, but it is not psychoanalytic.

Of all those who preceded transactional analysis, Alfred Adler comes the closest to talking like a script analyst.

> If I know the goal of a person I know in a general way what will happen. I am in a position to bring into their proper order each of the successive movements made. . . . We must remember that the person under observation would not know what to do with himself were he not oriented toward some goal . . . which determines his lifeline

. . . the psychic life of man is made to fit into the fifth act like a character drawn by a good dramatist . . . every psychic phenomenon, if it is to give us any understanding of a person, can only be grasped and understood if regarded as a preparation for some goal . . . an attempt at a planned final compensation and a (secret) life plan . . . the life plan remains in the unconscious, so that the patient may believe that an implacable fate and not a long-prepared and long-meditated plan for which he alone is responsible, is at work. . . . Such a man concludes his account and reconciles himself with life by constructing one or a number of "if-clauses." "If conditions had been different . . ."

The only exceptions which a script analyst would take to these statements are (1) that the life plan is usually not unconscious; (2) that the person is by no means solely responsible for it; and (3) that the goal and the manner of reaching it (the actual transactions, word for word) can be predicted much more precisely than even Adler claimed.[7]

Recently, R. D. Laing, the British psychiatrist, has described in a radio broadcast a view of life which is amazingly similar, even in its terminology, to the theory discussed in this book. For example, he uses the word "injunction" for strong parental programing.[8] Since, at this writing, he has not yet published these ideas, it is not possible to evaluate them properly.

Far older than all these, however, are the script analysts of ancient India, who based their prognostications largely on astrology. As the *Panchatantra* very aptly says, about 200 B.C.E.:

> These five are fixed for every man
> Before he leaves the womb:
> His length of days, his fate, his wealth,
> His learning, and his tomb.[9]

We need only make some slight changes to bring this up to date.

> These five are taken from your sires,
> Six summers from the womb:
> Your length of days, your fate, your wealth,
> Your learning, and your tomb.

NOTES

[1] For a discussion of the use of transactional analysis in the theater, see Schechner, R. "Approaches to Theory/Criticism." *Tulane Drama Review* 10: Summer 1966, pp. 20–53. Also Wagner, A. "Transactional Analysis and Acting." Ibid. 11: Summer 1967, pp. 81–88, and Berne, E. "Notes on Games and Theater," in the same issue, pp. 89–91.

[2] Wagner, A. "Permission and Protection," *The Drama Review* 13: Spring 1969, pp. 108–110, incorporates some of the more recent advances. For the direct application of transactional script theory to dramatic scripts, see the same issue pp. 110–114: Steiner, C. M. "A Script Checklist," and Cheney, W. D. "Hamlet: His Script Checklist." Both articles are reprinted from the *Transactional Analysis Bulletin* (Vol. 6, April, 1967, and Vol. 7, July, 1968).

[3] For a historical consideration of one aspect of "good guys" and "bad guys," see my article "The Mythology of Dark and Fair: Psychiatric Use of Folklore," *Journal of American Folklore* 1–12, 1959.

This gives a bibliography of about 100 items, including a few of the early psychoanalytic articles on fairy tales.

Geza Roheim is the most prolific writer on the folk tales of primitive people. See Roheim, G., *Psychoanalysis and Anthropology.* International Universities Press, New York, 1950.

[4] "Sleeping Beauty" or "Briar Rose" again comes from Andrew Lang's *Blue Fairy Book* and the Grimms. There is an expanded version, with sinister illustrations by Arthur Rackham, which is also very popular.

[5] For further information about the recent use of fairy tales in psychiatry, see Heuscher, J. *A Psychiatric Study of Fairy Tales.* C. C. Thomas, Springfield, 1963. This gives an existential symbolic interpretation. D. Dinnerstein's analysis of the story of "The Little Mermaid" (*Contemporary Psychoanalysis* 104–112, 1967), uses a "maturational" approach which involves some of the elements related to the evolution of a script.

Most directly connected with script analysis, however, is the work of H. Dieckmann, who relates fairy tales to the life patterns of his patients in a systematic way. See Dieckmann, H. "Das Lieblingsmärchen der Kindheit und seine Beziehung zu Neurose und Persönlichkeit." *Praxis der Kinderpsychologie und Kinderpsychiatrie* 6:202–208, August–September, 1967. Also *Märchen und Träume als Helfer des Menschen.* Bonz Verlag, Stuttgart, 1966.

[6] Cf. Flugel, J. C.: *The Psychoanalytic Study of the Family.* Hogarth Press, London, 1921.

[7] The bibliography for the historical background of the script concept is as follows:

Adler, A. "Individual Psychology" in *The World of Psychology,* ed. G. B. Levitas, George Braziller, New York, 1963.

Campbell, J. *The Hero With A Thousand Faces.* Pantheon Books, New York, 1949.

Erikson, E. *Childhood and Society.* W. W. Norton & Company, New York, 1950.

Freud, S. *Beyond the Pleasure Principle.* International Psychoanalytical Press, London, 1922.

Glover, E. *The Technique of Psycho-Analysis.* International Universities Press, New York, 1955.

Jung, C. G. *Psychological Types.* Harcourt, Brace & Company, New York, 1946.

Rank, O. *The Myth of the Birth of the Hero.* Nervous and Mental Disease Monographs, New York, 1910.

[8] First used in this connection by C. M. Steiner (*Transactional Analysis Bulletin* 5:133, April 1966).

[9] *Panchatantra,* trans. A. W. Ryder. University of Chicago Press, 1925, p. 237. Although these fables are dated back to 200 B.C.E., this version is from a manuscript of A.D. 1199, probably from the Hebrew codex. The five-book original is lost, but many of the tales are repeated in the four-book medieval *Hitopadesa.* Some date the Sanskrit original as late as A.D. 300.

11.

SOCIAL ENCOUNTERS: The Staging of the Self-Esteem

Ernest Becker

Usually we think of man's life in society as a rather routine thing, people going about their business so that the work can be done, saying what they have to say on the job or at the union hall. Even if we know about roles and statuses, how they structure social life, we tend to consider the whole thing as matter-of-fact; there shouldn't be much at stake in social encounters, since everything is fairly well pre-coded and automatic. So many of us may think—and we would be wrong. Ever since the early sociologists discovered that man was dependent on society for the fashioning of his self, his identity, we began to turn our attention to what was really going on. We began to understand that the individual's view of himself depended hopelessly on the general reflection he received back from society. Durkheim, Simmel, Cooley, James, Mead, and recently, Goffman, have provided us with a subtly detailed picture of the fact that man makes a pact with society in the preservation and creation of himself. *The fundamental task that every society on earth must face is truly monumental.* Society must protect its person-objects at their sorest point: the fragile self-esteem of each and every member. In the social encounter *each member exposes for public scrutiny, and possible intolerable undermining, the one thing he needs most:* the positive self-valuation he has so laboriously fashioned. With stakes of this magnitude there can be nothing routine about social life. Each social encounter is a hallowed event.

The crucial problem of protecting one's self-esteem in hazardous social encounters is handled by society in the form of an intricate series of conventions. Goffman has coined the perfect word for these conventions—he calls them "face ritual." In the social encounter the individual entrusts his "face" to others, and has the right to expect that they will handle it gently. Face rituals are codes for interaction, and they serve this function of gentle handling.

Now, we cannot understand how crucial this process of face protection is unless we shed our old habits of understanding face as a kind of vanity, or as a curious preoccupation of a decrepit Chinese culture. We have to reorient our understanding of the word "face," as we did for the word "self-esteem." They are both grounded, in short, *in the basic anxiety-buffering function of the self-system,* and reflect crucial aspects of human adaptation.

Consider this simple diagram (Figure 1): Face is the positive feeling of self-

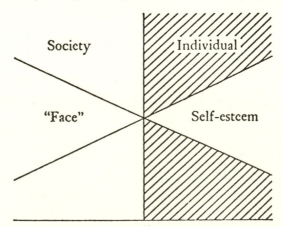

Society   Individual

"Face"   Self-esteem

Figure 1—"Face" is the vital self-esteem exposed to the
public for possible undermining.

warmth turned to the world for others' scrutiny *and potential sabotage*. Face is society's window to the core of the self. We can only fully appreciate the importance of face when we realize that *nothing goes deeper than the exposure of the self-esteem* to possible intolerable undermining in the social encounter.

This is the delicate charge that face rituals must protect. There are two claims that have to be met. On the one hand, society has a right to engage the self, to lay a social claim on it and include it in intercourse with similar selves. This is the major claim which permits social action. On the other hand, each individual has the right to keep others at a distance, and insist on his body privacy, his separateness, the simple fact that he is a person. The self must submit to being socially engaged, if this engagement is done with proper deference to the self-esteem. The everyday conventions that we know, the salutations, farewells, facile compliments, quick formal smiles of acknowledgment—punctuated in our culture by a "Hi"—are rituals of presentation whereby contact is made between selves. It may be permissible to make a social overture to the self by briefly adjusting another's tie or by brushing something off his shoulder—acts whereby we lay a social claim on his self. But we cannot encroach too much on the private selves of others; certain codified avoidances must be maintained: we cannot blow someone else's nose. There is a delicate tension to be maintained in social life, between avoiding and approaching others, a recognition and respect for the self, and a tacit claim on it. The individual helps maintain this delicate balance by a necessary degree of self-containment; there are times when one must be silent—a silence infused with separateness, yet with a willingness to be approached.

When we are slighted by a "snub" we are simply protesting that someone did not acknowledge the social existence of our self. The "Hi" makes electric contact, and fuses two discrete selves into a social unity. The problem of deference is an extremely touchy one precisely because self-esteem is at stake. We must exercise a social claim on each other, and yet not seem to manipulate. The simple act of engaging someone by offering him a seat is fraught with possibilities of bungling. Rituals of farewell are delicately sensitive because here the self is being released from a social situation. The release must be gentle, and not an ejection into isolation. . . .

As Goffman has so elegantly put it: society is tasked to show the self proper deference; the individual must maintain a certain demeanor. The double-sided process of social ceremony and self-governance is the theatrical drama for which the child has been laboriously trained. Let us not forget that the process of socialization is the fashioning of a skillful performer. The child is trained in all the subtle qualities necessary to maintain a proper tension between approaching others and avoiding them. We are familiar with training in deportment, dress, and bearing. The child is taught to be perceptive, to have dignity, considerateness, and poise: his self, in other words, is fashioned *in his own awareness,* he is taught to have feelings attached *to* himself. This attitude of self-regard makes itself felt in the social context. In one of Zola's novels a mother, training her daughter in husband-seeking, shouts, "Be conscious of your body!"

Less obvious are the qualities which make us mindful of the selves of others, as well as of our own. We are used to considering qualities like honor and pride basic to man's nature. And so they are. Without them, social performance could not go on. If we are properly proud, we have learned not to submerge others with what may be uncomfortable private data. We may tell our boss that we are ill, but we will not tell him the shape and color of our stool. To have learned honor is to know when to refrain from encompassing others with one's inappropriate designs. It is this overflow that we call "privatizing" the social context. A fellow commuter must be spared the gleefully imparted confidence that one is going to get by without paying a fare. In order for society to function, we must be trained to handle each other lightly and well. Man must make provision for the utmost sensitivity in social intercourse. Goffman goes so far as to say that this fine social sensitivity is what we mean when we speak of "universal human nature." Certainly it is a development of the very first step by which man distinguished himself from his subhuman cousins: the re-placement of sensitivity to mere power by sensitivity to symbolic status. . . .

Thus society provides that certain transactions with the self will be studiously avoided. It respects not only the body privacy but also an area slightly beyond it: to the aura that Georg Simmel saw each of us possessing. Ceremonials for avoidance provide for a psychic as well as for a physical distance. They imply that the self is personal. On the other hand, ceremonials for engaging the self imply that, if prop-erly approached, the self cannot refuse to be social. We may politely decline a seat someone has offered, with the excuse that we have been sitting all day. We refuse the gesture but we acknowledge the validity of the social claim. We cannot kick the chair over and remain silent. Now, it is obvious that neither of these processes could occur at all if there were no integral performance selves. Therefore, a fundamental obligation for social living is that the individual *have a self*. There must be some-thing socially transactable. . . .

The Self as a Locus of Linguistic Causality

The psychiatrist Harry Stack Sullivan liked to use the term "self-system" instead of the Freudian divisions of the psyche, because he saw that you cannot arbitrarily chop up the child's total ongoing action and experience. For Sullivan, this self-sys-tem was largely a *linguistic device* fashioned by the child to conciliate his world. Words are basic to the formation of his self, and words are the only way he can con-trol his environment. This is a powerful formulation, because it permits us to under-stand that what we term "personality" is largely a locus of word possibilities. When we expose our self-esteem to possible undermining by others in a social situa-tion, we are exposing a linguistic identity to other loci of linguistic causality. We have no idea what words are going to spout forth from another's self-system. The self-system, in this sense, is an ideational, linguistic device, in a continual state of modification and creation. We sit comfortably in our armchairs pouring forth con-ventional symbolic abstractions. In this shadowy monotone we exercise and modify our fragile selves, while our pet cat sits purringly by, convinced probably that we are only purring too.

After the child has fashioned a transactable self his work has hardly begun. He must then learn to use the ritual rules for social interaction. Children are notoriously termed "cruel"—the only way we find of expressing the idea that they have not yet learned to use the face-preserving social conventions. Probably the reason for the child's blustering early encounters is that he still basks in the parental omnipotence, and has no need to protect *himself* in the social situation, and therefore no thought to handling others gently. "Cripple!" "Fatty!" "Four-Eyes!" He sees the selves of others as something to be overcome, but not yet to be appeased in his own interest. His self-esteem is still dependent upon ministrations from the adult and not yet from society at large. We can only consider the socialization process complete when the child has learned to interact outside the family. The early peer group contacts are crucial in learning to transact with others, to protect their selves and to maintain one's own. "If you keep calling my doll ugly, I won't come play over at your house tomorrow." This is not a threat, but a plea for gentle handling, an enjoinder to exercise mutuality.

Sociologists insist on the importance of early training in role-playing. The child plays at various adult roles and learns the proper lines for each part—husband, wife, policeman, robber. By the time he grows up, he is already skilled at assuming the identity of some of the major figures in the cultural plot. But there is a more subtle side to early role-playing. The child learns to put forth and sustain a self and learns to modify the demands of that self, as well as to evaluate the performance of his peers. *He learns that there are certain reactions to his cues that he can discount.* We all remember, hopefully, at least one person with whom we could compare our performance favorably in early peer interaction, and feel properly social at a very early age. There was always one "sore loser" who filled us with a sense of social self-righteousness. "Ya, ya, you're a sore loser!" The child learns thereby to sustain his own valued self in the face of negative responses: there are those, he finds, whose evaluation he can ignore, who use improperly personal gambits in the social situation. He learns that there exists a privatization of the social context: an unwarranted handling by someone else of the child's own properly presented self. "Wasn't *I* right?" is a plea for reassurance that one is sustaining the social plot with proper mastery. To fail to learn this simple fact is to remain a center of error in a constantly correct world. It is a terrifying thought.

If the self is primarily a linguistic device, and the identity of the self primarily the experience of control over one's powers, one fundamental conclusion is inescapable. To present an infallible self is to present one which has unshakable control over words. It is amazing how little we realize this even after Dale Carnegie's unambiguous message: "It matters not what you *mean:* you and those around you become according to what you *say.*" This simple and crucial fact for understanding human behavior stares us so disarmingly in the face that we pass on to more involved and less important things. The proper word or phrase, properly delivered, is the highest attainment of human interpersonal power. The easy handling of the verbal context of action gives the only possibility of direct exercise of control over others.

We already saw that this fact is central to the development of the ego, how magically the child gets his gratification if he learns the right words. The word, a mere sound, miraculously obliges the adult to do one's bidding; it brings food and warmth, and closeness. The word which pleases the angry adult transforms him before one's eyes into a smiling, appreciative protector. So it is no wonder that in our adult life we carry over some of this early enchantment with the magical efficacy of words, this conviction that everything in the universe can hang delicately on the proper sound: and so, many people shrink at "using God's name in vain"; and others feel the impending ruin of society when they hear unbridled cursing. People who have an "obsessive-compulsive" character are often preoccupied with just the right utterance, just the right choice of words, and are perpetually uneasy over a potential slip of the tongue. But there are very few of us who have not at some time felt that we could probably really destroy a rival or a particularly hated person, if we delivered just the right curse, with the proper amount of vehement concentration. Primitives especially believe in the magical power of sound. A word can take form and kill; it enters the air and becomes embodied into the evil wish it expresses. When we use a four-letter word for copulation, we recapture some of this concretization: the word takes on the immediacy of the act itself. Usually we use four-letter words in situations where we have no control, where we feel vague and aimless—as in military life. Continual cursing seems to give us tangibility, decisiveness; it brings us back strongly into the world. It is an aspect of the natural "sadistic" technique. . . . We protest against the artificial and the conventional, against man-made rules and laws, by affirming the priority of bodily products and processes.

The efficacy of words, then, has from the beginning been at the very basis of our adaptation to anxiety, and respect for this talent is what the adult retains. This is the background to that marvelous feeling of power that comes with the simplest utterance: "I'm *terribly* sorry," "Good show!" "*Good* to see you!" With these simple phrases we frame the context for interaction. It is now up to our interlocutor to sustain our sincerity, to put forth the proper answer, to maintain the rhythm of the lines. The parents' early enjoinder "Say 'thank you' to the man" is not an inculcation of obsequiousness. It is an exercise in control: it is now up to "the man" to frame an appropriate response or to end the social situation gracefully. Words are the only tools we have for confident manipulation of the interpersonal situation. By verbally setting the tone for action by the proper ceremonial formula, we permit complementary action by our interlocutor. Not only do we permit it; we *compel* it, if he is to sustain his face. By properly delivering our lines we fulfill our end of the social bargain, and oblige the other to fulfill his in turn.

We are uncomfortable in strange groups and subcultures largely because we cannot frame the appropriate verbal context for sustaining the action or the ceremonial. We do not hear cues familiar to us, nor can we easily give those that make for smooth transitions in conversation. The English invariably discomfort Americans because they seem to be saying just the right thing at the right time, and in the same language, but it is so unfamiliar: when they confidently terminate an interaction with a hearty "Cheers," the American simply feels strange and uneasy. . . .

Take the fascination of youth for the theater. Goethe considered acting in one's youth an indispensable preparation for adult life. Theatrical acting is a vicarious freedom of *acting control* of a situation. It demonstrates perfectly how control can be gained merely by properly saying the right things. Perfect acting is a unique exercise in omnipotence, gained simply by infallible command of the script. By impeccable wielding of deference and demeanor the actor is at the same time undisputed director of his destiny. It is impossible to be undermined when one properly controls the verbal context of action. Learning a foreign tongue sometimes conveys the experiencing of the sheer power-control aspects of language. The individual finds that he is capable of utterances which usher others into appropriate complementary action, but which utterances, because they are new (and in a foreign tongue) he at first experiences as unreal and ego-alien. It is then that he can best "watch himself perform," and see and feel in action the power aspects of language. . . .

By using word ceremonial properly the individual can navigate without fear in a threatening social world. He can even ignore the true attitudes of others, as long as he can get by them with the proper ritual formulas of salutation, sustaining conversation, farewells, and so on. The actor has only to be sure of the face-saving ritual rules for interaction. Everyone is permitted the stolid self-assurance that comes with minute observation of unchallengeable rules—we can all become social bureaucrats.

However, there is a more subtle aspect to this mutual protection of fragile self-esteem. We have already touched on it: not only do words enable us to protect ourselves by confidently manipulating the interpersonal situation; also, by verbally setting the tone for action by the proper ritual formula, we permit complementary action by our interlocutor. That is, the ability to use formulas with facility actually implies the power to manipulate others indirectly, by providing the symbolic context for their action. We know this only too well, at least subconsciously. We need only reflect on the inordinate amount of time we spend in anguished self-recrimination over having failed merely to say the right thing at a given point in a conversation. Self-torture for having let power slip from one's grasp is pitiless: "If only I'd said *that!* Oh, if *only* I'd said that!" . . .

Even the slave enjoys power by skillfully using the obsequious formulas of deference appropriate to his status. These ingratiating and respectful expressions for engaging others in anxiety-free fashion are his only tools for manipulating the interpersonal situation. They are proved methods of control. What is more, by doing his part in permitting the action to continue he actually calls the tune for his superior, even from his inferior position. Thus, an army officer may exclaim to his sergeant, "Stop 'sirring' me!" It is a protest against being manipulated by an overly constrictive social definition of one's identity. One is too easily being put in another's box. The delight with which young recruits learn all the military jargon testifies to the pervasive feeling of power that accompanies proper definition of the situation for action: "Private Johnson reporting, sir!" not only creates the context for action, but at the same time *provides the motivation to act*. We sustain one another with properly placed verbal formulas.

We saw that the fundamental task of culture is to constitute the individual as an object of primary value in a world of meaning. Without this, he cannot act. Now, the proper exercise of ritual formulas provides just this. The actor can feel himself an object of primary value, motivated to act in a mutually meaningful situation.

"Private Johnson reporting, sir!" affirms the self, the proper motivation, and the life meaning which forever is. And when we permit our interlocutor as well as ourself to act in a fabric of shared meaning, we provide him with the possibility of self-validation. As we act meaningfully in pursuit of agreed goals we exercise our self-powers as only they can be exercised. This is vitally important. It is easy to see the reverse side of this same coin: namely, that if we bungle the verbal context for action, if we deliver the wrong lines at the wrong time, we frustrate the possibility of meaningful action and unquestioned motivation. "P-P-P-P-Private Johnson reporting, s-s-s-sir!" not only arrests all movement on stage but also undermines word power where it is most useful: in its expediency. Directness is self-convincing. For any animal, meaning dies when action bogs down; for man, it suffices that *verbal action* bog down in order for meaning to die. And so, unflinching mastery of the lines actually serves to *create* meaning by providing an unequivocal context for action. The leader who, after a short whispered outline plan of attack, shouts, "Let's go men!" with proper gravity and conviction, says much more than simply that. He implies that of all times and all places, this is the situation that man should want most to be in; and that " to go" into the attack is unquestionably the greatest, most meaningful act that one could hope to perform. Thus, the word not only sustains us by outlining a context of action in which we can be meaningfully motivated. It also "creates" us, in a sense, by infusing our action with meaning. That is, as we act meaningfully we exercise our powers and create our identity.

And so we see that not only is motivation reinforced by the flawless performance, but agreement in values is also cemented by the mutuality of performance. The actors are quickened in their commitment: man *lives* the cultural fiction. The linguistic self-system is an ideational device in continued movement–scanning, questioning, assimilating. It needs reinforcement and something to feed on. As the individual exercises his creative powers in the social encounter, and basks in the radiation of fabricated meaning, his identity is revealed *to himself*. He forms himself into a meaningful ideational whole, receiving affirmations, banishing contradictions. Remember the inner-newsreel. We carry around the symbols of our self-worth in our consciousness, most of the time subliminally running a film of our identity; and often we inwardly mutter the sound track as we pass along the street: "I am a doctor," "I am a doctor." This is not an egotistic self-titillation, but rather a rehearsal and self-revelation of the only meaning we can know—the status-cues which guide our action. We want to know how to perform onstage, and can only use the symbolic cues for performance that society provides us with. We train our performance by the social prescriptions for our role: "I feel like spitting, but a doctor cannot spit in front of others." *First* we discover who society says we are: *then* we build our identity on performance in that part. If we uphold our part in the performance, we are rewarded with social affirmation of our identity. It is hardly an exaggeration, then, to say that we are *created* in the performance. If we bungle the performance, show that we do not merit the part, we are destroyed—not figuratively, but literally. The financiers who plunged from tall buildings when their fortunes had been wiped out in 1929 were not reacting irrationally. . . . their selves were wrapped up in numbers in bank books, and when these numbers plunged to zero they were already dead. Now we can understand further that what they had really lost were the credentials for their particular performance parts, and thus their identity.

And so we can understand that there is another side to the social credo. "Let us all protect each other so that we can carry on the business of living." Man is a social creator as well as a social creature. By the social exercise of linguistic power man creates his own identity and reinforces that of others. In this sense, identity is simply the measure of power and participation of the individual in the joint cultural staging of self-enhancing ceremony. Only by proper performance in a social context does the individual fashion and renew himself by purposeful action in a world of shared meaning. Loneliness is not only a suspension in action and stimulation, it is a moratorium on self-acquaintance. It is a suspension in the very fashioning of identity; cut off from one's fellows, one cannot add his power to the enhancing of cultural meaning or derive his just share of it. Social ceremonial is a joint theatrical staging whose purpose it is to sustain and create meaning for all its members.

Subtler Aspects of the Social Creation of Meaning

If social encounters are largely a theatrical staging, part of the basic training of the players will be an inordinate sensitivity to cues. We want to know that everyone is playing correctly. Goffman says:

> As members of an audience it is natural for us to feel that the impression the performer seeks to give may be true or false . . . valid or 'phony'. So common is this doubt that . . . we often give special attention to *features of the performance that cannot be readily manipulated.*
> "When we discover that someone with whom we have dealings is an impostor and out-and-out fraud, we are discovering that he did not have the right to play the part he played, that he was not an accredited member of the relevant status (1959, p. 58).

Status, remember, is a social technique for facilitating action. It divides our social environment into a behavioral map, and by living according to the positional cues, our actions take on the only meaning they can have. Our alertness to the performance of others, therefore, is an expression of our concern over sustaining the underlying meaning of the plot. Goffman continues:

> . . . Paradoxically, the more closely the imposter's performance approximates the real thing, the more intensely we may be threatened, for a competent performance by someone who proves to be an impostor may weaken in our minds the moral connections between legitimate authorization . . . and capacity to play (1959, p. 58).

In other words, we must feel that the performer *deserves* his status, and if he didn't deserve it he wouldn't be able convincingly to play it. . . . In every culture man is alert to the discovery of fraud because it implies the basic legitimacy of the plot he is playing in. That is why we devour the cues in every performance, searching for conviction, for unshakable veridicality. The performance takes on such a life-and-death flavor precisely because life-meaning is being created. This is why it is important for each actor to bring to the social scene his own special dramatic talent, whereby the quality of the performance is enriched. It would be impossible to overinsist on the importance of this talent for social life. It is probably the most subtle and most important area of social creativity—a creativity in which everyone takes part, and in which there are the widest differences in skill. Part of our talent in this creativeness is our inordinate sensitivity to cues, both verbal and nonverbal, kinesic and unconscious. The inferences upon which our lines are based must be gathered from as many cues as possible, if we are to judge accurately and perform creatively in a given part.

Ansel Strauss points out (1959, p. 59) that each person has to assess three things about another. He must be alert to a myriad of cues to determine:

1. The other's general intent in the situation.
2. The other's response toward *himself*.
3. The other's response or feelings toward me, the recipient or observer of his action.

This interweaving, observes Strauss, of signs of intent, of self-feeling, and of feeling toward the other, must be exceedingly complex in any situation. Why is the assessment of these three things so important? Simply because this trilogy allows one to fulfill his "social human nature"—it allows him to exercise those unique capacities into which he has been schooled. The adept performer should be able to:

1. Save his own face (protect his fragile self-esteem) against unwarranted attack or privatization.
2. Prepare the appropriate lines that may be necessary to protect the other's self-esteem, if the other inadvertently makes a *gaffe*. Part of one's social obligation is to protect the other person, as well as oneself, against undermining in the social context.
3. Frame creative and convincing lines that carry the interaction along in the most meaningful, life-enhancing fashion. Or, wanting that, try to get out of the interaction gracefully, and at the other's expense. (Goffman is the acknowledged modern master at detailing the subtleties of these manoeuvres.)

A person's response toward himself, his self-alert, critical eye, is a transaction with what Sullivan so beautifully called his "fantastic auditor." Other psychoanalysts call it the "observing ego." We direct our performance to this imaginary judge, who sets the standards for it and keeps us in line, saying just the right things. Now and again, we slip out of the alert censorship of our "fantastic auditor," as when we explode into a mess of uncontrolled nonsense. When we watch another perform we think that we can see how he feels about himself. Actually, we don't see this at all; we can have little idea how he "feels about himself." What we do see is how smoothly the individual is staging himself, controlling his performance. We do not like to see another who is too absorbed in his own staging at the expense of convincing delivery of the lines. This kind of stage ineptitude is like performance in a high school play, where self-conscious actors deliver stilted, halting, unconvincing lines, or overly fluent ones. When we talk about someone who is "phony" we mean that his staging of himself is overly obvious. He is unconvincing because he allows *us* to see *his* efforts at delivering the right lines.

. . . The adolescent may see in the courtesy of manners a certain deceit. But the whole question of feigned politeness is integral to good performance. "Hypocrisy" is an unfairly negative expression for an adaptation to a social situation despite our feelings. We mask our private thoughts and sentiments to allow action to go forward. If these thoughts are inappropriate, masking them performs a vital social function: it allows the objective elements of the situation to hold sway. Instead of submerging the social context with our own private perceptions, we facilitate it by responding to its exigencies as cleanly as possible. . . .

Of course, the masking of inappropriate elements is never sure, precisely because the social encounter is not (in our culture, anyway) completely rigid and structured. One wants to come out of it somewhat aggrandized in his own image, and so he has to overextend himself. Part of the delicate subtlety of the encounter is its potential for increasing the value of the self in one's own eyes. This is what the social psychologists call "status-forcing." But one needs to be a most skillful performer to come out of an interaction better than he came in. He needs to have an acute sensitivity to the manifold cues, deliver the proper lines necessary to sustain his image and that of the others; he must enhance the cultural meaning as well as the personal meaning of all the selves concerned. . . .

We would expect this where people are thrown together without rigid ceremonial rules for protecting against privatization. A similar phenomenon occurs when a "line" is used: to employ a "line" usually means trying to get something out of an interaction that is grossly at the other person's expense. In traditional society there is less of this because cues are more dependable, and the situation tightly structured. There is very little "line" that one can employ on a date that is chaperoned, for instance. "Line" is a probing for advantage in the absence of standardized prescriptions for behavior, an attempt to emerge from the fluid interaction much better than one came in. Of course, every interaction has this creative element, the possibility of emerging from it somewhat enhanced in one's feeling of warmth about oneself.

This enhancement need not derive solely from success in forcing one's status in an encounter. Every performance has another creative element: by presenting uniquely creative lines the actor obliges his interlocutor to cope with the unexpected, also in a creative fashion. Each individual presents his own unique version of cultural meaning, as it is reworked and fashioned in his linguistic self-system. By constantly fabricating the unexpected, we edge our egos to new assimilative mastery. After all, the individual who can be counted on to give us exactly that ceremonial proper to each situation is the one we call a crashing bore. He doesn't inspire us to grow by coping with the unexpected.

One of the impetuses to the fragmentation of society into subgroups is that they provide some respite from the continual strain on creative alertness of the self-system. In the subgroup, conversation is familiar, automatic, untaxing for the most part. In some primitive societies "joking relationships" are established between certain individuals. These people, when they meet, engage in an unashamed mockery, teasing, and joking that is denied to others. Joking relationships seem to be established at points of tension in the social system—among inlaws, for example—and relieve the individuals of the strain of meeting these encounters, and the necessity of facilitating them creatively. Joking carries the encounter along automatically, and also provides for release of tension. . . .

Cooley, that great observer of human nature, very early saw what was at stake in social life—that it was a dramatistic creation of meaning, and not simply an ant-like, mechanistic scurrying. Each group works something into the drama: as Cooley put it, the status identifications of certain groups "has the effect of a conspiracy to work upon the credulity of the rest of the world" (1922, p. 353). This is not only to convince others of something that is not there, but to bring into social life a display of new meaning. The whole drama is thereby enriched in complexity. And this enrichment can take place not only by what is said, but by what is implied and unsaid. As that other brilliant observer of the subtleties of social life—Georg Simmel—remarked, one of the truly great inventions of mankind was the secret. The secret brings conviction into the social drama because it adds a dimension of mystery to it. Cooley observed with beautiful insight that von Moltke was "silent in six languages." The implication is that this gave him an awesome aura of depth: six languages, unspoken, are a tremendous reservoir of meaningful potential. Silence fascinates us because it implies that we carry something genuine around inside. Secrets and silences make life more real: the individual, self-absorbed and inwardly musing, taking himself very seriously, radiates a contagious aura: the tacit communication that the serious and the meaningful *exist*. And this is the conviction without which we cannot live with proper dedication.

Our earliest experiences of this take place when we are children, and when our queries or monologues are met with silence by our parents. Whatever we say seems so little relevant and important when it is met by a powerful silence on the part of those who give meaning to our acts. Our verbalizations seem superficial, and the inner world of our silent parents seems pregnant with meaning. . . . Part of our basic training in humanization is a sensitivity to two worlds, the inner and the outer, and for a symbolic animal the inner world is the truly complex and mysterious one. Silence captivates us precisely because we presume that thinking is going on. When we see a silent ape or dog, the idea may occur to us: "I wonder whether he is thinking anything?"—only to be rapidly dismissed as absurd. His silence intrigues us only in the split second that we assume that thought and silence are joined together. Silence without thought we dismiss as meaningless. In our dealings with humans, silence conveys a conviction of meaning only because we infer that *thought sequences* are being entertained. Silence is convincing because if confronts us with a marvelous organic creation whose whole life-identity is inseparable from thought sequences, silently entertained. Therefore, we can feel that the culturally constituted plan for action has a deeper than merely man-made significance. It is embodied in a tangible, organic *thing,* and not merely in airy words or thoughts. This is what captivates us in capable, self-assured people of few words. They give us living testimonial to the propriety of our symbolic designs. Madison Avenue advertisers know these things supremely well: how many magnificent heads they show us, silently contemplating trifling consumer products. So we might say that pregnant silence is at the same time the most facile, as well as one of the highest, esthetic achievements. . . .

A certain amount of silence, of course, is necessary simply to carry the play. The lines would lose their meaning if they did not emanate from a background of silence, but were to continue to fill the air at all times. When we engage the self we want to know that we are engaging something real—something that might just as well *not need to be* engaged, that was real and meaningful *within itself*. This is one reason constant talkers annoy us. To say that they "lack depth" is simply to affirm that silence is part of a good performance, because it implies that a genuine self exists apart from and beyond the immediate encounter. If I were to write a manual on seduction for adolescent young men, the first and foremost precept would be: Keep your mouth shut. But silence is not a facile talent for everybody: many people feel they have to talk in order to keep the interaction moving, and in order to discover and validate their identity. For them, silence is constricting and undermining.

One thing we can conclude at this point—and it should be very sobering, even unsettling—and that is that man's meaning hangs by a ludicrously fragile thread, such as a proper amount of silence. Most of us never realize the artifacts that make symbolic life believable, the flimsy stuff out of which man draws conviction and self-aggrandizement. Much depends on what the actor can pull off, as Cooley said, how one affects the credulity of others. And the main thing that gives conviction to social performance is self-conviction on the part of the actor. Key men in corporation and diplomatic posts are routinely chosen because they have this quality. The self, after all, is largely an attitude of self-regard, inculcated into the child during his socialization: "Don't let anyone bully you; tell them you're Sam Jones' boy."

. . . The psychoanalysts have added rich evidence to support our earliest sociological insights into these fascinating matters. When we add up the insights from both fields we have a fairly clear picture of what goes into the phenomenon of "natural leadership." A pattern of mothering feeds into the self-system of the child a boundless self-regard. He is taught that he can do no wrong, that he is to be an indomitable locus of causality destined to enrich the world. This gives him "an intense self, a militant, gloating 'I' "—as Cooley again so beautifully put it (1922, p. 328). When he grows up he convinces by his conviction, and we do not doubt for a moment that life is rich with meaning. Furthermore, he may use us to help create it. By putting forth a convincing self, the actor obliges others to a more careful deference. The strong self forces others to make an effort at performance that may often be beyond their means. Thus, the aura of his infallibility is enforced as their performance stumbles or becomes painfully effortful. This painful effort then generates a further conviction of meaningfulness in which all those around the leader can share. No wonder the leader radiates such power: not only does he embody it in himself, in his aura of self-reliant strength, but he also creates it in his interpersonal performance. We succumb to the leader because we want to share in this power and will accept any that is doled out to us. Again we can judge very clearly where man has departed from his subhuman cousins. We share the same awe and fear of power as the baboons, or any animal that is transcended by nature and by the strength of others. But in order for this power to truly captivate us, it has to be generated in the creation of meaning and in social performance, and not simply in brute animal strength. We may fear the bully, and may admire physical strength; but unless the bully also broods, and unless the strength serves a symbolic design, we will not sit in its shadow.

And so we may conclude that we are *metteurs en scène* not only in the fabrication of our inner-newsreels, but also in the action of our social world; we not only edit the images of our films with great skill, but also fashion our spoken lines. Some are more fortunately endowed to set the implicit tone for the performance because they present a model self. The less fortunate are obliged to dance a lifetime to the performance cues of others. Of course, we understand that each culture and even subgroup has its own model for commanding the most meaningful performance in its plot. In South India even a timid child who resembles Hanuman the monkey god is destined to have a favored part in the plot. In Western films the self must above all be silent and self-sufficient, but capable of exploding into brutal murder while maintaining a disarming smile. The Western hero, in fact, provides the best proof that sustaining a convincing self is the basis for enhancing cultural meaning. With nothing but penetrating eyes, charged silence, and an IQ of 80, why does this character thrill audiences to the core? The Western hero conveys little more—but nothing less—than unshakable conviction that underneath it all there is genuine meaning in man's action. The particular conspiracy to be worked on the world is preordained for each cultural plot. But in each case the object of social cynosure can be confident that he will be sustained by all others, if he plays his part well.

But what if he does not? What if the individual presents an unconvincing or even repugnant self? What happens if he does not deliver his lines correctly, if he fails to sustain his own face and that of others, if he digs obtrusively into his nose, or salivates nonchalantly? What happens, in sum, if by his performance he *undermines* the precariously constituted cultural meaning from which everyone draws the vital sustenance of motivation and value? This is the critical characteristic of those we term "abnormal," and presents a major problem in the study of society.

12.

ON FACE-WORK: An Analysis of Ritual Elements in Social Interaction

Erving Goffman

Every person lives in a world of social encounters, involving him either in face-to-face or mediated contact with other participants. In each of these contacts, he tends to act out what is sometimes called a *line*—that is, a pattern of verbal and nonverbal

Reprinted by special permission from The William Alanson White Psychiatric Foundation Inc., *Psychiatry* (1955) 18: 213–231 © 1955 by The William Alanson White Psychiatric Foundation.

acts by which he expresses his view of the situation and through this his evaluation of the participants, especially himself. Regardless of whether a person intends to take a line, he will find that he has done so in effect. The other participants will assume that he has more or less willfully taken a stand, so that if he is to deal with their response to him he must take into consideration the impression they have possibly formed of him.

The term *face* may be defined as the positive social value a person effectively claims for himself by the line others assume he has taken during a particular contact. Face is an image of self delineated in terms of approved social attributes—albeit an image that others may share, as when a person makes a good showing for his profession or religion by making a good showing for himself.[1]

A person tends to experience an immediate emotional response to the face which a contact with others allows him; he cathects his fact; his "feelings" become attached to it. If the encounter sustains an image of him that he has long taken for granted, he probably will have few feelings about the matter. If events establish a face for him that is better than he might have expected, he is likely to "feel good"; if his ordinary expectations are not fulfilled, one expects that he will "feel bad" or "feel hurt." In general, a person's attachment to a particular face, coupled with the ease with which disconfirming information can be conveyed by himself and others, provides one reason why he finds that participation in any contact with others is a commitment. A person will also have feelings about the face sustained for the other participants, and while these feelings may differ in quantity and direction from those he has for his own face, they constitute an involvement in the face of others that is as immediate and spontaneous as the involvement he has in his own face. One's own face and the face of others are constructs of the same order; it is the rules of the group and the definition of the situation which determine how much feeling one is to have for face and how this feeling is to be distributed among the faces involved.

A person may be said to *have*, or *be in*, or *maintain* face when the line he effectively takes presents an image of him that is internally consistent, that is supported by judgments and evidence conveyed by other participants, and that is confirmed by evidence conveyed through impersonal agencies in the situation. At such times the person's face clearly is something that is not lodged in or on his body, but rather something that is diffusely located in the flow of events in the encounter and becomes manifest only when these events are read and interpreted for the appraisals expressed in them.

The line maintained by and for a person during contact with others tends to be of a legitimate institutionalized kind. During a contact of a particular type, an interactant of known or visible attributes can expect to be sustained in a particular face and can feel that it is morally proper that this should be so. Given his attributes and the conventionalized nature of the encounter, he will find a small choice of lines will be open to him and a small choice of faces will be waiting for him. Further, on the basis of a few known attributes, he is given the responsibility of possessing a vast number of others. His coparticipants are not likely to be conscious of the character of many of these attributes until he acts perceptibly in such a way as to discredit his possession of them; then everyone becomes conscious of these attributes and assumes that he willfully gave a false impression of possessing them.

Thus while concern for face focuses the attention of the person on the current activity, he must, to maintain face in this activity, take into consideration his place in the social world beyond it. A person who can maintain face in the current situation is someone who abstained from certain actions in the past that would have been difficult to face up to later. In addition, he fears loss of face now partly because the others may take this as a sign that consideration for his feelings need not be shown in the future. There is nevertheless a limitation to this interdependence between the current situation and the wider social world: an encounter with people whom he will not have dealings with again leaves him free to take a high line that the future will discredit, or free to suffer humiliations that would make future dealings with them an embarrassing thing to have to face.

A person may be said to *be in wrong face* when information is brought forth in some way about his social worth which cannot be integrated, even with effort, into the line that is being sustained for him. A person may be said to *be out of face* when he participates in a contact with others without having ready a line of the kind participants in such situations are expected to take. The intent of many pranks is to lead a person into showing a wrong face or no face, but there will also be serious occasions, of course, when he will find himself expressively out of touch with the situation.

When a person senses that he is in face, he typically responds with feelings of confidence and assurance. Firm in the line he is taking, he feels that he can hold his head up and openly present himself to others. He feels some security and some relief—as he also can when the others feel he is in wrong face but successfully hide these feelings from him.

When a person is in wrong face or out of face, expressive events are being contributed to the encounter which cannot be readily woven into the expressive fabric of the occasion. Should he sense that he is in wrong face or out of face, he is likely to feel ashamed and inferior because of what has happened to the activity on his account and because of what may happen to his reputation as a participant. Further, he may feel bad because he had relied upon the encounter to support an image of self to which he has become emotionally attached and which he now finds threatened. Felt lack of judgmental support from the encounter may take him aback, confuse him, and momentarily incapacitate him as an interactant. His manner and bearing may falter, collapse, and crumble. He may become embarrassed and chagrined; he may become shamefaced. The feeling, whether warranted or not, that he is perceived in a flustered state by others, and that he is presenting no usable line, may add further injuries to his feelings, just as his change from being in wrong face or out of face to being shamefaced can add further disorder to the expressive organization of the situation. Following common usage, I shall employ the term *poise* to refer to the capacity to suppress and conceal any tendency to become shamefaced during encounters with others.

In our Anglo-American society, as in some others, the phrase ''to lose face'' seems to mean to be in wrong face, to be out of face, or to be shamefaced. The phrase ''to save one's face'' appears to refer to the process by which the person sustains an impression for others that he has not lost face. Following Chinese usage, one can say that "to give face" is to arrange for another to take a better line that he might otherwise have been able to take,[2] the other thereby gets face given him, this being one way in which he can gain face.

As an aspect of the social code of any social circle, one may expect to find an understanding as to how far a person should go to save his face. Once he takes on a self-image expressed through face he will be expected to live up to it. In different ways in different societies he will be required to show self-respect, abjuring certain actions because they are above or beneath him, while forcing himself to perform others even though they cost him dearly. By entering a situation in which he is given a face to maintain, a person takes on the responsibility of standing guard over the flow of events as they pass before him. He must ensure that a particular *expressive order* is sustained—an order that regulates the flow of events, large or small, so that anything that appears to be expressed by them will be consistent with his face. When a person manifests these compunctions primarily from duty to himself, one speaks in our society of pride; when he does so because of duty to wider social units, and receives support from these units in doing so, one speaks of honor. When these compunctions have to do with postural things, with expressive events derived from the way in which the person handles his body, his emotions, and the things with which he has physical contact, one speaks of dignity, this being an aspect of expressive control that is always praised and never studied. In any case, while his social face can be his most personal possession and the center of his security and pleasure, it is only on loan to him from society; it will be withdrawn unless he conducts himself in a way that is worthy of it. Approved attributes and their relation to face make of every man his own jailer; this is a fundamental social constraint even though each man may like his cell.

Just as the member of any group is expected to have self respect, so also he is expected to sustain a standard of considerateness; he is expected to go to certain lengths to save the feelings and the face of others present, and he is expected to do this willingly and spontaneously because of emotional identification with the others and with their feelings.[3] In consequence, he is disinclined to witness the defacement of others.[4] The person who can witness another's humiliation and unfeelingly retain a cool countenance himself is said in our society to be "heartless," just as he who can unfeelingly participate in his own defacement is thought to be "shameless."

The combined effect of the rule of self-respect and the rule of considerateness is that the person tends to conduct himself during an encounter so as to maintain both his own face and the face of the other participants. This means that the line taken by each participant is usually allowed to prevail, and each participant is allowed to carry off the role he appears to have chosen for himself. A state where everyone temporarily accepts everyone else's line is established.[5] This kind of mutual acceptance seems to be a basic structural feature of interaction, especially the interaction of face-to-face talk. It is typically a "working" acceptance, not a "real" one, since it tends to be based not on agreement of candidly expressed heart-felt evaluations, but upon a willingness to give temporary lip service to judgments with which the participants do not really agree.

The mutual acceptance of lines has an important conservative effect upon encounters. Once the person initially presents a line, he and the others tend to build their later responses upon it, and in a sense become stuck with it. Should the person radically alter his line, or should it become discredited, then confusion results, for the participants will have prepared and committed themselves for actions that are now unsuitable.

Ordinarily, maintenance of face is a condition of interaction, not its objective. Usual objectives, such as gaining face for oneself, giving free expression to one's true beliefs, introducing depreciating information about the others, or solving problems and performing tasks, are typically pursued in such a way as to be consistent with the maintenance of face. To study face-saving is to study the traffic rules of social interaction; one learns about the code the person adheres to in his movement across the paths and designs of others, but not where he is going, or why he wants to get there. One does not even learn why he is ready to follow the code, for a large number of different motives can equally lead him to do so. He may want to save his own face because of his emotional attachment to the image of self which it expresses, because of his pride or honor, because of the power his presumed status allows him to exert over the other participants, and so on. He may want to save the others' face because of his emotional attachment to an image of them, or because he feels that his coparticipants have a moral right to this protection, or because he wants to avoid the hostility that may be directed toward him if they lose their face. He may feel that an assumption has been made that he is the sort of person who shows compassion and sympathy toward others, so that to retain his own face, he may feel obliged to be considerate of the line taken by the other participants.

By *face-work* I mean to designate the actions taken by a person to make whatever he is doing consistent with face. Face-work serves to counteract "incidents"—that is, events whose effective symbolic implications threaten face. Thus poise is one important type of face-work, for through poise the person controls his embarrassment and hence the embarrassment that he and others might have over his embarrassment. Whether or not the full consequences of face-saving actions are known to the person who employs them, they often become habitual and standardized practices; they are like traditional plays in a game or traditional steps in a dance. Each person, subculture, and society seems to have its own characteristic repertoire of face-saving practices. It is to this repertoire that people partly refer when they ask what a person or culture is "really" like. And yet the particular set of practices stressed by particular persons or groups seems to be drawn from a single logically coherent framework of possible practices. It is as if face, by its very nature, can be saved only in a certain number of ways, and as if each social grouping must make its selections from this single matrix of possibilities.

The members of every social circle may be expected to have some knowledge of face-work and some experience in its use. In our society, this kind of capacity is sometimes called tact, *savoir-faire,* diplomacy, or social skill. Variation in social skill pertains more to the efficacy of face-work than to the frequency of its application, for almost all acts involving others are modified, prescriptively or proscriptively, by considerations of face.

If a person is to employ his repertoire of face-saving practices, obviously he must first become aware of the interpretations that others may have placed upon his acts and the interpretations that he ought perhaps to place upon theirs. In other words, he must exercise perceptiveness.[6] But even if he is properly alive to symbolically conveyed judgments and is socially skilled, he must yet be willing to exercise his perceptiveness and his skill; he must, in short, be prideful and considerate. Admittedly, of course, the possession of perceptiveness and social skill so often leads to their application that in our society terms such as politeness or tact fail to distinguish between the inclination to exercise such capacities and the capacities themselves.

I have already said that the person will have two points of view—a defensive orientation toward saving his own face and a protective orientation toward saving the others' face. Some practices will be primarily defensive and others primarily protective, although in general one may expect these two perspectives to be taken at the same time. In trying to save the face of others, the person must choose a tack that will not lead to loss of his own; in trying to save his own face, he must consider the loss of face that his action may entail for others.

In many societies there is a tendency to distinguish three levels of responsibility that a person may have for a threat to face that his actions have created. First, he may appear to have acted innocently: his offense seems to be unintended and unwitting, and those who perceive his act can feel that he would have attempted to avoid it had he foreseen its offensive consequences. In our society one calls such threats to face *faux pas, gaffes,* boners, or bricks. Secondly, the offending person may appear to have acted maliciously and spitefully, with the intention of causing open insult. Thirdly, there are incidental offenses; these arise as an unplanned but sometimes anticipated by-product of action—action the offender performs in spite of its offensive consequences, although not out of spite. From the point of view of a particular participant, these three types of threat can be introduced by the participant himself against his own face, by himself against the face of the others, by the others against their own face, or by the others against himself. Thus the person may find himself in many different relations to a threat to face. If he is to handle himself and others well in all contingencies, he will have to have a repertoire of face-saving practices for each of these possible relations to threat.

The Basic Kinds of Face-Work

The avoidance process.—The surest way for a person to prevent threats to his face is to avoid contacts in which these threats are likely to occur. In all societies one can observe this in the avoidance relationship [7] and in the tendency for certain delicate transactions to be conducted by go-betweens.[8] Similarly, in many societies, members know the value of voluntarily making a gracious withdrawal before an anticipated threat to face has had a chance to occur.[9]

Once the person does chance an encounter, other kinds of avoidance practices come into play. As defensive measures, he keeps off topics and away from activities that would lead to the expression of information that is inconsistent with the line he is maintaining. At opportune moments he will change the topic of conversation or the direction of activity. He will often present initially a front of diffidence and composure, suppressing any show of feeling until he has found out what kind of line the others will be ready to support for him. Any claims regarding self may be made with belittling modesty, with strong qualifications, or with a note of unseriousness; by hedging in these ways he will have prepared a self for himself that will not be discredited by exposure, personal failure, or the unanticipated acts of others. And if he does not hedge his claims about self, he will at least attempt to be realistic about them, knowing that otherwise events may discredit him and make him lose face.

Certain protective maneuvers are as common as these defensive ones. The person shows respect and politeness, making sure to extend to others any ceremonial treatment that might be their due. He employs discretion; he leaves unstated facts that might implicitly or explicitly contradict and embarrass the positive claims made by others.[10] He employs circumlocutions and deceptions, phrasing his replies with careful ambiguity so that the others' face is preserved even if their welfare is not.[11] He employs courtesies, making slight modifications of his demands on or appraisals of the others so that they will be able to define the situation as one in which their self-respect is not threatened. In making a belittling demand upon the others, or in imputing uncomplimentary attributes to them, he may employ a joking manner, allowing them to take the line that they are good sports, able to relax from their ordinary standards of pride and honor. And before engaging in a potentially offensive act, he may provide explanations as to why the others ought not to be affronted by it. . . .

When a person fails to prevent an incident, he can still attempt to maintain the fiction that no threat to face has occurred. The most blatant example of this is found where the person acts as if an event that contains a threatening expression has not occurred at all. He may apply this studied nonobservance to his own acts—as when he does not by any outward sign admit that his stomach is rumbling—or to the acts of others, as when he does not "see" that another has stumbled.[12] . . .

A more important, less spectacular kind of tactful overlooking is practiced when a person openly acknowledges an incident as an event that has occurred, but not as an event that contains a threatening expression. If he is not the one who is responsible for the incident, then his blindness will have to be supported by his forbearance; if he is the doer of the threatening deed, then his blindness will have to be supported by his willingness to seek a way of dealing with the matter, which leaves him dangerously dependent upon the cooperative forbearance of the others.

. . . *The corrective process.*—When the participants in an undertaking or encounter fail to prevent the occurrence of an event that is expressively incompatible with the judgments of social worth that are being maintained, and when the event is of the kind that is difficult to overlook, then the participants are likely to give it accredited status as an incident—to ratify it as a threat that deserves direct official attention—and to proceed to try to correct for its effects. At this point one or more participants find themselves in an established state of ritual disequilibrium or disgrace, and an attempt must be made to re-establish a satisfactory ritual state for them. I use the term *ritual* because I am dealing with acts through whose symbolic component the actor shows how worthy he is of respect or how worthy he feels others are of it. The imagery of equilibrium is apt here because the length and intensity of the corrective effort is nicely adapted to the persistence and intensity of the threat.[13] One's face, then, is a sacred thing, and the expressive order required to sustain it is therefore a ritual one.

The sequence of acts set in motion by an acknowledged threat to face, and terminating in the re-establishment of ritual equilibrium, I shall call an *interchange*.[14] Defining a message or move as everything conveyed by an actor during a turn at taking action, one can say that an interchange will involve two or more moves and two or more participants. Obvious examples in our society may be found in the sequence of "Excuse me" and "Certainly," and in the exchange of presents or visits. The interchange seems to be a basic concrete unit of social activity and provides one natural empirical way to study interaction of all kinds. Face-saving practices can be usefully classified according to their position in the natural sequence of moves that comprise this unit. Aside from the event which introduces the need for a corrective interchange, four classic moves seem to be involved.

There is, first, the challenge, by which participants take on the responsibility of calling attention to the misconduct; by implication they suggest that the threatened claims are to stand firm and that the threatening event itself will have to be brought back into line.

The second move consists of the offering, whereby a participant, typically the offender, is given a chance to correct for the offense and re-establish the expressive order. Some classic ways of making this move are available. On the one hand, an attempt can be made to show that what admittedly appeared to be a threatening expression is really a meaningless event, or an unintentional act, or a joke not meant to be taken seriously, or an unavoidable, "understandable" product of extenuating circumstances. On the other hand, the meaning of the event may be granted and effort concentrated on the creator of it. Information may be provided to show that the creator was under the influence of something and not himself, or that he was under the command of somebody else and not acting for himself. When a person claims that an act was meant in jest, he may go on and claim that the self that seemed to lie behind the act was also projected as a joke. . . .

As a supplement to or substitute for the strategy of redefining the offensive act or himself, the offender can follow two other procedures: he can provide compensations to the injured—when it is not his own face that he has threatened; or he can provide punishment, penance, and expiation for himself. These are important moves or phases in the ritual interchange. Even though the offender may fail to prove his innocence, he can suggest through these means that he is now a renewed person, a person who has paid for his sin against the expressive order and is once more to be trusted in the judgmental scene. Further, he can show that he does not treat the feelings of the others lightly, and that if their feelings have been injured by him, however innocently, he is prepared to pay a price for his action. Thus he assures the others that they can accept his explanations without this acceptance constituting a sign of weakness and a lack of pride on their part. Also, by his treatment of himself, by his self-castigation, he shows that he is clearly aware of the kind of crime he would have committed had the incident been what it first appeared to be, and that he knows the kind of punishment that ought to be accorded to one who would commit such a crime. The suspected person thus shows that he is thoroughly capable of taking the role of the others toward his own activity, that he can still be used as a responsible participant in the ritual process, and that the rules of conduct which he appears to have broken are still sacred, real, and unweakened. An offensive act may arouse anxiety about the ritual code; the offender allays this anxiety by showing that both the code and he as an upholder of it are still in working order.

After the challenge and the offering have been made, the third move can occur: the persons to whom the offering is made can accept it as a satisfactory means of re-establishing the expressive order and the faces supported by this order. Only then can the offender cease the major part of his ritual offering.

In the terminal move of the interchange, the forgiven person conveys a sign of gratitude to those who have given him the indulgence of forgiveness.

The phases of the corrective process—challenge, offering, acceptance, and thanks—provide a model for interpersonal ritual behavior, but a model that may be departed from in significant ways. For example, the offended parties may give the offender a chance to initiate the offering on his own before a challenge is made and before they ratify the offense as an incident. This is a common courtesy, extended on the assumption that the recipient will introduce a self-challenge. Further, when the offended persons accept the corrective offering, the offender may suspect that this has been grudgingly done from tact, and so he may volunteer additional corrective offerings, not allowing the matter to rest until he has received a second or third acceptance of his repeated apology. Or the offended persons may tactfully take over the role of the offender and volunteer excuses for him that will, perforce, be acceptable to the offended persons.

. . . It is plain that emotions play a part in these cycles of response, as when anguish is expressed because of what one has done to another's face, or anger because of what has been done to one's own. I want to stress that these emotions function as moves, and fit so precisely into the logic of the ritual game that it would seem difficult to understand them without it.[15] In fact, spontaneously expressed feelings are likely to fit into the formal pattern of the ritual interchange more elegantly than consciously designed ones.

Making Points–The Aggressive Use of Face-Work

Every face-saving practice which is allowed to neutralize a particular threat opens up the possibility that the threat will be willfully introduced for what can be safety gained by it. If a person knows that his modesty will be answered by others' praise of him, he can fish for compliments. If his own appraisal of self will be checked against incidental events, then he can arrange for favorable incidental events to appear. If others are prepared to overlook an affront to them and act forbearantly, or to accept apologies, then he can rely on this as a basis for safely offending them. He can attempt by sudden withdrawal to force the others into a ritually unsatisfactory state, leaving them to flounder in an interchange that cannot readily be completed. Finally, at some expense to himself, he can arrange for the others to hurt his feelings, thus forcing them to feel guilt, remorse, and sustained ritual disequilibrium.[16]

When a person treats face-work not as something he need be prepared to perform, but rather as something that others can be counted on to perform or to accept, then an encounter or an undertaking becomes less a scene of mutual considerateness than an arena in which a contest or match is held. The purpose of the game is to preserve everyone's line from an inexcusable contradiction, while scoring as many points as possible against one's adversaries and making as many gains as possible for oneself. An audience to the struggle is almost a necessity. The general method is for the person to introduce favorable facts about himself and unfavorable facts about the others in such a way that the only reply the others will be able to think up will be one that terminates the interchange in a grumble, a meager excuse, a face-saving I-can-take-a-joke laugh, or an empty stereotyped comeback of the "Oh yeah?" or "That's what you think" variety. The losers in such cases will have to cut their losses, tacitly grant the loss of a point, and attempt to do better in the next interchange. Points made by allusion to social class status are sometimes called snubs; those made by allusions to moral respectability are sometimes called digs; in either case one deals with a capacity at what is sometimes called "bitchiness."

In aggressive interchanges the winner not only succeeds in introducing information favorable to himself and unfavorable to the others, but also demonstrates that as interactant he can handle himself better than his adversaries. Evidence of this capacity is often more important than all the other information the person conveys in the interchange, so that the introduction of a "crack" in verbal interaction tends to imply that the initiator is better at footwork than those who must suffer his remarks. However, if they succeed in making a successful parry of the thrust and then a successful riposte, the instigator of the play must not only face the disparagement with which the others have answered him but also accept the fact that his assumption of superiority in footwork has proven false. He is made to look foolish; he loses face. Hence it is always a gamble to "make a remark." The tables can be turned and the aggressor can lose more than he could have gained had his move won the point. Successful ripostes or comebacks in our society are sometimes called squelches or toppers; theoretically it would be possible for a squelch to be squelched, a topper to be topped, and a riposte to be parried with a counterriposte, but except in staged interchanges this third level of successful action seems rare.[17]

The Choice of Appropriate Face-Work

When an incident occurs, the person whose face is threatened may attempt to reinstate the ritual order by means of one kind of strategy, while the other participants may desire or expect a practice of a different type to be employed. When, for example, a minor mishap occurs, momentarily revealing a person in wrong face or out of face, the others are often more willing and able to act blind to the discrepancy than is the threatened person himself. Often they would prefer him to exercise poise,[18] while he feels that he cannot afford to overlook what has happened to his face and so becomes apologetic and shamefaced, if he is the creator of the incident, or destructively assertive, if the others are responsible for it.[19] Yet on the other hand, a person may manifest poise when the others feel that he ought to have broken down into embarrassed apology—that he is taking undue advantage of their helpfulness by his attempts to brazen it out. Sometimes a person may himself be undecided as to which practice to employ, leaving the others in the embarrassing position of not knowing which tack they are going to have to follow. Thus when a person makes a slight *gaffe*, he and the others may become embarrassed not because of inability to handle such difficulties, but because for a moment no one knows whether the offender is going to act blind to the incident, or give it joking recognition, or employ some other face-saving practice.

Cooperation in Face-Work

When a face has been threatened, face-work must be done, but whether this is initiated and primarily carried through by the person whose face is threatened, or by the offender, or by a mere witness,[20] is often of secondary importance. Lack of effort on the part of one person induces compensative effort from others; a contribution by one person relieves the others of the task. In fact, there are many minor incidents in which the offender and the offended simultaneously attempt to initiate an apology.[21] Resolution of the situation to everyone's apparent satisfaction is the first requirement; correct apportionment of blame is typically a secondary consideration. Hence terms such as tact and *savoir-faire* fail to distinguish whether it is the person's own face that his diplomacy saves or the face of the others. Similarly, terms such as *gaffe* and *faux pas* fail to specify whether it is the actor's own face he has threatened or the face of other participants. And it is understandable that if one person finds he is powerless to save his own face, the others seem especially bound to protect him. For example, in polite society, a handshake that perhaps should not have been extended becomes one that cannot be declined. Thus one accounts for the *noblesse oblige* through which those of high status are expected to curb their power of embarrassing their lessers,[22] as well as the fact that the handicapped often accept courtesies that they can manage better without.

Since each participant in an undertaking is concerned, albeit for differing reasons, with saving his own face and the face of the others, then tacit cooperation will naturally arise so that the participants together can attain their shared but differently motivated objectives.

One common type of tacit cooperation in face-saving is the tact exerted in regard to face-work itself. The person not only defends his own face and protects the face of the others, but also acts so as to make it possible and even easy for the others to employ face-work for themselves and him. He helps them to help themselves and him. Social etiquette, for example, warns men against asking for New Year's Eve dates too early in the season, lest the girl find it difficult to provide a gentle excuse for refusing. . . .

Tact in regard to face-work often relies for its operation on a tacit agreement to do business through the language of hint—the language of innuendo, ambiguities, well-placed pauses, carefully worded jokes, and so on.[23] The rule regarding this unofficial kind of communication is that the sender ought not to act as if he had officially conveyed the message he has hinted at, while the recipients have the right and the obligation to act as if they have not officially received the message contained in the hint. Hinted communication, then, is deniable communication; it need not be faced up to. It provides a means by which the person can be warned that his current line or the current situation is leading to loss of face, without this warning itself becoming an incident.

Another form of tacit cooperation, and one that seems to be much used in many societies, is reciprocal self-denial. Often the person does not have a clear idea of what would be a just or acceptable apportionment of judgments during the occasion, and so he voluntarily deprives or depreciates himself while indulging and complimenting the others, in both cases carrying the judgments safely past what is likely to be just. The favorable judgments about himself he allows to come from the others; the unfavorable judgments of himself are his own contributions. This "after you, Alphonse" technique works, of course, because in depriving himself he can reliably anticipate that the others will compliment or indulge him. Whatever allocation of favors is eventually established, all participants are first given a chance to show that they are not bound or constrained by their own desires and expectations, that they have a properly modest view of themselves, and that they can be counted upon to support the ritual code. . . .

A person's performance of face-work, extended by his tacit agreement to help others perform theirs, represents his willingess to abide by the ground rules of social interaction. Here is the hallmark of his socialization as an interactant. If he and the others were not socialized in this way, interaction in most societies and most situations would be a much more hazardous thing for feelings and faces. The person would find it impractical to be oriented to symbolically conveyed appraisals of social worth, or to be possessed of feelings—that is, it would be impractical for him to be a ritually delicate object. And as I shall suggest, if the person were not a ritually delicate object, occasions of talk could not be organized in the way they usually are. It is no wonder that trouble is caused by a person who cannot be relied upon to play the face-saving game.

The Ritual Roles of the Self

So far I have implicitly been using a double definition of self: the self as an image pieced together from the expressive implications of the full flow of events in an undertaking; and the self as a kind of player in a ritual game who copes honorably or dishonorably, diplomatically or undiplomatically, with the judgmental contingencies of the situation. A double mandate is involved. As sacred objects, men are subject to slights and profanation; hence as players of the ritual game they have had to lead themselves into duels, and wait for a round of shots to go wide of the mark before embracing their opponents. Here is an echo of the distinction between the value of a hand drawn at cards and the capacity of the person who plays it. This distinction must be kept in mind, even though it appears that once a person has gotten a reputation for good or bad play this reputation may become part of the face he must later play at maintaining.

Once the two roles of the self have been separated, one can look to the ritual code implicit in face-work to learn how the two roles are related. When a person is responsible for introducing a threat to another's face, he apparently has a right, within limits, to wriggle out of the difficulty by means of self-abasement. When performed voluntarily these indignities do not seem to profane his own image. It is as if he had the right of insulation and could castigate himself qua actor without injuring himself qua object of ultimate worth. By token of the same insulation he can belittle himself and modestly underplay his positive qualities, with the understanding that no one will take his statements as a fair representation of his sacred self. On the other hand, if he is forced against his will to treat himself in these ways, his face, his pride, and his honor will be seriously threatened. Thus, in terms of the ritual code, the person seems to have a special license to accept mistreatment at his own hands that he does not have the right to accept from others. Perhaps this is a safe arrangement because he is not likely to carry this license too far, whereas the others, were they given this privilege, might be more likely to abuse it.

Further, within limits the person has a right to forgive other participants for affronts to his sacred image. He can forbearantly overlook minor slurs upon his face, and in regard to somewhat greater injuries he is the one person who is in a position to accept apologies on behalf of his sacred self. This is a relatively safe prerogative for the person to have in regard to himself, for it is one that is exercised in the interests of the others or of the undertaking. Interestingly enough, when the person commits a *gaffe* against himself, it is not he who has the license to forgive the event; only the others have that prerogative, and it is a safe prerogative for them to have because they can exercise it only in his interests or in the interests of the undertaking. One finds, then, a system of checks and balances by which each participant tends to be given the right to handle only those matters which he will have little motivation for mishandling. In short, the rights and obligations of an interactant are designed to prevent him from abusing his role as an object of sacred value.

Spoken Interaction

Most of what has been said so far applies to encounters of both an immediate and mediated kind, although in the latter the interaction is likely to be more attenuated, with each participant's line being gleaned from such things as written statements and work records. During direct personal contacts, however, unique informational conditions prevail and the significance of face becomes especially clear. The human tendency to use signs and symbols means that evidence of social worth and of mutual evaluations will be conveyed by very minor things, and these things will be witnessed, as will the fact that they have been witnessed. An unguarded glance, a momentary change in tone of voice, an ecological position taken or not taken, can drench a talk with judgmental significance. Therefore, just as there is no occasion of talk in which improper impressions could not intentionally or unintentionally arise, so there is no occasion of talk so trivial as not to require each participant to show serious concern with the way in which he handles himself and the others present. Ritual factors which are present in mediated contacts are here present in an extreme form.

In any society, whenever the physical possibility of spoken interaction arises, it seems that a system of practices, conventions, and procedural rules comes into play which functions as a means of guiding and organizing the flow of messages. An understanding will prevail as to when and where it will be permissible to initiate talk, among whom, and by means of what topics of conversation. A set of significant gestures is employed to initiate a spate of communication and as a means for the persons concerned to accredit each other as legitimate participants.[24] When this process of reciprocal ratification occurs, the persons so ratified are in what might be called a *state of talk*—that is, they have declared themselves officially open to one another for pupurposes of spoken communication and guarantee together to maintain a flow of words. A set of significant gestures is also employed by which one or more new participants can officially join the talk, by which one or more accredited participants can officially withdraw, and by which the state of talk can be terminated.

A single focus of thought and visual attention, and a single flow of talk, tends to be maintained and to be legitimated as officially representative of the encounter. The concerted and official visual attention of the participants tends to be transferred smoothly by means of formal or informal clearance cues, by which the current speaker signals that he is about to relinquish the floor and the prospective speaker signals a desire to be given the floor. An understanding will prevail as to how long and how frequently each participant is to hold the floor. The recipients convey to the speaker, by appropriate gestures, that they are according him their attention. Participants restrict their involvement in matters external to the encounter and observe a limit to involvement in any one message of the encounter, in this way ensuring that they will be able to follow along whatever direction the topic of conversation takes them. Interruptions and lulls are regulated so as not to disrupt the flow of messages. Messages that are not part of the officially accredited flow are modulated so as not to interfere seriously with the accredited messages. Nearby persons who are not participants visibly desist in some way from exploiting their communication position and also modify their own communication, if any, so as not to provide difficult interference. A particular ethos or emotional atmosphere is allowed to prevail. A polite accord is typically maintained, and participants who may be in real disagreement with one another give temporary lip service to views that bring them into agreement on matters of fact and principle. Rules are followed for smoothing out the transition, if any, from one topic of conversation to another.[25]

These rules of talk pertain not to spoken interaction considered as an ongoing process, but to *an* occasion of talk or episode of interaction as a naturally bounded unit. This unit consists of the total activity that occurs during the time that a given set of participants have accredited one another for talk and maintain a single moving focus of attention.[26]

The conventions regarding the structure of occasions of talk represent an effective solution to the problem of organizing a flow of spoken messages. In attempting to discover how it is that these conventions are maintained in force as guides to action, one finds evidence to suggest a functional relationship between the structure of the self and the structure of spoken interaction.

The socialized interactant comes to handle spoken interaction as he would any other kind, as something that must be pursued with ritual care. By automatically appealing to face, he knows how to conduct himself in regard to talk. By repeatedly and automatically asking himself the question, ''If I do or do not act in this way, will I or others lose face?'' he decides at each moment, consciously or unconsciously, how to behave. For example, entrance into an occasion of spoken interaction may be taken as a symbol of intimacy or legitimate purpose, and so the person must, to save his face, desist from entering into talk with a given set of others unless his circumstances justify what is expressed about him by his entrance. Once approached for talk, he must accede to the others in order to save their face. Once engaged in conversation, he must demand only the amount of attention that is an appropriate expression of his relative social worth. Undue lulls come to be potential signs of having nothing in common, or of being insufficiently self-possessed to create something to say, and hence must be avoided. Similarly, interruptions and inattentiveness may convey disrespect and must be avoided unless the implied disrespect is an accepted part of the relationship. A surface of agreement must be maintained by means of discretion and white lies, so that the assumption of mutual approval will not be discredited. Withdrawal must be handled so that it will not convey an improper evaluation.[27] The person must restrain his emotional involvement so as not to present an image of someone with no self-control or dignity who does not rise above his feelings.

The relation between the self and spoken interaction is further displayed when one examines the ritual interchange. In a conversational encounter, interaction tends to proceed in spurts, an interchange at a time, and the flow of information and business is parcelled out into these relatively closed ritual units.[28] The lull between interchanges tends to be greater than the lull between turns at talking in an interchange, and there tends to be a less meaningful relationship between two sequential interchanges than between two sequential speeches in an interchange.

This structural aspect of talk arises from the fact that when a person volunteers a statement or message, however trivial or commonplace, he commits himself and those he addresses, and in a sense places everyone present in jeopardy. By saying something, the speaker opens himself up to the possibility that the intended recipients will affront him by not listening or will think him forward, foolish, or offensive in what he has said. And should he meet with such a reception, he will find himself committed to the necessity of taking face-saving action against them. Furthermore, by saying something the speaker opens his intended recipients up to the possibility that the message will be self-approving, presumptuous, demanding, insulting, and generally an affront to them or to their conception of him, so that they will find themselves obliged to take action against him in defense of the ritual code. And should the speaker praise the recipients, they will be obliged to make suitable denials, showing that they do not hold too favorable an opinion of themselves and are not so eager to secure indulgences as to endanger their reliability and flexibility as interactants.

Thus when one person volunteers a message, thereby contributing what might easily be a threat to the ritual equilibrium, someone else present is obliged to show that the message has been received and that its content is acceptable to all concerned or can be acceptably countered. This acknowledging reply, of course, may contain a tactful rejection of the original communication, along with a request for modification. In such cases, several exchanges of messages may be required before the interchange is terminated on the basis of modified lines. The interchange comes to a close when it is possible to allow it to do so—that is, when everyone present has signified that he has been ritually appeased to a degree satisfactory to him.[29] A momentary lull between interchanges is possible, for it comes at a time when it will not be taken as a sign of something untoward.

In general, then, a person determines how he ought to conduct himself during an occasion of talk by testing the potentially symbolic meaning of his acts against the self-images that are being sustained. In doing this, however, he incidentally subjects his behavior to the expressive order that prevails and contributes to the orderly flow of messages. His aim is to save face; his effect is to save the situation. From the point of view of saving face, then, it is a good thing that spoken interaction has the conventional organization given it; from the point of view of sustaining an orderly flow of spoken messages, it is a good thing that the self has the ritual structure given it.

I do not mean, however, to claim that another kind of person related to another kind of message organization would not do as well. More important, I do not claim that the present system is without weaknesses or drawbacks; these must be expected, for everywhere in social life a mechanism or functional relation which solves one set of problems necessarily creates a set of potential difficulties and abuses all its own. For example, a characteristic problem in the ritual organization of personal contacts is that while a person can save his face by quarreling or by indignantly withdrawing from the encounter, he does this at the cost of the interaction. Furthermore, the person's attachment to face gives others something to aim at; they can not only make an effort to wound him unofficially, but may even make an official attempt utterly to destroy his face. Also, fear over possible loss of his face often prevents the person from initiating contacts in which important information can be transmitted and important relationships re-established; he may be led to seek the safety of solitude rather than the danger of social encounters. He may do this even though others feel that he is motivated by "false pride"—a pride which suggests that the ritual code is getting the better of those whose conduct is regulated by it. Further, the "after you, Alphonse" complex can make the termination of an interchange difficult. So, too, where each participant feels that he must sacrifice a little more than has been sacrificed for him, a kind of vicious indulgence cycle may occur—much like the hostility cycle that can lead to open quarrels—with each person receiving things he does not want and giving in return things he would rather keep. Again, when people are on formal terms, much energy may be spent in ensuring that events do not occur which might effectively carry an improper expression. And on the other hand, when a set of persons are on familiar terms and feel that they need not stand on ceremony with one another, then inattentiveness and interruptions are likely to become rife, and talk may degenerate into a happy babble of disorganized sound.

The ritual code itself requires a delicate balance, and can be easily upset by anyone who upholds it too eagerly or not eagerly enough, in terms of the standards and expectations of his group. Too little perceptiveness, too little *savoir-faire*, too little pride and considerateness, and the person ceases to be someone who can be trusted to take a hint about himself or give a hint that will save others embarrassment. Such a person comes to be a real threat to society; there is nothing much that can be done with him, and often he gets his way. Too much perceptiveness or too much pride, and the person becomes someone who is thin-skinned, who must be treated with kid gloves, requiring more care on the part of others than he may be worth to them. Too much *savoir-faire* or too much considerateness, and he becomes someone who is too socialized, who leaves the others with the feeling that they do not know how they really stand with him, nor what they should do to make an effective long-term adjustment to him.

In spite of these inherent "pathologies" in the organization of talk, the functional fitness between the socialized person and spoken interaction is a viable and practical one. The person's orientation to face, especially his own, is the point of leverage that the ritual order has in regard to him; yet a promise to take ritual care of his face is built into the very structure of talk.

Face and Social Relationships

When a person begins a mediated or immediate encounter, he already stands in some kind of social relationship to the others concerned, and expects to stand in a given relationship to them after the particular encounter ends. This, of course, is one of the ways in which social contacts are geared into the wider society. Much of the activity occurring during an encounter can be understood as an effort on everyone's part to get through the occasion and all the unanticipated and unintentional events that can cast participants in an undesirable light, without disrupting the relationships of the participants. And if relationships are in the process of change, the object will be to bring the encounter to a satisfactory close without altering the expected course of development. This perspective nicely accounts, for example, for the little ceremonies of greeting and farewell which occur when people begin a conversational encounter or depart from one. Greetings provide a way of showing that a relationship is still what it was at the termination of the previous coparticipation, and, typically, that this relationship involves sufficient suppression of hostility for the participants temporarily to drop their guards and talk. Farewells sum up the effect of the encounter upon the relationship and show what the participants may expect of one another when they next meet. The enthusiasm of greetings compensates for the weakening of the relationship caused by the absence just terminated, while the enthusiasm of farewells compensates the relationship for the harm that is about to be done to it by separation.[30]

It seems to be a characteristic obligation of many social relationships that each of the members guarantees to support a given face for the other members in given situations. To prevent disruption of these relationships, it is therefore necessary for each member to avoid destroying the others' face. At the same time, it is often the person's social relationship with others that leads him to participate in certain encounters with them, where incidentally he will be dependent upon them for supporting his face. Furthermore, in many relationships, the members come to share a face, so that in the presence of third parties an improper act on the part of one member becomes a source of acute embarrassment to the other members. A social relationship, then, can be seen as a way in which the person is more than ordinarily forced to trust his self-image and face to the tact and good conduct of others.

The Nature of the Ritual Order

The ritual order seems to be organized basically on accommodative lines, so that the imagery used in thinking about other types of social order is not quite suitable for it. For the other types of social order a kind of schoolboy model seems to be employed: if a person wishes to sustain a particular image of himself and trust his feelings to it, he must work hard for the credits that will buy this self-enhancement for him; should he try to obtain ends by improper means, by cheating or theft, he will be punished, disqualified from the race, or at least made to start all over again from the beginning. This is the imagery of a hard, dull game. In fact, society and the individual join in one that is easier on both of them, yet one that has dangers of its own.

Whatever his position in society, the person insulates himself by blindnesses, half-truths, illusions, and rationalizations. He makes an "adjustment" by convincing himself, with the tactful support of his intimate circle, that he is what he wants to be and that he would not do to gain his ends what the others have done to gain theirs. And as for society, if the person is willing to be subject to informal social control—if he is willing to find out from hints and glances and tactful cues what his place is, and keep it—then there will be no objection to his furnishing this place at his own discretion, with all the comfort, elegance, and nobility that his wit can muster for him. To protect this shelter he does not have to work hard, or join a group, or compete with anybody; he need only be careful about the expressed judgments he places himself in a position to witness. Some situations and acts and persons will have to be avoided; others, less threatening, must not be pressed too far. Social life is an uncluttered, orderly thing because the person voluntarily stays away from the places and topics and times where he is not wanted and where he might be disparaged for going. He cooperates to save his face, finding that there is much to be gained from venturing nothing.

Facts are of the schoolboy's world—they can be altered by diligent effort but they cannot be avoided. But what the person protects and defends and invests his feelings in is an idea about himself, and ideas are vulnerable not to facts and things but to communications. Communications belong to a less punitive scheme than do facts, for communications can be by-passed, withdrawn from, disbelieved, conveniently misunderstood, and tactfully conveyed. And even should the person misbehave and break the truce he has made with society, punishment need not be the consequence. If the offense is one that the offended persons can let go by without losing too much face, then they are likely to act forbearantly, telling themselves that they will get even with the offender in another way at another time, even though such an occasion may never arise and might not be exploited if it did. If the offense is great, the offended persons may withdraw from the encounter, or from future similar ones, allowing their withdrawal to be reinforced by the awe they may feel toward someone who breaks the ritual code. Or they may have the offender withdrawn, so that no further communication can occur. But since the offender can salvage a good deal of face from such operations, withdrawal is often not so much an informal punishment for an offense as it is merely a means of terminating it. Perhaps the main principle of the ritual order is not justice but face, and what any offender receives is not what he deserves but what will sustain for the moment the line to which he has committed himself, and through this the line to which he has committed the interaction.

Throughout this paper it has been implied that underneath their differences in culture, people everywhere are the same. If persons have a universal human nature, they themselves are not to be looked to for an explanation of it. One must look rather to the fact that societies everywhere, if they are to be societies, must mobilize their members as self-regulating participants in social encounters. One way of mobilizing the individual for this purpose is through ritual; he is taught to be perceptive, to have feelings attached to self and a self expressed through face, to have pride, honor, and dignity, to have considerateness, to have tact and a certain amount of poise. These are some of the elements of behavior which must be built into the person if practical use is to be made of him as an interactant, and it is these elements that are referred to in part when one speaks of universal human nature.

Universal human nature is not a very human thing. By acquiring it, the person becomes a kind of construct, built up not from inner psychic propensities but from moral rules that are impressed upon him from without. These rules, when followed, determine the evaluation he will make of himself and of his fellow-participants in the encounter, the distribution of his feelings, and the kinds of practices he will employ to maintain a specified and obligatory kind of ritual equilibrium. The general capacity to be bound by moral rules may well belong to the individual, but the particular set of rules which transforms him into a human being derives from requirements established in the ritual organization of social encounters. And if a particular person or group or society seems to have a unique character all its own, it is because its standard set of human-nature elements is pitched and combined in a particular way. Instead of much pride, there may be little. Instead of abiding by the rules, there may be much effort to break them safely. But if an encounter or undertaking is to be sustained as a viable system of interaction organized on ritual principles, then these variations must be held within certain bounds and nicely counterbalanced by corresponding modifications in some of the other rules and understandings. Similarly, the human nature of a particular set of persons may be specially designed for the special kind of undertakings in which they participate, but still each of these persons must have within him something of the balance of characteristics required of a usable participant in any ritually organized system of social activity.

NOTES

[1] For discussions of the Chinese Conception of face, see the following: Hsien Chin Hu, "The Chinese Concept of 'Face,' " *American Anthropologist,* 1944, n.s. 46:45–64. Martin C. Yang, *A Chinese Village* (New York, Columbia University Press, 1945), pp. 167–72. J. Macgowan, *Men and Manners of Modern China* (London, Unwin, 1912), pp. 301–12. Arthur H. Smith, *Chinese Characteristics* (New York, Felming II. Revell Co., 1894), pp. 16–18. For a comment on the American Indian conception of face, see Marcel Mauss, *The Gift,* tr. Ian Cunnison (London, Cohen & West, 1954), p. 38.

[2] See, for example, Smith, footnote 1; p. 17.

[3] Of course, the more power and prestige the others have, the more a person is likely to show consideration for their feelings, as H. E. Dale suggests in *The Higher Civil Service of Great Britain* (Oxford, Oxford Univ. Press, 1941), p. 126*n*. "The doctrine of 'feelings' was expounded to me many years ago by a very eminent civil servant with a pretty taste in cynicism. He explained that the importance of feelings varies in close correspondence with the importance of the person who feels. If the public interest requires that a junior clerk should be removed from his post, no regard need be paid to his feelings; if it is a case of an Assistant Secretary, they must be carefully considered, within reason; if it is a Permanent Secretary, his feelings are a principal element in the situation, and only imperative public interest can override their requirements."

[4] Salesmen, especially street "stemmers," know that if they take a line that will be discredited unless the reluctant customer buys, the customer may be trapped by considerateness and buy in order to save the face of the salesman and prevent what would ordinarily result in a scene.

[5] Surface agreement in the assessment of social worth does not, of course, imply equality; the evaluation consensually sustained of one participant may be quite different from the one consensually sustained of another. Such agreement is also compatible with expression of differences of opinion between two participants, provided each of the disputants shows "respect" for the other, guiding the expression of disagreement so that it will convey an evaluation of the other that the other will be willing to convey about himself. Extreme cases are provided by wars, duels, and barroom fights, when these are of a gentlemanly kind, for they can be conducted under consensual auspices, with each protagonist guiding his action according to the rules of the game, thereby making it possible for his action to be interpreted as an expression of a fair player openly in combat with a fair opponent. In fact, the rules and etiquette of any game can be analyzed as a means by which the image of a fair player can be expressed, just as the image of a fair player can be analyzed as a means by which the rules and etiquette of a game are sustained.

[6] Presumably social skill and perceptiveness will be high in groups whose members frequently act as representatives of wider social units such as lineages or nations, for the player here is gambling with a face to which the feelings of many persons are attached. Similarly, one might expect social skill to be well developed among those of high station and those with whom they have dealings, for the more face an interactant has, the greater the number of events that may be inconsistent with it, and hence the greater the need for social skill to forestall or counteract these inconsistencies.

[7] In our own society an illustration of avoidance is found in the middle- and upper-class Negro who avoids certain face-to-face contacts with whites in order to protect the self-evaluation projected by his clothes and manner. See, for example, Charles Johnson, *Patterns of Negro Segregation* (New York, Harper, 1943), ch. 13. The function of avoidance in maintaining the kinship system in small preliterate societies might be taken as a particular illustration of the same general theme.

[8] An illustration is given by K. S. Latourette, *The Chinese: Their History and Culture* (New York, Macmillan, 1942): "A neighbor or a group of neighbors may tender their good offices in adjusting a quarrel in which each antagonist would be sacrificing his face by taking the first step in approaching the other. The wise intermediary can effect the reconciliation while preserving the dignity of both" (vol. 2: p. 211).

[9] In an unpublished paper Harold Garfinkel has suggested that when the person finds that he has lost face in a conversational encounter, he may feel a desire to disappear or "drop through the floor," and that this may involve a wish not only to conceal loss of face but also to return magically to a point in time when it would have been possible to save face by avoiding the encounter.

[10] When the person knows the others well, he will know what issues ought not to be raised and what situ-

ations the others ought not to be placed in, and he will be free to introduce matters at will in all other areas. When the others are strangers to him, he will often reverse the formula, restricting himself to specific areas he knows are safe. On these occasions, as Simmel suggests, ". . . discretion consists by no means only in the respect for the secret of the other, for his specific will to conceal this or that from us, but in staying away from the knowledge of all that the other does not expressly reveal to us." See *The Sociology of Georg Simmel* (Kurt H. Wolff, tr. and ed.) (Glencoe, Ill., Free Press, 1950), pp. 320–21.

[11] The Western traveler used to complain that the Chinese could never be trusted to say what they meant but always said what they felt their Western listener wanted to hear. Ths Chinese used to complain that the Westerner was brusque, boorish, and unmannered. In terms of Chinese standards, presumably, the conduct of a Westerner is so gauche that he creates an emergency, forcing the Asian to forgo any kind of direct reply in order to rush in with a remark that might rescue the Westerner from the compromising position in which he had placed himself. (See Smith, footnote 1; ch. 8, "The Talent for Indirection.") This is an instance of the important group of misunderstandings which arise during interaction between persons who come from groups with different ritual standards.

[12] A pretty example of this is found in parade-ground etiquette which may oblige those in a parade to treat anyone who faints as if he were not present at all.

[13] This kind of imagery is one that social anthropologists seem to find naturally fitting. Note, for example, the implications of the following statement by Margaret Mead in her "Kinship in the Admiralty Islands," *Anthropological Papers of the American Museum of Natural History,* 34:183–358: "If a husband beats his wife, custom demands that she leave him and go to her brother, real or officiating, and remain a length of time commensurate with the degree of her offended dignity" (p. 274).

[14] The notion of interchange is drawn in part from Eliot D. Chapple, "Measuring Human Relations," *Genetic Psychol. Monographs* (1940) 22:3–147, especially pp. 26–30, and from A. B. Horsfall and C. A. Arensberg, "Teamwork and Productivity in a Shoe Factory," *Human Organization* (1949) 8:13–25, especially p. 19. For further material on the interchange as a unit see E. Goffman, "Communication Conduct in an Island Community," unpublished Ph. D. dissertation, Department of Sociology, University of Chicago, 1953, especially chs. 12 and 13, pp. 165–95.

[15] Even when a child demands something and is refused, he is likely to cry and sulk not as an irrational expression of frustration but as a ritual move, conveying that he already has a face to lose and that its loss is not to be permitted lightly. Sympathetic parents may even allow for such display, seeing in these crude strategies the beginnings of a social self.

[16] The strategy of maneuvering another into a position where he cannot right the harm he has done is very commonly employed but nowhere with such devotion to the ritual model of conduct as in revengeful suicide. See, for example, M. D. W. Jeffreys, "Samsonic Suicide, or Suicide of Revenge Among Africans," *African Studies* (1952) 11:118–22.

[17] In board and card games the player regularly takes into consideration the possible responses of his adversaries to a play that he is about to make, and even considers the possibility that his adversaries will know that he is taking such precautions. Conversational play is by comparison surprisingly impulsive; people regularly make remarks about others present without carefully designing their remarks to prevent a successful comeback. Similarly, while feinting and sandbagging are theoretical possibilities during talk, they seem to be little exploited.

[18] Folklore imputes a great deal of poise to the upper classes. If there is truth in this belief it may lie in the fact that the upper-class person tends to find himself in encounters in which he outranks the other participants in ways additional to class. The ranking participant is often somewhat independent of the good opinion of the others and finds it practical to be arrogant, sticking to a face regardless of whether the encounter supports it. On the other hand, those who are in the power of a fellow-participant tend to be very much concerned with the valuation he makes of them or witnesses being made of them, and so find it difficult to maintain a slightly wrong face without becoming embarrassed and apologetic. It may be added that people who lack awareness of the symbolism in minor events may keep cool in difficult situations, showing poise that they do not really possess.

[19] Thus, in our society, when a person feels that others expect him to measure up to approved standards of cleanliness, tidiness, fairness, hospitality, generosity, affluence, and so on, or when he sees himself as someone who ought to maintain such standards, he may burden an encounter with extended apologies for his failings, while all along the other participants do not care about the standard, or do not believe the

person is really lacking in it, or are convinced that he is lacking in it and see the apology itself as a vain effort at self-elevation.

[20] Thus one function of seconds in actual duels, as well as in figurative ones, is to provide an excuse for not fighting that both contestants can afford to accept.

[21] See, for instance, Jackson Toby, "Some Variables in Role Conflict Analysis," *Social Forces* (1952) 30:323–37: "With adults there is less likelihood for essentially trivial issues to produce conflict. The automatic apology of two strangers who accidentally collide on a busy street illustrates the integrative function of etiquette. In effect, each of the parties to the collision says, 'I don't know whether I am responsible for this situation, but *if* I am, you have a right to be angry with me, a right that I pray you will not exercise.' By defining the situation as one in which both parties must abase themselves, society enables each to keep his self-respect. Each may feel in his heart of hearts, 'Why can't that stupid ass watch where he's going?' But overtly *each plays the role of the guilty party* whether he feels he has been miscast or not" (p. 325).

[22] Regardless of the person's relative social position, in one sense he has power over the other participants and they must rely upon his considerateness. When the others act toward him in some way, they presume upon a social relationship to him, since one of the things expressed by interaction is the relationship of the interactants. Thus they compromise themselves, for they place him in a position to discredit the claims they express as to his attitude toward them. Hence in response to claimed social relationships every person, of high estate or low, will be expected to exercise *noblesse oblige* and refrain from exploiting the compromised position of the others.

Since social relationships are defined partly in terms of voluntary mutual aid, refusal of a request for assistance becomes a delicate matter, potentially destructive of the asker's face. Chester Holcombe, *The Real Chinaman* (New York, Dodd, Mead, 1895), provides a Chinese instance: "Much of the falsehood to which the Chinese as a nation are said to be addicted is a result of the demands of etiquette. A plain, frank 'no' is the height of discourtesy. Refusal or denial of any sort must be softened and toned down into an expression of regretted inability. Unwillingness to grant a favor is never shown. In place of it there is seen a chastened feeling of sorrow that unavoidable but quite imaginary circumstances render it wholly impossible. Centuries of practice in this form of evasion have made the Chinese matchlessly fertile in the invention and development of excuses. It is rare, indeed, that one is caught at a loss for a bit of artfully embroidered fiction with which to hide an unwelcome truth" (pp. 274–75).

[23] Useful comments in some of the structural roles played by unofficial communication can be found in a discussion of irony and banter in Tom Burns, "Friends, Eenemies, and the Polite Fiction," *Amer. Sociol. Rev.* (1953), 18:654–62.

[24] The meaning of this status can be appreciated by looking at the kinds of unlegitimated or unratified participation that can occur in spoken interaction. A person may overhear others unbeknownst to them; he can overhear them when they know this to be the case and when they choose either to act as if he were not overhearing them or to signal to him informally that they know he is overhearing them. In all of these cases, the outsider is officially held at bay as someone who is not formally participating in the occasion. Ritual codes, of course, require a ratified participant to be treated quite differently from an unratified one. Thus, for example, only a certain amount of insult from a ratified participant can be ignored without this avoidance practice causing loss of face to the insulted persons; after a point they must challenge the offender and demand redress. However, in many societies apparently, many kinds of verbal abuse from unratified participants can be ignored, without this failure to challenge constituting a loss of face.

[25] For a further treatment of the structure of spoken interaction see Goffman, footnote 14.

[26] I mean to include formal talks where rules of procedure are explicitly prescribed and officially enforced, and where only certain categories of participants may be allowed to hold the floor—as well as chats and sociable talks where rules are not explicit and the role of speaker passes back and forth among the participants.

[27] Among people who have had some experience in interacting with one another, conversational encounters are often terminated in such a way as to give the appearance that all participants have independently hit upon the same moment to withdraw. The disbandment is general, and no one may be conscious of the exchange of cues that has been required to make such a happy simultaneity of action possible. Each participant is thus saved from the compromising position of showing readiness to spend further time with someone who is not as ready to spend time with him.

[28] The empirical discreteness of the interchange unit is sometimes obscured when the same person who provides the terminating turn at talking in one interchange initiates the first turn at talking in the next. However, the analytical utility of the interchange as a unit remains.

[29] The occurrence of the interchange unit is an empirical fact. In addition to the ritual explanation for it, others may be suggested. For example, when the person makes a statement and receives a reply at once, this provides him with a way of learning that his statement has been received and correctly received. Such "metacommunication" would be necessary on functional grounds even were it unnecessary on ritual ones.

[30] Greetings, of course, serve to clarify and fix the roles that the participants will take during the occasion of talk and to commit participants to these roles, while farewells provide a way of unambiguously terminating the encounter. Greetings and farewells may also be used to state, and apologize for, extenuating circumstances—in the case of greetings for circumstances that have kept the participants from interacting until now, and in the case of farewells for circumstances that prevent the participants from continuing their display of solidarity. These apologies allow the impression to be maintained that the participants are more warmly related socially than may be the case. This positive stress, in turn, assures that they will act more ready to enter into contacts than they perhaps really feel inclined to do, thus guaranteeing that diffuse channels for potential communication will be kept open in the society.

13.

STAGE FRIGHT AND THE PROBLEM OF IDENTITY

Stanford M. Lyman and Marvin B. Scott

"All the world's a stage" has become a sociological as much as a Shakespearean observation for describing the nature of social life. And yet, curiously, the dramatic stage is virtually unique as the one area of social life where the potentially treacherous task of sustaining a reality is a conscious concern, and where the dangers of failure are so omnipresent that the participants continually suffer from acute anxiety. If in fact all the world were a stage, it would be a tale told by an idiot—a world of Hobbesian disorder.

Consider a world where the following experiences were permanent features of everyday life. Referring to his own performance anxiety, violinist Mischa Elman describes stage fright as "a consciousness of one's own limitations, at a moment when limitations of any sort place a barrier between what one wants to do and what one can do." [1] And actress Gertrude Lawrence reported on her own stage fright by noting: "These attacks of nerves seem to grow worse with the passing years. It's inexplicable and horrible and something you'd think you'd grow out of rather than into." [2]

Stage fright is manifested in forms familiar to the ordinary man as well as the actor in terms of motor and emotional disturbance.[3] Goffman provides a fairly complete inventory of the phenomenon in his discussion of embarrassment:

> Blushing, fumbling, stuttering, an unusually low or high-pitched voice, quavering speech or breaking of the voice, sweating, blanching, blinking, tremor of the hand, hesitating, or vacillating movement, absentmindedness and malapropisms . . . here are also symptoms of a subjective kind: constriction of the diaphragm, a feeling of wobbliness, consciousness of strained and unnatural gestures, a dazed sensation, dryness of the mouth, and tenseness of the muscles.[4]

Although embarrassment and stage fright are closely related as to the physical symptoms each produces, they differ analytically. Embarrassment occurs spontaneously when an individual's identity claims unexpectedly come under attack.[5] Stage fright, on the other hand, is generated in one of two ways: knowing in advance that a situation will open one to total inspection of self, or anticipating that a slip or flaw will suddenly thrust one into a position that invites challenges to a claimed identity, or both.

The phenomenon of stage fright highlights a fundamental problem of ordinary social interaction, namely, the problem of sustaining an identity.[6] And the dramatic stage provides the paradigm case of this problem.

Onstage, an actor may portray Winston Churchill, Jesus or Abraham Lincoln. Although the audience is aware that such a portrayal is "only" an impersonation, the spectators sharpen rather than relax their critical faculties and the smallest discrepancy between the ideal and the actual presentation is evaluated negatively. Below the surface of the audience's manifest consciousness, there seemingly bubbles a deep-seated resentment at the sight of a person claiming to be someone else. If this claim is going to be made, the audience seems to be saying, then the claimant had better be beyond reproach in his representation. And this attitude is prevalent not only with respect to the dramatic stage but also in everyday life.

In everyday life people frequently make claims (or are thought to be making claims) of being certain kinds of persons. In a typical case, the individual succeeds in carrying the burden of proof to substantiate his claim. But if a challenge to one's identity claims is anticipated, the condition for stage fright is activated. Thus, fellow interactants often constitute an audience possessed of powers of scrutiny and judgment, powers that might be applied to a person's identity claims with damaging results.

In everyday life a system of rules governs the operation of social interaction. These rules are understood by ordinary persons as the "recipes-for-living" that "everyone knows." [7] Among these rules are those of rectitude and relevance which indicate just what is proper and officially noticeable during the course of any interaction and just what is improper and irrelevant. One such rule involves norms of tact. Thus, when an individual makes a slip or commits a boner or a gaffe, his partners in the interaction disattend from these minor failings, make light of them, or accept without criticism an apology offered. Without such exercises of tact social interaction would be a treacherous state of affairs, always fraught with potentialities for unrelieved embarrassment, destruction of the mutually established sense of reality, or unresolvable questions of identity. In short, without such rules, humans would be immobilized for interaction in ordinary life.[8]

As adults, humans need little instruction in these rules. Rather, they serve as "background expectancies" or the taken-for-granted features of everyday life that are known in common by all *bona fide* members of the society. Such rules are problematic for children and often unknown to aliens, who in the processes of socialization and acculturation come to adopt and employ them as part of their own routine perspectives and as signs that they are indeed becoming full-fledged members of the society. Continuous violation of such rules by a person might earn him a label "troublemaker," or a stigma "Don't invite him; he always makes me uncomfortable," or render him eligible for clinical investigation. Onstage, however, such rules are relaxed, and individuals may legitimately become engrossed in slips that destroy the projected reality.

The dramatic stage is operating properly when its inhabitants successfully communicate to an audience a contrived construction of reality—the plot. The theater, unlike a confidence game and many small group experiments, demands that the audience engage in a voluntary deception: "the actor acts what he is not and the audience knows this." [9] However, the audience exacts a heavy price for this self-deception—nothing less than role perfection itself. "If the actor is good, he must be able to convince both audience and himself of the reality of his performance. When he succeeds, all ties to such non-play realities as his *other* roles are cut off, and he has reached the highest achievement of his profession." [10] Although role segmentation appears to be a feature of all urban industrial societies,[11] nowhere is it perfected so well as on the dramatic stage, where for the duration of the performance, and sometimes beyond, actor and character must merge.

Within the framework of the theatrical stage, then, slips and flaws are seriously attended; and unlike most offstage encounters in everyday life, performances are expected to occur with qualities of perfection not ordinarily achieved. Since total congruency is assumed as the definition of the theatrical situation, the rules of tact and disattendance prevailing under ordinary conditions are revoked and rules requiring perfection substituted. And since stage actors know that they will be judged in accordance with these extraordinary rules of conduct during a performance, they are apprehensive.

Our contention is that stage fright arises precisely from the fact that the contrived performance differs from ordinary life in one crucial respect: the rules requiring tact and disattendance from slips are revoked, and thus the actor must mobilize that perfection of verbal and muscular control not usually expected in everyday life. In short, by studying the dramatic stage—its characteristics and its attendant anxieties—we can call attention to its equivalents in ordinary life to learn more about the conditions that generate stage fright in normal relationships.

The Dramatic Frame and Stage Fright

The theater provides and demands a frame of meaning [12] whereby the audience engages in voluntary self-deception. Once the audience enters into this frame, it will—for the duration of the performance—accept as real the events portrayed within the frame.

There are virtually no limits to the self-deceiving reality that the audience will accept once it has entered the dramatic frame. . . .

Limitations on the dramatic frame, then, are not set by the imaginative capacities of the audience. Rather they are set by the scenario itself. The scenario sets the limits within which the actors conduct themselves. Necessarily, the scenario requires a compression of time and space so that the duration and place of the drama can be enacted in a few hours on a stage. Onstage the entire range of action is admitted into the frame of meaningful events. Every gesture—a scratch, a tic, a lurching forward—is open not merely to observation, but more importantly to interpretation. Each action, verbal and physical, is an element of dramatic reality being communicated during the performance.

From the point of view of the audience each actor is negotiating the identity of a character. The audience is in a state of hyperconsciousness, which alerts it to scrutinize each gesture for its apparent and subtle characterological meaning. Detecting some element of puzzlement or incongruity, the audience is triggered into an even more enhanced state of watchfulness.

One slip or small mishap can weaken the entire dramatic reality, leaving the audience tense. The audience is aware of frame danger and waits for rescue, or a failure of rescue, to occur. During this period, some in the audience may give audial recognition to their state of awareness by "flooding out," laughing, gasping, or catcalling. Once a slip occurs, the actor is tensed and his heightened anxiety can lead to just what he does not desire—yet another slip. That is, audience tenseness can be communicated to the performers leading to a further raising of anxiety levels and more errors. Thus the very first slip must be avoided. The requirement for mobilization of self to avoid the first slip is what lies at the heart of stage fright.

Otherwise put, the stage requires what we shall call the "rule of congruency." According to this rule each act and object present in the performance must be accounted for in terms of that performance.[13] Each actor must be on guard to communicate in character, while the audience gleans character identity from each staged action or interprets some of them as noticeable and disconfirming slips.

The theatrical frame, we are suggesting, has certain properties that lend themselves to both actor and audience becoming spontaneously engrossed in errors and mishaps. Aside from the rule of congruency, consider that what happens onstage is knowingly rehearsed. The audience's anticipation of a perfect performance is rooted in the everyday expectation that when people can rehearse what they are going to do, they ought to do it better than under conditions of spontaneity. The preacher in his pulpit, for instance, is expected to perform better under this circumstance than when appearing in ordinary encounters. The opportunity to practice in private what will be performed in public is assumed to provide the opportunity for perfection.

Actors themselves recognize the value of rehearsal in reducing the chance for errors onstage and in discovering for themselves the identity of the character to be portrayed. Lynn Fontanne reports that after the regular rehearsals at the theater, she rehearses again at home with her costar husband Alfred Lunt:

> [We] work and work at home and slowly you get into the character of the person you are playing—the walk, the gestures . . . gradually I become more and more acquainted with her and then as the days go by I sink deeper and deeper into her, discovering traits and things about her I did not know existed when I began to rehearse.[14]

An even more extreme version of the actor's attempt to merge himself with the character to be portrayed is found in the example of Edwin Booth. He would not only mentally construct exactly how the character looked and felt but also how the other characters looked and felt. When portraying Shylock, a particularly difficult role for which he worked years to master, he could not stand to have the actress playing Jessica standing in the wings within his range of vision:

> I go into that scene with a clear picture of Jessica. My own flesh and blood has betrayed me . . . I am deserted . . . I am hopeless—alone. I charge my voice with Shylock's agony, and then look up and see you—my daughter—standing [in the wings] before me, come back to me. My picture breaks up! I lose the scene! [15]

. . . For all its vaunted virtues, however, rehearsal does not eliminate stage fright. Seasoned actors as well as neophytes suffer from pre-performance anxieties, a fact which sometimes comes as a shock (as well as a source of stage fright itself) to new thespians. . . .

That frequency of performance alone does not eliminate stage fright suggests that we must look further into the nature of stage performance to ferret out the complex etiology of this phenomenon.

The Stage As An Environment

The stage is determinedly uneventful: it is a particular form of interaction in which the location of persons and objects is fixed by pre-established rules. Because the stage is, in this sense, an ecological environment, its rules of relevance differ from that of ordinary life. We may distinguish the crucial relevances for the stage under the headings "territories," "props," and "body." [16]

Territories

Staged dramas require that the actor performs in the most dramatically advantageous position available to the character that he is portraying. Ordinary life is never quite so exacting; an everyday encounter of considerable emotional significance may proceed without perfected locations for each interactant. On the stage, however, location is so important that chalked spots are often written on the stage floor to cue the actors to the proper position. Failure to position oneself properly or inability to move with poise to the right place at the right time are sources of anxiety for actors and causes for mirth or other frame-destructive reactions on the part of the audience.

The stage presents actors with an ecological problem only occasionally encountered in everyday life: namely, onstage the actor must sustain the relationship required by the plot of the play between himself and the other characters—while simultaneously communicating to the ever-watchful but nonparticipating audience.

The actor's precise location on the stage is thus often crucial. Not only must he talk to the conversational partner of the scene, but also audibly and visually for the audience to see what he means. Since not only sound but also facial gesture (and especially that of the eyes and mouth) communicate, the actor has to be both audially and visually available to the audience. Stage fright in this sense occurs when an actor imagines that he will—or in fact does—commit an ecological *faux pas* and is unable immediately to rescue himself from the damage.

Props

The stage is an arena of illusion in which both actors and audience agree to accept what is on the stage as actually being what it represents for the duration of the performance. Thus the "box" composed of wood, metal and wire represents the rooms of Willy Loman's home in Arthur Miller's *Death of a Salesman*. But it is precisely because the stage has transformed wood and wire into a temporarily working representation of reality that stage performances are hazardous. Ordinarily a door can be slammed without the walls of the house collapsing, stairs can be ascended without giving way beneath the weight of the person upon them, and ceilings can be expected to retain their horizontal stability at their pre-established height. On the stage, however, none of these can simply be taken for granted. The actor portraying the outraged husband may be expected to storm out of the room, slamming the door behind him, and leaving his wife weeping; but the slammed door should communicate only his anger, not sound the death knell of the house itself. The illusion of the prop-contrived reality must be maintained throughout the performance. Actions that suggest or reveal the actual nature of the props constitute frame destruction of the most irretrievable sort. To destroy the illusion here is to destroy all.

. . . Besides such fixed props as doors and walls, movable objects (or chattels) present a source of danger not usually experienced in everyday life. In every social situation there is some kind of equipment to manipulate. Ordinarily the ability to start or stop, move, or control the action of the equipment regularly associated with one's environment is a signal of self. In this respect social actors formulate at least two general but extreme orientations toward the equipment one regularly handles; first, there is a high order of skill presumed to lodge in the individual primarily because of the frequency with which he handles the item; or second, there is a very low order of skill, approximating motor incapacity or extreme clumsiness and also indicating a character type which seems unable to master the mechanical world. And for most persons, it is believed, the handling of everyday pieces of equipment—automobiles, cigarette lighters, ashtrays, keys and coins—falls into a broad middle range, efficient enough to admit of being able to operate in the modern world with only occasional flaws and failures.

On the stage, however, handling movable and mechanical equipment presents problems far more extraordinary than their offstage counterparts. Objects that are to be picked up, moved, discovered, or destroyed must be available for use at the correct time and in the right place. While in an actual living room the search for an ashtray or a notebook might not interrupt ongoing proceedings, a similar search on-stage—unless part of the plot—must not occur. Indeed, should an object necessary to the plot of a play be misplaced, the actor must not only make do without it but also contrive a suitable subterfuge to avoid audience awareness of the error.

Stage fright with respect to props may take the form of motor incapacity. The normal musculature appears to be frozen, and the actor is immobilized. Or he might get an attack of "the shakes," preventing appropriate handling of quite ordinary items, such as cigarette lighters, glasses, or telephones. Immobilization or shakiness may accelerate and exacerbate the original fear so that the anticipated flaw becomes realized. This in turn may generate a generalized fear which creates the very conditions for continuous errors and heightened fears.

Onstage, even clothing can serve as a source of danger. All clothing worn on the stage is officially a costume, that is, a garment appropriate to the character portrayed and not necessarily suitable to the actor wearing it. The actor must solve the problem of suiting the manner of its wear to the character, not to himself. In every-day life, of course, clothing can come undone, tear, or—by body movement—conceal or disclose aspects of the body and emotional states. Onstage the actor must keep clothing under perfect control not only in the ordinary sense of wear and tear, but also in the manner of its display.

Body

. . . In addition to the perfection of his stage location and handling of props, the actor has to control all those physical and vocal peculiarities that in everyday life are part of his own personal character, but which may be intrusive or discrediting to the character he is portraying onstage.

Thus in everyday concerns the frame of self-presentation assumes a wide variety of imperfections that are disattended, especially if they are irrelevant to the central features of one's role performance. A doctor's nervous tic is ruled out as irrelevant to his performance in removing a wart from the patient's foot; a lawyer's obesity bears no relation to his defense of an accused shop lifter; and a physics teacher's limp does not prevent him from lecturing on astronomy. But the nervous tic of the stage doctor, the excessive weight of the stage lawyer, and the limp of the stage professor are rich in inferential meaning—which the audience expects to be revealed to them. The doctor's nervous tic is but an external sign of his evil designs; the lawyer's fatness indicates a generally jolly disposition temporarily held in abeyance as he manfully defends his client; the professor's limp will eventually "explain" his interest in space exploration, a compensation for mobility interference on earth.

In short, to present a visible imperfection without explanation is to create frame confusion in the story line. While such imperfections may be tolerated as such during the early portions of the drama, if they remain unexplained (or uninterpretable) at the end, audiences will experience a sense of incompleteness, mystification, or even fraud: the imperfection was presented; therefore, it should have been accounted for in the drama.

Although in everyday life people will accept (albeit grudgingly sometimes) that looks deceive, an audience will not so easily acquiesce to that proposition. Type casting meets the audience's desire to have congruency between appearance and reality. And this includes, of course, congruence in the relation of feigned appearance and the final curtain revelation of who the character "really" was.

. . . A special case of complex and confused relationships between physical appearance and social reality arises in racially conscious societies. In the past American Negro actors have been relegated to a large assortment of stereotyped "Negro" roles. Negroes who wished to widen their repertoire and to include traditional "white" roles had to leave the country for such opportunity,[17] or might "pass" as whites if they were sufficiently light-skinned. But when racial barriers are relaxed the appearance of Negroes in conventional white roles sometimes occasions mirth or amazement. Thus a Negro child, upon seeing a Negro Santa Claus for the first time, remarked to her mother: "That sure is a funny Santa Claus. I mean he's not *white.*" [18]

Special problems of performance anxiety—relating to identity, stereotypes and social consequences—face Negro actors in times of transition in racial relations. These problems and anxieties, though probably affecting the performance, extend beyond it into controversies over what kind of status visibility Negroes should exhibit on stage and screen. Thus Hattie McDaniels replied to an attack on her for accepting Hollywood roles as a domestic: "It is better getting $7,000 a week playing a servant than $7 a week *being* one." [19] And Negro film star Sidney Poitier has been accused of building his successful career by sacrificing his screen sexuality and manliness (and by symbolic extension, the manliness of all Negro males in America).[20] The portrayal of racially stigmatized people by members of their own racial group results in anxieties having to do with appropriate and socially tactful (and also tactical) representation.

Beyond physical appearance and the control of physical or cultural stigmas is body movement itself. Onstage the body must be in readiness to act the part, and perfect control of its movements must be maintained throughout the performance. In everyday life individuals can retire from the social scene to restore or repair the body and then return to regular activities. For actors onstage, however, this can only be done surreptitiously and at some hazard to the play itself. In addition, offstage, the movement of arms, legs, head and trunk need not be in perfect coordination with the role being enacted; onstage, it must be. . . .

Stage Fright in Everyday Life

Stage fright is likely to be a feature of a situation during the *critical performance* of a claimed identity. Typically the occasion for this is a testing situation in which the identity claimed will be recognized and legitimated by persons in a position to provide some reward or payoff, such as admission into the circle of those who have established their claim to the identity, a new job or promotion, or the hand of a girl in marriage. Persons about to perform at such times not infrequently experience stage fright, even if the task itself is one with which they are quite familiar and is one which they perform with skill and *savoir-faire* on non-critical occasions.

. . . Critical performances are usually those that test the relationship between rehearsal and stage performance. Off the dramatic stage they include the first full-fledged engagement of a person with the activities with which he identifies himself. For an entrepreneur the test is whether he can actually meet his first payroll; for a doctor, whether he can diagnose his first patient; for a young husband, whether he can sexually satisfy his new wife.

When the critical performance occurs in the presence of higher-status others, the lower-status person is likely to experience anxiety over whether and in what manner he should acknowledge the real differences that separate him from the higher-status person. The problem is further complicated when the higher-status person commands the status inferior to, in effect, be "at ease." In such situations the status inferior tends to experience a kind of "frame confusion" whereby he is never sure whether the interaction he is engaged in is something other than what the status superior says it is. Thus when a monarch goes among his people and urges them to honestly tell him their grievances, when a school principal invites the students in for a "gloves off" chat, or when the colonel requests that his lieutenant candidly evaluate the colonel's battle plan—in each situation, the status inferior experiences uncertainty, anxiety and identity confusion.

On some occasions the tables are turned and higher-status persons are critically tested in the presence of inferiors. Such occasions generate a particularly acute anxiety since the performance occurs before an attentive, even hyperconscious audience, seeking to discover a single flaw by which they can discredit not only the performer himself, but also the status group which he represents and, by extension, the entire social order.

At such times the performer experiences an excruciating awareness that upon his shoulders, for a few moments, there rests history itself.

. . . Besides critical performances and interaction with status superiors and inferiors, problems of stage fright emerge during "first time" situations. That is, some performances must be carried off smoothly without prior rehearsal. The problem for those engaged in the activity is how to give off an air of dexterity and grace without having had any experience.

. . . While many activities combine first time performance with expectations of skill and savoir-faire, we must distinguish between those that are linked by knowledge and rehearsal to be followed by a testing performance and those for which knowledge is available but practice forbidden. Thus, as an example of the first point, lawyers with first cases have not only their general law background but also experience in moot court. But at least two activities often require smooth performances with no previous experience: surrendering one's virginity and death. Each is, so to speak, for the first and last time.[21]

Yet the manner of the performance is crucial since upon it may hang the fate of a relationship or the moral history of a life. Although virginity may excuse a bride from skill in her first attempts at sexual intercourse, apprehension and fear may be taken as a sign of lack of love or as indifference. Where virginity is culturally important, a woman undergoes stage fright precisely because of the special scrutiny with which her wedding night performance will be judged.

Death, too, often invokes an unrehearsed performance [22] before doctors, executioners, relatives and history. In other words, in the moments before it occurs a person may become frightened not only at the prospects of what death itself entails, but at the meaning of his own terminal performance. Executions profoundly tax the principal actors' capacities to cope with performance anxiety. The noble bearing of a condemned man just before his execution may win him plaudits that outweigh the heinous crime for which he has been sentenced.[23] For some men, then, nothing becomes them like their deaths, and their fears over just this may generate stage fright. Thus persons condemned to hang sometimes express fear that the loss of sphincter control concomitant with rope strangulation is too embarrassing to bear.

Certain roles—for example, the "understudy" and the parvenu—are vulnerable to the plight of stage fright to the extent that they share structural similarities with "first time" situations. The understudy, both onstage and in everyday life, is aware that many stand ready to challenge his credentials to give a performance. Thus, when a substitute teacher appears, students become active in testing the credibility of her identity claim. And to buoy up the stage confidence of the substitute teacher, the school principal and others make special efforts to reassure the "understudy" of her capacities to handle the situation. Among professional actors, the ritual everywhere is to offer the understudy moral support and boost confidence with flowers and good wishes to "break a leg."

Stage fright over claimed identity also arises for parvenus. Parvenus, aware of the precariousness of their identity claims, will frequently plan or search for coping mechanisms that hide their identity-betraying stage fright. Moreover, societies in which traditional values or legal norms are in transitional or fluctuating states provide numerous situations for trying out new identities under hazardous conditions. First-time users of marijuana, for example, who are not familiar with or sure about the emotional control measures available to them when high, fear that their mental state will be visible to disapproving non-users.[24] In general, contemporary society is systematically producing a vast assortment of parvenu statuses, making stage fright a more common problem in everyday life.[25]

Coping Strategies

With respect to stage fright, three general kinds of coping strategies are available. First, there are those strategies that prevent stage fright from emerging. Here is the place for rehearsals and practice. But we have already noted that in some situations—executions, wedding nights for virgins, and so on—no practice can occur and thus, in the absence of this coping device, we may expect some overt evidence of stage fright. Aside from rehearsals, stage fright may be nipped in the bud, so to speak, by anxiety-reducing redefinitions of the performance situation. Nudist camps, for example, try to relieve patrons and visitors of undue concern about their unclothed state by establishing rules prohibiting staring, sex talk, body contact, and nude dancing.[26]

The second kind of strategy for coping with stage fright is that which contains it and prevents it from erupting into behavior that may disrupt a performance or discredit the identity of the performer. One technique for reducing the effects of stage fright on performer and audience is for the performer to disarm both by lightly calling attention to his own anxieties. Thus, the new bank manager, making his maiden speech before the toastmaster's club, may begin by saying that his knees are knocking so loudly that he wonders if his voice can be heard. Other small, self-deprecating remarks by speakers act to reduce tension and save face by inviting audience sympathy.

A related coping device is the performer's employment of a confederate to buoy up sagging stage confidence. The simplest example is that in which a mother or tutor instructs a novice performer to fix his gaze on her all during the performance with an implied promise that a confidence-maintaining countenance will be returned throughout. A more subtle employment of the same technique is the use of a friend as an agent of silent collusive communication in moments of stress, so that the anxious performer knows that there is at least one person in the audience who by his facial expression and eye contact will supply him with moral support.

Beyond interpersonal techniques are all those physical objects that may be used to hide the presence of stage fright from an audience. A lectern prevents the audience from seeing the trembling hands and quivering knees of the public speaker. Some lecturers confess to an inordinate anxiety whenever they know that they will have to perform without the protections afforded by this wooden barrier. In a similar sense a teacher may be relieved of the anxiety that her pupils are allowing their eyes to wander to the body regions exposed to them when she sits behind her desk by having the front of the desk covered; but a young mini-skirted lady may suffer in silent agony when she is afforded no equal protection at a cocktail party and must remember to always cross her legs when seated. The presence or absence of a screen by which a performer may hide the most manifest signs of his own anxieties or those portions of the anatomy which when scrutinzed subject him or her to embarrassment constitutes a major element in the generation or inhibition of stage fright itself.[27]

A third kind of coping strategy involves employing rescue devices when stage fright has manifested itself in such a manner that the performance has been disrupted. Sometimes the restorative measures are not employed by the immobilized performer himself, but by fellow performers or the audience. Thus when one stage actor has "frozen" and cannot carry off his part, another actor may quickly construct lines to "save" the scene. Similarly, in a wedding ceremony, the usher whose hands are trembling so that he cannot light the altar candles may be assisted by a priest, altar-boy, or guest. At times the entire audience restores the confidence of a totally frightened performer by a spontaneous sympathetic approval. . . .

The experienced actor knows that he can often rescue a potentially disastrous scene by an ad lib, a joke, or some other hasty but effective scissors-and-paste over the cracked theatrical frame. Indeed, it is for this reason, probably, that the experienced stage actor suffers less anxiety over his own stage fright than the tyro performer or neophyte. The experienced actor, however, may be motivated by concerns other than the salvage of a scene when he employs ad libs and new constructions within the characterological portrayal. To begin with, he may ad lib to add zest to his performance. If lines are too well anticipated, an actor learns, the performance may become flat.

. . . *Ad libs* and other innovative activities on the stage, then, can have a variety of functions beyond that of saving the performance. They can indicate an actor's poise under pressure, a test of his *sang-froid* (his "coolness," to use a contemporary idiom).[28] In this sense, *ad libs* and improvisations on the stage can be a cause for as well as a rescue from slips and errors. And the actor who must anticipate his own ability to present or respond to the unexpected onstage, can suffer stage fright therefrom. The actor knows he must put on a performance for his fellow actor as an infrastructure to the performance he does for the audience; that is, a frame of action is placed within the larger frame of dramatic presentation. In terms of its total consequences, to fail in the inner frame may be quite as disastrous as to fail in the outer one. In short, coping devices are often two-edged swords.

Conclusions

Within the framework of the theatrical stage, slips and flaws are seriously attended, and unlike most offstage encounters in everyday life, performances are expected to occur with qualities of perfection not ordinarily achieved. Since total congruency is assumed as the definition of the theatrical situation, the rules of conduct prevailing under conditions of fragmented congruency—that is, the rules of conduct to which ordinary persons ordinarily subscribe—are revoked and rules requiring perfection substituted instead. And since stage actors know that they will be judged in accordance with these extraordinary rules of conduct during a performance, they are apprehensive. Consequently, the actor, as Sir Alec Guinness has observed, is totally exposed: "He's vulnerable from head to toe, his total personality is exposed to critical judgment—his intellect, his bearing, his whole appearance. In short, his ego.[29]

Stage fright is also a phenomenon of everyday life. We may expect stage fright to emerge whenever an event or performance itself is important. Importance is usually socially defined although there are idiosyncratic variations and individual innovations in the defining process. In general, however, we may expect that jockeys will experience greater performance anxiety when riding in the Kentucky Derby than in ordinary races; that a Jewish mother will be more acutely self-conscious at her son's Bar Mitzvah than on any other Saturday in the synagogue; and that a young man will more likely exhibit stage fright on his wedding night than on subsequent occasions of sexual intercourse with his wife.

A more complex situation generating stage fright involves the social composition of the audience. As a hypothesis we may suggest that both dramatic and social actors will experience a heightened sense of stage fright in proportion to the social status and valuable rewards available from the audience. To mention an extreme case of this point, we might expect the war hero to show greater anxiety at the ceremony in which he received the Congressional Medal of Honor than on the battlefield where he carried out the deeds to merit it.[30] In addition to the status and power of an audience, there is the question of its size. For some persons a performance that can be carried out with grace and skill before a few becomes impossible in front of seated hundreds.

Neophytes and the neophyte status is another strategic research site for the study of stage fright. The neophyte is about to perform for the first time in a role that calls for certain skills never yet publicly tested. Neophytes, unlike experienced performers, are unaware of the relationship between rehearsal and performance, and thus cannot know what connection exists between their private practicing and their public performance. In addition, there are some situated neophyte statuses: for example, wedding nights for virgins, for which perfect performance may be expected without any prior rehearsal. Rehearsal or not, the neophyte status may be perceived as one characterized by apprehension based upon the expectation of perfection in a never-before-performed task.

Besides the neophyte status, there are those categories of persons whose identity is potentially discreditable and who, therefore, have a vested interest in masking the stigmatizable elements of their self-presentation.[31] Examples include ex-mental patients, passing homosexuals, and professional check forgers.[32] Such types, unlike ordinary persons, must be alive to those elements in their daily and regular performances which might give them away. And it is among such discreditable types that heightened apprehensiveness is to be found as well, perhaps, as strategies for coping with flaws in behavior.

Such persons are commonly labeled as "paranoids." [33] Thus homosexuals, sensitive Negroes and cripples exhibit anxieties about their image and their fate suggesting that a pervasive fear governs their lives. This fear, we contend, is stage fright of the same order as that experienced by dramatic actors in the theater and social actors in unusual situations. But in the case of the stigmatized, the fear is permanent, based on the continuous feeling of being onstage as a performer—always under surveillance, everywhere being looked over for just those tell-tale slips that will betray the identity which he has voluntarily assumed or which he has involuntarily acquired.

But one need not look to extreme cases to witness stage fright in everyday life. Much of the so-called anxiety of the modern age is essentially due to stage fright. We live in a pluralistic society where increasingly identity claims are made problematic. In other words, we are suggesting that our society is evolving into one where individuals are continually being faced with the necessity of mobilizing their interactional performances, a society where individuals are aware that their identity claims are being temporarily honored—until further notice. If so, the twin plights of tension management and mobilization of the self for purposes of information control become a problem not only for the stigmatized but increasingly for all men. And the coping mechanisms already alluded to appear to us as becoming dominant features of interpersonal relations.

What we are suggesting finally is that the age-old debate between art and life is more complex than has been recognized. For most, the sense of artistic performance is experienced occasionally and briefly; for a few it is a matter of professional skills, experienced in settings clearly marked out as theater; but for some, especially the stigmatized, art does not imitate life, but becomes it. And a pervasive fear haunts those for whom their very existence is theater.

NOTES

[1] Rose Heylbut, "How to Abolish Fear Before Audiences," *Etude,* 57 (January, 1939), p. 12.

[2] Lewis Funke, "Always in the Wings—the Shakes," *New York Times Magazine,* May 17, 1964, p. 20.

[3] The symptoms, causes and prevention of stage fright, while neglected by sociologists, has received some attention in the psychological literature. See, for example, C. W. Lomas, "The Psychology of Stage Fright," *Quarterly Journal of Speech,* 23 (1937), pp. 35–44; M. Dickens, "An Experimental Study of Certain Physiological, Introspective and Rating Scale Techniques for the Measurement of Stage Fright," *Speech Monographs,* 18 (1951), pp. 251–259; T. Clevenger, Jr., "A Synthesis of Experimental Research in Stage Fright," *Quarterly Journal of Speech,* pp. 134–145. For an overview see Jon Eisenson, *et al., The Psychology of Communications,* N.Y.: Appleton-Century-Crofts, 1963, chapter 18, pp. 320–327.

[4] Erving Goffman, "Embarrassment and Social Organization," *American Journal of Sociology,* 62 (November 1956), p. 264.

[5] *Ibid.;* see also Edward Gross and Gregory Stone, "Embarrassment and the Analysis of Role Requirements," *American Journal of Sociology,* 69 (July, 1964), pp. 1–15.

[6] This is the central problem examined in Erving Goffman's *Presentation of Self in Everyday Life,* Garden City, N.Y.: Anchor, 1959. Sheldon L. Messinger and associates, "Life as Theater" in *Sociology and Everyday Life,* edited by Marcello Truzzi, Englewood Cliffs, N.J.: Prentice-Hall, 1968), have charged Goffman with reifying his dramaturgical approach. That is, in everyday life, Messinger argues, persons are not really engaged in the conscious employment of stagecraft to project identities. It is our position that in certain situations—those, for example, that are depicted in this paper—Goffman's normative model constitutes in fact an empirical description of social reality. Beyond this, we would suggest that increasingly American society is evolving into one where its social members are consciously engaged in the employment of stagecraft to construct and sustain identities. For a general discussion on the construction and maintenance of identity, see Anselm Strauss, *Mirrors and Masks,* Glencoe: The Free Press, 1959.

[7] See Alfred Schutz, "Commonsense and Scientific Interpretations of Human Action," in *Collected Papers, I,* edited by Maurice Natanson, The Hague: Martinus Nijhoff, 1962; also Harold Garfinkel, *Studies in Ethnomethodology,* Englewood Cliffs, N.J.: Prentice-Hall, 1967.

[8] For a general discussion, see Erving Goffman, "Fun in Games," in *Encounters,* Indianapolis, Indiana: Bobbs-Merrill, 1961.

[9] Odd Ramsoy, *Social Groups as Systems and Subsystems.* N.Y.: Free Press of Glencoe, 1963, p. 53.

[10] *Ibid.*

[11] Louis Wirth, "Urbanism as a Way of Life," *American Journal of Sociology,* 44 (July, 1938), pp. 1–24. The point, of course, was made earlier by Georg Simmel, "The Metropolis and Mental Life," in *Sociology of Georg Simmel,* edited by Kurt Wolff, New York: The Free Press, 1950, pp. 413–414.

[12] On the concept of "frame" or "frame of meaning," see Goffman, "Fun in Games," *op. cit.*

[13] This point is fully developed by Goffman, *Presentation of Self in Everyday Life, op. cit.,* pp. 3–76.

[14] Lewis Funke and John E. Booth, *Actors Talk About Acting, II,* New York: Avon, 1961, p. 35.

[15] Quoted in Garff B. Wilson, *A History of American Acting,* Bloomington: Indiana University Press, 1966, p. 77.

[16] Those concepts are employed by Gross and Stone, *op. cit.,* in their analysis of embarrassment.

[17] Thus the distinguished nineteenth century Negro Shakespearean actor Ira Aldridge could not win an audience in the United States, but he succeeded admirably in England and Ireland. See Richard Bardolph, *The Negro Vanguard,* New York: Vintage, 1961, p. 79.

[18] Reported in Herb Caen's column, *The San Francisco Chronicle,* December 19, 1967, p. 27.

[19] Langston Hughes, "The Negro and American Entertainment," in *The American Negro Reference Book,* edited by John P. Davis, Englewood Cliffs, N.J.: Prentice-Hall, p. 847.

[20] See Calvin C. Hernton, *White Papers for White Americans,* Garden City, N.Y.: Doubleday, 1966, pp. 53–70.

[21] In a sense this is not strictly accurate. Both the presence of virginity and the absence of life are socially defined and may vary within and between societies and classes. Moreover, both virgin status and death can be feigned. We are here concerned with the actor's orientation toward his situation and in each of these instances, we believe, the actors are experiencing a never-before, never-again situation.

[22] Two studies of dying are worthy of mention in this respect. Barney Glaser and Anselm Strauss, *Awareness of Dying,* Chicago: Aldine, 1965; *Time for Dying,* Chicago: Aldine, 1968. See also David Sudnow, *Passing On,* Englewood Cliffs, N.J.: Prentice-Hall, 1967.

[23] See Erving Goffman, "Where the Action Is," in *Interaction Ritual,* Garden City, N.J.: Doubleday Anchor, 1967, especially pp. 229–233.

[24] See Howard S. Becker, *Outsiders,* N.Y.: The Free Press, 1963, pp. 41–58.

[25] The civil rights movement has generated many new statuses and the attendant anxieties in their performances. Consider the personal description (Merril Proudfoot, *Diary of a Sit-In,* New Haven: College and University Press, 1964, pp. 1–2) of stage fright by a white college professor attempting his first sit-in in the company of a Negro student:

> When I made that promise to Robert Becker three months ago, I did not expect that I would ever have to keep it. Yet at 11:15 this morning I found myself—a white, bespectacled college professor at the usually conservative age of thirty-six—advancing to my baptism of fire as a sit-in demonstrator! With me was Robert Becker, a tall dignified Negro youth who is president of the student body of our college. As we approached the basement lunch counter in Rich's, the city's largest department store, Becker showed no fear; I was secretly terrified. . . .
>
> The seat of my personality had shifted to the solar plexus. "Could I possibly be the fellow, I who gets nervous indigestion when I have to make an announcement in chapel, who has got himself involved in this situation?" I was asking myself. "Now have you got enough nerve to go through with it, or are you going to let your student understand that you are a coward?" I sauntered in after Becker, trying to look like an ordinary customer, but I could not have felt more self-conscious had my skin been coal-black.

[26] See Martin S. Weinberg, "The Nudist Management of Respectability," in *Deviance and Respectability,* edited by Jack Douglas, N.Y.: Basic Books, 1970, pp. 375–403.

[27] For a general discussion of screening devices and other "involvement shields," see Erving Goffman, *Behavior in Public Places,* New York: The Free Press of Glencoe, 1963, pp. 176–178 and *passim.*

[28] See Stanford M. Lyman and Marvin B. Scott, "Coolness in Everyday Life," in *Sociology and Everyday Life, op. cit.,* pp. 93–101, reprinted as Chapter 6 in this book.

[29] Runke, *op. cit.,* p. 20.

[30] For a case in point, see Ralph G. Martin, *Boy from Nebraska,* New York: Harper and Brothers, 1946, p. 198.

[31] Goffman, *Stigma, op. cit.*

[32] For the case of the check forger, see Edwin H. Lemert, *Human Deviance, Social Problems, and Social Control,* Englewood Cliffs, N.J.: Prentice-Hall, 1967, pp. 109–134.

[33] For further discussion, see Marvin B. Scott and Stanford M. Lyman, "Paranoia, Homosexuality and Game Theory," *Journal of Health and Social Behavior,* 9 (September, 1968), pp. 179–187, reprinted as Chapter 3 in this book.

14.

THE FIDDLE FACTOR:

Social Binding Functions of Distractions

Robert R. Smith and Robert W. Hawkes

INTRODUCTION

Although the literature of communication research is rich in studies of communication effects, there is a paucity of studies concerning the factors which facilitate effective communication. In this paper we analyze a set of these facilitating phenomena. We are not interested in the direct relationship between given communication inputs and their effects; rather, we are interested in selecting from the ambience of the communication act.

In collecting samples of such behavior, the authors noted that much behavior related to communication seemed to serve the dual purpose of reducing personal anxiety and strengthening interpersonal bonds. The non-communicative yet functional character of these behaviors led the authors to term them "fiddles." [1]

FIDDLES: A DEFINITION

The fiddle factor is a specifiable set of catalytic-like phenomena which facilitate the relations between communication inputs and their effects. We call fiddles catalytic phenomena because they are not inherent parts of communication inputs nor of their effects; they simply allow and enhance the relations between them. Fiddling is a non-instrumental activity which allows an instrumental goal to be achieved. Briefly stated, a fiddle is a minor diversionary activity, not the primary "purpose" of a person or group which (a) places people in a cooperative relationship, whether in a voluntary task or play, (b) obligates neither person to relate beyond the time involved in the diversion, (c) invites agreement or mutual satisfaction and (d) creates interpersonal bonds not justified by other factors in the relationship.

Learning and the Fiddle

It is important to distinguish between learning to fiddle and fiddling while learning. Learning to fiddle involves a number of both conscious and unconscious processes. In general, learning to fiddle takes place in two ways (1) by trial and error and (2) through conscious imitation. Not all fiddles work equally well for everyone. The majority of acquired fiddles are observed and imitated through those psychological processes known as incidental learning. Many fiddles are learned as a

Reprinted by permission from *The Journal of Communications*, Vol. XXII, 1972.

consequence of psychological processes which are either unconscious or semi-conscious. These are intuitions or insights in which the individual suddenly finds himself with a successful fiddle after no apparent preparation.

Playing with a fountain pen while in conversation can be an example of a fiddle which is learned as a consequence of "the a-ha" effect, while learning to smoke is a fiddle which is often learned as a consequence of deliberate imitation.

Although numerous varieties of fiddles may be identified, the authors have selected six common types for discussion and illustration.[2]

FIDDLE I: FIDGET FIDDLES

A fidget fiddle is the most easily identified of the common varieties of fiddles. Its function is simply to release anxiety. Examples found in everyday experience are the lady who plays with her hair while talking of something of importance to her, the man who loads his pipe and repeatedly lights it, apparently content to repeat the lighting process and not bothered by the failure of the pipe to stay lit. Doodling or playing with a pen are also fidget fiddles. They facilitate communication by reducing anxiety surrounding the situation.

Freud and the Fidget Fiddle

According to the psychodynamic interpretation of personality there is no sharp break between normal and abnormal characteristics of personality. Indeed, they run along a smooth continuum. Abnormal behavior can be vaguely specified as that behavior which interferes with an individual's attempts to achieve mature life goals. There is behavior which the psychiatrist may interpret as symptomatic of neurosis but which in reality is serving the very productive function of relieving anxieties and tensions and allowing closer rapport among individuals. Thus, people who play with their keys, beads, or ball-point pens may be exhibiting mild forms of sexual behavior. These *may* be seen as symptoms of deep underlying neuroses, or they may simply be sexually oriented fidget fiddles which serve to reduce tensions and thereby help to bring about social closeness.

Development Stages and Fiddle Selection

According to Freud even the most mature person has remnants of each developmental stage (oral, anal, phallic and genital) left in his psyche [4, 8]. We suggest two propositions that influence an individual's fiddle selection. (1) An individual may confront various sources of tensions and anxieties. He will select that type of fiddle which will best relieve the particular type of tension or anxiety he may be undergoing. (e.g., A housewife who has not completed all of her spring cleaning may, instead of sitting down after dinner to have a conversation, clear the dishes while having the conversation.) (2) Some individuals get mildly fixated in one of the stages. This mild fixation will influence their fiddle selection. An individual mildly fixated in the oral stage will use, as an almost universal fiddle, cigarette smoking.

FIDDLE II: CONVERSATIONAL FIDDLES

There are numerous topics of conversation which are of little concern to the speakers and on which disagreement may not be a serious block to the development of variety of interpersonal relations [10]. Conversation about the weather, for instance, binds the participants because all are subjected to it. If one person claims to like cloudy days while the other prefers sunshine, the difference is not a point of contention but rather an opportunity for further exploration of each other without risking exposure of more anxiety-laden attitudes.[3] Topics such as sex and drugs, although somewhat more anxiety-producing than the weather, may perform a social-binding function if the participants in a conversation about them are in basic agreement. Politics and religion are notably awkward fiddles because they involve revealing something that may be regarded as important by the persons concerned, and because agreement is difficult to reach. In the authors' experience religion and politics are socially binding only when there is mutual agreement not to discuss them. "I never discuss religion." "Neither do I." "Only leads to arguments." "What do you think of the new town swimming pool?" [4]

Conversational fiddles are most effective when they involve topics in which little expertise is necessary. In fact, an expert may be a bad fiddler on those topics which fall within his expertise. A physician, for instance, is the wrong person with whom to fiddle on the topic of a flu epidemic. He will present too much information, preach, or resent the use of his expertise without pay. Two persons with no medical background, however, may fiddle pleasantly for many minutes about the dangers of flu, their experiences with it, and the failure of new drugs to combat it. . . . Conversational fiddles allow the participants to converse easily, yet drop out of the conversation at any point without offending the other party. They allow the exploration of the other's experience, seeking common interests without making any commitment of interest or intent.

FIDDLE III: RITUAL FIDDLES

A minor task repeated often, demanding little attention and involving two or more persons is a ritual fiddle. A nurse may find it difficult to inquire directly about a patient's health. If she enlists the patient's assistance in holding a piece of equipment, or in taking his temperature, informal conversation flows and the desired information is easily obtained. A mother may find it difficult to ask what seems to be bothering her teenage daughter. If she brushes her daughter's hair, she is likely to find that the ritual promotes the primary, but anxiety-laden communication.

The host who asks a shy guest to help out by passing drinks and the boss who asks a member of his group for an evaluation of a problem of little importance are both using ritual fiddles.[5]

The ritual fiddle concerns a routine action which is quickly understood by all concerned because it is familiar. It concerns formalized behavior involving contact with others. By aligning the persons concerned so that they are both committed to the success of the ritual, a basis of agreement and shared experience is achieved. To have "good manners" is, to some extent, simply to command a variety of fiddles and to use them with skill. . . .

FIDDLE IV: ORCHESTRAL FIDDLES

The fiddles considered up to this point have been fiddles used by individuals to facilitate social interaction. There are large-scale fiddles, used by groups as facilitating devices, which cannot be undertaken by individual members of a group in isolation. We have chosen to term these group activities "orchestral fiddles." The term was chosen because the group, in order to fiddle successfully, must work in unison with effective leadership and with the necessary administrative support. We will not belabor the orchestral metaphor further, but the reader who cares to pursue it will find that it fits in many details. The orchestral fiddle, then, is a group activity undertaken by a more-or-less skilled and disciplined group in order to achieve a secondary goal which is usually unspecified.

Examples of the orchestral fiddle are found in our common experience. Church dinners, for instance, are characteristically undertaken not to nourish the needy, or for sacerdotal participation, but rather to bring members of the church together in a low-anxiety, pleasant situation. Cocktail parties are seldom devoted to "serious drinking," but rather to the equally serious business of meeting and influencing other people. Yet it is doubtful if the second, unspoken goal would be achieved if there were no drinks, hors d'oeuvres and an agreement about appropriate behavior.

Persons participating in an orchestral fiddle may use many of the interpersonal fiddles described above. One may fidget fiddle with a cigarette at an orchestral fiddle such as a cocktail party. It should be noted, however, that each orchestral fiddle has a limited variety of ritual, conversational and fidget fiddles appropriate to it. A ritual fiddle such as flirtation, while appropriate for an orchestral fiddle fraternity dance, might be a bit subtle for use at an orchestral event such as a Fourth of July parade, and gauche if used at a church dinner. The success of an orchestral fiddle is determined, to some extent, by the success with which the organizers provide firm guidelines about the kinds of interpersonal fiddles appropriate to the occasion. The absence of such guidelines may be the source of anxiety destructive of the orchestral fiddle. For instance, a young faculty member who is uncertain whether he may smoke while attending a tea at the college president's home is not likely to participate effectively until he has either fiddled with a cigarette or found an acceptable substitute fiddle.

Orchestral fiddles, which may be thought of as contrived events for groups with a secondary purpose, play a large part in our lives. They are tangentially related to those happenings Daniel Boorstin [1] has termed "pseudo-events." Unlike pseudo-events, however orchestral fiddles deceive nobody with their importance. Few people would argue that homecoming, Thanksgiving, the Elks picnic and such events are intrinsically valuable. Their values derive from their usefulness in bringing people together for a different purpose (making new friends, reasserting the value of old ties).

Orchestral fiddles are characteristically undemanding of the participants. Mere presence, and conventional participation in the appropriate fiddles is sufficient to make one a successful orchestral fiddler. The criterion of success is typically "did you enjoy yourself?" Successful orchestral fiddles are sufficiently distracting and pleasant in themselves so that the achievement of secondary goals (meeting potential clients, tennis partners, or establishing one's identity with a group) is usually not mentioned.

Orchestral fiddles may be used by teachers to improve classes. Fidget fiddles, such as doodling, may be used by individual students. Teachers may use such fiddles as the ritual closing of the door at the beginning of class or the pledge of allegiance to the flag, to prepare the group for the activity which follows. Sometimes teachers overly concerned with classroom order, respect for rank or with the task at hand, may stifle constructive fiddling.[6] . . .

FIDDLE V: THE TASK FIDDLE

Closely related to the orchestral fiddle is the task fiddle: a nominal task undertaken to allow social interaction which promotes solidarity of the group.

Military unit-level training is characterized by the heavy use of task fiddles. Task fiddles, combined with rewards for success (weekend passes or relief from guard detail if the "enemy" is defeated) are valuable in creating bonds which may be necessary in future situations.

Many fraternal or community organizations undertake charitable works of various kinds (collecting contributions, selling token items, sponsoring events for the poor or handicapped). The aim of these events is typically two-fold: (1) to give some semblance of purpose to meetings which may be primarily undertaken for reasons not likely to win public approval (to "make contact," for instance is too closely related to indolence to be widely accepted as a reason for a group; it is more likely to succeed in that aim if it is also a task group), and (2) to accomplish as much as is conveniently possible for a good cause.

One of the unwritten rules of many charitable groups is that members may raise money, but are not expected to contribute. This avoids embarrassment for members who cannot afford large contributions, but it also suggests that the amount collected—the task—is less important than the activity of collecting it.

Task fiddles are usually evaluated specifically in terms of task performance. Group solidarity is promoted in direct proportion to success in the task taken on by the group. Single-task groups which succeed and wish to go on face a crisis in selecting a new task [13]. It must be closely related to the original task and provide similar rewards or the group will lose its sense of solidarity. The best tasks are recurring, such as fund appeals and political campaigns.

FIDDLE VI: STRATEGIC FIDDLES

Occasionally, a person or group may be given a problem or task of little importance to the one making the assignment. If the aim is to find out how the person will perform or to gather similar data, the assignment is a strategic fiddle.

Examples of the strategic fiddle are commonplace: the executive who sends a new man to a difficult client "to see how he does"; the teacher who wishes to group children and gives them tasks in which skills relevant to the grouping are used.

Generally, any task which is assigned so that the observer may learn more about the persons concerned is a strategic fiddle. Strategic fiddles may take the form of news leaks arranged by a public official, ambiguous instructions aimed at revealing the aims or preferences of the persons being instructed, or test cases before regulatory groups.

The strategic fiddle is distinct from all others in that, whereas all other fiddles depend upon cooperation and mutually understood standards, the strategic fiddle depends for its success upon withholding information from at least some of the people concerned in it. . . .

Cohesiveness and the Fiddle Factor

Cohesiveness, often defined as the resultant of all those forces which keep an individual in a group, is influenced strongly by the fiddles used by group members.

A number of operational variables have been found which influence the degree of cohesiveness including "liking of task." By creating a pleasant task, researchers have found that interaction rates are high among members of the group and that this interaction is characterized by friendliness. This "liking of task" is a strategic fiddle which is employed by the experimenter in order to produce a highly cohesive group. He in turn can then study the effects of a highly cohesive group on its members.[7]

THEORETICAL AND RESEARCH IMPLICATIONS

We assume that each individual personality can be viewed as a unified dynamic whole. This assumption, from Gestalt psychology, implies that all of the elements of an individual personality are linked together in a pattern. Although no two personalities are precisely the same in their configurations, they nevertheless share many common elements and many common dimensions. They also share many sub-configurations of elements and dimensions even though the total personality configurations differ.

The fiddle factor operates to produce interpersonal congruence between or among individual personalities. This is done primarily by evoking sub-configurations between or among the individual personalities. It is possible for the fiddle factor to evoke similar sub-configurations between and among personalities which have no apparent connection to the issue or task at hand. The task can be facilitated through this process because the common sub-configurations evoked minimize interpersonal anxiety. This process can be described as a tendency towards irrelevant interpersonal consistency. It has been described as the achievement of co-linearity of cognitive dimensions [12]. In this paper we extend the concept to include affective dimensions as well.

. . . There are some activities which serve as fiddles for some people. The same activities may not work or may be dysfunctional for other people. . . .

NOTES

[1] The term "distraction" was not used because of its negative connotations. English and English give, as the first definition of distractions, "an undesired shift of attention." See Horace B. English and Ava C. English, *A Comprehensive Dictionary of Psychological and Psychoanalytical Terms* (David McKay, 1958). Since fiddles are positive and functional, it would have distorted the term to call them distractions.

[2] The list of fiddles identified in this article is not exhaustive, but simply includes the most common types. Some fiddles were omitted because they are uncommon, some because we have not satisfied ourselves that they are not sub-categories of other types. For instance, the catalytic fiddle—an event which draws a group together, minimizing their differences, producing a willingness to act—seems to be an important part of political behavior, particularly when the groups concerned are informal, not particularly cohesive and lack structure. A successful leader of such groups apparently needs to be skilled in the use of the catalytic fiddle. We have not pursued it because it is less frequently encountered in everyday experience than the other fiddles described in this paper. We are indebted to Everett R. Spencer, Jr., for calling our attention to it.

[3] See the discussion of the "Sounding Out" process in J. D. Thompson and W. McEwen [15] *Sociological Review*, February 1958, vol. 23.

[4] The individual's obligation to maintain spontaneous involvement in the conversation and the difficulty of doing so place him in a delicate position. See Erving Goffman [5:105].

[5] Ritual denotes those aspects of prescribed formal behavior which have no direct technological consequence. The prescription is ordinarily provided by cultural tradition, but may in some cases be a spontaneous invention of the individual [7:607]. English and English [3:467] mention "the elaborate cleaning, filling, and lighting of a pipe under mild stress conditions" as a ritual, although the present authors consider this a fidget fiddle, reserving the term ritual for interpersonal behavior.

[6] Somewhat the same thing might be said of the profession of psychiatry. Clients do not fiddle with their analysts. There is a meaning in everything, including the current state of the weather. Fiddling is, by definition, a positive, productive activity; psychiatrists are, by training, focused on the pathological. Educators and psychiatrists both frequently overlook the value of facilitating behavior. Planned fiddling, in the classroom and on the analyst's sofa, might be productive for all concerned.

[7] Apart from laboratory manipulation, people invent attractive and pleasant tasks which allow them to get together to secure closer interpersonal relationships. This may be termed deliberately planned cohesiveness. Studies of such naturally occurring cohesiveness phenomena can be linked directly to the laboratory work to produce an even more compelling theory. Cohesiveness has been defined as "the resultant of all the forces acting on all the members to remain in the group." See D. Cartwright and A. F. Zander [2:74].

REFERENCES

1. Boorstin, Daniel J. *The Image or What Happened to the American Dream,* New York: Atheneum Press, 1962.
2. Cartwright, Dorwin, and Alvin Zander. "Group Cohesiveness: Introduction." In *Group Dynamics: Research and Theory* (edited by Dorwin Cartwright and Alvin Zander). Evanston, Ill.: Row, Peterson, 1960.
3. English, Horace B., and Ava C. English. *A Comprehensive Dictionary of Psychological and Psychoanalytical Terms.* New York: Longmans, Green and Co., 1958.
4. Freud, Sigmund. "Development of the Libido and Sexual Organizations." In *A General Introduction to Psychoanalysis.* New York: Boni and Liveright, 1924.
5. Goffman, Erving. "Alienation from Interaction." In *Communication and Culture* (edited by A. E. Smith). Holt, Rinehart and Winston, 1966.

6. Goffman, Erving. *The Presentation of Self in Everyday Life*. Garden City, N.Y.: Doubleday, 1959.

7. Gould, Julius, and William Kolb. *Dictionary of the Social Sciences*. Glencoe, Ill.: Free Press, 1964.

8. Hall, Calvin. *A Primer of Freudian Psychiatry*. Cleveland, O.: World Publishing Co., 1954.

9. Hall, Edward T. *The Silent Language*. Garden City, N.Y.: Doubleday, 1959.

10. Meerloo, J. A. M. *Conversation and Communication: A Psychological Inquiry into Language and Human Relations*. New York: International Universities Press, 1952.

11. Myers, Michele Toleda. "Transfer Effects of T-Group Training." ETC., 27:465–472, 1970.

12. Runkel, P. J. "Cognitive Similarity in Facilitating Communication." *Sociometry*, 19:178–191, 1956.

13. Sills, David. "The Succession of Goals." In *The Volunteers*. Glencoe, Ill.: Free Press, 1958, pp. 253–268. Also in *Complex Organizations: A Sociological Reader*, 2nd edition, by Amitai Etzioni. New York: Holt, Rinehart and Winston, 1969, pp. 175–187.

14. Simmel, Georg. *Sociology of Religion* (translated by Curt Rosenthal). New York: Philosophical Library, 1959.

15. Thompson, J. D., and W. J. McEwen. "Organizational Goals and Environment: Goal Setting as an Interaction Process." *American Sociological Review*, 23:23–31, 1958.

Part Three

Mass Communications as Drama

O NE OF THE MOST important features of modern society is the proliferation of the mass media of communications. The ''new media'' have been hailed as the instrument of expanded consciousness and condemned as the destroyer of old values and manipulator of human aspirations. The nature and impact of the mass media have come under great scholarly scrutiny. We have selected for this section work that touches on our theme: people and events, as presented through the ''filter'' of the mass media, take on dramatic qualities. In television news, for instance, events are often ''condensed'' into a dramatic unity, giving them qualities which may have little to do with the ''reality'' of the event. News is drama, not truth. Indeed, the presence of the mass media often affects the actions of the participants in an event, usually in a dramatic direction. The writings presented here explore those aspects of mass media that tend to make them, or what is communicated through them, dramatic.

The first piece is drawn from William Stephenson's *Play Theory of Mass Communications*. Stephenson, relying on the historian Huizinga's notion of *homo ludens,* distinguishes between ''communications-pain'' and ''communications-pleasure'' as distinct features of modern life. The former concerns work, effort, production; the latter deals with play, fun, interludes, entertainment. Painful communications occur in those areas of life involving ''social control,'' e.g., discipline, information, cooperation and so on. However, much of mass communications involves ''convergent selectivity,'' playful, disinterested activity outside of, apart from, indeed free of, the painful restraints of social control. In that sense, newsreading, radio listening or television viewing is escapism, involvement in a fantasy world that is play. The implications of this are enormous. Politics, for example, must be communicated as entertainment, as pleasure, and therefore what ''goes over" is the dramatic performance! Drama is fun, play, outside of the work-world of pain; hence a speech or convention or other event that is not organized and presented for its pleasurable impact on the audience may fail. The mass media thereby transform *events* into *drama*, by either dramatic organization in the presentation of an event, or by dramatic condensation of the medium itself. A political convention may be organized by the party managers to be dramatic (e.g., the Republican convention of 1972), or may be "condensed" as drama by the medium "gatekeepers" (the Democratic convention of 1968). In either case, the event is translated into something exciting, hopefully entertaining, but clearly dramatic for the audience.

The psychological process of the translation of reality into drama is dealt with in the piece by Walter Lippmann, drawn from his classic *Public Opinion.* Largely through the diverse information drawn from the mass media, people make "pictures," or images, in their heads that constitute their own "fictional" construct of what really is. From this "map" of the world men develop "pseudo-environments" which gives the larger world meaning and structure. The world, then, is given dramatic meaning by this symbolic condensation of information into an understandable unity. A vast war becomes not a complex process of many forces and participants, but rather a personal duel between a Churchill and a Hitler. Complex social processes are then made understandable: a stock market crash, a legislative struggle, an earthquake, are all given dramatic form. Our interpretative "pseudo-environment" is a dramatic environment.

The impact of the mass media on American culture is explored by historian Daniel Boorstin. Our expectations about the world have led to the development of the "pseudo-event," a synthetic, staged occurrence that provides the "stuff" of the mass audience. Increasingly, the realities of social life in the United States are replaced by the dramatic structure of the mass media and the demands for entertainment by their audience. Hence, the MacArthur tour acquires a dramatic structure in the mass media that it did not actually have. The political campaign comes not to be a discussion of issues and programs, but rather an exercise in controlled dramatic performance in settings designed to be entertaining. The convention, for example, is choreographed to eliminate conflict and debate, and to be entertaining to a prime-time television audience; a democratic institution is transformed into a pseudo-event. Pseudo-events, then, are a product of the mass media, which put a premium on dramatic performance and entertainment by elite actors and transform social events into drama.

The selection by sociologist Lloyd Warner is drawn from his presently neglected work on the "symbolic life" of a large American community, disguised as "Yankee City." Warner here is dealing with the extent to which a lower-class Irish roughneck builds his image, and thereby his career, through the mass media. "Biggy Muldoon" becomes a political hero to many of the humble in Yankee City through what was reported to them in the mass media. His baiting of the rich, his high-living style, his eternal combat with other institutions, all were communicated and enlarged by the local newspapers, and ordinary people could be amused and get vicarious pleasure from his activities. For most, Muldoon's activities were part of a drama—an elite drama that occurred in a realm of life they had no direct contact with, and could only imagine through media condensation of reality *into* drama. Biggy became a symbolic leader, a hero who was larger than life, and who acted in a dramatic realm apart from the mundane concerns and rules of everyday life. He was a creature of the media, who both used and was used by the mass communications that spawned him.

The article by Donald Horton and R. Richard Wohl explores a distinctive and crucial feature of the new mass media: the degree to which these media—especially television—give the illusion of intimate contact between performer and audience, what the authors call "para-social interaction." The media actor who develops an intimate style (an Arthur Godfrey or Dave Garroway) is termed a "persona." The "persona" is a dramatic performer who utilizes a medium to communicate a kind of "pseudo-relationship" that appears to be intimate, personal and spontaneous. Hence one of the illusions perpetuated by the mass media is that of intimate contact with the performer, indeed of close participation in events observed on them. Women have cried when a favorite character on a television soap opera "dies"; many get a sense of participation—of "being there"—in talk show conversations. Political advertising in campaigns now stresses the presentation of the style, the personality, the "image" of the candidate through "para-social" methods. The terminology used—planned spontaneity, fake honesty, simulated candor—suggests the degree to which the relationship is staged, and where the illusion is again mistaken for the actual.

The matter of communicating intention is the subject of the piece by George Gordon from his books *Persuasion: The Theory and Practice of Manipulative Communication.* Intention as a quality of communication transcends the medium of drama and the instrument chosen to distribute the communication. It is a crucial feature in any examination of mass communication, since it is "an objective designed to intrude upon another person's logical or psychological processes." Hence intentions become important to the dramatic structure in the mass media, "centering on the way (or ways) that given audiences perceive the intentions of communicators and their communications," as in the communication of propaganda. Gordon discusses both conscious and unconscious intentions and their relation to behavior in human transactions emphasizing Kenneth Burke's categories of the unconscious.

The articles in this section suggest that, for one reason or another, much (if not most) of what is communicated through the mass media is, one way or another, dramatic. The implications and questions which arise from this insight are many. What, for example, is it *about* a medium of mass communications that makes it dramatic? Is the medium itself the message, or is it simply used that way? Is mass "communications-pleasure" by definition dramatic? In any case, the reader may get the idea that the mass media are deliberately dramatic, or even downright "phony." Is this true, or is it simply that the nature of mass communications as we use them lead to dramatic activity? Are mass communications simply the modern extensions of the Greek drama of the *polis?* After all, is not drama itself mass communications?

15.

PLAY THEORY

William Stephenson

Social scientists have been busy, since the beginnings of mass communication research, trying to prove that the mass media have been sinful where they should have been good. The media have been looked at through the eyes of morality when, instead, what was required was a fresh glance at people existing in their own right for the first time. It is my thesis that the daily withdrawal of people into the mass media in their after hours [1] is a step in the *existential* direction, that is, a matter of subjectivity which invites freedom where there had been little or none before.

In this connection we must develop ideas which give the play theory of mass communication a firm theoretical basis. Among these the idea of *communication-pleasure* is of first importance.

Play

Modern thinking about play for our purposes begins with Huizinga's *Homo Ludens*.[2] I began my own applications of Huizinga's theory in 1958 and others had clearly been busy at the same time, including Szasz,[3] Caillois,[4] and Plath.[1] Most people distinguish play and leisure from work; leisure time is our free time, time for recreation, hobbies, or self-cultivation. Work deals with reality, with earning a living, with production. Play, on the contrary, is largely unproductive except for the self-satisfaction it provides.

There are, of course, thousands of games, toys, and ways of playing in leisure time in every culture and era of man and many explanations have been offered for man's tendencies to express himself in play. Huizinga's viewpoint, and the one I follow, sees play in terms of culture; the study of play, in short, has become the concern of cultural anthropology, as Plath's work on the "after hours" of the modern Japanese testifies. Culture, according to Huizinga, depends on play; rather, the spirit of play is essential to the development of culture. Many of our games, toys, and customs are residues of earlier phases of our culture and lie outside the evolving cultural process, but much of what characterizes current culture is rooted still in play—in law, stagecraft, military "science," debate, politics, liturgy, academic learning, prosody, business conduct, marriage rules, and much else—all forming the civilization in which we live. Scholars before Huizinga considered play a degradation of real living, a waste of time, a meaningless mask. To Huizinga, on the contrary, playing is a source of culture, giving rise to useful conventions that permit culture to evolve and stabilize—it teaches loyalty, competitiveness, and patience (the Chinese *wan*): "To the degree that he is influenced by play, man can check the monotony, determinism, and brutality of nature. He learns to construct order, conceive economy, and establish equity" [4] (p. 58).

Clearly very tricky matters are at issue as to what is play and what work. Our own distinction between them turns on what is fantasy and in some sense unreal, which is play, and what is real in the world, which is work.

Playing is *pretending*, a stepping outside the world of duty and responsibility. Play is an *interlude* in the day. It is not ordinary or real. It is *voluntary* and not a task or moral duty. It is in some sense *disinterested*, providing a temporary satisfaction. Though attended to with seriousness, it is not really important. The British, for example, would never cry when their team loses a match; Americans do. Games in Britain, though played seriously, are never confused with the serious things of life. Play is enjoyed, no matter who wins. It is astonishing to observe how often winning a fortune in a lottery or football pool (in England) makes no difference to the lucky person's way of life—he just goes about his daily work as a plumber or porter as before. Play is *secluded*, taking place in a particular place set off for the purpose in time or space: it has a beginning and an end. The child goes into a corner to play house. And play is a free activity; yet it absorbs the player completely. The player is unself-conscious if he plays with proper enjoyment.

Play has been explained by psychologists as abreactive, wish-fulfillment, instinctive, and much else. All that seems certain is that it is "fun," as Huizinga [2] remarked.

Caillois [8] differs from Huizinga somewhat in his account of play and games; he agrees that play is free, is subject to rules, is an interlude, is often uncertain about its ends, is unreal (as against real life), and is unproductive—except in lotteries and betting, which can be either highly lucrative or ruinous. A man may win a fortune at roulette or lose his proverbial shirt at cards. But even here the play is still the thing; as I observed above, a man may win a fortune in a football pool and then go about his daily work as though nothing had happened—this is most telling for play, which is always detached from "real life." Caillois distinguishes between four classes of play: *agon* (the agonistic principle of games involving two sides, as in football), *alea* (games of dice, roulette, lotteries, etc.), *mimicry* (acting, pretending), and *ilinx* (producing dizziness, as by swings, roundabouts, etc.). Much in play is a combination of two or more of these basic forms. There are also, Caillois indicates, at least three main ways of playing. *Paideia* is primitive, pure play of carefree gaiety, uncontrolled fantasy, and the like. *Ludus* is formal play, as in games with rules and conventions, requiring patience or the development of skill. *Wan* is the quietly sensual Chinese way of playing, as when jade is caressed to polish it, or with every subtle sniff or touch at issue, as in the sacred Hindu book of *Kama-Sutra*. Thousands of customs, devices, and occasions are employed to gratify playing in every culture of the world, in all its history.

Although there are hundreds of words for this or that aspect of playing, the general concept itself is little represented in any language. There is no common Indo-European word for play; the Greeks had a specific name for each child's game and different words for childish games, contests, and ritual plays. The Chinese languages have separate words for fun in the sense of romping, jesting, trifling, finger-ing things, sniffing pleasurably, and the like activities; for gambling, playing with dice, dancing, and so on; and for formal games. The Japanese have a definite gen-eral word for play function, covering recreation, relaxing, pastimes, amusements, jaunts, gambling, idling, playing the fool, imitating, jugglery, aesthetic tea-party-ing, and the like. And whereas Greek has numerous words for play functions, Latin has only *iudus, ludere,* meaning illusion or semblance, and this applies to children's games, recreation, contests, theatrical and liturgical presentations, and games of chance. I call my theory of mass communication the *ludic* theory, but for the sake of euphony I take a liberty with Latin and coin the word *ludenic* for play theory. It is so used in my paper dealing with newsreading.[5]

Relevance to Mass Communication

It is of course obvious that mass communication serves to inform as well as to en-tertain, but for theoretical purposes it is wise to distinguish that part of mass com-munication dealing with work (and therefore with reality, such as concerns the weather, farm information, shipping news, educational projects, and the like) from that concerned with leisure-time pursuits. Schramm [6] does not make this separation in his proposals for developing mass communications in the new countries of the world—with serious harm, in my opinion, to all concerned. Schramm sees a direct causal relation between mass communication and national development. It informs nations of their five-year plans; it "raises the goals, spreads the news, widens their acceptance," and thus raises the level of development in every nation. It fosters "nation-ness," Schramm reports, and the growth of loyalties. It helps to teach skills, literacy, and technology. It extends markets. It prepares people to play their roles in a country and among nations. All of this looks like hard work. It would seem better to maintain the distinction between this work and the pleasure-time pur-suits of rising (or any other) nations.

Mass communication in its play aspects may be the way a society develops its culture—the way it dreams, has its myths, and develops its loyalties; what it does in the way of inculcating work may be quite a different matter. What kind of a culture is it, for example, that thinks only of learning, production, and work? The Ameri-can, who knows all about work and technology, may be the least able to see what is required for the entertainment and play of a country, and therefore for its culture.

The Daily "Fill"

Hyman [7] observes that social and political communication in all countries, especially the newly developing ones, is apt to be brief; it is set in a daytime "fill" of entertainment material which is nonpolitical and might be quite unreal in social respects (as when Congolese enjoy an American Western movie). Soviet radio pro-grams transmit the basic Communist values, but the propaganda is an interlude in a daytime program of music and similar entertainment; 50 per cent of radio broadcast-ing is serious music.[8] Mystical Arab music is broadcast for hours on end in the

Middle East, in the intervals of which there is news and propaganda. Hyman suggests that apart from the obvious fact that people could scarcely be expected to listen all day to pretentious monologs on reforms, the "fill" serves a positive function: it keeps an audience available for the coming short messages of reform. The hint is taken from modern marketing, "Pleasant packaging pays!" The "fill" of mass communication is therefore not seen as flight from reality, escapism, or the like; nor is it debasing or seducing the masses as critics suppose. Hyman sees it as a "buffer" against conditions which would otherwise be anxiety-inducing. Without question a constant barrage of political propaganda would find few listeners or viewers or, if it found many, would arouse deep anxieties in an unsettled world.

Hyman does not propose that the "fill" can teach people to accept pleasure and to make free choices about minor matters of taste. He proposes, instead, that the principle of preselection should be looked at essentially as a defensive mechanism. People in the United States, for example, are confronted with massive offerings of subject matter—there is the voluminous *New York Times* Sunday edition; and TV, radio, magazines, movies, and journals are constantly harassing everyone. There is, Hyman suggests, a "blend" of such mass content, of a relatively constant kind under given circumstances: one copy of the *New York Times* is very like any other. The story "mix" of a murder or two, a civic scandal, a dope or other addict, is much the same in every edition of the New York *Daily News*. This "blend" or "mix," Hyman notes, might account for two sets of facts: ". . . the Western public doesn't suddenly change many of its topical opinions as a result of a particular exposure but, at the same time, the media do mold the rather odd ways some see the political world and relate to it" [7] (p. 147).

The individual, Hyman concludes, has to maintain his own viewpoint (his own values) in terms of this daily bombardment of news. According to Hyman the individual cannot possibly respond to all of this fare and therefore becomes preselective about it out of self-defense. This is a rather negative way of looking at things, but it is true that people react in the world in terms of their own interests and that they perceive (or, strictly, *apperceive*) most of the world around them in relation to these interests and values.

These ideas have direct connections with play theory. The daily "mix" is repetitious, like a child's game played over and over with variations on a familiar theme. In its content the individual can muse, at random if he is of a childlike mind, but skillfully with measured steps if he is well developed in ludenic respects. The "mix" is the way a person has to think of the wider world around him, so that he will be able to talk to himself and others about it; and in the process he does, of course, "learn" something to argue about for a day, he acquires a taste for this or that, and he is generally able to hold his head a little higher because of the daily incursion into the "mix" that suits him. On the other hand, what is molded by the mass media should not be confused too readily with what is poured first into the mold by introjected beliefs, which are subject to social and not to mass communication controls.

Thus, without denying what can be described as an informational function to the mass media I agree with Hyman that this (however important it may be) is only an interlude in the almost full-time function of the mass media in general, and of the press in particular, to entertain mass audiences. But whereas this is soporific for Hyman, a way to keep the masses quiet or more receptive to the sudden shots of propaganda given to them as "news" or the like, I take a more generous view of the actual function of such mass entertainment. To begin with, I do not think of it as merely entertainment in a non-ego-involving sense, but at its best as a highly developed form of subjective play. I go a little further: though it is true that a person's selfhood is formed largely in relation to social controls,[9] I want to look at the possibility that new aspects of self arise out of subjective play, such as that fostered by mass communication.

Schramm's Theory of Pleasure

We can take it for granted that people find mass communication, on the whole, enjoyable. Schramm [10] has speculated about the source of this enjoyment and proposes in his well-known theory of newsreading that the pleasure stems from two principles. When people read the news, certain of their impulses, needs, wishes, or wants are gratified, and the enjoyment is the feeling of pleasure so engendered. Sometimes the pleasure is immediate and sometimes it is delayed. The two are discussed as immediate and delayed reward. News about crime, corruption, accidents, disasters, sports, recreation, and social events provides immediate pleasure; news about public affairs, economics, social problems, science, education, public health, and so on gives delayed pleasure. Kingsbury and Hart [11] had suggested a similar division, many years earlier, into the "feebly socialized" newsreader and the "socialized"—the former no doubt having immediate enjoyment and the latter delayed. Schramm associated his two principles with Freud's pleasure and reality principles, respectively.

This, however, was scarcely fair to psychoanalysis because Freud's pleasure principle had reference to deeply unconscious mechanisms, whereas at least much of the immediate pleasure in newsreading is quite open and aboveboard. Schramm considered, even so, that from sensational news, crime, disasters, and news about entertainment and social events, newsreaders received immediate rewards: they could enjoy the pleasures of crime or sex, for example, vicariously ("shivering with the axe-murder" as Schramm put it, and gloating at the voluptuous blow-up of the queen of the call girls). This suggests, of course, that people prone to such vicarious pleasures are "feebly socialized"; their preoccupations are with accidents, crime, sex, and so on, because of their own unassuaged hostilities, aggressions, and sex-starved lives.

Reading about public affairs, however, and all the more intellectual or aesthetic subjects such as economics, literature, religion, art, and politics was considered by Schramm to be governed more by delayed reward. Indeed, the immediate reading about such matters, Schramm suggested, is apt to be unpleasant, annoying, or even alarming. To read of any world crisis is scarcely a delight for educated peace-loving men; news about the national debt and taxes is unlikely to please the hardheaded economic man; and news on the incidence of cancer in old age is scarcely likely to warm the hearts of elderly newsreaders. All such reading, Schramm supposed, requires the intelligent or socialized reader to endure immediate pain; but the end result would be pleasure because the "threat" provided by such news items prepares the reader the better to meet the future. So one dies of cancer the better pleased for hearing about it long before! Clearly this is nonsense. What is in error is the assumption that people are necessarily self-involved in such news items at the time of reading. If they are, the result will be unpleasure. If they are not, then the black news is just news like any other, no less or no more interesting.

What indeed are we to mean by being self-involved? I find it necessary to distinguish two meanings for our purpose. To see one's photograph unexpectedly in the newspaper is definitely self-involving in the sense that it matters to us, as self, to our sense of pride, conceit, or the like. But when one is absorbed in doing something, like reading a newspaper intently, all sense of self is absent; afterwards you may say how much you enjoyed it, but at the time there was no self-reference, no pride, no vanity, no sense of oneself, no wish, no being-with-anything, no intrusion of the self upon the news. How, then, is the self at issue in such absorption? Note that what is at issue is not deep concentration, such as one needs to read a book; it is merely quiet absorption in the news. Indeed it can now be no secret that in such absorption one is being highly subjective, and that the report afterwards about it is that one has enjoyed it! It is more like being in a trance than being in touch with reality.

For Schramm, however, the feebly socialized were out of touch with reality, whereas the socialized—those subject to delayed rewards—were regarded as serious-minded, reading the news with their thoughts on "the world of surrounding reality to which he can adapt only by hard work." The truth could be quite the other way around.

Schramm provides evidence to show that the more education a person has had, the more he is inclined to read "reality" news. The more uneducated, the more he is likely to prefer vicarious pleasures. Similarly, New Englanders and people from the eastern states are more "reality" oriented, and Deep Southerners, more "vicarious." But this merely indicates that as people become better educated, they may take more stock of public and international affairs.

The Pleasure Principle Reconsidered

Freud's principle is worth attention, however, for reasons not associated with Schramm's use of it but with out own theory of mass communication.

Freud wrote about the pleasure and reality principles in a brief paper called "Formulations Regarding the Two Principles in Mental Functioning." [12] Mankind's mental life began, Freud argued, in fantasy; the oldest primary mental process was the pleasure-pain principle, that is, a "waking tendency to shut out painful experiences." We strive, fundamentally, for pleasure and to avoid pain. This was the hedonic process at work before any consciousness of the person and before any awareness of self. It is little use arguing, in terms of this principle, that the "feebly socialized" are shutting out thought of the "real" world of international tensions, taxes, and so on, preferring instead to bask in the vicarious pleasure of comics, crime, and sex. Freud's primary principle does not apply directly to such conscious matters at all. The truth is likely to be rather different: the "feebly socialized" person is probably unaware of the trials ahead in international crises and similar "painful" matters, which the socialized person knows about and yet still prefers to read about.

Freud's second principle, concerning a later stage in development of the individual, maintains that fantasy cannot produce real gratifications, so that the individual is forced to strive not only for what is pleasant but for what is real, even if unpleasant. This is the *reality principle*.

The principles were conceived by Freud as primary processes, operating at almost a physiological level (*id* processes), before the individual has any awareness of self. The process of repression is similarly lowly placed. But as the person develops consciousness, the process of attention, memory, judgment, and thinking arise, replacing the primary mechanisms. The latter, however, are very tenacious—the organism finds it difficult to give up pleasure and to face realities, and the individual represses when he could better face the facts. For this reason two new psychological functions were postulated by Freud. One was *reality-testing,* in which consciousness and self take part; and the other was *fantasy-making,* in which, though consciousness and self are involved, there is a closer relation to the primary processes, to repression and to instinctual life, as in daydreaming and in the play of children. Repression is quite effective in fantasy-making, which is again free of reality-testing. One can understand how important these considerations are for any theory which relates the entertainment of the masses to childlike play.

Such are the principles on which Schramm based his theory of newsreading. Fantasy-making, and the primary processes of pleasure-pain, corresponds to immediate reward; in newsreading of this kind, wishes and fantasies are used to avoid unhappiness and unpleasant ideas. The reality principle corresponds to more conscious control and to delayed reward; the concern is with what is *useful* in life. But here too the pleasure principle is not altogether abandoned; it is merely deferred—a momentary pleasure, wish, or fantasy is given up in order to gain an assured pleasure later on. Thus, the religious person forgoes the pleasures of this world for greater joys in heaven. The growth of one's ego and self is characterized by reality-testing; the person grows into selfhood by conquering his primitive pleasure processes.

Thus, analysis of Schramm's self-evident fact suggests that, theoretically, we must expect signs of repression among the feebly socialized, since wishes and fantasies are at issue. With socialized readers we must expect, instead, much stronger ego-development, better judgment, greater thinking powers, a more elaborate memory.

Now it may well be true that the feebly socialized are more prone to fantasy, wishes, and repressions, to judge by their somewhat morbid interest in the sensational—crime, sex, accidents, divorces, and so on. But this cannot be taken for granted. Their more socialized fellow citizens could be even more repressed, differing from the others in the *kind* of fantasy they have rather than in its amount. Freud, of course, thought that really normal people, living by reality-testing, would be fantasy-free; the more fantasies one has, he assumed, the more neurotic one is. But can we regard the masses of the feebly socialized as neurotic in any way? Clearly not by ordinary standards. There is little doubt, however, about the richer intellects and greater knowledge of more socialized individuals—it is indeed likely that people who have been to college are more ego-developed (or something of the kind) than people who failed to graduate from a high school.

Paralleling the two meanings I have distinguished for self-involvement above, there are two for the word "pleasure." The one concerns our moods of elation, joy, sorrow, and the like; the other is retrospective, as when we say that we were so absorbed in an activity, so engrossed in it, that we "enjoyed" it. In the latter case the person may not have been experiencing any particular feelings—on the contrary he may have been so absorbed that he lost all sense of himself in the process. Thus, as I have said earlier, when people say they enjoy reading a newspaper, sheer absorption may be involved and not feelings at all.

These thoughts should lead us to be cautious about any too facile regard of a term like "pleasure." The pleasure-pain principle has indeed been considerably tempered, in recent years, by considerations like the above. Fenichel,[13] a well-known psychoanalyst, has replaced the pleasure-pain principle (as a primary process), by one of *functional pleasure*. This is the exercise of a function, not for gratification of instinct or other primitive impulses but in some ego-developed sense. The child enjoys reading the same story over and over, not out of some deeper fantasies, but out of a sense of mastery over the external world by repeated exercise of the function. Similarly the person who reads a newspaper "with enjoyment" may be involved not in gratification of pleasurable fantasies or wishes, of sex or crime, but in a sense of mastery and achievement over them. *Others* are shot, robbed or raped— but not the newsreader—and one's enjoyment lies in the constant affirmation of one's mastery over these everyday threats. I have no evidence pointing in this direction, but no doubt there are times when readers gloat over the downfall of others.

Still another viewpoint from the most far-reaching school of thought in psychoanalysis rejects Freud's primary principles altogether. Fairbairn,[14] and Klein before him,[15] supposed that the individual is primarily object-seeking, not pleasure-seeking. This looks at the individual from the standpoint of how he is influenced by what he takes into himself (primary introjection), rather than from what is instinctual in him to start with (the id). What matters is what the child eats, so to speak, what it smells and touches, not what is libidinal in it to start with. According to this view, pleasure-seeking is merely a safety valve, doing little for the individual other than to stop him from exploding altogether. But there is a long chain of connections from early object introjections to the pleasure-seeking behavior of the feebly socialized. Indeed, in all the discussions so far, whether about the primary processes, Fenichel's *mastery* conception, or Fairbairn's just mentioned, complicated developmental matters in which the self is everywhere involved are at issue, rather than ultimate *processes* only. We need Langer's [16] reminder about the fallacy of reductionism: "There is a wide-spread and familiar fallacy, known as the 'genetic fallacy,' which arises from the historical method in philosophy and criticism: the error of confusing the *origin* of a thing with its *import*, of tracing the thing to its most primitive form and then calling it merely this archaic phenomenon'' [16] (pp. 201–2). Schramm saved himself from this fallacy in his theory of reward in newsreading because he clearly recognized ego-identifications in it, and it is to this point that attention has now to be turned.

Szasz's Theory

We need a better theory of pleasure than Schramm had to work with; for this a beginning has been made by the psychiatrist Szasz,[17] who presents what he calls some conceptual ''models'' for it. He begins with the reminder that pleasure is a *concept,* and not a feeling or mood experience. The whole wide range of phenomena to which the concept of pleasure applies requires four very different definitions for the word.

There is, first, pleasure at a physiological, id, or economic level; the term is used in connection with the reduction of physiological need, as when hunger is appeased and satisfaction results. Psychoanalysts have used the word at this level in the past—the id alone is involved, without the mediation of the self. Freud's initial understanding of anxiety, too, was at this level; it was conceived as a discharge of affect which had been repressed, involving no conscious mind, no ego-involvement. It was a process of energy-like displacements. (He later modified this view, but it is doubtful whether it was ever fully abandoned.) The modern psychiatrist, like Szasz, wants to use the word ''pleasure'' at other than this process level—to lift it into conscious levels of mentation. Szasz remarks that this has already been done for the concepts of guilt and shame: ''Up to now only the latter (shame, guilt, etc.) have been approached in terms of ego-functions, signals and communications, and our understanding of pleasure has remained rooted in physiological and Id-oriented concepts.'' [17]

A second use of the term ''pleasure'' is in connection with its associations with objects. The child is gratified with an empty bottle—when it is satisfied with food, and up to a point even when it is hungry. In the latter case the pangs of hunger, a painful matter, are replaced by the associated pleasure of an empty bottle to suck. Already, it seems, the child is playing; the point arises again whether the child has an awareness of what it is doing, that is, that it is conscious of the deception, or whether purely mechanical matters, or processes, are at issue. If it is aware, this is a very different state of affairs from that which supposes that the child is motivated by a search for pleasure and avoidance of pain *as processes.* If aware, the child is controlling objects for its own purposes. This involves its self. The facts are not reducible to those of process only. Similarly for much else discussed in process terms: what is more likely to be at issue is not *persuasion, anxiety, reward,* or the like, as processes, but relationships between the self and things, as actions or behavior. When it is said that what the world is suffering from is a lack of love (''there is not enough love in the world''), this does not mean not enough affect or feeling of love, conscious or otherwise (of love ladled out by the gallon so to speak) but not enough actions of a certain kind—for example, of tolerance for others, concern for the poor, interest in suffering, joy in the pleasures of living, and the like, in all of which the self is everywhere involved. We have constant need of a reminder that this is so. It is all too easy to slip into the mistake of talking about a process when in fact what is at issue is an attitude of self in relation to things around it.

A third use of the term "pleasure" is the familiar one attributing it to objects: food itself is said to be pleasant, as though it has pleasure in it like vitamins and proteins. Wealth, adornments, possessions, are satisfying in themselves—so we think. But, again, it is only when the person adopts a certain attitude toward them that they are pleasant. No art gives pleasure per se, nor is a jewel, or a lover's body, a pleasure per se. In all cases the person behaves toward the objects in some way—which may indeed be far removed from anything that could be called pleasure as a mood, or as something which on later reflection we attribute to the objects, saying how pleasing they are, what pleasures they hold, what a treasure, what a delight. At the time the actions were being experienced they may have been quite astonishing, erotic, sensual, "off the beam," unbounded, sadistic, grasping, and much else indeed. But afterwards we say we enjoyed it.

A fourth use for the word "pleasure" introduced by Szasz he called *communication-pleasure*. When two people meet and converse, they may say afterwards how much they enjoyed it. They have been talking in a complex way, now serious, now in fun, now at cross-purposes, now with gusto, in intricate interaction. The talk serves no apparent purpose as far as one can see; one person is not necessarily trying to convince the other, to subdue the other, to get anything out of the other. They are not trying to please one another—nor is the one in some remote degree having fantasy about the other, or seeking to seduce, influence, or in any way become involved in the other's purposes. Afterwards, they both say how pleasant it was. This is communication-pleasure: its characteristic is that the two so talking are not expecting anything. Quite different from it is communication which is meant to bring about a change in one or both persons talking—such as a command for action, a cry for help, a demand. Such we might call "communication-pain."

Thus, communication-pleasure, parodied by smugness and self-satisfaction, is contrasted with communication-unpleasure or -pain—which alone is apt to bring about action and change in the status quo. It is well known that unfavorable affects can bring about social change, and the wily advertiser knows that his job is half done if he can make the consumer dissatisfied with what he has. Communication-pleasure calls for no action: communication-unpleasure is a command for action.

Thus, the self is involved in all but the first of the four uses of the concept of pleasure. But there is a profound difference in the way the self enters into pleasure compared with its involvement in pain. In the latter there is a *loss* of self, in the former a *gain* in self. One would like to "hide one's head" in shame. The guilty person becomes suspicious, furtive, or confined—"secret guilt by silence is betrayed." But communication-pleasure is attended by a gain of self, a feeling that somehow it "did one good," that one's stature is increased; something is added to the self. This is *after* the event. Our two happy talkers, for example, male and female, both young, talk without expectancy of anything. There is not an implication of a wish or desire—and yet, afterwards, both go their ways with higher heads and a gain of self. Some people achieve in this way a profound contentment, a prolonged well-being and serenity. It is not in the least necessary to suppose that this is reached only by way of complex Schramm's early formulation to this: *newsreading is a communication-pleasure, sans reward.*

Our theory more generally therefore is to the effect that mass communication, where it concerns entertainment, is characteristically a matter of communication-pleasure. It brings no material gain and serves no "work" functions, but it does induce certain elements of self-enchantment. . . .

Work and Play

For theoretical reasons it is important to distinguish sharply between the concepts of work and play. I shall consider all work to be communication-pain (work gets something done), and all play to be communication-pleasure (play is just fun). Moreover, I shall consider all social control to veer toward communication-pain, and all convergent selectivity to veer toward communication-pleasure.

This is the essential simplification of our theory. I am well aware of many contradictions in relation to it. Some people work for the fun of it; others work hard at having a good time. Social controls are put upon us in our cultures by customs, institutions, and creeds, which are all couched in play and are therefore enjoyed. But it is precisely the purpose of such play to give communication-pleasure and thus to soften the hard realities of control and work by a leavening of enjoyment.

We shall see politics from the public viewpoint, for example, as *play*. The diplomats and politicians do the work; the public merely has something given to it to talk about, to give them communication-pleasure. Much of religion is play, too; people dress up in their Sunday clothes and go to church, there to sing and praise. During weekdays they go to work, not entirely unmindful of the precepts and hymns of Sunday but not exactly indifferent either to the hard realities of making a living.

The separation of these two areas, play versus work, is of course schematic and theoretical. The ordinary man does not find it difficult to distinguish between his work and his play. But his distractors confound matters. He is told that he should work for the joy and glory of it; that his work should be his play; that some play at work, and others work at play. For my part reality and work alike concern actions, attended more by pain than pleasure. So the "ploughman homeward plods his weary way," and the seamstress "with fingers weary and worn, with eyelids heavy and red" epitomizes labor. It is the taskmaster who asks us to work for joy, and the devout who say that work is worship—*laborare est orare*. Most of us, left alone, prefer the enjoyment of play.

. . . These ramifications of our theory into culture take us outside our immediate interest, except insofar as the concept of *social character* (and therefore also of national character) has to be developed as a matter of communication-pleasure. It will be suggested that social character is how we discourse in common in after-work, or in outside-of-work situations. That is, social character is merely what we have conversations about. As such it is communication-pleasure, a sort of unending bull-session. It involves self-psychology rather than ego-psychology.

Synopsis of the Theory

   . . . Play theory applies to all customary institutions, whether of state, church, court, school, college, factory, or home. I see the role of the mass media, compared with these playful culture-forming institutions, as serving two purposes. One is to give people something to talk to each other about, to foster their mutual socialization. Q-factors, approximating as they do to inner talk—as a sort of conversation with oneself and thus also to one's conversation with others—are scientific models of sociability. Here the term is used technically to mean attitudes adopted to maximize sociable interaction *for its own sake,* a "play form" such as Simmel [18] discussed, or such as Huizinga [2] described more widely. For my part I accept the viewpoint that mass communication may influence customs, as play. Its purpose can be to "normalize manners" (as Toeplitz [19] puts the matter), to suggest to the masses certain standards of conduct, to provide for the leisure of such peoples, to make life easier for them. I see nothing oppressive or nefarious in this. On the contrary, it is beneficial. The classical study by Warner and Henry [20] of the audience for daytime radio "soap operas" showed how clearly supportive these programs were for the hard-pressed housewives who listened to them every day.

   The other purpose of mass communication is to "rock the boat," to be in the forefront of change in status quo conditions. The press, traditionally, has served revolution and revolt. It is important to notice that it is difficult to change basic beliefs, though in a revolution that is perhaps exactly what happens willy-nilly. It takes a cataclysmic event, however, to bring this about. The achievement of mass communication lies in the way it short-circuits older beliefs, substituting new values for them.

   In the latter respect I keep in mind the role of *social control* on the one side, upon which all our institutions are based, and of *convergent selectivity* on the other, with which mass communication is more particularly concerned. Social controls are subserved by deeply internalized beliefs which are difficult, if not impossible, to change. Convergent selective conditions concern trivial matters in comparison with the above. One's religious faith is a matter of social control and belief; one's wish for a Coke is more likely to involve convergency. Social controls involve ethical needs and moral injunctions—the problems are in the realm of the public good. There is little but communication-pleasure in attendance upon convergent wants; communication-pleasure is in many respects what our theory is about.

BIBLIOGRAPHY

1. Plath, D. W. *The After Hours: Modern Japan and the Search for Enjoyment.* Berkeley and Los Angeles: University of California Press, 1964.
2. Huizinga, J. *Homo ludens.* Paperback edition, Boston: Beacon Press, 1950.
3. Szasz, T. S. *The Myth of Mental Illness.* New York: Hoeber-Harper, 1961.

4. Caillois, R. *Man, Plan, and Games.* Glencoe, Ill.: Free Press, 1961.
5. Stephenson, W. "The Ludenic Theory of Newsreading," *Journalism Quarterly,* XLI (1964), 367–74.
6. Schramm, W. *Mass Media and National Development.* Stanford: Stanford University Press, 1964.
7. Hyman, H. "Mass Media and Political Socialization: The Role of Patterns of Communication." In L. W. Pye (ed.), *Communications and Political Development,* chap. 8. Princeton: Princeton University Press, 1963.
8. Inkeles, A. *Public Opinion in Soviet Russia.* Cambridge, Mass.: Harvard University Press, 1951.
9. LaPiere, R. T. *A Theory of Social Control.* New York: McGraw-Hill, 1954.
10. Schramm, W. "The Nature of News," *Journalism Quarterly,* XXVI (1949), 259–69.
11. Kingsbury, S. M., and Hart, H. *Newspapers and the News.* New York: Putnam, 1937.
12. Freud, S., "Formulations Regarding the Two Principles in Mental Functioning." In *Collected Papers,* Vol. IV, chap. 1. London: Hogarth Press, 1925.
13. Fenichel, O. *The Psychoanalytic Theory of Neurosis.* New York: Norton, 1945.
14. Fairbairn, W. R. D. *Psychoanalytic Studies of Personality.* London: Tavistock, 1952.
15. Klein, M. *Developments in Psychoanalysis, 1921–1945.* London: Hogarth, 1948.
16. Langer, S. K. *Philosophy in a New Key.* New York: American Library of World Literature, 1951.
17. Szasz, T. S. *Pain and Pleasure.* New York: Basic Books, 1957.
18. Simmel, G. *The Sociology of George Simmel.* Translated by K. Woett. Glencoe, Ill.: Free Press, 1950.
19. Toeplitz, K. T. "Mass Culture." Review of an article, No. 34 of Cultural Review (Poland). Translated and reprinted in Atlas, May, 1963, pp. 307–89.
20. Warner, W. L., and Henry, W. E. "The Radio Day Time Serial: A Symbolic Analysis," Genetic Psychological Monographs, XXXVII (1948), 3–71.

16.

THE WORLD OUTSIDE AND THE PICTURES IN OUR HEADS

Walter Lippmann

There is an island in the ocean where in 1914 a few Englishmen, Frenchmen, and Germans lived. No cable reaches that island, and the British mail steamer comes but once in sixty days. In September it had not yet come, and the islanders were still talking about the latest newspaper which told about the approaching trial of Madame Caillaux for the shooting of Gaston Calmette. It was, therefore, with more than usual eagerness that the whole colony assembled at the quay on a day in mid-September to hear from the captain what the verdict had been. They learned that for over six weeks now those of them who were English and those of them who were French had been fighting in behalf of the sanctity of treaties against those of them who were Germans. For six strange weeks they had acted as if they were friends, when in fact they were enemies.

But their plight was not so different from that of most of the population of Europe. They had been mistaken for six weeks, on the continent the interval may have been only six days or six hours. There was an interval. There was a moment when the picture of Europe on which men were conducting their business as usual, did not in any way correspond to the Europe which was about to make a jumble of their lives. There was a time for each man when he was still adjusted to an environment that no longer existed. All over the world as late as July 25th men were making goods that they would not be able to ship, buying goods they would not be able to import, careers were being planned, enterprises contemplated, hopes and expectations entertained, all in the belief that the world as known was the world as it was. Men were writing books describing that world. They trusted the picture in their heads. And then over four years later, on a Thursday morning, came the news of an armistice, and people gave vent to their unutterable relief that the slaughter was over. Yet in the five days before the real armistice came, though the end of the war had been celebrated, several thousand young men died on the battlefields.

Looking back we can see how indirectly we know the environment in which nevertheless we live. We can see that the news of it comes to us now fast, now slowly; but that whatever we believe to be a true picture, we treat as if it were the environment itself. It is harder to remember that about the beliefs upon which we are now acting, but in respect to other peoples and other ages we flatter ourselves that it is easy to see when they were in deadly earnest about ludicrous pictures of the world. We insist, because of our superior hindsight, that the world as they needed to know it, and the world as they did know it, were often two quite contradictory things. We can see, too, that while they governed and fought, traded and reformed in the world as they imagined it to be, they produced results, or failed to produce any, in the world as it was. They started for the Indies and found America. They diagnosed evil and hanged old women. They thought they could grow rich by always selling and never buying. A caliph, obeying what he conceived to be the Will of Allah, burned the library at Alexandria.

. . . Great men, even during their lifetime, are usually known to the public only through a fictitious personality. Hence the modicum of truth in the old saying that no man is a hero to his valet. There is only a modicum of truth, for the valet, and the private secretary, are often immersed in the fiction themselves. Royal personages are, of course, constructed personalities. Whether they themselves believe in their public character, or whether they merely permit the chamberlain to stage-manage it, there are at least two distinct selves, the public and regal self, the private and human. The biographies of great people fall more or less readily into the histories of these two selves. The official biographer reproduces the public life, the revealing memoir the other. The Charnwood Lincoln, for example, is a noble portrait, not of an actual human being, but of an epic figure, replete with significance, who moves on much the same level of reality as Aeneas or St. George. Oliver's Hamilton is a magnificent abstraction, the sculpture of an idea, "an essay" as Mr. Oliver himself calls it, "on American union." It is a formal monument to the statecraft of federalism, hardly the biography of a person. Sometimes people create their own façade when they think they are revealing the interior scene. The Repington diaries and Margot Asquith's are a species of self-portraiture in which the intimate detail is most revealing as an index of how the authors like to think about themselves.

But the most interesting kind of portraiture is that which arises spontaneously in people's minds. When Victoria came to the throne, says Mr. Strachey, "among the outside public there was a great wave of enthusiasm. Sentiment and romance were coming into fashion; and the spectacle of the little girl-queen, innocent, modest, with fair hair and pink cheeks, driving through her capital, filled the hearts of the beholders with raptures of affectionate loyalty. What, above all, struck everybody with overwhelming force was the contrast between Queen Victoria and her uncles. The nasty old men, debauched and selfish, pigheaded and ridiculous, with their per-petual burden of debts, confusions, and disreputabilities—they had vanished like the snows of winter, and here at last, crowned and radiant, was the spring."

. . . Joffre was compounded out of the victory won by him, his staff and his troops, the despair of the war, the personal sorrows, and the hope of future victory. But beside hero-worship there is the exorcism of devils. By the same mechanism through which heroes are incarnated, devils are made. If everything good was to come from Joffre, Foch, Wilson, or Roosevelt, everything evil originated in the Kaiser Wilhelm, Lenin, and Trotsky. They were as omnipotent for evil as the heroes were omnipotent for good. To many simple and frightened minds there was no political reverse, no strike, no obstruction, no mysterious death or mysterious conflagration anywhere in the world of which the causes did not wind back to there personal sources of evil.

World-wide concentration of this kind on a symbolic personality is rare enough to be clearly remarkable, and every author has a weakness for the striking and irre-futable example. The vivisection of war reveals such examples, but it does not make them out of nothing. In a more normal public life, symbolic pictures are no less governant of behavior, but each symbol is far less inclusive because there are so many competing ones. Not only is each symbol charged with less feeling because at most it represents only a part of the population, but even within that part there is in-finitely less suppression of individual difference. The symbols of public opinion, in times of moderate security, are subject to check and comparison and argument. They come and go, coalesce and are forgotten, never organizing perfectly the emo-tion of the whole group. There is, after all, just one human activity left in which whole populations accomplish the union sacrée. It occurs in those middle phases of a war when fear, pugnacity, and hatred have secured complete dominion of the spirit, either to crush every other instinct or to enlist it, and before weariness is felt.

At almost all other times, and even in war when it is deadlocked, a sufficiently greater range of feelings is aroused to establish conflict, choice, hesitation, and compromise. The symbolism of public opinion usually bears, as we shall see, the marks of this balancing of interest. Think, for example, of how rapidly, after the ar-mistice, the precarious and by no means successfully established symbol of Allied Unity disappeared, how it was followed almost immediately by the breakdown of each nation's symbolic picture of the other: Britain the Defender of Public Law, France watching at the Frontier of Freedom, America the Crusader. And think then of how within each nation the symbolic picture of itself frayed out, as party and class conflict and personal ambition began to stir postponed issues. And then of how the symbolic pictures of the leaders gave way, as one by one, Wilson, Clemenceau, Lloyd George, ceased to be the incarnation of human hope, and became merely the negotiators and administrators for a disillusioned world.

Whether we regret this as one of the soft evils of peace or applaud it as a return to sanity is obviously no matter here. Our first concern with fictions and symbols is to forget their value to the existing social order, and to think of them simply as an important part of the machinery of human communication. Now in any society that is not completely self-contained in its interests and so small that everyone can know all about everything that happens, ideas deal with events that are out of sight and hard to grasp. Miss Sherwin of Gopher Prairie is aware that a war is raging in France and tries to conceive it. She has never been to France, and certainly she has never been along what it now the battlefront. Pictures of French and German soldiers she has seen, but it is impossible for her to imagine three million men. No one, in fact, can imagine them, and the professionals do not try. They think of them as, say, two hundred divisions. But Miss Sherwin has no access to the order of battle maps, and so if she is to think about the war, she fastens upon Joffre and the Kaiser as if they were engaged in a personal duel. Perhaps if you could see what she sees with her mind's eye, the image in its composition might be not unlike an eighteenth-century engraving of a great soldier. He stands there boldly unruffled and more than life size, whith a shadowy army of tiny little figures winding off into the landscape behind. Nor it seems are great men oblivious to these expectations. M. de Pierrefeu tells of a photographer's visit to Joffre. The General was in his "middle class office, before the worktable without papers, where he sat down to write his signature. Suddenly it was noticed that there were no maps on the walls. But since according to popular ideas it is not possible to think of a general without maps, a few were placed in position for the picture, and removed soon afterwards."

. . . When an Attorney General, who has been frightened by a bomb exploded on his doorstep, convinces himself by the reading of revolutionary literature that a revolution is to happen on the first of May, 1920, we recognize that much the same mechanism is at work. The war, of course, furnished many examples of this pattern: the casual fact, the creative imagination, the will to believe, and out of these three elements, a counterfeit of reality to which there was a violent instinctive response. For it is clear enough that under certain conditions men respond as powerfully to fictions as they do realities, and that in many cases they help to create the very fictions to which they respond. Let him cast the first stone who did not believe in the Russian army that passed through England in August, 1914, did not accept any tale of atrocities without direct proof, and never saw a plot, a traitor, or a spy where there was none. Let him cast a stone who never passed on as the real inside truth what he had heard someone say who knew no more than he did.

In all these instances we must note particularly one common factor. It is the insertion between man and his environment of a pseudo-environment. To that pseudo-environment his behavior is a response. But because it *is* behavior, the consequences, if they are acts, operate not in the pseudo-environment where the behavior is stimulated, but in the real environment where action eventuates. If the behavior is not a practical act, but what we call roughly thought and emotion, it may be a long time before there is any noticeable break in the texture of the fictitious world. But when the stimulus of the pseudo-fact results in action on things or other people, contradiction soon develops. Then comes the sensation of butting one's head against a stone wall, of learning by experience, and witnessing Herbert Spencer's tragedy of the murder of a Beautiful Theory by a Gang of Brutal Facts, the discomfort in short of a maladjustment. For certainly, at the level of social life, what is called the adjustment of man to his environment takes place through the medium of fictions.

By fictions I do not mean lies. I mean a representation of the environment which is in lesser or greater degree made by man himself. The range of fiction extends all the way from complete hallucination to the scientists' perfectly self-conscious use of a schematic model, or his decision that for his particular problem accuracy beyond a certain number of decimal places is not important. A work of fiction may have almost any degree of fidelity, and so long as the degree of fidelity can be taken into account, fiction is not misleading. In fact, human culture is very largely the selection, the rearrangement, the tracing of patterns upon, and the stylizing of, what William James called "the random irradiations and resettlements of our ideas." The alternative to the use of fictions is direct exposure to the ebb and flow of sensation. That is not a real alternative, for however refreshing it is to see at times with a perfectly innocent eye, innocence itself is not wisdom, though a source and corrective of wisdom.

For the real environment is altogether too big, too complex, and too fleeting for direct acquaintance. We are not equipped to deal with so much subtlety, so much variety, so many permutations and combinations. And although we have to act in that environment, we have to reconstruct it on a simpler model before we can manage with it. To traverse the world men must have maps of the world. Their persistent difficulty is to secure maps on which their own need, or someone else's need, has not sketched in the coast of Bohemia.

The analyst of public opinion must begin then, by recognizing the triangular relationship between the scene of action, the human picture of that scene, and the human response to that picture working itself out upon the scene of action. It is like a play suggested to the actors by their own experience, in which the plot is transacted in the real lives of the actors, and not merely in their stage parts. The moving picture often emphasizes with great skill this double drama of interior motive and external behavior. Two men are quarreling, ostensibly about some money, but their passion is inexplicable. Then the picture fades out and what one or the other of the two men sees with his mind's eye is reënacted. Across the table they were quarreling about money. In memory they are back in their youth when the girl jilted him for the other man. The exterior drama is explained: the hero is not greedy: the hero is in love.

A scene not so different was played in the United States Senate. At breakfast on the morning of September 29, 1919, some of the senators read a news dispatch in the *Washington Post* about the landing of American marines on the Dalmatian coast. The newspaper said:

FACTS NOW ESTABLISHED

The following important facts appear already *established*. The orders to Rear Admiral Andrews commanding the American naval forces in the Adriatic, came from the British Admiralty via the War Council and Rear Admiral Knapps in London. The approval or disapproval of the American Navy Department was not asked. . . .

WITHOUT DANIELS' KNOWLEDGE

Mr. Daniels was admittedly placed in a peculiar position when cables reached here stating that the forces over which he is presumed to have exclusive control were carrying on what amounted to naval warfare without his knowledge. It was fully realized that the *British Admiralty might desire to issue orders to Rear Admiral Andrews* to act on behalf of Great Britain and her Allies, because the situation required sacrifice on the part of some nation if D'Annunzio's followers were to be held in check.

It was further realized that *under the new league of nations plan foreigners would be in a position to direct American Naval forces in emergencies* with or without the consent of the American Navy Department. . . . etc. (Italics mine).

The first senator to comment is Mr. Knox of Pennsylvania. Indignantly he demands investigation. In Mr. Brandegee of Connecticut, who spoke next, indignation has already stimulated credulity. Where Mr. Knox indignantly wishes to know if the report is true, Mr. Brandegee, a half minute later, would like to know what would have happened if marines had been killed. Mr. Knox, interested in the question, forgets that he asked for an inquiry, and replies. If American marines had been killed, it would be war. The mood of the debate is still conditional. Debate proceeds. Mr. McCormick of Illinois reminds the Senate that the Wilson administration is prone to the waging of small unauthorized wars. He repeats Theodore Roosevelt's quip about "waging peace." More debate. Mr. Brandegee notes that the marines acted "under orders of a Supreme Council sitting somewhere," but he cannot recall who represents the United States on that body. The Supreme Council is unknown to the Constitution of the United States. Therefore Mr. New of Indiana submits a resolution calling for the facts.

So far the senators still recognize vaguely that they are discussing a rumor. Being lawyers they still remember some of the forms of evidence. But as red-blooded men they already experience all the indignation which is appropriate to the fact that American marines have been ordered into war by a foreign government and without the consent of Congress. Emotionally they want to believe it, because they are Republicans fighting the League of Nations. This arouses the Democratic leader, Mr. Hitchcock of Nebraska. He defends the Supreme Council: it was acting under the war powers. Peace has not yet been concluded because the Republicans are delaying it. Therefore the action was necessary and legal. Both sides now assume that the report is true, and the conclusions they draw are the conclusions of their partisanship. Yet this extraordinary assumption is in a debate over a resolution to investigate the truth of the assumption. It reveals how difficult it is, even for trained lawyers, to suspend response until the returns are in. The response is instantaneous. The fiction is taken for truth because the fiction is badly needed.

A few days later an official report showed that the marines were not landed by order of the British Government or of the Supreme Council. They had not been fighting the Italians. They had been landed at the request of the Italian Government to protect Italians, and the American commander had been officially thanked by the Italian authorities. The marines were not at war with Italy. They had acted according to an established international practice which had nothing to do with the League of Nations.

The scene of action was the Adriatic. The picture of that scene in the senators' heads at Washington was furnished, in this case probably with intent to deceive, by a man who cared nothing about the Adriatic, but much about defeating the League. To this picture, the Senate responded by a strengthening of its partisan differences over the League.

. . . The world that we have to deal with politically is out of reach, out of sight, out of mind. It has to be explored, reported, and imagined. Man is no Aristotelian god contemplating all existence at one glance. He is the creature of an evolution who can just about span a sufficient portion of reality to manage his survival, and snatch what on the scale of time are but a few moments of insight and happiness. Yet this same creature has invented ways of seeing what no naked eye could see, of hearing what no ear could hear, of weighing immense masses and infinitesimal ones, of counting and separating more items than he can individually remember. He is learning to see with his mind vast portions of the world that he could never see, touch, smell, hear, or remember. Gradually he makes for himself a trustworthy picture inside his head of the world beyond his reach.

Those features of the world outside which have to do with the behavior of other human beings, in so far as that behavior crosses ours, is dependent upon us, or if interesting to us, we call roughly public affairs. The pictures inside the heads of these human beings, the pictures of themselves, of others, of their needs, purposes, and relationship, are their public opinions. Those pictures which are acted upon by groups of people, or by individuals acting in the name of groups, are Public Opinion with capital letters.

. . . I argue that representative government, either in what is ordinarily called politics, or in industry, cannot be worked successfully no matter what the basis of election, unless there is an independent expert organization for making the unseen facts intelligible to those who have to make the decisions. I attempt, therefore, to argue that the serious acceptance of the principle that personal representation must be supplemented by representation of the unseen facts would alone permit a satisfactory decentralization, and allow us to escape from the intolerable and unworkable fiction that each of us must acquire a competent opinion about all public affairs. It is argued that the problem of the press is confused because the critics and the apologists expect the press to realize this fiction, expect it to make up for all that was not foreseen in the theory of democracy, and that the readers expect this miracle to be performed at no cost or trouble to themselves. The newspapers are regarded by democrats as a panacea for their own defects, whereas analysis of the nature of news and of the economic basis of journalism seems to show that the newspapers necessarily and inevitably reflect, and therefore, in greater or lesser measure, intensify, the defective organization of public opinion. My conclusion is that public opinions must be organized for the press if they are to be sound, not by the press as is the case today. This organization I conceive to be in the first instance the task of a political science that has won its proper place as formulator, in advance of real decision, instead of apologist, critic, or reporter after the decision has been made. I try to indicate that the perplexities of government and industry are conspiring to give political science this enormous opportunity to enrich itself and to serve the public.

17.

FROM NEWS GATHERING TO NEWS MAKING:
A Flood of Pseudo-Events

Daniel J. Boorstin

The simplest of our extravagant expectations concerns the amount of novelty in the world. There was a time when the reader of an unexciting newspaper would remark, "How dull is the world today!" Nowadays he says, "What a dull newspaper!" When the first American newspaper, Benjamin Harris' *Publick Occurrences Both Forreign and Domestick,* appeared in Boston on September 25, 1690, it promised to furnish news regularly once a month. But, the editor explained, it might appear oftener "if any Glut of Occurrences happen." The responsibility for making news was entirely God's—or the Devil's. The newsman's task was only to give "an Account of such considerable things as have arrived unto our Notice."

. . . Of course, this is now a very old-fashioned way of thinking. Our current point of view is better expressed in the definition by Arthur MacEwen, whom William Randolph Hearst made his first editor of the San Francisco *Examiner:* "News is anything that makes a reader say, 'Gee whiz!' " Or, put more soberly, "News is whatever a good editor chooses to print."

We need not be theologians to see that we have shifted responsibility for making the world interesting from God to the newspaperman. We used to believe there were only so many "events" in the world. If there were not many intriguing or startling occurrences, it was no fault of the reporter. He could not be expected to report what did not exist.

Within the last hundred years, however, and especially in the twentieth century, all this has changed. We expect the papers to be full of news. If there is no news vis-

---

Reprinted by permission of Daniel J. Boorstin from *The Image: A Guide to Pseudo Events in America,* Harper Colophon, 1964.

ible to the naked eye, or to the average citizen, we still expect it to be there for the enterprising newsman. The successful reporter is one who can find a story, even if there is no earthquake or assassination or civil war. If he cannot find a story, then he must make one—by the questions he asks of public figures, by the surprising human interest he unfolds from some commonplace event, or by "the news behind the news." If all this fails, then he must give us a "think piece"—an embroidering of well-known facts, or a speculation about startling things to come.

This change in our attitude toward "news" is not merely a basic fact about the history of American newspapers. It is a symptom of a revolutionary change in our attitude toward what happens in the world, how much of it is new, and surprising, and important. Toward how life can be enlivened, toward our power and the power of those who inform and educate and guide us, to provide synthetic happenings to make up for the lack of spontaneous events. Demanding more than the world can give us, we require that something be fabricated to make up for the world's deficiency. This is only one example of our demand for illusions.

Many historical forces help explain how we have come to our present immoderate hopes. But there can be no doubt about what we now expect, nor that it is immoderate. Every American knows the anticipation with which he picks up his morning newspaper at breakfast or opens his evening paper before dinner, or listens to the newscasts every hour on the hour as he drives across country, or watches his favorite commentator on television interpret the events of the day. Many enterprising Americans are now at work to help us satisfy these expectations. Many might be put out of work if we should suddenly moderate our expectations. But it is we who keep them in business and demand that they fill oui consciousness with novelties, that they play God for us.

The new kind of synthetic novelty which has flooded our experience I will call "pseudo-events." The common prefix "pseudo" comes from the Greek word meaning false, or intended to deceive. Before I recall the historical forces which have made these pseudo-events possible, have increased the supply of them and the demand for them, I will give a commonplace example.

The owners of a hotel, in an illustration offered by Edward L. Bernays in his pioneer *Crystallizing Public Opinion* (1923), consult a public relations counsel. They ask how to increase their hotel's prestige and so improve their business. In less sophisticated times, the answer might have been to hire a new chef, to improve the plumbing, to paint the rooms, or to install a crystal chandelier in the lobby. The public relations counsel's technique is more indirect. He proposes that the management stage a celebration of the hotel's thirtieth anniversary. A committee is formed, including a prominent banker, a leading society matron, a well-known lawyer, an influential preacher, and an "event" is planned (say a banquet) to call attention to the distinguished service the hotel has been rendering the community. The celebration is held, photographs are taken, the occasion is widely reported, and the object is accomplished. Now this occasion is a pseudo-event, and will illustrate all the essential features of pseudo-events.

This celebration, we can see at the outset, is somewhat—but not entirely—

misleading. Presumably the public relations counsel would not have been able to form his committee of prominent citizens if the hotel had not actually been rendering service to the community. On the other hand, if the hotel's services had been all that important, instigation by public relations counsel might not have been necessary. Once the celebration has been held, the celebration itself becomes evidence that the hotel really is a distinguished institution. The occasion actually gives the hotel the prestige to which it is pretending.

It is obvious, too, that the value of such a celebration to the owners depends on its being photographed and reported in newspapers, magazines, newsreels, on radio, and over television. It is the report that gives the event its force in the minds of potential customers. The power to make a reportable event is thus the power to make experience. One is reminded of Napoleon's apocryphal reply to his general, who objected that circumstances were unfavorable to a proposed campaign: "Bah, I make circumstances!" The modern public relations counsel—and he is, of course, only one of many twentieth-century creators of pseudo-events—has come close to fulfilling Napoleon's idle boast. "The counsel on public relations," Mr. Bernays explains, "not only knows what news value is, but knowing it, he is in a position to *make news happen*. He is a creator of events."

The intriguing feature of the modern situation, however, comes precisely from the fact that the modern news makers are not God. The news they make happen, the events they create, are somehow not quite real. There remains a tantalizing difference between man-made and God-made events.

A pseudo-event, then, is a happening that possesses the following characteristics:

(1) It is not spontaneous, but comes about because someone has planned, planted, or incited it. Typically, it is not a train wreck or an earthquake, but an interview.

(2) It is planted primarily (not always exclusively) for the immediate purpose of being reported or reproduced. Therefore, its occurrence is arranged for the convenience of the reporting or reproducing media. Its success is measured by how widely it is reported. Time relations in it are commonly fictitious or factitious; the announcement is given out in advance "for future release" and written as if the event had occurred in the past. The question, "Is it real?" is less important than, "Is it newsworthy?"

(3) Its relation to the underlying reality of the situation is ambiguous. Its interest arises largely from this very ambiguity. Concerning a pseudo-event the question, "What does it mean?" has a new dimension. While the news interest in a train wreck is in *what* happened and in the real consequences, the interest in an interview is always, in a sense, in *whether* it really happened and in what might have been the motives. Did the statement really mean what it said? Without some of this ambiguity a pseudo-event cannot be very interesting.

(4) Usually it is intended to be a self-fulfiling prophecy. The hotel's thirtieth-anniversary celebration, by saying that the hotel is a distinguished institution, actually makes it one.

In the last half century a larger and larger proportion of our experience, of what we read and see and hear, has come to consist of pseudo-events. We expect more of them and we are given more of them. They flood our consciousness. Their multiplication has gone on in the United States at a faster rate than elsewhere. Even the rate of increase is increasing every day. This is true of the world of education, of consumption, and of personal relations. It is especially true of the world of public affairs which I describe in this chapter.

A full explanation of the origin and rise of pseudo-events would be nothing less than a history of modern America. For our present purposes it is enough to recall a few of the more revolutionary recent developments.

The great modern increase in the supply and the demand for news began in the early nineteenth century. Until then newspapers tended to fill out their columns with lackadaisical secondhand accounts or stale reprints of items first published elsewhere at home and abroad. The laws of plagiarism and of copyright were undeveloped. Most newspapers were little more than excuses for espousing a political position, for listing the arrival and departure of ships, for familiar essays and useful advice, or for commercial or legal announcements.

Less than a century and a half ago did newspapers begin to disseminate up-to-date reports of matters of public interest written by eyewitnesses or professional reporters near the scene. The telegraph was perfected and applied to news reporting in the 1830's and '40's. Two newspapermen, William M. Swain of the Philadelphia *Public Ledger* and Amos Kendall of Frankfort, Kentucky, were founders of the national telegraphic network. Polk's presidential message in 1846 was the first to be transmitted by wire. When the Associated Press was founded in 1848, news began to be a salable commodity. Then appeared the rotary press, which could print on a continuous sheet and on both sides of the paper at the same time. The New York *Tribune*'s high-speed press, installed in the 1870's, could turn out 18,000 papers per hour. The Civil War, and later the Spanish-American War, offered raw materials and incentive for vivid up-to-the-minute, on-the-spot reporting. The competitive daring of giants like James Gordon Bennett, Joseph Pulitzer, and William Randolph Hearst intensified the race for news and widened newspaper circulation.

These events were part of a great, but little-noticed, revolution—what I would call the Graphic Revolution. Man's ability to make, preserve, transmit, and disseminate precise images—images of print, of men and landscapes and events, of the voices of men and mobs—now grew at a fantastic pace. The increased speed of printing was itself revolutionary. Still more revolutionary were the new techniques for making direct images of nature. Photography was destined soon to give printed matter itself a secondary role. By a giant leap Americans crossed the gulf from the daguerreotype to color television in less than a century. Dry-plate photography came in 1873; Bell patented the telephone in 1876; the phonograph was invented in 1877; the roll film appeared in 1884; Eastman's Kodak No. 1 was produced in 1888; Edison's patent on the radio came in 1891; motion pictures came in and voice was first transmitted by radio around 1900; the first national political convention widely broadcast by radio was that of 1928; television became commercially important in 1941, and color television even more recently.

Verisimilitude took on a new meaning. Not only was it now possible to give the actual voice and gestures of Franklin Delano Roosevelt unprecedented reality and intimacy for a whole nation. Vivid image came to overshadow pale reality. Sound motion pictures in color led a whole generation of pioneering American moviegoers to think of Benjamin Disraeli as an earlier imitation of George Arliss, just as television has led a later generation of television watchers to see the Western cowboy as an inferior replica of John Wayne. The Grand Canyon itself became a disappointing reproduction of the Kodachrome original.

The new power to report and portray what had happened was a new temptation leading newsmen to make probable images or to prepare reports in advance of what was expected to happen. As so often, men came to mistake their power for their necessities. Readers and viewers would soon prefer the vividness of the account, the "candidness" of the photograph, to the spontaneity of what was recounted.

Then came round-the-clock media. The news gap soon became so narrow that in order to have additional "news" for each new edition or each new broadcast it was necessary to plan in advance the stages by which any available news would be unveiled. After the weekly and the daily came the "extras" and the numerous regular editions. The Philadelphia *Evening Bulletin* soon had seven editions a day. No rest for the newsman. With more space to fill, he had to fill it ever more quickly. In order to justify the numerous editions, it was increasingly necessary that the news constantly change or at least seem to change. With radio on the air continuously during waking hours, the reporters' problems became still more acute. News every hour on the hour, and sometimes on the half hour. Programs interrupted any time for special bulletins. How to avoid deadly repetition, the appearance that nothing was happening, that news gatherers were asleep, or that competitors were more alert? As the costs of printing and then of broadcasting increased, it became financially necessary to keep the presses always at work and the TV screen always busy. Pressures toward the making of pseudo-events became ever stronger. News gathering turned into news making.

The "interview" was a novel way of making news which had come in with the Graphic Revolution. Later it became elaborated into lengthy radio and television panels and quizzes of public figures, and the three-hour-long, rambling conversation programs. Although the interview technique might seem an obvious one—and in a primitive form was as old as Socrates—the use of the word in its modern journalistic sense is a relatively recent Americanism. The Boston *News-Letter*'s account (March 2, 1719) of the death of Blackbeard the Pirate had apparently been based on a kind of interview with a ship captain. . . .

Historians of journalism date the first full-fledged modern interview with a well-known public figure from July 13, 1859, when Horace Greeley interviewed Brigham Young in Salt Lake City, asking him questions on many matters of public interest, and then publishing the answers verbatim in his New York *Tribune* (August 20, 1859). The common use of the word "interview" in this modern American sense first came in about this time. Very early the institution acquired a reputation for being contrived. "The 'interview,' " *The Nation* complained (January 28, 1869), "as at present managed, is generally the joint product of some humbug of a hack politician and another humbug of a reporter." A few years later another magazine editor called the interview "the most perfect contrivance yet devised to make journalism an offence, a thing of ill savor in all decent nostrils."

Many objected to the practice as an invasion of privacy. After the American example it was used in England and France, but in both those countries it made much slower headway.

Even before the invention of the interview, the news-making profession in America had attained a new dignity as well as a menacing power. It was in 1828 that Macaulay called the gallery where reporters sat in Parliament a "fourth estate of the realm." But Macaulay could not have imagined the prestige of journalists in the twentieth-century United States. They have long since made themselves the tribunes of the people. Their supposed detachment and lack of partisanship, their closeness to the sources of information, their articulateness, and their constant and direct access to the whole citizenry have made them also the counselors of the people. Foreign observers are now astonished by the almost constitutional—perhaps we should say supra-constitutional—powers of our Washington press corps.

Since the rise of the modern Presidential press conference, about 1933, capital correspondents have had the power regularly to question the President face-to-face, to embarrass him, to needle him, to force him into positions or into public refusal to take a position. A President may find it inconvenient to meet a group of dissident Senators or Congressmen; he seldom dares refuse the press. That refusal itself becomes news. It is only very recently, and as a result of increasing pressures by newsmen, that the phrase "No comment" has become a way of saying something important. The reputation of newsmen—who now of course include those working for radio, TV, and magazines—depends on their ability to ask hard questions, to put politicians on the spot; their very livelihood depends on the willing collaboration of public figures. . . .

The live television broadcasting of the President's regular news conferences, which President Kennedy began in 1961, immediately after taking office, has somewhat changed their character. Newsmen are no longer so important as intermediaries who relay the President's statements. But the new occasion acquires a new interest as a dramatic performance. Citizens who from homes or offices have seen the President at his news conference are then even more interested to hear competing interpretations by skilled commentators. News commentators can add a new appeal as dramatic critics to their traditional role as interpreters of current history. Even in the new format it is still the newsmen who put the questions. They are still tribunes of the people.

The British Constitution, shaped as it is from materials accumulated since the middle ages, functions, we have often been told, only because the British people are willing to live with a great number of legal fictions. The monarchy is only the most prominent. We Americans have accommodated our eighteenth-century constitution to twentieth-century technology by multiplying pseudo-events and by developing professions which both help make pseudo-events and help us interpret them. The disproportion between what an informed citizen needs to know and what he can know is ever greater. The disproportion grows with the increase of the officials' powers of concealment and contrivance. The news gatherers' need to select, invent, and plan correspondingly increases. Thus inevitably our whole system of public information produces always more "packaged" news, more pseudo-events.

A trivial but prophetic example of the American penchant for pseudo-events has long been found in our *Congressional Record*. The British and French counterparts, surprisingly enough, give a faithful report of what is said on the floor of their deliberative bodies. But ever since the establishment of the *Congressional Record* under its present title in 1873, our only ostensibly complete report of what goes on in Congress has had no more than the faintest resemblance to what is actually said there. Despite occasional feeble protests, our *Record* has remained a gargantuan miscellany in which actual proceedings are buried beneath undelivered speeches, and mountains of the unread and the unreadable. Only a national humorlessness—or sense of humor—can account for our willingness to tolerate this. Perhaps it also explains why, as a frustrated reformer of the *Record* argued on the floor of the Senate in 1884, "the American public have generally come to regard the proceedings of Congress as a sort of variety performance, where nothing is supposed to be real except the pay."

The common "news releases" which every day issue by the ream from Congressmen's offices, from the President's press secretary, from the press relations offices of businesses, charitable organizations, and universities are a kind of *Congressional Record* covering all American life. And they are only a slightly less inaccurate record of spontaneous happenings. To secure "news coverage" for an event (especially if it has little news interest) one must issue, in proper form, a "release." The very expression "news release" (apparently an American invention; it was first recorded in 1907) did not come into common use until recently. There is an appropriate perversity in calling it a "release." It might more accurately be described as a "news holdback," since its purpose is to offer something that is to be held back from publication until a specified future date. The newspaperman's slightly derogatory slang term for the news release is "handout," from the phrase originally used for a bundle of stale food handed out from a house to a beggar. . . .

The release is news pre-cooked, and supposed to keep till needed. In the well-recognized format (usually mimeographed) it bears a date, say February 1, and also indicates, "For release to PM's February 15." The account is written in the past tense but usually describes an event that has not yet happened when the release is given out. The use and interpretation of handouts have become an essential part of the newsman's job. The National Press Club in its Washington clubrooms has a large rack which is filled daily with the latest releases, so the reporter does not even have to visit the offices which give them out. . . .

The general public has become so accustomed to these procedures that a public official can sometimes "make news" merely by departing from the advance text given out in his release. When President Kennedy spoke in Chicago on the night of April 28, 1961, early editions of the next morning's newspapers (printed the night before for early-morning home delivery) merely reported his speech as it was given to newsmen in the advance text. When the President abandoned the advance text, later editions of the Chicago *Sun-Times* headlined: "Kennedy Speaks Off

Cuff . . .'' The article beneath emphasized that he had departed from his advance text and gave about equal space to his off-the-cuff speech and to the speech he never gave. Apparently the most newsworthy fact was that the President had not stuck to his prepared text.

We begin to be puzzled about what is really the "original" of an event. The authentic news record of what "happens" or is said comes increasingly to seem to be what is given out in advance. More and more news events become dramatic performances in which "men in the news" simply act out more or less well their prepared script. The story prepared "for future release" acquires an authenticity that competes with that of the actual occurrences on the scheduled date.

In recent years our successful politicians have been those most adept at using the press and other means to create pseudo-events. President Franklin Delano Roosevelt, whom Heywood Broun called "the best newspaperman who has ever been President of the United States," was the first modern master. While newspaper owners opposed him in editorials which few read, F.D.R. himself, with the collaboration of a friendly corps of Washington correspondents, was using front-page headlines to make news read by everybody. He was making "facts"—pseudo-events—while editorial writers were simply expressing opinions. It is a familiar story how he employed the trial balloon, how he exploited the ethic of off-the-record remarks, how he transformed the Presidential press conference from a boring ritual into a major national institution which no later President dared disrespect, and how he developed the fireside chat. Knowing that newspapermen lived on news, he helped them manufacture it. And he knew enough about news-making techniques to help shape their stories to his own purposes.

Take, for example, these comments which President Roosevelt made at a press conference during his visit to a Civilian Conservation Corps camp in Florida on February 18, 1939, when war tensions were mounting:

> I want to get something across, only don't put it that way. In other words, it is a thing that I cannot put as direct stuff, but it is background. And the way—as you know I very often do it—if I were writing the story, the way I'd write it is this—you know the formula: When asked when he was returning [to Washington], the President intimated that it was impossible to give any date; because, while he hoped to be away until the third or fourth of March, information that continues to be received with respect to the international situation continues to be disturbing, therefore, it may be necessary for the President to return [to the capital] before the third or fourth of March. It is understood that this information relates to the possible renewal of demands by certain countries, these demands being pushed, not through normal diplomatic channels but, rather, through the more recent type of relations; in other words, the use of fear of aggression.

F.D.R. was a man of great warmth, natural spontaneity, and simple eloquence, and his public utterances reached the citizen with a new intimacy. Yet, paradoxically, it was under his administrations that statements by the President attained a new subtlety and a new calculatedness. On his production team, in addition to newspapermen, there were poets, playwrights, and a regular corps of speech writers. Far from detracting from his effectiveness, this collaborative system for producing the impression of personal frankness and spontaneity provided an additional subject of newsworthy interest. Was it Robert Sherwood or Judge Samuel Rosenman who contributed this or that phrase? How much had the President revised the draft given him by his speechwriting team? Citizens became nearly as much interested in how a particular speech was put together as in what it said. And when the President spoke, almost everyone knew it was a long-planned group production in which F.D.R. was only the star performer.

Of course President Roosevelt made many great decisions and lived in times which he only helped make stirring. But it is possible to build a political career almost entirely on pseudo-events. Such was that of the late Joseph R. McCarthy, Senator from Wisconsin from 1947 to 1957. His career might have been impossible without the elaborate, perpetually grinding machinery of "information" which I have already described. And he was a natural genius at creating reportable happenings that had an interestingly ambiguous relation to underlying reality. Richard Rovere, a reporter in Washington during McCarthy's heyday, recalls:

> He knew how to get into the news even on those rare occasions when invention failed him and he had no unfacts to give out. For example, he invented the morning press conference called for the purpose of announcing an afternoon press conference. The reporters would come in—they were beginning, in this period, to respond to his summonses like Pavlov's dogs at the clang of a bell—and McCarthy would say that he just wanted to give them the word that he expected to be ready with a shattering announcement later in the day, for use in the papers the following morning. This would gain him a headline in the afternoon papers: "New McCarthy Revelations Awaited in Capital." Afternoon would come, and if McCarthy had something, he would give it out, but often enough he had nothing, and this was a matter of slight concern. He would simply say that he wasn't quite ready, that he was having difficulty in getting some of the "documents" he needed or that a "witness" was proving elusive. Morning headlines: "Delay Seen in McCarthy Case—Mystery Witness Being Sought."

He had a diabolical fascination and an almost hypnotic power over news-hungry reporters. They were somehow reluctantly grateful to him for turning out their product. They stood astonished that he could make so much news from such meager raw material. Many hated him; all helped him. They were victims of what one of them called their "indiscriminate objectivity." In other words, McCarthy and the newsmen both thrived on the same synthetic commodity.

Senator McCarthy's political fortunes were promoted almost as much by newsmen who considered themselves his enemies as by those few who were his friends. Without the active help of all of them he could never have created the pseudo-events which brought him notoriety and power. Newspaper editors, who self-righteously attacked the Senator's "collaborators," themselves proved worse than powerless to cut him down to size. Even while they attacked him on the editorial page inside, they were building him up in front-page headlines. Newspapermen were his most potent allies, for they were his co-manufacturers of pseudo-events. They were caught in their own web. Honest newsmen and the unscrupulous Senator McCarthy were in separate branches of the same business.

In the traditional vocabulary of newspapermen, there is a well-recognized distinction between "hard" and "soft" news. Hard news is supposed to be the solid report of significant matters: politics, economics, international relations, social welfare, science. Soft news reports popular interests, curiosities, and diversions: it includes sensational local reporting, scandalmongering, gossip columns, comic strips, the sexual lives of movie stars, and the latest murder. Journalist-critics attack American newspapers today for not being "serious" enough, for giving a larger and larger proportion of their space to soft rather than to hard news.

. . . What this can mean in a particular case is illustrated by the tribulations of a certain hard-working reporter who was trying to do his job and earn his keep at the time when the Austrian Treaty of 1955 came up for debate in the Senate. Although it was a matter of some national and international importance, the adoption of the Treaty was a foregone conclusion; there would be little news in it. So, in order to make a story, this reporter went to Senator Walter George, Chairman of the Senate Foreign Relations Committee, and extracted a statement to the effect that under the Treaty Austria would receive no money or military aid, only long-term credits. "That became my lead," the reporter recalled. "I had fulfilled the necessary function of having a story that seemed to be part of the next day's news."

The next day, the Treaty came up for debate. The debate was dull, and it was hard to squeeze out a story. Luckily, however, Senator Jenner made a nasty crack about President Eisenhower, which the reporter (after considering what other wire service reporters covering the story might be doing) sent off as an "insert." The Treaty was adopted by the Senate a little after 3:30 P.M. That automatically made a bulletin and required a new lead for the story on the debate. But by that time the hard-pressed reporter was faced with writing a completely new story for the next day's morning papers.

> But my job had not finished. The Treaty adoption bulletin had gone out too late to get into most of the East Coast afternoon papers except the big city ones like the Philadelphia *Evening Bulletin*, which has seven editions. I had to find a new angle for an overnight to be carried next day by those P.M.'s which failed to carry the Treaty story.
>
> They don't want to carry simply a day-old account of the debate. They want a "top" to the news. So, to put it quite bluntly, I went and got Senator Thye to say that Jenner by his actions was weakening the President's authority. Actually, the Thye charge was more lively news than the passage of the Austrian Treaty itself. It revealed conflict among the Senate Republicans. But the story had developed out of my need for a new peg for the news. It was not spontaneous on Thye's part. I had called seven other Senators before I could get someone to make a statement on Jenner. There is a fair criticism, I recognize, to be made of this practice. These Senators didn't call me. I called them. I, in a sense, generated the news. The reporter's imagination brought the Senator's thinking to bear on alternatives that he might not have thought of by himself.
>
> This can be a very pervasive practice. One wire service reporter hounded Senator George daily on the foreign trade question until he finally got George to make the suggestion that Japan should trade with Red China as an alternative to dumping textiles on the American market. Then the reporter went straightway to Senator Knowland to get him to knock down the suggestion. It made a good story, and it also stimulated a minor policy debate that might not have got started otherwise. The "overnight" is the greatest single field for exploratory reporting for the wire services. It is what might be called "milking the news."

The reporter shrewdly adds that the task of his profession today is seldom to compose accounts of the latest events at lightning speed. Rather, it is shaped by "the problem of packaging.'' He says: "Our job is to report the news but it is also to keep a steady flow of news coming forward. Every Saturday morning, for example, we visit the Congressional leaders. We could write all the stories that we get out of those conferences for the Sunday A.M.'s but we don't. We learn to schedule them in order to space them out over Sunday's and Monday's papers.''

An innocent observer might have expected that the rise of television and on-the-spot telecasting of the news would produce a pressure to report authentic spontaneous events exactly as they occur. But, ironically, these, like earlier improvements in the techniques of precise representation, have simply created more and better pseudo-events.

When General Douglas MacArthur returned to the United States (after President Truman relieved him of command in the Far East, on April 11, 1951, during the Korean War) he made a "triumphal" journey around the country. He was invited to help Chicago celebrate "MacArthur Day" (April 26, 1951) which had been proclaimed by resolution of the City Council. Elaborate ceremonies were arranged, including a parade. The proceedings were being televised.

A team of thirty-one University of Chicago sociologists, under the imaginative direction of Kurt Lang, took their posts at strategic points along the route of the MacArthur parade. The purpose was to note the reactions of the crowd and to compare what the spectators were seeing (or said they were seeing) with what they might have witnessed on television. This ingenious study confirmed my observation that we tend increasingly to fill our experience with contrived content. The newspapers had, of course, already prepared people for what the Chicago *Tribune* that morning predicted to be "a triumphant hero's welcome—biggest and warmest in the history of the middle west.'' Many of the actual spectators jammed in the crowd at the scene complained it was hard to see what was going on; in some places they waited for hours and then were lucky to have a fleeting glimpse of the General.

But the television perspective was quite different. The video viewer had the advantage of numerous cameras which were widely dispersed. Television thus ordered the events in its own way, quite different from that of the on-the-spot confusion. The cameras were carefully focused on "significant" happenings—that is, those which emphasized the drama of the occasion. For the television watcher, the General was the continuous center of attraction from his appearance during the parade at 2:21 P.M. until the sudden blackout at 3:00 P.M. Announcers continually reiterated (the scripts showed over fifteen explicit references) the unprecedented drama of the event, or that this was "the greatest ovation this city has ever turned out." On the television screen one received the impression of wildly cheering and enthusiastic crowds before, during, and after the parade. Of course the cameras were specially selecting "action" shots, which showed a noisy, waving audience; yet in many cases the cheering, waving, and shouting were really a response not so much to the General as to the aiming of the camera. Actual spectators, with sore feet, suffered long periods of boredom. Many groups were apathetic. The video viewer, his eyes fixed alternately on the General and on an enthusiastic crowd, his ears filled with a breathless narrative emphasizing the interplay of crowd and celebrity, could not fail to receive an impression of continuous dramatic pageantry.

The most important single conclusion of these sociologists was that the television presentation (as contrasted with the actual witnessing) of the events "remained true to form until the very end, interpreting the entire proceedings according to expectations. . . . The telecast was made to conform to what was interpreted as the pattern of viewers' expectations." Actual spectators at the scene were doubly disappointed, not only because they usually saw very little (and that only briefly) from where they happened to be standing, but also because they knew they were missing a much better performance (with far more of the drama they expected) on the television screen. "I bet my wife saw it much better over television!" and "We should have stayed home and watched it on TV" were the almost universal forms of dissatisfaction. While those at the scene were envying the viewers of the pseudo-event back home, the television viewers were, of course, being told again and again by the network commentators how great was the excitement of being "actually present."

Yet, as the Chicago sociologists noted, for many of those actually present one of the greatest thrills of the day was the opportunity to be on television. Just as everybody likes to see his name in the newspapers, so nearly everybody likes to think that he can be seen (or still better, with the aid of videotape, actually can see himself) on television. Similarly, reporters following candidates Kennedy and Nixon during their tours in the 1960 Presidential campaign noted how many of the "supporters" in the large crowds that were being televised had come out because they wanted to be seen on the television cameras.

Television reporting allows us all to be the actors we really are. Recently I wandered onto the campus of the University of Chicago and happened to witness a tug of war between teams of students. It was amusing to see the women's team drench the men's team by pulling them into Botany Pond. Television cameras of the leading networks were there. The victory of the women's team seemed suspiciously easy to me. I was puzzled until told that this was not the original contest at all; the real tug of war had occurred a day or two before when telecasting conditions were not so good. This was a re-enactment for television.

On December 2, 1960, during the school integration disorders in New Orleans, Mayor de Lesseps S. Morrison wrote a letter to newsmen proposing a three-day moratorium on news and television coverage of the controversy. He argued that the printed and televised reports were exaggerated and were damaging the city's reputation and its tourist trade. People were given an impression of prevailing violence, when, he said, only one-tenth of 1 per cent of the population had been involved in the demonstration. But he also pointed out that the mere presence of telecasting facilities was breeding disorder. "In many cases," he observed, "these people go to the area to get themselves on television and hurry home for the afternoon and evening telecasts to see the show." At least two television reporters had gone about the crowd interviewing demonstrators with inflammatory questions like "Why are you opposed to intermarriage?" Mayor Morrison said he himself had witnessed a television cameraman "setting up a scene," and then, having persuaded a group of students to respond like a "cheering section," had them yell and demonstrate on cue. The conscientious reporters indignantly rejected the Mayor's proposed moratorium on news. They said that "Freedom of the Press" was at stake. That was once an institution preserved in the interest of the community. Now it is often a euphemism for the prerogative of reporters to produce their synthetic commodity.

In many subtle ways, the rise of pseudo-events has mixed up our roles as actors and audience—or, the philosophers would say, as "object" and as "subject." Now we can oscillate between the two roles. "The movies are the only business," Will Rogers once remarked, "where you can go out front and applaud yourself." Nowadays one need not be a professional actor to have this satisfaction. We can appear in the mob scene and then go home and see ourselves on the television screen. No wonder we become confused about what is spontaneous, about what is really going on out there!

New forms of pseudo-events, especially in the world of politics, thus offer a new kind of bewilderment to both politician and newsman. The politician (like F.D.R. in our example, or any holder of a press conference) himself in a sense composes the story; the journalist (like the wire service reporter we have quoted, or any newsman who incites an inflammatory statement) himself generates the event. The citizen can hardly be expected to assess the reality when the participants themselves are so often unsure who is doing the deed and who is making the report of it. Who is the history, and who is the historian?

An admirable example of this new intertwinement of subject and object, of the history and the historian, of the actor and the reporter, is the so-called news "leak." By now the leak has become an important and well-established institution in American politics. It is, in fact, one of the main vehicles for communicating important information from officials to the public.

A clue to the new unreality of the citizen's world is the perverse new meaning now given to the word "leak." To leak, according to the dictionary, is to "let a fluid substance out or in accidentally: as, the ship leaks." But nowadays a news leak is one of the most elaborately planned ways of emitting information. It is, of course, a way in which a government official, with some clearly defined purpose (a leak, even more than a direct announcement, is apt to have some definite devious purpose behind it), makes an announcement, asks a question, or puts a suggestion. It might more accurately be called a *"sub rosa* announcement," an "indirect statement," or "cloaked news."

The news leak is a pseudo-event par excellence. In its origin and growth, the leak illustrates another axiom of the world of pseudo-events: pseudo-events produce more pseudo-events. I will say more on this later.

With the elaboration of news-gathering facilities in Washington—of regular, planned press conferences, of prepared statements for future release, and of countless other practices—the news protocol has hardened. Both government officials and reporters have felt the need for more flexible and more ambiguous modes of communication between them. The Presidential press conference itself actually began as a kind of leak. President Theodore Roosevelt for some time allowed Lincoln Steffens to interview him as he was being shaved. Other Presidents gave favored correspondents an interview from time to time or dropped hints to friendly journalists. Similarly, the present institution of the news leak began in the irregular practice of a government official's helping a particular correspondent by confidentially giving him information not yet generally released. But today the leak is almost as well organized and as rigidly ruled by protocol as a formal press conference. Being fuller of ambiguity, with a welcome atmosphere of confidence and intrigue, it is more appealing to all concerned. The institutionalized leak puts a greater burden of contrivance and pretense on both government officials and reporters.

In Washington these days, and elsewhere on a smaller scale, the custom has grown up among important members of the government of arranging to dine with select representatives of the news corps. Such dinners are usually preceded by drinks, and beforehand there is a certain amount of restrained conviviality. Everyone knows the rules: the occasion is private, and any information given out afterwards must be communicated according to rule and in the technically proper vocabulary. After dinner the undersecretary, the general, or the admiral allows himself to be questioned. He may recount "facts" behind past news, state plans, or declare policy. The reporters have confidence, if not in the ingenuousness of the official, at least in their colleagues' respect of the protocol. Everybody understands the degree of attribution permissible for every statement made: what, if anything, can be directly quoted, what is "background," what is "deep background," what must be ascribed to "a spokesman," to "an informed source," to speculation, to rumor, or to remote possibility.

Such occasions and the reports flowing from them are loaded with ambiguity. The reporter himself often is not clear whether he is being told a simple fact, a newly settled policy, an administrative hope, or whether perhaps untruths are being deliberately diffused to allay public fears that the true facts are really true. The government official himself (who is sometimes no more than a spokesman) may not be clear. The reporter's task is to find a way of weaving these threads of unreality into a fabric that the reader will not recognize as entirely unreal. Some people have criticized the institutionalized leak as a form of domestic counter-intelligence inappropriate in a republic. It has become more and more important and is the source today of many of the most influential reports of current politics.

. . . Pseudo-events spawn other pseudo-events in geometric progression. This is partly because every kind of pseudo-event (being planned) tends to become ritualized, with a protocol and a rigidity all its own. As each type of pseudo-event acquires this rigidity, pressures arise to produce other, derivative, forms of pseudo-event which are more fluid, more tantalizing, and more interestingly ambiguous. Thus, as the press conference (itself a pseudo-event) became formalized, there grew up the institutionalized leak. As the leak becomes formalized still other devices will appear. Of course the shrewd politician or the enterprising newsman knows this and knows how to take advantage of it. Seldom for outright deception; more often simply to make more "news," to provide more "information," or to "improve communication."

For example, a background off-the-record press conference, if it is actually a mere trial balloon or a diplomatic device (as it sometimes was for Secretary of State John Foster Dulles), becomes the basis of official "denials" and "disavowals," of speculation and interpretation by columnists and commentators, and of special interviews on and off television with Senators, Representatives, and other public officials. Any statement or non-statement by anyone in the public eye can become the basis of counter-statements or refusals to comment by others. All these compound the ambiguity of the occasion which first brought them into being.

Nowadays the test of a Washington reporter is seldom his skill at precise dramatic reporting, but more often his adeptness at dark intimation. If he wishes to keep his news channels open he must accumulate a vocabulary and develop a style to conceal his sources and obscure the relation of a supposed event or statement to the underlying facts of life, at the same time seeming to offer hard facts. Much of his stock in trade is his own and other people's speculation about the reality of what he reports. He lives in a penumbra between fact and fantasy. He helps create that very obscurity without which the supposed illumination of his reports would be unnecessary. A deft administrator these days must have similar skills. He must master "the technique of denying the truth without actually lying."

These pseudo-events which flood our consciousness must be distinguished from propaganda. The two do have some characteristics in common. But our peculiar problems come from the fact that pseudo-events are in some respects the opposite of the propaganda which rules totalitarian countries. Propaganda—as prescribed, say, by Hitler in *Mein Kampf*—is information intentionally biased. Its effect depends primarily on its emotional appeal. While a pseudo-event is an ambiguous truth, propaganda is an appealing falsehood. Pseudo-events thrive on our honest desire to be informed, to have "all the facts," and even to have more facts than there really are. But propaganda feeds on our willingness to be inflamed. Pseudo-events appeal to our duty to be educated, propaganda appeals to our desire to be aroused. While propaganda substitutes opinion for facts, pseudo-events are synthetic facts which move people indirectly, by providing the "factual" basis on which they are supposed to make up their minds. Propaganda moves them directly by explicitly making judgments for them.

In a totalitarian society, where people are flooded by purposeful lies, the real facts are of course misrepresented, but the representation itself is not ambiguous. The propaganda lie is asserted as if it were true. Its object is to lead people to believe that the truth is simpler, more intelligible, than it really is. "Now the purpose of propaganda," Hitler explained, "is not continually to produce interesting changes for a few blasé little masters, but to convince; that means, to convince the masses. The masses, however, with their inertia, always need a certain time before they are ready even to notice a thing, and they will lend their memories only to the thousandfold repetition of the most simple ideas." But in our society, pseudo-events make simple facts seem more subtle, more ambiguous, and more speculative than they really are. Propaganda oversimplifies experience, pseudo-events over-complicate it.

At first it may seem strange that the rise of pseudo-events has coincided with the growth of the professional ethic which obliges newsmen to omit editorializing and personal judgments from their news accounts. But now it is in the making of pseudo-events that newsmen find ample scope for their individuality and creative imagination.

In a democratic society like ours—and more especially in a highly literate, wealthy, competitive, and technologically advanced society—the people can be flooded by pseudo-events. For us, freedom of speech and of the press and of broadcasting includes freedom to create pseudo-events. Competing politicians, competing newsmen, and competing news media contest in this creation. They vie with one another in offering attractive, "informative" accounts and images of the world. They are free to speculate on the facts, to bring new facts into being, to demand answers to their own contrived questions. Our "free market place of ideas" is a place where people are confronted by competing pseudo-events and are allowed to judge among them. When we speak of "informing" the people this is what we really mean.

Until recently we have been justified in believing Abraham Lincoln's familiar maxim: "You may fool all the people some of the time; you can even fool some of the people all the time; but you can't fool all of the people all the time." This has been the foundation-belief of American democracy. Lincoln's appealing slogan rests on two elementary assumptions. First, that there is a clear and visible distinction between sham and reality, between the lies a demagogue would have us believe and the truths which are there all the time. Second, that the people tend to prefer reality to sham, that if offered a choice between a simple truth and a contrived image, they will prefer the truth.

Neither of these any longer fits the facts. Not because people are less intelligent or more dishonest. Rather because great unforeseen changes—the great forward strides of American civilization—have blurred the edges of reality. The pseudo-events which flood our consciousness are neither true nor false in the old familiar senses. The very same advances which have made them possible have also made the images—however planned, contrived, or distorted—more vivid, more attractive, more impressive, and more persuasive than reality itself.

We cannot say that we are being fooled. It is not entirely inaccurate to say that we are being "informed." This world of ambiguity is created by those who believe they are instructing us, by our best public servants, and with our own collaboration. Our problem is the harder to solve because it is created by people working honestly and industriously at respectable jobs. It is not created by demagogues or crooks, by conspiracy or evil purpose. The efficient mass production of pseudo-events—in all kinds of packages, in black-and-white, in technicolor, in words, and in a thousand other forms—is the work of the whole machinery of our society. It is the daily product of men of good will. The media must be fed! The people must be informed! Most pleas for "more information" are therefore misguided. So long as we define information as a knowledge of pseudo-events, "more information" will simply multiply the symptoms without curing the disease.

The American citizen thus lives in a world where fantasy is more real than reality, where the image has more dignity than its original. We hardly dare face our bewilderment, because our ambiguous experience is so pleasantly iridescent, and the solace of belief in contrived reality is so thoroughly real. We have become eager accessories to the great hoaxes of the age. These are the hoaxes we play on ourselves.

Pseudo-events from their very nature tend to be more interesting and more attractive than spontaneous events. Therefore in American public life today pseudo-events tend to drive all other kinds of events out of our consciousness, or at least to overshadow them. Earnest, well-informed citizens seldom notice that their experience of spontaneous events is buried by pseudo-events. Yet nowadays, the more industriously they work at "informing" themselves the more this tends to be true.

. . . Recent improvements in vividness and speed, the enlargement and multiplying of news-reporting media, and the public's increasing news hunger now make Lippmann's brilliant analysis of the stereotype the legacy of a simpler age. For stereotypes made experience handy to grasp. But pseudo-events would make experience newly and satisfyingly elusive. In 1911 Will Irwin, writing in *Collier's,* described the new era's growing public demand for news as "a crying primal want of the mind, like hunger of the body." The mania for news was a symptom of expectations enlarged far beyond the capacity of the natural world to satisfy. It required a synthetic product. It stirred an irrational and undiscriminating hunger for fancier, more varied items. Stereotypes there had been and always would be; but they only dulled the palate for information. They were an opiate. Pseudo-events whetted the appetite; they aroused news hunger in the very act of satisfying it.

In the age of pseudo-events it is less the artificial simplification than the artificial complication of experience that confuses us. Whenever in the public mind a pseudo-event competes for attention with a spontaneous event in the same field, the pseudo-event will tend to dominate. What happens on television will overshadow what happens off television. Of course I am concerned here not with our private worlds but with our world of public affairs.

Here are some characteristics of pseudo-events which make them overshadow spontaneous events:

(1) Pseudo-events are more dramatic. A television debate between candidates can be planned to be more suspenseful (for example, by reserving questions which are then popped suddenly) than a casual encounter or consecutive formal speeches planned by each separately.

(2) Pseudo-events, being planned for dissemination, are easier to disseminate and to make vivid. Participants are selected for their newsworthy and dramatic interest.

(3) Pseudo-events can be repeated at will, and thus their impression can be re-enforced.

(4) Pseudo-events cost money to create; hence somebody has an interest in disseminating, magnifying, advertising, and extolling them as events worth watching or worth believing. They are therefore advertised in advance, and rerun in order to get money's worth.

(5) Pseudo-events, being planned for intelligibility, are more intelligible and hence more reassuring. Even if we cannot discuss intelligently the qualifications of the candidates or the complicated issues, we can at least judge the effectiveness of a television performance. How conforting to have some political matter we can grasp!

(6) Pseudo-events are more sociable, more conversable, and more convenient to witness. Their occurrence is planned for our convenience. The Sunday newspaper ap-

pears when we have a lazy morning for it. Television programs appear when we are ready with our glass of beer. In the office the next morning, Jack Paar's (or any other star performer's) regular late-night show at the usual hour will overshadow in conversation a casual event that suddenly came up and had to find its way into the news.

(7) Knowledge of pseudo-events—of what has been reported, or what has been staged, and how—becomes the test of being "informed." News magazines provide us regularly with quiz questions concerning not what has happened but concerning "names in the news"—what has been reported in the news magazines. Pseudo-events begin to provide that "common discourse" which some of my old-fashioned friends have hoped to find in the Great Books.

(8) Finally, pseudo-events spawn other pseudo-events in geometric progression. They dominate our consciousness simply because there are more of them, and ever more.

By this new Gresham's law of American public life, counterfeit happenings tend to drive spontaneous happenings out of circulation. The rise in the power and prestige of the Presidency is due not only to the broadening powers of the office and the need for quick decisions, but also to the rise of centralized news gathering and broadcasting, and the increase of the Washington press corps. The President has an ever more ready, more frequent, and more centralized access to the world of pseudo-events. A similar explanation helps account for the rising prominence in recent years of the Congressional investigating committees. In many cases these committees have virtually no legislative impulse, and sometimes no intelligible legislative assignment. But they do have an almost unprecedented power, possessed now by no one else in the Federal government except the President, to make news. Newsmen support the committees because the committees feed the newsmen: they live together in happy symbiosis. The battle for power among Washington agencies becomes a contest to dominate the citizen's information of the government. This can most easily be done by fabricating pseudo-events.

A perfect example of how pseudo-events can dominate is the recent popularity of the quiz show format. Its original appeal came less from the fact that such shows were tests of intelligence (or of dissimulation) than from the fact that the situations were elaborately contrived—with isolation booths, armed bank guards, and all the rest—and they purported to inform the public.

The application of the quiz show format to the so-called "Great Debates" between Presidential candidates in the election of 1960 is only another example. These four campaign programs, pompously and self-righteously advertised by the broadcasting networks, were remarkably successful in reducing great national issues to trivial dimensions. With appropriate vulgarity, they might have been called the $400,000 Question (Prize: a $100,000-a-year job for four years). They were a clinical example of the pseudo-event, of how it is made, why it appeals, and of its consequences for democracy in America.

In origin the Great Debates were confusedly collaborative between politicians and news makers. Public interest centered around the pseudo-event itself: the lighting, make-up, ground rules, whether notes would be allowed, etc. Far more interest was shown in the performance than in what was said. The pseudo-events spawned in turn by the Great Debates were numberless. People who had seen the shows read about them the more avidly, and listened eagerly for interpretations by news commentators. Representatives of both parties made "statements" on the probable effects of the debates. Numerous interviews and discussion programs were broadcast exploring their meaning. Opinion polls kept us informed on the nuances of our own and other people's reactions. Topics of speculation multiplied. Even the question whether there should be a fifth debate became for a while a lively "issue."

The drama of the situation was mostly specious, or at least had an extremely ambiguous relevance to the main (but forgotten) issue: which participant was better qualified for the Presidency. Of course, a man's ability, while standing under klieg lights, without notes, to answer in two and a half minutes a question kept secret until that moment, had only the most dubious relevance—if any at all—to his real qualifications to make deliberate Presidential decisions on long-standing public questions after being instructed by a corps of advisers. The great Presidents in our history (with the possible exception of F.D.R.) would have done miserably; but our most notorious demagogues would have shone. A number of exciting pseudo-events were created—for example, the Quemoy-Matsu issue. But that, too, was a good example of a pseudo-event: it was created to be reported, it concerned a then-quiescent problem, and it put into the most factitious and trivial terms the great and real issue of our relation to Communist China.

The television medium shapes this new kind of political quiz-show spectacular in many crucial ways. Theodore H. White has proven this with copious detail in his *The Making of the President: 1960* (1961). All the circumstances of this particular competition for votes were far more novel than the old word "debate" and the comparisons with the Lincoln-Douglas Debates suggested. Kennedy's great strength in the critical first debate, according to White, was that he was in fact "debating" at all, but was seizing the opportunity to address the whole nation; while Nixon stuck close to the issues raised by his opponent, rebutting them one by one. Nixon, moreover, suffered a handicap that was serious only on television: he has a light, naturally transparent skin. On an ordinary camera that takes pictures by optical projection, this skin photographs well. But a television camera projects electronically, by an "image-orthicon tube" which has an x-ray effect. This camera penetrates Nixon's transparent skin and brings out (even just after a shave) the tiniest hair growing in the follicles beneath the surface. For the decisive first program Nixon wore a make-up called "Lazy Shave" which was ineffective under these conditions. He therefore looked haggard and heavy-bearded by contrast to Kennedy, who looked pert and clean-cut.

This greatest opportunity in American history to educate the voters by debating the large issues of the campaign failed. The main reason, as White points out, was the compulsions of the medium. "The nature of both TV and radio is that they abhor silence and 'dead time.' All TV and radio discussion programs are compelled to snap question and answer back and forth as if the contestants were adversaries in an intellectual tennis match. Although every experienced newspaperman and inquirer knows that the most thoughtful and responsive answers to any difficult question come after long pause, and that the longer the pause the more illuminating the thought that follows it, nonetheless the electronic media cannot bear to suffer a pause of more than five seconds; a pause of thirty seconds of dead time on air seems interminable. Thus, snapping their two-and-a-half-minute answers back and forth, both candidates could only react for the cameras and the people, they could not think.'' Whenever either candidate found himself touching a thought too large for two-minute exploration, he quickly retreated. Finally the television-watching voter was left to judge, not on issues explored by thoughtful men, but on the relative capacity of the two candidates to perform under television stress.

Pseudo-events thus lead to emphasis on pseudo-qualifications. Again the self-fulfilling prophecy. If we test Presidential candidates by their talents on TV quiz performances, we will, of course, choose presidents for precisely these qualifications. In a democracy, reality tends to conform to the pseudo-event. Nature imitates art.

We are frustrated by our very efforts publicly to unmask the pseudo-event. Whenever we describe the lighting, the make-up, the studio setting, the rehearsals, etc., we simply arouse more interest. One newsman's interpretation makes us more eager to hear another's. One commentator's speculation that the debates may have little significance makes us curious to hear whether another commentator disagrees.

Pseudo-events do, of course, increase our illusion of grasp on the world, what some have called the American illusion of omnipotence. Perhaps, we come to think, the world's problems can really be settled by "statements," by "Summit" meetings, by a competition of "prestige," by overshadowing images, and by political quiz shows.

Once we have tasted the charm of pseudo-events, we are tempted to believe they are the only important events. Our progress poisons the sources of our experience. And the poison tastes so sweet that it spoils our appetite for plain fact. Our seeming ability to satisfy our exaggerated expectations makes us forget that they are exaggerated.

18.

MASS MEDIA: The Transformation of a Political Hero

W. Lloyd Warner

Mask for a Hero

Biggy Muldoon's fight with Hill Street was played before two highly interested audiences. The local ones, the citizens of Yankee City, consisted of those who participated as actors in the drama and those who, acting as a kind of chorus, watched

---

Reprinted by permission from *The Living and the Dead: A Study of the Symbolic Life of Americans*, Yale University Press, 1959.

and commented as the plot unfolded. Among them were the Hill Street crowd, the lace-curtain Irish, and the ordinary little people, Yankee and ethnic, who lived down by the river. For the national audience Yankee City itself, through the symbols of the mass media, became a stage where a human drama of intense interest was being played, yet no one of the audience was directly involved. Each vicariously experienced what happened by reading about it in the great metropolitan papers and magazines, seeing it in a newsreel, or hearing it over the radio. Biggy became a topic of dinner-table conversation, barbershop gossip, a part of gay and ribald talk in the speakeasies throughout the nation.

The Yankee City audience at first viewed him as one kind of character in the plot: a public personality fashioned by events and through experiences with members of the town. Later they saw him and the other members of his drama in a different light, characters whose lines had been rewritten by the national media of communication. Here he became something more than he had been and was applauded accordingly. The local effect of this outside influence was considerable. It was felt directly, for about half the newspapers sold in Yankee City came from metropolitan sources.

To the local audience, despite its laughter, this was a serious play, a tragedy or a drama of triumph according to the time and necessities of those who watched. If so minded, they could laugh, and laugh hard, when Biggy made his opponents ridiculous; but beneath the laughter, and often beside it, were anxious feelings that what was happening demanded sober consideration. The responsibilities of the citizen were involved in what should be felt about each event.

For the audience in the world beyond Yankee City, Biggy's drama was either light comedy or slapstick. The hero could be liked and enjoyed by everyone because he laid his paddle across the fat posteriors of the rich, upset the self-respect of the respectable, and dumped their power and authority on the floor. Yet no one needed to feel responsible for what happened; everyone could have fun. Childhood fantasies of kicking adult authority in the pants, of breaking loose from subordination and the restraint of respectability, were vicariously felt. For the general audience Biggy was the little guy, the "small fry" in them, still rebelling against the jail-like constraints of adult responsibility. He was also the embodiment of their distrust and concern about the rigid moral attitudes of the middle class. But above all he was a symbol of revolt against the imposition of these moral restraints by the powerful middle class; through him, without fear of punishment, they had a good time raising hell before the pained gaze of the respectable.

In Yankee City a part of the figure of Biggy Muldoon was inescapably true, real, an actual person—but in Memphis or Peoria or Pittsburgh he was a glorious clown or a figure of light comedy, though still the hero of the show and a man his audience could respect. They liked and trusted him as "an honest man doing his damnedest." Second thoughts that might arise in the minds of the serious about not wanting "that kind of thing to happen in my town" could be easily dropped because Biggy was not there. For many, perhaps most, it was easy to say, "what this town of ours needs is a Biggy Muldoon, maybe he'd stir things up and get rid of the damned stuffed shirts and crooked politicians who are running things." For such people in Yankee City the trouble with Biggy was that he was in Yankee City.

For many in both audiences Biggy's actions, his friends, and his enemies had been transformed into something more than a drama by the metropolitan papers and national mass media. Perhaps the whole might be called a contemporary collective ritual, its participants characters in a collective rite in which everyone symbolically participated. The characters under different names have appeared in thousands of plays and legends and stories, told straight or with humor, that everyone has heard and seen. The hero, dominant and positive symbol of countless folktales—lodged securely in everyone's pleasant private fantasies and the mythical embodiment of a people's hopes—as champion of the oppressed goes forth to battle. He attacks the position of the powerful few and of those who arouse the fears and anxiety of the many. Those in power fight back, and with their superior weapons capture the hero, incarcerate him, and for a time defeat and disgrace him. But one knows that by his indomitable courage and herculean determination, and with the help of the little people, he will once again attack the fortresses of the mighty, in the end defeating his enemies and winning a great victory for the common people. This drama, continuously modified to meet the needs of the time, older than the records of history, is a public fantasy deeply embedded in the conscious imagery of all Americans.

For a brief time, in the heyday of Biggy's fame, Yankee City became one of the many small stages where America watches the current but passing heroes of the national scene act out a drama whose cast and plot express the varying sentiments, values, and symbolic themes of our people and the system of social relations which organizes and controls us. Through newspapers, magazines, radio, and motion picture, events in that city were conveyed to the world in the form of a drama which did not necessarily correspond in cold fact to what those events and persons really were; nor did its representations present an exact image of the social world of Yankee City.

The contemporary storytellers whose mass art maintains the living continuity of myth and legend in our society and contributes to the integration and persistence of the culture work under far more difficult circumstances than storytellers of the bygone days. Formerly, fables, legends, and myths could be told as if they were true—because they *should* be true, and the imaginations and fantasies of their audiences unquestioningly accepted them. Heroes and villains and their plots and solutions conformed to traditional convention, and for the audience as well as the storyteller who entertained them, defined the proper role of each character and determined how these symbolic beings should be related to each other. The artist and the members of his audience, although different persons, were products of the same social matrix, with closely corresponding beliefs, values, and expectancies about each other and the world in which they lived. The symbols and themes used to arouse anxiety or assuage fear, and the masks and ritualistic plots of the drama which evoked the hopes and fears of their audiences, needed only the artistry of the entertainers and the sanction of conformity to the conventions of the culture to be assured eager acceptance.

The audience believed a tale or a drama was true and conformed to *their* reality if it fell within the confines of sanctioned collective representations. The close fit of the private image and the public symbol provided the conviction of reality while arousing the private emotions of the individual and at the same time controlling them. The collective representations were evaluated beliefs sanctioned by the whole moral and social order. Their private fantasies being controlled more fully by the collective representations of their society, early storytellers easily projected their private imagery on the tales they told and into the folk dramas they presented. Their own private images often were no more than minute individual variations of those in the public domain. Consequently the need of evidence, of induction and rational empirical testing, was greatly reduced.

Today the reporter is trained to be objective, accurate, and to get the facts about the people and events that make a news story. The more recently developed mass media use these same criteria and insist on rules of evidence as guides for their field men who report on current events. The instant repercussions of a modern libel law, as well as the potential embarrassments inherent in a modern system of communications only too ready to point out and publish any discrepancies of fact, sharpen this rule.

Despite the intrusion of modern canons of accuracy and the infusion of the spirit of rationality into newspapers and other mass media, a casual listing of the prevailing selection of stories and the simplest analysis of the criteria of a "good story" that will hold readers and perhaps build circulation demonstrate that the "objective" coverage of what happens every day to the people of the world is dominated by the basic wishes, the hopes and fears, the non-logical symbolic themes and folk beliefs of the people who buy and read the papers. The degree of rationality and accuracy exhibited in the news stories of a paper or magazine is in direct relation to the degree of rational values of its audience. The audiences of mass media vary by age, sex, education, social class, urbanity, and many other social characteristics. Those who have been trained to respect rationality and objective reporting and to expect accurate coverage of events usually read papers and magazines which carry more stories of this character and have corresponding policies. Even these papers print news accounts often filled with evocative, non-logical symbols rather than logical and empirical ones—symbols arousing the feelings and cultural beliefs of the reader rather than pointing out the factual flow of human actions in the event reported.

The fact is, the contemporary newsman must tell his story much as did his progenitors. His tale must arouse and hold the interest of his readers; he must hold out the same kind of symbols to their fears and hopes as did his predecessors. There must be villains and heroes in every paper, and the story lines must conform to the usage of suspense, conflict, the defeat of evil, and the triumph of good that have guided the good sense and artistry of past storytellers and controlled their audience's ability to respond.

But today the reporter must put the mark of empirical truth on the story—over the whole of his plot, its *dramatis personae,* and its solutions—as if it all really happened. He must believe (or pretend) that the facts, rather than the story, speak for themselves. Although the events of the news story may have all occurred in the form in which they are set forth, the relations of the major and minor characters, the arrangement of the incidents, and the symbols used to refer to them must be part of the storyteller's art. The news report is consequently composed of fact combined

with the thematic materials supplied by the reporter and the conventions and traditions of his profession as well as those of his readers and his society. An exact correspondence between the scientific reality of what has actually happened and the story
of what is supposed to have happened is not necessarily a test of the story's capacity
to convince its readers. The mask of empirical truth is often present only for the easier acceptance of the non-logical "truths" of contemporary popular arts. The empirical facts of an event for those who write and read may be no more than a passing
illustration of the deeper evocative "truths" of the nonlogical symbols of our culture.

Biggy Muldoon and the Mass Media

The symbolic transformation of Biggy began with the paid advertisements he
placed in the local paper when he first challenged his enemies to answer his charges
of injustice and foul play. He thus unknowingly began his public transformation
from the inconsequential boy from the wrong side of the tracks to the American citizen who has not been given a fair chance. In one of his first political ads Biggy told
everyone that all he wanted was an opportunity to show his "true worth." Later he
said that his enemies, the high and mighty "codfish aristocrats," were conspiring to
destroy the rightful chance of every American to be somebody. "There is a little
crowd of bankers and aristocrats in this old town," he reiterated throughout the
campaign, "who don't want anybody else to have a chance but themselves. They
have run this town long enough. They don't want me to have a chance. That's what
the row has been. They've ridden me." When he became mayor he added, "Now,
I'm going to ride them. I'll repeal their zoning law and go after that permit."

He told the people along the river and anyone who would listen that the zoning
law his opponents used to stop him from putting the gas station on Hill Street was a
law to protect the people on Hill Street, not the people of Riverbrook. The clammers
(almost entirely Yankee and lower-lower-class) were being deprived of their livelihood, he said, because no one had come to their assistance; but he, Biggy, would be
their champion, lead them, and force the state to purify the polluted waters of the
river and make their clams fit for sale and human consumption.

These efforts were the first suggestion of his transformation into the hero who
championed the poor. But as Biggy himself has said, it is doubtful if they would
have been sufficient to elect him. Just before the election a further development in
his symbolic transformation occurred which lifted him out of himself and made him
something more than the man, Biggy Muldoon. This was the story, previously mentioned, which appeared first in the metropolitan press, then in hundreds of other
papers, thus beginning the transformation of Biggy into a real public hero. It
changed the campaign of local fact and fancy into what was also a battle between
positive and negative national stereotypes, symbols now identified with Biggy
which both friends and enemies tried to use to capture the imagination and votes of
the people. The story was published in a Boston paper a few days before the election, a two-column, front-page news item with Biggy's picture, recounting the in-

cidents—now dated by a year or so—of the circus posters, the chamber pots, and the house of Hill Street. It will be remembered that outwardly, until the mayoralty election, his acts in themselves, dramatic as they were, had done little to advance Biggy's political aspirations. It is certain that very few persons thought of what he had done on Hill Street as important enough to make him a successful candidate for the highest political position in the community. Yet the emotional foundations for this had been established.

. . . He became a symbolic figure of pleasure, of permissiveness. With him millions could vicariously rebel against the restraints of their environment and have a good time. Although he did not drink, prohibiting people from having a drink was not to him a "noble experiment"; he was for everyone's drinking as much as he wanted. He swore and enjoyed gambling with his friends. He liked to have fun. For his great audience he was a "good guy" and a "straight-shooter"—not a hypocrite or a stuffed shirt.

Lady's Favorite and Masculine Symbol

. . . One of the most striking symbolic transformations of Biggy Muldoon, followed his recognition by the national mass media, was his masculine role and his relation to women. It will be remembered that at the time of his election his reputation was such that he felt it necessary to declare publicly, "I'm supposed to be a woman-hater, that's the bunk," and that with the Navy in the Caribbean he had been forced to "jump out of a second-story window to keep my independence."

Editors and those who controlled other mass media soon got the feel of Biggy's potentialities as a sexual symbol. Within a month or two he was being played up as a judge of beautiful women, a man in search of a beautiful bride, an authority on female attractiveness. The businessmen who put on such attractions as beauty contests, marathons, and burlesque shows saw in him a figure that would appeal to male and female alike as a man who knew his way around and was attractive to women. He was regarded by both sexes as a he-man, "not a pretty boy you see in the movies, but a two-fisted guy." Biggy became a powerful masculine sexual symbol for many in the great audience. For the women he was something more than the bad boy who said girls were "like puppy dogs"; multitudes of letters, coyly or openly erotic, poured in on him.

In America the cluster of meanings about the big two-fisted, strong young male who knows what he wants and sets out to get it always evokes positive feeling among many as to his sexuality and potency. In the fantasies of his mass audience Biggy was soon transformed and served as symbol of the untamed male, the great muscular "brute." He became still another example of the libidinal male found in the literature of the superior such as *The Hairy Ape, Lady Chatterley's Lover,* and Robinson Jeffers' "Roan Stallion," or in popular novels, movies, and radio as the truck driver and the husky sailor; or in folk myth and ballad as expressed in the powerful sexuality of the subordinate white or Negro male. Symbolically he was to many the anarchal monad, the free man, free from weakening middle-class morality. In fact, even in middle-class terms Biggy was in many respects a well-reared, proper boy; he was not loose sexually any more than he was loose in other areas of his deportment. His mother's training had stayed with him. He did not drink or smoke and, though not ascetic, his conduct with women was scrupulous and careful. But the women who wrote him from all over the United States saw and responded to another Biggy—the symbolic one created by the press.

. . . Biggy the man, living and acting out his life in Yankee City, had largely disappeared in the enlarged and greatly modified heroic mold into which his life had been re-formed by the public press and other mass media. Although each part of the popular figure was founded on elements of fact, the few quotations from the letters of his public make clear that his meanings for them, although intensely personal, express the collective values, the hopes and fears, the wishes and anxieties of the American people.

Economic, Social, and Symbolic Factors in a Hero's Career

. . . Biggy fought a successful fight as a common man and an underdog against the highly placed powerful people at the top of the social heap. The figure of little David, champion of the little people, attacking the giant Goliath is but one of thousands of similar symbols that permeate every aspect of our sacred and secular life. From the secular extreme of such recent favorites as Mickey Mouse and the Three Little Pigs and their animated nonsense to that of the sacred Lowly One attacking the power of the highly placed Jews, multitudes of our symbols express the wishes, beliefs, and values of a people hungering for a lowly champion, who, as their representative, can treat the high and mighty with the scorn and contempt they are believed to deserve and can righteously defeat or slay these "evil enemies of the people." A champion in America, however, must be forever on his guard to be more the common man than champion, lest his followers look for new Davids to slay him—the old David—who for them has become a new Goliath.

Biggy won his fight to degrade and commercialize the mansion and its environment. He succeeded in translating them from status symbols, which evoked superior feelings related to the way of life of the elite, into purely economic symbols needing only the value of money for their possession. The house was moved to a poor-status area and divided into apartments inappropriate for the superior. Its location and lovely garden became a service station, one in the chain of a great petroleum corporation.

After the place was sold, his violence was no longer so easy to connect with the underdog's attack on his superiors. The sale removed his struggle from the public arena, where he was the little man fighting entrenched wealth and the champion performing extraordinary deeds in the service of his fellows, and reduced it to the level of a private economic transaction. Maybe the spectacle had been fun to watch, but the symbol of the struggle of right and wrong, good and evil, poor and rich, the many versus Hill Street, had been removed. When the house became a large roll of bills in Biggy's pocket, everyone could cheer for his triumph, but the power of the money now became part of Biggy's own meaning. His new position demanded a different style of behavior. In some ways he now dramatically represented some of the very things and values he had assailed. The attack on the mansion implicitly made him one of the people; the translation of it into money made him explicitly a man of wealth.

. . . Having achieved economic success, Biggy conformed to the powerful rags-to-riches motif which is a basic tenet of Americans. The myth of ultimate success and the creation of the symbolic role of the successful man who rises from lowly beginnings to greatness and final heights is a necessary part of the apparatus of our social and status system. To live as normal and respected citizens, most Americans must either internalize this myth and make it a part of themselves or in some fashion achieve an acceptable peace with it. Otherwise they face social attack and possible destruction. A man without ambition needs to explain himself.

Biggy was able to translate his own attitudes, intentions, and behavior into simple but highly powerful symbols with which most people in Yankee City (and the United States) could sympathetically identify. They were rudimentary symbols carrying a great emotional impact anyone could understand, symbols that aroused laughter in the electorate rather than anger.

The reasons for his later defeat are numerous, diverse, and difficult to determine; the principal ones, however, can be stated. The signs and symbols of the mass media, unless constantly refreshed with new meanings, rapidly become shopworn and no longer attractive to their audiences. In simple terms, the same man in the same variety act frequently repeated soon becomes tiresome. On radio or television the audience can turn him off or try another station. When a character on a local scene loses his appeal the editors of the press turn the main spotlight elsewhere to another set of fresh events. These factors operated in Biggy's decreasing popularity and the waning use of him as a symbol by the mass media.

But more fundamentally, the role of hero with Biggy in charge as a master of ceremonies who could make fun of his enemies, with the Hill Street mansion as a prop for his public spectacle, had changed for the most part to that of clown or, for those who had learned to hate him, villain, because he had threatened and endangered their self-respect and their position in the community. From the beginning of his rise to fame he was never free from the implication that much of his behavior was funny and he himself ridiculous.

. . . Biggy refused to obey the ordinary rules that guide most people in their efforts to advance themselves in the social heap. He believed in middle-class economic values and morality but rebelled against middle- and upper-class social values; yet he still wanted to be mobile and achieve recognition even to being President of the United States. However, he did not want to pay the price of learning how to do it. He attacked the whole system controlling the rise of a successful man, and his attacks created conflicts that could not be resolved within the ordinary functioning of the system.

To be successful in our society a man and his family who are socially mobile must be willing and able to translate their economic gains into status symbols acceptable to the social levels above them. Neither Biggy nor his mother was willing even to attempt to do this. On the contrary, they defined their active goals for advancement in the community in strictly economic terms and violently attacked everyone at the superior levels who was playing the game according to the social rules. Their behavior was too deviant not to arouse the anxieties and hostility of those around them. Had Biggy and his mother been able to introduce their own values, beliefs, and consequent behavior into Yankee City they would have constituted a threat to the whole system, for the basic values on which contemporary society rests run counter to what they attempted to do. Mother and son knew and followed the rules for the economic game as conventionally defined in America: they worked hard, saved and invested their money in property, and as good entrepreneurs they bought cheap and sold dear. They accumulated a small fortune and thus conformed to the traditional rags-to-riches pattern, from immigrant poor to wealthy Americans. But here they stopped. They not only refused to transform their accumulated wealth into symbols of social status and into social status itself, but also refused to make their behavior conform to standards set by those who were placed above them; in fact, they attacked and tried to destroy the symbols of status and, instead of submitting to higher authority, attempted to defeat and subordinate it.

The destruction of the Hill Street mansion and the substitution of a filling station, with all the prior and subsequent behavior related to that hostile act, explicitly expressed this conflict in values. Neither Biggy nor his mother *wanted* to translate their economic rise into social mobility. They usually looked upon the symbols of the superior, the mansion and its gardens, the elm-lined dwelling area of Hill Street, as economic rather than social objects; but whenever they felt them to be something more than objects of trade they deliberately misused them to attack the power and prestige of the upper and upper-middle classes. Clearly, they were aware that these objects represented something more than economic items. Their use of them, although exactly the opposite of that intended, demonstrates that they, too, felt them to be status symbols.

Biggy achieved his immediate goal and realized his intentions partly because neither he nor his mother wanted to do what had to be done if they were to rise socially, and they steadily ridiculed and lampooned the successful Irish who had accepted conventional ways of gaining the respect of their fellows and finding worth in themselves. They called such people by the derogatory term of "lace-curtain Irish" as well as other names less mentionable. The deep hostility of each to authority seemingly made them incapable of accepting the standards of a status society.

When Biggy defeated his enemies in the superior classes he translated his victory into an economic triumph. When he sold his filling station to the Standard Oil Company he detached the controversial symbol of the house and garden from himself and thereby proclaimed himself conqueror of the Hill Streeters, but by the same act transformed the social symbol of the mobile lower-class man's triumph into the cold realities of a financial statement. There can be no doubt that in the values of his lower-class and common-man following he gained a great victory. Many admired and envied his financial achievement and his ability to defeat his tormentors, but once he had attained his goal he separated himself from the powerful symbol that had brought him their attention.

Biggy's continual attacks on political authority and on the status system forced people toward either open revolt against the system—too frightening for most of them to sustain—or annoyance, embarrassment, and finally confusion and weariness. His following changed constantly. At one time some would be close in his counsels, then they would be out and often his enemies. At some moments he would have a tight little clique that would work closely with him, at others no more than two or three people. Essentially he is a very lonely man. People are afraid of him.

Our political order permits ambitious individuals a choice among a number of possible career routes. They can accept the present world for what it is; they can attack its weaknesses and abuses and attempt to improve parts of the structure to conform to the precepts of justice and morality; or they can challenge the whole social and political order and attempt to substitute a new system for the old. This last inevitably incurs the application of violent sanctions against those who lead such revolutionary movements, yet such roles are provided for, recognized, and grudgingly accepted by our society. In the larger sense, they are theoretically necessary for the successful operation of the political community, for our society is built on a premise of free and reasonable individuals making choices for the collectivity. Men who choose the path of revolution reassert the right of others to think and act as individuals free from restraint and demonstrate that our political precepts are in fact possible. At the same time, most revolutionaries are object lessons proving that such choice can overreach itself and that there are sensible boundaries beyond which reasonable and patriotic men must not go.

In politics Biggy was a social and not an economic rebel. He was not the conventional political or economic revolutionary. Yet he was attacking one of the foundations of American society, our status order. Psychologically he was always in revolt and consequently found it impossible to adjust himself to a situation where he was the man with authority and political power. While mayor he sometimes confused his following by continuing in revolt against what in fact was his own power. For a while he aroused more anxiety and increased more tension than he could release. After his election his fighting, though still highly regarded by some, embarrassed and frightened many, particularly when he fought some of his own people and created disorder in his own ranks. Many of his followers no longer felt easy with him; their champion had become a potential threat to their sense of security. Increasing fear in Biggy's social group restrained and limited action. This was not necessarily his fault, but possibly a function of the loose social structure of the lower groups and of the aggression of people attracted to his cause. There was also increasing fear of Biggy because of his attack on the moral shortcomings of those he knew. Although supposedly very permissive, he attacked the moral imperfections of those around him, asking embarrassing questions or referring to incidents involving cowardice, drunkenness, infidelity, and other disapproved behavior.

The champion of the people, the martyr, the traitor, the villain, fool, and clown—all roles Biggy played or was forced to play—express in ideal form some of the values and beliefs we have about ourselves. They exaggerate the petty acts, the minor observances and infractions of the rules, which are part of our own behavior. Human conduct and all the values and beliefs which order it are enlarged in such roles to heroic and godlike proportions. These symbolic figures stretch our ordinary feelings about good and evil, impulse and restraint, order and individual freedom, to their ultimate extremes.

The good citizen who becomes the martyr, who sacrifices his life for the moral principles which maintain and sustain a nation, the hero who at great risk and with utter abnegation of self conquers the wicked foes of his country, the evil man who leads his people to destruction or betrays them to an enemy, and the ridiculous impulsive fellow who knocks over the chairs of constituted authority while chasing well-formed blondes through the halls of respectable hotels—all are human figures enlarged beyond life size into symbols which evoke basic feelings about ourselves and our social world. They release and free us, yet bind and control us, for they take us beyond ourselves and permit us to identify with the ideals of our culture. The sacred ideals of godhood are never more than one step beyond; sometimes they are immediate and present, for in human history heroes often become gods.

The cultural values of a people themselves supply the powerful symbols which, properly molded, become the plot and story of a life or mystic hero, a villain or a fool. The cultural hero is an attractive and powerful symbol with which to identify; he easily arouses those who listen. To outsiders who are not personally concerned his story is only a story, but to those involved the drama of a champion struggling against his and their antagonists is not a story but "reality." The most fantastic legends, the most curious fables, can be believed once the "reality" of the political hero has been established in the feelings and beliefs of his followers, while—equally true—the most scurrilous and impossible tales of iniquity are faithfully credited by those who feel the "reality" of his reported evil acts.

Villain and hero, idealizations of the interdependent, dual forces of good and evil, make vice and virtue manifest in sensuous, perceptible human form. When this happens fantasy reshapes reality, the non-rational, mythic symbols dominate the logical and empirical ones, and the semi- and unconscious inward images emotionally control the outer concepts of empirical fact. Men can hate and love, and take pleasure in doing it. It's holiday time for everyone. If actual holidays are not publicly declared and real processions formed to celebrate the love of a hero, they take place in the informal actions, beliefs, and excitement of the people. Sometimes a generation later those who were not originally present, in their effort to recapture and participate in the emotional excitement of yesterday, formally declare a holiday dedicated to the dead hero. But the intense pleasures experienced in worshiping him usually remain as dead as he is; only the feeling of moral worth can be revived when they celebrate his birthday. Now and then the work of a great artist, poet, or dramatist, or the folk drama of a people, succeeds momentarily in helping a new generation to experience the excitement felt by an older one when their hero walked on earth.

In the heat of political battle Biggy Muldoon, Huey Long, Al Smith, Senator McCarthy, Franklin Roosevelt and, in generations past, Andrew Jackson, Abraham Lincoln, and others, each to his own degree has captured the imagination of the people and in his own time has been transfigured into the human symbols of good or evil, sainthood or villainy. The cold propositions of reason can prevail only when the myths of today's heroes no longer arouse the wishes and fears of those who love and hate them; even then their legends become the canonized myths and moral representations necessary for the persistence and cultural continuity of their society. The symbol of Abraham Lincoln as clown and villain are dead with the fears and hatreds of the past, but the sanctified myth of Old Abe, whose wit defeated his enemies, whose laughter carried him and his nation through the bitter and fearful hours of defeat and impending disaster, lives on in the lives of all Americans, and with it the folk legends of the powerful body which outwrestled the town bully—the big and humble man who rose from the backwoods and the river bottoms to greatness, yet stayed common just like everybody else. The evidence and reasoned propositions composing the most objective research are easily fitted into the moral assumptions and values, the social logics, of the Lincoln myth.

Biggy Muldoon is not, nor does he claim to be, an Abraham Lincoln or an Andrew Jackson. But he and other Americans who have enjoyed and suffered transfiguration by mass media into symbols with power to evoke hatred and love share the necessary psychological and social attributes which are the materials needed by their countrymen for the substance of their collective myths.

To understand Biggy, it helps to view him as if he were the hero of a tragic drama who had the power, because of the precepts and underlying assumptions of the social context where he strove for success, to achieve partial, but never complete, victory. There were always present the latent but well-established factors which would defeat his aspirations for greater achievement and ultimate triumph. Although "time desireless" had shown him to be a courageous man who fought without fear, Fate, in the form of social reality and the inner world of his personality, temporarily at least defeated his aspirations. The strong man of classical drama, believing he is unjustly treated, pursues the dictates of his own ego, but in doing so finds he has violated part of the code of his group. Muldoon, the strong man, knowing he was a good man unjustly treated, following the urge of his ego, strove for success using some of the accepted rules of his society; but he, too, violated some of the basic rules of his group.

Perhaps such a man as Biggy Muldoon will never again appear in Yankee City or even in America, but others will come forward to play the role of hero or champion of the downtrodden, or the common man who challenges the select few and slays the dragon. Some of these will rise to national positions, but they will achieve the highest levels only when they learn how to conform to the basic beliefs and values of the group. When they fail, sometimes it will be caused by their inability to adjust their basic beliefs and values to those that govern American society.

19.

MASS COMMUNICATION AND PARA-SOCIAL
INTERACTION: Observations on Intimacy at a Distance

Donald Horton and R. Richard Wohl

One of the striking characteristics of the new mass media—radio, television, and the movies—is that they give the illusion of face-to-face relationship with the performer. The conditions of response to the performer are analogous to those in a primary group. The most remote and illustrious men are met *as if* they were in the circle of one's peers; the same is true of a character in a story who comes to life in these media in an especially vivid and arresting way. We propose to call this seeming face-to-face relationship between spectator and performer a *para-social relationship*.

In television, especially, the image which is presented makes available nuances of appearance and gesture to which ordinary social perception is attentive and to which interaction is cued. Sometimes the 'actor'—whether he is playing himself or performing in a fictional role—is seen engaged with others; but often he faces the spectator, uses the mode of direct address, talks as if he were conversing personally and privately. The audience, for its part, responds with something more than mere running observation; it is, as it were, subtly insinuated into the program's action and internal social relationships and, by dint of this kind of staging, is ambiguously transformed into a group which observes and participates in the show by turns. The more the performer seems to adjust his performance to the supposed response of the audience, the more the audience tends to make the response anticipated. This simulacrum of conversational give and take may be called *para-social interaction*.

Para-social relations may be governed by little or no sense of obligation, effort, or responsibility on the part of the spectator. He is free to withdraw at any moment. If he remains involved, these para-social relations provide a framework within which much may be added by fantasy. But these are differences of degree, not of kind, from what may be termed the ortho-social. The crucial difference in experience obviously lies in the lack of effective reciprocity, and this the audience cannot normally conceal from itself. To be sure, the audience is free to choose among the relationships offered, but it cannot create new ones. The interaction, characteristically, is one-sided, nondialectical, controlled by the performer, and not susceptible of mutual development. There are, of course, ways in which the spectators can make their feelings known to the performers and the technicians who design the programs, but these lie outside the para-social interaction itself. Whoever finds the experience unsatisfying has only the option to withdraw.

Reprinted by special permission of The William Alanson White Psychiatric Foundation Inc., *Psychiatry* (1956) 19: 215–229 © 1956 by The William Alanson White Psychiatric Foundation Inc.

What we have said so far forcibly recalls the theatre as an ambiguous meeting ground on which real people play out the roles of fictional characters. For a brief interval, the fictional takes precedence over the actual, as the actor becomes identified with the fictional role in the magic of the theatre. This glamorous confusion of identities is temporary: the worlds of fact and fiction meet only for the moment. And the actor, when he takes his bows at the end of the performance, crosses back over the threshold into the matter-of-fact world.

Radio and television, however—and in what follows we shall speak primarily of television—are hospitable to both these worlds in continuous interplay. They are alternately public platforms and theatres, extending the para-social relationship now to leading people of the world of affairs, now to fictional characters, sometimes even to puppets anthropomorphically transformed into "personalities," and, finally, to theatrical stars who appear in their capacities as real celebrities. But of particular interest is the creation by these media of a new type of performer: quizmasters, announcers, "interviewers" in a new "show-business" world—in brief, a special category of "personalities" whose existence is a function of the media themselves. These "personalities," usually, are not prominent in any of the social spheres beyond the media.[1] They exist for their audiences only in the para-social relation. Lacking an appropriate name for these performers, we shall call them *personae*.

The Role of the Persona

The persona is the typical and indigenous figure of the social scene presented by radio and television. To say that he is familiar and intimate is to use pale and feeble language for the pervasiveness and closeness with which multitudes feel his presence. The spectacular fact about such personae is that they can claim and achieve an intimacy with what are literally crowds of strangers, and this intimacy, even if it is an imitation and a shadow of what is ordinarily meant by that word, is extremely influential with, and satisfying for, the great numbers who willingly receive it and share in it. They "know" such a persona in somewhat the same way they know their chosen friends: through direct observation and interpretation of his appearance, his gestures and voice, his conversation and conduct in a variety of situations. Indeed, those who make up his audience are invited, by designed informality, to make precisely these evaluations—to consider that they are involved in a face-to-face exchange rather than in passive observation. When the television camera pans down on a performer, the illusion is strong that he is enhancing the presumed intimacy by literally coming closer. But the persona's image, while partial, contrived, and penetrated by illusion, is no fantasy or dream; his performance is an objectively perceptible action in which the viewer is implicated imaginatively, but which he does not imagine.

The persona offers, above all, a continuing relationship. His appearance is a regular and dependable event, to be counted on, planned for, and integrated into the routines of daily life. His devotees 'live with him' and share the small episodes of his public life—and to some extent even of his private life away from the show. Indeed, their continued association with him acquires a history, and the accumulation of shared past experiences gives additional meaning to the present performance. This bond is symbolized by allusions that lack meaning for the casual observer and appear occult to the outsider. In time, the devotee—the "fan"—comes to believe that he "knows" the persona more intimately and profoundly than others do; that he "understands" his character and appreciates his values and motives.[2] Such an accumulation of knowledge and intensification of loyalty, however, appears to be a kind of growth without development, for the one-sided nature of the connection precludes a progressive and mutual reformulation of its values and aims.[3]

The persona may be considered by his audience as a friend, counselor, comforter, and model; but, unlike real associates, he has the peculiar virtue of being standardized according to the "formula" for his character and performance which he and his managers have worked out and embodied in an appropriate "production format." Thus his character and pattern of action remain basically unchanged in a world of otherwise disturbing change. The persona is ordinarily predictable, and gives his adherents no unpleasant surprises. In their association with him there are no problems of understanding or empathy too great to be solved. Typically, there are no challenges to a spectator's self—to his ability to take the reciprocal part in the performance that is assigned to him—that cannot be met comfortably. This reliable sameness is only approximated, and then only in the short run, by the figures of fiction. On television, Groucho is always sharp; Godfrey is always warm-hearted.

The Bond of Intimacy

It is an unvarying characteristic of these "personality" programs that the greatest pains are taken by the persona to create an illusion of intimacy. We call it an illusion because the relationship between the persona and any member of his audience is inevitably one-sided, and reciprocity between the two can only be suggested. There are several principal strategies for achieving this illusion of intimacy.

Most characteristic is the attempt of the persona to duplicate the gestures, conversational style, and milieu of an informal face-to-face gathering. This accounts, in great measure, for the casualness with which even the formalities of program scheduling are treated. The spectator is encouraged to gain the impression that what is taking place on the program gains a momentum of its own in the very process of being enacted. Thus Steve Allen is always pointing out to his audience that "we never know what is going to happen on this show." In addition, the persona tries to maintain a flow of small talk which gives the impression that he is responding to and sustaining the contributions of an invisible interlocutor. Dave Garroway, who has mastered this style to perfection, has described how he stumbled on the device in his early days in radio.

> Most talk on the radio in those days was formal and usually a little stiff. But I just rambled along, saying whatever came into my mind. I was introspective. I tried to pretend that I was chatting with a friend over a highball late in the evening. . . . Then—and later—I consciously tried to talk to the listener as an individual, to make each listener feel that he knew me and I knew him. It seemed to work pretty well then and

later. I know that strangers often stop me on the street today, call me Dave and seem to feel that we are old friends who know all about each other.[4]

In addition to creating an appropriate tone and patter, the persona tries as far as possible to eradicate, or at least to blur, the line which divides him and his show, as a formal performance, from the audience both in the studio and at home. The most usual way of achieving this ambiguity is for the persona to treat his supporting cast as a group of close intimates. Thus all the members of the cast will be addressed by their first names, or by special nicknames, to emphasize intimacy. They very quickly develop, or have imputed to them, stylized character traits which, as members of the supporting cast, they will indulge in and exploit regularly in program after program. The member of the audience, therefore, not only accumulates an historical picture of "the kinds of people they really are," but tends to believe that this fellowship includes him by extension. As a matter of fact, all members of the program who are visible to the audience will be drawn into this by-play to suggest this ramification of intimacy.

Furthermore, the persona may try to step out of the particular format of his show and literally blend with the audience. Most usually, the persona leaves the stage and mingles with the studio audience in a question-and-answer exchange. In some few cases, and particularly on the Steve Allen show, this device has been carried a step further. Thus Allen has managed to blend even with the home audience by the maneuver of training a television camera on the street outside the studio and, in effect, suspending his own show and converting all the world outside into a stage. Allen, his supporting cast, and the audience, both at home and in the studio, watch together what transpires on the street—the persona and his spectators symbolically united as one big audience. In this way, Allen erases for the moment the line which separates persona and spectator.

In addition to the management of relationships between the persona and performers, and between him and his audience, the technical devices of the media themselves are exploited to create illusions of intimacy.

> For example [Dave Garroway explains in this connection], we developed the "subjective-camera" idea, which was simply making the camera be the eyes of the audience. In one scene the camera—that's you the viewer—approached the door of a dentist's office, saw a sign that the dentist was out to lunch, sat down nervously in the waiting room. The dentist returned and beckoned to the camera, which went in and sat in the big chair. "Open wide," the dentist said, poking a huge, wicked-looked drill at the camera. There was a roar as the drill was turned on, sparks flew and the camera vibrated and the viewers got a magnified version of sitting in the dentist's chair—except that it didn't hurt.[5]

All these devices are indulged in not only to lure the attention of the audience, and to create the easy impression that there is a kind of participation open to them in the program itself, but also highlight the chief values stressed in such "personality" shows. These are sociability, easy affability, friendship, and close contact—briefly, all the values associated with free access to and easy participation in pleasant social interaction in primary groups. Because the relationship between persona and audience is one-sided and cannot be developed mutually, very nearly the whole burden of creating a plausible imitation of intimacy is thrown on the persona and on the show of which he is the pivot. If he is successful in initiating an intimacy which his audience can believe in, then the audience may help him maintain it by fan mail and by the various other kinds of support which can be provided indirectly to buttress his actions.

The Role of the Audience

At one extreme, the "personality" program is like a drama in having a cast of characters, which includes the persona, his professional supporting cast, nonprofessional contestants and interviewees, and the studio audience. At the other extreme, the persona addresses his entire performance to the home audience with undisturbed intimacy. In the dramatic type of program, the participation of the spectator involves, we presume, the same taking of successive roles and deeper empathic involvements in the leading roles which occurs in any observed social interaction.[6] It is possible that the spectator's "collaborative expectancy" [7] may assume the more profound form of identification with one or more of the performers. But such identification can hardly be more than intermittent. The "personality" program, unlike the threatrical drama, does not demand or even permit the esthetic illusion—that loss of situationl reference and self-consciousness in which the audience not only accepts the symbol as reality, but fully assimilates the symbolic role. The persona and his staff maintain the para-social relationship, continually referring to and addressing the home audience as a third party to the program; and such references remind the spectator of his own independent identity. The only illusion maintained is that of directness and immediacy of participation.

When the persona appears alone, in apparent face-to-face interaction with the home viewer, the latter is still more likely to maintain his own identity without interruption, for he is called upon to make appropriate responses which are complementary to those of the persona. This 'answering' role is, to a degree, voluntary and independent. In it, the spectator retains control over the content of his participation rather than surrendering control through identification with others, as he does when absorbed in watching a drama or movie.

This independence is relative, however, in a twofold sense: First, it is relative in the profound sense that the very act of entering into any interaction with another involves *some* adaptation to the other's perspectives, if communication is to be achieved at all. And, second, in the present case, it is relative because the role of the persona is enacted in such a way, or is of such a character, that an *appropriate* answering role is specified by implication and suggestion. The persona's performance, therefore, is open-ended, calling for a rather specific answering role to give it closure.[8]

The general outlines of the appropriate audience role are perceived intuitively from familiarity with the common cultural patterns on which the role of the persona is constructed. These roles are chiefly derived from the primary relations of friendship and the family, characterized by intimacy, sympathy, and sociability. The audience is expected to accept the situation defined by the program format as credible, and to concede as "natural" the rules and conventions governing the actions performed and the values realized. It should play the role of the loved one to the persona's lover; the admiring dependent to his father-surrogate; the earnest citizen to his fearless opponent of political evils. It is expected to benefit by his wisdom, reflect on his advice, sympathize with him in his difficulties, forgive his mistakes, buy the products that he recommends, and keep his sponsor informed of the esteem in which he is held.

Other attitudes than compliance in the assigned role are, of course, possible. One may reject, take an analytical stance, perhaps even find a cynical amusement in refusing the offered gambit and playing some other role not implied in the script, or view the proceedings with detached curiosity or hostility. But such attitudes as these are, usually, for the one-time viewer. The faithful audience is one that can accept the gambit offered; and the functions of the program for this audience are served not by the mere perception of it, but by the role-enactment that completes it.

The Coaching of Audience Attitudes

Just how the situation should be defined by the audience, what to expect of the persona, what attitudes to take toward him, what to 'do' as a participant in the program, is not left entirely to the common experience and intuitions of the audience. Numerous devices are used in a deliberate "coaching of attitudes," to use Kenneth Burke's phrase.[9] The typical program format calls for a studio audience to provide a situation of face-to-face interaction for the persona, and exemplifies to the home audience an enthusiastic and 'correct' response. The more interaction occurs, the more clearly is demonstrated the kind of man the persona is, the values to be shared in association with him, and the kind of support to give him. A similar model of appropriate response may be supplied by the professional assistants who, though technically performers, act in a subordinate and deferential reciprocal relation toward the persona. The audience is schooled in correct responses to the persona by a variety of other means as well. Other personae may be invited as guests, for example, who play up to the host in exemplary fashion; or persons drawn from the audience may be maneuvered into fulfilling this function. And, in a more direct and literal fashion, reading excerpts from fanmail may serve the purpose.

Beyond the coaching of specific attitudes toward personae, a general propaganda on their behalf flows from the performers themselves, their press agents, and the mass communication industry. Its major theme is that the performer should be loved and admired. Every attempt possible is made to strengthen the illusion of reciprocity and rapport in order to offset the inherent impersonality of the media themselves. The jargon of show business teems with special terms for the mysterious ingredients of such rapport: ideally, a performer should have "heart," should be "sincere"; [10] his performance should be "real" and "warm." [11] The publicity campaigns built around successful performers continually emphasize the sympathetic image which, it is hoped, the audience is perceiving and developing.[12]

The audience, in its turn, is expected to contribute to the illusion by believing in it, and by rewarding the persona's "sincerity" with "loyalty." The audience is entreated to assume a sense of personal obligation to the performer, to help him in his struggle for "success" if he is "on the way up," or to maintain his success if he has already won it. "Success" in show business is itself a theme which is prominently exploited in this kind of propaganda. It forms the basis of many movies; it appears often in the patter of the leading comedians and in the exhortations of MC's; it dominates the so-called amateur hours and talent shows; and it is subject to frequent comment in interviews with "show people." [13]

Conditions of Acceptance of the Para-Social Role by the Audience

The acceptance by the audience of the role offered by the program involves acceptance of the explicit and implicit terms which define the situation and the action to be carried out in the program. Unless the spectator understands these terms, the role performances of the participants are meaningless to him; and unless he accepts them, he cannot 'enter into' the performance himself. But beyond this, the spectator must be able to play the part demanded of him; and this raises the question of the compatibility between his normal self—as a system of role-patterns and self-conceptions with their implicated norms and values—and the kind of self postulated by the program schema and the actions of the persona. In short, one may conjecture that the probability of rejection of the proffered role will be greater the less closely the spectator 'fits' the role prescription.

To accept the gambit without the necessary personality 'qualifications' is to invite increasing dissatisfaction and alienation—which the student of the media can overcome only by a deliberate, imaginative effort to take the postulated role. The persona himself takes the role of his projected audience in the interpretation of his own actions, often with the aid of cues provided by a studio audience. He builds his performance on a cumulative structure of assumptions about their response, and so postulates—more or less consciously—the complex of attitudes to which his own actions are adapted. A spectator who fails to make the anticipated responses will find himself further and further removed from the base-line of common understanding. [14] One would expect the 'error' to be cumulative, and eventually to be carried, perhaps, to the point at which the spectator is forced to resign in confusion, disgust, anger, or boredom. If a significant portion of the audience fails in this way, the persona's "error in role-taking" [15] has to be corrected with the aid of audience research, "program doctors," and other aids. But, obviously, the intended adjustment is to some average or typical spectator, and cannot take too much account of deviants.

The simplest example of such a failure to fulfill the role prescription would be the case of an intellectual discussion in which the audience is presumed to have certain basic knowledge and the ability to follow the development of the argument. Those who cannot meet these requirements find the discussion progressively less comprehensible. A similar progressive alienation probably occurs when children attempt to follow an adult program or movie. One observes them absorbed in the opening scenes, but gradually losing interest as the developing action leaves them behind. Another such situation might be found in the growing confusion and restiveness of some audiences watching foreign movies or "high-brow" drama. Such resistance is also manifested when some members of an audience are asked to take the opposite-sex role—the woman's perspective is rejected more commonly by men than vice versa—or when audiences refuse to accept empathically the roles of outcasts or those of racial or cultural minorities whom they consider inferior.[16]

It should be observed that merely witnessing a program is not evidence that a spectator has played the required part. Having made the initial commitment, he may "string along" with it at a low level of empathy but reject it retrospectively. The experience does not end with the program itself. On the contrary, it may be only after it has ended that it is submitted to intellectual analysis and integrated into, or rejected by, the self; this occurs especially in those discussions which the spectator may undertake with other people in which favorable or unfavorable consensual interpretations and judgments are arrived at. It is important to enter a qualification at this point. The suspension of immediate judgment is probably more complete in the viewing of the dramatic program, where there is an esthetic illusion to be accepted, than in the more self-conscious viewing of "personality" programs.

Value of the Para-Social Role for the Audience

What para-social roles are acceptable to the spectator and what benefits their enactment has for him would seem to be related to the systems of patterned roles and social situations in which he is involved in his everyday life. The values of a para-social role may be related, for example, to the demands being made upon the spectator for achievement in certain statuses. Such demands, to pursue this instance further, may be manifested in the expectations of others, or they may be self-demands, with the concomitant emergence of more or less satisfactory self-conceptions. The enactment of a para-social role may therefore constitute an exploration and development of new role possibilities, as in the experimental phases of actual, or aspired to, social mobility.[17] It may offer a recapitulation of roles no longer played—roles which, perhaps, are no longer possible. The audience is diversified in terms of life-stages, as well as by other social and cultural characteristics; thus, what for youth may be the anticipatory enactment of roles to be assumed in the future may be, for older persons, a reliving and reevaluation of the actual or imagined past.

The enacted role may be an idealized version of an everyday performance—a 'successful' para-social approximation of an ideal pattern, not often, perhaps never, achieved in real life. Here the contribution of the persona may be to hold up a magic mirror to his followers, playing his reciprocal part more skillfully and ideally than do the partners of the real world. So Liberace, for example, outdoes the ordinary husband in gentle understanding, or Nancy Berg outdoes the ordinary wife in amorous complaisance. Thus, the spectator may be enabled to play his part suavely and completely in imagination as he is unable to do in actuality.

If we have emphasized the opportunities offered for playing a vicarious or actual role, it is because we regard this as the key operation in the spectator's activity, and the chief avenue of the program's meaning for him. This is not to overlook the fact that every social role is reciprocal to the social roles of others, and that it is as important to learn to understand, to decipher, and to anticipate their conduct as it is to manage one's own. The function of the mass media, and of the programs we have been discussing, is also the exemplification of the patterns of conduct one needs to understand and cope with in others as well as of those patterns which one must apply to one's self. Thus the spectator is instructed variously in the behaviors of the opposite sex, of people of higher and lower status, of people in particular occupations and professions. In a quantitative sense, by reason of the sheer volume of such instruction, this may be the most important aspect of the para-social experience, if only because each person's roles are relatively few, while those of the others in his social worlds are very numerous. In this culture, it is evident that to be prepared to meet all the exigencies of a changing social situation, no matter how limited it may be, could—and often does—require a great stream of plays and stories, advice columns and social how-to-do-it books. What, after all, is soap opera but an interminable exploration of the contingencies to be met with in "home life?" [18]

In addition to the possibilities we have already mentioned, the media present opportunities for the playing of roles to which the spectator has—or feels he has—a legitimate claim, but for which he finds no opportunity in his social environment. This function of the para-social then can properly be called compensatory, inasmuch as it provides the socially and psychologically isolated with a chance to enjoy the elixir of sociability. The "personality" program—in contrast to the drama—is especially designed to provide occasion for good-natured joking and teasing, praising and admiring, gossiping and telling anecdotes, in which the values of friendship and intimacy are stressed.

It is typical of the "personality" programs that ordinary people are shown being treated, for the moment, as persons of consequence. In the interviews of nonprofessional contestants, the subject may be praised for having children—whether few or many does not matter; he may be flattered on his youthful appearance; and he is likely to be honored the more—with applause from the studio audience—the longer he has been "successfully" married. There is even applause, and a consequent heightening of ceremony and importance for the person being interviewed, at mention of the town he lives in. In all this, the values realized for the subject are those of a harmonious, successful participation in one's appointed place in the social order. The subject is represented as someone secure in the affections and respect of others, and he probably senses the experience as a gratifying reassurance of social solidarity and self-confidence. For the audience, in the studio and at home, it is a model of appropriate role performance—as husband, wife, mother, as "attractive" middle age, "remarkably youthful" old age, and the like. It is, furthermore, a demonstration of the fundamental generosity and good will of all concerned, including, of course, the commercial sponsor.[19] But unlike a similar exemplification of happy sociability in a play or a novel, the television or radio program is real; that is to say, it is enveloped in the continuing reassurances and gratifications of objective responses. For instance there may be telephone calls to "outside" contestants, the receipt and acknowledgement of requests from the home audience, and so on. Almost every member of the home audience is left with the comfortable feeling that he too, if he wished, could appropriately take part in this healing ceremony.

Extreme Para-Sociability

For the great majority of the audience, the para-social is complementary to normal social life. It provides a social milieu in which the everyday assumptions and understandings of primary group interaction and sociability are demonstrated and reaffirmed. The "personality" program, however, is peculiarly favorable to the formation of compensatory attachments by the socially isolated, the socially inept, the aged and invalid, the timid and rejected. The persona himself is readily available as an object of love—especially when he succeeds in cultivating the recommended quality of "heart." Nothing could be more reasonable or natural than that people who are isolated and lonely should seek sociability and love wherever they think they can find it. It is only when the para-social relationship becomes a substitute for autonomous social participation, when it proceeds in absolute defiance of objective reality, that it can be regarded as pathological.[20]

The existence of a marginal segment of the lonely in American society has been recognized by the mass media themselves, and from time to time specially designed offerings have been addressed to this minority.[21] In these programs, the maximum illusion of a personal, intimate relationship has been attempted. They represent the extreme development of the para-social, appealing to the most isolated, and illustrate, in an exaggerated way, the principles we believe to apply through the whole range of "personality" programs. The programs which fall in this extreme category promise not only escape from an unsatisfactory and drab reality, but try to prop up the sagging self-esteem of their unhappy audience by the most blatant reassurances. Evidently on the presumption that the maximum of loneliness is the lack of a sexual partner, these programs tend to be addressed to one sex or the other, and to endow the persona with an erotic suggestiveness.[22]

Such seems to have been the purpose and import of *The Lonesome Gal,* a short radio program which achieved such popularity in 1951 that it was broadcast in ninety different cities. Within a relatively short time, the program spread from Hollywood, where it had originated, across the country to New York, where it was heard each evening at 11:15.[23]

The outline of the program was simplicity itself. After a preliminary flourish of music, and an identifying announcement, the main and only character was ushered into the presence of the audience. She was exactly as represented, apparently a lonesome girl, but without a name or a history. Her entire performance consisted of an unbroken monologue unembarrassed by plot, climax, or denouement. On the continuum of para-social action, this is the very opposite of self-contained drama; it is, in fact nothing but the reciprocal of the spectator's own para-social role. The Lonesome Gal simply spoke in a throaty, unctuous voice whose suggestive sexiness belied the seeming modesty of her words.[24]

From the first, the Lonesome Gal took a strongly intimate line, almost as if she were addressing a lover in the utter privacy of some hidden rendezvous:

> Darling, you look so tired, and a little put out about something this evening. . . . You are worried, I feel it. Lover, you need rest . . . rest and someone who understands you. Come, lie down on the couch, relax, I want to stroke your hair gently . . . I am with you now, always with you. You are never alone, you must never forget that you mean everything to me, that I live only for you, your Lonesome Gal.

At some time in the course of each program, the Lonesome Gal specifically assured her listeners that these endearments were not being addressed to the hale and handsome, the clever and the well-poised, but to the shy, the withdrawn—the lonely men who had always dreamed, in their inmost reveries, of finding a lonesome girl to comfort them.

The world is literally full of such lonesome girls, she urged; like herself, they were all seeking love and companionship. Fate was unkind, however, and they were disappointed and left in unrequited loneliness, with no one to console them. On the radio, the voice was everybody's Lonesome Gal:

> Don't you see, darling, that I am only one of millions of lonely girls. I belong to him who spends his Sundays in museums, who strolls in Central Park looking sadly at the lovers there. But I am more fortunate than any of these lovers, because I have you. Do you know that I am always thinking about you? . . . You need someone to worry about you, who will look after your health, you need me. I share your hopes and your disappointments. I, your Lonesome Gal, your girl, to whom you so often feel drawn in the big city where so many are lonely. . . .

The Lonesome Gal was inundated with thousands of letters tendering proposals of marriage, the writers respectfully assuring her that she was indeed the woman for whom they had been vainly searching all their lives.

As a character in a radio program, the Lonesome Gal had certain advantages in the cultivation of para-social attachments over television offerings of a similar tenor. She was literally an unseen presence, and each of her listeners could, in his mind's eye, picture her as his fancy dictated. She could, by an act of the imagination, be almost any age or any size, have any background.

Not so Miss Nancy Berg, who began to appear last year in a five-minute television spot called *Count Sheep*.[25] She is seen at 11 A. M. each weekday. After an announcement card has flashed to warn the audience that she is about to appear, and a commercial has been read, the stage is entirely given over to Miss Berg. She emerges in a lavishly decorated bedroom clad in a peignoir, or negligee, minces around the room, stretches, yawns, jumps into bed, and then wriggles out again for a final romp with her French poodle. Then she crawls under the covers, cuddles up for the night, and composes herself for sleep. The camera pans down for an enormous close-up, and the microphones catch Miss Berg whispering a sleepy "Goodnight." From out of the distance soft music fades in, and the last thing the viewers see is a cartoon of sheep jumping over a fence. The program is over.

There is a little more to the program than this. Each early morning, Miss Berg is provided with a special bit of dialogue or business which, brief though it is, delights her audience afresh:

Once, she put her finger through a pizza pie, put the pie on a record player and what came out was Dean Martin singing "That's Amore." She has read, with expression, from "Romeo and Juliet," "Of Time and the River," and her fan mail. She has eaten grapes off a toy ferris-wheel and held an imaginary telephone conversation with some one who, she revealed when it was all over, had the wrong number.[26]

Sometimes she regales her viewers with a personal detail. For instance, she has explained that the dog which appears on the show is her own. Its name is "Phaedeaux," she disclosed coyly, pronounced "Fido."

It takes between twenty and twenty-six people, aside from Miss Berg herself, to put this show on the air; and all of them seem to be rather bemused by the success she is enjoying. Her manager, who professes himself happily baffled by the whole thing, tried to discover some of the reasons for this success in a recent interview when he was questioned about the purpose of the show:

> Purpose? The purpose was, Number 1, to get a sponsor; Number 2, to give people a chance to look at a beautiful girl at 1 o'clock in the morning; Number 3, to do some off-beat stuff. I think this girl's going to be a big star, and this was a way to get attention for her. We sure got it. She's a showman, being slightly on the screwball side, but there's a hell of a brain there. She just doesn't touch things—she caresses things. Sometimes, she doesn't say anything out loud, maybe she's thinking what you're thinking.[27]

The central fact in this explanation seems to be the one which touches on Miss Berg's ability to suggest to her audience that she is privy to, and might share, their inmost thoughts. This is precisely the impression that the Lonesome Gal attempted to create, more directly and more conversationally, in her monologue. Both programs were geared to fostering and maintaining the illusion of intimacy which we mentioned earlier in our discussion. The sexiness of both these programs must, we think, be read in this light. They are seductive in more than the ordinary sense. Sexual suggestiveness is used probably because it is one of the most obvious cues to a supposed intimacy—a catalytic for prompt sociability.

Such roles as Miss Berg and the Lonesome Gal portray require a strict adherence to a standardized portrayal of their "personalities." Their actual personalities, and the details of their backgrounds, are not allowed to become sharply focused and differentiated, for each specification of particular detail might alienate some part of the audience, or might interfere with rapport. Thus, Miss Berg, despite the apparent intimacy of her show—the audience is invited into her bedroom—refuses to disclose her "dimensions," although this is a piece of standard information freely available about movie beauties.

The Lonesome Gal was even more strict regarding personal details. Only once did she appear in a public performance away from her radio show. On that occasion she wore a black mask over her face, and was introduced to her "live" audience on the same mysteriously anonymous terms as she met her radio audience. Rumor, however, was not idle, and one may safely presume that these rumors can current to provide her with a diffuse glamour of a kind which her audience would think appropriate. It was said that she lived in Hollywood, but that she originally came from Texas, a state which, in popular folklore, enjoys a lively reputation for improbabilities and extravagances. Whispers also had it that French and Indian blood coursed in her veins, a combination all too likely to suggest wildness and passion to the stereotypes of her listeners. For the rest, nothing was known of her, and no further details were apparently ever permitted.

The Image as Artifact

The encouragement of, not to say demand for, a sense of intimacy with the persona and an appreciation of him as a "real" person is in contradiction to the fact that the image he presents is to some extent a construct—a façade—which bears little resemblance to his private character. The puritanical conventions of the contemporary media make this façade a decidedly namby-pamby one. With few exceptions, the popular figures of radio and television are, or give the appearance of being, paragons of middle-class virtue with decently modest intellectual capacities. Since some of them are really very intelligent and all of them are, like the rest of us, strong and weak, good and bad, the façade is maintained only by concealing discrepancies between the public image and the private life.

The standard technique is not to make the private life an absolute secret—for the interest of the audience cannot be ignored—but to create an acceptable façade of private life as well, a more or less contrived private image of the life behind the contrived public image. This is the work of the press agent, the publicity man, and the fan magazine. How successfully they have done their work is perhaps indicated by the current vogue of magazines devoted to the "dirt" behind the façade.[28]

Public preoccupation with the private lives of stars and personae is not self-explanatory. Sheer appreciation and understanding of their performances as actors, singers, or entertainers does not depend upon information about them as persons. And undoubtedly many members of the audience do enjoy them without knowing or caring to know about their homes, children, sports cars, or favorite foods, or keeping track of the ins and outs of their marriages and divorces. It has often been said that the Hollywood stars—and their slightly less glamorous colleagues of radio and television—are modern "heroes" in whom are embodied popular cultural values, and that the interest in them is a form of hero-worship and vicarious experience through identification. Both of these interpretations may be true; we would emphasize, however, a third motive—the confirmation and enrichment of the para-social relation with them. It may be precisely because this is basically an illusion that such an effort is required to confirm it. It seems likely that those to whom para-social relationships are important must constantly strive to overcome the inherent limitations of these relationships, either by elaborating the image of the other, or by attempting to transcend the illusion by making some kind of actual contact with him.

Given the prolonged intimacy of para-social relations with the persona, accompanied by the assurance that beyond the illusion there is a real person, it is not surprising that many members of the audience become dissatisfied and attempt to establish actual contact with him. Under exactly what conditions people are motivated to write to the performer, or to go further and attempt to meet him—to draw from him a personal response—we do not know. The fan phenomenon has been studied to some extent,[29] but fan clubs and fan demonstrations are likely to be group affairs, motivated as much by the values of collective participation with others as by devotion to the persona himself. There are obvious social rewards for the trophies of contact with the famous or notorious—from autographs to handkerchiefs dipped in the dead bandit's blood—which invite toward their possessor some shadow of the attitudes of awe or admiration originally directed to their source. One would suppose that contact with, and recognition by, the persona transfers some of his prestige and influence to the active fan. And most often such attempts to reach closer to the persona are limited to letters and to visits. But in the extreme case, the social rewards of mingling with the mighty are foregone for the satisfaction of some deeply private purpose. The follower is actually "in love" with the persona, and demands real reciprocity which the para-social relation cannot provide.

. . . The new mass media are obviously distinguished by their ability to confront a member of the audience with an apparently intimate, face-to-face association with a performer. Nowhere does this feature of their technological resources seem more forcefully or more directly displayed than in the "personality" program. In these programs a new kind of performer, the persona, is featured whose main attribute seems to be his ability to cultivate and maintain this suggested intimacy. As he appears before his audience, in program after program, he carries on recurrent social transactions with his adherents; he sustains what we have called para-social interaction. These adherents, as members of his audience, play a psychologically active role which, under some conditions, but by no means invariably passes over into the more formal, overt, and expressive activities of fan behavior.

As an implicit response to the performance of the persona, this para-social interaction is guided and to some extent controlled by him. The chief basis of this guidance and control, however, lies in the imputation to the spectator of a kind of role complementary to that of the persona himself. This imputed complementary role is social in character, and is some variant of the role or roles normally played in the spectator's primary social groups. It is defined, demonstrated, and inculcated by numerous devices of radio and television showmanship. When it has been learned, the persona is assured that the entire transaction between himself and the audience—of which his performance is only one phase—is being properly completed by the unseen audience.

Seen from this standpoint, it seems to follow that there is no such discontinuity between everyday and para-social experience everyday and para-social experience as is suggested by the common practice, among observers of these media, of using the analogy of fantasy or dream in the interpretation of programs which are essentially dramatic in character. The relationship of the devotee to the persona is, we suggest, experienced as of the same order as, and related to, the network of actual social relations. This, we believe, is even more the case when the persona becomes a common object to the members of the primary groups in which the spectator carries on his everyday life. As a matter of fact, it seems profitable to consider the interaction with the persona as a phase of the role-enactments of the spectator's daily life.

. . . In essence, therefore, we would like to expand and capitalize on the truism that the persona and the "personality" programs are part of the lives of millions of people, by asking how both are assimilated, and by trying to discover what effects these responses have on the attitudes and actions of the audiences who are so devoted to and absorbed in this side of American culture.

NOTES

[1] They may move out into positions of leadership in the world at large as they become famous and influential. Frank Sinatra, for example, has become known as a "youth leader." Conversely, figures from the political world, to choose another example, may become media "personalities" when they appear regularly, Fiorello LaGuardia, the late Mayor of New York, is one such case.

[2] Merton's discussion of the attitude toward Kate Smith of her adherents exemplifies, with much circumstantial detail, what we have said above. See Robert K. Merton, Marjorie Fiske, and Alberta Curtis, *Mass Persuasion; The Social Psychology of a War Bond Drive;* New York, Harper, 1946; especially Chapter 6.

[3] There does remain the possibility that over the course of his professional life the persona, responding to influences from his audience, may develop new conceptions of himself and his role.

[4] Dave Garroway as told to Joe Alex Morris, "I Lead a Goofy Life," *The Saturday Evening Post,* February 11, 1956; p. 62.

[5] Reference footnote 4; p. 64.

[6] See, for instance: George H. Mead, *Mind, Self and Society;* Chicago, Univ. of Chicago Press, 1934. Walter Coutu, *Emergent Human Nature;* New York, Knopf, 1949. Rosalind Dymond, "Personality and Empathy," *J. Consulting Psychol.* (1950) 14:343–350.

[7] Burke uses this expression to describe an attitude evoked by formal rhetorical devices, but it seems equally appropriate here. See Kenneth Burke, *A Rhetoric of Motives;* New York, Prentice-Hall, 1950; p. 58.

[8] This is in contrast to the closed system of the drama, in which all the roles are predetermined in their mutual relations.

[9] Kenneth Burke, *Attitudes Toward History Vol. 1;* New York, New Republic Publishing Co., 1937; see, for instance, p. 104.

[10] See Merton's acute analysis of the audience's demand for "sincerity" as a reassurance against manipulation. Reference footnote 2: pp. 142–146.

[11] These attributes have been strikingly discussed by Mervyn LeRoy, a Hollywood director, in a recent book. Although he refers specifically to the motion-picture star, similar notions are common in other branches of show business. "What draws you to certain people?" he asks. "I have said before that you can't be a really fine actress or actor without heart. You also have to possess the ability to project that heart, that feeling and emotion. The sympathy in your eyes will show. The audience has to feel sorry for the person on the screen. If there aren't moments when, rightly or wrongly, he moves the audience to sympathy, there's an actor who will never be big box-office." Mervyn LeRoy and Alyce Canfield, *It Takes More Than Talent;* New York, Knopf, 1953; p. 114.

[12] Once an actor has succeeded in establishing a good relationship with his audience in a particular kind of dramatic role, he may be "typed" in that role. Stereotyping in the motion-picture industry is often rooted in the belief that sustained rapport with the audience can be achieved by repeating past success. (This principle is usually criticized as detrimental to the talent of the actor, but it is a *sine qua non* for the persona whose professional success depends upon creating and sustaining a plausible and unchanging identity.) Sometimes, indeed, the Hollywood performer will actually take his name from a successful role; this is one of the principles on which Warner Brothers Studios selects the names of some of its ac-

tors. For instance, Donna Lee Hickey was renamed Mae Wynn after a character she portrayed, with great distinction, in *The Caine Mutiny*. See "Names of Hollywood Actors," *Names* (1955) 3:116.

[13] The "loyalty" which is demanded of the audience is not necessarily passive or confined only to patronizing the persona's performance. Its active demonstration is called for in charity appeals, "marathons," and "telethons"; and, of course, it is expected to be freely transferable to the products advertised by the performer. Its most active form is represented by the organization of fan clubs with programs of activities and membership obligations, which give a continuing testimony of loyalty.

[14] Comedians on radio and television frequently chide their audience if they do not laugh at the appropriate places, or if their response is held to be inadequate. The comedian tells the audience that if they don't respond promptly, he won't wait, whereupon the audience usually provides the demanded laugh. Sometimes the chiding is more oblique, as when the comedian interrupts his performance to announce that he will fire the writer of the unsuccessful joke. Again, the admonition to respond correctly is itself treated as a joke and is followed by a laugh.

[15] Coutu, reference footnote 6; p. 294.

[16] See, for example, W. Lloyd Warner and William E. Henry, "The Radio Day Time Serial: A Symbolic Analysis," *Genetic Psychol. Monographs* (1948) 37:3–71, the study of a daytime radio serial program in which it is shown that upper-middle-class women tend to reject identification with lower-middle-class women represented in the drama. Yet some people are willing to take unfamiliar roles. This appears to be especially characteristic of the intellectual whose distinction is not so much that he has cosmopolitan tastes and knowledge, but that he has the capacity to transcend the limits of his own culture in his identifications. Remarkably little is known about how this ability is developed.

[17] Most students of the mass media occupy a cultural level somewhat above that of the most popular programs and personalities of the media, and necessarily look down upon them. But it should not be forgotten that for many millions indulgence in these media is a matter of looking up. Is it not also possible that some of the media permit a welcome regression, for some, from the higher cultural standards of their present status? This may be one explanation of the vogue of detective stories and science fiction among intellectuals, and might also explain the escape downward from middle-class standards in the literature of "low life" generally.

[18] It is frequently charged that the media's description of this side of life is partial, shallow, and often false. It would be easier and more profitable to evaluate these criticisms if they were formulated in terms of role-theory. From the viewpoint of any given role it would be interesting to know how well the media take account of the values and expectations of the role-reciprocators. What range of legitimate variations in role performance is acknowledged? How much attention is given to the problems arising from changing roles, and how creatively are these problems handled? These are only a few of the many similar questions which at once come to mind.

[19] There is a close analogy here with one type of newspaper human-interest story which records extreme instances of role-achievement and their rewards. Such stories detail cases of extreme longevity, marriages of especially long duration, large numbers of children; deeds of heroism—role performance under "immpossible" conditions; extraordinary luck, prizes, and so on.

[20] Dave Garroway, after making the point that he has many "devout" admirers, goes on to say that "some of them . . . were a bit too devout." He tells the story of one lady "from a Western state" who "arrived in Chicago [where he was then broadcasting], registered at a big hotel as Mrs. Dave Garroway, opened several charge accounts in my name and established a joint bank account in which she deposited a large sum of money. Some months later she took a taxi to my hotel and informed the desk clerk she was moving in. He called a detective agency that we had engaged to check up on her, and they persuaded her to return home. Since then there have been others, but none so persistent." Reference footnote 4; p. 62.

[21] This group presumably includes those for whom "Lonely Hearts" and "Pen Pal" clubs operate.

[22] While the examples which follow are of female personae addressing themselves to male audiences, it should be noted that for a time there was also a program on television featuring *The Continental*, who acted the part of a debonair foreigner and whose performance consisted of murmuring endearing remarks to an invisible female audience. He wore evening clothes and cut a figure in full conformity with the American stereotype of a suave European lover.

[23] This program apparently evoked no very great amount of comment or criticism in the American press, and we are indebted to an article in a German illustrated weekly for details about the show, and for the

verbatim quotations from the Lonesome Gal's monologue which we have retranslated into English. See "Ich bin bei dir, Liebling . . . Weltbild Welibild (Munich), March 1, 1952; p. 12.

[24] This is in piquant contrast to the popular singers, the modesty of whose voice and mein is often belied by the sexiness of the words in the songs they sing.

[25] The details relating to this show are based on Gilbert Millstein, "Tired of it All?" *The New York Times Magazine,* September 18, 1955; p. 44. See also "Beddy-Bye," *Time,* August 15, 1955; p. 45.

[26] *The New York Times Magazine,* reference footnote 25.

[27] *The New York Times Magazine,* reference footnote 25.

[28] Such magazines as *Uncensored* and *Confidential* (which bears the subtitle, "Tells the Facts and Names the Names") enjoy enormous circulations, and may be thought of as the very opposite of the fan magazine. They claim to "expose" the person behind the persona.

[29] M. F. Thorp, *America at the Movies;* New Haven, Yale Univ. Press, 1939. S. Stansfeld Sargent, *Social Psychology:* New York, Ronald Press, 1950. K. P. Berliant, "The Nature and Emergence of Fan Behavior" (unpublished M.A. Thesis, Univ. of Chicago).

20.

Communicating Intention

George N. Gordon

. . . The author has . . . written elsewhere about intentions calling them by a more general rubric, "objectives of communication." [1] In the broad study of communications, it is, however, surprising to discover how little attention has been given intention. Much consideration has, one imagines, been euphemized away in studies of motivation in general, or subsumed into such abused terms as "propaganda," "education," "public relations," "public information," "press relations," and their kin. In the first place, a communicator is usually assumed either to *have* intentions or *not* to have them. (The wisdom of the Victorian virginal query "What are your intentions, sir?" presumes that the suitor *must* have *some sort* of intentions.) In the second place, *if* one has intentions, it is also generally understood that a communicator may (if he wishes) simply and directly articulate them. Or, if an auditor is clever or has a proper method, he may infer them backwards, from message to composer's frontal lobes.

Intention is probably a quality of all communication, just as "motivation" (as the word is usually used by psychologists) is involved with all behavior—as long as the communication and/or the behavior involves human beings. [2] This cause and effect assumption (and assumption it is) rests at the heart of our behavioral sciences, some of our philosophies, and nearly every useful generalization that has ever been

---

Reprinted by permission from *Persuasion: The Theory and Practice of Manipulative Communication,* Hastings House, 1971.

offered about communications. Like motivations, intentions may, of course, be extremely obscure, both to persons sending or receiving a communication, and may, as in the instance of blushing or belching, function entirely beyond the control of the former. As also observed previously, many types of intention, again like motivations, may operate in that dim universe we so glibly label "the unconscious."

The qualitative question that the concept of intentions forces us to ask about human transactions is "Why?" And this question is frequently far more difficult to answer than it should be. Accordingly, we usually credit intention with a psychological power that is, on its face, unmistakable in a communication at the focus of our attention; that is, we note *overt* intention as intention.[3] *Covert* intention we often credit with nothing, or (if we are so oriented), with everything, as convention demands at the time.

The Framework of Intention

One of the few serious considerations of intention *per se* (not in a part of some other discussion) has appeared in the writings of J. A. Richards. His description of what function intention serves in poetry, in fact, is so concise that it deserves direct quotation:

> Finally . . . there is the speaker's intention, his aim, *conscious or unconscious,* the effect he is endeavoring to promote. Ordinarily he speaks for a purpose, and his purpose modifies his speech. The understanding of it is part of the whole business of apprehending his meaning. Unless we know what he is trying to do, we can hardly estimate the measure of his success. Yet the number of readers who admit such considerations might make a faint-hearted writer despair. Sometimes, of course, he will purpose no more than to state his thoughts or to express his feelings . . .
>
> Frequently his intention operates through and satisfies itself in a combination of other functions. Yet it has effects not reducible to their effects. It may govern the stress laid upon points in the argument . . . . It controls the "plot" in the largest sense of the word, and is at work whenever the author is "hiding his hand." And it has especial importance in dramatic and semi-dramatic literature . . . .[4]

As a quality of communication which transcends both the mediums employed (narrative, picture or drama) and the instrument chosen to distribute the communication, intention accordingly seems more vital operationally than as the critical tool Richards discussed above, an insight that he himself seems to recognize in the full course of his writings. Thanks to his acumen, the student is able to generalize the notion of intention to cover nearly the total field of human communication, no matter how expressed. The mechanistically oriented may wish to understand intention as the basic coloration of the various facets of human interactions. Merely to *state* (or *be*) is, to a degree, to imply an objective from a communications viewpoint, if one is effectively stating that he is a person and has an identity in a given culture at a certain moment.[5] This basic coloration is then overlaid with many other hues—some visible to the naked eye, some requiring special illumination—which, while they are usually in flux, signal in behavior (as audited by others) certain human objectives.

. . . Let us note the report in a recent best seller on how political figures are merchandised on television these days. The writer quotes an idealistic freelance film maker who was employed to make campaign spots for a candidate and party, both of which he despised. Talking about the political specialties with whom he is forced to work, he says, "Oh, I don't know. The effect is (insidious), but I don't know what we are in our intent. If we were really being charlatans, we would give much more study to the psychological part . . . But these people aren't that smart. They're fools in fact . . . That's because they don't *know* what they're after. Their product is amorphous—it has to be amorphous—because so are they . . . I mean the Nixon people with their identical expressions and their identical dark suits . . ." [6]

The point of the book—that politicians may these days be merchandised like products sold on television—is moot. But the point that the film maker comes upon is equally as trenchant and important, namely, that even under conditions which ostensibly provide the clearest of objectives for communication (getting a man elected to the American presidency), the framework of intention, while ever-present, is nevertheless obscure, subject to forces and counter-forces and sometimes appears at cross purposes with itself to a knowledgeable outside observer. The speaker knows that the framework is there, in fact, what it is supposed to support, and yet the behaviors of the communicators appear to him indecisive, unclear, and, in his words, "amorphous," despite their eventual prospects of "success" in making good their intention.

. . . To prove by any reliable method that the intentional framework is, indeed, omnipresent in communications is not possible. It is another assumption, based upon a faith in what observation, reason, and some psychological evidence tells us. It is (and has always been) also accepted as an assumption in most artistic criticism—once the crude notion of "art for its own sake" has been passed over by a critic, a move that he must make, unless he merely wants to repeat a phrase in Latin.

What our recognition of the framework accomplishes for us at this point may be summed up in the provisional conclusion that persuasion is not a class of human intercourse separable (in most instances) from other kinds of communication. It is instead the degree and direction of an already present quality, that of intention. Whether or not all human communication may therefore fairly be termed "persuasive" is another matter, requiring a fuller knowledge of the multitude of human "plots" with their infinite number of relationships in which men are involved, a knowledge that no mind will ever contain. To guess, however, that a great percentage of it may be properly called "persuasive" is relatively safe. What we mean is simply that *the intention present in a communication is clear or potent or meaningful enough to be recognized by some auditor (if only an observer) as designed to intrude upon another person's logical or psychological processes. . . .*

Intention and Consciousness

One might think that the separation of conscious from unconscious objectives of communication is a relatively simple matter, and so it was before the present age of psychoanalysis. This ubiquitous phenomenon of our time and place, although diminishing as a form of high fashion and cocktail party chatter, has put an enormous strain upon the whole concept of motivation and helped thoroughly to confuse the matter of intention. Those of us who have done our time (and paid our price) on the psychoanalytic couch know from personal experience how the matter of intention concerning any of our behaviors—or thoughts—may be peeled off from layer to layer to layer of interpretation when we are faced with nondirective silence of a skilled analyst or his monosyllables like "Eh?" or "So?" [7]

The *theory* of the unconscious is, of course, the primary culprit. . . . Freud brought a new type of systematic thought to the concept of the unconscious, related it fundamentally to the metaphor and symbol (to what end we have noted in the previous chapter), and articulated a theory of mind that was sophisticated enough to contain the paradox of a motivational reservoir that could be neither seen, heard, felt, tasted, intuited, nor brought to consciousness directly. The Freudian contribution was heroic and formidable, no matter what the objections of his detractors, if merely by virtue of its influence on art, literature and criticism during the first half of the current century—to say nothing of its more ambiguous function in psychotherapy.[8]

Because the ambiguities surrounding the idea of consciousness bear so critically upon intention (and therefore upon the ultimate process of persuasion), let us examine them more closely than the usual psychoanalytic perspective permits. Psychoanalysis is, after all, primarily intended to be a therapeutic device, despite other services to which it has been called. Freud wisely chose to discuss most of his insights into the unconscious in the format of the case study, and most training given psychoanalysts today centers upon processes in their own unconsciouses or those of their patients. In other words, the problem of consciousness is usually regarded as the dynamic activity of an organism or agent, not primarily as an inevitable part of human experience. Even the generalized unconscious processes identified by Freud were named after agents (or people) drawn from the drama, not identified as abstract dispositions.[9]

Kenneth Burke, however, has manfully described eight manifestations of the unconscious, heavily dependent, of course, upon Freud, and quite useful in application to the notion of intent, largely because they shade for us the usual tendency to sever strictly conscious and unconscious phenomena one from the other as if they were a totally different class of considerations in black and white, a tendency also of many psychoanalysts. Human motivations, unfortunately, admit of few simplistic formulae, particularly those relating to *genus,* for two apparent reasons: 1.) the variability of perception and feeling from individual to individual, and 2.) the interdependence of functions which entwine neurological, physical, emotional, mental and environment factors together. Only in extremely simple matters (reflex reactions, for instance) or among very simple people (some behavioral psychologists, for instance) are such complexities avoided.

Burke's categories, in essence, are: [10]

1. The unconscious processes of the body, including all the activities of growth, repair, metabolism, etc., as well as those functions involved in perception, automatic muscle activities, and certain facets of our thought processes that are probably organic but of which we are unaware.
2. Past experiences, either those that have been forgotten or repressed from our own

living, or those that may be vestigial in our human state and have been passed on to us by culture or hereditary factors which we cannot bring to consciousness.

3. Past experiences of which we are unaware or have been forgotten but that may be recalled to memory, given the proper association or stimulus.
4. Unconscious material which is the part of a subpersonality that we at one time assumed (or presently assume) when drugged or exposed to stress or indulging in artistic fancy.
5. The unconscious meaning and motivations intrinsic to symbols which are used consciously, the presence of which we are unaware of but, nevertheless, feel "right" in a given situation.
6. One's "societal unconscious" (the author's phrase, not Burke's), a sort of Hegelian antithesis to conscious behavior; the unnoticed generalized reaction to all intended, motivated behavior, best described by Marxian notion of class consciousness that implies, also, a concept of class unconsciousness (as in the case of the "bourgeois mind" that cannot perceive the true dynamics of social reality).
7. The unconscious manifestations we like to term "intuition," or (sometimes) "instinct," but which are probably really flashes of highly sophisticated, complex judgment (like the "stroke of genius" that revealed the unconscious to Freud) sometimes called a "creative flash."
8. We all operate, at times, on an unconscious level of sheer stupidity, more happily called "error," "ignorance," "uncertainty" and "confusion" by Burke.

How many of these categories may now be severed *absolutely* from their associations with consciousness? The reader must answer this question for himself,[11] and will naturally use himself as the agent for his conclusion. If he is not blinded by some form of doctrine, he will notice that the conscious and unconscious do not cleave from each other as neatly as he was told in psychology class, or as dramatists and writers often ask us to believe.

The Jekyll Hyde story (in which the doctor remains aware of the behavior of this bestial alter-ego) indicates how great was Robert Louis Stevenson's psychological sophistication, apparently sharper than that of his contemporary, Oscar Wilde in *The Picture of Dorian Gray,* in which the decaying portrait does not directly affect Dorian's person until he stabs it and kills himself. Or perhaps Wilde's commentary on Victorian depravity (and doubtless his own emotions) was even a little wiser than Stevenson's retelling of what is, in fact, a classical theme. Both stories, however, prod with considerable prescience the mutuability of the conscious and nonconscious experiences of their central characters, who represent neither heroes nor villains but simply people like the authors themselves, fancifully extenuated into fascinating parables.

Unconscious intentions may be manifest in a number of ways, all relevant to communications. First, an individual (or group) may have articulated a conscious objective but actually be motivated by an unconscious one—a matter of degree rather than kind. Most professional actors, for instance, excuse their appearances in trash as the noble pursuit of pelf, while, in fact, many of them enjoy any kind of theatrical excursion. An entire nation may have articulated aims of the loftiest sort concerning the substitution, in its schools, of vocational for liberal education, and actually be responding to the pressure of labor unions to keep child labor out of the market.

Are such contradictions hypocritical or dishonest? They may be in certain instances, but, once again, we cannot judge. An advertising copywriter may consciously enjoy the breakfast cereal he is lionizing in prose and harbor unconscious resentments towards the product *only* because he has to sing its praises. On the other hand, he may receive some kind of gratification from thinking himself a prostitute, while unconsciously he loves what he is doing. Or he may, both consciously and unconsciously, enjoy or despise his work. In any case, he does it; and his finished products are likely to be similar, regardless of his intentions. The matter of conscious or unconscious intent is, from a moral point of view, irrelevant except to the man himself.

Second, an illusion of conscious intent may be employed to dissemble a *real* conscious intent that in turn articulates perfectly with an unconscious intent. Here we may list "campaign promises" intended to get a politician elected, which is exactly what he is after. Again, we are speaking of provisional matters; it is not naïve to assume that politicians frequently fool themselves consciously with their own campaign rhetoric. Self-deception is a form of intent but operates often through short periods of time.

Third, in the absence of any evidence to the contrary, a communication may have an entirely unconscious intent. The "body English" that seems mysteriously to notify a member of the opposite sex that he or she attracts one may be just this sort of communication—although the limited vocabulary of the "English" may be learned quickly and also employed consciously as a signal system.[12] Such involuntary messages (not necessarily sexual) seem the common property of all societies, and their contents vary with the cultures no matter how simple the realm of discourse, for reasons yet to be discovered by behavioral scientists. But, once again, the margins of the unconscious in such discourse have been far from clearly drawn.

The Focus of Intent

It is difficult for many students of communications to comprehend the degree to which intention may modify the meaning of a given communication, in spite of the fact that most of us in informal situations either use statements of intention to influence our actions, or imply intentions from others that we then construe as the content of what they are trying to communicate to us. Examples include teachers who refuse, for instance, to believe that they are influenced in their grading of students (particularly on subjective tests) by what they assume a particular student's intentions to be. The home economics faculty of a major university once created a storm because an academic department was about to bestow a doctorate (in a sociologically oriented discipline) upon a man who had created a national reputation as an unorthodox nutrition expert. His intentions, they reasoned, for wanting a Ph.D. degree were bad. They assumed he merely wanted to be called "doctor," and, therefore, they also assumed that his scholarship must be faulty, his sponsor corrupt and the academic department in which he worked beneath contempt. The fact that he was an excellent student and had written a competent dissertation meant little to them in the light of what they considered the man's intentions to be.

Those of us who have tried to argue with policemen to the effect that we did not intend to light a cigarette in the subway, or drive over a speed limit know, roughly, that sometimes, under some circumstances, the intent we manage to get others to perceive in *us* may modify their behavior. To return to our Victorian virgin, there is some likelihood that she will submit to her seducer, if he can convince her that his intentions are to marry her. While intention is certainly neither a medium nor an instrument of communication, its influence on the nature of interpersonal activities is obviously critical. What is often misunderstood is where the proper focus of interest should be placed in communication and what should be at the primary attention of the observer or analyst of communications relevant to the communication process in which he is involved, as well as the reasons for the communication.

Historians, biographers, novelists, dramatists and some psychologists often lead us astray in this regard, because they are interested only in the motivational factors surrounding the intention of communications and no other possibilities, conscious or unconscious, inherent in them. The intention of Edward R. Murrow's famous television broadcast in 1952 on his *See It Now* program concerning the witch hunting activities of Joseph McCarthy was obviously to discredit the junior senator from Wisconsin, as his competent biographer observes.[13] The intention of Hamlet's coaching of the players was unquestionably to "catch the conscience of the king." The intention of Franklin Roosevelt's promise in 1940 to the "mothers and fathers of America" that Americans would not die in "foreign wars" was undoubtedly to win what looked as if it might be a close presidential election.

Judging these communications (and communicators) in their perspectives above, we are led to ask two relevant questions regarding intentions: Were they conscious or unconscious? Were they true objectives—that is, honest or dishonest? In all cases, they were conscious; in all cases they were true or honest, as far as we know (granting that FDR was the political animal we have been led to believe).

Another aspect of intention concerning them, however, comes to us by way of certain experimental data from the discipline of social psychology. One must be extremely wary of such data for a number of reasons irrelevant here, but these particular studies—and others like them—are revealing both conceptually and in what they show about the behaviors of the subjects involved in them. They result largely from a number of studies performed by psychologist Carl Hovland and various associates in the 1950's.[14]

While Hovland arrived at no breath-taking conclusions, he did articulate the notion of "source credibility" which is, in effect, the force in a communication that a *perception of intent* (right, wrong or irrelevant) has upon the nature (in this case the believability) of a message at hand. While his results (and theorizing) indicate quite specifically that if the content of a message is believed for itself, its source is rarely questioned, more ambiguous communications are judged by criteria relating to the "trustworthiness" of the source. In other words, credibility depends upon the implications of intention.

In one of his experiments, Hovland exposed a group of students to a series of magazine articles on various subjects attributed to different "high credibility" and "low credibility" sources. He and Weiss report, "Under the conditions of this experiment, neither the acquisition nor the retention of *factual information* appears to be affected by the trustworthiness of the source. But changes in opinion are significantly related to the trustworthiness of the source used in communications." [15] Other experimental and theoretical work has also shown that the so-called "prestige" of a communicator affects the way in which messages of various kinds are interpreted. [16]

Data such as these have been available for a considerable time and are usually construed as warnings to writers and propagandists to dress up the trustworthiness of their sources, or to cloak some devious confidence scheme in the prestige of a celebrity or status symbol. They have rarely been considered as significant statements concerning the perception of intention and its relationship to the manner in which transactions of meaning are modified by it. Nor have they been considered in anything but cursory fashion as a component of various kinds of communications under differing conditions, not merely newspaper items, magazine articles, slogans and other convenient experimental material handed to college students in test situations.

Both notions of this sort are suggested here: First, the main focus of attention to any sort of communication (on the part of the communicator or an auditor) is not the nature of the communication but usually how it is likely to be construed. Second, such constructions may attend every type of communication imaginable, although the historian, biographer, novelist, dramatist and some psychologists are then at a loss to explain how this internal process may work, except to admit that different people see things in different ways.

To many, Murrow's motives at the time of the McCarthy broadcast were self-serving and self-aggrandizing. Hamlet's motives, to King Claudius, were devilish; the Lord knows what the Players thought (although Tom Stoppard, an unusual playwright, takes a magnificent guess [17]). Roosevelt's promise (or implied promise) to keep America out of World War II was a solemn pledge to some. That *most* people believed one intent or another in each of these instances is irrelevant; observing the functions of the qualities of communications does not constitute popularity contests or political exercises decided by majority vote. The important point for the student of persuasion is the many possibilities which the focus of intention may have, *considering the nature of the perceptions of the individual who responds to the stimulus involved.*

Elsewhere the writer has considered and discussed "misread objectives," [18] too facile a notion to explain the variability of the perception of intention, once the focus is turned upon the *recipient* of a communication. The process is far more subtle psychologically than the mere tendency to impose expectations (or selective criteria) upon communications and perceive them accordingly—the conventional explanations of such misreadings. This tendency, it appears on second thought, is discovered not only in so-called communications behavior, but is obviously (so obviously that it is often missed) a qualifying element of all perceptions and of all people, places and things, as well as messages, and of objects and actions and animals as well. To speak, therefore, of selective perception is to speak of *all* perception as it always functions, not to describe *one* form or peculiarity of normal or average perception, as one judges either or both.

In these terms, then, may a building have an intention? May a can of beans on a supermarket shelf? May a statue, a gerbil, a telephone, a calendar, a barometer? Of course they may, depending upon the perceptual disposition *of the individual observing them*. To a hungry man, a sandwich is to eat (a critical point in the study of persuasion to which we shall return later). To some, a cat is to stroke, as the children's book observes. To others, it is to recoil from. And to still others, it is to sneeze and break out in hives because of. Depending, therefore, upon how we direct the focus of observation, the quality of intention of any message may be relevant or irrelevant to our concerns, depending upon what we are looking at and what part of consciousness we audit it with.

Any simpler observation than this one (those, for instance, accepted in much contemporary behavioral science), are entirely inadequate for a holistic view of the communication of intention in a many-faceted cultural field including, often, situations in which vast numbers of individuals are exposed to single messages with possibly ambiguous—or hidden—intentions.[19] What is less significant about an intention than its motive, is the way in which it is perceived. And this perception is variable among different people. It may even vary for the same individual within a short period of time. Most pat psychological formulae, therefore, by which we presently judge the power of intention do not accord with empirical observation, except in limited, experimental settings that realistically describe a behavior process *up to a point*. They are far more useful, usually, as springboards for conjecture than evidences of cause and effect.

Manifestation of Intention

Our study of persuasion is, in some respects, almost entirely an inquiry into the nature of intention and into its focus and its effects, considering particularly the multi-faceted perceptions of the attentions of others and, most important, what people in contemporary cultures are likely to *do* in response to them. This latter consideration almost constitutes a description of the process of persuasion as a form of human behavior: simply the behavioral manifestations that occur as the result of how individuals regard the intentions of others in interacting with them. Students of the process place these transactions in classes of behaviors usually called "communications," and are especially interested in them when the intentions are purveyed to large audiences by means of one of the techniques for devices associated with disseminating narratives, pictures or re-enactments.

. . . In most arts, the more obtrusive an intention, the less likely is the work of art, frequently, to first enhance that objective and second, to communicate successfully on a cognitive or emotional level.[20] Of course, obtrusiveness and the degree to which it manifests itself anywhere is not a precise concept. It is frequently judged in reverse, from effect to cause. If a persuasive communication fails to persuade, *and* the intention seems overstated, we may assume that it was, in this instance, obtrusive. Yet, under some circumstances, judgment may be applied to this matter without reasoning backwards.

The inappropriate obtrusiveness of intention into communication may be understood as operating on a scale from "no intrusion" to "complete dominance." The objective of the communication must then be located somewhere on this scale. The famous film *Bonnie and Clyde* had intentions. They are all locatable on a continuum. So did the controversial play, *The Deputy*. Now, each of these communications must be held up to particular audiences to which they were exposed in order to judge the degree of obtrusiveness of the intentions. This will also tell us the degree to which these communications probably succeeded in "moving" their spectators.

In the case of *Bonnie and Clyde,* if we assume that the objective was to stimulate empathy by means of filmic violence (one possible objective), it succeeded admirably, considering the young, excitable, emotionally vulnerable audiences to which such types of movies appeal. *The Deputy,* on the other hand, as an anti-Catholic polemic (a fair summation, probably, of the intention of its American production), was largely an irrelevant and overly didactic intellectual exercise to most of the reasonably educated, older people who witnessed it. Its failure to carry through its intention, therefore, had to do largely with the over-emphasis, over-statement and the spurious cultural logic of that intent shown in the drama.

Conclusion

 . . . Intention in communications is closely related to all forms of motivation in the flax of social life. It is a quality which, although it appears much like a medium of communication, transcends immediately perceptible characteristics of the three mediums communications and is formulated in many different ways. It is not a *class* of human transaction but an *objective,* designed to intrude upon another person's logical or psychological processes.

Unconscious intentions are frequent and are related to the numerous kinds of unconscious behavior it is possible to observe (or feel) in human transactions. Some of these are related strictly to Freudian notions of unconscious; some are not. Combinations of unconscious and conscious intentions reveal interesting insights into how and why people regard certain communications the way they do, and whether or not a communication is likely to achieve its objective. From a theoretical perspective, the problem of intent is largely psychological, centering on the way (or ways) that given audiences perceive the intentions of communicators and their communications. A good deal of experimental (and some theoretical) data exist upon the various curiosities visible in this process. What they accomplish, at present, is to force the re-evaluation of the once generally accepted concept of "selective perception" (and other theories) to explain why certain individuals do or do not respond to the intention of certain kinds of persuasive messages.

Intention also plays a critical role in artistic, affective and emotional communications, often intruding into them in such a degree that their own didactic purposes are somehow negated or reversed. Didactic trends have appeared all through the history of art and letters and are with us at present, particularly in education. In the latter field, they are currently shifting toward a naïve but positivistic (and therefore highly quantifiable) trend towards shifting the intentional aspects of all schooling towards the articulation and measurement of certain kinds of observable cognitive terminal behaviors, especially those that may most easily be graded by machines. In both art and education, evidence exists of wide misconstruction and misunderstanding of the quality of intention and of its role in communication and persuasion.

NOTES

[1] See George N. Gordon, *Languages of Communications* (G.N.G., LC), pp. 204–218.

[2] I shall leave to Arthur C. Clarke and his colleagues in the field of technological make believe the problem of whether computers—or similar instruments—may have intentions. For an amusing treatment of this notion, note the "character" of Hal in his *2001, A Space Odyssey* (New York: New American Library, 1968), or the film or both.

[3] I have previously suggested—and will not emphasize it here—that *artlessly* framed intentions in discourse are frequently all we are talking about when we refer to "objectives" or "intentions," and that artful ones—even those that are downright commercial—often slip by unnoticed. Such artlessness is, of course, frequently what commercial communicators think they are striving for, calling it "product indentification," or lionizing the nuisance value of some artless advertisement. See G.N.G., LC, pp. 206–207.

[4] Richards, *Practical Criticism,* pp. 182–183.

[5] Certain analysts of interpersonal communications claim that from a metacommunications viewpoint (that is, communications about communications), it is impossible for anyone *not* to communicate, because the very act of remaining silent "says" something about the individual involved. On its own level of analysis—and delimiting its application only to certain special instruments of communications under certain conditions—this observation is certainly true and valuable, perhaps, to students of communications breakdowns in mental illness, patient-therapist relationships and human relations gambits. See Paul Watzlawick, Janet II. Beavin, Don D. Jackson, *Pragmatics of Human Communication* (New York: W. W. Norton Co., 1967), pp. 48–51.

[6] Joe McGinnis, *The Selling of the President* (New York: Trident Press, 1969), p. 116.

[7] Let me recommend highly here (for nearly everything but its jejune, contrived ending) "Joyce MacIver's" novel, *The Frog Pond* (New York: George Braziller, 1961), that I read *before* an extensive bout with psychoanalysis and, at that time, dismissed as fanciful sensationalism. I have since re-read it and now think it is an excellent, realistic and delightfully irreverent item of cultural history.

[8] A good layman's approach to this topic is J. P. Chaplin, *The Unconscious* (New York: Ballantine Books, 1960). Chaplin, a non-therapeutically oriented psychologist at the University of Vermont has, in a number of books, dealt effectively with obtuse psychological matters in clear English.

[9] The most familiar are the Oedipus and Electra complexes, but by the time one finishes with Freud's followers in this labeling process, one has run through much Greek mythology, Shakespeare and the Bible. The agent is omnipresent.

[10] These categories have been modified from those of Burke, *op. cit.,* pp. 67–72.

[11] Burke's purpose in devising this list is to make a similar point, namely that the unconscious need not be invariably related to the Freudian notion of repression, as it was by Freud and so often is at present by psychoanalysts.

[12] The oddest such system (usually employed unconsciously) was pointed out to me some years ago by a Freudian psychiatrist, and both study and experience tend to confirm it. The signal of sexual excitation from certain women sitting with crossed legs is the repeated rapid swinging of the top leg creating thereby a certain amount of genital stimulation. The swinging occurs at the time the male (usually) object of attraction is *speaking,* and it stops when his voice stops. Confirmation of the validity of this neuromuscular manifestation of intention requires research more intensive than I am competent to give it. See

the amusing article on the work (mainly) of Dr. Ray Birdwhistell on body communication in Flora Davis, "The Way We Speak 'Body Language,' " *The New York Times Magazine,* May 31, 1970, pp. 8–9, 29, 31, 32, 33, 41–42, and the more questionable propositions in the dubious book, Julius Fast, *Body Language* (New York: M. Evans and Co., Inc., 1970).

[13] Alexander Kendrick, *Prime Time* (Boston: Little, Brown and Co., 1969), pp. 50–54.

[14] See Carl Hovland, Irving L. Janis, and Harold Kelley, *Communication and Persuasion* (New Haven: Yale University Press, 1953), pp. 19–55, and Carl I. Hovland and Walter Weiss, "The Influence of Source Credibility on Communications Effectiveness" in Daniel Katz (ed.), *Public Opinion and Propaganda* (New York: The Dryden Press, 1954), pp. 337–347.

[15] Hovland and Weiss, *op. cit.,* p. 345.

[16] See Helen Block Lewis, "An Experiment on the Operation of Prestige Suggestion" in Guy E. Swanson. *et. al., Readings in Social Psychology* (New York: Henry Holt and Co., 1952), pp. 18–29.

[17] See Tom Stoppard, *Rosencrantz and Guildenstern are Dead* (New York: The Grove Press, Inc. 1967). "We're tragedians, you see," says the Player, "We follow directions—there is no *choice* involved. The bad end unhappily, the good unluckily. That is what tragedy means," (p. 80) when the plot of Hamlet's drama is criticized by Guildenstern.

[18] See G.N.C., LC, pp. 215–217, and the notation there that pertinent material on the distortion of apperception can be found in Bernard Berelson and Gary Steiner, *Human Behavior* (New York: Harcourt, Brace and World, Inc., 1964), pp. 183–187, 530–532.

[19] Vance Packard, for instance, made much of the supposed intentions of advertisers and motivational researchers in *The Hidden Persuaders* (New York: David McKay, Inc., 1957), and sold a lot of books. His well-meant warnings seem today considerably overstated, not because advertisers are any less covetous than he implies, but because translating these intentional into subliminal appeals is far more difficult to accomplish than Packard was led to believe by the glib behavioral "scientists" (a word loosely used in this context) that advertising agencies consult on these arcane matters.

[20] This phenomenon is somewhat like "the law (of) Reversed Effect," which is by no means a "law" and is definitely not *regularly* applicable to any class of communications, although intentions may often "boomerang" in various ways. See J.A.C. Brown, *The Techniques of Persuasion* (Baltimore: Penguin Books, 1963), pp. 80–81. Also note the more extensive discussion of the "boomerang" in various ways. See J.A.C. Brown, *The Techniques of Persuasion* (Baltimore: Penguin Books, 1963), pp. 80–81. Also note the more extensive discussion of the "boomerang" of intentional communications in Robert K. Merton, *Social Theory and Society and Social Structure,* Enlarged Edition (New York: The Free Press, 1968), pp. 571–578, in Merton's discussion (written in collaboration with Paul F. Lazarsfeld) of radio and film propaganda as they appeared to the eyes of sociologists some years ago.

Part Four

Public Dramas

I T IS AN AXIOM of the theatre that dramatic presentation typically occurs "on-stage," perceptually separated from the audience which observes the symbolic action. In that sense, staged drama has always been "public," enacted before a "mass" audience. It is not difficult, accordingly, to see why many social and political events have the features of drama, and indeed can most adequately be described as theatre. Under this category we may subsume many kinds of collective or community activity: group life, politics as enacted by elites, specific social and political events such as conventions, rallies, or confrontations, rituals and ceremonies. The articles included in this section explore various kinds of "sociodramas."

The piece by sociologist Joseph Gusfield is the concluding chapter of his influential work concerning a "symbolic crusade," the social movement in America against alcohol that culminated in the Eighteenth Amendment. He argues that social movements can often be explained as "symbolic" actions concerned with the distribution of status in society. Hence the Temperance movement became a vehicle for the symbolic expression of traditional values for those segments of society declining in political power. For Gusfield, the movement coalesced around a symbolic and therefore dramatic conception of political issues; implicitly, then, we may infer that group activities stemming from that conception tended to be dramatic. Further, it was the action itself, the symbolic expression, that was significant to the actors; the psychological rewards were derived from dramatic activity in the movement itself. Status politics, since it focuses on symbolic rather than tangible rewards, tends to acquire dramatic conceptions and actions. Gusfield's work is a genuine contribution to the study of social movements, and his dramatistic interpretation can be applied to many other "status" groups: the Radical Right and Left, the women's movement, the American Independent Party and so on.

We noted above that Gusfield grounded dramatic social action in a subjective element, symbolic conceptions. Dan Nimmo traces the origin of political action to *images,* subjective "knowledge" with which we give symbolic meaning to our environment. Political images thus provide the basis for dramatic conceptions and thereby dramatic enactments in politics. Political actors, like actors in other social contexts, are caught in a drama, and attempt to convey "impressions" to other actors in the drama and to the audience. The audience can participate in the dramas of politics through "symbolic play," a vicarious experience of the dramatic actions of elite actors. Nimmo is dealing with the most difficult of subjects—the relationship between subjective and objective reality—and introduces the notion that dramas occur because of that relationship.

The public dramas of "public men" and the images they present to audiences are discussed by Orrin Klapp. He focuses on the "dramatic domain" of elite encounters that are witnessed through the mass media. Dramatic confrontations condense complex issues for the audience to symbolic leaders who personify or identify the conflicts. There are various types of roles in such dramatic contexts, most obviously heroes, villains and fools. They become these by their qualities to an appropriate audience, but they cannot maintain these identities alone. Drama implies conflict or quest, and it requires some natural or social object against which they must joust: Hillary climbing Everest, Kennedy "facing" Wallace, Churchill against Hitler. For Klapp, the outcome of elite dramas is often not predetermined: if one can perform under pressure, one can "steal the show."

The article by Richard Merelman is an explicit attempt to ground the "dramaturgy of politics" in dramatic theory. Using concepts drawn from the theatre—catharsis, suspense, etc.—he attempts to catalog those areas of political life where such dramatic "techniques" come into play. Political campaigns, for example, invite the use of dramatic technique because of the necessity of communicating a message to a perceived audience. Hence, the candidate can succeed by "adroit self-projection" through the use of such devices as climax, peripety and unmasking. For instance, "peace was at hand" in Vietnam just before the 1972 election, a curious convergence of negotiative and electoral climaxes. In American campaigns, the use of peripety is well-known: the "log cabin" appeal, running against the "special interests," the populist identification, all appeal to the idea of the humble taking on the mighty and winning. Merelman concludes with a plan for the convergence of dramatic and sociological categories across the "two cultures," a major aim of this text.

One of the major areas of social drama is ceremony and ritual, "obligatory scenes" that provide for symbolic celebration of social values and social integration. The study of the coronation of Elizabeth II by Edward Shils and Michael Young focuses on the meaning of such an event for the society, and concludes that it was a "great act of national communion." Such ritual serves as a "reminder" of the sacred values that hold a diverse society together, by bestowing upon an individual the mantle of legitimacy, symbolically personifying the values in the Queen. The function of social dramas for stability have not been fully explored, but certainly the integrative powers of inaugurations, commencements, various "rites of passage," funerals, marriages and the like must be considerable.

Not all such social ceremonials are "positive" in the sense of bestowing a superior status on an individual. Some social dramas degrade or lower the status of the individual, indeed sometimes even deny that the person in question exists. Harold Garfinkel here attempts to develop a paradigm of the "degradation ceremony" and its uses for the public regulation of deviance. Through a dramatic structure, the community thus expresses its moral indignation towards an individual. The military ceremony of "drumming out," for example, strips the individual of his status in the organization (by literally removing the symbols of rank and affiliation), asserts the values and power of the organization by demonstrating what kinds of behavior it does and does not approve of (approves of bravery, disapproves of cowardice), and finally denies the existence of the individual offender (the troops all do an about-face as he leaves). Garfinkel provides one of the few systematic treatments of such dramatic events.

Finally, we include a short selection from Norman O. Brown's speculative work on the implications of Freud, *Love's Body*. These notions are of interest here because they conceive of public life as theatre. In a sense, Brown is concerned with the psychology of representation: what does the public leader "represent"? He envisions a theatre wherein the "public person" acts for the community on the stage of history, with a Freudian explanation of the relationship. The psychology of theatre—in whatever context—remains a relatively unexplored area of inquiry, and Brown's suggestions (as well as others in this section) hopefully will stimulate research in this area. What does drama mean to the actors and to the audience? What is the function of public dramaturgy for a social order? In what sense are certain public enactments dramatic?

21.

A DRAMATISTIC THEORY OF STATUS POLITICS

Joseph R. Gusfield

Political action has a meaning inherent in what it signifies about the structure of the society as well as in what such action actually achieves. We have argued that Prohibition and Temperance have operated as symbolic rather than as instrumental goals in American politics. The passage of legislation or the act of public approval of Temperance has been as significant to the activities of the Temperance movement as has the instrumental achievement of an abstinent society. The agitation and struggle of the Temperance adherents has been directed toward the establishment of their norms as marks of social and political superiority.

The distinction between political action as significant per se and political action as means to an end is the source of the theory underlying our analysis of the Temperance movement. We refer to it as a dramatistic theory because, like drama, it represents an action which is make-believe but which moves its audience. It is in keeping with Kenneth Burke's meaning of dramatism, "since it invites one to consider the matter of motives in a perspective that, being developed from the analysis of drama, treats language and thought primarily as modes of action." [1] It is make-believe in that the action need have no relation to its ostensible goal. The effect upon the audience comes from the significance which they find in the action as it represents events or figures outside of the drama.

Throughout the analysis of Temperance we have referred to the symbolic nature of Temperance goals. Our theory is further dramatistic in its perspective on political action as symbolic action, as action in which "the object referred to has a range of meaning beyond itself." [2]

. . . The dramatistic approach has important implications for the study of political institutions. These will be analyzed in this chapter, in the light of our study of the Temperance movement. Governments affect the distribution of values through symbolic acts, as well as through the force of instrumental ones. The struggle to control the symbolic actions of government is often as bitter and as fateful as the struggle to control its tangible effects. Much of our response to political events is in terms of their dramatic, symbolic meaning.

This is especially the case where elements of the status order are at issue. The distribution of prestige is partially regulated by symbolic acts of public and political figures. Such persons "act out" the drama in which one status group is degraded and another is given deference. In seeking to effect their honor and prestige in the society, a group makes demands upon governing agents to act in ways which serve to symbolize deference or to degrade the opposition whose status they challenge or

Reprinted by permission from *Symbolic Crusade: Status Politics and the American Temperance Movement,* University of Illinois Press, 1966.

who challenge theirs. We have seen this in the ways that Temperance goals symbolized victory or defeat for the devout native American Protestant.

This view of social status as a political interest enables us to solve some of the ambiguities about noneconomic issues and movements with which we began our study. It also provides us with a useful addition to the economic and the psychological modes of analysis current in the study of political and social movements.

SYMBOLIC ISSUES IN POLITICS

The State and the Public

Following Max Weber, it has become customary for sociologists to define the state as the legitimate monopolizer of force.[3] A major defect of this view, however, is that it minimizes the extent to which governments function as representatives of the total society. Other organizations or institutions claim to represent the values and interests of one group, subculture, or collectivity within the total social organization. Government is the only agency which claims to act for the entire society. It seeks its legitimation through the claim that it is effected with a "public interest" rather than with a special, limited set of goals. Much of the effective acceptance of government as legitimate rests upon the supposition that it is representative of the total society, that it has the moral responsibility "to commit the group to action or to perform coordinated acts for its general welfare." [4]

The public and visible nature of governmental acts provides them with wider consequences for other institutions than is true of any other area of social life. The actions of government can affect the tangible resources of citizens but they can also affect the attitudes, opinions, and judgments which people make about each other.

It is readily apparent that governments affect the distribution of resources and, in this fashion, promote or deter the interest of economic classes. The passage of a minimum wage law does affect the incomes of millions of laborers and the profits of thousands of owners of capital. The Wagner Labor Relations Act and the Taft-Hartley Act have changed the conditions of collective bargaining during the past 26 years. Tariff laws do influence the prices of products. While these legislative actions may not direct and control behavior as much as was contemplated in their passage, they nevertheless find their *raison d'être* as instruments which have affected behavior to the delight of some and the dismay of others. They are instruments to achieve a goal or end through their use.

That governmental acts have symbolic significance is not so readily appreciated, although it has always been recognized. We see the act of recall of an ambassador as an expression of anger between one government and another. We recognize in the standardized pattern of inaugural addresses the gesture toward consensus after the strain of electoral conflict. These acts, of ambassadorial recall and of presidential oratory, are not taken at face value but as devices to induce response in their audiences, as symbolic of anger or of appeal for consensus.

Not only ritual and ceremony are included in symbolic action. Law contains a great deal which has little direct effect upon behavior. The moral reform legislation embodying Temperance ideals has largely been of this nature, as have other reforms, such as those directed against gambling, birth control, and prostitution. The impact of legislation on such problems as civil rights, economic monopoly, or patriotic loyalties is certainly dubious. While we do not maintain that Temperance legislation, and the other legislation cited, has had no effect on behavior, we do find its instrumental effects are slight compared to the response which it entails as a symbol, irrespective of its utility as a means to a tangible end.

Nature of the Symbol

In distinguishing symbolic from instrumental action we need to specify the way in which a symbol stands for something else. It is customary in linguistic analysis to distinguish between "sign" and "symbol." [5] The former points to and indicates objects or experiences to our senses. The latter represents objects and events apart from any sensory contacts. Thus the ringing of the doorbell is a sign that someone is at the front door. The word "doorbell" is a symbol, as is the concept of "democracy." Our usage is not linguistic in this sense,[6] but literary. We are concerned with the multiplicity of meanings which the same object or act can have for the observer and which, in a society, are often fixed, shared, and standardized. The artist and the writer have developed language and visual art with the use of symbols as major tools of communication. Religious institutions have developed a rich culture around the use of objects whose meanings are symbolic. The wine and wafer of the Mass are but one example of objects which embody a multiple set of meanings for the same person at the same time.

This distinction between instrumental and symbolic action is, in many ways, similar to the difference between denotative and connotative discourse. In denotation, our eyes are on the referent which, in clear language, is the same for all who use the term. Instrumental action is similar in being oriented as a means to a fixed end. Connotative references are more ambiguous, less fixed. The symbol is connotative in that "it has acquired a meaning which is added to its immediate intrinsic significance." [7]

It is useful to think of symbolic acts as forms of rhetoric, functioning to organize the perceptions, attitudes, and feelings of observers. Symbolic acts "invite consideration rather than overt action." [8] They are persuasive devices which alter the observer's view of the objects. Kenneth Burke, perhaps the greatest analyst of political symbolism, has given a clear illustration of how a political speech can function rhetorically by the use of language to build a picture contradicting the instrumental effects of political action. For example, if action is proposed or performed which will offend the businessman, language is produced in speeches which glorify the businessman. In this context, language functions to persuade the "victim" that government is not really against him. It allays the fears and "softens the blow." Burke refers to this technique as "secular prayer." It is the normal way in which prayer is used, "to sharpen up the pointless and blunt the too sharply pointed." [9]

It is not only language which is utilized in symbolic fashion by political agents.

Any act of government can be imbued with symbolic import when it becomes associated with noninstrumental identifications, when it serves to glorify or demean the character of one group or another. Ceremony and ritual can become affected with great significance as actions in which the political agent, as representative of the society, symbolizes the societal attitude, the public norm, toward some person, object, or social group. Law, language, and behavior can all function ceremonially. They persuade men to a form of thought or behavior rather than force them to it. "The officer who doubts the obedience of his men may meet the situation by raising his voice, adopting a truculent tone, and putting on a pugnacious swagger." [10] This, too, is a form of rhetoric, of persuasive art.

Types of Political Symbolism

We find it useful to distinguish between two forms of political symbolism: *gestures of cohesion* and *gestures of differentiation*. The first type, gestures of cohesion, serve to fix the common and consensual aspects of the society as sources of governmental support. They appeal to the unifying elements in the society and the grounds for the legitimacy of the political institution, irrespective of its specific officeholders and particular laws. They seek to mobilize the loyalties to government which may exist above and across the political conflict of parties, interest groups, and factions. National holidays, inaugural addresses, and the protocols of address and behavior are ways in which the President of the United States attempts this function in his actions and words. The coronation of the monarch in Great Britain represents a highly ritualized method of symbolizing legitimacy.[11]

Gestures of differentiation point to the glorification or degradation of one group in opposition to others within the society. They suggest that some people have a legitimate claim to greater respect, importance, or worth in the society than have some others. In such gestures, governments take sides in social conflicts and place the power and prestige of the public, operating through the political institution, on one side or the other. The inauguration ceremonies of two presidents can be used as illustrations. In his 1953 inaugural, Dwight Eisenhower prefaced his address with a short, personally written prayer. Commenting on this freely, a WCTU officer remarked approvingly, "Imagine that prayer written in the morning in an offhand way! It's the finest thing we've had in years from a president's lips." This gesture placed government on the side of the traditionalist and the devout and separated it from identification with the secularist and freethinker.

. . . Such gestures of differentiation are often crucial to the support or opposition of a government because they state the character of an administration in moralistic terms. They indicate the kinds of persons, the tastes, the moralities, and the general life styles toward which government is sympathetic or censorious.[12] They indicate whether or not a set of officials are "for people like us" or "against people like us." It is through this mechanism of symbolic character that a government affects the status order.

STATUS AS A PUBLIC ISSUE

Deference Conferral

In what sense can the prestige of a status group be a matter at issue? Conflicts about the appropriate deference to be shown can, and do, exist. Currently the relations between whites and Negroes in the United States are examples of a status system undergoing intensive conflict. An issue, however, is a proposal that people can be for or against. A public issue has status implications insofar as its public outcome is interpretable as conferring prestige upon or withdrawing it from a status group.

Desegregation is a status issue par excellence. Its symbolic characteristics lie in the deference which the norm of integration implies. The acceptance of token integration, which is what has occurred in the North, is itself prestige-conferring because it establishes the public character of the norm supporting integration. It indicates what side is publicly legitimate and dominant. Without understanding this symbolic quality of the desegregation issue, the fierceness of the struggle would appear absurd. Since so little actual change in concrete behavior ensues, the question would be moot if it were not for this character as an act of deference toward Negroes and of degradation toward whites.

Unlike the desegregation question, many public issues are confrontations between opposed systems of moralities, cultures, and styles of life. Examples of these are issues of civil liberties, international organizations, vivisection, Sunday "blue laws," and the definition and treatment of domestic Communism. Probably the clearest of such issues in American public life has been the one studied in this book, the issue of restrictive or permissive norms governing drinking. Status issues indicate, by their resolution, the group, culture, or style of life to which government and society are publicly committed. They answer the question: On behalf of which ethnic, religious, or other cultural group is this government and this society being carried out? We label these as *status issues* precisely because what is at issue is the position of the relevant groups in the status order of the society. Such issues polarize the society along lines of status group differentiation, posing conflicts between divergent styles of life. They are contrasted with *class issues,* which polarize the society along lines of economic interests.[13]

Status issues function as vehicles through which a noneconomic group has deference conferred upon it or degradation imposed upon it. Victory in issues of status is the symbolic conferral of respect upon the norms of the victor and disrespect upon the norms of the vanquished. The political institution or public is thus capable of confirming or disconfirming the individual's conception of his place in the social order.[14] Such actions serve to reconstitute the group as a social object by heaping shame or honor upon it through the support or rejection displayed toward its tastes, values, and customs. When the indignation of the abstinent toward the drinker is publicly confirmed by prohibitory legislation it is, in Harold Garfinkel's analysis of degradation ceremonies, an act of public denunciation: "We publicly deliver the curse: 'I call upon all men to bear witness that he is not as he appears but is otherwise and *in essence* of a lower species.' " [15]

Symbolic properties of deference and degradation can be involved in a wide range of issues and events. They may be implicated as a major theme in some issues or as a peripheral element in other issues, where the groups and themes are more directly those of specific economic interests. David Riesman and Ruel Denney have given us an excellent analysis of American football as a carrier of symbols which served to heighten the prestige of some social groups at the expense of the degradation of others.[16] The victories of Knute Rockne and Notre Dame over the previous championship teams of the Ivy League symbolized the growing social and educational equality of the non-Protestant middle-class Midwest vis-à-vis the Protestant upper-class East. Fans could identify themselves with football teams as carriers of their prestige, whether or not they were college graduates themselves. Knute Rockne was football's equivalent of Al Smith in politics.

Status Interests

Precisely because prestige is far from stable in a changing society, specific issues can become structured as tests of status when they are construed as symbols of group moralities and life styles. A civil liberties issue, such as domestic Communism, takes much of its affect and meaning from the clashes between traditionalized and modernist groups in American culture. Elements of educational sophistication, religious secularism, or political liberalism may appear as alien, foreign, and in direct contradiction to the localistic ways of life of the traditional oriented culture. Issues of civil liberties become fields on which such cultural and educational groups fight to establish their claims to public recognition and prestige.

In his analysis of McCarthyism, Peter Vierick has referred to just this kind of process in characterizing the attack on officials in the State Department. Vierick placed one source of this attack in the feeling of degradation which the Midwestern, agricultural, middle class felt at political domination by the aristocracy of the Eastern seaboard, educated at Ivy League schools and so prominent in State Department affairs. They symbolized the State Department personnel as "striped-pants diplomats" and "cookie-pushers." "Against the latter (the Foreign Service—ed.) the old Populist and La Follette weapon against diplomats of 'you internationalist Anglophile snob' was replaced by 'you egghead security risk.' " [17]

In the struggle between groups for prestige and social position, the demands for deference and the protection from degradation are channeled into government and into such institutions of cultural formation as schools, churches, and media of communication. Because these institutions have power to affect public recognition, they are arenas of conflict between opposing status groups. Their ceremonial, ritual, and policy are matters of interest for status groups as well as for economic classes.

It is in this sense that status politics is a form of interest-oriented politics. The enhancement or defense of a position in the status order is as much an interest as the protection or expansion of income or economic power. The activities of government, as the most public institutions, confer respect upon a given style of life or directly upon a specific group. For this reason questions of institutional support of tastes, morals, and other aspects of life styles have consequences for the prestige of persons. Where status anxieties exist, they are then likely to be represented in the form of symbolic issues through which they are resolved.

To see that government, as do other institutions, is a prestige-granting agency is to recognize that status politics is neither extraordinary nor an irrational force in American history. Seymour Lipset appears to be quite mistaken when he writes, "Where there are status anxieties, there is little or nothing which a government can do." [18] Governments constantly affect the status order. During the 1930's the Democratic Party won many votes by increasing the number of Jews and Catholics appointed to state and federal judgeships. Such jobs did little to increase the total number of jobs open to these ethnic and religious groups. They did constitute a greater representation and through this a greater recognition of the worth of these groups. In this sense they were rituals of prestige enhancements, just as Andrew Jackson's inauguration symbolized the advent of the "common man" to power and prestige by the fact that rough men in boots strode across the floors of the White House.

It is just this consequence of the Temperance movement for the public designation of respectability that we have seen throughout this study. We have been interested in the efforts of Temperance people to reform the habits of others. While such efforts have indeed been motivated by the desire to perfect others in accordance with the reformer's vision of perfection, they have also become enmeshed in consequences affecting the distribution of prestige. Temperance issues have served as symbols around which groups of divergent morals and values have opposed each other.[19] On the side of Temperance there has been the rural, orthodox Protestant, agricultural, native American. On the side of drinking there has been the immigrant, the Catholic, the industrial worker, and the secularized upper class. In more recent years the clash has pitted the modernist and the urbanized cosmopolitans against the traditionalists and the localities, the new middle classes against the old.

When Temperance forces were culturally dominant, the confrontation was that of the social superior. He sought to convert the weaker members of the society through persuasion backed by his dominance of the major institutions. Where dominance of the society is in doubt, then the need for positive governmental and institutional action is greater. The need for symbolic vindication and deference is channeled into political action. What is at stake is not so much the action of men, whether or not they drink, but their ideals, the moralities to which they owe their public allegiance.

POLITICAL MODELS AND STATUS POLITICS [20]

Our analysis of symbolic acts has implications for traditional theories of American politics. In attempting to understand political processes and movements sociologists, political scientists, and psychologists have operated with two major models of political motivation. One model has been drawn from economic action and reflects the struggle for economic interests. This model we have designated *class politics*. The other model has been drawn from clinical psychology and reflects a view of politics as an arena into which "irrational" impulses are projected. The latter model, which we have called *psychological expressivism,* has been utilized by others to describe movements of status politics. Our use of a model of symbolic action has been intended to distinguish movements of status politics from both economic interest on the one hand, and psychological expressivism on the other. . . .

Class Politics and the Pluralistic Model

The view of the political process as a balance of economic forces organized as classes has led to a compromise model of political actions. The pluralistic model assumes a multiple number of specific interest groups whose demands conflict with and contradict each other. Farmers, bankers, skilled workers, unskilled workers, and professionals are represented through pressure groups and occupational associations. Political decisions are resultants of the compromises mediated between the various groups in accordance with the distribution of political power. Each group tries to get as much as they can but accepts partial losses in return for partial gains.

Compromise and the model of the political arena as one of mutually cooperating yet antagonistic groups presupposes a "political culture" in which victory and defeat are only end points on a continuum. An expediential attitude of calculation and exchange must govern the trading and bargaining. The language and imagery of compromise is drawn to a considerable extent from the marketplace, where monetary transactions enable interaction to be expressed in measurable quantities and mutual advantages. We "meet people halfway," develop political programs that are "deals," and operate through political parties talked about as "brokers of interests."

The "rules of the game" governing pluralistic politics are sharply antithetical to the "poor loser," the "sorehead," the intolerant ideologue who considers himself morally right and all others morally evil. He cannot accept the legitimacy of an institution in which even partial defeat occurs. For him politics is not a search for benefits in his work and life but a battleground between forces of good and evil. He reacts with passion in ways which contradict the rules of pluralistic politics. He rejects the presupposition that everybody in the political arena has a legitimate right to get something and nobody has a legitimate right to get everything. He typifies the moralizer in politics, described by Riesman. . . .

Psychological Expressivism as a Model of Status Politics

The analytical scheme of pluralistic politics is most applicable to movements of class politics and instrumental action. Movements such as Prohibition, civil rights, religious differences, and educational change are puzzles to the sociologist and political scientist precisely because they cannot be analyzed in instrumental terms. Their goals and major images appear "irrational" and unrelated to the content of their aims. Being puzzles, a resort is often made to schemes which stress the impulsive, uncontrolled elements of spontaneous and unconscious behavior. Thus Lipset writes of status discontents as one source of rightist extremism: "It is not surprising therefore that political movements which have successfully appealed to status resentments have been irrational in character and have sought scapegoats which conveniently serve to symbolize the status threat." [21]

The essential idea in psychological expressivism is that the adherence to the movement is explainable as an expression of the adherent's personality. "Thus the mass man is vulnerable to the appeal of mass movements which offer him a way of overcoming the pain of self-alienation by shifting attention away from himself and by focussing it on the movement." [22] Unlike instrumental action, which is about conflicts of interest, the substance of political struggles in expressive politics is not about anything because it is not a vehicle of conflict but a vehicle of catharsis—a purging of emotions through expression. The analysis of politics as expressive takes on the attributes of magic, as in Malinowksi's classic definition: "Man, engaged in a series of practical activities, comes to a gap . . . passive inaction, the only thing dictated by reason, is the last thing in which he can acquiesce. His nervous system and his whole organism drive him to some substitute activity." [23]

If we utilize only the two models of instrumental actions and psychological expressivism we tend to divide political and social movements into two categories—the rational and the irrational. Status politics . . . gets readily classified as "irrational": "Therefore, it is the tendency of status politics to be expressed more in vindictiveness, in sour memories, in the search for scapegoats, than in realistic proposals for concrete actions." [24] Between instrumental and expressive politics there is no bin into which the symbolic goals of status movements can be analytically placed. Our usage of symbolic politics is an effort to provide such a bin.

Symbolic Politics and Status Interests

The consequences of interpreting status movements in the language of psychological expressivism is that the analyst ignores the reality of the status conflict. Expressive politics cannot be referred back to any social conflict which is resolved by the action taken. It is not a vehicle through which conflicts are mediated or settled. We have tried to show, in the instance of the Temperance movement, that the attempt to utilize political action was not only expressive but was a way of winning a concrete and very real struggle over the distribution of prestige in American society.

Discontents that arise from the status order are often as sharp and as powerful as those that emerge in the struggles over income and employment. In a society of diverse cultures and of rapid change, it is quite clear that systems of culture are as open to downward and upward mobility as are occupations or persons. Yesterday's moral virtue is today's ridiculed fanaticism. As the cultural fortunes of one group go up and those of another group go down, expectations of prestige are repulsed and the ingredients of social conflict are produced.

The dramatistic approach we have used in this study includes language but is by no means only a linguistic analysis. It is applicable to acts of legislation, such as Prohibition or fluoridation, to court decisions, and to official ceremony. Arguments about symbolic action are real in the sense that men's regard for respect, honor, and prestige is real. We do live in a forest of symbols, and within that forest there is disagreement, conflict, and disorder.

We are not maintaining a symbolic approach to politics as an alternative to instrumental or expressive models. We conceive of it as an addition to methods of analysis but an addition which can best help us understand the implications of status conflicts for political actions and, vice versa, the ways in which political acts affect the distribution of prestige. Most movements, and most political acts, contain a mixture of instrumental, expressive, and symbolic elements. The issues of style, which have troubled many social scientists in recent years, have not lent themselves well to political analysis. Those issues which have appeared as "matters of principle" now appear to us to be related to status conflicts and understandable in symbolic terms.

. . . A political model that ignores symbolic action in politics would exclude an important category of governmental action. It is a major way in which conflicts in the social order are institutionalized as political issues. Groups form around such issues, symbols are given specific meaning, and opposing forces have some arena in which to test their power and bring about compromise and accommodation, if possible. This is precisely what the issues of Prohibition and Temperance have enabled the status groups involved as Wets and Drys to accomplish. Turning status conflicts into political conflicts is precisely what Lasswell seems to have meant when he described politics as "the process by which the irrational bases of society are brought out into the open." [25]

. . . We live in a human environment in which symbolic gestures have great relevance to our sense of pride, mortification, and honor. Social conflicts and tensions are manifested in a disarray of the symbolic order as well as in other areas of action. Dismissing these reactions as "irrational" clouds analysis and ignores the events which have significance for people. Kenneth Burke has pointed out the pejorative implications which emerge when noninstrumental usages are described as "magical." He distinguishes between poetic language, which is action for its own sake, scientific language, which is a preparation for action, and rhetorical language, which is inducement to action or attitude. If you think of acts as either magical or scientific there is no place to classify symbolic acts of the kind we have been considering, where an interest conflict is resolved but in noninstrumental symbolic terms. Consequently, a great deal of political activity is dismissed as ritual, magic, or irrational waste when "it should be handled in its own terms as an aspect of what it really is: Rhetoric." [26]

THE VOLATILITY OF STATUS POLITICS

Issues invested with status interests are not easily handled by political institutions oriented to the model of a pluralistic class politics. In American politics such issues are likely to be most difficult to regularize within the structure of the American political framework. Their volatile nature is further accentuated by recent changes in American culture and society which make such issues emerge even more explosively than they have in the past.

Status Conflict and the Political Process

It is the issues of morals and style, of religious belief and ethnic loyalties which searches for political harmony most often implore be kept out of politics. Such pleas are recognition of the intensity with which status loyalties and aspirations prevent the operation of the culture of bargaining, compromise, and detached trading so necessary for a pluralistic politics. The introduction of status issues cuts deeply at the sources of political consensus by converting political questions into moral ones.

The language of status issues, essential to their symbolic import, is the language of moral condemnation. In the confrontation of one culture with another, each seeks to degrade the other and to build its own claims to deference. The sources of conflict are not quantitative ones of the distribution of resources. Instead they are differences between right and wrong, the ugly and the beautiful, the sinful and the virtuous. Such issues are less readily compromised than are quantitative issues. When politicians argue about the definition of sin instead of being uniformly opposed to it, then the underlying political consensus is itself threatened.

The discontents generated by social change become fixed upon groups which are in status opposition. Each becomes the symbol of the other's obstacle in objectifying its view of its proper position. Each seeks to wrest from the other the admission of its place in the order. An issue like fluoridation, for example, carries the status struggle between the culturally modern and cosmopolitan middle classes and the culturally fundamentalist and localistic old middle classes.

The association of an issue with the styles of life of its supporters enhances the tendency of political issues to turn into matters of "face," freezing the adherents to a given program and further diminishing the possibilities of compromise or graceful defeat. When participants have become committed to a "line" which makes retreat and compromise immoral, discontinuance of the stance will be more painful than if they had entered with a bargaining orientation. In the former case, they invested their egos. In part, compromise is possible at all because the parties to the action will help each other maintain the illusion that a victory has been achieved. In human encounters, as Goffman has shown, parties to the interaction help maintain each other's "face." People mutually accept each other's lines—the consistent pattern of acts expressing the actor's evaluation of himself and the participants. The hostess covers over the embarrassment of the guest who has just broken a new and expensive piece of glassware by minimizing the importance of the breakage. She maintains the guest's "face" as a considerate person and permits him to "erase" the act by mumbling apologies. "Should the person radically alter his line, or should it become discredited, then confusion results, for the participants will have prepared and committed themselves for actions that are now unsuitable." [27]

Status conflicts, however, involve just such "face-smashing" operations. The pretense that one's values and morals are prestigious and powerful is undermined whenever public actions contradict such assertions. Loss of face becomes degrading. Since status conflicts involve opposition between styles of life, it is necessary to break the "face" of the opponent by degrading his cultural content. Ego is invested in status claims and degradation is keenly felt. The inability of the forces of

North and South to reach compromise on the eve of the Civil War is a good illustration of how investment in a line made compromise less possible. ". . . after years of strife the complex issues between the sections assumed the form of a conflict between *right* and *rights*. . . . They suggested things which cannot be compromised." [28]

Political Structure and Status Politics

The institutionalization of status conflicts occurs less frequently than the institutionalization of class conflicts. Class organization develops out of stable, institutional positions in the occupational and economic structures. Labor unions, businessmen's associations, professional organizations are constructed on the basis of institutional roles and statuses. The organization of conflict associations is a necessary step in the structuring of conflict relationships. It enables political accommodations to be worked out among contending groups. Institutional ties operate both to promote the formation of "pressure groups" and to integrate the occupant into organizations on this basis.

. . . The exclusion of status elements from institutionalized politics imparts an erratic, highly emotional, and disturbing character to such issues when they do find their way into politics. They emerge in highly diffuse forms. The separation of the issue from any specific party location destroys the control of the institution, the political party system, over it. Support in the form of sentiments are just as likely to come from one class as another, from Republicans as well as Democrats. Since status issues are likely to be highly symbolic, the absence of fixed political connotations enables people to provide their own connotations. In this fashion a bewildering array of diverse groups can become attached to any set of symbols when they lack clear location in the political spectrum. Almost every major social segment in the United States has been included by some writer as one of the major supports of Senator Joseph McCarthy. Pro-McCarthyism has been attributed to highly diverse and often conflicting groups, sometimes by the same author. Neo-Populists, Catholics, anti-Catholics, isolationists, downwardly mobile people, upwardly mobile people, Protestant fundamentalists, small businessmen, and industrial workers have all been held "responsible" for McCarthyism.[29] This "looseness" is seldom the case with economic issues.

Status constituencies, however, are looser collections of adherents than are economic interest groups. Formed out of sentiments rather than concrete, objectified interests, commitment is less structured. The organization is less able to speak for its constituency, less able to "deal" with opposing groups in the negotiations on which the model of class politics has been built. The constituency of doctors is more clearly represented by the American Medical Association than the constituency of birth control adherents is represented by the Association for Planned Parenthood.

. . . Temperance has receded as an issue of paramount significance in American life. It is highly doubtful that the status conflicts which it represented have disappeared from the American scene. The quest for an honored place in society is likely to persist. Social changes are likely to continue to upset old hierarchies and develop new aspirations. Cultural transformations are to be expected and resistance to them is almost certain. Status politics is neither a new nor a transient aspect of American society.

NOTES

[1] Kenneth Burke, *A Grammar of Motives* (New York: Prentice-Hall, 1945), p. xxii.

[2] M. H. Abrams, quoted in Maurice Beebe (ed.), *Literary Symbolism* (San Francisco: Wadsworth Publishing Co., 1960), p. 18.

[3] Max Weber, *Theory of Social and Economic Organization,* tr. A. M. Henderson and Talcott Parsons (New York: Oxford University Press, 1947), p. 156. "The claim of the modern state to monopolize the use of force is as essential to it as its character of compulsory jurisdiction and of continuous organization." This definition is open both to the objection discussed above and to the inadequacy of singling out "force" as a major method of compulsion. Other institutions compel behavior by effective means other than violence, such as the ecclesiastical controls of a priesthood or the employment powers of management. The phenomena of "private governments" is not included in Weber's definition but the only ground of exclusion which is sociologically significant is the public character of governing bodies.

[4] Frances X. Sutton, "Representation and the Nature of Political Systems," Comparative Studies in Society and History, 2 (October, 1959), 1–10, at 6. Sutton points out that in primitive societies the political officers are often only representatives to other tribes rather than agents to enforce law.

[5] See the discussion of signs and symbols in Susanne K. Langer, *Philosophy in a New Key* (Baltimore, Md.: Penguin Books, 1948), pp. 45–50.

[6] Neither is our usage to be equated with the discussion of symbolic behavior used in the writings of the symbolic interaction school of social psychology, best represented by the works of George H. Mead. The idea of symbolic behavior in that context emphasizes the linguistic and imaginative processes as implicated in behavior. It is by no means contrary to our usage of symbols but the context is not specifically literary. The symbolic interactionists call attention to the fact that objects are given meanings by the systems of concept formation. We emphasize one aspect of this process.

[7] Talcott Parsons, *The Social System* (Glencoe, Ill.: The Free Press, 1954), p. 286.

[8] Phillip Wheelwright, *The Burning Fountain* (Bloomington: Indiana University Press, 1954), p. 23.

[9] Burke, *op. cit.,* p. 393. My debt to Burke's writings is very great. He has supplied the major conceptual and theoretical tools for bridging literary and political analysis. In addition to *A Grammar of Motives,* see his *Attitudes Toward History* (Los Altos, Calif.: Hermes Publications, 1959), and *Permanence and Change* (New York: New Republic, Inc., 1935). Two sociologists, heavily influenced by Burke, have been extremely useful in developing attention to symbolic behavior in the sense used here. They are Erving Goffman, whose works are cited throughout this study, and Hugh D. Duncan, *Language and Literature in Society* (Chicago: University of Chicago Press, 1953).

[10] Harold Lasswell, "Language of Politics," in Ruth Anshen (ed.), *Language* (New York: Harper and Bros., 1957), pp. 270–284, at 281.

[11] Edward Shils and Michael Young have studied the consensual effects of the coronation ceremony in England. See their "The Meaning of the Coronation," *Sociological Review,* 1, n.s. (December, 1953), 63–81. The use of ritual and ceremony to establish social cohesion and social control through historical pagents and holidays in modern society is studied empirically in W. Lloyd Warner, *The Living and the Dead* (New Haven, Conn.: Yale University Press, 1959), esp. Pts. I and II. These aspects of "political religion" have received comparatively little attention from students of modern societies although most recognize the importance of such rituals and would agree with Hugh Duncan that "Any institution can 'describe' the way it wants people to act but only as it develops rites, ceremonies and symbols for communication through rite in which people can act does it rise to power." Duncan, *op. cit.,* p. 18.

[12] Another example of this symbolic process in political issues can be found in the conflicts over city

manager plans. Development of city manager government is usually supported by middle-class voters and opposed by the lower socioeconomic groups. The impersonal, moralistic, and bureaucratized "good government" is much closer to standards of conduct typical in middle classes. The machine politician is closer to the open, personalized, and flexible government that represents the lower-class systems of social control. The issue of the city manager poses the two subcultures against each other. One study of the advent of city manager government reported that the first thing the new council did was to take away jobs from Catholic employees and, under merit employment, give them to Protestants. The city manager people celebrated their political victory with a banquet at the Masonic hall. See the discussion in Martin Meyerson and Edward Banfield, *Politics, Planning and the Public Interest* (Glencoe, Ill.: The Free Press, 1955), pp. 290–291.

[13] Essentially the same distinction is made by students of the voting process. Berelson, Lazarsfeld, and McPhee distinguish between issues of style ("ideal" issues) and issues of position ("material" issues). Bernard Berelson, Paul Lazarsfeld, and William McPhee, *Voting* (Chicago: University of Chicago Press, 1959), p. 184.

[14] ". . . the individual must rely on others to complete the picture of him . . . each individual is responsible for the demeanour image of himself and deference image of others, so that for a complete man to be expressed, individuals must hold hands in a chain of ceremony, each giving deferentially with proper demeanor to the one on the right what will be received deferentially from the one on the left." Erving Goffman, "The Nature of Deference and Demeanor," *American Anthropologist,* 58 (June, 1956), 473–502, at 493. Goffman's writings constitute an important discussion of deference and degradation ceremonies in interpersonal interaction. In addition to the article cited above see *The Presentation of Self in Everyday Life* (New York: Doubleday Anchor Books, 1959), and *Encounters* (Indianapolis, Ind.: Bobbs-Merrill, 1961).

[15] Harold Garfinkel, "Conditions of Successful Degradation Ceremonies," *American Journal of Sociology,* 61 March, 1956), 420–424, at 421.

[16] David Riesman and Ruel Denney, "Football in America," *The American Quarterly,* 3 (Winter, 1951), 309–325.

[17] Peter Vierick, "The Revolt Against the Elite," in Daniel Bell (ed.), *The New American Right* (New York: Criterion Books, 1955), pp. 91–116, at 103.

[18] Seymour Lipset, "The Sources of the Radical Right," in *ibid,* pp. 166–234, at 168.

[19] This is evident in Lee Benson, *The Concept of Jacksonian Democracy* (Princeton, N.J.: Princeton University Press, 1961), esp. Ch. 9. Benson's work appeared too late to have been used in earlier sections of the book. It provides valuable evidence for the role of moral issues, and especially Temperance, in developing party loyalties in New York state in the 1840's. Using the concept of negative reference groups, Benson shows that economic interests played less of a role than did religious, cultural, and moral differences as influences on voting. Voters tended to see the two major parties as linked to one or another ethnocultural group.

[20] Some of the matters discussed in this section are treated in greater detail in my "Mass Society and Extremist Politics," *American Sociological Review,* 27 (February, 1962), 19–30.

[21] Lipset, *op. cit.,* p. 168.

[22] William Kornhauser, *The Politics of Mass Society* (Glencoe, Ill.: The Free Press, 1959), p. 112

[23] Bronislaw Malinowski, *Magic, Science and Religion* (New York: Doubleday Anchor Books, 1954; orig. pub., 1925), p. 79.

[24] Richard Hofstadter, "The Pseudo-Conservative Revolt," in Bell (ed.), *op. cit.,* pp. 33–55, at 44.

[25] Harold Lasswell, *Psychopathology and Politics* (Chicago: University of Chicago Press, 1930), p. 184.

[26] Kenneth Burke, *A Rhetoric of Motives* (New York: Prentice-Hall, 1950), p. 42.

[27] Erving Goffman, "On Face-Work," *Psychiatry,* 18 (August, 1955), 213–231, at 216.

[28] Avery O. Craven, "The Civil War and the Democratic Process," in Kenneth Stampp (ed.), *The Causes of the Civil War* (Englewood Cliffs, N.J.: Prentice-Hall, 1959), pp. 150–152, at 152.

[29] See the array of theories and groups in Bell, *op. cit.*

22.

THE DRAMA, ILLUSION AND REALITY
OF POLITICAL IMAGES

Dan Nimmo

People have subjective knowledge of political objects. On the basis of such knowledge, which we have called *images*, they give meaning to political signs. These signs are *symbols* representing their environment. . . . Looking at the dramatic, illusionary, and realistic aspects of political images will afford an opportunity to summarize major points as to images of politics.

The Dramatic Qualities of Political Imagery

The view that human behavior is dramatic action has a long and rich tradition.[1] By probing that tradition, one can isolate the principal qualities of dramatic action relevant for dealing with political images.

There is a simple but crucial distinction made in dramatistic theories of behavior—the distinction between motion and action. *Motion* consists of the mere physical movement of any object or being, as when a rock rolls or dust blows. *Action,* however, differs from motion in that an act consists both of physical movement and of the subjective significance of the movement for the person committing it, or for some observer. *Action* is motion plus subjective significance, but "action cannot be reduced to motion:"

> The man who designs a computer is acting. The computer that he designs can but move. Though the process of the computer can throw light upon its designer, they do not provide a terminology adequate for the defining of its maker. That's the crux of the Dramatistic position.[2]

In politics we find an example of the motion-action distinction in voting. Pulling the lever on a voting machine is motion; the voter's sense of why he is moving that lever makes it an act: "insofar as a vote is cast without adequate knowledge of its consequences, one might even question whether it should be classed as an activity at all; one might rather call it passive, or perhaps sheer motion (what the behaviorists would call a Response to a Stimulus)."[3] The automatic obligation some Americans feel regarding voting, while thinking that elections have little or no effect upon policy making, . . . is evidence that voting is some times motion rather than action. Yet, so long as discharging a civic duty gives meaning to voting, it is an act beyond mere motion.

But how do we give meaning to the things we do? How do we make actions of our motions? . . . We represent objects through our images and by communicating

Dan Nimmo, *Popular Images of Politics: A Taxonomy,* © 1974, pp. 131–155. Reprinted by permission of Prentice-Hall, Inc., Englewood Cliffs, New Jersey.

images through symbols. By symbols we communicate what objects and events mean to us. Since those symbols do mean something to us, a meaning that rests upon our images of the world, the symbols we use to achieve material gain, make judgments, and express ourselves are actions in themselves (i.e., these symbols are meaningful in themselves), as well as means to an end. Put in the language of the dramatistic view, human behavior consists of symbolic acts that make up theatrical performances, that is, people presenting themselves to each other to influence their mutual impressions of one another and their joint expectations of what must be done to sustain the performance.

To get a better picture of the nature of dramatic performance consider the words of heavyweight boxer Muhammad Ali (then Cassius Clay), on the eve of his 1964 bout with the reigning champion, Sonny Liston:

> This fight with Liston is truly a command performance. And that's exactly the way I planned it. . . . Where do you think I would be next week if I didn't know how to shout and holler and make the public sit up and take notice? I would be poor, for one thing, and I would probably be down in Louisville, Ky., my home town, washing windows and saying 'yes suh' and 'no suh' and knowing my place. . . . When I walk into a room where he [Liston] is and see him staring at me with that mean, hateful look, I want to laugh, but then I think maybe it's not so funny. I'm pretty sure the way he acts is just a pose, the same way I have a pose, but that look of his still shakes me. I wonder what's really going on in that head of his. . . .[4]

The relationship between images and performances is circular: our performances define our self- and public images; those definitions set the conditions and expectations of others' performances toward us; our impressions of their performances and what they think of us helps us confirm, reject, or disconfirm our self-images; and this, in turn, establishes the limits of our return performance before them (the verbal and nonverbal messages we transmit and the settings in which we transmit them). In other words, what a person does toward others restricts or enhances what he can and will choose to do in the future. Life and politics, in this sense, is drama. People do not relate toward one another *as if* engaged in dramatic performances. They are caught up in a drama: "the proposition 'things move, persons act,' is literal." [5]

Dramatistic theory, then, conceives of the individual as a performer who manages the impressions people have of him by playing various roles. Moreover, from the dramatistic perspective all of us are members of the cast. We are "on-stage"; i.e., through motivated role performances we present images for audiences to observe, interpret, and respond to. Our performances take place in particular settings, and we use several media and props to convey the impressions appropriate to our roles. In theatrical parlance the key elements of any performance are the act (or acts), actor, motive, role, scene, and vehicle for addressing an audience.[6]

Two recent Presidents of the United States presenting policies toward the war in Vietnam illustrate the dramatic elements in political action. In the 1964 presidential campaign (the scene) Lyndon Johnson (the actor) performing in the role of a campaigner seeking reelection (motive) promised in campaign speeches (vehicle) that his administration sought "no wider war" (symbolic act). He raised the public (audience) expectation that there would be no massive commitment of American ground forces in Southeast Asia. Yet, from his perspective as President once reelected (a different role), he deemed that practical conditions made such a commitment necessary. Hence, to sustain his performance, now as President rather than campaigner, he sent troops to Vietnam to "contain" the war (symbolic act), not to widen it. In 1968 another actor in the role of capaigner, Richard Nixon, proclaimed a desire to extricate the United States from Vietnam by a "plan" to bring "peace with honor" and without surrender (symbolic act). Upon occupying the Presidency (his new role) he announced graduated troop withdrawals (symbolic act) and "Vietnamization" of the war to replace the United States in a fighting role with South Vietnamese forces. Later, in keeping with this performance, the President said the 1970 invasion of Cambodia was undertaken to shorten rather than prolong the war by destroying enemy supply bases; similarly resumption of bombing of North Vietnam in 1971–72 was necessary to "hasten" the day of American withdrawal. Then, in the dual role of President as Campaigner in 1972, Nixon created the expectation of a cease fire in Vietnam either before or shortly after election day. In both cases the Presidents' declarations of peaceful intentions heightened demands from other actors (members of the U.S. Senate, antiwar groups, the North Vietnamese, and others) for quick withdrawal.

There are a number of ways to look at these two performances. One can attribute error to both Presidents and say that they were overly optimistic about the possibilities for peace. Or one can say that both presidential candidates purposely misled the American People. The dramatistic analyst, however, would argue that these performances illustrate how political images evoked in one dramatic setting and for one dramatic purpose ("we seek no wider war" and "peace with honor" as campaign messages) affect political action by shaping what an audience expects about goals and, what is of equal importance, by structuring the rhetorical context within which politicians reach and publicize political decisions.[7] In the dramatistic perspective neither Johnson nor Nixon could be charged with deliberate deceit. Rather, the very *drama* of running for President constitutes a framework of popular expectations that a politician should have peaceful intentions which, given his image of an ethical performance in the role of presidential contender, he sincerely declares. Once President the dramatic scene, role, and motives change even though other dramatic elements (actor, media, and audience) remain. In short, there is a logic for each dramatic performance; the logic of campaigning for the presidency is not the logic of being president. Yet the images a candidate commits himself to in one role carry over to influence his role performance in the presidential drama.

Dramatic performances therefore are not inherently deceitful, pretentious, faked, or acted out by charlatans. In studying "life as theatre" the dramaturgic analyst "seeks to describe the ways in which 'impressions' are created, sustained, and ruptured under the condition that the actor is 'unconscious' or only dimly 'conscious' that this is part of the business he is in." [8] A dramatistic approach does not assert that politics is deception or that politicians are confidence men. This approach is merely a device to emphasize that the *images* people have of politics, politicians, and the mass are, in themselves, *actions* that establish the contours of leader-follower relationships; they are actions that stem from *and* determine motives, but the motives themselves are inherently neither good nor bad, conscious nor unconscious. But the subtleties of politics make it hard to be precise about who is on stage and who is in the audience.

. . . To be sure, the performers we see when we go to the theatre do several things to remind us that we are witnessing a play. They use exaggerated gestures, take bows, and appear in public outside their stage roles. But in political dramas we seldom get such clues. If politicians have characters different from those they portray on stage, we are rarely privy to the back stage where they appear. As members of the mass audience, as Shakespeare wrote, "the play's the thing"; and participation in politics for most of us is limited to being members of that mass audience.[9]

In sum, the dramatistic viewpoint regards all social relationships as dramatic action. A person in a social drama (be he in a political setting, religious ceremony, business-labor negotiation, marital contract, or even in the bedroom) performs in accordance with the impression he wishes to leave on his audience. While on-stage the logic of the dramatic performance guides and controls his relations to other performers and spectators.

The Political Uses of Drama

. . . Leaders use personification, identification, ceremonies, public denunciation, and dramatic confrontation . . . and style, rhetoric, para-social interaction, and play—all are aspects of image communication with dramatic overtones. Which ones of many possible dramatic devices people use in politics depends upon several factors, but principally upon the actors, audience, issues, setting, and media.

Two considerations affect the *political actor's* choice of dramatic mechanisms. One is whether a politician can adapt his political style to certain performances. Can a leader take advantage of his appearance and forensic abilities to capitalize on the opportunities afforded by unfolding political dramas? President Franklin Roosevelt was one politician who could. Although confined to a wheel chair by poliomyelitis, he stood when making a public address, thus giving the impression of a man with indomitable strength and courage who could lead America out of the Great Depression and through World War II. Moreover, his speeches were even prepared by a dramatist, Robert E. Sherwood (the writer of a successful 1930s drama, *Abe Lincoln in Illinois*). In his "fireside chats" (radio addresses to the American public from the informal setting of his White House study), Roosevelt employed many of the devices conducive to cementing a parasocial relationship with his audience.

In addition to possessing an advantageous political style, the politician's penchant for performing leads to his use of certain dramatic devices. In the 1964 Democratic national convention President Lyndon Johnson employed suspense as a dramatic mechanism. In what was basically a cut-and-dried nominating convention he played cat-and-mouse with the press and hinted at several possibilities regarding the selection of a running mate; the President contrived to wait until the last minute to announce personally to delegates that Hubert Humphrey was his vice-presidential preference.

The *spectators* to a dramatic performance are not a passive audience. Since they read meanings into the performance, their expectations help determine the expressions an actor uses to influence the audience's impressions of him. If audience expectations permit, reinforce, or even demand it, an actor can deliberately "play" to his audience. On the night of an election, for example, candidates who know they have been soundly defeated maintain an optimistic front, go to their campaign headquarters and assure supporters that things will change when the "late returns are in," and withhold any concession statement until all hopes for victory are lost. The electoral winner in the drama goes through "rites of passage" by following a definite scenario to demonstrate to one and all that he is exchanging the role of partisan contender for that of public official. He makes a gracious acceptance speech, praises the gentlemanly conduct of his opponent, asks both his supporters and opponents for help, and dedicates himself to public service. He takes the oath of office in a formal inaugural ceremony; usually the more important his role is to the governmental drama, the more elaborate the ritual (compare, for example, the inauguration of a President or Governor with the swearing in of a city councilman). Finally, he addresses his entire constituency in his inaugural speech, no longer as a divisive partisan but as a unifying political authority. This marks the end of his passage from partisan to winner to public servant. Both victor and vanquished perform as the audience expects regardless of what may be their private feelings: "Whether an honest performer wishes to convey the truth or whether a dishonest performer wishes to convey a falsehood, both must take care to enliven their performances with appropriate expressions, exclude from their performances expressions that might discredit the impressions being fostered, and take care lest the audience impute unintended meanings." [10]

Certain *issues* generally encourage the use of dramatic devices. Some issues involve concrete matters dividing candidates and voters while others are ambiguous moral and ethical questions on which there is a broad consensus. The latter yield dramatic possibilities. It is relatively easy to dramatize one's stand against the "drug traffic," "organized crime," or "labor racketeers." By playing the hero against symbolically defined forces of evil, a leader confronts wrong, denounces wrongdoers, and professes to stamp out sin wherever he sees it. Thomas E. Dewey, twice nominated as Republican presidential candidate, took advantage of ethical issues; he came to national prominence for his dramatic confrontations with criminals as New York City's district attorney. Ralph Nader has built a national reputation on such issues as safety, quality, and environmental protection; regularly denouncing manufacturers of automobiles, electrical appliances, detergents, and others, he identifies himself as the leader of a crusade to protect the consumer against unsafe, low-quality, polluting products.

Some *political settings* are more conducive to dramatic performances than others. A partisan political convention, for example, is particularly suited because of its avowed symbolism honoring legendary folk heroes (such as Abraham Lincoln and Thomas Jefferson), and opportunities for conflict, dramatic encounters, and public denunciations. Congressional hearings also hold dramatic possibilities. In public hearings such as the 1973 Senate inquiry into the Watergate affair congressional leaders interrogate witnesses, identify with popular figures, denounce villians, and label partisan opponents as fools. Debates, filibusters, and votes in the U.S. Senate are scenes of high drama (witness the drama of the Senate vote failing to convict President Andrew Johnson after impeachment proceedings following the Civil War or the more recent roll calls rejecting President Richard Nixon's appointments of Clement F. Haynsworth in 1969 and G. Harrold Carswell in 1970 to the Supreme Court). And, the judiciary with its adversary system, elaborate ritual, clear definitions of roles, and courtroom props such as flags, elevated bench, and witness stand provides an ideal stage for political drama.

. . . Few political scenes involve such dramatic exploitation as political campaigns. A case in point was the presidential campaign of 1952 which took place in the setting of the unpopular Korean War. Neither candidate, Republican Dwight Eisenhower nor Democrat Adlai Stevenson, had definite plans for ending that war, but Eisenhower dramatized his willingness to try by promising that, if elected, "I will go to Korea." The announcement employed several dramatic devices:

> His offer had overtones of peripety; i.e., the single plain man would wage war directly against the overwhelming power of bureaucratic mechanics. It also personified the war by indicating that leaders like Eisenhower himself could be held directly responsible and that the war was not doomed by an impersonal fate to drag on hopelessly. These factors produced a level of identification with Eisenhower that any candidate could envy. Finally, the promise set up a ready-made climax composed of those moments when Eisenhower would actually arrive in Korea to survey the situation. How could an electorate on the verge of voting deny itself such an attractive climax by voting for Stevenson? [11]

All of the *media of communication* . . . have dramatic uses. Roosevelt's fireside chats, the 1960 Kennedy-Nixon debates, televised hearings of congressional committees into the conduct of the Vietnam war—all served as vehicles for politicians who influenced the inferences audiences made about them. The stock-in-trade of many newspaper columnists consists of exploiting dramatic devices, particularly "unmasking" public figures to expose their "real" characters and motives. In late 1971 India and Pakistan waged a brief but costly war in which India victoriously liberated East Pakistan and assisted in establishing the newly independent state of Bangladesh. In that war the Nixon Administration assumed a public stance generally opposed to India. In early 1972 newspaper columnist Jack Anderson published material from classified government memoranda allegedly revealing the ways U.S. policy makers contrived to blame India for the war. Anderson's efforts to unmask the Nixon administration created an image of duplicity whether such deception actually existed or not. In the 1972 presidential campaign the same Jack Anderson endeavored to unmask the then Democratic vice-presidential nominee, Senator Thomas Eagleton, as an alcholic who had been arrested for driving while intoxicated. Not being able to prove those charges, Anderson offered a dramatic apology to Eagleton on national television. (The controversy surrounding Eagleton, pertaining to his previous hospitalization for emotional stress, nevertheless led to his resignation from the Democratic ticket.)

. . . Some *events* seem almost destined for dramatic presentation. The disclosure in 1971 of a classified 47-volume, 7000-page study of U.S. involvement in the Vietnam war is an apt example. Known as the "Pentagon Papers" (a symbol with connotations that the report was a product of a civilian-military elite), the study implied that decisions to escalate the war in Vietnam were made well before seeking public support for involvement of American forces. Many people concluded that the American public and Congress had been deceived into believing that no massive commitments would be made. Summaries of the report were published in both *The New York Times* and *The Washington Post* after it had been leaked to the newspapers by "unidentified sources." The U.S. Department of Justice asked the newspapers to return the documents and halt publication as injurious to the "defense interests of the U.S." When the *Times* refused to comply the Justice Department sought a court order against publication. A dramatic confrontation of principles and personages ensued. Members of the news fraternity argued that publication was protected by the people's right to a "free press" and "freedom of information." Government officials responded that the right of "executive privilege" and interests of "national security" were paramount. Within twelve days of the publication of the first installment of the "Pentagon Papers," the case reached the Supreme Court which ruled that the government had failed to justify its case for a permanent injunction against publication. In the meantime Daniel Ellsberg, a former Pentagon aide and at the time a research associate of Massachusetts Institute of Technology, revealed that he had leaked the documents to the press. Subsequently he was indicted, but not convicted, for a violation of the Espionage Act for his unauthorized possession of documents related to national defense.

The controversy over publication of the "Pentagon Papers" had all the ingredients of high political drama. First, the actors in the encounter were clearly identified and symbolized—the "press" (acting on behalf of the "public") versus the "government." Second, the symbols of press and public represented powerful political interests, *The New York Times* and *The Washington Post* versus the past policies of Lyndon B. Johnson and the current policies of President Richard Nixon, Secretary of Defense Melvin Laird, and other administration officials. Third, what began as a conflict between relatively narrow interests, quickly became a symbolic confrontation of principle (the "right of a free press" versus the "national interest"). Fourth, the drama unfolded through several vehicles—in newspapers, magazines, books, and on radio and television—and on several stages—in Congress, in the Supreme Court, and in the Presidency. Fifth, the dramatic mechanism of *peripety* appeared (the situation in which a nobody becomes important or a celebrity falls from grace); to some Daniel Ellsberg became the hero of the antiwar movement while to others he typified the disloyal, radical intellectual. Sixth, the drama played out very quickly. Within a few days after the Supreme Court decision, news of the controversy faded from the headlines; it had been stripped of its dramatic overtones because the suspense and secrecy were gone, dramatic encounters ceased, and a climax had been reached. Finally, the drama of the "Pentagon Papers" illustrates how small is the actual attentive audience for even the most widely publicized political issues; at the height of the controversy, and on the day the Supreme Court announced its decision, a nationwide Gallup Poll revealed only 55 percent of respondents were even aware of the existence of the publication of the papers! [12]

THE ILLUSIONS IN POLITICAL IMAGERY

If political imagery is dramatic, then it shares with drama one other distinguishing quality—make-believe. Especially in considering the evaluative and expressive uses of political images, we have emphasized that images often have no goal beyond themselves; people have some images of politics which they find satisfying even though those images don't assist them in tangible ways. Political symbols, ceremonies, rituals, encounters, and other dramatistic devices are often means to an end, but frequently they are simply enjoyable in their own right. But where there is dramatic performance for its own sake, there is also the possibility that participants may mistake pretending for reality, and thus enter into a world of fantasy and illusion. All of this is not to say people don't respond to facts. They do. However, they are the facts *as they imagine them*. People perceive and interpret facts in accordance with their images and as those facts are presented through symbols. If the images are so private that they don't match what is "out there" (however that can be determined) or if the symbols communicate political fictions, then political imagery may be illusionary. In the discussion that follows we examine two tendencies in political imagery, conceived as dramatic action, that illustrate illusionary properties. These tendencies at the personal and social levels contrast politics as symbolic play with efforts to achieve social order.

Politics as Symbolic Play

. . . There are aspects of the development and communication of political images that contribute to a make-believe and playlike quality of politics. . . . We distinguish between play and imitation in a person's formation of political images. . . . If his mental pictures of the world are confined to mimicking the objects and persons in his environment (if, in other words, he unthinkingly accommodates, or modifies, his images to match new experiences), he is engaged in imitation; but, if he simply assimilates new stimuli into what he has already learned so that new information, data, and experiences have no influence on what he does or thinks, he is in symbolic play. Symbolic play involves protection of the self-image against threatening influences. In symbolic play, information about the environment may entertain and titillate but will not assist a person to adapt to changing conditions. We also know that such play influences image communication; . . . that is, people pay attention to messages they agree with and interact most with people they like or people who are like themselves. If they acquire political information from the media, it is to reinforce their political images, not to alter them. Moreover, much of popular attention to politics stems from a disinterested, voluntary, playlike search for pleasurable ways to express self-images; consequently people turn to political messages for restorative as well as reinforcing reasons.[13]

In addition to these play elements in politics, we also point to other aspects of political images that suggest its make-believe quality. The development of the cognitive content of political images lags behind affective development . . . Children learn loyalty to their political community before they are able to differentiate their nation from others; they place trust in the President and local policeman before understanding what these officials do; they build an affective tie to the political party of their parents long before knowing what differences there are in party positions on policies. And, as adults, people in the mass hold political opinions that have only minimal information behind them, respond to the personal style of leaders more quickly than to political experience, and have stronger emotional than rational links with political figures, issues, and events . . .

For the individuals who comprise the mass, therefore, politics is a playful, expressive drama by which they air needs to be with others, needs to be liked, self-acceptance and self-doubts, aggressions, love, and hate.[14] If the theatrical qualities of political images add up to play the implication is that the development of popular images of politics somehow gets arrested at a precausal and premoral stage. Consequently, instead of facilitating our adaptation to our environments by providing us with accurate perceptions of what the world is like, our political images impress the world with what *we* are like—or at least what we express ourselves as being like. If politics is built upon such illusions associated with symbolic play at the personal level, what consequences does this have for politics as a process of social order?

Politics as Social Order

There are two contrasting conceptions of how political images contribute to the regulation of social conflict. One states that images are manipulated as tools of social control; the other makes the assumption that images are elements of subjective play, and that political arrangements depend less upon the manipulation of symbols by leaders than upon the collective satisfactions people obtain from negotiating and holding similar images. These two conceptions overlap in several respects, but let us examine each separately.

We can label the first conception of the function of politics in achieving social order as that of *social control*.[15] It rests upon the view that societies are collectivities of people organized into hierarchies of different ranks, classes, and status. The *form* of hierarchy reflects human differences and transcends societies generally. There is always a potential for disorder in any particular hierarchy because people disobey, are disloyal, cheat, fight, steal, etc. Man employs his distinctive symbol-using, imagining capacity in the name of hierarchy. Through symbols he sanctifies a given social order (and its expression through hierarchy). The hierarchy is grounded in symbols representing what he believes is the intrinsic nature of man, society, and God. Note, for example, the pertinent references in the American *Declaration of Independence,* a document written to reject one hierarchical order and replace it with another; the dissolution of political bonds is justified on the basis of the "laws of nature and of nature's God," "a decent respect to the opinions of mankind," and a series of truths taken as "self-evident." Meaningful symbols such as these supply the language for the social drama that upholds, destroys, or changes the principles of the existing social order.

Politics plays a crucial role in preserving order, because political authorities portray government to people in ways that dramatize its legitimacy. They accomplish this by manipulating the politically relevant images people have learned to love and cherish, images that have been transmitted from generation unto generation—ways of life, social customs, religious faiths, and political doctrines.

The techniques of social control are by now familiar to us. Leaders endeavor to personify the highest ideals of the community, both while in public office and while trying to attain it: "The local candidate for township engineer assures us that his party will save the city, which in turn will save the nation, which in turn will save the free world, until finally we are saving Christian civilization by voting the local surveyor into office. Such 'mountings' always end in God, and thus, by inference, if we vote for the candidate, we vote for God." [16] Or a leader stages social dramas convincing followers of his majesty and power and identifying himself with the sacred social order: "We observe carefully how rulers stage themselves before different audiences, ranging from the office staff of the boss of a small local institution to the elaborate social dramas in which an emperor, king, or president acts out principles of social order. . . . When the followers have been taught to believe deeply in great transcendent principles which uphold social order, they watch carefully to see that their leaders play their roles in keeping with such principles." [17]

If there are threats to social order political rulers use symbols to convince citizens that dissidents are guilty of "sins" against the prevailing hierarchy of people, customs, and faiths. A favorite dramatic ploy is to find a scapegoat, the symbol of some person or social group to blame for social disturbances. Hence, Hitler placed the blame for social unrest in post-World War I Germany upon the "Jew." The use of the scapegoat device is not restricted to nondemocratic regimes; it is found at all times and places. Taken aback by protests against the 1970 invasion of Cambodia during the Vietnam war the President of the United States referred to student protesters as "bums" in informal remarks but later tempered the reference by stating it applied not to all protesters but only those that "burn buildings," "engage in violence," and "terrorize their fellow students and terrorize the faculty."

The essential feature of social control is that people learn images that support a given social order. Their deep and abiding loyalties to those images and to the social order they represent give leaders an opportunity to manipulate appropriate symbols to enforce obedience to the regime, laws, and authorities. As necessary, political authorities combine propagandistic appeals with threats of force. Some rulers enforce social order by constraint, i.e., by threatening to deprive a population of something deemed valuable such as freedom or wealth. Others achieve social order through inducement—the promise of some indulgence such as greater wealth, physical well-being, respect, or affection. Most combine constraints with inducements, but the degree of deprivation and inducement varies considerably. Deprivation may be as mild as a token tax or as severe as property confiscation, and inducements vary from the promise of the President's autographed photo to a lucrative defense contract. A high degree of constraint and/or inducement results in coercion, whereas a low degree of both constitutes choice.[18]

Contrasted with the social control conception of order is that of *convergent selectivity*. . . . Convergent selectivity consists of individuals (each making a choice independently and freely for himself with minimal constraint) reaching a consensus on goals, products, issues, political candidates, or whatever. Whereas the social control conception regards mass opinion as a product of deliberate organization and manipulation by propagandistic appeals, the convergent selectivity view regards people as absorbed in mass communication for pleasurable subjective play. Hence, the choices they make, whether in the market-place or political arena, are personally pleasing. In social control the object is to get people to arrive at common decisions (thus enhancing social order) by mobilizing them through symbol manipulation; in convergent selectivity "the object is to let each person choose something different for himself" so that social order flows from the convergence of freely made individual choices.[19]

In both the social control and convergent selectivity conceptions popular images of politics are basic to social order. In social control politicians mobilize images in support of the political community, its regime, and its leaders by clever manipulation of the symbols that people respond to with meaning. Preservation of social order depends upon political elites who can accurately gauge and guide public sentiment through symbolic appeals. The hierarchy of the social order is thus marked by clear divisions: "Throughout human history the upper strata of society leaned more toward symbolic activities, the lower strata engaged more in physical action, and the middle classes were in trade. The upper classes achieved their aims through control of information and physical coercion; the lower classes used passive resistance (strike) or violence (revolution); and the middle classes used credit and price manipulation."[20]

Convergent selectivity counters the hierarchical view. The preservation of social order does not rest with symbol-manipulating elites but results from freely acting individuals making common choices. To be sure, elites still play a significant role in the social drama. But instead of making decisions and enforcing them through propaganda and/or coercion, their role is more akin to the mass merchandiser, i.e., the elites suggest alternatives and compete for support through advertising. Unlike propaganda, advertising does not address itself to the group, but to single individuals: advertising "characteristically wants to sell *one* old piano to *one* person."[21] It transmits possibilities rather than factual information (whether that information be "disinterested" and objective as in education or "interested" and biased as in propaganda).[22] The target of advertising is not the individual in his group setting but the independent, free man before his television set or reading his newspaper who knows he "only goes around once in life" so he must get as much "gusto" from it as he can. Advertising speaks to individual subjectivity and is "concerned with the ways of imparting a desired meaning to a newly created set of symbols or of adding new meaning to already existing symbols."[23]

Certainly, we live in an era in America of emphasis on the convergent selectivity view. Armed with data from public opinion polls and experimental studies of popular images, advertising agencies build sales campaigns for laundry soaps, toothpastes, deodorants, or automobiles to appeal to each person's unique hope for "a whiter, brighter wash," fear of tooth decay, or desire to be "cool and dry." Automobile advertising, for instance, urges each prospective car buyer to purchase a vehicle appropriate to his particular personality. Research indicates there is a high degree of congruency between a car owner's perception of his automobile and himself, that "automobiles are often expressions of the owner's image of self." [24] But, advertising is not confined to the sale of commercial products; few candidates for public office enter electoral contests without the services of professional image-makers and even such public agencies as the U.S. Army turn to mass advertising for stepping-up recruiting, telling young Americans that "We Want to Join You!"

The convergent selectivity conception thus recognizes the capacities of individuals in mass society for symbolic play. It accepts the premise that free individuals try to enhance their self-images and respond to symbols they find pleasurable rather than to those that promise only social communion. When a sufficient number of individuals in mass society converge in their selection of pleasurable symbols, convergent selectivity may foster social order. But, contrasted with social control, order rests upon more than just the manipulation of symbols by elites. Something must be added to augment convergent selectivity as a device for achieving social order. There must be the opportunity for people to make free choices from a diverse, rich, variegated set of alternatives from which to choose. It is not enough to say that people may choose any soap they please. There must be many different soaps available to choose from. When it comes to consumer goods in mass society, the number and variety of alternatives depend upon several factors—levels of national economic development, types of economic controls upon production and sales, the size and diversity of the consumer audience, etc. With political "goods," however, range of choice is limited in most regimes. This is precisely what concerns critics of contemporary politics. Indeed, one argument goes so far as to say that *the very image that there is choice in contemporary political regimes is the most fundamental mass illusion of our times.* . . .

NOTES

[1] The view dates back prior to the ancient Greeks but is put most clearly by Shakespeare in Act II, Scene VII, of *As You Like It* in the oft-quoted passage,

> "All the world's a stage
> And all the men and women merely players;
> They have their exits and their entrances;
> And one man in his time plays many parts."

The tradition is most apparent in the following: George Herbert Mead, *Mind, Self, and Society* (Chicago: University of Chicago Press, 1934); Kenneth Burke, *A Grammar of Motives* (Englewood Cliffs, N.J.: Prentice-Hall, 1945); an example of an explicit attempt to employ dramaturgical analysis in political studies is Joseph R. Gusfield, *Symbolic Crusade* (Urbana: University of Illinois Press, 1966); a critique of the approach can be found in Patricke Johns Heine, *Personality in Social Theory* (Chicago: Adline Publishing, 1971), pp. 58–66.

[2] Kenneth Burke, "Dramatism," in Lee Thayer, ed., *Communication: Concepts and Perspectives* (Washington: Spartan Books, 1967), p. 329.

[3] Burke, *A Grammar of Motives,* p. xx; see also Haorld D. Lasswell and Abraham Kaplan, *Power and Society* (New Haven: Yale University Press, 1950), p. 10.

[4] Cassius Clay, "I'm a Little Special," *Sports Illustrated,* February 24, 1964, p. 14; a detailed account of the dramatic performances in everyday living can be found in Erving Goffman, *The Presentation of Self in Everyday Life* (New York: Doubleday, 1959), pp. 1–76.

[5] Burke, "Dramatism," p. 331.

[6] Compare Burke, *A Grammar of Motives*, p. xv.

[7] Hugh Dalziel Duncan, *Symbols in Society* (New York: Oxford University Press, 1968), p. 48.

[8] Sheldon L. Messinger et al., "Life as Theater: Some Notes on the Dramaturgic Approach to Social Reality," *Sociometry*, Vol. 25 (1962), 106.

[9] James N. Rosenau, *The Dramas of Politics* (Boston: Little, Brown, 1973).

[10] Goffman, *The Presentation of Self in Everyday Life*, p. 66; a detailed description of the rites of passage in American politics can be found in William C. Mitchell, *The American Polity (New York: Free Press, 1962), pp. 132–39.*

[11] Richard M. Merelman, "The Dramaturgy of Politics," *Sociological Quarterly*, Vol. 2 (Spring 1969), 232.

[12] News Release, American Institute of Public Opinion, July 2, 1971.

[13] Jean Piaget, *Play, Dreams, and Imitation in Childhood* (New York: Norton, 1962), pp. 147–212; Brian Sutton-Smith, "Piaget on Play: A Critique," *Psychological Review*, Vol. 73 (1966), 104–10; Mihaly Csikszentmihalyi and Stith Bennet, "An Exploratory Model of Play," *American Anthropologist*, Vol. 73 (February 1971), *45–58; William Stephenson, The Play Theory of Mass Communication* (Chicago: University of Chicago Press, 1967); Gerhart D. Wiebe, "Two Psychological Factors in Media Audience Behavior," *Public Opinion Quarterly*, Vol. 33 (Winter *1969–1970), 523–*36.

[14] Steven R. Brown and John D. Ellithorp, "Emotional Experiences in Political Groups: The Case of the McCarthy Phenomenon," *American Political Science Review*, Vol. 64 (June 1970), 349–66. Robert E. Lane, *Political Thinking and Consciousness* (Chicago: Markham, 1969).

[15] Duncan, *Symbols in Society*.

[16] Hugh Dalziel Duncan, *Communication and Social Order* (New York: Oxford University Press, 1962), pp. 139–40.

[17] Duncan, *Symbols in Society*, p. 203.

[18] Lasswell and Kaplan, *Power and Society*, p. 97.

[19] Stephenson, *The Play Theory of Mass Communication*, p. 2.

[20] Jurgen Ruesch, "The Social Control of Symbolic Systems," *Journal of Communication*, Vol. 17 (September 1967), 289.

[21] Stephenson, *The Play Theory of Mass Communication*, p. 35.

[22] Terence H. Qualter, *Propaganda and Psychological Warfare* (New York: Random House, 1962), pp. 26–31.

[23] Ruesch, "The Social Control of Symbolic Systems," p. 278.

[24] Al E. Birdwell, "A Study of the Influence of Image Congruence on Consumer Choice," *Journal of Business*, Vol. 41 (January 1968), 87–88.

23.

DRAMATIC ENCOUNTERS

Orrin Klapp

Public men are understandably wary of dramatic encounters—televised debates, pointed questions, and personal challenges. In one city, twelve mayoralty primary candidates were invited to the same banquet to explain their positions. Of those who

Reprinted from Orrin Klapp, *Symbolic Leaders: Public Dramas and Public Men*, Minerva Press, 1968. Reprinted by permission of the author and Aldine Publishing Company.

came, we can imagine that some had mixed feelings and poor digestions, for they knew they would not only get publicity but be put "on the spot"; they knew, also, that such a free-for-all was potentially very dangerous; but they came. A public man has to pretend to like confrontations, or at least he must not seem reluctant to face them. Yet the question is fair: Why should a program or a reputation, perhaps the work of years, be casually jeopardized merely to satisfy some person or group? There is always more risk for a "big" man than for a small one in challenging encounters; the former has much to lose, while the latter may have everything to gain. The trouble with a dramatic confrontation is that, unlike a mere "appearance" or "presentation," [1] one puts himself and his prestige into the scales for a contest or comparison with somebody else, and in so doing may confer the gift of prestige on his opponent and meanwhile subject himself to a role crisis.

A political candidate is aware of this vast difference between a speech or a TV appearance and a confrontation. People with unstable personalities may expose themselves recklessly, so their careers are a tapestry of scandalous and ludicrous albeit interesting, incidents; [2] politicians are more likely to try to avoid dangerous encounters and to accept only those that are favorable, meanwhile maintaining the pose that they would meet anyone anywhere. Their wariness comes from their recognition of the risks in the dramatic domain; they know that peculiar laws operate in it and that great role changes can come from minor incidents. . . .

. . . This chapter will analyze some of the things that any good tactical politician may be considering: the peculiar laws of the dramatic domain, some types of dramatic encounters, and the principles that seem to govern their income.

PECULIAR LAWS OF THE DRAMATIC DOMAIN

One of the peculiarities of the dramatic domain is that a public drama cannot be confined to the billed performers; almost anyone can steal the show. Nor does it require remarkable abilities or achievements. Even a lunatic threatening a crowd or a desperate man about to jump off a roof is, for the moment, the star (if not the hero) of the show. Someone who is merely antic or colorful can take the spotlight away from a dull man, however important the latter may be. Entertainers are alert to such possibilities [3] and often object to being billed with animals or children or people who are funnier than they. Subtle theatrical techniques can be used to command attention,[4] and a public man, if he does not use them, should at least be sure that they are not used against him. The gist of this is that the star can be forgotten by a shift of attention. How can a public man protect himself from losing attention just when he needs it most? Will expensive TV time and full press coverage guarantee that the audience will not be watching something else?

Another peculiarity of the dramatic realm is that an insignificant person can easily challenge and jeopardize a more important person. The considerateness with which a public speaker answers a person in the audience—or, on the other hand, the sharpness with which an apparently innocent questioner is "put down"—is likely to result not from the innate courtesy or discourtesy of the speaker but from his awareness of threat and his defensiveness. Every teacher knows that a small person can challenge an important person in a way that has a curious advantage for the smaller.

The "upstart" or "smart alec" has no prestige to lose, and any score he can make on the "big shot" benefits him tremendously. On the other hand, the most the bigger man can do is "put down" the upstart and return things to the status quo; he gets little credit for his victory. While the big man may have experience, power, and self-confidence on his side, he has to put into the wager more than it is worth to him. Politicians, knowing this, avoid confrontations that can do them no good and only benefit their rivals. . . .

This danger to the big man and advantage to the underdog is sometimes attributed to democratic ideology, or to the fact that the common man finds it easier to identify with someone at his own level than with someone above. But even people of high status and aristocratic bias can identify with underdogs. More fundamentally, then, a dramatic prejudice in favor of upsets seem to be a built-in feature of drama itself.

A third peculiarity of the dramatic realm is that there are no strict logical limitations on what can become important to audiences; almost any kind of contest, struggle, predicament, or contretemps can be meaningful, even a frog race. It would be a mistake to suppose that incidents have to be significant in a moral, intellectual, or material sense to hold the attention of the public. The only requirement is that a person (or animal) in whom the public is capable of being interested engage in an action that has conflict, suspense, and other features of "human interst." [5] This means that trivial events—a movie scandal, a personal feud—can be blown up out of proportion to their true merit, can become *causes célèbres,* that mere gestures (Thoreau refusing to pay a one-dollar tax, Sewell Avery being carried out bodily from the Montgomery Ward plant, Khrushchev banging his shoe) can be as important as real deeds. Pygmies then become giants. Dramatic encounters double the magnitude of any event; people who have no tangible stake in what is happening become aroused and inflamed by the fate of a hero, villain, or victim; things that would ordinarily have been insignificant suddenly become terrbly important. On the other hand, bureaucracy suffers from want of drama (unless it, too, becomes a fool or villain.) However important it may be intrinsically, it usually seems uninteresting or comic; therefore it cannot get a fair hearing in the court of public opinion. Because of such disproportions, we may say that the scale of public events is topsy-turvy.

The very essence of drama—the high point of its most important scenes—is usually a confrontation in which parties are thrown on their mettle, reveal and expose themselves, drop their defenses, call on their personal resources to meet a crisis. *Spontaneity* is maximized. On stage, a script takes care of this, but in real life spontaneity means unexpected behavior and consequences; no one knows quite what will happen; mistakes, contretemps, or foolish roles are likely. A demagogue tries to create encounters that he can handle and his opponent cannot; witness Khrushchev, clowning, blustering, browbeating, probing into his enemy's defenses looking for a soft spot.[6] . . .

Another potent risk-producing factor of drama is the close-up—not merely of audience with actor (made embarrassingly intimate by modern photography and high-fidelity equipment) but between the parties in personal encounter. Two giants can exist in separate fables, but bring them together and one is likely to appear smaller than the other. It is so for public men; their scale is changed by mere juxtaposition. Actors know this well and choose partners and positions on stage accordingly. If two persons stand chest-to-chest or eye-to-eye with each other, it is likely that one of them will suffer; whereas, if they perform at separate times and places, only experts can rate the differences and a "match race" to settle things is avoided. So public men should take care about whom they are matched with, billed with, or even stand next to.

Yet another hazard is the enormous importance of timing, of the right role at the right time. One can "play the hero" a moment too soon or too late and be the biggest kind of fool. The successful hero steps into a situation at exactly the moment when audience expectation and the plot call for such a part; things have gotten as bad as possible for the victim, and the crisis has been properly developed; suspense and interest are at a maximum, so no one is tired of the situation; and the balance has become so precarious that it can easily be tipped in his favor. If a man manages to do things, it is hard to imagine how he can fail to become socially significant. On the other hand, many good deeds and worthy enterprises have failed because the time was not ripe or the ratio of forces was unfavorable. Both tragedy and comedy hinge on precarious considerations like these.

In addition, the pressure of the audience favors certain parts and outcomes. If conflict arises, people need to define a "good guy" and a "bad guy"; they will look for cues or merely cast these parts arbitrarily (as we often do at sporting contests). An audience also usually favors underdogs and victims and is very quick to find a fool, to laugh at anything funny. The man who steps into a situation, may find a part handed to him—he may unexpectedly find himself on stage, as a performer or as the subject of a joke he had not anticipated. Such pressures may seem "unfair," but it is hard to keep the proceedings sensible and objective when the atmosphere becomes dramatic.

The more general observation follows, then, that in drama outcome does not equal input. One man alone, however sincere and even if he is physically successful in what he sets out to do, cannot guarantee what his act will mean or what roles will be assigned to him and others as a result of his action. The factors that determine these consequences are outside the scope of any individual actor and do not bear a precise relationship to the phsical forces mobilized or the real nature of the elements employed. A very large army, for example, could seem small and belittled in spite of its power or a noble deed could emerge as villainy. There is a capricious power in drama that might almost be called magical, for it produces astounding results from apparently insufficient means and causes changes in character like a chameleon.

We see this capriciousness in examples of "quixotic" characters, whose historical roles have unexpected outcomes. I refer here to a man of independent will and idealistic purpose who goes to an extreme that society defines as villainous or foolish, though he is in his own eyes a crusader doing good. His determined adherence to principle throws him out of joint with his times and leads him to the extreme necessary to produce a villain or fool. Certain men, we know, whether from idealism or hot-headedness, are likely to go to excess in fighting for what they believe. They will stand against public opinion even when there seems to be no hope,[7] they become diehards and fanatics, and they are ready to act on their own view regardless of what others think. Harry S. Truman's statement suggests that he could easily play a role: "I shall continue to do what I think is right whether anybody likes it or not." [8]

The important thing, however, is that though quixotic characters are ready to act as heroes, they cannot determine the role that history will thrust upon them. For one thing, they are either blind or indifferent to others' definitions; they see the drama only in their own terms. When their good intentions carry them to extremes that others will not follow, they cannot understand why the world becomes angry or ridicules them. When such men are "lucky," like John Brown and General Custer, they are approved by history with a sort of grudging recognition of their admirable stubbornness. But when they are unlucky, their very persistence and idealism provide some of the worst desperadoes and most laughable fools, such as John Wilkes Booth, who has often been compared with Brutus,[9] except that his drama had a different outcome.

. . . The real question of dramatic outcome involves factors having little to do with personal input, with what a man is or intends to be. The pertinent questions are these: Did he act at the right psychological moment? Did he have the spotlight? What was the mood of the audience? Did he carry his role well before the audience? Was he suitably cast for the part? Was the plot pattern favorable? Who played the parts against him, and how did they carry off their parts? If these factors are changed, all kinds of remarkable things can happen to the public character of a man.

In brief, the peculiarities of the dramatic domain are these; (1) almost anyone can steal the show, (2) a small part has an advantage over a larger one, (3) almost any kind of struggle or issue can become important, (4) spontaneity in dramatic crises and encounters favors unexpected outcomes, (5) there is great risk in close-ups, (6) timing is enormously important, (7) audience need and expectation can press hero, villain, fool, and victim roles on people and favor certain kinds of outcomes, and (8) the same kinds of character and motive (especially those called "quixotic") can elicit widely varying definitions, depending on the situation. Because of such peculiarities in the dramatic domain, outcome is not equal to input in any realistic, logical, or personal sense; one cannot predict from the input of a drama (character, deeds, or intentions) what the outcome will be. The power and "magic" of drama originate from other sources.

Let us now look more closely at several types of dramatic confrontations and their outcomes.

TYPES OF DRAMATIC ENCOUNTER

For most practical purposes, there are seven important role alternatives for a public man in dramatic confrontations, ranging from a popular "hit" to downright defeat. Once he commits himself, he may come out in any of these ways.

1. Honorific Ceremonial Meetings

The safest encounter is an honorific ceremony where important people, such as the heads of states or other organizations, meet under conditions of elaborate courtesy. . . . "Face" and rank are carefully maintained. No one does anything out of place; if an exchange occurs, it is all positive, with no loss to anybody; it involves mutual compliments, recognition, gifts. The audience warmly identifies with one or both parties. . . .

2. Hero-making Confrontations

Hero-making confrontations are inherently risky but potentially more rewarding than honorific meetings. Three common modes can be distinguished: the benefactor, the winner in a test, and the defeat of the martyr.

The safest confrontation for a hero is with a needy party, to whom he generously makes a gift and who is in an inferior position and is showing gratitude. There is no contest between principals; indeed, the recipient may be a helpless victim. Leaders, patrons, aristocratic classes, and political bosses try to play such a role to the public. In Argentina, Eva Perón played guardian angel to working girls, unwed mothers, and the like, establishing herself as a kind of patron saint as well as reinforcing her husband's regime. . . .

Yet even such relationships between benefactor and recipient can get out of hand. One major risk is that the needy party will not show appropriate gratitude and thus make it hard for the benefactor to play his role without incurring suspicion that there is something wrong with him rather than with the recipient. (This has apparently happened in nations that view American foreign aid in terms of "ugly" Americans.) Another risk is that a competitor will steal the show with an even more exciting gift, thus making the would-be benefactor look reluctant or cheap. . . .

The second type of hero-making confrontation—the test—is of course more risky because it requires the subject to emerge as victor in a show of strength after committing himself fully. Such an encounter is safe only with a "setup," an opponent who looks dangerous but really is unable to compete effectively. Thus, a famous news picture shows Mayor Fiorello La Guardia of New York smashing slot machines in a police raid in 1934. He cuts a fine figure, poised over the wicked machines wielding a sledge hammer, rather like Richard the Lion-Hearted with his two-handed sword. Though there is no reason to suppose that La Guardia avoided real encounters, it was much safer for him to attack machines than publicly to rebuke a live gambler.

Within the test category are at least three subpatterns: (1) the battle of rival champions, (2) the defeat of a villain (whose wickedness points up the goodness of the hero), and (3) a David-Goliath encounter in which a little man upsets a big man.

The battle of champions is illustrated by President John F. Kennedy's historic confrontation with Roger Blough, chairman of the board of United States Steel Corporation, on April 12, 1962. The chairman called on the President to inform him of an arbitrary raise in the price of steel. The President soon thereafter, in a press conference, denounced the steel industry for irresponsibility and selfishness and threatened legal and political reprisals. Within forty-eight hours, the steel industry backed down, cancelling its price increases. Said *Time:*

> The ferocity of his attack on steel alienated and angered many a businessman . . . [but] there could be no doubt that John Kennedy had won a popular victory. Beyond question, the great majority of Americans reacted angrily to U.S. Steel's price-increase announcement. That reaction was instinctive, and Kennedy exploited it skillfully. . . . He had made the steelmen look like Milquetoasts.[10]

Though Kennedy charged villainy on the part of the steel industry, actually this was a contest between champions of rival corporate power blocs—big government versus big business. It had all the qualities of a good contest; a personal encounter between two powerful men, a conflict of wills, and a test of strength and prestige. Kennedy acted with the sturdy stance of King Arthur swinging his great sword, and Blough was obliged to back off. Blough's dramatic alternatives were to act as a villain (which he did not accept; his behavior was in no way discreditable, though some blamed him for bad timing and judgment), as the rival champion of equal strength who loses, or as the weak knight [11] who is disgraced and made a fool. While his role had aspects of all these alternatives, it was mainly the second that emerged. Kennedy also risked failure, which could have made him look like a fool (risking the power of the Presidency against a mere group of corporations and being outfoxed); the wrong tactics might have cast him as a bully, coward, swaggerer, or stuffed shirt. Blough had to be big enough to test Kennedy's mettle (there is no glory in an encounter with a stooge, a weak or humble person, or a fool) yet not big enough to overthrow him. It was very important also how Blough reacted; a more colorful man—a cantankerous Sewell Avery, a big-talking Diamond Jim Brady, a wisecracking Will Rogers—might have stolen the show. And, of course, the whole thing might have happened in some other way (by committees, trial balloons, or private correspondence) so that no actual confrontation would have occurred.

The second test pattern, the defeat of a villain, is safer for the "hero" because there is no sympathy to swing to the opponent if the tables should be turned. Almost any good effort against a villain receives some credit; a knockout is, of course, a "hit." The badness and strength of the villain make the hero look all the better (whereas to defeat a good man inevitably leaves the audience with some ambivalent regret). When the pattern is at its best, the hero catches a villain red-handed and at the height of a crisis, knocks him down, and carries off the prize or restores the threatened welfare. Ideally, a villain helps by confirming his own status: admitting guilt, fighting unfairly, running away, performing treachery or cruelty, and other acts well known in melodrama. President Kennedy did not have a very good villain in Roger Blough, but he had a better one in Premier Khrushchev, in the confrontation over the missile bases in Cuba in October, 1962, which followed classic lines. Here, it might almost be said, was Perseus arriving to face the dragon or Achilles girding himself to do battle for the Greeks, and the dragon backed off and withdrew his missiles, giving dramatic victory to the hero.[12] . . .

The third hero-making test pattern, that of David and Goliath, requires that a small hero be pitted against a large villain. It is well illustrated by Martin Luther King's organization of the strike against the bus companies of Montgomery, Alabama, forcing them to modify their "Jim Crow" rules. The success of an obscure Baptist minister against the bus companies and against powerful white resistance put him in the role of David against the Goliath of segregation, which he then hit with the stone of non-violent resistance, again and again.

Ironically, another illustration is provided by an enemy of integration, Governor Ross Barnett of Mississippi, a dull political prospect who managed by a series of confrontations with the United States government to make himself a local hero and thus brighten his outlook. In an article entitled "Now He's a Hero," *Time* tells how his defiance of the federal government, for a time blocking the registration of James Meredith in the University of Mississippi, brought a "dizzying turnabout" in his political prospects.[13] We may analyze this role with profit. Prior to the event, his reputation had been that of a confirmed racist with some reputation for Christian piety (he had taught Sunday school and had vetoed a bill to raise the alcohol limit of wine), but he was a rather disappointing governor, who had a reputation as a "do-nothing." A chance to dramatize himself came with the decision of the Department of Justice to make a test case of James Meredith's entrance at the University of Mississippi. Barnett's transfiguration took place as a series of confrontations in which he defied the Goliath of the federal government as a threat to states' rights. First came a private meeting, on September 20, 1962, in which, as self-appointed registrar of the university, he rejected Meredith and the federal court order supporting his application for admission. This called some attention to him as a man who had succeeded in defying the law, but the second encounter, at the doorway of Room 1007 of the capitol building with Chief U.S. Marshall James McShane, on September 25, was more crucial. The door swung open with "theatrical timing" as Meredith appeared, backed by McShane and an aide. There stood the Governor. The officers tried "fumblingly" to hand Barnett some court orders, which he refused. Then he read off a proclamation denying Meredith admission to the university. The federal officer, James Doar, made "one last, limp try":

> "Do you refuse to permit us to come in this door?" he asked.
> *Barnett:* "Yes, sir."
> *Doar:* "All right. Thank you."
> *Barnette:* "I do that politely."
> *Doar:* "Thank you. We leave politely." [14]

Thus the federal government backed down. It is entirely possible that the encounter could have come out favorably for the government with more adroit handling. As it was, the federal officers were made to look inept, clumsy, and even timid; they were apparently balked by the stand of one valiant man. If they had circumvented or defeated the Governor in some way, they could have stolen his thunder.

The third encounter, next day, was also a dramatic loss to the federal forces, though Barnett, because of a missed plane, was unable to capitalize on it personally. Now the man blocking the way was Lieutenant Governor Paul B. Johnson, who stood at the doorway of the university, backed by about twenty state policemen and a dozen sheriffs.

As before, McShane and Doar tried pleading, urging, arguing, demanding and waving court orders—all in vain. Now McShane tried using his muscles. Several times he pushed a meaty shoulder against highway patrolmen. . . . But he was outnumbered twenty to one by the troopers, some of them pretty husky too, and his scufflings with them were utterly futile, merely adding a dash of absurdity to the proceeding.

The fourth encounter, September 27, was between a motor cavalcade of marshalls and a small army of some 200 state policemen backed by sheriffs, deputies, and a mob. Again the federal forces, seeing the impossibility of making progress without serious bloodshed, withdrew. "The decision to pull back was sensible, but it looked embarrassingly like a retreat." There then followed a lull, during which President Kennedy made a speech and a federal court found Barnett guilty of contempt *in absentia,* threatening him with a 10,000-dollar-a-day fine and confinement. The Governor, seeing the handwriting on the wall, desisted, and the episode was over. He had already made himself a hero and "could quit well ahead." Why should he be a martyr to satisfy a few fanatics? [15]

An appraisal of this episode shows that the four encounters were defeats, practically and dramatically, for the federal govermnet, that Barnett gained corresponding credit, and that the court decision lacked the qualities of an encounter and so was not a defeat for Barnett. President Kennedy, probably fortunately, stayed out of all this personally, though if he had confronted Barnett it might have created a new pattern of drama (though one of doubtful advantage to the President). The most important thing to be noted was a buildup of forces on each side from one encounter to another that continuously operated to the disadvantage of the government. The federal forces were not strong or adroit enough to win easily. Yet, if they had built up their power and overridden the Governor and his forces, they would have offered a good opportunity of martyrdom to the rebels; while by backing off, they looked weak, hesitant, even foolish (in the comic frustration of a large by a small force). How could they have won without seeming to be Goliaths (bullies) who overcame valiant little men? Almost any kind of private or indirect dealing, it seems, would have been dramatically better for the federal government than allowing Barnett to benefit from these favorable scenes. I am not qualified to suggest alternative diplomatic tactics, but clearly the public ratio of forces was dramatically bad for the government, even though Barnett in his relation to Meredith (as a single man without federal support) was a bully oppressing the weak (at least in northern eyes). The public encounter with Barnett should have been managed with a ratio of forces that did not offer heroism or martyrdom to the defiant party. You cannot win dramatically by flouting this ratio.

. . . If you cannot win, you can lose heroically; and this sometimes makes a better symbol than a victory. This is especially the case for the martyr role, the third and most costly hero-making route. The defeat or suffering endured by the hero is taken as a sign that, although he has lost, the cause itself will win, if only out of the loyalty of such men or the improved morale of those who remember and follow him. In contrast, a victim role, though it gets public sympathy, is not nearly so valuable; the essential difference is that it comes by accident. The martyr role must emerge from a seemingly voluntary choice for the good of the cause. One could not, for example, impose martyrdom on a fleeing victim, though if he turned and stood he might easily win the role.

The great advantage of non-violent resistance, as practiced by Hindus under Gandhi or Negroes following Martin Luther King, is that it invites martyrdom, so to speak, as a second choice to victory. It is, then, a dramatic strategy that cannot lose; the resister, being passive, is extremely hard to see as a villain, while the opponent, whether he wins or not, can hardly avoid being cast as an aggressor by an open-minded audience. The catch, of course, as practitioners well know, is in the self-control of the resister, since, if he displays the least aggressiveness, he enters the ordinary arena where he can quite as easily become a villain as a hero, and his advantage is gone.

It is not absolutely necessary to have a villain in a martyr drama; Colonel Gorgas' volunteers in the fight against malaria, for example, were martyrs, though malaria parasites could be called villains only by some stretch of the imagination. But, if the villain is present, he must play his part correctly. For example, if he overwhelms the hero without allowing him time to display fortitude and choice, he is more likely to create a mere victim, or, if he fails to be sufficiently cruel and unfair (as, for example, did Pontius Pilate), he does not make a very good persecutor and robs the martyr of his melodramatic advantage. If we begin to feel sorry for the bad guy, the affair is more likely to seem tragic than melodramatic.[16] From the standpoint of casting martyrs, then, it is partly a matter of finding a suitable villain—one who will accept his part and play it with vindictive glee, showing no remorse and not spoiling the scene by being human.

3. Villain-making Encounters

It is sufficient to point out here two patterns [17] of villainy: the oppression of a weaker party and the cowardly attack.

The behavior of Eugene "Bull" Conner of Birmingham, Alabama, enormously helped Martin Luther King's civil rights cause:

> Conner became an international symbol of blind, cruel Southern racism. When King sent out his marchers, Conner had them mowed down by streams from fire hoses. Shocking news photos splashed across the pages of the world's press—of a young Negro sent sprawling by a jet of water, of a Negro woman pinioned to the sidewalk with a cop's knee at her throat, of police dogs lunging at fleeing Negroes. With that, millions of people—North and South, black and white—felt the pangs of segregation and, at least in sympathy, joined the protest movement.[18]

The other villain-making pattern is also conveniently illustrated from the civil rights struggle in the unseen assassins who shot Medgar Evers, Negro leader, in the back, or those who bombed the Baptist church in Birmingham, Alabama, on September 15, 1963, killing four Negro children. These events, though the criminals were not caught, supplied a vivid image of the kind of person involved in such villainy; nor was there any mistaking the surge of national and world feeling for the Negro cause that followed these acts. The villains could not have done more damage to their own cause if they had used bombs and bullets on their own ranks.

In such dramas, almost any unsuspecting, helpless victim is sufficient. Of course, the height of the villainy is greatly increased if the one attacked is a popular hero; this puts the villain into a status like that of John Wilkes Booth, Judas, Mordred, or Delilah. . . .

4. Fool-making Encounters

Another dramatic possibility, of course, is to be made a fool, either by one's own action or by someone else's. . . . Comic mishaps . . . can rob a performer of serious consideration unless he can turn them to his own advantage, perhaps by accepting the clown role, or by turning the tables so cleverly that the audience is more impressed by his agility than by what he intended to do in the first place. If he takes himself too seriously or lacks sufficient wit to turn it to his advantage, a public man can be in difficulty when the show turns to comedy.

While anyone can make a fool of himself merely by acting in an undignified fashion, he is likely to be made a fool by somebody else in one of two ways: a joke that he cannot turn back against the jester or a defeat by a small obstacle or a grossly inferior party. The first situation is exemplified by a "hot foot" perpetrated on a sleeping victim or a heckling wisecrack that makes a speaker lose his temper and his good judgment. The second is illustrated by the comic frustration of a large force by a small force (the mouse outwitting the elephant, a large man getting himself locked in a telephone booth). A jester can literally try to put his opponents in such situations, or he can depict them by stories, remarks, cartoons, rumors, and so on. In a later chapter some of these fool-making tactics and situations will be examined.

The main thing that keeps comedy from being used more widely in public life is that it requires more wit than does melodrama. And, in general, people protect themselves from comic predicaments rather better than they do from melodramas, where there is a tendency for sincere people to rush in. But if public men began paying gagmen as much as top comedians pay television scriptwriters, we might see a new and livelier era in politics.

5. Becoming a Victim

The role of victim falls to many people whether or not they choose it. The role has added pathos to public careers—Franklin Roosevelt's paralysis; the loss of sons by Coolidge, Lindbergh, and Nelson Rockefeller; Wilson's stroke during his battle with Senate enemies. It has pulled some men out of trouble and pushed others into trouble. It is a symbolic advantage of a sort; the least it can do is quiet criticism for a time, since, whether or not critics actually feel sorry for the victim, they do not want it to appear that they are "hitting a man when he is down."

. . . If we ask what constitutes a good victim, the first inference . . . is that certain kinds of objects are especially likely to attract sympathy. Differences in culture plainly make a great difference in this regard; perhaps the most shocking thing one can do in England is mistreat a dog, while such action would cause little stir in the Philippines. But, once allowance is made for such cultural biases, the ratio of apparent forces assumes its due importance. The second inference, judging by folktales and dramas everywhere, is that smallness or weakness in anything or anyone that makes it helpless and unable to fight back is a prime quality of a good victim. . . . Third, we may infer that style of encounter is significant—passivity, meekness, innocence, gentleness, feminity, versus aggressiveness and the modes of villainy. Here the villain makes his contribution by taking all the blame on himself and leaving all the sympathy to the other; should the victim have any fault, it is easily forgotten because the villain is so much worse. Fourth, magnitude of misfortune makes a difference. The event must approach disaster; it must not be the kind of thing that happens to us all. Finally, it is crucial that the trouble be suffered but not chosen, since otherwise the public may say that the victim brought it all on himself.[19] The victim should not do much to help himself or seem capable of remedying the situation, otherwise he will rob the misfortune of its diastrous quality—and, incidentally, he may then steal the show from any hero who might try to save him (if the drowning man swims with the lifeguard, neither gets much credit).

The victim, then, has two dramatic partners: a hero, who is going to get him out of trouble, and the villain, who got him into trouble in the first place. The moral is that, if one is going to have anything to do with a victim, it had better be as hero rather than as villain

6. The Tragic Role

The tragic role is not as important as it might be in American public life for the simple reason that it is too hard to achieve. The popular mind in this country runs along comic and melodramatic rather than tragic lines, tending most often to create villains, fools, victims, or martyrs out of the potential material.[20] Lincoln, Wilson, and McKinley are sometimes cited as tragic Presidents; yet none of the disasters that struck them was strictly tragic. Wilson and McKinley were victims, and even Lincoln's assassination was a classic melodrama, one that could hardly have been more lurid if Harriet Beecher Stowe herself had worked on the script.[21] There is loose talk about the "tragedy" of this or that, especially in newspapers, but actually very few well-known people do achieve tragedy in public images, though we may not rule it out as a possibility.

For a public drama to develop along tragic lines, it would require a hero close enough to villainy to be deeply and consciously at fault for the misfortunes that he brings on himself and others, yet noble enough, for all that—in fortitude and dignity, at least—to command the sympathy if not the admiration of the audience. He must not have a clearly worthy cause or his misfortune will seem a martyrdom; he must come close to the martyr role in choosing his fate or he will seem merely a helpless victim of disaster. Those who oppose or persecute him may be villains to some extent; but if they are too evil—or he paints them so—the pattern descends to melodrama and he loses his tragic character. If he falls off this knife-edge, he becomes one of the simpler types that we have been discussing. Indeed, without a master dramatist to guide him, how is a public person to manage such a role?

The answer may be that it does not matter, that it is academic to try to define the conditions of a public tragic role since there is not enough advantage in it to warrant trying to attain it, though it could come by accident. Such a role, being ambivalent, cannot mobilize an audience in the way of simpler types. It may be, indeed, that the only advantage of a tragic role would be to provide interesting material for biographers.

7. Draw or Loss without Discredit

Finally, we may distinguish the confrontation pattern of holding one's own, of defeat without discredit, coming off honorably without victory, as when knights of King Arthur's Round Table, after breaking a few lances, part without deciding the issue. It is found in the surrender of General Robert E. Lee to General Ulysses S. Grant, for each had made such a good fight that the outcome seemed almost accidental—a Roland and Oliver type of encounter, in which two champions rest on their swords and declare (or discover) themselves friends. Each had proved the other's mettle, and the loser shared honors with the victor. Another version of defeat with honor is for a ''comer''—a young aspirant new to professional or public life—to hold his own against a more important opponent. His showing is not only good publicity but indicates his potential for better things. . . .

CONCLUSION

I have thus outlined seven outcomes of dramatic confrontation: (1) honorific ceremony, (2) hero-making (benefactor, winner, and martyr), (3) villain-making, (4) fool-making, (5) victim-making, (6) tragic, and (7) loss or draw without discredit. . . . Judging from these, what can be said about the principles that seem to govern? Surely there is more involved than merely the force exerted or the success of the outcome, for one can win materially yet lose dramatically.

The single most important factor in any dramatic encounter is the apparent ratio of forces. This ratio has much to do not only with how the event will actually turn out but with who will be hero, villain, fool, or victim and where audience sympathy will turn. Too great a preponderance of force on one side sets the stage for a villain who is using an unfair advantage or, if defeat looms, for a fool who could not win even when the cards were stacked in his favor. A David-and-Goliath situation is created, and the smaller party gets a role choice of hero or victim; the larger party has the possibility of victory with small credit but runs a very real chance of being villain or fool, and such an encounter is, for him, a poor bargain.[22] Apparent force, of course, is the key factor. It does not matter how many aces you have up your sleeve or tanks or henchmen hidden away; you must not display your true strength too obviously. Too large a display at the outset of a drama may make one look fearsome (as a villain), fearful (as a coward), or grandiose and pompous (as a stuffed shirt riding to his fall). For that reason, the movie hero usually underplays his strength before knocking out the bad guy,[23] and the cartoon Popeye eats his can of spinach only at the last. Buildups at the beginning are for villains and fools.

It seems plain that restraint in the early stages of an encounter has a number of consequences: (1) it avoids having the hero seem overconfident (the public welcomes the deflation of a stuffed shirt); (2) it casts the opponent as the "heavy" or the "bully"; (3) it arouses sympathy for a nice guy getting the worst of it until his wrath, valor, or potency is kindled; (4) it builds up suspense and deepens crisis; and (5) it maximizes the swing from looming defeat to victory, thus giving the audience the most exciting of emotional sleighrides. Of course, we presume a "win" or a martyr outcome; otherwise the would-be hero, instead of showing restraint, had better not appear at all.

The practical moral is that the public man, if he wishes to be popular, and regardless of how well laid his plans, how clever his tactics, or how great his resources, should always seem to act with a fair or somewhat disadvantageous ratio of force. He thus avoids being set up as a villain by would-be martyrs or impudent challengers. If defeat comes for him, with a safe ratio of forces he has the dramatic "outs" of the martyr or victim or of defeat with honor. He avoids (without being obvious about it) confrontations with small or unworthy antagonists who can only make him look bad as villain or fool. . . .

Another principle that emerges from the cases discussed is that the style of performance is of great importance, though not as important as the ratio of forces. It does not matter what you do substantively so much as how you do it. The advantage of non-violent resistance, for example, is that its style makes it almost impossible to define the aggressor as a villain; the worst he can be called is "troublemaker." He is, however, naturally eligible for victim and martyr roles. Certain qualities of style (unfairness, sneakiness, bluster, arrogance) help create a villain in the mind of the audience, just as other qualities (modesty, fairness, straightforwardness, pluck) set up a hero within an appropriate ratio of forces. Again, pomposity, clumsiness, timidity, levity, or antic behavior cast one—whatever his substantive deeds—as fool, if only because the audience becomes predisposed to laugh at anything that happens to him. But style alone, without an appropriate ratio of forces, cannot govern. . . .

Seeking key factors should not obscure the importance of the drama as a whole, the mutual effects of the roles of all actors as action proceeds through scenes, development, and turns.

NOTES

[1] Compare Jacqueline Kennedy's famous televised tour of the White House, which, though a smash hit, was not a confrontation but a solo performance and therefore comparatively safe. Had she undertaken a discussion or an argument with another lady about the history, art, and style of the White House, she might have glorified her partner and also subjected herself to a confrontation that could have meant "win or lose" for both.

[2] See Myrick Land, *The Fine Art of Literary Mayhem* (New York: Holt, Rinehart and Winston, 1963).

[3] In the movie, "The Road to Hong Kong," starring Bob Hope and Bing Crosby, Peter Sellers had a small part as a doctor in a delightful five-minute scene. During the shooting, Hope wisecracked, "Get rid of this man. He's too funny." (*McCall's,* August, 1963, p. 42.)

[4] Richard Burton found early in his career that by standing absolutely still on stage he could draw attention to himself and away from other actors.

[5] See Helen M. Hughes, *News and the Human Interest Story* (Chicago: University of Chicago Press, 1940).

[6] Premier Nikita Khrushchev of Russia has been called "the man of many faces." Whether making a toast at a banquet or joking with factory workers, he usually shows a nice consistency with the Soviet propaganda line of the moment. He is said to be a natural actor who can assume with zest the role suited to the occasion: the homespun, tipsy *muzhik,* the hard-headed businessman, the tough guy, the genial buffoon, the outraged puritan. He tries to force opponents into situations in which they look bad. (Eugene Lyons, "The Many Faces of Nikita Khrushchev," *Reader's Digest,* August, 1959, pp. 49–54.)

[7] John F. Kennedy's *Profiles in Courage* (New York: Harper, 1956) deals with cases like this.

[8] H. S. Truman, *Mr. President* (New York: Farrar, Strauss and Young, 1952), p. 288.

[9] "Many, I know—the vulgar herd—will blame me for what I am about to do, but posterity, I am sure, will justify me." (John Wilkes Booth, quoted in Izola Forrester, *This One Mad Act* [Boston: Hale, Cushman and Flint, 1937], p. 228; Francis Wilson, *John Wilkes Booth* [Boston: Houghton Mifflin, 1929], pp. 114, 116, 139, 183, 192, 193n.; Philip Van Doren Stern, *The Man Who Killed Lincoln* [New York: Literary Guild of America, 1939], pp. 70, 99, 135, 382–83.)

[10] April 20, 1962, p. 25.

[11] Epitomized in tales of King Arthur as Sir Kay, who is overthrown by boys and fools.

[12] The President personally offered a challenge to Russia by discussing on television the danger to the United States from the missile sites and the encounter of Soviet and U.S. ships. The *New York Times* described the atmosphere in the capital as a "nightmare" during these days. After an unsuccessful bid to swap Cuban for Turkish bases, Khrushchev suddenly backed down, giving dramatic victory to Kennedy, who "emerged in the West as the hero of the crisis" (October 30, 1962).

[13] Though he could not, by law, succeed himself as governor, his new popularity at home made almost any other public office in the state seem open to him. (*Time,* October 5, 1962, p. 17.)

[14] *Time,* October 5, 1962, p. 15.

[15] *Time,* October 5, 1962, pp. 15–17.

[16] Melodramas are, by definition, black versus white, where the villain takes all the badness on himself and gives all the goodness to the hero; whereas, in tragedy, fault is always shared by the hero.

[17] For a survey of American patterns see my *Heroes, Villains and Fools,* chap. iii.

[18] *Time,* August 30, 1963, p. 12.

[19] Martyrdom, as an alternative, has already been discussed, but, for martyrdom, a significant cause must be evident. A suicide, to the American public, is a person who has lost the dramatic advantages of both victim and martyr. His death is meaningless, so he cannot be a martyr. He brought it on himself, so he cannot be a victim. On the other hand, Medgar Evers, the assassinated Negro leader, was not quite a perfect martyr and more a victim. He was too passive and helpless for it to be said that he had fully chosen his role, though it is true that he had announced his willingness to die for integration and his expectation that someone might kill him. However, comparison with perfect martyrs like Joan of Arc or Socrates, who explicitly chose their deaths and repeatedly rejected their chances to escape, make it clear why Evers' role was closer to victim than to martyr.

[20] I have come to the conclusion that average Americans do not know what tragedy is. My reasons are given in "Tragedy and the American Climate of Opinion," *Centennial Review,* 11 (1958), 396–413; also reprinted in John D. Hurrell, *Two Modern Tragedies* (New York: Scribner, 1961), and in Robert W. Corrigan, *The Form and Vision of Tragedy* (San Francisco: Chandler Publishing Company, 1965).

[21] Booth, if anyone, was the tragic character, with his Brutus-like role. The tragedy of Lincoln's career must be found, as Whitman saw, in the choice, direction, and course of the war itself—a nation rending itself and guilty of its own blood. In this sense, he was captain of a tragic ship.

[22] Perhaps this applies mainly to countries with the Anglo-American tradition of fair play and sympathy for the underdog, though I suspect that it is much more widespread, since the basic melodramatic and comic patterns can be found throughout world folklore and drama.

[23] One of the greatest of movie fights occured in "El Cid." It followed classic lines. When El Cid fights the champion of the rival king, he is knocked off his horse, then off his feet. Getting to his feet he backs away, apparently at the mercy of the brute strength of his opponent, who swings a heavy mace. Finally,

grasping a two-handed sword at the same time as his enemy, he finds himself on fair and equal terms. A furious exchange follows, in which El Cid knocks down his opponent, then with both hands plunges the sword through his prostrate form (pity is gone). El Cid lost the early rounds and then won by a knockout. Likewise, in classic Westerns, the hero shows restraint and gentility, even acting like a sissy, before he defeats the villain.

_____

24.

THE DRAMATURGY OF POLITICS

Richard M. Merelman

Any serious student of politics who nowadays takes it upon himself to introduce new conceptual frameworks, new priorities, and new terms into the study of politics should tread carefully indeed. The proliferation of theory and speculation in political science defies our capacity to absorb, integrate, synthesize, and choose. Ideally, perhaps, ours should be a period more of consolidation and careful exploitation of what we already have than of mad dashes after yet more abstruse, more ambitious, and more doubtful formulae. It is therefore with apprehension that I approach the question of the relationships between the political process and notions of the drama.[1] This unease is, however, not unmitigated. I do not propose that the considerations I put forth be taken as a theory; indeed, they have few of the characteristics of a theory. I merely mean to suggest, first, that in addition to its other characteristics politics incorporates specific dramatic characteristics because politicians use dramatic devices; that at some points in the political process these devices are particularly salient; that, therefore, it is useful to know some principles of dramatic construction in order to appreciate politics fully; and finally, that these dramatic devices must become part of the traditional categories we use to analyze politics.

I do not claim that the political process can be compared exactly to dramatic entertainment. Concepts which are similar by analogy are also different in important ways. Of course, the audience in the theater remains aware of its separation from the events on the stage.[2] Rare indeed is the theatergoer who mistakes the play for real life. The use of a proscenium stage emphasizes the distance between audience and performance, and the introduction of theater-in-the-round reduces this gulf more effectively technically than psychologically. Politics, on the other hand, is not a play at all, but a process which intimately affects the living conditions of large numbers over a long period of time. The artifice which is the play is a structured form of projection composed by a playwright. It is not, even when it attempts to be, a wholly realistic depiction of life,[3] but rather a highly selective arrangement of

Reprinted by permission from *Sociological Quarterly,* Vol. X, 1969.

plots, characters, and themes which has a beginning, middle, and some identifiable end. Political life is not as neat.[4]

All these qualifications are to the point; yet they do not touch the central problem. For we all know that dramas are not confined to theaters. Numerous events in real life evoke the same sorts of feelings we experience at the theater. Why is this so? The reason is that many of the dramaturgical techniques upon which the playwright relies in the theater are drawn from everyday social behavior. Indeed, as I hope to show, playwrights employ dramatic devices which occur in a variety of political situations. Before discussing these devices, however, let us look at three characteristics which are especially important in relating aspects of the theater to politics. First, and most fundamental, all drama is concerned with the conveyance of impressions to a group of auditors. Such impressions are meant to be accepted as truthful and credible. A play fails if it is unable to ''manage impressions'' successfully.[5] But the playwright in constructing a drama for presentation in the theater is only borrowing from social life, especially politics perhaps, the element of impression management. All politicians attempt to impress others with a certain evaluation of themselves. Indeed, one of the things we mean by ''power'' is the control over other people's responses which stems directly from their belief in our impression management. Both the politician and the actor specialize in conveying impressions to others for which, if they are to succeed in their respective fields, they must get acceptance. The politician uses the dramatic devices we shall be discussing to gain the acceptance essential to political power. The artifice required by theatrical productions need not blind us to this major simlarity between the theater and the political world.

Yet, it may be said, this fact is not enough to build a bridge. After all, if the politician must manage impressions successfully, so must we all. Perhaps I have cast a net too wide to catch only politics and drama. Yet, as Goffman points out, some statuses embody tasks which are especially well adapted to the use of dramaturgical techniques. He speaks specifically of the possibilities for dramatic manipulation lodged in the roles of prize fighter and surgeon.[6] We may wonder what makes these two roles productive of so much drama. In the first case, prize fighters often perform their roles before large audiences. In the second case, the surgeon often performs his role in matters which literally mean life and death. When we turn to the politician, we see both these factors at work. American politicians at the higher reaches of government deal increasingly with matters of life and death in both domestic and foreign affairs. American politicians are also expected to appear and perform before large audiences. When these two role characteristics are acted out simultaneously, as in the Cuban missile crisis, we become immediately aware of the dramatic impact of politics.

Finally, we may borrow again from the example of the prize fighter to indicate the element which is perhaps most important in making politics replete with dramatic devices. Prize fighters must engage in violent conflict in order to fulfill their roles successfully. This conflict grips a crowd in a variety of ways—through the elements of risk, danger, and jeopardy that are part of conflict; through the enjoyment of the sheer physical action involved in violence; and for other reasons which have their origins in ordinarily inaccessible layers of the personality.[7] The violence of the encounter, however, should not hide the subtler aspects of conflict at a prize fight. The psychological match between the handlers of the fighters, the collision of differing fighting styles, and the surges of personal courage by the fighters are all intimate parts of the encounter in the ring and produce many levels of conflict. In his turn, the playwright injects many forms of conflict, both physical and mental, into his play to hold audience interest as well as to accomplish his other purposes. Dramatic conflict is vital to a play's success because it performs so many functions. It highlights character, allows for the testing of ideas against each other, and moves the story along.[8] Conflict of an apparently different sort is a major feature of politics. The political process has been characterized as the means by which conflicts over the dispositions of social values are resolved.[9] However, such large-scale social conflicts force politicians to engage in interpersonal contests which perform the dramatic functions we have just discussed. Therefore interpersonal conflict over important matters before large audiences, with control contingent upon the management of impressions—these elements in conjunction encourage politicians to use the dramatic devices we shall be analyzing. However, each of these factors singly adds to the dramatic coloration of any political event, assuring that in most political circumstances some dramatic devices are being employed.

. . . The personality variable thus occupies an ambiguous, residual category in recent electoral analysis. Yet few would doubt that the exhibition of personality is important, especially in those deviant occurrences in which individuals or political groups are able to transcend the traditional alignment of political forces to shape events anew. As examples, one need only cite Huey Long who, as Sindler notes, broke through the traditional constellation of forces in Louisiana politics; [10] Douglas MacArthur, who produced the elements of mass support while circumventing much of the machinery of the Republican Party; and Estes Kefauver, who almost managed to parlay a coonskin cap and an unfruitful exposé of crime into a Vice-Presidential nomination despite the active opposition of powerful Democrats. I do not believe the rise of these leaders can be understood merely by reference to the "inherently" attractive qualities of the three men. Nor did these individuals derive their power primarily from organizational support. Rather, their political success was based primarily upon adroit self-projection through the use of the dramatic techniques we shall analyze. Because these personalities owe their rise in varying degrees to dramaturgical expertise, their cases illustrate most visibly the importance of dramatic mechanisms for all political leaders. Their examples demonstrate that the analysis of dramatic techniques is necessary to the greater understanding of the candidate variable in electoral analysis.

Finally, one need be no alarmist to realize that the growth of mass communications expands the scope for dramatic techniques in politics. Certainly, many politicians are aware of the dramatic potentialities offered them, as Herbert Waltzer indicates in his discussion of Lyndon Johnson's sensitivity to the dramatic potential of 1964 convention coverage.[11] The mass media provide the politician with greatly expanded opportunities for the dramatic arrangement of political events. The desire of the mass media to hold their audiences also exaggerates the importance of dramaturgy in politics. For example, Kurt and Gladys Lang document the extent to which television, to maximize viewer interest, inflated the extent of popular enthusiasm during MacArthur's arrival at Chicago in 1952.[12] Much, of course, has been made of the effects of the televised 1960 Presidential debates on the outcome of that election. These debates rewarded the performer who most clearly grasped the importance of the mass media in encouraging the use of dramatic techniques in politics.

Dramatic Mechanisms in Politics

Dramaturgical mechanisms are consciously and unconsciously adapted by political actors to their purposes. These devices appear in the structured ideologies that are the intellectual currency of the political process and in the more personal appeals of politicians. Let us introduce some of these mechanisms by analyzing the dramaturgical structure of political ideologies and the appeals of politicians.

Perhaps the simplest and best known devices provide a useful starting point. Social scientists have studied many functions of political ideologies.[13] Few, however, have perceived the dramatic framework of political ideologies or recognized the vital importance dramaturgical devices have in the ultimate success of these ideologies. Political ideologies provide the themes of political action, the points of conflict around which political action is to revolve. Their success is measured not only by the number of supporters they gain but, in the first instance, by their power to command the interest of large numbers over a considerable period. Therefore, inevitably, there are differences between political philosophies and political ideologies. It is not primarily by their divergent degrees of sophistication, as some commentators have thought, but by the dramatic functions of ideologies in social structures that ideology and philosophy are distinguished. How do political ideologies function dramatically?

Ideologies cast the world in dramatic terms by employing such dramaturgical techniques as personification, identification appeals, symbolism, catharsis, and suspense. Without each of these dramaturgical elements of ideological structure, we can expect little success for the ideology. Ideologies interpret some political forces as villains, others as heroes, others as fools. They thus personify political conflict. Personification is a process by which social processes are associated with visible groups or individuals, thereby providing greater impact for the ideology. The first step is to single out some kind of personified villains for ideological treatment, often by employing stereotypes to enhance dramatic power as well as for conceptual simplicity. In Marxism the forces of the market are personified in the actions of capitalists. Marxism then personifies its heroes as a righteous working class preparing to do battle with the forces represented by the capitalists. Marxism's fools are those workers who are seduced away from Communism by the blandishments of the capitalists; those Socialists who think it will be possible to avoid a final confrontation with the villains; and those others who have had moral and religious scruples foisted on them by the capitalists.

The more dramatically complete an ideology is, the more its fools will be as important as its villains and heroes. Hence, some Marxists fear that the future of Marxism hinges on the behavior of the gullible fools in its scenario; many conservative Republicans worry about the gullibility of passive Americans in the face of blandishments offered by the ''Eastern Liberal Establishment.'' The pivotal role of fools in political ideologies is closely related to the functions of fools in drama. In many plays, fools are used as unwitting instruments to destroy heroes.[14] This hero-villain-fool interplay forms the dramatic focus of most completely developed ideologies.

But personification is only the first requisite in constructing dramatically successful political ideologies and appeals. A second is identification. Political identification is an empathic process whereby large numbers come to view their own political destinies as tied up with an ideology in the political process or a political leader. Politicians follow two strategies to gain the identification of the public. Each of these strategies contradicts the other logically, but they are quite consistent dramatically. On the one hand, the political leader encourages support and identification by arguing that he represents an unstoppable political force. The ''wave of the future'' identification appeal is attractive because large numbers are impressed by the appearance of absolute certainty in politics and are willing to grant legitimacy to the self-confident. Such ''wave of the future'' arguments are especially inviting to those whom Hoffer has called ''true believers.'' On the other hand, in the short run political leaders often argue that they themselves are threatened by powerful opponents and that unless a reversal in fortunes occurs soon they will be lost. Furthermore, if they are lost their programs will be later in arriving. In election campaigns, typically, politicians claim that although what they stand for will ultimately triumph, they themselves are in danger because the polls show them to be in close races, their opponents have money and organizational support which they themselves do not have, and their opponents are campaigning unfairly. Here the politician makes use of the principle that a threat to ego ideals produces support and legitimacy for the program of the one threatened. The skillful juggling of these two strategies encourages identification with the political leader, his appeals, and his ideologies. Playwrights make both appeals easily visible by refining them in their plays. Who has not seen the melodrama in which the hero is endangered while his predicament is juxtaposed against the assurance that what he represents will eventually overcome whatever obstacles exist?

Much that has so far been said emphasizes the importance of building up the illusion of conflict to maximize dramatic impact in politics. However, political actors are also careful to blend into their appeals and ideologies elements of catharsis. Barnet, Berman, and Burto suggest that the major characteristics of catharsis are purgation and emotional release.[15] It is doubtful that any political appeal or ideology would be completely successful if it did not promise such ultimate relief from conflict or define some series of conditions under which conflict would no longer be necessary. The prospect of endless conflict is too forbidding to attract many enthusiasts. The defining conditions for conflict cessation are the cathartic points of the ideology or appeal. Of course, dramatists can build into their plays catharses at those moments when emotional release and the development of thematic conflict are most complementary. Such points are not so readily identified in politics, however. Therefore, politicians face a major problem in deciding when high levels of tension require reconciliation scenes designed to produce momentary catharsis. Such judgments presently divide aspects of the civil rights movement in the United States.[16]

Often politicians can provide temporary catharses for their followers without affecting their appeals or ideologies at all. Throughout the political process there exist rituals and customs which most participants feel bound to observe. These performances are nonpartisan in character and constitute, in dramatic terms, "obligatory scenes." According to Archer, "An obligatory scene is one which the audience . . . foresees and desires, and the absence of which it may with reason resent."[17] When political opponents participate together in such nonpartisan obligatory scenes—as they frequently perceive themselves forced to do—they may provide temporary relief for their committed followers who desire rehearsals of the reconciliation that is ultimately to come. They can also allay the fears of the uncommitted that conflict will be total. For these reasons, polities which have not succeeded in developing such integrative obligatory scenes are prone to serious internal disorders. A good example of such an obligatory scene is the symbolic reconciliation of American electoral opponents after the votes have been counted, with promises of support for the winner by the loser. When Senator Goldwater waited an uncommonly long time after the 1964 election results were clear to play this scene, he aroused rumbles of protest.[18] Not only are these ritualistic obligatory scenes useful as cathartic outlets for specific publics, but they also provide the system as a whole with temporary respites from internal conflict.

The dramatic characteristic of suspense is based on the flow of possibilities around the cathartic points in an ideology. Suspense could not exist were it not that supporters of ideologies knew that the arrival of the political catharsis promised by their ideology depended at least partially on the outcome of contemporary events. It is the interaction between a desired future and a threatening present which produces suspense and rivets attention on the political scene. The question which creates suspense is, "Will such and such a situation impede or contribute to the attainment of political catharsis?"

Success in eliciting public support for political ideologies and appeals rests partially on dramatic techniques other than those already discussed. Playwrights often signify the presence of particular themes by key symbols. One thinks of Chekhov's cherry orchard or Ibsen's wild duck. The manipulation of symbols permits an economy of action which intensifies the conveyance and heightens the impact of meanings. Mature ideologies are replete with symbols and rituals which can convey messages of significant emotional intensity. Examples of these symbols are special flags, salutes, gestures, insignia, and songs. Hence, we should not be surprised to find a correlation between the evocation of ideologies in politics and the appearance of dramatic rituals and symbols. The shorthand provided by symbolic manipulation permits both the actor and the politician to evoke rapidly a specific, highly partisan mood in their audiences. Such symbols have meanings that words cannot convey.

Three other dramatic techniques useful in political appeals also bear discussion—climax, peripety, and unmasking. Good plots in both the theater and politics often have a climax, a single short period in which the major conflicts of themes and personalities are resolved. The political system provides the politician some built-in climaxes, such as election nights, close votes in Congress, and Supreme Court decision days. However, these climaxes are primarily institutional, not personal. Therefore, the politician tries to create his own climaxes, sometimes legitimizing them by linking them to institutional climaxes, sometimes not. Of course, institutional and personal climaxes may be joined more or less easily from political system to political system. In Britain, for example, the time separating personal policy-making climaxes from one institutional climax, the election, can be relatively short. The party in power, having scored a policy-making coup, can call a general election immediately. In the United States, the time between personal and institutional climaxes in the electoral arena is not as flexible. However, the history of American politics indicates the extent to which Presidents attempt to reach their personal climaxes in policy-making right before they may be legitimized in the institutional climax of elections.[19]

One of the problems with staging climaxes in politics is that it is often very difficult to point to particular events as "key" to particular outcomes. This problem is especially acute in an incrementalist polity like that of the United States where—if Lindblom and Braybrooke are correct—decisions are often taken without any clear priority of goals, and problems are rarely cleanly resolved.[20] Nonetheless, politicians continually specify particular events as "crucial" to outcomes, although they themselves may not believe what they are saying. They make such claims in order to introduce the dramatic advantages of perceived climaxes into their appeals.

A second technique is that of peripety, the dramatic situation in which one individual suddenly declines from a favored position or rises from a low status. Greek tragedies made heavy use of the dramatic possibilities of this role reversal, as did Mark Twain in his novels *The Prince and the Pauper* and *Pudd'nhead Wilson*. These two kinds of role reversal, especially when operative simultaneously, rivet attention on the political scene. Politicians attempt to build peripety into their appeals by claiming that their opponents have more resources than they themselves have but are declining because of corruption or unpopularity, or by arguing that they themselves have risen from a disadvantaged situation. In a society which values upward mobility as much as does ours the use of peripety may be quite effective.[21]

A third important dramatic device employed in political appeals is unmasking. Unmasking is the exposure of what had appeared to be desirable as undesirable or what had appeared to be undesirable as desirable. The intimate link between unmasking and subsequent peripetal patterns is obvious. The technique will be most effective if two conditions are fulfilled:

1) The status of the unmasked object is drastically different after the unmasking.
2) The unmasking occurs quickly before a large audience.

An example of such an unmasking which formed a prerequisite to a peripetal rise in the political world is provided by the Alger Hiss-Richard Nixon confrontation. Nixon was able to unmask Hiss rapidly in public, thereby propelling himself into an expanding political career. The problem with the use of unmasking, as Nixon was subsequently to discover, is the question of evidence. Is there enough evidence to suggest that the individual one is attempting to unmask is what one says he is? Few unmasking appeals are as effective as was Nixon's. Still, much standard political rhetoric is filled with unmasking appeals, as evidenced by the frequency of "smear" charges in our political life. In all cases, attempted unmasking tries to re-structure the perceived identities of actors in the political process to the benefit of those performing the unmasking.

Unmasking strategies differ from political system to political system. In American politics, for example, the bases of disagreement between opponents are often rather narrow. For this reason, unmasking often involves attempts by both sides to magnify their differences. A favorite unmasking tactic among American politicians, therefore, is to label each other as "really" more "extremist" than their present identities may appear to make them.[22]

The elements of dramatic construction we have discussed help explain why political ideologies and political leaders may be successful or unsuccessful at particular times. Politicians are more likely to fail the less successful their personification of opponents, the less able they are in applying their identification appeals, the less suspense they can build into their appeals, the less credible their promises of catharsis, and the fewer the symbols and rituals they are able to manipulate. They will also fail if unable to arrange climactic scenes for themselves, unmask opponents, or employ peripetal appeals.

Many explanations of the rise and fall of Joseph McCarthy have been offered, but few have focused on the relationship between the conflict his appeals postulated and the acceptance of such a conflict by the public. Yet Stouffer indicates that at the height of McCarthy's power relatively few Americans were willing to accept the central hero-villain-fool personification in his ideology—that a large domestic Communist conspiracy was at work to undermine the foundations of American democracy.[23] It is at least partially possible that McCarthy's inability to uncover domestic Communists was responsible for his failure to produce a credible conflict for his audience. On the other hand, much of the failure of American Communism lies in the lack of credibility for its catharses as well as for its central conflict. Large numbers of Americans have been unconvinced that socializing productive processes and ultimately reducing the role of the state will bring about reconciliation and peace. Many feel that power struggles are inherent in the nature of social life.[24] . . .

Variables Conditioning the Political Uses of Dramatic Mechanisms

When will dramatic mechanisms be most effective and, therefore, most frequently employed in the political arena? Answers to this question are crucial. If this paper is to be taken as something more than an attempt to suggest that some traditional modes of political behavior can be understood completely only by the employment of dramatic theory, we must set forth a series of hypotheses which predict the appearance of dramatic behavior in politics. Personification, identification, suspense, symbolism, climax, peripety, unmasking, and catharsis will come into play in various combinations depending upon the political situation. Specifically, the major independent political variables that determine the uses and appearance of all these mechanisms are matters of issue, setting, group structure, and encounter.

Issues. Style issues encourage the appearance of dramatic mechanisms. Position issues do not. According to Froman, ''. . . style issues are those issues concerning moral and ethical questions which tend, in our terminology, to be 'fuzzy' and difficult to pin down to a particular meaning. . . . Position issues, on the other hand, have a more concrete meaning. They are . . . closer to reality and more easily translated into measurable units of analysis.'' [25] An example of a position issue is the allocation of quotas for agricultural products under federal legislation. An example of a style issue is the legitimacy or moral status of federal controls in the agricultural sector.

Because their stands on style issues go far toward defining their identities, individuals do not find it easy to compromise in style issue disagreements. Furthermore, the ambiguity surrounding style issues allows wide leeway for individuals to externalize their private conflicts. The introduction of externalized private motives raises the intensity of any disagreement. Also, the murky, often contradictory status of crucial definitions in style issue controversies makes compromise even more difficult. For all these reasons, therefore, style issues usually exist in a heated emotional environment fraught with conflict.[26] Conflict, as we have seen, is a major requisite for the use of dramaturgical techniques. Indeed, the high levels of conflict over style issues encourage the introduction of whole ideologies largely composed of such issues, the arrival of forceful climaxes when it appears that one set of protagonists is winning, and the consequent commensurate level of catharsis when the issue appears resolved.

Position issues, because they involve measurable quantities and seem primarily technical, do not lend themselves to dramatic handling. The technicality of such issues makes them unfit for consumption by large audiences. Often they can be resolved easily by professional specialists, whose codes frown upon the introduction of apparently extraneous dramaturgical techniques which obfuscate the issue at hand. Furthermore, the bench marks that measurability provides encourage a compromising, bargaining style of interaction where technical acceptability rather than dramatic success becomes the goal toward which participants move.

The initially small audience for position issues suggests that style appeals must be incorporated if the introduction of dramaturgical mechanisms is to succeed. An example of an issue which is naturally position, but has become infused by style considerations, is flouridation. The normally technical question of water supply components has become enmeshed in a controversy over the imposition of central planning on local communities, the autonomy of the individual in health matters, and the invasion of privacy. Opponents of fluoridation can thus employ peripetal appeals by claiming that they are standing up for the ''little man'' against entrenched, powerful government bureaucrats.[27] Occasionally, exteme elements in the opposition to fluoridation can also attempt to unmask the scheme as a Communist plot. The dynamics of the transition from low-keyed position issue to explosive style issue are unclear. Nonetheless, while it is probable that the dramaturgical techniques we have described are also important in the transition to a style issue conflict, they are definitely crucial to the outcome of that conflict.

Issues which are not easily fitted into existing political cognitive maps or which defy normal political alignments encourage the appearance of dramatic mechanisms. Such issues lie temporarily "free," uncontrolled by traditional political organizations. Therefore, they often attract political "dark horses" or novices out of favor with organizational leaders, who hope to enhance their own power. These mavericks cannot rely on a stable core of organizational support to guarantee them public visibility, however. Instead, they must dramatize free issues to produce an impact on the public. But the initial successes of maverick leaders may put free issues in a form institutions such as political parties can handle. For this reason, dark horses later on will have to fight off the incursions of established institutions. The best strategy for such leaders is to use the support gained by their initial appeals as a means of keeping the issue for themselves and away from institutions.

. . . Political issues which divide former allies will encourage the use of dramatic mechanisms. Political realignment brings forth dramaturgical techniques because, as Simmel shows, conflict is at its most bitter between those formerly closest to each other.[28] During periods of realignment former friends become opponents, in the process attempting to unmask each other. Such attempts become cruder and more brutal—approaching the simplest form of unmasking, vilification—the more disturbing the realignment. Conflicts over style issues internal to a political group often provoke realignment, and such issues, as we have seen, encourage the resort to dramaturgy. These style issues will be composed of esoteric symbols historically associated with the disturbed group. Because of their historical and emotional significance, these symbols cannot be abandoned, but become instead prizes which participants in the realignment attempt to retain for themselves and deny to their new opponents. Attempts will be made to label others as villains, dupes, and heroes in the question at hand, and the unsettled nature of political alignments will provide many opportunities to stage peripetal comebacks, climactic scenes, and speeches of victory designed to produce catharsis. Finally, such realignments normally produce entirely new ideologies as recently discovered friends and enemies attempt to rationalize their novel relations.

Settings. Bureaucracies discourage the use of dramaturgy in political appeals to the public. Bureaucracies regularize political procedures and impose a set of more or less inflexible roles and rules on organizational participants. If political leaders are to make use of dramatic mechanisms in communicating to their publics, they must circumvent the inflexibilities of their party bureaucracies. Furthermore, bureaucracies as mechanisms depersonalize authority, thereby making decision-making less visible to the public. Leaders committed to the bureaucracy are, therefore, also committed to less visible decision-making. The effective use of dramatic mechanisms to communicate to the public, on the other hand, demands that decision-making be traceable to particular individuals and relatively visible to the public. For these reasons, politicians interested in dramatizing their own power—or enhancing it—must contrive or make the most of situations which are highly visible and those in which important decisions seem to be in process. This tension between the internal norms of bureaucracy and the external demands of dramaturgy become most evident when normally bureaucratic organizations are forced into situations where hierarchical controls cannot operate easily. Political nominating conventions are good examples of the phenomenon. Because of the visibility of nominating procedures and the importance of outcomes, bureaucratic leaders are occasionally unable to prevent maverick politicians from successfully employing dramatic appeals, such as a call for public decision-making or an unmasking charge that invisible bosses illegitimately control convention activity.[29] In other words, nominating conventions temporarily weaken hierarchical controls and give politicians leeway to employ dramatic appeals to their publics. It is therefore understandable why party professionals should fear both open party conventions and, even more, party primary elections.[30]

Occasionally a short-circuiting of any kind of institutionalized procedure comprises in itself a dramatically successful public appeal, but only if it makes use of many dramatic mechanisms. For example, candidate Eisenhower's promise to ignore the institutionalized niceties of diplomatic intercourse and personally "go to Korea" if elected was a great dramatic stroke.[31] His offer had overtones of peripety; i.e., the single, plain man would wage war directly against the overwhelming power of bureaucratic mechanics. It also personified the war by indicating that leaders like Eisenhower himself could be held directly responsible and that the war was not doomed by an impersonal fate to drag on hopelessly. These factors produced a level of identification with Eisenhower that any candidate would envy. Finally, the promise set up a ready-made climax composed of those moments when Eisenhower would actually arrive in Korea to survey the situation. How could an electorate on the verge of voting deny itself such an attractive climax by voting for Stevenson? [32] It should be obvious, however, that without the assurance both of public attention and of public power to reward short-circuiting, the tactic may quite possibly backfire.

. . . *Groups*. Dramaturgical techniques in public appeals will be resorted to more often in groups which feel themselves threatened than in secure groups. Threatening political situations produce emotion-laden style issues which encourage the resort to dramaturgy. Also, as many psychologists have demonstrated, individual or group insecurity often causes stereotyping, a process in which the forces of opposition are personified with dangerous simplicity. Stereotyping then activates other dramatic elements such as peripety, attempts to invoke symbolism, and efforts to produce climaxes and to promise catharsis. Most often, insecure groups attempt to make sense of the threats which surround them by suggesting that they are the victims of a conspiracy, but that though currently the underdogs they will eventually triumph. The quasi-mythical character of this interpretation stems directly from its employment of dramaturgical techniques.

Perception of threat also encourages the resort to dramatic techniques, because threats undercut traditional institutional structures of control. Leaders accustomed to working within the institutional apparatus of the organization may find it difficult to mobilize their energies to meet stressful conditions. The less applicable their settled procedures are to the resolution of the crisis, the more likely it becomes that the entire institutional mechanism will be discredited with them. Once this process has occurred, new flexibility permits those leaders who are skilled in the use of dramatic methods to rise to power by employing dramatic appeals to those inside and outside the organization. At a certain point in the crisis, institutional leaders will have been weakened to the point at which the first dramatic appeals occur, often in the form of what might be termed an "internal security plot."

In this "internal security plot" emerging leaders attempt to link institutional leaders to the external threat, suggesting that the latter are knowing parties to it and are, in fact, conspirators in league with the enemy. The dramatic power of this appeal is great, mostly because it makes use of so many of the mechanisms we have already explored. It employs the unmasking device as an explanatory vehicle. That is, it suggests that the major sources of difficulty can be removed through an unmasking. It traces the source of difficulties to individuals within the organization, thereby producing greater impact than would an analysis of the threat stressing the importance of outsiders. Members of the organization can now expect to see public confrontations of accusers and accused. These confrontations are likely to produce climaxes of significant impact after which, if the accusers are correct, some momentary catharsis may be expected because the perceived sources of danger will have been removed. The success of this appeal depends on its explanatory and prescriptive characteristics. It is easy to believe that leaders within the organization are responsible, for they are in positions of power. Furthermore, it is feasible to remove them, whereas it may not be so easy to get at the dangers posed by other groups.

Illegitimate groups will be particularly likely to employ dramatic appeals to their followers and to the public at large. This proposition follows as a kind of corollary of the one above, because illegitimate groups often perceive themselves as threatened by their opposition. But, in addition, such organizations are likely to see a drastic incompatibility between their own goals and the goals of legitimate groups within their political environment. Dramatic mechanisms will revolve around this incompatibility. At some point, the dialectic in such groups will focus on alternatives in facing the environment. One set of leaders may argue that the group must moderate its goals to gain legitimacy; however, in so doing, they encourage their opponents within the organization to brand them as traitors and to produce unmasking appeals to the membership. The moderates may defend themselves by claiming that the diehards envisage nothing but continued conflict while their course holds out the only hope for some kind of catharsis. The introduction of these dramatic appeals is caused by the strategic problems of the illegitimate group.

Further, resort to dramatic mechanisms will be greater in illegitimate groups because such groups often have trouble settling on an accepted set of operating procedures. Instead, illegitimate groups are subjected to outside sanctions which often force new working procedures on them.[33] This organizational flux assures that dramatic appeals will find an easy hearing. In addition, illegitimate organizations are often composed of individuals psychologically and spiritually alienated from their society.[34] Often, psychological misfits are the earliest and most dedicated recruits. Such individuals—Lasswell's agitator types, for example—are both prone to resort to dramaturgical techniques themselves and to respond to such appeals. The only hope for group survival in this case is that an organizational genius—a Lenin, for example—will gain sufficient control to force procedural discipline on the organization. It is worthy of note, however, that whether disciplined or not secret organizations seem especially prone to the use of internal dramatic appeals. Strict secrecy encourages the fear of conspiracies within the organization, whereas a freer flow of information tends to mitigate the dramatic possibilities of conspiracies.

. . . Heterogeneous groups produce more use of dramaturgical techniques than homogeneous groups under normal conditions. Homogeneous groups are usually composed of relative equals, and equals are more likely than unequals to share similar viewpoints on the proper goals and tactics of the group. Differences in goals and methods are more likely in heterogeneous groups. In order to reach common understandings and bridge this possibly dangerous gap, heterogeneous groups resort to dramatic techniques directed against other groups. Leaders of such groups try to solidify their own organization by producing dramaturgical attacks on other organizations. Indeed, because of the differing perspectives of unequals, many encounters in a heterogeneous group may be limited to entirely safe, ritualistic denunciations of other groups and serve little policymaking function. If so, the organization will soon suffer both external and internal stress unless policy-making devices can be improvised which surmount this difficulty.

. . . *Encounters.* Both short and prolonged encounters encourage resort to dramatic techniques. Encounters of intermediate length do not. The shorter a confrontation, the less likely it is that dramatic mechanisms must withstand scrutiny from a variety of viewpoints and be subjected to tests of truth. Dramatic versions of reality, therefore, will be accepted as the truth because more prosaic, factual versions of reality take too long to assemble and convey. Furthermore, in short encounters the individuals most likely to gain attention are those who can use dramaturgical techniques effectively; their histrionic talents bring them rapidly to public attention. Finally, when interaction must be brief, participants formerly unknown to each other are forced to rely on cues about their fellows which are relatively superficial—manner, gesture, bearing. Such aspects of personality can often be most effectively displayed through the introduction of the dramatic mechanisms which have already been discussed. Participants can personify issues at hand in the confrontation, invoke symbolism, construct versions of the confrontation which involve elements of peripety and unmasking, and provide cathartic relaxation—all of which actions appear to elevate the individual, producing in his auditors what may be a false sense of his seeming nobility.

Long encounters, on the other hand, are extremely tiring. In addition, such encounters when they involve policy choices would not be long without significant conflicts. As time drags on, participants find it progressively more difficult to focus clearly on the position aspects of the issues at hand. Faced with a need to produce a policy and progressively less able to make the fine distinctions required by the complexity of issues, participants may well look elsewhere for direction and resolution. Often, dramaturgical techniques can be used to produce for dulled minds a relatively simple, highly attractive picture of the problem, thereby bringing an end to the exhausting encounter. Thus, encounters which turn out to be excessively long are prime candidates for the introduction of successful dramaturgical mechanisms.

. . . In summation, dramatic techniques are likely to come into play when style issues are involved, when free issues attract maverick politicians to dramatize them, and when an issue forces political realignment. Dramatic mechanisms are also more likely to be found when encounters between leaders and audiences occur uncontrolled by bureaucracy, when partisan arenas are the seats of encounters, when groups feel themselves threatened—especially when they are illegitimate within their environment—and when groups are actually in decline. Under most conditions, we will find more dramaturgy in heterogeneous than in homogeneous groups. Finally, brief or very long encounters are also likely to produce dramatic techniques.

Conclusion: The Role of Dramatic Theory in the Study of Politics

It seems clear that dramatic theory can provide us with a perspective on politics that highlights formerly obscured aspects of the political process. It is even possible to use dramatic theory to produce testable hypotheses about varying kinds of political behavior. Yet, the writer confesses a lingering dissatisfaction which may be discussed briefly in conclusion. This dissatisfaction is caused by the still uneasy fit between notions of dramatic form and analyses of the political process. Why is this fit loose?

First, discussions of politics which one wishes to illuminate through an application of dramatic theory run into difficulties with dramatic theory itself. The state of dramatic theory—indeed, the whole field of aesthetics—leaves a systematic reader depressed. As Robert Lane notes, theories of literature, of which dramatic theory is a branch, agree little on fundamental definitions, modes of inquiry, or goals for research.[35] There are virtually as many answers to the questions "What do we mean by drama?" and "What is it that makes a drama great?" as there are commentators on drama.

Furthermore, what answers there are come couched in metaphysical terminology or in vague aphorisms which themselves function as little more than rhetoric. One need not claim that dramatic theory—or aesthetics generally—must become a science in order to argue that those who write on dramatic form should agree on a set of terms so that they can talk with each other sensibly. In this essay I have spoken about a number of dramatic mechanisms which are specific enough that dramatic theorists agree on their meaning. This restriction has allowed me to set forth some fairly operational hypotheses about politics. But until theorists of drama do more than agree on the meaning of specific dramatic devices, until they produce theories of the entire dramatic process which approach the criteria of the social scientist, it will remain a formidable task to put dramatic theory to work in the study of politics. Nor will it improve the situation to argue that the nature of the phenomena at which dramatic theory looks is simply not amenable to the criteria the social scientist erects. That argument is an a priori dismissal which requires a demonstration yet to be made. The fact that social and natural scientists presently talk far more to each other than to humanists does not necessarily prove that social scientists have little in common with humanists. The gap between the "two cultures" is caused as much by a failure of will and energy as it is by incompatible phenomena.

Secondly, few social scientists have taken the trouble to use the tools of their own trade in the analysis of drama or recognized that dramas can be considered ideal types of human behavior which can provide clues to the real world of phenomena. But there are obvious guideposts which can point social scientists in the correct direction to remedy this situation. Sociologists borrowed the concept of role unconsciously, from the drama and put it to fruitful use in sociology. Why should they find it impossible to explore the implications of dramatic role structure for sociological role theory, in the process bringing notions of the drama directly into the social sciences? Common terms bespeak potentially common phenomena and theory. It may be argued that the Parsonian influence on sociology has inhibited the exploration of dynamic, noninstitutional behavior. Yet, a movement in sociology—resting upon economic exchange theory—concerns itself with social interaction both inside and outside institutions.[36] The exchanges of behavior which this theory discusses may be applied quite fruitfully to notions of dramatic form. Thus, the tools for the enterprise do exist.

One of these tools, small group analysis, provides a bridge between sociological concerns with group structure and the interest of psychologists in the effects of personality on group functioning. Small group analysis can easily be applied to interactions in the drama in an effort to gain insight into human behavior. Other branches of psychology can also make a contribution. Learning theory, dealing with questions of perception, motivation, and cognitive structure, can benefit greatly from the way in which the drama produces audience response. Drama is a highly controlled form of communication, which depends entirely for its success on the interaction between its messages and its audience. Is it impossible that theorists of communication and information can learn something about efficient modes of communication by analyzing the structure of successful drama? Finally, those psychologists interested in problems of personality structure and emotional behavior share interests with the theorist of drama. Each is concerned with "identification," "catharsis," "stereotypes." Indeed, each of the staple motives of drama—love, aggression, morality—is a concern of the psychologist. Therefore, once he recognizes that political interaction employs dramaturgy, tools of social science are available with which the political scientist can tighten the fit between the study of politics and the study of drama.

NOTES

[1] Most of the thinking about dramatic theory which informs this paper is drawn from the following sources: Eric Bentley, *The Life of the Drama* (New York: Atheneum, 1964); Walter Kerr, *How Not to Write A Play* (New York: Simon and Schuster, 1955); Constantin Stanislavski, *Building a Character*, Trans. Elizabeth Reynolds Hapgood (New York: Theatre Art Books, 1949); William Archer, *Playmaking* (New York: Dodd, Mead, 1928); Sylvan Barnet, Morton Berman, and William Burto (eds.), *Aspects of the Drama* (Boston: Little, Brown and Co., 1962); Allardyce Nicoll, *The Theatre and Dramatic Theory* (New York: Barnes and Noble, 1962); J. L. Styan, *The Elements of Drama* (Cambridge:

Cambridge University Press, 1960); and Lajos Egri, The Art of Dramatic Writing (New York: Simon and Schuster, 1965).

[2] Nicoll, op. cit., chap. 1.

[3] When it gets too close to life, argues Kerr, it is bound to fail as a play. Kerr, op. cit., chap. 8.

[4] For a more complete catalog of the differences between drama and politics, see Vernon Van Dyke, Political Science: A Philosophical Analysis (Stanford: Stanford University Press, 1960), pp. 14–15.

[5] I borrow the term from Erving Goffman, The Presentation of Self in Everyday Life (Garden City: Anchor Books, 1959), passim.

[6] Ibid.

[7] For suggestions on this point, see Harold D. Lasswell, Psychopathology and Politics (New York: The Viking Press, 1960), chap. 10; Leonard Berkowitz, Aggression (New York: McGraw-Hill, 1962); and John Dollard et al., Frustration and Aggression (New Haven: Yale University Press, 1939).

[8] Compare Klapp: "The very essence of drama—the high point of its most important scenes—is usually a confrontation in which parties are thrown on their mettle, reveal and expose themselves, drop their defenses, call on their personal resources to meet a crisis." Orrin Klapp, Symbolic Leaders (Chicago: Aldine Publishing Co., 1964), p. 70.

[9] David Easton, The Political System (New York: Knopf, 1953), chap. 5.

[10] Allen Sindler, Huey Long's Louisiana (Baltimore: Johns Hopkins University Press, 1956), chap. 2.

[11] Herbert Waltzer, "In the Magic Lantern: Television Coverage of the 1964 National Conventions," Public Opinion Quarterly, 30:33–54 (Spring, 1966). Waltzer writes:
"President Johnson personally supervised the preparations for his party's 1964 convention. . . . He rescheduled the showing of a film tribute to the late President Kennedy, to be introduced by his brother, Robert F. Kennedy, from before to after the nomination of a vice-presidential candidate, to avoid a televised outburst of delegate and gallery support for Robert Kennedy, whom he had scratched from his list of those acceptable to him as a running mate. When the convention lost its pace and movement, President Johnson created the excitement of a tradition-breaking appearance before the convention to state his 'recommendation' for a vice-presidential nominee. In so doing, he drew the cameras away from the squabbling over contested seats and the demonstrators for civil rights, obtained for himself an added evening of exposure during prime television time and sought to create sufficient excitement to carry the audience through the last two days of the convention. The following evening, when he appeared again on the rostrum to deliver his acceptance speech, he removed his watch from his wrist, pointed at the time, and silenced the cheering convention so that he might be heard during maximum televiewing time" (p. 51).
On the sensitivity of campaign managers to dramatic matters, see Stephen C. Shadegg, How to Win an Election (New York: Taplinger Publishing Co., 1964), passim.

[12] Kurt and Gladys Lang, "The Unique Perspective of Television and Its Effect: A Pilot Study," American Sociological Review, 18:3–12 (1953).

[13] For some of the more recent thinking on the subject, see M. Brewster Smith, Jerome S. Bruner, and Robert W. White, Opinions and Personality (New York: Wiley, 1956); Robert E. Lane, Political Ideology (New York: The Free Press of Glencoe, 1962); and Daniel Katz, "The Functional Approach to the Study of Attitudes," Public Opinion Quarterly, 24:163–205 (Summer, 1960).

[14] One of the best examples of the use of a fool figure to destroy a hero occurs in Budd Schulberg's On the Waterfront. Terry Malloy, clearly a fool figure at the outset, destroys at the villains' behest a hero in the community. The story follows Malloy as he matures from a fool into a hero.

[15] Barnet, Berman, and Burto, op. cit., pp. 266–67. They define suspense as "Uncertainty, often characterized by anxiety." Ibid., p. 261.

[16] Advocates of "black power" argue that there must be no symbolic reconciliation yet, but that further tension, suspense, and conflict are necessary instead. Others seem to suggest that momentary reconciliation is now desirable.

[17] Archer, op. cit., p. 227.

[18] There are, however, many obligatory scenes which are demanded by partisan audiences as well. As we shall see, these obligatory scenes intensify conflict and produce an outpouring of dramatic appeals.

[19] In some cases, Presidents have deliberately produced climaxes designed to injure them temporarily in the hope of using the climax for future gain. The strategy was successfully employed by President Truman when he called back the 80th Congress into special session just before the 1948 Presidential cam-

paign. Truman knew the Congress would rebuke all his major proposals, giving him a negative climax he could take to the country.

[20] For a development of their argument, see David Braybrooke and Charles Lindblom, *A Strategy of Decision* (New York: The Free Press of Glencoe, 1963), Parts 1 and 2.

[21] For an historical examination of images of upward mobility, see Irvin G. Wyllie, *The Self-Made Man in America* (New York: The Free Press of Glencoe, 1966).

[22] In other polities, interestingly, unmasking occurs in the opposite way. In France, for example, candidates attempt to show that their opponents are not really as radical and leftist as they claim to be. This is indicated by the continued concern of French parties to get seats on the left in the Assembly and for moderately conservative parties to use the term "radical" in their names as was true of the extremely bourgeois Radical Party in the Third and Fourth Republics.

[23] Samuel Stouffer, *Communism, Conformity, and Civil Liberties* (Gloucester, Mass.: Peter Smith, 1963), chap. 3.

[24] For example, in the Minnesota Public Opinion Poll 213 conducted in March, 1962, 81 per cent of the respondents agreed with the statement, "Human nature being what it is, there will always be war and conflict." (Data kindly supplied by the Roper Public Opinion Center, Williamstown, Mass.)

[25] Lewis A. Froman, *People and Politics* (Englewood Cliffs, N.J.: Prentice-Hall, 1962), pp. 24–25.

[26] For a discussion of style issues, see Edelman, *op. cit.*, chap. 1.

[27] Widely approved symbols, such as the "little man" as an object of protection, which are available to all political participants regardless of personal ideology, probably have to be connected with position issues in order to convert the latter into style issues suitable for dramatic handling.

[28] Georg Simmel, *Conflict and the Web of Group Affiliations,* Trans. Kurt Wolff and Reinhard Bendix (New York: The Free Press of Glencoe, 1964), pp. 45–48.

[29] A good recent case in point is the 1966 New York State Democratic Nominating Convention. Appeals to prove that the Democratic Party was not "boss-controlled" resulted in the surprising nomination for Lt. Governor of Howard Samuels, a man quite unacceptable to such leaders of the party as Robert Kennedy and Frank O'Connor. Their choice, Orrin Lehman, was rapidly shunted aside by the delegates.

[30] I do not mean to imply that no dramaturgical techniques are used within bureaucracies. Other kinds of dramaturgical mechanisms flourish in bureaucracies.

[31] For an indication of how unconsciously dramatic appeals may be made to mass audiences, see Hughes' account of the genesis of Eisenhower's promise. Emmet john Hughes, *The Ordeal of Power* (New York: Atheneum, 1963), pp. 32–35.

[32] Here again is a good example of a candidate's linking personal political climaxes to institutional climaxes in order to make his dramatic impact greater. Indeed, Eisenhower made mass enjoyment of his personal political climax dependent upon a favorable outcome to a prior institutional climax.

[33] For example, the chaotic conditions among groups opposed to the Russian Czarist machine were not only brought about by differences in doctrine, but also by circulation between opposition group and Czarist jail cell or exile.

[34] See, for example, Gabriel Almond, *The Appeals of Communism* (Princeton: Princeton University Press, 1954), chaps. 9 and 10.

[35] See Lane's polemic aimed at literary criticism, demanding it produce theory that the social scientist and the humanist can both use. Robert E. Lane, *The Liberties of Wit* (New Haven: Yale University Press, 1961).

[36] See, for example, Blau, *op. cit.;* and George Homans, *Social Behavior: Its Elementary Forms* (New York: Harcourt, Brace and World, 1961). Much of this work stems from the exchange theory in Parson's macro-sociology. See Talcott Parsons, *The Social System* (Glencoe: The Free Press, 1951), chap. 3.

25.

THE MEANING OF THE CORONATION

Edward Shils and Michael Young

The heart has its reasons which the mind does not suspect. In a survey of street parties in East London nothing was more remarkable than the complete inability of people to say why they thought important the occasion they were honouring with such elaborate ritual, and the newspapers naturally took for granted the behaviour on which this essay is a comment. What is perhaps more strange is that on the monarchy, at a Coronation or any other time, political science and philosophy too are silent. About this most august institution there is no serious discussion at all.

Some political scientists, as if sure that the end of so many nineteenth century reformers has been achieved, tend to speak as if Britain is now an odd kind of republic,[1] which happens to have as its chief functionary a Queen instead of a President. It seems that even the most eminent scholars lose their sureness of touch when they enter the presence of Royalty. Sir Ivor Jennings has nothing to say in his volume on *Parliament*,[2] and in his *Cabinet Government*,[3] pausing only to note that the Sovereign still possesses considerable influence on legislation and that the King is also an important part of the 'social structure', he gives nearly all his space on this subject to an historical treatment of the Victorian period. The late Professor Harold Laski was more discerning, even though his preferences belong to the more rationalistic phase of recent intellectual history. 'Eulogy of its habits', he says, speaking of the monarchy, 'has reached a level of intensity more comparable with the religious ecstasy of the seventeenth century, when men could still believe in the divine right of kings, than of the scientific temper of the twentieth, which has seen three great imperial houses broken, and the King of Spain transformed into a homeless wanderer'.[4] For the rest, while lightly attributing this change in attitude to the imperial propaganda conducted since Victoria was proclaimed Empress of India, he too devotes himself to constitutional history, with special reference to the tangled events of 1911 and 1931. Recent British political philosophy is as applicable to a repbulic as it is to a monarchy, whose place in a modern society is a subject most studiously avoided.[5]

Kingsley Martin is almost the only modern political writer to concern himself [6] with the theme to which Walter Bagehot gave such prominence when he set out in 1867 to trace 'how the actions of a retired widow and an unemployed youth become of such importance'.[7] Bagehot firmly recognized that the role of the Crown was not so much constitutional as 'psychological.' He supported the monarchy for the precise reason that republicans opposed it: because it enabled the educated ten

Reprinted from Edward Shils, *Center and Periphery: Essays in Macro-Sociology,* University of Chicago Press, © 1975 by The University of Chicago. All rights reserved. This material appeared in a different form in the *Sociological Review,* Vol. 1, 1953.

thousand to go on governing as before. By commanding their unbounded loyalty, it tamed the uncouth 'labourers of Somersetshire' who, in their simplicity, needed a person to symbolize the State. In this way 'the English Monarchy strengthens our government with the strength of religion. . . . It gives now a vast strength to the entire constitution, by enlisting on its behalf the credulous obedience of enormous masses.' [8] . . .

The careful avoidance of the monarchy's role in British life appears, to the authors of this essay, to be the consequence of an 'intellectualist' bias. It is avoided because the monarchy has its roots in man's beliefs and sentiments about what he regards as sacred. The decline in the intensity of religious belief, especially in the educated classes, has produced an aversion towards all the sentiments and practices associated with religion. They do not acknowledge the somewhat alarming existence of these sentiments within themselves and refuse to admit that these are at work in others. They are acknowledged only when they are derogated as 'irrational' [9]—a charge which is both true and misleading, because it serves to dismiss them from further consideration.

The frequency with which the Coronation was spoken of by ordinary people as an 'inspiration',[10] and as a 'rededication' of the nation, only underscores the egregiousness of the omission. This essay, using the Coronation as a point of departure, seeks to advance, in some slight measure, the analysis of a neglected subject.

In all societies, most of the adult members possess some moral standards and beliefs about which there is agreement. There is an ordering and assessment of actions and qualities according to a definite, though usually unspoken, conception of virtue. The general acceptance of this scale of values, even though vague and inarticulate, constitutes the general moral consensus of society. Only philosophical intellectuals and prophets demand that conduct be guided by explicit moral standards. In the normal way, the general moral standards are manifested only in concrete judgments, and are seldom abstractly formulated. Persons who conduct themselves in accordance with rigorous and abstract schemes of moral value, who derive and justify every action by referring it to a general principle, impress most others as intolerable doctrinaires. To the doctrinaires, of course, the ordinary man is even more shocking; they would shake the *homme moyen sensuel* from his spiritual slothfulness and elevate him to a higher plane on which he would act knowingly only in the service of the highest good. To the doctrinaire, to the ideological intellectual, the ordinary sociable man is a poor thing—narrow, unprincipled, unmoral. The ordinary man is, of course, by no means as poor a thing as his educated detractors pretend. He too is a moral being, and even when he evades standards and dishonours obligations, he almost always concedes their validity. The revivalist reassertion of moral standards in highly individualistic frontier groups, or among detribalized primitive societies in the process of yielding before the pressure of a modern economy, are instances of the respect vice pays to virtue. The recourse to the priestly confessor and the psychoanalyst testify to the power of moral standards even in situations where they are powerless to prevent actual wrongdoing.

We do not claim that men always act in conformity with their sense of values, nor do we claim that the measure of agreement in any society, even the most consensual, is anywhere near complete. Just as no society can exist without moral consensus, without fairly far-reaching agreement on fundamental standards and beliefs, so is every society bound to be the scene of conflict. Not only is there a clash of interests, but moral and intellectual beliefs too are in collision. Yet inter-twined with all these conflicts are agreements strong enough to keep society generally peaceful and coherent.

What are these moral values which restrain men's egotism and which enable society to hold itself together? A few can be listed illustratively: generosity, charity, loyalty, justice in the distribution of opportunities and rewards, reasonable respect for authority, the dignity of the individual and his right to freedom. Most people take these values so much for granted that argument about them seems neither necessary nor possible. Their very commonplaceness may seem to place them at the very opposite pole from the sacred. Yet these values are part of the substance of the sacred, and values like them have sacred attributes in every society.

Life in a community is not only necessary to man for the *genetic* development of his human qualities. Society is necessary to man as an object of his higher evaluations and attachments, and without it man's human qualities could not find expression.[11] The *polis* or community is not just a group of concrete and particular persons; it is, more fundamentally, a group of persons acquiring their significance by their embodiment of values which transcend them and by their conformity with standards and rules from which they derive their dignity. The sacredness of society is at bottom the sacredness of its moral rules, which itself derives from the presumed relationship between these rules in their deepest significance and the forces and agents which men regard as having the power to influence their destiny for better or for worse.

Man, as a moral creature with the capacity to discriminate among degrees of rightness and wrongness, feels not only safe but also terribly unsafe in the presence of the abstract symbols of these moral rules. *This is one reason why there is a recurrent need in men to reaffirm the rightness of the moral rules by which they live or feel they ought to live.* The reaffirmation of the moral rules of society serves to quell their own hostility towards these rules and also reinstates them in the appropriate relations with the greater values and powers behind the moral rules.

The need to reaffirm the moral rules comes then, not only from their sacred character, which require that they and their sources be respected in the most serious manner, but also from the struggle against morality being continuously enacted in the human mind. Dr. Ernest Jones, in a perceptive essay,[12] has pointed to the fundamental ambivalence in the attitude to authority—first towards the parents, then towards the wider authorities of State and Church, and finally towards the rules which emanate from these authorities. This ambivalence can be overcome in a number of ways of which reaction-formation and displacement are the most prominent. In order to curb an impulse to contravene a moral law, men will sometimes put all their energy into the fulfillment of the contrary impulse. Connection with the symbols of morality or proximity to them helps in this exertion and reinforces the strength which the individual can muster from his own resources to keep the moral law uppermost. It re-establishes the preponderance of positive devotion to the moral rules to enter into contact with them in their purest form. Contact with them in their most sacred form—as principles, or when symbolized in ritual activities, or when preached in moving sermons or speeches—renews their potency and makes the individual feel that he is in 'good relations' with the sacred, as well as safe from his own sacrilegious tendencies.

If this argument be accepted, it is barely necessary to state the interpretation of the Coronation which follows from it: that the Coronation was the ceremonial occasion for the affirmation of the moral values by which the society lives. It was an act of national communion. In this we are merely restating the interpretation, in a particular context, of a more general view (which can apply to Christmas, Independence Day, Thanksgiving Day, May Day, or any other great communal ritual) expressed by a great sociologist. 'There can be no society,' said Durkheim, 'which does not feel the need of upholding and reaffirming at regular intervals the collective sentiments and the collective ideas which make its unity and its personality. Now this moral remaking cannot be achieved except by the means of reunions, assemblies and meetings where the individuals, being closely united to one another, reaffirm in common their common sentiments; hence come ceremonies which do not differ from regular religious ceremonies, either in their object, the results which they produce, or the processes employed to attain these results. What essential difference is there between an assembly of Christians celebrating the principal dates of the life of Christ, or of Jews remembering the exodus from Egypt or the promulgation of the decalogue, and a reunion of citizens commemorating the promulgation of a new moral or legal system or some great event in the national life?' [13]

The Coronation is exactly this kind of ceremonial in which the society reaffirms the moral values which constitute it as a society and renews its devotion to those values by an act of communion.

In the following pages, this interpretation of the Coronation will be illustrated by a brief analysis of the Service itself and of some aspects of public participation in it.

The Coronation Service itself is a series of ritual affirmations of the moral values necessary to a well-governed and good society. The key to the Coronation Service is the Queen's promise to abide by the moral standards of society. The whole service reiterates their supremacy above the personality of the Sovereign. In her assurance that she will observe the canons of mercy, charity, justice and protective affection, she acknowledges and submits to their power. When she does this, she symbolically proclaims her community with her subjects who, in the ritual—and in the wider audience outside the Abbey—commit themselves to obedience within the society constituted by the moral rules which she has agreed to uphold.

This intricate series of affirmations is performed in the elaborate pattern which makes up the Coronation ceremony.

The Recognition

When the Archbishop presents the Queen to the four sides of the 'theatre', he is asking the assembly to reaffirm their allegiance to her not so much as an individual as the incumbent of an office of authority charged with moral responsibility and for which she has the preliminary qualifications of a *blood-tie*. The 'People' who signify their willingness to 'do homage and service' were once the actual members and representatives of the Estates whose participation was necessary for the security of the realm. Now, those within the Abbey, although many of great power stand among them, are no longer its exclusive possessors. The 'homage and service' of the entire society is far more important than it was in earlier Coronations and their offering is no more than a dramatic concentration of the devotion which millions now feel.

The Oath

The Queen is asked whether she will solemnly promise and swear to govern the people of the United Kingdom and the Dominions and other possessions and territories in accordance with their respective laws and customs. When she does so, she clearly acknowledges that the moral standards embodied in the laws and customs are superior to her own personal will. The Queen agrees to respect justice and mercy in her judgments, and to do her utmost to maintain the laws of God and the true profession of the Gospel. In doing this, she acknowledges once more the superiority of the transcendent moral standards and their divine source, and therewith the sacred character of the moral standards of British society.

Apart from the momentary appearance of the Moderator of the General Assembly of the Church of Scotland, the Church of England administers the entire ceremony (though the Duke of Norfolk—a Roman Catholic—organised it), and yet there is no indication that this was regarded as anomaly in a country where only a small proportion of the population actively adheres to that church. Britain is generally a Christian country, it is certainly a religious country, in the broad sense, and in the Coronation Service the Church of England served the vague religiosity of the mass of the British people without raising issues of ecclesiastical jurisdiction or formal representation. As with so much else in the Coronation Service, behind the archaic façade was a vital sense of permanent contemporaneity.

Presenting the Holy Bible

When the Moderator presents the Bible to the Queen, the Archbishop says that this act is performed in order to keep Her Majesty 'ever mindful of the Law'. The Bible is a sacred object which contains in writing the fundamental moral teachings of the Christian society. Since this Bible is to go with her always, her moral consciousness is to be kept alive by means of continuous contact with the Book in which God's will is revealed. As the Moderator says, 'Here is Wisdom; This is the royal Law;[14] These are the lively Oracles of God'. The Bible which is handed to the Queen is not simply a closed and final promulgation of moral doctrine. It is the 'lively Oracles of God', in which moral inspiration and stimulus for the mastery of constantly emerging new events are to be found. The Bible is the vessel of God's intention, a source of continuous inspiration in the moral regulation of society.

The Anointing

When the Queen is divested of her regalia, she is presented as a frail creature who has now to be brought into contact with the divine, and thus transformed into a Queen, who will be something more and greater than the human being who has received the previous instruction. When the Queen sits in the saintly King Edward's Chair she is anointed by the Archbishop with consecrated oil which sanctifies her in her regal office. When he makes the cross on both her hands, her breast and the crown of her head, he places her in the tradition of the Kings of Israel and of all the rulers of England. He anoints her saying 'And as Solomon was anointed king by Zadok the priest and Nathan the prophet, so be thou anointed, blessed, and consecrated Queen over the Peoples.' It is not merely an analogy; it is a symbolization of reality, in conformity with sacred precedent. She shows her submission before the Archbishop as God's agent, kneeling before him while he implores God to bless her.

Presenting the Sword and the Orb

The Queen is then told that she will be given power to enforce the moral law of justice and to protect and encourage those whose lives are in accordance with the law. She is commanded to confirm what is in good order, and to restore to order what has fallen away from it. The sword is an instrument of destruction. It is as dangerous as the sacred foundations of the moral rules themselves and its terrible power, for evil, as well as good, must never be forgotten by the Queen. To stress this dual potentiality of authority, it is, throughout the rest of the ceremony, carried naked before her by the peer who redeemed it. In this way, the terrible responsibilities and powers of royal authority are communicated to the Queen and the people. The people are thus made aware of the protection which a good authority can offer them when they themselves adhere to the moral law, and of the wrathful punishment which will follow their deviation. She is next invested with the bracelets of sincerity and wisdom and is dressed in the Robe Royal, which enfolds her in righteousness. With these dramatic actions, she is transformed from a young woman into a vessel of the virtues which must flow through her into her society. Thus transformed, she is reminded of the wide sphere of her power, and of the responsibilities for its moral and pious use, by the Orb which she takes in her hand and places on the altar which is the repository of the most sacred objects. In doing this, she resanctifies her own authority. She is told to execute justice but never to forget mercy.

The Benediction

The communal kernel of the Coronation becomes visible again in the Benediction when the duties of the subjects are given special prominence by the Archbishop. In his blessing, he says: 'The Lord give you faithful Parliaments and quiet Realms; sure defence against all enemies; fruitful lands and a prosperous industry;

wise counsellors and upright magistrates; leaders of integrity in learning and labour; a devout, learned, and useful clergy; honest, peaceable, and dutiful citizens'. The circle of obligation is completed: the Queen to God's rule, and to her subjects in the light of God's rule, and then, her subjects to her by the same standard.

The Coronation Service and the Procession which followed were shared and celebrated by nearly all the people of Britain. In these events of 2nd June the Queen and her people were, through radio, television and press and in festivities throughout the land, brought into a great nation-wide communion. Not only the principals and the spectators inside the Abbey, but the people outside also, participated in the sacred rite. There is no doubt about the depth of the popular enthusiasm. Only about its causes is there disagreement. Some claim that it is the product of commercially interested publicity, others that it is the child of the popular press, others simply dismiss it as hysteria or 'irrationality'. There are those who claim (with rather more justice) that the involvement in the Coronation was no more than an expression of an ever-present British love of processions, uniforms, parades and pageants. Still others see the whole affair as a national 'binge', or an opportunity for millions of people to seize the occasion for a good time. The youth and charm of the Queen and the attractiveness of her husband and children are also cited to explain the absorption of the populace.

Which of these explanations is correct? All of them, it seems to us, are at best partial answers. They all overlook the element of communion with the sacred, in which the commitment to values is reaffirmed and fortified. As we said earlier, the rationalistic bias of educated persons in the present century, particularly those of radical or liberal political disposition, is liable to produce abhorrence towards manifestations of popular devotion to any institution which cannot recommend itself to secular utilitarianism.

The collision between the latter viewpoint and the devoted gravity of the popular attitude was revealed most strikingly in the uproar which followed the publication of Mr. David Low's cartoon in the *Manchester Guardian* on 3rd June. This cartoon showed a Blimp-like figure, 'the morning after', a paper crown awry on his head, the remains of the tinsel and crepe paper of a gay party littered about him, a television receiver in the corner and over it all a grim reminder that £100,000,000 had been spent on the spree. It was in the radical 'debunking' tradition. It called forth a storm of denunciation. Moral sentiments had been affronted by Mr. Low's frivolity at a time when they were at a high pitch of seriousness.[15] . . .

The solemn sense that something touching the roots of British society was involved found expression in many other ways as well. An experienced observer of the London crowd said that the atmosphere on 1st June was like that of Armistice Day 1918 and of VE and VJ Days 1945: there was an air of gravity accompanied by a profound release from anxiety. The extraordinary stillness and tranquillity of the people on the route all through the early morning of 2nd June was noted by many who moved among them. Churches received many persons who came to pray or to meditate in the quiet, and in at least one famous London church—All Hallows Barking—communion services were held every hour.

Just as the Coronation Service in the Abbey was a religious ceremony in the conventional sense, so then the popular participation in the service throughout the country had many of the properties of the enactment of a religious ritual. For one thing, it was not just an extraordinary spectacle, which people were interested in as individuals in search of enjoyment. The Coronation was throughout a collective, not an individual experience.

W. Robertson Smith in his great work, *Lectures on the Religion of the Semites,* [16] points out that acts of communion (of which the Coronation can be regarded as an example) are never experienced by individuals alone: they are always communal occasions. They are acts of communion between the deity or other symbols of the highest values of the community, and persons who come together to be in communion with one another through their common contact with the sacred. The fact that the experience is communal means that one of the values, the virtue of social unity or solidarity, is acknowledged and strengthened in the very act of communion.

The greatly increased sensitivity of individuals to their social ties, the greater absorption of the individual into his group and therewith into the larger community through his group found expression not only on the procession route but in the absent people as well, notably through their families. The family, despite the ravages of urban life and despite those who allege that it is in dissolution, remains one of the most sinewy of institutions. The family tie is regarded as sacred, even by those who would, or do, shirk the diffuse obligations it imposes. The Coronation, like any other great occasion which in some manner touches the sense of the sacred, brings vitality into family relationships. The Coronation, much like Christmas, was a time for drawing closer the bonds of the family, for re-asserting its solidarity and for re-emphasizing the values of the family—generosity, loyalty, love—which are *at the same time* the fundamental values necessary for the well being of the larger society. When listening to the radio, looking at the television, walking the streets to look at the decorations, the unit was the family, and neither mother nor father were far away when their children sat down for cakes and ice-cream at one of the thousands of street and village parties held that week. Prominent in the crowds were parents holding small children on their shoulders and carrying even smaller ones in cradles. In all towns over the country, prams were pushed great distances to bring into contact with the symbols of the great event infants who could see or appreciate little. It was as if people recognized that the most elementary unit for entry into communion with the sacred was the family, not the individual.

The solidarity of the family is often heightened at the cost of solidarity in the wider community. Not so at the Coronation. On this occasion one family was knit together with another in one great national family through identification with the monarchy. A general warmth and congeniality permeated relations even with strangers. It was the same type of atmosphere, except that it was more pronounced, that one notices at Christmas time when, in busy streets and crowded trains, people are much more warm-hearted, sympathetic and kindly than they are on more ordinary occasions. Affection generated by the great event overflowed from the family to outsiders, and back again into the family. One correspondent of the *Manchester Guardian,* reporting the Coronation procession, observed: 'The Colonial contingents sweep by. The crowd loves them. The crowd now loves everybody.' Antagonism emerged only against people who did not seem to be joining in the great event or treating with proper respect the important social values—by failing, for example, to decorate their buildings with proper splendour. A minor example of the increase in communal unity was the police report that, contrary to their expectations, the pickpockets, usually an inevitable concomitant of any large crowd, were entirely inactive during Coronation Day.

. . . Something like this kind of spirit had been manifested before—during the Blitz, the Fuel Crisis of 1947, the London smog of 1952, even during the Watson—Bailey stand in the Lord's Test or Lock's final overs at the Oval—and to some extent the broad reasons were probably the same. There was a vital common subject for people to talk about; whatever the individual's speciality, the same thought was uppermost in his mind as in everyone else's, and that made it easier to overcome the customary barriers. But not less important than the common subject is the common sentiment of the sacredness of communal life and institutions. In a great national communion like the Coronation, people became more aware of their dependence upon each other, and they sensed some connection between this and their relationship to the Queen. Thereby they became more sensitive to the values which bound them all together. Once there is a common vital object of attention, and a common sentiment about it, the feelings apt for the occasion spread by a kind of contagion. Kindness, met with on every side, reinforces itself, and a feeling of diffuse benevolence and sympathy spreads; under these circumstances the individual loses his egoistic boundaries and feels himself fused with his community.

The need to render gifts and sacrifices, so central in religious ceremonies, was also apparent in various forms. Many persons sent gifts directly to the Queen, and the vast scale of individual and collective gifts to persons known and unknown has been the occasion of much comment. Very many municipalities arranged 'treats for old folks', local authorities gave gifts to school children and gift-giving within and between families was very widespread. The joint viewing of the Coronation Service and Procession on the television called forth many presentations. The universal decorations attest not merely to the sense of festivity but also to the disposition to offer valuable objects on such an occasion of entry into contact with the sacred values of society. Low's cartoon in the *Manchester Guardian* certainly portrayed one aspect of the truth when he saw the whole thing as 'one gigantic binge'. But it was not just a 'good time' or an 'opportunity for a good time', as some persons grudgingly said in justification for giving themselves up to the Coronation. There was an orgy, in a certain sense, but it was not just one of self-indulgence. Students of comparative religion have shown that an orgy following an act of communion with the sacred is far from uncommon. It aids the release of tension and reduces the anxiety which intense and immediate contact with the sacred engenders. Moreover, what appears to be simply an orgy of self-indulgence is often one of indulgence with goods which have been consecrated or which have some sacred, communally significant properties.

Surcease from drabness and routine, from the commonplaceness and triviality of daily preoccupation, is certainly one reason for the exaltation. There is surely wisdom in the remark of a philosophical Northern villager: 'What people like is the sheer excess of it. We lead niggling enough lives these days. Something a bit lavish for a change is good for the soul.' [17] But he did not go far enough. The British love of processions, of uniforms, and ceremonial is not just simple-minded gullibility— it is the love of proximity to greatness and power, to the charismatic person or institution which partakes of the sacred. The crowds who turned out to see the Queen, who waited in the rain in quiet happiness to see the Queen and her soldiers, were waiting to enter into contact with the mighty powers who are symbolically and to some extent, really responsible for the care and protection of their basic values and who on this day had been confirmed in these responsibilities. The crowds who clamoured for the Queen outside Buckingham Palace or who lined the streets on the days following Coronation Day when she made her tours of London were not just idle curiosity-seekers. They were, it is probably true, looking for a thrill but it was the thrill of contact with something great, with something which is connected with the sacred, in the way that authority which is charged with obligations to provide for and to protect the community in its fundamental constitution is always rooted in the sacred.

. . . The combination of constitutional monarchy and political democracy has itself played a part in the creation and maintenance of moral consensus, and it is this part which we shall now briefly consider. The late John Rickman and Ernest Jones have argued that the deep ambivalence towards authority and towards moral rules has promoted the widespread acceptance of the monarchy in Britain and in other countries where constitutional monarchy has become firmly established. Whereas the lands where personal or absolute monarchy prevailed were beset by revolution, countries of constitutional monarchy became politically stable and orderly, with a vigorously democratic political life. Hostility against authority was, it is said, displaced from royalty onto the leaders of the opposition party and even onto the leaders of the government party. Constitutional monarchies and their societies were fortified by drawing to themselves the loyalties and devotion of their members while avoiding the hostility which is always, in varying measure, engendered by submission to morality. When protected from the full blast of destructiveness by its very *powerlessness,* royalty is able to bask in the sunshine of an affection unadulterated by its opposite. The institution of the constitutional monarchy is supported by one of the mechanisms by which the mind defends itself from conflict, namely, by the segregation of mutually antagonistic sentiments, previously directed towards a single object, onto discrete and separate objects.[18]

It might therefore be said that the vigour of British political life is actually rendered possible by the existence of the constitutional monarchy. But the aggressiveness which is channelled into the political arena is in its turn ameliorated and checked by the sentiments of moral unity which the Crown helps to create. Here it is not only the symbolism of the Crown but also the painstaking probity of Kings George V and VI in dealing with the Labour Party, both when it was in opposition and when it formed the Government, which have helped to weld the Labour Party and its following firmly into the moral framework of the national life.

An effective segregation of love and hatred, when the love is directed towards a genuinely love-worthy object, reduces the intensity of the hatred as well. Just as the existence of a constitutional monarchy softens the acerbity in the relations between political parties, so it also lessens the antagonism of the governed towards the reigning government. Governments are well known to benefit whenever the virtues of Royalty are displayed.[19] It appears that the popularity of the Conservative Administration was at least temporarily increased by the Coronation, and at the time much newspaper speculation centred on the question whether Mr. Churchill would use the advantage to win a large majority for his Party at a General Election.

Thus we can see that the image of the monarch as the symbolic custodian of the awful powers and beneficent moral standards is one weighty element in moral consensus. But the monarch is not only symbol. Personal qualities are also significant. Hence it is appropriate at this point to refer to the role of the Royal Family in attaching the population to the monarchy. Walter Bagehot said: 'A family on the throne is an interesting idea also. It brings down the pride of sovereignty to the level of petty life.'[20] More and more has this become true since then. Where once to mention the family of the King, like Charles II or George IV, would have provoked laughter, it is now common form to talk about the Royal Family. The monarchy is idealised not so much for the virtue of the individual sovereign as for the virtue which he expresses in his family life.

Devotion to the Royal Family thus does mean in a very direct way devotion to one's own family, because the values embodied in each are the same. When allowance is also made for the force of displacement, if it is accepted that a person venerates the Sovereign partly because he is associated, in the seat of the emotions, with the wondrous parents of phantasy, and if it is accepted that there is also a sort of re-displacement at work, whereby the real parents and wives and children are thought of more highly because they receive some of the backwash of emotion from their Royal counterparts,[21] it is easy to see that the emotional change is a reciprocal one, and all the more powerful for that. Some aspects of this relationship become clear in the Christmas broadcast in which the Sovereign year after year talks about the Royal Family, the millions of British families, and the nation as a whole, as though they are one.[22] On sacred occasions, the whole society is felt to be one large family, and even the nations of the Commonwealth, represented at the Coronation by their prime ministers, queens, and ambassadors, are conceived of as a 'family of nations'.

In other ways the monarchy plays on more ordinary occasions the same kind of role as it does at a Coronation—only in a far less spectacular way. Thus British society combines free institutional pluralism with an underlying moral consensus. The universities, the municipalities, the professional bodies, the trades unions, the business corporations—all seek to enforce and protect their internal standards and to fend off external encroachment. Yet they coexist and cooperate in a remarkable atmosphere of mutual respect and relative freedom from acrimony. There are many reasons for this (which we hope to treat more elaborately and with adequate documentation in subsequent publications). In the present context we wish only to stress the unifying function of the monarchy and the orders of society which derive their legitimacy from connection with it. Every corporate body which has some connection with the sacred properties, the *charisma,* of the Crown thereby has infused into it a reminder of the moral obligations which extend beyond its own corporate boundaries. It is tied, so to speak, to the central value system of the society as a whole through its relationship with Royalty.

There are the Royal Charters, the patronage of charities, the inaugural ceremonies of hospitals and ships, gardens and factories. The monarchy is the one pervasive institution, standing above all others, which plays a part in a vital way comparable to the function of the medieval Church as seen by Professor Tawney—the function of integrating diverse elements into a whole by protecting and defining their autonomy.[23]

Even where the monarchy does not assume ceremonial offices of the type just referred to, the function of holding together the plurality of institutions is performed in some measure by the peerage and the system of honours. In all institutions and professions, all forms of individual achievement and merit are recognized and blessed by this system. The outstanding actors and poets, doctors and scientists, leaders of trade unions and trade associations, scholars and sportsmen, musicians and managers, the brave, the brilliant and the industrious, all receive confirmation of their conformity with the highest standards of society by an honour awarded by the Sovereign. The Sovereign acts as agent of the value system, and the moral values of the society are reinforced in the individuals honoured.

To sum up: A society is held together by its internal agreement about the sacredness of certain fundamental moral standards. In an inchoate, dimly perceived, and seldom explicit manner, the central authority of an orderly society, whether it be secular or ecclesiastical, is acknowledged to be the avenue of communication with the realm of the sacred values. Within its society, popular constitutional monarchy enjoys almost universal recognition in this capacity, and it is therefore enabled to heighten the moral and civic sensibility of the society and to permeate it with symbols of those values to which the sensitivity responds. Intermittent rituals bring the society or varying sectors of it repeatedly into contact with this vessel of the sacred values. The Coronation provided at one time and for practically the entire society such an intensive contact with the sacred that we believe we are justified in interpreting it as we have done in this essay, as a great act of national communion.

NOTES

[1] The virtual disappearance of republican sentiment is obvious. John Gollan (*Communist Review,* June 1953) and Emrys Hughes, M.P., are indeed unorthodox. The current Labour attitude was expressed by Mr. Attlee in the House of Commons on 9 July, 1952. Speaking against sweeping economies in Royal expenditure, he said 'It is a great mistake to make government too dull. That, I think, was the fault of the German Republic after the First World War. They were very drab and dull; the trouble was that they let the devil get all the best tunes.' See also Sir Stafford Cripps (*Hansard,* 17 December 1947).

[2] 'Of the King we need say nothing. His part in the process of legislation has become little more than formal.' *Parliament.* Cambridge, 1939, p. 3.

[3] *Cabinet Government.* Cambridge, 1947.

[4] *Parliamentary Government in England.* Allen & Unwin, London, 1938, p. 389.

[5] Sir Ernest Barker scarcely refers to Monarchy in his *Reflections on Government* (Oxford, 1942) and passes over it entirely in his brief 'Reflections on English Political Theory' (*Political Studies,* I, I. Oxford, 1953. pp. 6–12.)

[6] *The Magic of Monarchy.* Nelson, London, 1937. The article by J. G. Weightman, 'Loyal Thoughts of an Ex-Republican', and other articles in the June 1953 issue of *The Twentieth Century* must also rank as shining exceptions.

[7] *The English Constitution.* Oxford, 1936, p. 30.

[8] Op. cit. pp. 35, 39.

[9] See, for instance, Percy Black, *The Mystique of Modern Monarchy.* Watts, London, 1953.

[10] Not only in Britain and the Commonwealth. Sebastian Haffner speaks of the way in which the Coronation has 'taken hold of the public consciousness of America, France and Germany. . . . There is, instead, an absorbed participation which almost, momentarily, removes the barriers of statehood—as if these foreign countries were celebrating, with mourning or rejoicing, great events in their own ruling Houses, or as if the British Monarchy had become a common possession of the Western world at large.' *The Twentieth Century,* June 1953, p. 418.

[11] *The Politics of Aristotle,* trans. by Sir Ernest Barker, Oxford, 1946, p. 2.

[12] Jones, Ernest. 'The Psychology of Constitutional Monarchy' in *Essays in Applied Psychoanalysis,* Vol. I. Hogarth, London, 1951.

[13] *Elementary Forms of Religious Life.* Allen & Unwin. London. 1915, p. 427. Cf. also Radcliffe-Brown, A. R., *The Andaman Islanders,* Cambridge, 1922, Ch. V.

[14] It is the law which is to govern Royalty, and only in this way does it refer to the law made by Royalty for the government of society.

[15] Durkheim, to whose understanding of the function of great communal rituals we have already referred, designated the side of life which includes action on behalf of or in accordance with the sacred moral values as 'la vie serieuse'. Durkheim might have been referring to the 'Low crisis' when he wrote: 'What social danger is there in touching a tabooed object, an impure animal or man, in letting the sacred fire die down, in eating certain meats, in failure to make the traditional sacrifice over the graves of parents, in not exactly pronouncing the ritual formula, in not celebrating certain holidays, etc.? We know, however, what a large place in the repressive law of many peoples ritual regimentation, etiquette, ceremonial, and religious practices play'. . . . 'An act is criminal when it offends strong and defined states of the collective conscience.' *The Division of Labor in Society.* Macmillan, New York, 1933, pp. 72; 80.

[16] *Lectures on the Religion of the Semites,* Black, London, 1927.

[17] *Manchester Guardian,* 3 June 1953.

[18] Anna Freud. *The Ego and the Mechanisms of Defence.* Hogarth, London, 1937.

[19] The Secretary of the Labour Party once told one of the authors of this essay that he had always been confident that Labour would win the hotly contested Gravesend by-election in 1947 because the then Princess Elizabeth had been married a short time before.

[20] Op. cit., p. 34.

[21] One of the authors, during an interview in a London slum district, asked a mother the age of her small son. 'Just the same age as Prince Charles' she replied, looking at him with a smile of pride and love.

[22] We have mentioned above the significance of the reconciliation between the intellectuals and the monarchy as part of the general re-acceptance of society by the intellectuals. With respect to the family, the change is equally impressive. Who among the figures of the high intelligentsia would now accept the critical views on the family of Shaw, Wells, Havelock Ellis, Edward Carpenter, D. H. Lawrence or the Bertrand Russell of the 1920's? Who among well known British intellectuals today would be sympathetic with H. G. Wells' pronouncement?: 'The family can remain only as a biological fact. Its economic and educational autonomy are inevitably doomed. The modern state is bound to be the ultimate guardian of all children, and it must assist, replace or subordinate the parents as supporter, guardian and educator; it must release all human beings from the obligation of mutual proprietorship and it must refuse absolutely to recognize or enforce any kind of sexual ownership.' *Experiment in Auto-Biography,* Vol. II. Gollancz and Cresset Press, London, 1934, p. 481.

26.

CONDITIONS OF SUCCESSFUL DEGRADATION CEREMONIES

Harold Garfinkel

Any communicative work between persons, whereby the public identity of an actor is transformed into something looked on as lower in the local scheme of social types, will be called a "status degradation ceremony." Some restrictions on this definition may increase its usefulness. The identities referred to must be "total" identities. That is, these identities must refer to persons as "motivational" types rather than as "behavioral" types,[1] not to what a person may be expected to have done or to do (in Parsons' term,[2] to his "performances") but to what the group holds to be the ultimate "grounds" or "reasons" for his performance.[3]

The grounds on which a participant achieves what for him is adequate understanding of why he or another acted as he did are not treated by him in a utilitarian manner. Rather, the correctness of an imputation is decided by the participant in accordance with socially valid and institutionally recommended standards of "preference." With reference to these standards, he makes the crucial distinctions between appearances and reality, truth and falsity, triviality and importance, accident and essence, coincidence and cause. Taken together, the grounds, as well as the behavior that the grounds make explicable as the other person's conduct, constitute a person's identity. Together, they constitute the other as a social object. Persons identified by means of the ultimate "reasons" for their socially categorized and socially understood behavior will be said to be "totally" identified. The degradation ceremonies here discussed are those that are concerned with the alteration of total identities.

It is proposed that only in societies that are completely demoralized, will an observer be unable to find such ceremonies, since only in total anomie are the conditions of degradation ceremonies lacking. Max Scheler [4] argued that there is no society that does not provide in the very features of its organization the conditions sufficient for inducing shame. It will be treated here as axiomatic that there is no society whose social structure does not provide, in its routine features, the conditions

Reprinted by permission from *American Journal of Sociology,* Vol. LXI, 1956, University of Chicago Press, © by The University of Chicago.

of identity degradation. Just as the structural conditions of shame are universal to all societies by the very fact of their being organized, so the structural conditions of status degradation are universal to all societies. In this framework the critical question is not whether status degradation occurs or can occur within any given society. Instead, the question is: Starting from any state of a society's organization, what program of communicative tactics will get the work of status degradation done?

First of all, two questions will have to be decided, at least tentatively: *What are we referring to behaviorally when we propose the product of successful degradation work to be a changed total identity?* And *what are we to conceive the work of status degradation to have itself accomplished or to have assumed as the conditions of its success?*

Degradation ceremonies fall within the scope of the sociology of moral indignation. Moral indignation is a social affect. Roughly speaking, it is an instance of a class of feelings particular to the more or less organized ways that human beings develop as they live out their lives in one another's company. Shame, guilt, and boredom are further important instances of such affects.

Any affect has its behavioral paradigm. That of shame is found in the withdrawal and covering of the portion of the body that socially defines one's public appearance—prominently, in our society, the eyes and face. The paradigm of shame is found in the phrases that denote removal of the self from public view, i.e., removal from the regard of the publicly identified other: "I could have sunk through the floor; I wanted to run away and hide; I wanted the earth to open up and swallow me." The feeling of guilt finds its paradigm in the behavior of self-abnegation—disgust, the rejection of further contact with or withdrawal from, and the bodily and symbolic expulsion of the foreign body, as when we cough, blow, gag, vomit, spit, etc.

The paradigm of moral indignation is *public* denunciation. We publicly deliver the curse: "I call upon all men to bear witness that he is not as he appears but is otherwise and *in essence* [5] of a lower species."

The social affects serve various functions both for the person as well as for the collectivity. A prominent function of shame for the person is that of preserving the ego from further onslaughts by withdrawing entirely its contact with the outside. For the collectivity shame is an "individuator." One experiences shame in his own time.

Moral indignation serves to effect the ritual destruction of the person denounced. Unlike shame, which does not bind persons together, moral indignation may reinforce group solidarity. In the market and in politics, a degradation ceremony must be counted as a secular form of communion. Structurally, a degradation ceremony bears close resemblance to ceremonies of investiture and elevation. How such a ceremony may bind persons to the collectivity we shall see when we take up the conditions of a successful denunciation. Our immediate question concerns the meaning of ritual destruction.

In the statement that moral indignation brings about the ritual destruction of the person being denounced, destruction is intended literally. The transformation of identities is the destruction of one social object and the constitution of another. The transformation does not involve the substitution of one identity for another, with the terms of the old one loitering about like the overlooked parts of a fresh assembly, any more than the woman we see in the department-store window that turns out to be a dummy carries with it the possibilities of a woman. It is not that the old object has been overhauled; rather it is replaced by another. One declares, *"Now,* it was otherwise in the first place."

The work of the denunciation effects the recasting of the objective character of the perceived other: The other person becomes in the eyes of his condemners literally a different and *new* person. It is not that the new attributes are added to the old "nucleus." He is not changed, he is reconstituted. The former identity, at best, receives the accent of mere appearance. In the social calculus of reality representations and test, the former identity stands as accidental; the new identity is the "basic reality." What he is now is what, "after all," he was all along.[6]

The public denunciation effects such a transformation of essence by substituting another socially validated motivational scheme for that previously used to name and order the performances of the denounced. It is with reference to this substituted, socially validated motivational scheme as the essential grounds, i.e., the *first principles,* that his performances, past, present, and prospective, according to the witnesses, are to be properly and necessarily understood.[7] Through the interpretive work that respects this rule, the denounced person becomes in the eyes of the witness a different person.

How can one make a good denunciation?[8]

To be successful, the denunciation must redefine the situations of those that are witnesses to the denunciation work. The denouncer, the party to be denounced (let us call him the "perpetrator"), and the thing that is being blamed on the perpetrator (let us call it the "event") must be transformed as follows:[9]

1. Both event and perpetrator must be removed from the realm of their everyday character and be made to stand as "out of the ordinary."

2. Both event and perpetrator must be placed within a scheme of preferences that shows the following properties:

A. The preferences must not be for event A over event B, but for event of *type* A over event of *type* B. The same typing must be accomplished for the perpetrator. Event and perpetrator must be defined as instances of a uniformity and must be treated as a uniformity throughout the work of the denunciation. The unique, never recurring character of the event or perpetrator should be lost. Similarly, any sense of accident, coincidence, indeterminism, chance, or monetary occurrence must not merely be minimized. Ideally, such measures should be inconceivable; at least they should be made false.

B. The witnesses must appreciate the characteristics of the typed person and event by referring the type to a dialectical counterpart. Ideally, the witnesses should not be able to contemplate the features of the denounced person without reference to the counterconception, as the profanity of an occurrence or a desire or a character trait, for example, is clarified by the references it bears to its opposite, the sacred.

The features of the mad-dog murderer reverse the features of the peaceful citizen. The confessions of the Red can be read to each the meanings of patriotism. There are many contrasts available, and any aggregate of witnesses this side of a complete war of each against all will have a plethora of such schemata for effecting a "familiar," "natural," "proper," ordering of motives, qualities, and other events.

From such contrasts, the following is to be learned. If the denunciation is to take effect, the scheme must not be one in which the witness is allowed to elect the preferred. Rather, the alternatives must be such that the preferred is morally required. Matters must be so arranged that the validity of his choice, its justification, is maintained by the fact that he makes it.[10] The scheme of alternatives must be such as to place constraints upon his making a selection "for a purpose." Nor will the denunciation succeed if the witness is free to look beyond the fact that he makes the selection for evidence that the correct alternative has been chosen, as, for example, by the test of empirical consequences of the choice. The alternatives must be such that, in "choosing," he takes it for granted and beyond any motive for doubt that not choosing can mean only preference for its opposite.

3. The denouncer must so identify himself to the witnesses that during the denunciation they regard him not as a private but as a publicly known person. He must not portray himself as acting according to his personal, unique experiences. He must rather be regarded as acting in his capacity as a public figure, drawing upon communally entertained and verified experience. He must act as a bona fide participant in the tribal relationships to which the witnesses subscribe. What he says must not be regarded as true for him alone, not even in the sense that it can be regarded by denouncer and witnesses as matters upon which they can become agreed. In no case, except in a most ironical sense, can the convention of true-for-reasonable-men be invoked. What the denouncer says must be regarded by the witnesses as true on the grounds of a socially employed metaphysics whereby witnesses assume that witnesses and denouncer are alike in essence.[11]

4. The denouncer must make the dignity of the supra-personal values of the tribe salient and accessible to view, and his denunciation must be delivered in their name.

5. The denouncer must arrange to be invested with the right to speak in the name of these ultimate values. The success of the denunciation will be undermined if, for his authority to denounce, the denouncer invokes the personal interests that he may have acquired by virtue of the wrong done to him or someone else. He must rather use the wrong he has suffered as a tribal member to invoke the authority to speak in the name of these ultimate values.

6. The denouncer must get himself so defined by the witnesses that they locate him as a supporter of these values.

7. Not only must the denouncer fix his distance from the person being denounced, but the witnesses must be made to experience their distance from him also.

8. Finally, the denounced person must be ritually separated from a place in the legitimate order, i.e., he must be defined as standing at a place opposed to it. He must be placed "outside," he must be made "strange."

These are the conditions that must be fulfilled for a successful denunciation. If they are absent, the denunciation will fail. Regardless of the situation when the denouncer enters, if he is to succeed in degrading the other man, it is necessary to introduce these features.[12]

Not all degradation ceremonies are carried on in accordance with publicly prescribed and publicly validated measures. Quarrels which seek the humiliation of the opponent through personal invective may achieve degrading on a limited scale. Comparatively few person at a time enter into this form of communion, few benefit from it, and the fact of participation does not give the witness a definition of the other that is standardized beyond the particular group or scene of its occurrence.

The devices for effecting degradation vary in the feature and effectiveness according to the organization and operation of the system of action in which they occur. In our society the arena of degradation whose product, the redefined person, enjoys the widest transferability between groups has been rationalized, at least as to the institutional measures for carrying it out. The court and its officers have something like a fair monopoly over such ceremonies, and there they have become an occupational routine. This is to be contrasted with degradation undertaken as an immediate kinship and tribal obligation and carried out by those who, unlike our professional degraders in the law courts, acquire both right and obligation to engage in it through being themselves the injured parties or kin to the injured parties.

Factors conditioning the effectiveness of degradation tactics are provided in the organization and operation of the system of action within which the degradation occurs. For example, timing rules that provide for serial or reciprocal "conversations" would have much to do with the kinds of tactics that one might be best advised to use. The tactics advisable for an accused who can answer the charge as soon as it is made are in contrast with those recommended for one who had to wait out the denunciation before replying. Face-to-face contact is a different situation from that wherein the denunciation and reply are conducted by radio and newspaper. Whether the denunciation must be accomplished on a single occasion or is to be carried out over a sequence of "tries," factors like the territorial arrangements and movements of persons at the scene of the denunciation, the numbers of persons involved as accused, degraders, and witnesses, status claims of the contenders, prestige and power allocations among participants, all should influence the outcome.

In short, the factors that condition the success of the work of degradation are those that we point to when we conceive the actions of a number of persons as group-governed. Only some of the more obvious structural variables that may be expected to serve as predicters of the characteristics of denunciatory communicative tactics have been mentioned. They tell us not only how to construct an effective denunciation but also how to render denunciation useless.

NOTES

[1] These terms are borrowed from Alfred Schutz, "Common Sense and Scientific Interpretation of Human Action," *Philosophy and Phenomenological Research,* Vol. XIV, No. 1 (September, 1953).
[2] Talcott Parsons and Edward Shils, "Values, Motives, and Systems of Action," in Parsons and Shils (eds.), *Toward a General Theory of Action* (Cambridge: Harvard University Press, 1951).

[3] Cf. the writings of Kenneth Burke, particularly *Permanence and Change* (Los Altos, Calif.: Hermes Publications, 1954), and *A Grammar of Motives* (New York: Prentice-Hall, Inc., 1945).

[4] Richard Hays Williams, "Scheler's Contributions to the Sociology of Affective Action, with Special Attention to the Problem of Shame," *Philosophy and Phenomenological Research,* Vol. II, No. 3 (March, 1942).

[5] The man at whose hands a neighbor suffered death becomes a "murderer." The person who passes on information to enemies is really, i.e., "in essence," "in the first place," "all along," "in the final analysis," "originally," an informer.

[6] Two themes commonly stand out in the rhetoric of denunciation: (1) the irony between what the denounced appeared to be and what he is seen now really to be where the new motivational scheme is taken as the standard and (2) a re-examination and redefinition of origins of the denounced. For the sociological relevance of the relationship between concerns for essence and concerns for origins see particularly Kenneth Burke, *A Grammar of Motives.*

[7] While constructions like "substantially a something" or "essentially a something" have been banished from the domain of scientific discourse, such constructions have prominent and honored places in the theories of motives, persons, and conduct that are employed in handling the affairs of daily life. Reasons can be given to justify the hypothesis that such constructions may be lost to a group's "terminology of motives" only if the relevance of socially sanctioned theories to practical problems is suspended. This can occur where interpersonal relations are trivial (such as during play) or, more interestingly, under severe demoralization of a system of activities. In such organizational states the frequency of status degradation is low.

[8] Because the paper is short, the risk must be run that, as a result of excluding certain considerations, the treated topics may appear exaggerated. It would be desirable, for example, to take account of the multitude of hedges that will be found against false denunciation; of the rights to denounce; of the differential apportionment of these rights, as well as the ways in which a claim, once staked out, may become a vested interest and may tie into the contests for economic and political advantage. Further, there are questions centering around the appropriate arenas of denunciation. For example, in our society the tribal council has fallen into secondary importance; among lay persons the denunciation has given way to the complaint to the authorities.

[9] These are the effects that the communicative tactics of the denouncer must be designed to accomplish. Put otherwise, in so far as the denouncer's tactics accomplish the reordering of the definitions of the situation of the witnesses to the denunciatory performances, the denouncer will have succeeded in effecting the transformation of the public identity of his victim. The list of conditions of this degrading effect are the determinants of the effect. Viewed in the scheme of a project to be rationally pursued, they are the adequate means. One would have to choose one's tactics for their efficiency in accomplishing these effects.

[10] Cf. Gregory Bateson and Jurgen Ruesch, *Communication: The Social Matrix of Psychiatry* (New York: W. W. Norton & Co., 1951), pp. 212–27.

[11] For bona fide members it is not that these are the grounds upon which we are agreed but upon which we are *alike,* consubstantial, in origin the same.

[12] Neither of the problems of possible communicative or organizational conditions of their effectiveness have been treated here in systematic fashion. However, the problem of communicative tactics in degradation ceremonies is set in the light of systematically related conceptions. These conceptions may be listed in the following statements:

1. The definition of the situation of the witnesses (for ease of discourse we shall use the letter S) always bears a time qualification.

2. The S at t_2 is a function of the S at t_1. This function is described as an operator that transforms the S at t_1.

3. The operator is conceived as communicative work.

4. For a successful denunciation, it is required that the S at t_2 show specific properties. These have been specified previously.

5. The task of the denouncer is to alter the S's of the witnesses so that these S's will show the specified properties.

6. The "rationality" of the denouncer's tactics, i.e., their adequacy as a means for effecting the set of transformations necessary for effecting the identity transformation, is decided by the rule that the orga-

nizational and operational properties of the communicative net (the social system) are determinative of the size of the discrepancy between an intended and an actual effect of the communicative work. Put otherwise, the question is not that of the temporal origin of the situation but always and only how it is altered over time. The view is recommended that the definition of the situation at time 2 is a function of the definition at time 1 where this function consists of the communicative work conceived as a set of operations whereby the altered situation at time 1 is the situation at time 2. In strategy terms the function consists of the program of procedures that a denouncer should follow to effect the change of state S_{t1} to S_{t2}. In this paper S_{t1} is treated as an unspecified state.

27.

SELECTIONS FROM LOVE'S BODY

Norman O. Brown

. . . Personality is *persona,* a mask. The world is a stage, the self a theatrical creation: "The self, then, as a performed character, is not an organic thing that has a specific location, whose fundamental fate is to be born, to mature, to die: it is a dramatic effect arising diffusely from a scene that is presented." The self does not belong to its possessor. "He and his body merely provide the peg on which something of a collaborative manufacture will be hung for a time. The means for producing and maintaining selves do not reside inside the peg . . . There will be a team of persons whose activity on stage in conjunction with available props will constitute the scene from which the performed character's self will emerge, and another team, the audience, whose interpretive activity will be necessary for this emergence."

It is all psychodrama. The symptom is a dramatized wish; neurosis endows reality with a special meaning and a secret significance. "I have a little dog and they want to take it away from me." "The dog was his disease, his personality, and his penis." Sickness is all shamming, role-playing, acting-out. And so is therapy; in the transference, the patient is acting out, reënacting, new editions of old conflicts. Social groups are theatrical groups, for group therapy. . . .

. . . A PERSON, is he, *whose words or actions are considered, either as his own, or as representing the words or actions of another man . . .* . When they are considered as his owne, then he is called a *Naturall Person:* And when they are considered as representing the words and actions of another, then is he a *Feigned* or *Artificiall person."* A person is always a feigned or artificial person, *persona ficta.* A person is never himself but always a mask; a person never owns his own person, but always represents another, by whom he is possessed. And the other that one is, is

Reprinted by permission from *Love's Body,* Random House, 1966.

always ancestors; one's soul is not one's own, but daddy's. This is the meaning of the Oedipus Complex.

. . . From the primitive mask to the modern personality, through three intermediate reorganizations of the theater: Roman law, Stoic ethics, Christian theology.

. . . Roman law, the Roman jurists say, is concerned with three things only, persons, things, and actions. Roman law is a set of rules for a new theater of judicial and political process, the *respublica* or public realm. "The organization of the *polis,* physically secured by the wall around the city and physiognomically guaranteed by its law—lest the succeeding generations change its identity beyond recognition—is a kind of organized remembrance. It assures the mortal actor that his passing existence and fleeting greatness will never lack the reality that comes from being seen, being heard, and, generally, appearing before an audience." "Action, in so far as it engages in founding and preserving political bodies, creates the condition for remembrance, that is, for history." "That is why the theater is the political art par excellence." Solon and Thespis, these two, are one: a new theatricality, a new histrionic sensibility.

Action is what takes place in front of the camera, with the lights turned on, to throw the rest of reality into darkness (scotomisation, repression); action takes place in Plato's cave. Those for whom not to be seen is non-existence are not alive; and the kind of existence they seek, the immortality they seek, is spectral; to be seen is the ambition of ghosts, and to be remembered the ambition of the dead. The public realm is the stage for heroic action, and heroes are spectres of the living dead. The passport which grants access to the public realm, which distinguishes master from slave, the essential political virtue, is the courage to die, to commit suicide, to make one's life a living death. "One must pay dearly for immortality: one has to die several times while still alive." . . .

Heroic individualism is identification with ancestors in a new space and a new time: the new space is the public realm; the new time is history. Greek Tragedy is the imitation of an actor; Roman real action, as opposed to the childish stage plays of the Greeks, is what takes place on the stage of history. Identification with ancestors, instead of being an occasional ritual, is now a life destiny, is enacted in a whole life (of public service). Instead of the cyclic recurrence of a temporary role, the historical personage offers a continuous performance and achieves a continuous existence; not for a moment but for all time; an individual embodiment of the ancestral soul or dream. . . .

. . . Representation, or personality: for these two notions are one; for the Essence of the Commonwealth is (to define it) *"One Person, of whose Acts a great Multitude, by Mutuall Covenants one with another, have made themselves every one the Author."* And "a Multitude of men are made *One* Person, when they are by one man, or one Person, Represented." Representation is the essence of the social contract: "To conferr all their power and strength upon one Man, or upon one Assembly of men, that may reduce all their wills, by a plurality of voices, unto one Will: which is as much as to say, to appoint one Man, or Assembly of men, to bear their Person." The essence of representation is the mysterious relation, "bearing the Person of them all." . . .

. . . "A Multitude of men are made *One* Person." The idea of a people is the idea of a corporation, and the idea of a corporation is the idea of a juristic person. "This is more than Consent, or Concord: it is a reall Unitie of them all, in one and the same Person." Out of many, one: a logical impossibility; a piece of poetry, or symbolism; an enacted or incarnate metaphor; a poetic creation. The Commonwealth is "an Artificiall Man," a body politic, "in which, the *Soveraignty* is and Artificall *Soul;* the Magistrates, and other *Officers* of Judicature and Execution, artificiall *Joynts,*" etc. Does this "Artificiall Man," this "Feigned or Artificiall Person," make "a real Unitie of them all"? Are juristic persons real, or only legal fictions, *personae fictae?* "Analogy with the living person and shift of meaning are the essence of the mode of legal statement which refers to corporate bodies." Is the shift of meaning real? Does the metaphor accomplish a metamorphosis? "The Pacts and Covenants, by which the parts of this Body Politique were at first made, set together, and united, resemble that *Fiat,* or the *Let us make man,* pronounced by God in the Creation." Or like that *hoc est corpus meum,* This is my body, pronounced by God in the Redemption. Is there a real transubstantiation? Is there a miracle in the communion of the mortal God, the great Leviathan; a miracle which gives life to the individual communicants also? For so-called "real," "living," "natural" persons, individual persons, are not natural but juristic persons, *personae fictae,* social creations, no more real than corporations. . . .

The Commonwealth is a Person; the representative, or *"Publique* Person," is a person. But "A PERSON is he, *whose words are considered, either as his own, or as representing the words or actions of another man . . .* a *Person,* is the same that an *Actor* is, both on the Stage and in common Conversation; and to *personate,* is to *Act,* or *Represent* himselfe, or an other; and he that acteth another is said to bear his Person, or act in his name; . . . and is called on diverse occasions, diversly: as a *Representer,* or *Representative,* a *Lieutenant,* a *Vicar,* an *Attorney,* a *Deputy,* a *Procurator,* an *Actor,* and the like." Political representation is theatrical representation. A political society comes into existence when it articulates itself and produces a representative; that is to say, organizes itself as a theater, addressed to a stage, on which their representative can perform. The "real Unitie of them all" is made out of the identification of the group with the actor on the stage. In Hobbes's words, "it is the *Unity* of the Representer, not the *Unity* of the Represented, that maketh the Person *One.*" In Freud's words, "I have in mind the situation of the most ancient Greek Tragedy. A company of individuals, named and dressed alike, surrounded a single figure, all hanging upon his words and deeds: they were the chorus and the impersonator of the Hero." "A primary group of this kind is a number of individuals who have substituted one and the same object for their ego ideal and have consequently identified themselves with one another in their ego.''

The stage produced by political articulation is the stage of history. "As a result of political articulation, we find human beings, the rulers, who can act for society, men whose acts are not imputed to their own persons but to the society as a whole.'' Representation is "the form by which a political society gains existence for action in history.'' The nations obtain access to the stage of history through their representatives, the kings who strut the stage. Voegelin illustrates from the *History of the Lombards* by Paulus Diaconus. The active history of the Lombards begins when the people decided that they no longer wanted to live in small federated tribes, and "established for themselves a king like the other nations.'' And the consequences of having a king is having a history, that is to say, wars; the purpose of which is to put down the historical action, the kings, of other peoples. First the Herules and next the Gepids were defeated and their power broken to the degree that "they no longer had a king.'' Peaceful existence, existence without historical action, needs no kingship: the Alans and Suebes preserved their kingship in Spain for a long time, "though they had no need of it in their undistrubed quiet.'' . . .

. . . A ritual approach is a historical approach. Ritual is, simply, a reenactment of the past. The great revolutions in human society are changes in the form of symbolic representation; reorganizations of the theater, of the stage for human action. The matter remains the same: the "seasonal pattern of ritual''; the basic dream; the old, old story; old unhappy far-off things—the matter of Troy, or Brittany, or Britain—which are also familiar matter of today; as in *Finnegan's Wake*. But the form changes, the form of the public enactment. In one of these great revolutions, the principle of representation itself emerges; there was a time before there were kings. "Up to this point we have been considering the seasonal ceremonies as rites performed collectively by the community as a whole. In course of time, however, the tendency grows up to concentrate them in a single individual who is taken to personify and epitomize the entire group. . . . Consequently all the things which were previously done by the group as a whole in order to ensure and maintain its existence, now tend to be done representatively by the king.'' The king incorporates the ritual; makes it a one-man show. . . .

. . . Political society articulates itself and produces a representative; and is then ready for history; tragedy; even as the chorus, the dance group, articulates itself and produces the hero, the dying god. The chorus has a leader of the dance; the Couretes, the young men of the war dance, having a Leading Man. More and more they differentiate him from themselves, make him their vicar. Their attitude becomes more and more one of contemplation. More and more they become spectators, of his action. Theatrically speaking, they become as audience; religiously speaking, they become worshippers; he becomes a god. Gradually they lose all sense that the god is themselves. "He is utterly projected.'' . . .

. . . In vicarious experience there is both identification and distance. The mediator is to keep reality at a distance, to keep the multitude in remote contact with reality. Hobbes saw the paradigm in Exodus XX, 18–19: "And all the people saw the thundering, and the lightnings, and the noise of the trumpet, and the mountain smoking; and when they saw it, they removed, and stood far off. And they said unto Moses, Speak thous with us, and we will hear: but let not God speak with us, lest we die." Representative institutions depend upon the distance separating the spectators from the actor on the stage; the distance which permits both identification and detachment which makes for a participation without action; which establishes the detached observer, whose participation consists in seeing and is restricted to seeing; whose body is restricted to the eyes. Everything which is merely seen is seen through a windowpane, distantly; and purely: a pure aesthetic experience. Representative institutions depend upon the aesthetic illusion of distance. . . .

Part Five

Organizational Dramaturgy

D RAMATURGY OCCURS in many social settings, but one area of life where it has been scrutinized by scholars is in organizations. The occurrence of organizational drama takes many forms, and this section collects some of the more insightful and titillating efforts in this area of inquiry. We do not include here the dramaturgy of the individual career, which has received exhaustive attention in many other works. The "on the make" Sammy Glick and the "organization man" have been portrayed many times elsewhere, probably because their activities are so thoroughly histrionic. Here we restrict our selections to those that deal with relational dramas of conflict within an organizational hierarchy, and not simply the private drama of ambition.

An overview of organizational drama is provided by Victor Thompson. People in organizational roles are often engaged in conflicts over power, status or authority, and therefore the degree to which one controls "impressions" in communications may be crucial in such struggles. Indeed, the hierarchy is maintained by dramaturgical performances by superiors that communicate their legitimate right to rule, and to thereby command inferiors. Hence, a corporate elite may come to use ritual and status symbols to communicate their superiority and right to deference. In order to advance up the hierarchy, impression management is at least as important as accomplishment. Thompson's treatment indicates that organizations are a veritable ecology of dramas.

The ecology of organizational dramas includes the control and use of territory— access to an office, a washroom, to leisure facilities and so on. Erving Goffman, in his study of "asylums," deals with the negotiation of space between patients and staff in a mental hospital. Physical control over an area, access to another, freedom from restraint in yet another, become critical to the patients, but a matter of authority and control by the staff. Territory itself becomes a matter of dramaturgical activity between conflict groups. The role of space in dramatic presentations, of the "proxemics" of organizational interaction, needs to be more fully explored.

Murray Edleman examines the extent to which political settings are used for dramaturgical presentations. Political settings are selected and utilized for their symbolic quality and for the extent to which a setting permits control of the definition of the situation. A president signing a civil rights act at the Lincoln Memorial is doing so in a symbolic setting; a surrender ceremony signed on a ship in the midst of the enemy fleet communicates their power over the setting. Hence the setting can be selected and arranged for maximum effect over the observers of it; a convention hall is transformed into a setting that communicates the patriotism, heritage and strength of a political party. Political actions, to be effective, must be congruent with the logic of the setting. An inauguration speech must be one of solemn celebration of community values and goals, consistent with the expectations and meaning of the setting. Organizational settings are therefore not merely functional but also symbolic, and provide the potential for dramaturgy.

Finally, the functions (and dysfunctions) of organizational dramaturgy are explored by Barney Glaser and Anselm Strauss with reference to death. Modern deaths often occur in an organizational setting, and awareness of dying, must be handled by both staff and patient to facilitate the smooth operation of the organization. Hence a "mutual pretense" develops in such situations, involving a set of avoidance reactions the authors term a "ritual drama." This permits the staff to continue their work and avoid any emotional involvement; it gets the patient used to "business as usual" and facilitates his acceptance of death as an integral part of the organizational setting. The mutual pretense of the actors concerned makes the setting an organizational drama, ending only with the demise of the patient.

Many features of modern organizational life contribute to the occurrence of dramaturgy in organization: the existence of status hierarchy, of formal relationships, of staff-client relations, of presentations in, and control of, settings and so on. The existence of large-scale organizations is one of the major features of modern life, and it behooves any viable theory of social organization to include the dramaturgical dimension in its considerations. The question must be asked: What are the features of formal organization that contribute to, perhaps even necessitate, the conduct of such dramas?

28.

DRAMATURGY

Victor Thompson

The Dramaturgical Aspect of Organizations

In a remarkable study, Erving Goffman has recently shown how the performance of their roles of various kinds involves people in impression management.[1] We must try to control the information or cues imparted to others in order to protect our representations of self and to control the impressions others form about us. We are all involved, therefore, in dramaturgy.

Although, for reasons given below, this chapter is principally concerned with dramaturgy in the hierarchy, we should mention briefly that specialization also has its dramaturgical side. Specialist dramaturgy seems to be particularly related to the problem of accreditation. The ubiquitous white coat of the medical doctor suggests that here is a man of fastidious cleanliness, the stethoscope dangling from his pocket suggests the great and mysterious range of his knowledge. The engineer's slide rule performs a similar function. If a specialist role is only weakly established, we should expect a dramaturgy of insecurity, with pompous self-importance, lack of communicativeness, etc.

As Goffman points out, the dramaturgical side of formal organizations has been neglected. Students have in the past been interested in the technical, the political, the structural, and the cultural aspects, but not this.[2] We believe that dramaturgical behavior in the bureaucratic organization is structurally related to its other and more familiar characteristics. Perceptions of leadership, status, and power depend heavily upon communication.[3] People will rate a position in a scale of leadership, status, or power at least partly in accordance with information they have about that position. The control of information, therefore, and the management of impressions, become important techniques in the struggle for authority, status, and power.

Legitimation of Authority Roles

We have argued . . . that a number of developments are challenging the legitimacy of hierarchical authority in bureaucratic organization. Particularly crucial is the gap which advancing specialization and technical complexity are creating between the right to take a specific action and the knowledge needed to do so. Cultural definitions of hierarchical rights and expectations of hierarchical role performance are increasingly at war with reality. The greater the discrepancy between the self-image projected, on the one hand, and reality, on the other, the greater the load placed upon sheer play acting. Dramaturgical skill has become increasingly essen-

Reprinted by permission from *Modern Organizations*, Alfred A. Knopf, 1963.

tial to the hierarchical role, and technical competence increasingly irrelevant.[4]

Discrepancies between role expectations and the technical imperatives related to goal accomplishment are generally hidden or at least disguised by fictions, myths, and "just-pretend" behavior which are quite general throughout our bureaucratic organizations. For instance, the inability of the organization to live with the superior's right to control communication leads inevitably to the development of elaborate informal channels of communication. The existence of these informal channels is often officially denied, or the superior's signature is put on the communication by rubber stamp to pretend that it came from him.[5] If these informal channels are depicted on organizational charts (they usually are not), dotted lines are used, indicating the taint of illegality about them. In general, any informal or unofficial arrangements are considered somewhat illegal and are undertaken surreptitiously.

The fact that those who are traditionally empowered to make all decisions cannot any longer have the range of knowledge necessary to do so brings about a good deal of pretense in organizational activities. In fact, much of the organization's work is done by surreptitious methods. Everyone is involved in "playing the game." Reality is hidden by "double talk." As Goffman points out,[6] "double-talk" communication may convey information between people inconsistent with their roles. One person in a relationship says one thing but means something else. The overt expression is consistent with the formal relationship, but the hidden meaning is not. The other person in the relationship may accept the hidden communication; or he may ignore it and accept the overt expression which is consistent with the relationship, which is "proper." A common example concerns breaking in a new boss. When an assistant must break in a new boss, he will have to convey instructions to his boss in a form which makes it appear overtly as though he were receiving these instructions from the boss. This kind of communication occurs in connection with matters outside a person's formal jurisdiction but depending upon him. It occurs when a subordinate tries to seize the direction of action or his superior tries to extend it to him. In this kind of situation, "double-talk" communication allows a subordinate to initiate lines of endeavor without giving explicit recognition to the implications this action has for the formal role relationship between him and his superior.[7]

Discrepancies between actual authority and expected authority inevitably arise, because organizationally defined competencies of centralized specialties conflict with the culturally defined rights of hierarchical position. The attempt is universally made to hide these discrepancies by simply denying them. Thus it is alleged that the central specialists, the "staff," only advise; they have no authority. If their advice comes in the form of a command, everyone is supposed to pretend that it comes from a higher executive, and sometimes provision is made to have his signature stamped on the more formal specialist commands. This "just-pretend" behavior also protects status-inflated self-images of those receiving specialist commands, a necessity since these commands are quite likely to come from lower-status people.[8]

The dramaturgical management of impressions about hierarchical positions and roles is no longer a sporadic affair depending upon the accidents of personality. It appears to be institutionally organized. That is to say, opportunities for hierarchical success in modern bureaucracy depend to a very large extent upon the ability and willingness to engage in impression management. Our contention is that this kind of behavior is essential as a device for maintaining the legitimacy of hierarchical roles in the face of advancing specialization. Although no leadership traits have been discovered, a definite executive type seems to be emerging.[9]

DRAMATURGY OF THE SUPERIOR

What are the impressions fostered by hierarchical dramaturgy? As would be expected, they are the heroic and charismatic qualities—the same ones that leadership-trait studies have been seeking. The impression is fostered that occupants of hierarchical positions are, of all people in the organization, the ablest, the most industrious, the most indispensable, the most loyal, the most reliable, the most self-controlled, the most ethical, which is to say, the most honest, fair, and impartial. Technical skill is not among these fostered impressions. Modern bureaucracy derogates technical skill or any great learning. To "get ahead," a person must give up his technical specialty.[10] By derogating the role of the specialist, the superior protects his own role in the hierarchy.

It is within this framework that the extreme busyness of persons in hierarchical positions is to be understood. Busyness suggests indispensability, as Riesman. Glazer, and Denney[11] have noted. It also suggests that the very busy person is of unusual importance to the organization and takes its interests more to heart than do others. The very busy person is felt to be more dependable and loyal than the others. Consequently, it is advisable for those who want to get ahead to load their briefcases when they leave at night, and perhaps to come in for a few hours on the week end.[12]

Impression management follows certain broad rules already supplied by the culture. Such audience rules as taking a person at his face value and not interfering with his performance when it is going on operate to everyone's advantage. Persons in high positions have some additional dramaturgical advantages in the form of hierarchical rights, especially their rights to deference. The status system is sustained by its own well worn dramaturgical apparatus, including familiar status symbols such as insignia, titles, and ceremonies; and office symbols such as private offices, rugs, and special furniture. "A name on the door rates a rug on the floor."[13]

Impression management requires that some attention be paid to the preparation of the audience.[14] For hierarchical presentations, the audience has already been prepared by the status system. The audience is trained to take cues at their face value, to show the proper appreciation for the performance. Status behavior protects the backstage area by teaching people to "keep their place." Information inconsistent with fostered impressions is kept secret. Status training has prepared the audience to exercise tact, and the performers to exercise tact with respect to tact. Both sides "play the game," thus protecting the performances from miscues, bad acting, *faux pas,* "scenes," etc.

An act has a better chance of coming off well when the audience is not too large and when the interaction is of short duration.[15] Superiors are therefore admonished to deal with subordinates individually and privately. The status system allows the hierarchical superior to choose his audience, the time, place, and duration of the performance, by giving the high-status person the initiative in interaction. He can usually begin and terminate the interview. This ability to control the timing of the interaction is particularly valuable in sustaining the impression of busyness and importance to the organization.[16]

The more background information possessed by the audience, the less likely it is that the performance will have an important influence.[17] The status system puts social distance between people so that the audience is not likely to have much background information about higher-status performers. Superiors are therefore advised not to become intimate with subordinates. "Don't go to lunch with the wrong person." The executive eats in an "executive dining room"; he has a private secretary disciplined in discretion; he has control of access to his office.[18] Finally, the status system provides a more or less elaborate set of staging devices or props as background for the management of impressions about the character and activities of persons occupying hierarchical roles.[19]

The point has been made that the general institutionalized system of deference, the "status system," provides a set of situational definitions of great value for the management of impressions on the part of persons in the hierarchy. Other general attitudes toward self-expression reinforce the status system in this respect. People generally believe there is a "sacred compatibility between the man and the job," [20] a sacred connection between the right to play a part and the capacity to do so. Since the person in a hierarchical position has the right to make "decisions," he is assumed to have the ability to do so.[21]

Furthermore, since it is generally assumed that a person should be accepted as what he claims to be, should be taken at face value and given the benefit of the doubt, advantageous definitions of any situations based upon technical performance are more difficult to secure than those based upon dramaturgy, upon impression management. It is easier to be what you say you are than what you do. In this connection, people seem to be more concerned with the right to give a performance than with the performance itself. Even though the performance is outstanding, if the person did not have the right to perform, he is severely criticized, perhaps even jailed as an imposter.[22] Conversely, even though the performance is of low quality, the right to give it will protect it from criticism. Here again the hierarchical role is fortunately situated, insofar as inability to perform will be masked by the undoubted right to do so. The same is true of well-established specialist roles, like that of the doctor, of the lawyer, or of the engineer.

THE MANAGEMENT TROUPE

Successful performances demand the loyalty of the performers, the solidarity of the performing team. Since the control of impressions requires the careful withholding and editing of information imparted to the audience, it is imperative that all members of the team be trustworthy, that they be discreet with regard to the facts relevant to the performance. This solidarity can be promoted by making the audience a "race apart," and particularly by demeaning the audience, by conceiving of it as being composed of people of lesser stature.[23] Demeaning the audience also protects the performers from their own deceit, both emotionally and morally—the deceit that the performers, or occupants of hierarchical roles, are superior, more dependable, more industrious, more loyal, and therefore more important to the organization.[24] The general dramaturgical framework provided by the status system serves the purpose of dehumanizing the audience of subordinates. They are mere lower-status employees, "subordinates," childlike creatures both unskilled and undependable, requiring "close supervision." The derogation of specialist roles serves the same purpose.

The loyalty of the performing team is assured by practicing rotation to avoid a sympathetic attachment to the audience. If a superior becomes too closely identified with his subordinates, he is regarded as "useless" to the management and must be removed or transferred.

More important than rotation in assuring the solidarity of the team is the careful selection of persons to be admitted to the team. Careful selection not only insures loyalty, but it also guarantees ability to perform the required routine. Furthermore, each member of the team is part of the staging props, background, or scenery against which the performance must be presented. Since much of the information conveyed to the audience is by visible rather than verbal symbols, the appearances and mannerisms of the performers cannot be overlooked.

Consequently, hierarchical roles cannot be filled by reference to technical qualifications alone. The real check is not a merit examination but a suitability interview, and for a person being considered for promotion, long and close observation by a superior. Various physical features have doomed persons to lower-level positions: [25] Physical appearance, dress, mannerisms, office behavior-all are important. Impressions fostered at work are probably as important as accomplishment. The person to be absorbed into the team must have shown his ability to create the impressions of busyness, loyalty, "sound judgment," etc.

It is especially important in the selection process to determine the discretion of the person to be admitted to the team. He must have no black spots on his record; and a good record is most easily achieved by "going along with the gang," by avoiding risky innovations or ideas. He must not appear too intellectual, nor too technically skilled; and he must at least appear to place the good of the team above his profession.[26]

Higher positions are frequently filled by the sponsorship system. Promising youngsters who appear to be "our kind" are carefully prepared for the later assumption of high managerial positions.[27] Persons selected for the team must possess "dramaturgical discipline." [28] They must be able to control their emotions, to be "on top" of their performance, and to control their hostilities. Control of face, voice, and gesture is central here.[29] Without dramaturgical discipline, the performer might make an improper disclosure or extend to the audience the status of team members.

Behavior away from work is no less important that behavior at work. An embarrassing disclosure in only one aspect of a person's role, in one routine among many, is likely to discredit the many other areas of activity in which he has nothing to conceal.[30] His church, his clubs, the location of his home, his children's school, his wife, his home life, all are matters which might discredit the desired impression as an upper-hierarchical-role occupant. And since the discrediting of one performer on the team might discredit the whole team's performance, all of these private matters become relevant in choosing a person for admission to the team. Undoubtedly, this consideration is an important reason for the deplored invasion of private life by modern organizations.

SUBORDINATE DRAMATURGY

Although we have stressed the management of impressions by superiors, subordinates must also engage in this kind of behavior. In general, subordinates must create the impression that they are awed by their superiors, that the latters' performance has gone off well. This is simply a reflection of their need to please the boss.[31] Subordinates must create the impression that they *need* to be told what to do; that they *need* to be told how to do it; and, in general, that they could not get along without the boss. Since the superior is presented as the initiating and creative force, subordinates must convey the impression that all of their ideas and actions are *his* actions. Since the superior is presented as the busiest and most important person, subordinates must create the impression that they understand that he has little time to deal with them and their relatively unimportant problems. Many subordinates, therefore, attempt communication with the boss infrequently and briefly. Interviews, telephone conversations, and memos may be few and brief.[32] Since the superior is presented as the person with the greatest intellectual and moral qualities, subordinates must create the impression that they feel awed and humble in his presence. As in the case with superordinate impression management, the status system aids subordinate impression management by keeping the audience and performers segregated and by protecting the backstage, with all of its performance-discrediting information. It is backstage that one finds out what subordinates really think about their superiors.

NOTES

[1] Erving Goffman: *The Presentation of Self in Everyday Life* (Garden City, New York: Doubleday & Company, Inc.; 1959).

[2] Ibid., pp. 239–40.

[3] See Robert F. Bales: "The Equilibrium Problem in Small Groups," in Talcott Parsons, Robert F. Bales, and Edward A. Shils: *Working Papers in The Theory of Action* (Glencoe, Illinois: The Free Press; 1953); Cecil A. Gibb: "Leadership," in Gardner Lindzey, ed.: *Handbook of Social Psychology* (Reading, Massachusetts: Addison-Wesley Publishing Company, Inc.; 1954) and the discussion of status ranking above in ch. iv. That perceptions of power may be dramaturgically manipulated is clearly indicated in John W. Thibaut and Harold H. Kelly: *The Social Psychology of Groups* (New York: John Wiley & Son, Inc.; 1959), pp. 122–4.

[4] See Alvin W. Gouldner: *Studies in Leadership: Leadership and Democratic Action* (New York: Harper

& Brothers; 1950), pp. 225–7. This statement refers only to the hierarchical aspect of any particular job, not its specialist aspect; however, as we have repeatedly stated, the specialist content becomes more and more attenuated as one goes up the hierarchy. "We sit at our desks all day," says a business chief executive, "While around us whiz and gyrate a vast number of special activities, some of which we only dimly understand. And for each of these activities there is a specialist. . . . But it has reached a point where the greatest task of the president is to understand enough of all these specialties so that when a problem comes up he can assign the right team of experts to work on it." John L. McCaffrey: "What Corporation Presidents Think about at Night," *Fortune* (September 1953), pp. 128 ff., quoted in C. Wright Mills: *The Power Elite* (New York: Oxford University Press, Inc.; 1957), p. 135.

The extent to which "management" has been specialized out of executive (management) positions can be illustrated by the special subjects discussed at an industrial management conference at Illinois Institute of Technology on February 5 and 6, 1959. The subjects included sales forecasts, preparing budgets, quality control, cost considerations, engineering economics, launching a new product, market surveys, wage incentives, operations research, data processing, new site selection, human engineering, production and inventory planning, automation, research and development expenditures, and new product selection. See the references in ch. viii, pp. 156-7, ft. nt. 8.

[5] The signature also acts as a surety that the source will not refuse to acknowledge the communication later.

[6] Op. cit., pp. 194-5.

[7] As Whyte says about junior subordinates: "Given minimum committeemanship skills, by an adroit question here and a modest suggestion there, he can call attention to himself and *still play the game." The Organization Man* (Garden City, New York: Doubleday & Company, Inc.; 1957), p. 168 (my italics). There is sometimes a special problem in presenting the results of work to others outside the unit. The superior's rights of communication and his claim of responsibility require that he make the presentation. Since he is less familiar with it than the others, a rather intricate business of prompting is often required. (Goffman refers to "staging cues"). Sign language and other secret communicative devices are then used, such as foot scraping, voice clearing, fidgeting, etc. See Goffman: op. cit., p. 185; also Victor A. Thompson: *The Regulatory Process in OPA Rationing* (New York: King's Crown Press; 1950), p. 311. See also Peter B. Hammond: "The Function of Indirection in Communication," in *Comparative Studies in Administration,* edited by the Staff of the Administrative Science Center, University of Pittsburgh (University of Pittsburgh Press; 1959).

[8] See above, ch. iii.

[9] It has been reported that employers now seem to look for an ideal "Hollywood type." Perrin Stryker, quoting Ann Hoff, the placement expert: "How Executive Get Jobs," *Fortune* (August 1953), p. 182. Shape of teeth and size of ears have disqualified men. (Ibid.) ". . . executives often project an air of competency and general grasp of the situation." Goffman: op. cit., p. 47. "More and more, the executive must act according to the role that he is cast for-the calm eye that never strays from the other's gaze, the easy, controlled laughter, the whole demeanor that tells onlookers that here certainly is a man without neurosis and inner rumblings," Whyte: op. cit., p. 172. For an essentially similar but somewhat unfriendly characterization, see Mills: op. cit., pp. 142-3.

[10] See ch. v and the references there cited on p. 98 in ft. nt. 5.

[11] David Riesman, Nathan Glazer, and Reuel Denney: *The Lonely Crowd* (Garden City, New York: Doubleday & Company, Inc.; 1953), pp. 307–8. Note that questions of how much "work" a person does, of "overwork," of reimbursable work are matters of cultural definition. Thus, for example, the work of the housewife is not so defined, and so she is tired out at night, yet suffers a sense of guilt for "having done nothing" all day, while her "overworked" husband is entitled to the children's and her sympathy when he comes home at night. (Ibid., pp. 300, 308.) People generally do not think of the long hours of the scientist in his lab or the writer at his desk as being "overwork." The specialist who spends his evenings reading works in the field of his special interest is not considered to have taken work home from the office. Then, of course, there is always the question of the usefulness of activities. One good idea may be much more valuable in relation to organizational goals than large amounts of *pro forma* memo writing or conference, board, or committee attendance. When the end result of activities is not a countable pile of objects, it is probably impossible to determine who works the "hardest," and the brilliant person may accomplish more with apparently less "work" than the less brilliant.

[12] See Whyte: op. cit., p. 158.

[13] See Chester Barnard: "Functions and Pathology of Status Systems in Formal Organizations," In William Foote Whyte, ed.: *Industry and Society* (New York: McGraw-Hill Book Co.; 1946); also Thompson: op. cit., p. 323.

[14] Goffman: op. cit., ch. vi.

[15] Ibid.

[16] See Thompson: op. cit., pp. 324—5. Modern bueaucratic telephone technique can be at least partly understood as a dramaturgical competition between two secretaries to see which can force the other's boss to come on the line first, thereby having to wait until the "busier" one is plugged in. Ibid., p. 323.

[17] Goffman: op. cit.

[18] Thus an executive can make a graceful gesture by instituting an "open door" policy, safe in the assurance that the status system will protect access to his office almost as well as a locked door.

[19] We refer to the symbols which make the status visible, discussed in ch. iv. In Goffman's dramaturgical terms, these symbols act as scenery and help make the performance impressive.

[20] Goffman: op. cit., pp. 46, 58–66. Performers usually foster this impression.

[21] Popular and journalistic interpretations of affairs are consistently based upon the identification of right and ability, resulting in a strange, charismatic, personalized interpretation of events as outcomes of high-level personal interactions. The assumed sacred compatibility between the man and the role acts as a legitimization of any *de facto* power or wealth. "He must be a very able man because he gets all that money," or "He must be the smartest man there because he is the boss." Thus, power and wealth are held to be their own justification. We do not need to go beyond their possession. Perhaps this kind of circularity was an ideological necessity at the time the middle class was struggling for power with feudalism. It has always created uncomfortable uncertainties in connection with out-and-out criminally obtained wealth and power. It also encourages phantasies and wishful thinking about lucky windfalls ("when my ship comes in"), perhaps encourages crime, and certainly encourages give-away shows on TV.

[22] Goffman: op. cit., p. 59. He says the better the impostor's performance, the more we feel threatened because the situation challenges the assumed sacred relation between the man and the role.

[23] Note the reported hidden ridicule of Chinese prison guards and interrogators by American prisoners in the Korean War. E. H. Schein: "The Chinese Indoctrination Program for Prisoners of War," *Psychiatry,* Vol. XIX (1956), pp. 149–72.

[24] See Goffman: op. cit., pp. 214–15. When the performers are subordinate to the audience, as employees are in the performances they must present to superiors, derogation of the audience serves the additional purpose of recapturing the performers' self-respect. "But secret derogation seems to be much more common than secret praise, perhaps because such derogation serves to maintain the solidarity of the team, demonstrating mutual regard at the expense of those absent and compensating, perhaps, for the loss of self-respect that may occur when the audience must be accorded accommodative face-to-face treatment." (Ibid., p. 171.) The manipulative approach fails to realize that the subordinate's behavior is also a performance, that subordinates control managerial impressions. Because of this interrelation, direct knowledge of employee moral or regard for management can rarely be obtained. Instead, inferences must be drawn from various indices, such as absenteeism, turnover, output, etc. Inferences drawn from output are particularly liable to be in error. See Whyte: op. cit., pp. 63–4; and James G. March and Herbert A. Simon: *Organizations* (New York: John Wiley & Sons, Inc.; 1958), pp. 47–8.

[25] See pp. 142–3 ft. nt. 9, above.

[26] It has often been reported that professional and technical specialists are vaguely distrusted by managements. It is feared, probably with good reason, that they might not go "all the way down the line" for the organization, especially if its demands conflicted with their professional code of conduct. See Gouldner: op. cit., pp. 225–7; Whyte: op. cit., pp. 164, 182: and Mills: op. cit., pp. 138–46. In an illustration of what he means by "responsibility," Barnard indicated he expects the loyal employee to put the good of the organization ahead of even the lives of family members. *The Functions of the Executive* (Cambridge: Harvard University Press; 1947), p. 269.

[27] The preference for middle- and upper-class individuals is understandable as a device for protecting the backstage. Despite the "open class myth," itself a legitimating ideology, the upper hierarchy is largely reserved for middle- and upper-class persons. Of the very top business executives in this country in 1951,

57 percent were the sons of businessmen, 14 percent the sons of professional people, 15 percent the sons of farmers, and only 12 percent the sons of wage earners: C. Wright Mills: op. cit., pp. 127–8. Of the 1952 executives under 50, only 2½ percent had wage-earner origins, "The Nine Hundred," *Fortune* (November 1952), pp. 132 ff. The social origins of top government executives are predominantly middle class. Reinhard Bendix: "Who are the Government Bureaucrats?," in Gouldner, ed.: op. cit., pp. 330–41.

[28] Goffman: op. cit., pp. 216–18. "Perhaps the focus of dramaturgical discipline is to be found in the management of one's face and voice." Ibid., p. 217.

[29] "In my judgment, confirmed by others whose opinion I respect, it is as a general rule exceedingly bad practice for one in a superior position to swear at or in the presence of those of subordinate or inferior status . . . I have known very few men who could do it without adverse reactions on their influence. I suppose the reason is that whatever lowers the dignity of a superior position makes it more difficult to accept difference of position." Chester Barnard: *Organization and Management* (Cambridge: Harvard University Press; 1949), pp. 73–4; quoted in Goffman: op. cit., p. 199. Actually, swearing in this situation is inconsistent with the lofty impression projected by the higher-status person.

[30] Goffman: op. cit., pp. 64–5. In this respect, note the destruction of Sherman Adams's image presented to the world by the minor and rather silly disclosures in regard to Bernard Goldfine.

[31] Harold Leavitt says any job is actually two jobs. "One is to carry out the assignment, to get the job done; the other . . . job is to please the superior." *Managerial Psychology* (Chicago: University of Chicago Press; 1958), p. 264.

[32] There is also the status-hungry "climber" who attempts a great deal of communication with superiors as a device for enhancing his status *vis-à-vis* his peers. One suspects that this kind of "pushy" behavior is not usually rewarded by co-optation into the "management team." See Robert K. Merton: "Continuities in the Theory of Reference Groups and Social Structure," in *Social Theory and Social Structure,* rev. ed. (Glencoe, Illinois: The Free Press; 1957).

29.

PLACES

Erving Goffman

. . . I turn now to the question of the setting, for if these activities of underlife are to occur, they must occur in some place or region.[1]

In Central Hospital, as in many total institutions, each inmate tended to find his world divided into three parts, the partitioning drawn similarly for those of the same privilege status.

First, there was space that was off-limits or out of bounds. Here mere presence was the form of conduct that was actively prohibited—unless, for example, the inmate was specifically "with" an authorized agent or active in a relevant service role. For example, according to the rules posted in one of the male services, the grounds behind one of the female services were out of bounds, presumably as a chastity measure. For all patients but the few with town parole, anything beyond the institution walls was out of bounds. So, too, everything outside a locked ward was off-limits for its resident patients, and the ward itself was off-limits for patients not resident there. Many of the administrative buildings and administrative sections of buildings, doctors' offices, and, with some variations, ward nursing stations were out of bounds for patients. Similar arrangements have of course been reported in other studies of mental hospitals:

> When the charge [attendant] is in his office, the office itself and a zone of about 6 square feet outside the office is off limits to all except the top group of ward helpers among the privileged patients. The other patients neither stand nor sit in this zone. Even the privileged patients may be sent away with abrupt authority if the charge or his attendants desire it. Obedience when this order occurs—usually in a parental form, such as "run along, now"—is instantaneous. The privileged patient is privileged precisely because he understands the meaning of this social space and other aspects of the attendant's position.[2]

Second, there was *surveillance space*, the area a patient needed no special excuse for being in, but where he would be subject to the usual authority and restrictions of the establishment. This area included most of the hospital for those patients with parole. Finally, there was space ruled by less than usual staff authority; it is the varieties of this third kind of space that I want to consider now.

The visible activity of a particular secondary adjustment may be actively forbidden in a mental hospital, as in other establishments. If the practice is to occur, it must be shielded from the eyes and ears of staff. This may involve merely turning away from a staff person's line of vision.[3] The inmate may smile derisively by half-turning away, chew on food without signs of jaw motion when eating is forbidden, cup a lighted cigarette in the hand when smoking is not permitted, and use a hand to conceal cigarette chips during a ward poker game when the supervising nurse passes through the ward. These were concealment devices employed in Central Hospital. A further example is cited from another mental institution:

> My total rejection of psychiatry, which had, after coma, become a fanatical adulation, now passed into a third phase—one of constructive criticism. I became aware of the peripheral obtuseness and the administrative dogmatism of the hospital bureaucracy. My first impulse was to condemn; later, I perfected means of maneuvering freely within the clumsy structure of ward politics. To illustrate, my reading matter had been kept under surveillance for quite some time, and I had at last perfected a means of keeping *au courant* without unnecessarily alarming the nurses and attendants. I had smuggled several issues of *Hound and Horn* into my ward on the pretext that it was a field-and-stream magazine. I had read Hoch and Kalinowski's *Shock Therapy* (a top secret manual of arms at the hospital) quite openly, after I had put it into the dust jacket of Anna Balakian's *Literary Origins of Surrealism*.[4]

In addition, however, to these temporary means of avoiding hospital surveillance, inmates and staff tacitly co-operated to allow the emergence of bounded physical spaces in which ordinary levels of surveillance and restriction were markedly reduced, spaces where the inmate could openly engage in a range of tabooed activities with some degree of security. These places often also provided a marked reduction in usual patient population density, contributing to the peace and quiet characteristic of them. The staff did not know of the existence of these places, or knew but either stayed away or tacitly relinquished their authority when entering them. Licence, in short, had a geography. I shall call these regions *free places*. We may especially expect to find them when authority in an organization is lodged in a whole echelon of staff instead of in a set of pyramids of command. Free places are backstage to the usual performance of staff-inmate relationships.

Free places in Central Hospital were often employed as the scene for specifically tabooed activities: the patch of woods behind the hospital was occasionally used as a cover for drinking; the area behind the recreation building and the shade of a large tree near the center of the hospital grounds were used as locations for poker games.

Sometimes, however, free places seemed to be employed for no purpose other than to obtain time away from the long arm of the staff and from the crowded, noisy wards. Thus, underneath some of the buildings there was an old line of cart tracks once used for moving food from central kitchens; on the banks of this underground trench patients had collected benches and chairs, and some patients sat out the day there, knowing that no attendant was likely to address them. The underground trench itself was used as a means of passing from one part of the grounds to another without having to meet staff on ordinary patient-staff terms. All of these places seemed pervaded by a feeling of relaxation and self-determination, in marked contrast to the sense of uneasiness prevailing on some wards. Here one could be one's own man.[5]

As suggested earlier, free places vary according to the numbers of persons who make use of them, and according to drawing region, that is, residence of users. Some free places in Central Hospital drew their users from only one ward. An instance of this was the toilet and the hall leading to it in the chronic male wards. Here the floor was stone and the windows had no curtains. It was here patients were sent who wanted to smoke, and here it was understood attendants would exercise little surveillance.[6] Regardless of the smell in this section of the ward, some patients elected to spend part of the day there, reading, looking out the window, or just sitting on the relatively comfortable toilet seats. In winter, the open-air porches of some wards came to have a similar status, some patients electing to be relatively cold in exchange for being relatively free of surveillance.

Other free places drew their users from a whole psychiatric service made up of one or more buildings. The disused sub-basement of one building in a chronic male service had been informally taken over by the patients, who had brought in a few chairs and a ping-pong table. There some members of the service spent the day under no one's authority. When attendants came to use the ping-pong table, they did so almost as patients' equals; attendants not prepared to sustain this kind of fiction tended to stay away.

In addition to ward and service free places, there were free places that drew patients from the whole hospital community. The partly wooded field behind one of the main buildings, providing an excellent hilltop view of the neighboring city, was one such place. (Families not connected with the hospital sometimes came to picnic here.) This area was important in the mythology of the hospital being *the* place where nefarious sexual activity was said to occur. Another community free place, oddly, was the guardhouse at the main entrance to the hospital grounds. It was heated during the winter, gave a view of those entering and leaving the hospital grounds, was close to ordinary civilian streets, and was a usable destination point for walks. The guardhouse was under the jurisdiction of police guards, not attendants, who—apparently because they were somewhat isolated from other hospital staff—tended to rely on sociable interaction with patients; a relatively free atmosphere prevailed.

Perhaps the most important community free place was the area immediately around the small free-standing shop that served as the patients' canteen, which was run by the Association of the Blind and included a few patients on its staff. Here patients and a few attendants passed the time of day around a few outdoor benches, lounging, gossiping, commenting on the state of the hospital, drinking coffee and soft drinks, and eating sandwiches. In addition to being a free place, this area had the added function of the town pump, that is, an informal center of information exchange.[7]

Another free place for some patients was the staff cafeteria, a building where patients were officially allowed to go if they had ground parole (or responsible visitors) and the money to pay for the food.[8] While many patients felt in awe of this place, and were uncomfortable when there, others managed to make very full use of it, exploiting the tacit understanding that here a patient was to be treated like anyone else. A handful of patients came for coffee after each meal on the ward, washing away the taste of a meal under ward conditions, mixing with student nurses and residents, and generally using the place as a social center—to such an extent that they were periodically banned from it.

It was evident that as patients progressed through the "ward system" to increasing privileges they tended to get access to free places that drew from wider and wider regions.[9] Further, the status of space was tied into the ward system, so that what was off-limits for a disobedient patient could come eventually to be a free space for an obedient one.[10] It should be also stated that a ward itself could become a free place, at least for the members of the relevant service. Thus, a few of the wards on one of the chronic services, and a discharge or convalescent ward on a male admission service, were "open" at the time of study. No staff or very little staff was assigned to these wards during the day, and hence these places were relatively free from surveillance. Since the admission service ward was also stocked with a pool table, magazines, TV, cards, books, and student nurses, an atmosphere of security, ease, and pleasure developed, likened by some patients to an army recreation hall.

Many types of assignment provided patients with free places, especially if work was done under the guidance of a specialist in the work instead of an attendant—for at such times the milieu of a work place tended to be maintained, and this marked a distinct freedom from authority and restraint as compared to ward life. This was so at the major scenes of industrial therapy, the laundry and the shoe shop. Obtaining a free place, then, was a principal way of working an assignment. For some patients the occupational-therapy room in the admission service, where woodworking was done, provided a free place. The basement where dance therapy was given also served in this way, especially for the group of young patients, of wide and leading reputation among fellow patients and staff, who formed a kind of stage company for producing dramatic and dance presentations, and who enjoyed long hours of training and rehearsal under the guidance of the well-liked dance therapist. During midperiod breaks, and for a few moments after the dance sessions, patients would, for example, wander into the anteroom off the dance chamber and, with cokes obtained from the machine, and cigarettes, sometimes contributed by the therapist, congregate around a piano, dancing a little, making a pass at a jitterbug step, chatting, and having what on the outside would be called an informal break. Compared to the lives many of these favored patients lived on the ward, these moments were incredibly soft, harmonious, and free from hospital pressure.

Although the provision of a free place was an incidental aspect of many assignments, it was apparently the main gain of some assignments. For example, off the insulin room adjoining the admission ward on one service was a small anteroom where nurses could lie down and where nourishment could be prepared for patients coming out of shock. The few patients who managed to get the job of helping in the insulin room could enjoy the quiet medical note sustained there and also some of the TLC that was given to those in shock; in the anteroom they could come out of the patient role, relax, smoke, polish their shoes, banter with the nurses, and make themselves coffee.

Free places in which tenure was not firmly established were to be found, some, paradoxically, in quite central parts of the buildings.[11] In one of the older buildings the main hallway onto which the administrative offices entered was large, high-ceilinged, and cool in summer; cutting into it at right angles was a hallway about twelve feet wide, leading, through a locked door, to wards. Benches lined both sides of this dark alcove, and there was a coke machine and phone booth. Throughout the main hallway and the alcove an administrative civil service atmosphere tended to prevail. Officially, patients were not supposed to "hang around" this alcove and in some cases were even cautioned against passing through the hallway. However, a few patients, well-known to the staff and having some trusty-like duties, were allowed to sit in the alcove, and during hot summer afternoons they could be found there, sometimes pressing their claim to the point of playing cards, and in general getting away from the hospital although sitting in one of the centers of it.

The vicarious consumption of free places was one of the most poignant instances of make-do in the hospital. Patients in seclusion would sometimes spend time looking out the outside window, when this was within reach, or out of the Judas hole in the door, vicariously following the activity on the grounds or in the ward. Some male patients in back wards would vie with each other for possession of a window sill; once obtained, the sill was used as a seat, the patient curling up in the window, looking outside through the bars, pressing the nose of his whole body up against the outside, and in this way somewhat removing himself from the ward and somewhat freeing himself from its territorial restrictions. Parole patients on the grounds would sometimes take the benches closest to the outside fence and spend time watching civilians walk and ride past the hospital, gaining thereby a minor sense of participation in the free world outside.

It may be suggested that the more unpalatable the environment in which the individual must live, the more easily will places qualify as free ones. Thus, in some of the worst wards, housing up to sixty patients, many "regressed," the problem of reduced personnel on the evening (4:00 to 12:00 P.M.) shift was met by herding all the patients into the day room and blocking the entrance so that every patient on the ward could be placed under the surveillance of one pair of eyes. This time corresponded with the departure of medical staff; with dusk (in winter), which was very apparent because the wards were ill-lit; and often, with the shutting of windows. At this time a pall fell on what was already a pall, and there was an intensification of negative affect, tension, and strife. A few patients, often ones willing to sweep down the floor, prepare the beds, and herd other patients to sleep, were allowed to stay outside of this pen and wander freely in the then-emptied hallways between the dormitory and the maintenance offices. At such times any place not in the day room took on a quiet tone, with a relatively unhostile staff definition of the situation prevailing. What was off-limits for the bulk of the patients became, through the same ruling, a free place for a select few.

The kind of free place considered until now is a categorical one: the patient who used the place had to appreciate that other patients, to whom he was not particularly related, would or could have access to it, too; exclusiveness and sense of ownership were not involved. In some cases, however, a group of patients added to their access to a free place the proprietary right to keep out all other patients, except when properly invited. We can speak here of group territories.[12]

Group territories seem very little developed in Central Hospital, appearing merely as extensions of rights regarding use of a particular space that are legitimately accorded patients. For example, one of the continued-treatment services had a glassed-in porch off one of the wards containing a pool table, a card table, TV, magazines, and other recreational equipment. Here attendants and well-established, long-term patients of the elder-statesman class mixed with sociable equality, talking over the news of the hospital and in general functioning as a sergeant majors' mess. An attendant might bring in his dog to show to others present, occasionally arrange fishing dates with town-parole patients, and consult the racing form with the group at large, kidding and joking about bets that had been or were to be placed. The poker game that attendants and patients played here on weekends brought the attendants somewhat into the power of the patients, as did the fact that here an attendant felt secure enough to eat openly food brought him from the patient kitchen—a use of patient food that was forbidden. Attendants could sanction noisy patients but could hardly do so without the tacit approval of the other patients present. Here was a clear case of fraternization, providing an interesting contrast to the kind of relationship that the medical psychiatric staff proffered those patients in whom they developed an interest. And here attendants and patients made a joint effort to keep patients from other services out of the room and, especially, out of the poker game.

Just as assignments that brought patients into close contact with the work milieu of the staff could provide a free place for these patients, so a place of this kind, restricted to a small number of patients officially assigned to it, could become a territory for them.[13] For example, one of the offices in the recreation building was assigned to a few patients who actively participated in producing the weekly patient paper. Here they could enjoy not only the work conditions of any small business office staff but also the expectation that other patients would not intrude without good reason. During the many occasions when no specific duty was pressing, a member of this group could sit back in a comfortable office chair, put his or her feet up on the desk, and quietly leaf through a magazine, enjoying a coke, cigarette, or other treat supplied by the generous recreational staff—a condition of privacy and control to be appreciated only against the background of usual hospital conditions.

The recreation building figured in another way as a group territory. About six patients were assigned to the building to help with domestic and janitorial tasks. In a tacit exchange for their work, they were accorded special rights. On Sunday, after they had washed down the floors and tidied up from the night before, and before the late-morning opening of doors, the place was theirs. They would brew coffee and take from the refrigerator the cakes and cookies saved from the previous occasion of helping out in the kitchen. From the manager's desk they were able to borrow, for a few hours, both of the Sunday papers which were regularly delivered to the building. For a couple of hours after clean-up, while other paroled patients were crowded around the door waiting to get in, these workers could luxuriate in an experience of quietness, comfort, and control. If one of them arrived late for work, he could press through the group at the door, and he alone would be let in by one of his fellow workers on the inside.

Although the guardhouse tended to be a free place for any patient with parole, there were places that similarly drew from the whole hospital but were not open to all patients. One of these was the little office of the staff member who managed the building in which the theater was housed. During rehearsals for plays, pageants, and the like—at which time the backstage of the theater and the "house" itself became a free place for the patient participants—this office was used by a small set of "campus wheels" as a well-protected place in which to eat lunch and gossip. The building caretaker, being much in contact with patients and little in contact with colleagues, as in the case of the guards, tended to play a marginal role between staff and patients and was accorded, at least by the campus wheels the respect and intimacy of not being treated as a staff person.

On a few of the wards, the group territory maintained by some patients came to be tacitly upheld by the ward staff. On these wards, where almost all the patients were regressed, senile, or organics, the few patients who were in contact were, in exchange for mopping the floor and keeping order, unofficially allotted a whole wing of the porch, which was closed off to the other patients by a barrier of chairs.

Some of the territorial jurisdictions developed by patients had a phased character. For example, the work assignment of five patients on a male chronic service was to help serve food to some patients incapable of the routine trip from ward to cafeteria. After serving these patients, the working patients would retire with the empty plates to a wash-up room attached to the ward. Just before or after doing this, however, they would be allowed a plate of food and a jug of milk, to be consumed on their own, at their own pace, in the ward kitchen. From the refrigerator in this room they would take some black coffee saved over from breakfast, reheat it, light up a tailor-made, and for about half an hour sit and relax in control of their own milieu. Even more fleeting claims to territories were to be found. For example, in the male admission service, on the ward to which depressed, excited, and brain-injury cases were brought, a few of the patients in relatively good contact would segregate themselves by a barrier of chairs in an effort to keep a corner of the day room free of grossly symptomatic fellow inmates.[14]

I have mentioned two kinds of places over which the patient has unusual control: free places and group territories. He shares the first with any patient and the second with a selected few. There remains private claim on space, where the individual develops some comforts, control, and tacit rights that he shares with no other patients except by his own invitation. I shall speak here of *personal territory*. A continuum is involved, with a veritable home or nest [15] at one extreme, and at the other a mere location or refuge site [16] in which the individual feels as protected and satisfied as is possible in the setting.

In mental hospitals and similar institutions the basic kind of personal territory is, perhaps, the private sleeping room, officially available to around five or ten per cent of the ward population. In Central Hospital such a room was sometimes given in exchange for doing ward work.[17] Once obtained, a private room could be stocked with objects that could lend comfort, pleasure, and control to the patient's life. Pin-up pictures, a radio, a box of paper-back detective stories, a bag of fruit, coffee-making equipment, matches, shaving equipment—these were some of the objects, many of them illicit, that were introduced by patients.

Patients who had been on a given ward for several months tended to develop personal territories in the day room, at least to the degree that some inmates developed favorite sitting or standing places and would make some effort to dislodge anybody who usurped them.[18] Thus, on one continued treatment ward, one elderly patient in contact was by mutual consent accorded a free-standing radiator; by spreading paper on top, he managed to be able to sit on it, and sit on it he usually did. Behind the radiator he kept some of his personal effects, which further marked off the area as his place.[19] A few feet from him, in a corner of the room, a working patient had what amounted to his "office," this being the place where staff knew they could find him when he was wanted. He had sat so long in this corner that there was a soiled dent in the plaster wall where his head usually came to rest. On the same ward, another patient laid claim to a chair that was directly in front of the TV set; although a few patients would contest this place, he generally could sustain his claim upon it.

Territory formation on wards has a special relation to mental disorder. In many civilian situations an equalitarian rule such as "first come, first served" prevails, and some disguise conceals another organizing principle, "strongest takes what he wants." This last rule operated to some extent on bad wards, just as the first rule did on good wards. Another dimension must be introduced, however. The alignment to ward life that many backward patients took, for whatever voluntary reason or from whatever involuntary cause, led them to remain silent and unprotesting and to move away from any commotion involving themselves. Such a person could be dislodged from a seat or place regardless of his size or strength. Hence, on the bad wards, a special pecking order of a sort occurred, with vocal patients in good contact taking favorite chairs and benches from those not in contact. This was carried to a point where one patient might force a mute one off a footrest, leaving the vocal patient with a chair *and* a footrest, and the mute patient with nothing at all—a difference that is not negligible considering the fact that except for breaks at mealtime some patients spent the whole of the day on these wards doing nothing but sitting or standing in one place.

Perhaps the minimum space that was built into a personal territory was that provided by a patient's blanket. In some wards, a few patients would carry their blankets around with them during the day and, in an act thought to be highly regressive, each would curl up on the floor with his blanket completely covering him; within this covered space each had some margin of control.[20]

As may be expected, a personal territory can develop within a free place or group territory. For example, in the recreation room of a chronic male service one of the two large wooden armchairs favorably situated close to the light and the radiator was regularly taken by an elderly respected patient, both patients and staff recognizing his right to it.[21]

One of the most elaborate illustrations of territory formation in a free place in Central Hospital occurred in the disused basement of one of the continued-treatment buildings. Here a few of the more intact rooms had been taken over by lower-echelon staff to use as supply rooms; thus there was a paint room and a room where grounds-care equipment was stored. In each of these rooms a patient helper held semi-official dominion. Pin-ups, a radio, a relatively soft chair, and supplies of hospital tobacco were to be found. A few of the remaining less usable rooms had been appropriated by aging long-term parole patients, each of whom had managed to stock his nest with something, if only a broken chair and stacks of old *Life* magazines.[22] In the rare event of any of these patients being needed during the day by a member of staff, a message would be sent directly to his basement office, not his ward.

In some cases, an assignment provided a personal territory. For example, the working patients who looked after their ward's clothing and supply room were allowed to stay in this room when no chores were to be done; and there they could sit or lie on the floor away from the alterations of commotion and pall in the day room.

NOTES

[1] The study of the social use of space has recently been restimulated by the work of animal ethologists such as H. Hediger and Konrad Lorenz. See, for example, the very interesting paper by Robert Sommer, "Studies in Personal Space," *Sociometry*, XXII (1959), pp. 247–60, and H. F. Ellenberger, "Zoological Garden and Mental Hospital," *Canadian Psychiatric Association Journal*, V (1960), pp. 136–49.

[2] Ivan Belknap, *Human Problems of a State Mental Hospital* (New York: McGraw-Hill, 1956), pp. 179–80.

[3] An American prison example may be cited from Alfred Hassler's *Diary of a Self-Made Convict* (Chicago: Regnery, 1954), p. 123:

"A few minutes later the guard makes his 'count,' at which time each man is supposed to be standing, fully dressed, at his door. Since the hack simply glances in at the window, however, it is a simple enough matter to slip one's shirt on and, by standing close to the door, give the desired impression."

[4] Carl Solomon, "Report from the Asylum," in G. Feldman and M. Gartenberg, eds., *The Beat Generation and the Angry Young Men* (New York: Dell Publishing Co., 1959), pp. 177–78.

[5] A fine example on board a frigate is provided by Melville, op. cit., pp. 305–7:

"Notwithstanding the domestic communism to which the seamen in a man-of-war are condemned, and the publicity in which actions the most diffident and retiring in their nature must be performed, there is yet an odd corner or two where you may sometimes steal away, and, for a few moments, almost be private.

"Chief among these places is the chains, to which I would sometimes hie during our pleasant homeward-bound glide over those pensive tropical latitudes. After hearing my fill of the wild yarns of our top, here would I recline—if not disturbed—serenely concocting information into wisdom.

"The chains designates the small platform outside of the hull, at the base of the large shrouds leading down from the three mast-heads to the bulwarks. . . . Here a naval officer might lounge away an hour after action, smoking a cigar to drive out of his whiskers the villainous smoke of the gunpowder. . . .

"But though the quarter-galleries and the stern-gallery of a man-of-war are departed, yet the chains still linger; nor can there be imagined a more agreeable retreat. The huge blocks and lanyards forming the pedestals of the shrouds divide the chains into numerous little chapels, alcoves, niches, and altars, where you lazily lounge—outside of the ship, though on board. But there are plenty to divide a good thing with you in this man-of-war. Often, when snugly seated in one of these little alcoves, gazing off to the horizon, and thinking of Cathay, I have been startled from my repose by some old quarter-gunner, who, having newly painted a parcel of match-tubs, wanted to set them to dry.

"At other times, one of the tattooing artists would crawl over the bulwarks, followed by his sitter; and then a bare arm or leg would be extended, and the disagreeable business of 'pricking' commence, right under my eyes; or an irruption of tars, with ditty-bags or sea-reticules, and piles of old trowsers to mend, would break in upon my seclusion, and, forming a sewing circle, drive me off with their chatter.

"But once—it was a Sunday afternoon—I was pleasantly reclining in a particularly shady and secluded little niche between two lanyards, when I heard a low, supplicating voice. Peeping through the narrow space between the ropes, I perceived an aged seaman on his knees, his face turned seaward, with closed eyes, buried in prayer."

[6] Toilets serve a similar function in other institutions, too. Kogon, op. cit., p. 51, provides a concentration-camp illustration: *"When a camp had been fully established, a washroom and open privy might be installed between each two wings. This was where the prisoners secretly smoked when they had the chance, smoking in the barracks being strictly forbidden."*

A prison instance may be cited from Heckstall-Smith, *op. cit.*, p. 28:

"In the mail bag shop, as in all prison workshops, there were lavatories where the men seemed to spend as much time as possible. They went to them for a surreptitious smoke or simply to sit so as to dodge work, for one seldom meets a man in prison who has the slightest interest in the work he is doing."

[7] Melville, op. cit., pp. 363–64, provides a naval example:

"In men-of-war, the galley, or cookery, on the gun-deck is the grand centre of gossip and news among the sailors. Here crowds assemble to chat away the half-hour elapsing after every meal. The reason why this place and these hours are selected rather than others is this: in the neighbourhood of the galley alone, and only after meals, is the man-of-war's man permitted to regale himself with a smoke."

In American small towns, the front of certain business establishments may serve in this way for categories of citizens; a good description is provided by James West, *Plainville, U.S.A.* (New York: Columbia University Press, 1945), "Loafing and Gossip Groups," pp. 99–107.

[8] This ruling is a good example of the humane and liberal policy maintained in Central Hospital in regard to certain aspects of hospital life. A hospital report could be constructed entirely from such liberalisms, and journalists have in fact done so. In reviewing a preliminary report of my study, the then First Assistant Physician suggested that, while he did not dispute any particular statement, he could match the overall result with equally true statements favorable to the hospital. And he could. The issue, however, is

whether a liberal feature of hospital administration touches the lives of only a handful of patients during a handful of moments, or whether it pertains to a crucial and recurrent feature of the social system governing central aspects of the lives of the bulk of the patients.

[9] In civil society, as previously suggested, a free place may be fed by individuals from a very broad area, as in the case of a city's parks. In London, up to the eighteenth century, that city fed harassed thieves into free places called "sanctuaries," which sometimes gave freedom from arrest. See L. O. Pike, *History of Crime in England* (2 vols.; London: Smith, Elder & Co., 1876), Vol. II, pp. 252–54.

[10] It may be added that some of the places that were off-limits for patients, such as the staff single-male living quarters, were, in fact, by virtue of such a ruling, places where staff could "relax," free of that constraint upon their behavior that the presence of patients invoked.

[11] It is an odd social fact that free places are often to be found in the immediate vicinity of officials, part of whose function is to exercise surveillance over broad physical regions. For example, winos in small towns sometimes congregate on the lawn of the county courthouse, enjoying there some rights of lounging assembly denied them in the main streets. See Irwin Deutscher, "The Petty Offender: A Sociological Alien," *Journal of Criminal Law, Criminology and Police Science*, XLIV (1954), p. 595, fn.

[12] A well-known example of territory was the division of Chicago into zones each controlled by a different gang. See, for example, John Landesco, *Organized Crime in Chicago*, Part III of the Illinois Crime Survey, 1929, p. 931:

"While the heavy casualties of the beer war did not lead to the extermination of gangsters, as many law-abiding citizens optimistically expected, they did induce the leading gangsters, for different reasons, to agree to peace terms which defined the territory within which each gang or syndicate might operate without competition and beyond which it should not encroach upon the territory of others." "A type of territory that has recently received attention is the delinquent's "turf."

The original concept of territory derives from ethology, especially ornithology; it refers to the area that an animal or pack of animals defends, usually against males of the same species. This area varies greatly in what it includes, with, at one extreme, only the nest or lair of the animal, and, at the other, the whole of the "home range," that is, the area within which the animal limits his regular movements. Within the home range there will be specialized localities: nurseries, drinking places, bathing places, rubbing posts, and so forth. See W. H. Burt, "Territoriality and Home Range Concepts as Applied to Mammals," *Journal of Mammology*, XXIV (1943), pp. 346–52; H. Hediger, *Studies of the Psychology and Behaviour of Captive Animals in Zoos and Circuses* (London: Butterworths Scientific Publications, 1955), pp. 16–18; C. R. Carpenter, "Territoriality: A Review of Concepts and Problems," in A. Roe and G. G. Simpson, eds., *Behavior and Evolution* (New Haven: Yale University Press, 1958), pp. 224–50. On the concept of territoriality I am indebted to Irven DeVore for help.

[13] These arrangements have been cited in other mental-hospital reports, for example, Belknap, *op. cit.*, p. 174: *"Both the toilet facilities and the clothes room and closets were forbidden territory except at authorized times to most patients. A selected group of patients, however, was allowed in the clothes room and, under certain circumstances, in the mop and broom room."*

Prisons of course are famous for such possibilities. A British example is provided by Heckstall-Smith, *op. cit.*, p. 70: *"Up in the Education Office I had plenty of opportunities of talking frankly and openly with the prison officials. Our position there was somewhat unique. We were very much trusted. We could come and go almost as we pleased and were under no direct supervision, working alone and carrying the keys of the office with us. Apart from being the most comfortable job in the prison—for in the office we had a wireless and, during the winter, a roaring fire—. . . ."*

[14] This kind of territory formation is, of course, very common throughout civil life. It can be observed in the enclosure arrangements at Ascot and the chair barriers improvised by musicians who have to play at weddings (see Howard S. Becker, "The Professional Dance Musician and His Audience," *American Journal of Sociology*, LVII [1951], p. 142).

[15] On the concept of "nesting," see E. S. Russell, *The Behaviour of Animals* (2nd ed., London: Arnold, 1938), pp. 69–73; Hediger, *op. cit.*, pp. 21–22.

The line between personal territories of the nestlike variety and group territories is sometimes hard to draw. For example, in the social world of American boys, a tree house, fort, or cave constructed in a boy's yard is likely to be his personal territory, his friends participating by invitation that can be withdrawn should relations deteriorate; the same edifice constructed on unclaimed land is likely to be collectively owned.

[16] Refuge sites are one of the specialized localities often within an animal's home range.

[17] Aside from the work price of a private room, there were other drawbacks. In most wards, private-room doors were kept locked during the day, so that the patient had to ask each time he wanted to be let in, and he had to suffer the refusal or look of impatience this often brought forth from the staff person with the key. Further, some patients felt these rooms were not as well ventilated as the large sleeping dormitories and subject to greater extremes of temperature, so that during the hottest months some patients made an effort to transfer temporarily out of their private rooms.

[18] Seating territories, famous from the light literature on clubs, are reported in mental-hospital material, for example, Johnson and Dodds, *op. cit.,* p. 72:

"I occupied these sleeping quarters for several months. In the daytime, we occupied a pleasant day room, large and well-polished with easy chairs. Sometimes we sat here for hours with no one speaking. There was no sound other than an occasional scuffle, when one of the older inhabitants took exception to the fact that some newcomer was occupying the chair which was her customary right."

[19] Wherever individuals have an anchored work place, such as an office desk, a ticket window, or a lathe, they tend, with time, to exude arrangements of comfort and control, speckling the immediate area with the stuff that homes are made of. I cite an example again from life in the orchestra pit, Ottenheimer, *op. cit.: "Once a show has settled into a run, the pit takes on a cozy, lived-in atmosphere. The men put up hooks on which to hang their horns during intermission, and racks and shelves for music, books, and other paraphernalia. One common practice is to fasten a small wooden box to the music stand with coat-hanger wire, as a convenient repository for paper, pencils, chewing gum, and eyeglasses. A particular homey touch was supplied in the string section of the "West Side Story" orchestra by pin-ups fastened (out of the audience's sight) to the inner side of the curtains that hung from the pit railing. Some men even brought little portable radios—usually to follow a favorite sport."*

[20] Ecological niches such as doorways and blanket tents can also be found among autistic children, as reported, for example, by Bruno Bettelheim, "Feral Children and Autistic Children," *American Journal of Sociology,* LXIV (1959), p. 458: *"Others, again, build themselves dens in dark corners or closets, sleep nowhere else, and prefer spending all day and all night there."*

[21] As an experiment, I waited for an evening when the second good chair had been moved to another part of the room and then, before this patient arrived, sat in his chair, attempting to give the appearance of someone innocently reading. When he arrived at his usual hour, he gave me a long, quiet look. I attempted to give the response of someone who didn't know that he was being looked at. Failing in this way to remind me of my place, the patient scanned the room for the other good chair, found it, and brought it back to its usual place next the one I was in. The patient then said in a respectful, unantagonistic tone: "Do you mind, son, moving over into that chair for me?" I moved, ending the experiment.

[22] A few patients attempted to construct such nests in wooded parts of campus grounds, but apparently grounds staff quickly disassembled these structures.

30.

POLITICAL SETTINGS AS SYMBOLISM

Murray Edelman

Although every act takes place in a setting, we ordinarily take scenes for granted, focussing our attention on actions. When certain special kinds of acts are to take place, however, a very different practice prevails. Great pains are taken to call at-

Reprinted by permission from The Symbolic *Uses of Politics,* University of Illinois Press 1967.

tention to settings and to present them conspicuously, as if the scene were expected either to call forth a response of its own or to heighten the response to the act it frames. Such accenting of settings typically accompanies theatrical performances, religious ceremonies, and the more common types of formal political actions.

Witnesses of political acts are likely to be sensitive to settings and to judge them as appropriate or inappropriate. The courtroom, the police station, the legislative chamber, the party convention hall, the presidential and even the mayoral office, the battleship or chamber in which the formal offer of surrender in war is accepted all have their distinctive and dramaturgical features, planned by the arrangers and actors in the event and expected by their audiences.

The occasional departure from what is appropriate only points up the centrality of setting to the political process. A motorist arrested in a small town for speeding should not be too surprised if he is escorted to a grocery store or other little shop where the local justice of the peace dispenses justice in shirtsleeves when he can get away from a customer. In this situation the motorist is at least as likely to be offended by the unaesthetic setting in which the wheels of government grind slowly as by his fine. A scene that is perfectly suitable for selling groceries becomes shocking when a formal governmental proceeding takes place in it.

That settings have a vital bearing upon actors, upon responses to acts, and especially upon the evocation of feeling and aesthetic reactions has always been fully recognized in the arts. In the drama, the opera, the ballet, in the display of paintings and in the performance of music setting is plotted and manipulated, just as it often is in the staging of governmental acts. The student of politics who wishes to analyze with some precision the bearing of settings upon the behavior of political elites and masses can probably learn even more from aesthetic theory than from anthropology and social psychology, though all of these make pertinent contributions.

The common element in the political settings mentioned here and in others that might have been mentioned is their contrived character. They are unabashedly built up to emphasize a departure from men's daily routine, a special or heroic quality in the proceedings they are to frame. Massiveness, ornateness, and formality are the most common notes struck in the design of these scenes, and they are presented upon a scale which focuses constant attention upon the difference between everyday life and the special occasion when one appears in court, in Congress, or at an event of historic significance.

We know something of the impact of the manifestly contrived setting, so designed as to make clear that it is framing a special performance and not ordinary life. Such backgrounds make for heightened sensitivity and easier conviction in onlookers, for the framed actions are taken on their own terms. They are not qualified by inconsistent facts in the environment. The creation of an artificial space or semblance thus sets the stage for a concentration of suggestions: of connotations, of emotions, and of authority. It is for this reason that Susanne Langer regards the creation of a semblance as vital to all the arts.[1] Through the creation of an artificial space a particular set of impressions and responses can be intensified, serving to condense and organize a wide range of connotations, free of the irrelevancies, distractions, and qualifications of which everyday life mainly consists.

Although a political setting is too rarely a work of art, some of the same psychological and symbolic consequences can be made to operate. The conspicuousness with which a setting is presented for observation and special attention in any social situation defines the degree to which an audience is being injected into an artificial universe or semblance. The latter in turn makes easier the functioning of evocative, condensation symbolism, as just indicated, and involves a corresponding diversion of attention from cognitive and rational analysis and manipulation of the environment. As examples of the two symbolic poles involved in this contrast we might cite on the one hand tribal ceremonies in a contrived setting of masks, totems, and formal dance, and, on the other hand, a mathematician or theoretical physicist working in his rather disorderly office or den, or, for that matter, a primitive tribesman carefully building himself a canoe. In the last two instances setting is not noticed as a frame at all, while the nature of the job forces constant attention upon cognitive manipulation of the environment or of referential symbols so as to produce a desired result. In the first example attention is diverted from the immediate environment and focused upon abstractions that powerfully grip emotions. They do so not because there is a demonstrable tie to desired results, as in logical or mathematical manipulation, but precisely because there is no tie to consequences at all, no means of verification. People are therefore free to assure each other that the symbol means what they all passionately want it to mean: rain, fertility, a good crop, or another shared need. There is no danger that reality will prove them all wrong because they are not observing reality; and if the future upsets their hopes, countermagic or a failure to comply rigidly with the prescribed ritual can be blamed. Social suggestion, not individual work and verification, becomes the stimulus of activity, and what is suggested is implicit in the setting. It compels attention, emotional release, and compliance because it promises to end a source of deep and common anxiety if there is profound and shared faith in the symbol, with every individual an instrument of the common interest rather than a cognitive and empirical manipulator of reality.

These background observations regarding the functions of settings, in art and in primitive social organization, help us understand the circumstances in which settings are conspicuously presented for attention in modern government. Setting, one notices, fades in and out of attention in intriguing correspondence with: (1) the importance of impressing a large audience, as distinct from the need to convince an individual through logical demonstration; (2) the intention of legitimizing a series of future acts (whose content is still unknown) and thereby maximizing the chance of acquiescence in them and of compliance with rules they embody; (3) the need to establish or reinforce a particular definition of the self in a public official. Comments already made bear upon the first of these functions of political settings, and other illustrations appear in the course of the chapter. The second and third functions are more specific, and each now calls for examination.

Kenneth Burke's insight that there is a rigid "ratio" between a dramatic setting and the quality of the acts that can take place within it and be regarded as appropriate offers a useful basis for the analysis of the tie between background and action. Several of his observations should be quoted:

> It is a principle of drama that the nature of acts and agents should be consistent with the nature of the scene. . . .[2]

From the motivational point of view, there is implicit in the quality of a scene the quality of the action that is to take place within it. This would be another way of saying that
the act will be consistent with the scene.[3]

. . . the stage-set contains the action *ambiguously* (as regards the norms of action)—
and in the course of the play's development this ambiguity is converted into a corresponding articulacy. The proportion would be: scene is to act as implicit is to explicit.
One could not deduce the details of the action from the details of the setting, but one
could deduce the quality of the action from the quality of the setting.[4]

The appropriateness of act to setting is normally so carefully plotted in the political realm that we are rarely conscious of the importance or ramifications of the tie
between the two. Burke's emphasis upon compatibility between the "quality" of
acts and their settings naturally points toward the desirability of specifying concrete
qualities if possible. Perhaps the most conspicuous kind of quality political scenes
suggest is the emotional context of the acts they enfold. The judicial bench and
chambers, formal, ornate, permanent and solid, lined with thick tomes, "prove"
the deliberateness, scholarliness, and judiciousness of the acts that take place in
them, even though careful study of some of these acts in a university or newspaper
office (different settings) may indicate they were highly arbitrary, prejudiced, or
casual. The severe, mobile setting of a military commander's camp in the field helps
establish for the public his assertiveness, hardness, and self-assurance, as do the
quality of his statements and communiques. Because the speeches are separable
from tactics and are addressed to a different audience, they help establish the setting
in this instance. When communiques embody craftsmanlike epitomes of the qualities we expect in a commander, they become memorable: "Nuts." "We have met
the enemy and they are ours." "Veni, vidi, vici." Formality and ornateness in
physical setting would be regarded here as evidence of incompetence, as would
scholarliness or slow weighing of alternatives in action.

That settings are addressed to different, wider audiences than acts is vital to the
significance of the transaction. Burke's formulation rather obscures this distinction,
but consideration of political acts and settings focuses attention upon it, and it con-
firms his main insight. The military commander's communiques and postures are
addressed to the civilian population in his own country and perhaps in other countries, including the enemy's; but his troop deployments and bombardments are
addressed to the bases of the enemy's military power, especially enemy troops.
Judicial settings and dicta are addressed to all those whose confidence in the competence and judiciousness of the judicial system is important, but court decisions are
addressed to litigants and to the accused. Setting helps legitimize an act for those
who might oppose or overturn it politically by establishing that it was not properly
or appropriately motivated.

Settings cannot, in fact, serve their function at all except as they are addressed to
mass audiences rather than face-to-face, interacting groups. An especially revealing
illustration of this fact can be found in the history of presidential press conferences
over the last thirty years. Superficially, and as presented by White House press
secretaries and most of the mass media, the trend has been steadily toward a closer
rapport between the President and the people. Franklin Roosevelt held closed meetings with reporters, with direct quotation usually forbidden and much information

labeled "background" and unpublishable. Eisenhower made much of his permission to record press conferences for later editing and broadcasting. Kennedy's Press Secretary claimed that his Chief moved even closer to the people by permitting live telecasts of press conferences.

When we apply to this trend our propositions about the psychological effects of settings, it becomes clear why the more perceptive observers and reporters have complained that the movement has in fact been in the direction of greater remoteness, less information, and far more contriving of impressions. The Roosevelt pattern permitted the President to convey information, to set off trial balloons, and to be fully responsive to questions when he wished to be, precisely because he did not have to concern himself with mass impressions. Interaction and information, not setting, were emphasized. There was accordingly more news and more data and close contact with reporters, though the President had then to rely on other devices, such as the fireside chat, to address mass audiences.

The television screen, presenting a live performance, creates not close contact but a semblance of close contact, and the distinction is crucial. Though the picture is in one's living room, the President is remote and in a frame, and he is patently offering a performance. Unlike the Chief Executive engaging in an exchange with reporters alone, his words are now unchallengeable and unchangeable. The reporters asking questions are themselves part of the setting. Like every dramatic performance, this one concentrates impressions and evocations, becoming its own justification. Instead of a channel of information, we have an instrument for influencing opinion and response. The setting, and the mass audience to respond to it, define the situation and the action.

In general, then, the focussing of attention on settings is itself evidence either that there is a conscious effort to manipulate meanings and mass response or that the setting is inappropriate to the action. Our statements about act-setting ratios are specifications of what audiences will find acceptable or unacceptable. A difference in the quality of scene and act produces shock or anger or anxiety or a suspicion that the actor is incompetent. It therefore threatens his continued incumbency. The act is not legitimized. In the continuous interaction between official actor and mass public, setting supplies both the norms or justification for the action and the limits beyond which mass restiveness and disaffection become increasingly probable.

As Duncan puts it, there are no neutral scenes.[5] As soon as a setting becomes a conscious object of attention it sets the stage for some general type of action, offering or reinforcing suggestions of its motivation. "Background" and "ground" are both synonymous and complementary.

It is possible to distinguish between a static and a dynamic political function of settings. The immediate setting of any act is likely to be widely characterized at once as either appropriate or inappropriate. This is true because the act occurs as part of a wider spatial and temporal background which makes one type of act and its immediate setting acceptable and other types unacceptable. Given the background of war a military leader is expected to fight, and his immediate headquarters are expected in turn to be appropriate to the emotional qualities of aggressiveness. Given a background of detente the military leader who makes aggressive statements becomes a center of controversy. He is not now expected either to be in the field or to speak as though he is, but rather to serve in a solid Pentagon building or university armory as an adjunct to peacetime social and governmental activity.

In this sense scenes and acts both reinforce and motivate each other and also are spatially and temporally dynamic. The setting in its widest sense creates the perspective from which mass audiences will view a challenge and thereby defines their response to it and the emotional aura which accompanies the response. No matter what the dynamics by which a business-as-usual aura comes into being, it thereafter defines the various specific acts and settings which governmental organs will find politically acceptable. Except for those immediately involved as participants, the general public of the 1920's was likely to see business as benign, the time as prosperous, the future as rosy, and the serious farm depression as not part of the scene. This wide background, framing what was visible and what was good and moving, in turn defined a Federal Trade Commission policy of encouragement of oligopoly and a presidential posture of laissez-faire.

A pragmatic definition of political setting, then, must recognize it as whatever is background and remains over a period of time, limiting perception and response. It is more than land, buildings, and physical props. It includes any assumptions about basic causation or motivation that are generally accepted.

That the politically relevant setting is not merely physical but also social in character is fundamental to symbol formation. As already noted, physical setting and the acts occurring within it are commonly judged as appropriate or inappropriate to a wider spatial and temporal setting which men cue each other to understand and accept. Mead suggests a view of setting very like that defined in the last paragraph when he writes, "The unity of the environment is that of organization of the conditions for the solution of the problem." [6]

In this connection the attitude of the ancient Greeks toward legislation is especially in point. As Hannah Arendt reminds us, the Greeks did not see the lawmaker as a politician, but rather as one who had to do his work before political activity could begin. "He therefore was treated like any other craftsman or architect and could be called from abroad and commissioned without having to be a citizen, whereas the right . . . to engage in the numerous activities which eventually went on in the *polis,* was entirely restricted to citizens." [7]

The laws create a space in which to act. . . . In adopting this view the Greeks recognized that to draft a law is not to reflect a public "will"; it is only through subsequent bargaining and administrative decision-making that values find some sort of realization in policy. To formulate a law is essentially a job of constructing a setting in the sense of building background assumptions and limits that will persist over time and influence the quality of political acts but not their content or direction. A statute may do this in several ways. It may state norms: either vague ones to which everyone will agree ("promote the public interest") or the norms of a controversial group which is thereby legitimized. It may define an ultimate objective toward which administrators or judges are to strive ("maintain high levels of employment"). It may even specify benefits or penalties in cardinal numbers or other very specific terms ($1.25 an hour minimum wage), while leaving to subsequent political interplay the determination of who is to be covered and who exempted. It often creates administrative agencies to act in the future, specifying in some form the mode of access various interests are to enjoy.[8]

All these acts of the statutory draftsman amount to a statement of the legitimate claims to recognition of various social groups. They are neither commands nor predictions of future action. They do, however, perform all the functions of settings in both their static and their dynamic senses.

The nature of the connection between setting and other influences upon action can be specified rather more fully, although further exploration of this relationship would be useful. Morris emphasizes the impossibility of action unless both a stimulus and a supporting environment are present: "the fact that behavior takes place within a supporting environment implies that the sign alone does not cause the response evoked, since the sign is merely one condition for a response-sequence in the given situation in which it is a sign. The dog upon hearing the buzzer does not seek food wherever it happens to be (though certain components of a food-response—such as salivation—may appear when the buzzer is heard). Only if a supporting environment is present will it seek food." [9]

The analogue for public policy formation is clear. Unless an appropriate political setting has been created, legitimizing a set of values and a mode of access, a group interest cannot be expressed in policy no matter how strong or widespread it may be. A unilateral presidential creation of a Fair Employment Practices Commission without sanctioning legislation is grudgingly tolerated so long as a wartime setting offers some sanction, but is promptly scuttled when this supporting environment fades. Presidential appeals for price and wage restraint are viewed as arbitrary intervention into private matters and routinely ignored unless managements and unions are themselves divided and ambivalent. Political decisions overtly reached through bargaining are commonly regarded as unsanctioned by an acceptable setting and are therefore unpopular with mass publics and resisted by them unless otherwise rationalized. Administrative acts, such as the presidential illustrations just cited, are frequently regarded as incompatible with the larger legislative and constitutional setting in which they occur, even though they may reflect quite accurately the immediate administrative background.

More common in recent American politics than a probing of the outer limits legitimized by settings is a predilection for staying so comfortably inside the limits that the main impression conveyed is one of craftsmanship in conforming to the prevailing political climate. Indeed, it has been clearly possible for presidents, majority leaders, and House speakers of the fifties and sixties to develop into an art the devising of public acts notable chiefly for their craftsmanlike conformity to the aura of the prevailing setting, but which are so trivial or inevitable that their major function is to preserve the leader's popularity. A leader who is regarded as the epitome of his times is necessarily an artful exponent of the quality of his setting. Such officials may sometimes arouse controversy, but this leadership style involves careful rationing of controversial issues to a number sufficient to maintain the impression of aggressiveness if it is fashionable, while lavishing militancy almost entirely upon issues for which it is not needed in the sense that the battle is already won.

Only very rarely can a person perceive the whole of even a physical setting at one time, and it is manifestly impossible to perceive a social setting in its full spatial and temporal extension. The question therefore arises how men, individually and collectively, normally take settings into account so that they may judge acts as compatible or incompatible with background. If the mechanism by which this is accomplished could operate only infrequently or under special conditions, then its influence upon political activity would be correspondingly limited.

Apparently, however, the mechanism is such that there is considerable opportunity for background to influence response to acts, for even a part of the setting evokes it. On this point Ogden and Richards say: "When a context has affected us in the past the recurrence of merely a part of the context will cause us to react in the same way in which we reacted before. A sign is always a stimulus similar to some part of an original stimulus and sufficient to call up an excitation similar to that caused by the original stimulus." [10]

There are many political applications of this principle. Lloyd Warner in his Yankee City study has given us examples of the ability of condensation symbols to evoke again the intense emotional aura of a setting with which the symbol is associated and thereby to influence the political value structures of people. He documents the manner in which a Memorial Day celebration, for example, called up the supporting environment of America's wars and reawakened some associations that had grown dim. [11] Alger Hiss has become associated for most Americans with the norms of the thirties or those of the era dominated by Senator McCarthy, and references to the Hiss case re-establish those settings. It is especially significant that the evoked settings need not have been physically experienced. Many Yankeee City residents of the 1940's and 1950's had not lived through the wars and the heroic era Memorial Day symbolized for them. There is, in fact, some question whether this America ever existed. The test of the political potency of a setting is a consensus on its norms and on the effects attached to them by a mass public, not the historical verifiability of the setting or the accuracy of the consensual perception.

In view of these effects of settings upon values and behavior it is to be expected that the same political act may be regarded as legitimate in one setting and shocking in another. Kenneth Burke offers a revealing illustration. He remarks that businessmen despise "in the wrangles of the politicians, the reflection of the policies they as businessmen demand. So that they can admire the cause in themselves while despising the symptom in their henchmen." While businessmen constantly praise their own commodity, "politicians compete by slandering the opposition. When you add it all up, you get a grand total of absolute praise for business and a grand total of absolute slander for politics." [12] Notice, however, that the praise in the one situation and the slander in the other are expected responses precisely because a higher moral standard is expected in public affairs than in private ones. Therefore an act that evokes a disapproving reaction when a public official performs it is regarded as shrewd business tactics in a private setting. Resort to misleading or meaningless rhetoric is differently evaluated in the two realms especially commonly.

We can also illustrate the point with narrower settings as the variables. Pritchett has nominated as "the most potent myth in American political life" the belief that the United States Supreme Court is a nonpolitical body.[13] Burke goes farther, declaring that the Court is the organ that comes closest in our democracy to possessing the attributes of patriarchalism.[14] Certainly, the Court, like the meeting of tribal elders or the sybil's cave, calls up an atmosphere in which some measure of suspension of individual criticism and considerable credibility are regarded as appropriate responses. This is at least relatively true, as compared to what is appropriate in response to legislative or congressional acts. The Court can accordingly pursue some policies which organs conventionally regarded as political cannot: declare school segregation illegal, for example, and uphold a great many of the civil and political rights of Communists. By the same token a political act viewed as directed against the Court, such as the 1937 Roosevelt plan for its enlargement, becomes symbolic parricide, while bills to rig the political make-up of legislative and administrative agencies are routinely viewed as quite conventional ploys in the political game.

Settings not only condition political acts. They mold the very personalities of the actors. As Sherif formulates it in a major text in social psychology: "the individual in any human grouping develops an ego which more or less reflects his social setting and which defines in a major way the very anchorages of his identity in relation to other persons, groups, institutions, etc. . . . disruption of these anchorages, or their loss, implies psychologically the breakdown of his identity. Such a disruption or loss of the individual's moorings is accompanied by anxiety or insecurity." [15] Markey, discussing nonreflective modes of action, declares: "Group situations are thus seen to present the social backgrounds and surroundings in which social influences, symbolic and nonsymbolic, direct and limit the kind of personality which may be developed." [16] We should expect, then, that a person's values, style of life and of political action, and expectations of others' roles would be shaped by his social setting, symbolic and nonsymbolic.

Certain elements of political self-definition influenced by social settings have been uniformly noticed by the writers on political psychology. Clearest, apparently, are the definition of the self as a participant in a stable, continuing order or as excluded from it (the feudal vassal and the modern displaced person are polar examples); as protected by prevailing institutions or as expendable (the big business entrepreneur abroad and the army enlisted man); as elite or as nonelite.

There is good evidence that an urban-industrial setting promotes a sense of political effectiveness. Lane's summary of several studies of the question declares: "A sense of political effectiveness is likely to be increased by association with industry, unions, and the complexity of urban living; it is negatively related to rural life and its less dense constituencies and greater face-to-face contact with politicians." [17] Relatively isolated living is apparently the key variable here. It is the quality and frequency of one's contacts with other people that seems to matter, not one's objective ability to influence policy. To be a part of an organization viewed as potent is evidently to derive some feeling of effectiveness. Especially revealing is the finding that such association is more important than personal contact with politicians. If government is viewed as remote and not directly approachable, faith in a mediating organization rather than in personal effort is understandable.

Other evidence of the crucial function of settings in shaping people's basic orientations toward politics appears in socialization studies. Differences among adults in political participation and orientation and in authoritarian dispositions quite clearly have their origin in part in childhood environment. The mother's educational level and such aspects of the family situation as income level and urban or rural background are especially influential. The adult behavior pattern established in most complete form by childhood setting is party affiliation because of the simplicity of the symbols involved and the easy possibility of direct indoctrination.[18]

A challenging hypothesis of a more specific kind about the relationship between family background and party identification has been offered by a psychiatrist:

> It is quite apparent that our political party affiliations are highly emotionally surcharged loyalties and that we often tend to perceive one party as hero and the other as villain; one as succorant and giving, the other retentive and refusing; one interested in the "common man," the other the instrumentality of "special interests." If the primary identifications are prototypic of the secondary one, the needs and wishes which were unfilled in childhood are irrationally transferred to the political party of our choice. We would then expect that a conflict between the maternal and paternal images in childhood would result in the conflict of voting choice.[19]

A significant difference in scope appears, then, between the settings that influence political acts and those that shape the self and its responses to political events and institutions. Political acts must be compatible with settings physically or symbolically expressive of particular *political* norms, legitimations, or postures. In identifying the backgrounds that shape personality, however, we turn chiefly to *nonpolitical* settings: to occupation, urban or rural character of the individual's surroundings, and family background. In the first instance we are explaining how mass publics as audiences view compatibility between act and scene. In the second instance we are explaining how people from particular demographic backgrounds mold themselves and hence their political gestures through the choice of significant others, whose roles they take.

If people's backgrounds are this important in shaping their values and responses, backgrounds have the most serious implications for policy formation. Patterns of social stratification, urbanization, industrialization, and authoritarian family behavior place severe limits upon the range of policies that will be popular or accepted. This factor must be considered, however, in conjunction with other symbolic interactions. It is often necessary for officials to overcome the limitations upon their maneuverability imposed by popular reactions through resort to legitimizing symbols. A government can neutralize a large part of its own population insistent upon a disarmament treaty by specifying as a prerequisite to disarmament seemingly reasonable conditions known in advance to be unacceptable to other countries involved in the negotiations: an inspection requirement, for example. Opponents of nuclear testing in the atmosphere can be mollified by repeated references to past testing or to plans for future testing by a potential enemy country.

One type of setting especially common in the political process stems directly from the inevitable prevalence in government of large bureaucracies. For reasons reviewed in the chapters on administrative symbolism large numbers of people asking benefits, favors, or what they regard as their rights from governmental bureaucracies are denied what they seek. Taking the roles of specific clienteles, bureaucratic organizations frequently are not responsive to larger and less well organized publics. Some of the reasons this lack of responsiveness is not more generally resented or protested are analyzed elsewhere; but setting often plays a significant part as well by creating an atmosphere that is forbidding and difficult to penetrate.

In some degree the forbidding aspect of the setting is physical. The long corridors, closed doors, unfamiliar bureau and section names, and succession of subordinates serving as screens to the presence of officials can create a Kafkaesque aura. As in *The Trial* and *The Castle* the atmosphere at once encourages timidity in the outsider seeking favors and foreshadows rebuffs from the insiders.

The petty bureaucrat, who more often than his superiors comes into direct contact with the unorganized clientele, is prone to complement the advantage offered by his physical setting with the invocation of an even more forbidding social setting symbolized in "the rules." These are unseen and untouchable and hence, like all dogma, not to be violated, altered, or questioned. Their invocation is a signal that discussion of the merits of the issue is out of place and profane, that what is involved is the transmission and conservation of a sacred tradition.[20] Reference to "the rules" therefore evokes a symbolic political setting that is extremely confining with respect to appropriate action and behavior on both sides.

The shaping of the self or personality is also involved. Petty bureaucrats (including policemen) are especially likely to behave dogmatically when anxious about defiance from clients or reversal or sanctions from hierarchical superiors.[21] The rules then serve them as legitimation of their inflexible behavior.

This frequently encountered political situation, while only one type of example, serves as an apt summary of my major observations about settings. Individual claimants of benefits or favors and minor bureaucrats intereact in the course of a long-standing pattern of behavior that ties policy to the interests of organized clientele groups. This larger temporal setting finds its immediate expression in a forbidding physical scene and in acts and speeches that evoke an untouchable and emotionally compelling "semblance" characterized by dogmatism and restriction. Thus do various conceptual and physical echelons of settings and acts fit into and complement each other; the entire background shapes personalities able to engage indefinitely in the type of inflexible behavior that is politically and symbolically appropriate.

NOTES

[1] Langer, *Feeling and Form,* pp. 46–48.

[2] Kenneth Burke, *A Grammer of Motives* (New York, 1945), p. 393.

[3] *Ibid.,* pp. 6–7.

[4] *Ibid.,* p. 7.

[5] Hugh D. *Duncan, Language and Literature in Society* (Chicago, 1953), p. 106.

[6] Anselm Strauss (ed.), *The Social Psychology of George Herbert Mead* (Chicago, 1934), p. 85.

[7] Hannah Arendt, *The Human Condition* (New York, 1959), pp. 169—170.

[8] For a detailed consideration of the significance of statutory mandates, see Murray Edelman, "Interest Representation and Policy Choice in Labor Law Administration," *Labor Law Journal*, Vol. 9 (March, 1958), pp. 218–226.

[9] Charles Morris, *Signs, Language and Behavior* (New York, 1946), p. 209.

[10] C. K. Ogden and I. A. Richards, *The Meaning of Meaning* (New York, 1952), p. 53.

[11] W. Lloyd Warner, *The Living and the Dead* (New Haven, Conn., 1959), Chap. 8.

[12] Kenneth Burke, *Attitudes Toward History* (New York, 1937), pp. 196–197.

[13] C. Herman Pritchett, *The Roosevelt Court* (New York, 1945), p. 4.

[14] Burke, *Attitudes Toward History*, pp. 59–61.

[15] Sherif, *An Outline of Social Psychology*, p. 105.

[16] John F. Markey, *The Symbolic Process and Its Integration in Children* (New York, 1928), p. 171.

[17] Robert E. Lane, *Political Life* (Glencoe, Ill., 1959), Part III.

[18] Herbert Hyman, *Political Socialization* (Glencoe, Ill., 1959), p. 47.

[19] C. W. Wahl in Eugene Burdick and Arthur J. Brodbeck, *American Voting Behavior* (Glencoe, Ill., 1959), p. 272.

[20] Bronislaw Malinowski, *Magic Science, and Religion and Other Essays* (New York, 1948), p. 93.

[21] For several analyses of the dynamics of this phenomenon by organizational theorists, see James G. March and Herbert A. Simon, *Organizations* (New York, 1958), pp. 36–47.

31.

THE RITUAL DRAMA OF MUTUAL PRETENSE

Barney G. Glaser and Anselm L. Straus

When patient and staff both know that the patient is dying but pretend otherwise— when both agree to act as if he were going to live—then a context of mutual pretense exists. Either party can initiate his share of the context; it ends when one side cannot, or will not, sustain the pretense any longer.

The mutual-pretense awareness context is perhaps less visible, even to its participants, than the closed, open, and suspicion contexts, because the interaction involved tends to be more subtle. On some hospital services, however, it is the predominant context. One nurse who worked on an intensive care unit remarked about an unusual patient who had announced he was going to die: "I haven't had to cope with this very often. I may know they are going to die, and the patient knows it, but (usually) he's just not going to let you know that he knows."

Once we visited a small Catholic hospital where medical and nursing care for the many dying patients was efficiently organized. The staff members were supported in their difficult work by a powerful philosophy—that they were doing everything possible for the patient's comfort—but generally did not talk with patients about death. This setting brought about frequent mutual pretense. This awareness context is also predominant in such settings as county hospitals, where elderly patients of low socioeconomic status are sent to die; patient and staff are well aware of imminent death but each tends to go silently about his own business.[1] Yet, as we shall see, sometimes the mutual pretense context is neither silent nor unnegotiated.

The same kind of ritual pretense is enacted in many situations apart from illness. A charming example occurs when a child announces that he is now a storekeeper, and that his mother should buy something at his store. To carry out his fiction, delicately cooperative action is required. The mother must play seriously, and when the episode has run its natural course, the child will often close it himself with a rounding-off gesture, or it may be concluded by an intruding outside event or by the mother. Quick analysis of this little game of pretense suggests that either player can begin; that the other must then play properly; that realistic (nonfictional) action will destroy the illusion and end the game; that the specific action of the game must develop during interaction; and that eventually the make-believe ends or is ended. Little familial games or dramas of this kind tend to be continual, though each episode may be brief.

For contrast, here is another example that pertains to both children and adults. At the circus, when a clown appears, all but the youngest children know that the clown is not real. But both he and his audience must participate, if only symbolically, in the pretense that he is a clown. The onlookers need do no more than appreciate the clown's act, but if they remove themselves too far, by examining the clown's technique too closely, let us say, then the illusion will be shattered. The clown must also do his best to sustain the illusion by clever acting, by not playing too far "out of character." Ordinarily nobody addresses him as if he were other than the character he is pretending to be. That is, everybody takes him seriously, at face value. And unless particular members return to see the circus again, the clown's performance occurs only once, beginning and ending according to a prearranged schedule.

Our two simple examples of pretense suggest some important features of the particular awareness context to which we shall devote this chapter. The make-believe in which patient and hospital staff engage resembles the child's game much more than the clown's act. It has no institutionalized beginning and ending comparable to the entry and departure of the clown; either the patient or the staff must signal the beginning of their joint pretense. Both parties must act properly if the pretense is to be maintained, because, as in the child's game, the illusion created is fragile, and easily shattered by incongruous "realistic" acts. But if either party slips slightly, the other may pretend to ignore the slip.[2] Each episode between the patient and a staff member tends to be brief, but the mutual pretense is done with terrible seriousness, for the stakes are very high.[3]

INITATING THE PRETENSE

This particular awareness context cannot exist, of course, unless both the patient and staff are aware that he is dying. Therefore all the structural conditions which contribute to the existence of open awareness (and which are absent in closed and suspicion awareness) contribute also to the existence of mutual pretense. In addition, at least one interactant must indicate a desire to pretend that the patient is not dying and the other must agree to the pretense, acting accordingly.

A prime structural condition in the existence and maintenance of mutual pretense is that unless the patient initiates conversation about his impending death, no staff member is required to talk about it with him. As typical Americans, they are unlikely to initiate such a conversation; and as professionals they have no rules commanding them to talk about death with the patient, unless he desires it. In turn, he may wish to initiate such conversation, but surely neither hospital rules nor common convention urges it upon him. Consequently, unless either the aware patient or the staff members breaks the silence by words or gestures, a mutual pretense rather than an open awareness context will exist; as, for example, when the physician does not care to talk about death, and the patient does not press the issue though he clearly does recognize his terminality.

The patient, of course, is more likely than the staff members to refer openly to his death, thereby inviting them, explicitly or implicitly, to respond in kind. If they seem unwilling, he may decide they do not wish to confront openly the fact of his death, and then he may, out of tact or genuine empathy for their embarrassment or distress, keep his silence. He may misinterpret their responses, of course, but for reasons suggested in previous chapters, he probably has correctly read their reluctance to refer openly to his impending death.

Staff members, in turn, may give him opportunities to speak of his death, if they deem it wise, without their directly or obviously referring to the topic. But if he does not care to act or talk as if he were dying, then they will support his pretense. In doing so, they have, in effect, accepted a complementary assignment of status—they will act with pretense toward his pretense. (If they have misinterpreted his reluctance to act openly, then they have assigned, rather than accepted, a complementary status.)

Two related professional rationales permit them to engage in the pretense. One is that if the patient wishes to pretend, it may well be best for his health, and if and when the pretense finally fails him, all concerned can act more realistically. A secondary rationale is that perhaps they can give him better medical and nursing care if they do not have to face him so openly. In addition, as noted earlier, they can rely on common tact to justify their part in the pretense. Ordinarily, Americans believe that any individual may live—and die—as he chooses, so long as he does not interfere with others' activities, or, in this case, so long as proper care can be given him.

To illustrate the way these silent bargains are initiated and maintained, we quote from an interview with a special nurse. She had been assigned to a patient before he became terminal, and she was more apt than most personnel to encourage his talking openly, because as a graduate student in a nursing class that emphasized psychological care, she had more time to spend with her patient than a regular floor nurse. Here is the exchange between interviewer and nurse:

INTERVIEWER: Did he talk about his cancer or his dying?
NURSE: Well, no, he never talked about it. I never heard him use the word cancer. . . .
INTERVIEWER: Did he indicate that he knew he was dying?

NURSE: Well, I got that impression, yes. . . . It wasn't really openly, but I think the day that his roommate said he should get up and start walking, I felt that he was a little bit antagonistic. He said what his condition was, that he felt very, very ill that moment.

INTERVIEWER: He never talked about leaving the hospital?

NURSE: Never.

INTERVIEWER: Did he talk about his future at all?

NURSE: Not a thing. I never heard a word. . . .

INTERVIEWER: You said yesterday that he was more or less isolated, because the nurses felt that he was hostile. But they have dealt with patients like this many many times. You said they stayed away from him?

NURSE: Well, I think at the very end. You see, this is what I meant by isolation . . . we don't communicate with them. I didn't, except when I did things for him. I think you expect somebody to respond to, and if they're very ill we don't . . . I talked it over with my instructor, mentioning things that I could probably have done; for instance, this isolation, I should have communicated with him . . .

INTERVIEWER: You think that since you knew he was going to die, and you half suspected that he knew it too, or more than half; do you think that this understanding grew between you in any way?

NURSE: I believe so . . . I think it's kind of hard to say but when I came in the room, even when he was very ill, he'd rather look at me and try to give me a smile, and gave me the impression that he accepted . . . I think this is one reason why I feel I should have communicated with him . . . and this is why I feel he was rather isolated. . . .

From the nurse's account, it is difficult to tell whether the patient wished to talk openly about his death, but was rebuffed; or whether he initiated the pretense and the nurse accepted his decision. But it is remarkable how a patient can flash cues to the staff about his own dread knowledge, inviting the staff to talk about his destiny, while the nurses and physicians decide that it is better not to talk too openly with him about his condition lest he "go to pieces." The patient, as remarked earlier, picks up these signals of unwillingness, and the mutual pretense context has been initiated. A specific and obvious instance is this: an elderly patient, who had lived a full and satisfying life, wished to round it off by talking about his impending death. The nurses retreated before this prospect, as did his wife, reproving him, saying he should not think or talk about such morbid matters. A hospital chaplain finally intervened, first by listening to the patient himself, then by inducing the nurses and the wife to do likewise, or at least to acknowledge more openly that the man was dying. He was not successful with all the nurses.

The staff members are more likely to sanction a patient's pretense, than his family's. The implicit rule is that though the patient need not be forced to speak of his dying, or to act as if he were dying, his kin should face facts. After all, they will have to live with the facts after his death. Besides, staff members usually find it less difficult to talk about dying with the family. Family members are not inevitably drawn into open discussion, but the likelihood is high, particularly since they themselves are likely to initiate discussion or at least to make gestures of awareness.

Sometimes, however, pretense protects the family member temporarily against too much grief, and the staff members against too immediate a scene. This may occur when a relative has just learned about the impending death and the nurse controls the ensuing scene by initiating temporary pretense. The reverse situation also occurs: a newly arrived nurse discovers the patient's terminality, and the relative smooths over the nurse's distress by temporary pretense.

THE PRETENSE INTERACTION

An intern whom we observed during our field work suspected that the patient he was examining had cancer, but he could not discover where it was located. The patient previously had been told that she probably had cancer, and she was now at this teaching hospital for that reason. The intern's examination went on for some time. Yet neither he nor she spoke about what he was searching for, nor in any way suggested that she might be dying. We mention this episode to contrast it with the more extended interactions with which this chapter is concerned. These have an episodic quality—personnel enter and leave the patient's room, or he occasionally emerges and encounters them—but their extended duration means that special effort is required to prevent their breaking down, and that the interactants must work hard to construct and maintain their mutual pretense. By contrast, in a formally staged play, although the actors have to construct and maintain a performance, making it credible to their audience, they are not required to write the script themselves. The situation that involves a terminal patient is much more like a masquerade party, where one masked actor plays carefully *to* another as long as they are together, and the total drama actually emerges from their joint creative effort.

A masquerade, however, has more extensive resources to sustain it than those the hospital situation provides. Masqueraders wear masks, hiding their facial expressions; even if they "break up" with silent laughter (as a staff member may "break down" with sympathy), this fact is concealed. Also, according to the rules ordinarily governing masquerades, each actor chooses his own status, his "character," and this makes his role in the constructed drama somewhat easier to play. He may even have played similar parts before. But terminal patients usually have had no previous experience with their pretended status, and not all personnel have had much experience. In a masquerade, when the drama fails it can be broken off, each actor moving along to another partner; but in the hospital the pretenders (especially the patient) have few comparable opportunities.

Both situations share one feature—the extensive use of props for sustaining the crucial illusion. In the masquerade, the props include not only masks but clothes and other costuming, as well as the setting where the masquerade takes place. In the hospital interaction, props also abound. Patients dress for the part of non-dying patient, including careful attention to grooming, and to hair and makeup by female patients. The terminal patient may also fix up his room so that it looks and feels "just like home," an activity that supports his enactment of normalcy. Nurses may respond to these props with explicit appreciation—"how lovely your hair looks this morning"—or even help to establish them, as by doing the patient's hair. We remember one elaborate pretense ritual involving a husband and wife who had won the nurses' sympathy. The husband simply would not recognize that his already comatose wife was approaching death, so each morning the nurses carefully prepared her for his visit, dressing her for the occasion and making certain that she looked as beautiful as possible.

The staff, of course, has its own props to support its ritual prediction that the patient is going to get well: thermometers, baths, fresh sheets, and meals on time! Each party utilizes these props as he sees fit, thereby helping to create the pretense anew. But when a patient wishes to demonstrate that he is finished with life, he may drive the nurses wild by refusing to cooperate in the daily routines of hospital life—that is, he refuses to allow the nurses to use their props. Conversely, when the personnel wish to indicate how things are with him, they may begin to omit some of those routines.

During the pretense episodes, both sides play according to the rules implicit in the interaction. Although neither the staff nor patient may recognize these rules as such, certain tactics are fashioned around them, and the action is partly constrained by them. One rule is that dangerous topics should generally be avoided. The most obviously dangerous topic is the patient's death; another is events that will happen afterwards. Of course, both parties to the pretense are supposed to follow the avoidance rule.

There is, however, a qualifying rule: Talk about dangerous topics is permissible as long as neither party breaks down. Thus, a patient refers to the distant future, as if it were his to talk about. He talks about his plans for his family, as if he would be there to share their consummation. He and the nurses discuss today's events—such as his treatments—as if they had implications for a real future, when he will have recovered from his illness. And some of his brave or foolhardy activities may signify a brave show of pretense, as when he bathes himself or insists on tottering to the toilet by himself. The staff in turn permits his activity. (Two days before he returned to the hospital to die, one patient insisted that his wife allow him to travel downtown to keep a speaking engagement, and to the last he kept up a lively conversation with a close friend about a book they were planning to write together.)

A third rule, complementing the first two, is that each actor should focus determinedly on appropriately safe topics. It is customary to talk about the daily routines—eating (the food was especially good or bad), and sleeping (whether one slept well or poorly last night). Complaints and their management help pass the time. So do minor personal confidences, and chatter about events on the ward. Talk about physical symptoms is safe enough if confined to the symptoms themselves, with no implied references to death. A terminal patient and a staff member may safely talk, and at length, about his disease so long as they skirt its fatal significance. And there are many genuinely safe topics having to do with movies and movie stars, politics, fashions—with everything, in short, that signifies that life is going on "as usual."

A fourth interactional rule is that when something happens, or is said, that tends to expose the fiction that both parties are attempting to sustain, then each must pretend that nothing has gone awry. Just as each has carefully avoided calling attention to the true situation, each now must avert his gaze from the unfortunate intrusion. Thus, a nurse may take special pains to announce herself before entering a patient's room so as not to surprise him at his crying. If she finds him crying, she may ignore it or convert it into an innocuous event with a skillful comment or gesture—much like the tactful gentleman who, having stumbled upon a woman in his bathtub, is said to have casually closed the bathroom door, murmuring "Pardon me, *sir.*" The mutuality of the pretense is illustrated by the way a patient who cannot control a sudden expression of great pain will verbally discount its significance, while the nurse in turn goes along with his pretense. Or she may brush aside or totally ignore a major error in his portrayal, as when he refers spontaneously to his death. If he is tempted to admit impulsively his terminality, she may, again, ignore his impulsive remarks or obviously misinterpret them. Thus, pretense is piled upon pretense to conceal or minimize interactional slips.

Clearly then, each party to the ritual pretense shares responsibility for maintaining it. The major responsibility may be transferred back and forth, but each party must support the other's temporary dominance in his own action. This is true even when conversation is absolutely minimal, as in some hospitals where patients take no particular pains to signal awareness of their terminality, and the staff makes no special gestures to convey its own awareness. The pretense interaction in this case is greatly simplified, but it is still discernible. Whenever a staff member is so indelicate, or so straightforward, as to act openly as if a terminal patient were dying, or if the patient does so himself, then the pretense vanishes. If neither wishes to destroy the fiction, however, then each must strive to keep the situation "normal." [4]

THE TRANSITION TO OPEN AWARENESS

A mutual pretense context that is not sustained can only change to an open awareness context. (Either party, however, may again initiate the pretense context and sometimes get cooperation from the other.) The change can be sudden, when either patient or staff distinctly conveys that he has permanently abandoned the pretense. Or the change to the open context can be gradual: nurses, and relatives, too, are familiar with patients who admit to terminality more openly on some days than they do on other days, when pretense is dominant, until finally pretense vanished altogether. Sometimes the physician skillfully paces his interaction with a patient, leading the patient finally to refer openly to his terminality and to leave behind the earlier phase of pretense.

Pretense generally collapses when certain conditions make its maintenance increasingly difficult. These conditions have been foreshadowed in our previous discussion. Thus, when the patient cannot keep from expressing his increasing pain, or his suffering grows to the point that he is kept under heavy sedation, then the enactment of pretense becomes more difficult, especially for him.

Again, neither patient nor staff may be able to avoid bringing impending death into the open if radical physical deterioration sets in, the staff because it has a tough job to do, and the patient breaks his pretense for psychological reasons, as when he discovers that he cannot face death alone, or when a chaplain convinces him that it is better to bring things out into the open than to remain silent. (Sometimes, however, a patient may find such a sympathetic listener in the chaplain that he can continue his pretense with other personnel.) Sometimes he breaks the pretense when it no longer makes sense in light of obvious physical deterioration.

Here is a poignant episode during which a patient dying with great pain and obvious bodily deterioration finally abandoned her pretense with a nurse:

> There was a long silence. Then the patient asked, "After I get home from the nursing home will you visit me?" I asked if she wanted me to. "Yes, Mary, you know we could go on long drives together. . . ." She had a faraway look in her eyes as if day-

dreaming about all the places she would visit and all the things we could do together. This continued for some time. Then I asked, "Do you think you will be able to drive your car again?" She looked at me, "Mary, I know I am daydreaming; I know I am going to die." Then she cried, and said, "This is terrible, I never thought I would be this way."

In short, when a patient finds it increasingly difficult to hang onto a semblance of his former healthy self and begins to become a person who is visibly dying, both he and the staff are increasingly prone to say so openly, whether by word or gesture. Sometimes, however, a race occurs between a patient's persistent pretense and his becoming comatose or his actual death—a few more days of sentience or life, and either he or the staff would have dropped the pretense.

Yet, a contest may also ensue when only one side wishes to keep up the pretense. When a patient openly displays his awareness but shows it unacceptably, as by apathetically "giving up," the staff or family may try to reinstate the pretense. Usually the patient then insists on open recognition of his own impending death, but sometimes he is persuaded to return to the pretense. For instance, one patient finally wished to talk openly about death, but her husband argued against its probability, although he knew better; so after several attempts to talk openly, the patient obligingly gave up the contest. The reverse situation may also occur: the nurses begin to give the patient every opportunity to die with a maximum of comfort—as by cutting down on normal routines—thus signaling that he should no longer pretend, but the patient insists on putting up a brave show and so the nurses capitulate.

We would complicate our analysis unduly if we did more than suggest that, under such conditions, the pretense ritual sometimes resembles Ptolemy's cumbersomely patched astronomical system, with interactants pretending to pretend to pretend! We shall only add that when nurses attempt to change the pretense context into an open context, they generally do this "on their own" and not because of any calculated ward standards or specific orders from an attending physician. And the tactics they use to get the patient to refer openly to his terminality are less tried and true than the more customary tactics for forcing him to pretend.

CONSEQUENCES OF MUTUAL PRETENSE

For the patient, the pretense context can yield a measure of dignity and considerable privacy, though it may deny him the closer relationships with staff members and family members that sometimes occur when he allows them to participate in his open acceptance of death. And if they initiate and he accepts the pretense, he may have nobody with whom to talk although he might profit greatly from talk. (One terminal patient told a close friend, who told us, that when her family and husband insisted on pretending that she would recover, she suffered from the isolation, feeling as if she were trapped in cotton batting.) For the family—especially more distant kin—the pretense context can minimize embarrassment and other interactional strains; but for closer kin, franker concourse may have many advantages.

. . . Oscillation between contexts of open awareness and mutual pretense can also cause interactional strains. We once observed a man persuading his mother to abandon her apathy—she had permanently closed her eyes, to the staff's great distress—and "try hard to live." She agreed finally to resume the pretense, but later relapsed into apathy. The series of episodes caused some anguish to both family and patient, as well as to the nurses. When the patient initiates the mutual pretense, staff members are likely to feel relieved. Yet the consequent stress of either maintaining the pretense or changing it to open awareness sometimes may be considerable. Again, both the relief and the stress affect nurses more than medical personnel, principally because the latter spend less time with patients.

But whether staff or patient initiates the ritual of pretense, maintaining it creates a characteristic ward mood of cautious serenity. A nurse once told us of a cancer hospital where each patient understood that everyone there had cancer, including himself, but the rules of tact, buttressed by staff silence, were so strong that few patients talked openly about anyone's condition. The consequent atmosphere was probably less serene than when only a few patients are engaged in mutual pretense, but even one such patient can affect the organizational mood, especially if the personnel become "involved" with him.

A persistent context of mutual pretense profoundly affects the more permanent aspects of hospital organization as well. (This often occurs at county and city hospitals.) Imagine what a hospital service would be like if all terminal patients were unacquainted with their terminality, or if all were perfectly open about their awareness-whether they accepted or rebelled against their fate.[5] When closed awareness generally prevails the personnel must guard against disclosure, but they need not organize themselves as a team to handle continued pretense and its sometimes stressful breakdown. Also, a chief organizational consequence of the mutual pretense context is that it eliminates any possibility that staff members might "work with" patients psychologically, on a self-conscious professional basis. This consequence was strikingly evident at the small Catholic hospital referred to a few pages ago. It is also entirely possible that a ward mood of tension can be set when (as a former patient once told us) a number of elderly dying patients continually communicate to each other their willingness to die, but the staff members persistently insist on the pretense that the patients are going to recover. On the other hand, the prevailing ward mood accompanying mutual pretense tends to be more serene—or at least less obviously tense—than when open suspicion awareness is dominant.

NOTES

[1] Robert Kastenbaum has reported that at Cushing Hospital, "a Public Medical Institution for the care and custody of the elderly" in Framingham, Massachusetts, "patient and staff members frequently have an implicit mutual understanding with regard to death . . . institutional dynamics tend to operate against making death 'visible' and a subject of open communication. . . . Elderly patients often behave as though they appreciated the unspoken feelings of the staff members and were attempting to make their demise as acceptable and unthreatening as possible." This observation is noted in Robert Kastenbaum. "The Interpersonal Context of Death in a Geriatric Institution," abstract of paper presented at the Seventeenth Annual Scientific Meeting, Gerontological Society (Minneapolis: October 29–31, 1964).

[2] I. Bensman and I. Garver, "Crime and Punishment in the Factory," in A. Gouldner and H. Gouldner (eds.), *Modern Society* (New York: Harcourt, Brace and World, 1963), pp. 593–96.

[3] A German communist, Alexander Weissberg, accused of spying during the great period of Soviet spy trials, has written a fascinating account of how he and many other accused persons collaborated with the Soviet government in an elaborate pretense, carried on for the benefit of the outside world. The stakes were high for the accused (their lives) as well as for the Soviet. Weissberg's narrative also illustrated how uninitiated interactants must be coached into their roles and how they must be cued into the existence of the pretense context where they do not recognize it. See Alexander Weissberg, *The Accused* (New York: Simon and Schuster, 1951).

[4] A close reading of John Gunther's poignant account of his young son's last months shows that the boy maintained a sustained and delicately balanced mutual pretense with his parents, physicians and nurses. John Gunther, *Death Be Not Proud* (New York: Harper and Bros., 1949). Also see Bensman and Gerver, *op. cit.*

[5] For a description of a research hospital where open awareness prevails, with far-reaching effects on hospital social structure, see Renée Fox, *Experiment Perilous* (New York: Free Press of Glencoe, 1959).

Part Six

Culture and History
as Drama

T HE LAST SECTION of this book deals with the most inclusive image of social drama: that the enactment and understanding of a historically extant culture is itself drama. A particular culture, it is argued, is held together by symbols—"collective representations," in Durkheim's term—which are guarded and interpreted by a cultural elite. These cultural "myths" are reaffirmed by their presentation in community ritual dramas of "secular consecration." Further, the socio-logic of that particular culture means that the myths must be enacted on the stage of history, must be followed to their "logical" conclusion. The "script" of each culture so dictates.

In another piece drawn from *The Living and the Dead,* Lloyd Warner discusses the symbolic structure of the "Yankee City" ter-centenary pageant. The "story" of the city was told in "dramatic scenes," tableaux that represented the heroes, events, groups, aspirations of that diverse collectivity. The past was "evoked" to place the present and the future in symbolic and temporal references with the flow and the meaning of history. Yankee City, like states, nations, indeed entire civilizations, thus reminded itself who it was, where it had been, and where it was going.

When a serious disturbance occurs in the history of a culture, identity problems result. This can lead to either dissolution or resolution. Kinser and Kleinman's brilliant essay on Germany explains their recent history in this way. The German loss of World War I and the subsequent dissolution of the Versailles Treaty and Weimar Republic loosed a search for coherence, for a "cultural metaphor" that restored the historical meaning of Germany. The Nazis triumphed because they restored the myth of cultural unity and direction of a "script" that appeared, at first, to be invigorating, but later became pathological. Thomas Mann neatly summed it up: "National Socialism means: 'I do not care for the social issue at all. What I want is the folk tale.' " The folk tale had its consequences in the drama of the "final solution" for both the villains and the heroes.

Associated with identity problems is the search for reality. In the last half century the documentary film has been defined as "the creative interpretation of reality." Reality is not treated as background but the very subject of these films. This concentration on milieu is a major attribute of the factual film's efforts to achieve a synthesis of the real environment and the forces that move through history and culture. Where the fictional film brought dramatic excitement to the screen, the film of fact, especially after the development of the "cinema-verité," or "direct cinema" techniques, established dramatic continuity, without plot or story line, by recording the "reality" inherent in human personality and human relationships. James Arnold discusses these claims of the documentary film, and the American search for reality, in his analysis of the present state of that medium.

The above definition of documentary may be misleading; because the question that immediately arises from the definition is: What is reality? Surely subtle and complex human relationships, with which many of the best fiction films deal, are also as much a part of reality as those other aspects generally probed by documentary makers. Fables, myths, and folk and fairy tales have their roots in reality. Krishna, Aladdin, Cinderella and Jack the Giant Killer all have their prototypes in real life. Therefore, in a sense, fables and myths are also creative interpretations of reality and all artists in all branches of non-abstract art are engaged in the same pursuit of reality which some have assigned exclusively to the makers of documentary films. In dealing with the drama and reality of the American culture and history many Americans have turned to Hollywood and the movies. It is this search for reality and the role of the movies that is the focal point of Pauline Kael's provocative essay on "Trash, Art, and the Movies."

The dramaturgical perspective applied to such sweeping events may well have its uses. One may justifiably be suspicious of holistic quasi-Hegelian notions being applied to explain a historical culture, but perhaps such attempts are unavoidable speculation. Do we not speak of a "sick society," of China being a "prisoner of her past," of the "American century," where "manifest destiny" led us to move westward across the Pacific? Does the American dramatic logic lead us inexorably to do certain things and refuse to do others? Can we escape or change our "script" any more than other cultures? Finally, does the drama of international "self-actualization" now being enacted between the Americans, Russians and Chinese lead to a final Armageddon? Is the drama of man's history inevitably tragic? It does seem clear that both elites and masses see cultural symbols and elite actions as dramatic; the only question is whether quiet dramas of peace will prove as "satisfying" as the more exciting and suspenseful dramas of conflict and war.

32.

THE RITUALIZATION OF THE PAST

Lloyd Warner

During the early period of our research, Yankee City celebrated the three-hundredth anniversary of its existence. Forty thousand people came from all over the country to be a part of the historic event. Natives gone to the West and to the great metropolitan cities returned home and others born elsewhere came there for this historic moment, many seeking ancestors and hoping to identify with a known and desirable past. The people of Yankee City had spent the major part of a year carefully preparing for this tercentenary celebration. Everyone was involved: the aristocracy of Hill Street, the clam-diggers of the river flats; Protestants, Catholics, and Jews; recent immigrants and the lineal descendants of the Puritan founders. Fine old houses and other places of prestige and pride throughout the city were selected and marked with permanent signs which told of their importance and significance.

Five days were devoted to historical processions and parades, to games, religious ceremonies, and sermons and speeches by the great and near great. At the grand climax a huge audience assembled to watch the townsmen march together "as one people" in a grand historical procession. This secular rite, through the presentation of concrete historical incidents, stated symbolically what the collectivity believed and wanted itself to be. Those who watched saw past events portrayed with symbolic choice and emphasis in the dramatic scenes of the tableaux which passed before them. At that moment in their long history the people of Yankee City as a collectivity asked and answered these questions: Who are we? How do we feel about ourselves? Why are we what we are? Through the symbols publicly displayed at this time when near and distant kin collected, the city told its story.

Forty-two dramatic scenes representing over three hundred years of history (1630–1930), beginning with an idyllic view of the continental wilderness—"the forest primeval, before man came"—and concluding with a war scene from contemporary times, passed before the official reviewing stand and the vast audience. Among the scenes were Governor Winthrop bringing the Charter of the colony, the landing of the founding fathers of Yankee City on the banks of the river, a local witch trial, as well as episodes from the French, Indian, Revolutionary, and other wars of American history. . . .

All had immediate significance for Yankee City, and most of the scenes were important in the history of the nation. Among the personages portrayed were Lafayette, George Washington, Benjamin Franklin, and William Lloyd Garrison.

Extraordinary care has been taken to make each scene historically correct. Local, state, and national histories were consulted by an expert committee to be sure that each occasion, each character, the actions depicted, the clothes worn, and the stage

Reprinted by permission from *The Living and the Dead,* Yale University Press, 1959.

settings were authentic. The Boston Museum of Fine Arts supervised the production of most of the floats, constructing authentic models of the historical characters and incidents.

The total sign context of the parade from the beginning "Before Man Came" until now, the very movement of the trucks that carried the floats, each vividly portraying things past, all showed time going by. "Events" from the distant but diminishing past moved toward the present in preordained "inevitability," supposedly bound to the imposed irreversibility of chronology. They came into the eyes and present worlds of the audience, then once more disappeared into the past like the historic events they represented. What was put in and left out, selected and rejected, became symbols which revealed something of the inner world of those involved and the present beliefs and values of the collectivity.

The great Procession passed before the dignitaries of an official reviewing stand who were the city's official representatives. Then, in effect, the collectivity officially accepted the significance of the signs that it had fashioned and now offered publicly to its ceremonial leaders: the sign-maker accepted his own signs in self-communion. On such a memorable occasion what meanings flowed from the past to be again part of the present? At the particular moment in time and place when the group see the symbols they have made and chosen, what are they saying to themselves? And to whom, other than themselves, are they speaking? This question is necessary, since what they say about themselves will be partly determined by the audience to whom they communicate it. The city's Tercentenary Committee made all this quite evident. On several occasions the chairman and others declared that the Procession would help to establish "understanding among citizens of diverse racial origins and points of view" and "teach our children the importance of our city's past." It was clear they were also talking to themselves, for they said, "We will learn of our own greatness and the important part we have played in this country's history."

Despite the successful use of expert knowledge, the authentic reconstruction of each event, and the overriding emphasis on evidence and fact, the significance of each event selected (and rejected) was not a matter of reference and rational sign behavior but of collective emotion and evocative symbolism. The story's plot, its characters, actions, minor and major episodes and their development, as well as the opinions and attitudes of the audience and the producers, were significant symbolic evidence which could be collected and analyzed. Each dramatic episode and the entire procession were examples of pure symbol. They were fabricated signs whose present meanings referred overtly and explicitly to past events in the life of the community and the nation. But beyond this, they were evocations and present products of the past emotional life of the group *as presently felt*. As symbols they were collective representations which conformed to Durkheim's classical definition of collective rites. Collective representations, he has said, are signs which express how "the group conceives itself in its relations with objects which affect it." Within their meanings is collective power individually felt, the condensation of the "innumerable individual" mentalities of past generations whose social interactions produced and maintained them. All societies uphold and reaffirm "at regular intervals the collective sentiments and collective ideas'' which help to maintain their unity. They achieve this unity at times by means ''of reunions, assemblies and meetings where individuals being closely united to one another reaffirm in common their common sentiments.''

More important than the rational and scientific, not to say Puritan, moral resolve to ''create understanding'' and teach by ''learning of their own greatness,'' the people of the community unknowingly revealed their non-rational, unconscious feelings and beliefs about themselves. In talking to themselves, in presenting their own signs to themselves, with their own meanings given to these signs as they were offered and accepted, revalued and reconceptualized, they were dealing with George Mead's ''significant symbol.'' They were saying not only what history is objectively, but what they now *wished* it all were and what they wished it were not. They ignored this or that difficult period of time or unpleasant occurrence or embarrassing group of men and women; they left out awkward political passions; they selected small items out of large time contexts, seizing them to express today's values. Thus, at times they denied or contradicted the larger flow of history and the intentions of yesterday's understanding, often repudiating beliefs and values that were once sanctioned or honored.

. . . The condensation of collective experience expressed in the forty-two tableaux was much greater than the condensation of an individual's dream, for the latter at best reflects only one lifetime, whereas the images of this procession dealt with a span of time which covered the total meaning of the lives of tens of thousands of individuals who had lived, died, and passed on their collective and individual significance to those now living. The forty-two dramatic scenes were intended to represent historical truth and recreate the past for three hundred years of experience—for the actions of thousands of men and women who had once lived, their accumulated total being many times the city's present census. This represents an incalculable number of events, of comings and goings, deaths and births, failures and triumphs, beginnings, endings, and continuities, which make up the lives of individuals who compose the living history of the group. Any one of these events, any one of the forgotten thousands, had a significant story whose meanings, properly unraveled and told, could inform today's people of their beginnings and their past. Yet most of them, both events and individuals, have disappeared without identifying trace. They have not been ''forgotten,'' for most of them were never remembered. Yet they were woven into the fabric of group life.

The Period of Preparation: the Secular Rites of Legitimation

The meanings and functions of (symbolic) drama, as everyone knows, range from the most sacred rituals of an established religion to those which are purely secular in character. The drama of the Mass at the altar of a Christ crucified, sacred processions on public streets, the tragedy and comedy of theater, the celebrational themes of thousands of festivals and fiestas, among them stern morality stories or those evoking licentious abandon, as well as the skits and trivialities of vaudeville, radio, and television, are among the many varieties. In each a story is dramatically portrayed, where the actions of a hero and other characters embody the values and beliefs communicated.

In the Yankee City celebration, to make the symbols chosen for the Procession perform the function of evoking the past—to make them believable and manifest to a diverse audience—was a most difficult task. How were the signs to be fashioned and presented so that they would mean something real and legitimate? It is our thesis that most of the period of preparation immediately preceding the Procession was itself an unintentional, informal, secular ritual of consecration. Supposedly entirely devoted to the examination and selection of historical facts referring to the past of Yankee City, and their transformation into authentic concrete form, the preparatory activities served primarily to perform this function in such a way that the audience could make the mental acts of affirmation necessary to accept the symbols as true. Faith in their scientific truth had to be established.

. . . There was a variety of ways theoretically available to those who produced the Procession to establish its symbols as real and legitimate. [140] Taking in the broad possibilities of cultures in general, the symbols used might have been consecrated by religious leaders invested with the power to mysteriously transmute them from ordinary into supernatural ones through rituals of sacred legitimation. Or at the secular level the belief system of the community might have been such that the organizers of the Tercentenary could have been invested with political power from an ultimate Leader, endowing them with this ability to establish faith; or with a political or economic doctrine, conformance to which would establish a sense of reality in the symbols. The symbols of the Procession might conceivably have involved belief in the conversion of ordinary men into extraordinary ones—for example, returned soldiers whose extraordinary courage, valor, and good luck in the face of death as champions of the people, or as defenders of the faith against the infidel, had changed them into heroes or martyrs whose meanings could be infused with the collectivity's values about its own survival.

To an extent this was true of the Procession; but its symbols and objects did not intrinsically carry *their own* proofs of validity. To evoke such meanings it was necessary to use and manipulate modern values and beliefs—to utilize ''scientific'' means. In a social world founded on Protestantism, the usages of sacred investment fail and the usual mystical ritual methods cannot accomplish such ends. The belief in the efficacy of the power of words and acts of ritual such as those of the Mass, which transform modern objects not only into transcendant signs of godhead but into God Himself, cannot be used. There can be no sacred icons, images of sacred investment, to speak the truths that need to be expressed. Nor is there a divinely or politically appointed authority capable of performing such acts of ritual consecration. No one would believe what he did. The souls of the ancestors cannot be called up ritually from the past to live in the present as they are in the totemic rites of simpler peoples. Something else needs to be done. The people of Yankee City, mostly Protestants and all skeptics in that they live in a modern science-based civilization, must settle for less—if not the souls of ancestors, then at least images that evoke for the living the spirit that animated the generations that embodied the power and glory of yesterday.

The techniques and authority of scientific reconstruction provided signs—incidents, costumes, settings, etc.—which supposedly referred to real things and happenings of the historical past. This faith established and the proper preparatory activities performed according to prescribed standards, the symbols—the accepted combinations of sign and meaning—could be and were legitimated. To the audience (since the signs could be believed) their meanings were true, and this being so, all or many of the evaluations and interpretations of events portrayed could also be accepted and believed. To understand this, let us begin our analysis of the preliminary (second) period to present the evidence.

The first official announcement by the Tercentenary Committee to arouse public interest and launch the collective activity which culminated in the great celebration eight months later, appeared in a front page story in the local paper. "The people of Yankee City are to have an opportunity," it said, "to hear Professor Albert Bushnell Hart of Harvard College, who will come here to speak of the significance of the Tercentenary Celebration and what other cities and towns are doing to observe the great event. All persons residing in Yankee City are invited to attend and get the advantage of Professor Hart's learning, as he is an historian of national reputation." It said further that he had written "a special article on the subject" in which he declared that the occasion "will be the greatest opportunity in 300 years for the people of Massachusetts *to take account of stock, to sum up what they have been doing and to set it forth* [italics mine]."

This first document in the official files kept by the chairman of the committee and used as evidence in our study also told the people of the city (as mentioned above) that a "proper observation" of the Tercentenary would not only be "worth while in showing the development of 300 years, but it will also have a valuable effect in *establishing among our own citizens of diverse racial origins and points of view and demonstrate their relationship and importance to community progress* [italics mine]."

To all races of traders, whether merchant princes of seagoing fifteenth-century Venice, eighteenth-century Yankee City, or their modern successors, taking stock and setting forth their wares to the customers has always been an exciting exercise. Balancing the books to show a profit and demonstrating the success of an enterprise to others as well as to those engaged in it, in fact and symbol, lie at the heart of their economies and moralities. Selling historic objects and symbolic events to tourist pilgrims seeking "culture" or to nostalgic natives returned to reinvest themselves and some of their money in the world which first made them is even more worthwhile and exciting to these men. "Establishing understanding" in this kind of customer is doubly worth-while, for it brings additional profits while teaching buyers of "diverse racial origins and points of view" the importance of the stock and their need to have it when it is set forth.

Two weeks after this announcement the elder statesman and keeper of the tribal knowledge came forth from Harvard and made his appearance in Yankee City. The great authority on American history reviewed the great events and "paid a noble and well deserved tribute to the Massachusetts character and mentality which sent so many famous men to the presidency, to the Senate and House of Representatives and to all parts of the country." He left his paper with the committee. For Yankee City and other Bay State communities it became a guide and source book for their programs. From its ultimate authority of science and learning first flowed the ability to believe.

Interestingly enough, considering the official desire to demonstrate the "relationship and importance" to the community's past of its ethnic citizens (almost half of the Yankee City population, most being Catholic), he did not speak at City Hall or a similar non-sectarian place but at Unitarian Hall, the meeting place of a very small, yet powerful, New England Protestant sect. With few exceptions those who attended were Unitarians, Episcopalians, Presbyterians, or Congregationalists. The executive committee of the Tercentenary was entirely so composed. The members of the subcommittee that selected the subjects for symbolic display and decided on the models for the floats and their suitability were entirely from the old-family aristocracy. Later, after these important decisions had been made, various groups chose the episodes they wished to sponsor. Included among sponsoring groups were "the citizens of French descent," "the Polish people," and "the Jewish community." Then came such sponsors as lodges, secret societies, and churches which represented citizens of "diverse racial origin," many from social ranks far below those who made the conceptual decisions. Only then was the committee greatly expanded to be sure "everyone is included," as everyone ultimately was, to guarantee the popular success of the collective rites.

After Professor Hart's departure the local historical authorities took over. Authenticity and extract reproduction of the events of history were the ideals dominating their efforts and purpose. The symbols had to be as objective and reliable as expert historical authorities and institutions could make them. The committee to select the events and choose the markers of historical sites included local historical authorities but consulted other authorities as well as local and national histories. These and other sources, such as the local historical societies, helped to ensure authenticity. Genealogical experts were employed; to increase the feeling of historic reality, descendants of original participants in the great events were interviewed and encouraged to re-enact the roles of their ancestors.

The Tercentenary stories appearing serially were written by a local citizen, as we have seen. The writer's family name was greatly respected by everyone; the family lineage went back to Yankee City's period of renown and was connected with important events portrayed in the Procession. The artist who directed the construction of most of the models was himself an authority on the history of the town and of New England and a member of the Boston Museum of Fine Arts. Moreover, he was a son of one of the aristocratic families of the city. Thus the directors strove for historical validity and reliability. In the rational aspect they were scientists, in spirit seeking to establish secular rather than sacred realities; non-rationally they were ritual functionaries consecrating and legitimizing a secular rite.

When the Washington parade occurred, initiating the Procession, it was in "exact" accordance with the preserved full account of this event. "Washington" came from Ipswich attended by people playing the roles of those who originally accompanied him. He was met on the steps of the great mansion where he had originally been received. The same speeches—fortunately preserved—were given and replied to in the words originally spoken.

Each float in the main procession was heralded by a placard with its date and description prosaically and rationally set down. Immediately following came the historic tableau, played by living men and women each costumed according to the period. At one level of understanding they were, except for their movement, display cases in a modern scientific museum—well-labeled, authentic representations of ethnological reality. Behind them was authority expressed in expert design and workmanship.

Clearly this almost obsessive effort for scientific realism was an exemplification of the mentality of the people and a need to satisfy some vitally important demand for certainty. They did not look for sacred authority, as did their ancestors, to prove whatever they were trying to demonstrate, but for secular authority. Although they spoke as heirs of their forebears, and Yankee and Puritan values were everywhere being expressed—in their manner of "taking stock," "summing up and setting forth," as well as in professions of scientific purpose—the emotionally symbolic factors operating were of greater significance.

From the learned essay of Professor Hart and the study and efforts of those who followed him flowed the prestige of higher learning and the power to capture popular contemporary faith in modern science. From the authority of the latter's signs and facts came the ability to believe that the committee and their experts on local history could re-create the past and make it manifest in the signs displayed in the Procession and on the highly valued objects of the community. The physical presence of the "high priest" himself among them, giving a "noble and well deserved tribute to the Massachusetts character and mentality" while telling them what they must do to praise themselves by telling nothing but the truth, increased their desire and their will to believe. The facts of history, symbolically recreated through scholarly knowledge and the skills of the arts, were the ultimate and absolute sources of belief. Those who knew them were sufficiently authoritative to make their symbols of history legitimate and believable. To themselves and to others the search for, and emphasis upon, scientific fact and its reproduction in authentic representations were, as we have said, in effect a modern scientific ritual of consecration.

For this ritual to be efficacious in legitimizing the endeavor and thus establishing faith in it, the action system involved had to conform to standards of objectivity, reliability, validity, and such other tests and judgments as will create in the minds of those concerned the feeling that they are in the presence of facts. The authority of "facts" could not be disregarded; their meanings had to be sought and understood. Once understood, they must carry ultimate weight. Thus the empirical symbols, in this case those of history, which refer to, and stand for, objective facts command very great respect in our society. The methods used to find and establish facts, and the outward signs necessary to create and reliably communicate their meanings, accumulate their own social power. Those who can manipulate these skills and whose delphic voices speak for facts and their meanings, once believed by their audience, possess a secular form of absolute power. At this moment in Yankee City, because the audience believed in scientific fact and skill and the authority of those who use them, they could identify with the images of what purported to be their individual and collective past and reaffirm their feelings and beliefs about what they were by faith in selected facts of history. Thus the whole period of preparation was a secular ritual of scientific consecration. Like priests at the altar, the members of the committee took ordinary things and, by the authority vested in them, transformed them into symbols of ultimate significance. The differences between priestly and "scientific" power are notable here because they throw further light on the problem of how the symbols of the Tercentenary were legitimized and made believable. The Christian priest, for example, performs a sacred ritual under the mystical power of God, and as his agent transforms ordinary things into elements of ritual significance which become, among other things, the symbols of an historic sacred event. He represents, and is authorized by, a church to perform this act. Ultimately he represents a community of men who believe in Christ. The ritual of the priest by intent and official pronouncement functions to make this transformation possible.

Secular rituals of consecration, although habitually functioning in our society, are not publicly recognized or authorized as such. If those engaged in the preparatory activities in Yankee City had believed that their intent was primarily to establish belief in their symbols—or, putting it speculatively, had their audience believed this was their primary purpose—it could not have succeeded. They needed to believe in the intrinsic power of historic fact and their ability to represent it. Their audience also needed to believe that the symbols of the Procession were invested with this ultimate factual authority. Then the ritual drama of the Procession could be accepted, because the creation of its symbols was *not* recognized as a form of secular consecration.

To see clearly that the symbolic function of this period of preparation was not so much historical reconstruction as ritual consecration to establish belief in the values of the symbols chosen one need only think what might have happened had Professor Hart—from Harvard and Cambridge, in Massachusetts—not been invited to establish the ideology and voice the values and beliefs of the Tercentenary. Suppose Professor Charles Beard of Columbia and New York City, author of the *Economic Interpretation of the Constitution,* had been requested to write the founding document for the Procession. Let us suppose he had made his own kind of speech, with his characteristic values and beliefs, to launch the celebration. It seems unlikely that the historical facts as he would see them could have become effective symbols in the Procession. The preparatory ritual of consecration would not have achieved its end, for the community could not have identified with it; or, having admitted his facts as true, could hardly have incorporated them into its system of beliefs and values as symbols of its faith. Moreover, what he and Hart as *persons* stood for, as well as their places of origin, would give the latter the mark of approval and acceptance and the former probable doubt and disapproval.

Further, a committee composed, let us say, of third-generation Irish Catholics, all of Yankee City, all rightly respected professional historians, and all devoted to their home town, could not have hoped to establish the faith necessary to make the symbols of the Procession carry authority. In brief, while scientific processes were part of, and necessary to, the preparation, and historic facts were indeed collected and arranged in symbolic form, they were the lesser part of the enterprise and perhaps necessary only because they successfully disguised its real nature.

We have given our attention only to the Procession signs; we must also examine the problem of the ritualization of the objects of the community. Later we shall give a full description of the objects marked throughout the city, their chronological distribution, and their factual and symbolic significance. Here we must hold to the problem of their ritual consecration and the differences involved between their legitimation and that of the signs of the Procession.

The same careful procedure was used to determine the dates and history of the various things marked; the dates when houses were built, the time of their occupancy by distinguished families, and their association with important happenings were all traced. The houses and other historic objects were surviving facts of a living past; the people, their activities, and the historic events were gone and could only be represented by descriptive signs in the Procession, but the dwellings and public places where persons or families had lived and great events had taken place were a part of contemporary Yankee City. The problem was to turn them into objects of special regard and ritual significance.

The historical markers placed before the houses were signs, as were those that accompanied the floats. But, supported by the authority of the Tercentenary, they changed objects of present utility into those of ritual significance. In terms of the broader theory, . . . they moved from objects and facts into "intermediate signs" standing for something else and expressing values other than what they were unto themselves. The markers were needed to make them historically legitimate. Those who now viewed them knew that they came from, and were authoritatively blessed by, their intimate association with the ancestors. But to accomplish this transformation so that the meanings attributed would turn them from present objects into signs of past significance, their historical contexts needed to be known and verified to permit confident acceptance. They could then evoke the proper feelings about the glories of the past. These authoritative signs allowed everyone to share in the investiture of significance put upon them by the Tercentenary ritual.

The Autonomous Word and the Autonomous Individual

In the collective rite celebrating three centuries of its life, the Yankee City that was symbolically presented to the world and for its own people's self-regard and esteem was a secular, not a sacred, society. When descendants of the Puritan ancestors who founded a theocracy repudiated the authority of the early fathers, they also renounced the spiritual primacy and ultimate authority of what was once a sacred order. The established church and the sacred mythology of the ancestors did not have symbols in the celebration which related men to God's authority on earth or to his mysteries in heaven. Bishops, evangelists, and divines were displayed, but as jewels to adorn the robes of a secular order. They were the "facts" of history, conceived within the secular matrix of values and beliefs from which historians bring their presentations about the truth of past time. The symbols, officially and in fact, were referential; their signs were marks that pointed to events of the Puritan past.

But nowhere in the entire pageant was there any sacred sign which demanded an act of faith about a sacred world of the past, through the holy men of Puritan history connecting men of today with the mysteries of the supernatural and Christian deity. The whole celebration was cast in rationalistic terms; all supernaturalism was suppressed. In its symbols the Puritans were no longer God's men; no miraculous intervention was celebrated; it was all secularly determined. Each great event in the symbols of the Procession was earthbound and morally determined by men. If God was present he was remote. If the Puritans of the past saw themselves as the children of Israel and their fate the working out of God's will, their descendants did not view them or themselves in this image.

It is significant that the event celebrated by Yankee City and the other seaboard towns to mark their "birthday" was Governor John Winthrop bringing the Charter to the Massachusetts Bay Colony; Winthrop, the bringer of the word "in the beginning" of the Procession, did not come with the Sacred Book. The word he brought was the Charter, an economic and political agreement among men.

More significantly, the Charter with its controlling words was meaningful in the Procession and the whole celebration because it was *moved* from England and brought to America where, being controlled by the ruling theocrats and magistrates and clergy, it was considered, then and now, as the symbolic source of the collectivity's autonomy. Still more significantly for purposes of symbolic theory, the word issued by royal authority to set up the legal conditions of the religious and economic experiment could be moved. By nature, in the beliefs of those who used it, the word, as it once had been in the early history of man, was no longer inherently one with the speaker and his context. The symbol as a written sign system could itself be moved and not lose its meaning (significance and power). It, too, could adventure beyond the confines of its physical place of origin.

Not only was the individual developing autonomy, but symbols themselves were becoming free and more autonomous. The autonomous symbol, made possible partly by the less perishable and more permanent marks of writing and partly by the attitudes of increasing acceptance of its validity in meaning and power beyond the place of its origin, once "turned loose" could ultimately go elsewhere. Its only boundaries, under ideal conditions, are the total environment of human interpreters. The symbols of oral speech and human gesture tend to be fixed and stationary; those outside man, beginning with writing and continuing in many of the new mass media, tend to be autonomous and to move with a life of their own.

Their autonomy may reach the point where the communication they carry may be directly received from a sender of three hundred or three thousand years ago. Delayed communication is a necessary characteristic of permanent signs. The effect of such communication on holding the generations of men together is immeasurable. Furthermore, if words and other such signs are free and capable of movement, then presumably each man is free to choose among them for their significances of his life, and each generation is partly liberated from the thralldom and absolute authority of the preceding generation, who alone once possessed the symbols of oral tradition. The contemporary generations of each society become the human environments to which the moving, autonomous signs of meaning have migrated—

these, too, like their human counterparts, to be assimilated or to remain impervious to the influence of their most recent setting. These sacred or secular objective symbols of the past or present, free from the control of their creators and their contexts of origin, as they move may radically change their meanings and the manner of their acceptance; the sacred word may become secular, or the secular marks of the economic and political agreement of the Charter become semisacred. The Puritan children of Israel coming to the Promised Land of New England in their own self-conceptions were a holy people directed by God and his Word, the Bible, and by Governor Winthrop who, like Moses, also had the Charter of Law on which the laws of men were founded. The words of the Charter, the symbol of free men and their symbol of autonomy, in the Procession also represented the beginnings of things as they now are and marked the change from a world without form to one of order.

The Bible, whose words carry different meanings for each of the churches, had no part in the general collectivity's pageant rites. Only in the sermons of the churches and a brief collective ceremony at a hill beyond the dwellings of the town after the celebration was over were the Bible and the sacred world allowed to enter the symbolism of the Tercentenary. As in life, the need for unity and agreement and the evolutions of history which had produced the religious diversity of the town, drove the marks and meanings of sacred life into the confined contexts of each church, and for some to the brief, unimportant ceremony on the hill.

We must return to our consideration of the *delayed, indirect,* and unintentional use of signs. In the literature the economic, political, and religious aspects of autonomous men have been stressed. . . . This is not enough. Above everything else this shift in the Western world's culture was related to the release of secular and sacred words from oral control and from the face-to-face control of their meaning and overwhelming power to influence action and behavior. When they were freed from the bodies of the users and were no longer bound by the necessities of direct action, in which mouths and ears create and consume perishable sounds and signs, a whole set of new possibilities developed. If men can symbolize saying-what-they-mean so that it is no longer a momentary act of attribution but something that persists in time, the possibilities are limitless for extending the number and kind of people to whom signs can be "sent" and who may be influenced *indirectly* by the sender.

In the simpler stages of man's life, for words and other objective signs to continue circulating in the limited environment of those who create and maintain them, it is of course necessary that individuals of each generation relearn and refashion them as signs of communal agreement as to what they mean and are signs of. It is said that words are exchanged in communication between the sender and receiver. More correctly, sender and receiver, when conversing, stimulate themselves with *socially selected sounds and silences.* As long as this verbal stimulation is labial and auditory and strengthened with the auxiliary gestures of an interpersonal and immediate context, those who know what the words are meant to convey and who choose to speak, or choose not to, are in positions of great strength. They have control over these vehicles of collective knowledge, which can be, and often are, of incalculable power. When they speak, those who cannot understand what is told them may be placed fortuitously in positions of helplessness. They do not have some of the tools necessary to control their environment; the others do. The control of the use of words demands that their meanings be known by the user, and he can choose to speak or not speak, hear or refuse to hear.

When words are written, being no longer dependent on the *immediate* organic environment where sounds and silences stimulate meaning in live organisms, several powerful new factors enter. Freed from immediacy, words can now go elsewhere, beyond the interpersonal context. The secret intimate written words of two people—for example, a love letter—freed from sound, may leave their first context and move into a space limited only by human environment and into a time limited only by mankind's survival. Those who use words in the present or future by the use of the written form of delayed communication may "converse" with the past. Delayed communication, which at times may be more accurately called continuing communication, between individuals of generations widely separated in time and space, is one of the important ways in which words are freed from their immediate controls and, thus circulating, become autonomous—move beyond the bounds of mortality (where to live they must be consumed) toward immortality.

Being still dependent as signs on human beings, they must be protected to attain full autonomy. The autonomy of each individual person is dependent on a social structure with values and beliefs which do not fix his position but allow him freedom to move from one social place to another, from one social context to others. So it is with words. When the morality which controls their proper use defines them autonomously, they can move more easily from context to context, from B.C. to A.D. In oral tradition, their meanings can move through time in a chain of live interaction from mouth to ear, from ear to mouth, within the continuing flow of human tissue, but unbroken generational continuity must be present.

The written word, an object whose form is an agreed-upon sign, is by nature so constituted that the objective part of the sign—the material object—does not need to be refashioned or recreated each time a new individual or a new generation uses it. If used, however, the meaning must be under the influence of intervening generations. The archaeologist may unearth unused inscribed tablets whose signs belong to a culture long forgotten and never before known to this civilization. Although the signs remain the same and the meanings intended have not passed through any transformation of changing belief and value, the receivers of this delayed communication have been influenced by the flux of cultural transition of perhaps a hundred generations. What they know and feel cannot be what those who invented the delayed message could have meant, even though the message comes directly from the forgotten source. In this sense the sign is autonomous—dependent, like the autonomous individual, on the values and beliefs of society for its freedom of movement. So long as its existence in the human mind is important, involving the value of wanting to find out what it meant to those who sent it, then within the human limits of such a term it has sign autonomy. And as such it is both free and bound—free to move within the limits of human mentality; bound to serve the meanings attributed by those who use it.

As such it also acts both as a conservative force, strengthening the hold of the past on the changing present, and as a liberalizing one, freeing the present generation from dependence upon oral transmission of the immediate older generation's interpretations of the sacred tradition. Not one, but a hundred generations are now sending their own delayed interpretations of what both they and we are. If a written sign like the Massachusetts Bay Charter or the Constitution of the United States has passed through continuing generations of interlocked interpreters, then not only is the original sign present as a whole, but the inscribed meanings are also directly sent to help distant ancestors communicate with their present "contemporaries." This is in fact the purpose of such a document as the Constitution, with its effort at "wise provision" for the future. The written sign loosens the control of time and modifies its effect upon us, for as we can now send words to the present and future, those in the past have been able to send directly these same signs of meaning to those born long after them. The signs of delayed communication have a quality of simultaneity about them—they "speak," we "listen," in the same moment of interpretation, as it were. Like receiving a telegram sent across the distances of a continent, to be read a brief moment later, reading these signs of distant meaning changes the significance of space and time. Through the unity of meaning between sender and receiver, the realities of time and space are transformed into *social* realities of meaningful nearness. "The" meaning that was "instantaneously" "put into" the signs which is the Charter, three centuries ago and a continent away, by the sign-maker, in the receiver's act of interpretation today in Yankee City can be "instantly" and "immediately" shared.

Thus the autonomous word, for instance, within the guarantees of freedom of speech and press to tell the truth, has a variety of meanings in Yankee City which have clashed. All played vital roles in the symbols of the Procession and in the historical events symbolized in the signs of this collective rite. The Word of the first settlers was in two forms: the Sacred Book which put them in direct communication with God through the literal signs of his Truth, and the secular Charter which Winthrop and the proprietors of the Massachusetts Bay Colony brought with them. Those early ancestors thus had the absolute power of the Word of God and the great but less powerful word of the secular covenant in their hands. As such, the Bible, the Holy Word, was the ultimate source of all authority; its truth was absolute. Those who controlled the interpretation of the scripture could be—and some were— theocratic tyrants, but since the truth was believed to be in the Word, directly communicated by God to those who were the instruments of his communication, this infallible Book, freed from the controls of an ecclesiastical hierarchy, potentially gave to each man who could read absolute autonomy and power. For there he could find the truth and, thus informed, be not only free to know it but duty bound to tell it to others. Each man might become his own private sect, at peace or war with all others.

Since it was believed that it was each man's duty to learn the truth and read the Scriptures, it was necessary that he learn to read and have immediate access to the Holy Word. From the very beginning, Massachusetts and Yankee City taught their young to read. Public schools were believed necessary, and they were publicly supported. Private academies were endowed and Harvard College founded, all primarily because of implicit faith in the written word, particularly the Sacred Word. The second float after Winthrop and his Charter was "The First Class at Harvard. Benjamin Woodbridge of Yankee City ranked highest in this class of nine . . ."

The social and symbolic processes which, through time, formed the symbols in the minds and hands of the modern symbol-makers to create the signs of the Procession representing things past and evoking and expressing contemporary beliefs and values about them, emerged from the most diverse sources. As such these signs of the past were given *delayed attribution of meaning*. The action of meaning took place over hundreds of years rather than in the immediacy of a moment. Meanings deriving from three hundred years, tens of thousands of hours, and millions upon millions of past words and events were condensed into a few brief hours and forty-two passing symbols. The condensation of the meanings of experience stored in the unconscious of one individual is slight compared to the condensation of social significance in the symbolic equipment of each generation and the special signs of historical works or rites used by collectivities to speak to themselves about their past.

Necessarily in such signs there is *displacement* of significance; necessarily many of the older meanings are no longer allowed explicit expression. Unconscious meanings, never permitted open expression even during the occurrence of an event, still seek and find covert acknowledgment. The older meanings of signs, implicit or explicit, rational or non-rational, also change their accent. Some retreat into somber obscurity, not being publicly acknowledged and celebrated; others once not publicly admitted come from their closets and parade before an approving multitude. Through time, as everyone knows, signs and symbols stand for something more—something less—something quite different—or cease to exist. New signs stand for old meanings, old ones for new—sometimes the opposite of what they once meant.

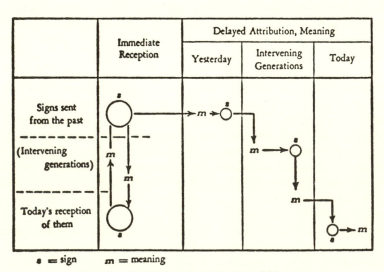

● = sign   *m* = meaning

Chart 1.   The Delayed Attribution of Meaning

Chart 1, "The Delayed Attribution of Meaning," depicts the major outline of this process. At the upper left are the signs sent from the past; below, in the same column, today's reception. At the top of the left-hand column the label "Immediate Reception" shows the situation when today's generation receives its signs directly from the long dead past. In this vertical column the circles representing signs are *directly* connected by two vertical arrows, the one pointing from the past to the present circle, indicating that the sign has been conveyed directly from the past without passing through the minds of intervening generations; the other pointing upward from present to past, indicating no more than past signs presently interpreted.

Beyond this column are the vertical columns from left to right: Yesterday, Intervening Generations, and Today. The circles and labels *m* and *s,* connected by arrows, depict no more than the passage of meaning *m* through the mental life of the generations.

The flow of signs, events, and their meanings depicted by the chart takes place, of course, in the interconnected organisms and species events which have composed the collectivity during the span involved. The flow of events through the social and status structures influences the content of each symbolic form. The continuing interpretation and reinterpretation of the events and the society in which they occur contribute an important share to the significance of symbols of the past wherever they are being used by the collectivity. The conceptualizations of what man is, what the world is, and what the supernatural is, flow through the social and status structure, influencing and being influenced by its changing values and stream of events. All of these—status and social structure, values and beliefs, and the events of time—persist and change and add to and subtract from the meanings of the past as they are caught and momentarily held in today's symbols. Logical or non-logical, rational or irrational, conscious or buried far below in the organic life of the species, adequately or not, they find expression in man's collective symbols.

The Non-logical Time and Space of the Species

The meanings of life were represented in the non-rational symbols of the Procession as events of ordered time which, moving out of the unknown toward, and into, a timeless region of earth and water, became the living time and space of Yankee City. There resting briefly, the significance of time developed into enduring importance in the recorded activities of the community. Then, at an ever-accelerated speed, we see the significant present move out beyond the city to the vast western distances, to the great metropolises, to the more important economic and social life of a powerful nation. The importance of time in Yankee City is not in the here and now but as it once was, in an enduring yesterday that has remained while present time has gone elsewhere. Since the end of the nineteenth century events are felt to be "too recent" and, while important, lack significance. They are not invested with the full social power of the mental life of the group. Yankee City is now enmeshed in the huge, dull world beyond it. Recent time in the meanings of the Procession lies sprawled and mired in the ordinary rounds of unimportant events. The splendor is gone; the power and the glory are elsewhere. Yankee City must go to them; they no longer come to Yankee City.

Within the non-rational feelings of today, time has run down. The spiritual and absolute certainty of the Protestant faith of the early fathers has been drained from the people, the great period has gone and only a diminished secular prestige remains. Yet as the nation grows into world greatness we, the people of Yankee City (the symbols of the Procession seem to say), who started and established things as they are, possess a unique kind of prestige shared only with those who were present when the Great Society came into being. Our present power is relatively weak, our contemporary prestige not conspicuous, but properly viewed in the context of the Great Society. To establish their claims as legitimate heirs and present holders of the great tradition, they who live elsewhere—the hundred-odd million—must come to us. In us the great tradition lives and our symbols legitimately express it.

Analysis of the forty-two scenes of the several time periods demonstrates that, although the whole Procession is a representation of the passage of time, and time as movement and change, in these same symbols there is also present a non-rational eternal finality. This static, unchanging, eternal quality has to do with the ultimate nature of man; it is in the fixed-forever of the species group. The eternal verities of the drama were in the unconscious assumptions that created it. By their sequential movement before the stationary reviewing stand, the scenes of the great Procession, precisely following each other chronologically, stressed the rational and linear qualities of time. But the symbolic conventions of such dramatic processions demand that the reviewing stand, those in it, and the public they represent, be still and rest in one place.

For that moment the lives of those who viewed the spectacle were suspended and timeless. In them the meanings of the Eternal City of St. Augustine were present. Coming from the past, time moved by them. The time-ordered events of the parade moved from the starting place in Yankee City through the streets of the city as *one* thing. The Procession itself, while trying to emphasize the rationality of time, played havoc with it. The meanings of objective time were non-rationally contradicted. Although first things came symbolically and logically first and the beginnings of history were spatially and logically at the beginning of the Procession, while last things appeared at the end, to those in the stationary reviewing stand their own time stood still. All the scenes were parts of one timeless thing.

In the feelings of the people, past and present life were one. Governor Winthrop and his Charter were of a piece with Greely, the ancient living hero, for they were of one substance. In this symbolic unity the simultaneity of 1630 and 1930 was non-rationally stressed. The great past of the ancestors was evoked and symbolically lived in the present. Many sensed this. On the first day of the celebration the minister of the oldest church, which traced its being to the beginnings, said to his congregation, "The Great Book of Life lies open before our generation; today, in the scenes we produce [its] notable characters seem again to walk our streets . . ." Those in the reviewing stand saw the forty-two scenes move as the "one Book of Life" across their vision, and pass on through the spaces of the city. In their diversity there was logical empirical time; within the non-rational meanings of their unity was the static, fixed quality of being. The timeless sense of species existence, felt as eternity, was present. The rationality of Durkheim's "Chart" depicting the points of time, and the deeply felt unconscious sense of total existence where, in Freud's findings, there is no time, were both present.

Despite the prevailing and perhaps necessary belief in the unitary character of time held by members of our culture, there are nevertheless many kinds of time. For our purposes we can divide them into what some philosophers have called objective and subjective time, forgetting their quarrels about one or the other being true, or all time being one or the other.

Objective time, as we said earlier, supposedly has to do with the world beyond man, particularly the movements of the earth, stars, and planets. Objective time is numbered and measured. We think we take account of it by the clock, calendar, and the instruments of the physicists and astronomers. We relate objective time to our social life and regulate much of our existence by clock and calendar. Events are accordingly timed and regulated. The individual, being part of this action context, learns and internalizes it and makes it part of himself. Such "objective" time concepts are then applied to social age status, to biological change, and to the transitional activities of the individual through the age statuses and the events of his life history. Days, weeks, months, and years, anchored to a birthday, produce a person forever measured by "objective" time, but by a time to which he and others also attribute human values. By this means the time of the individual and the society can be named and numbered.

The time symbols of the Procession were multiple and diverse. There was the objective time of chronology and verifiable historical references. Events of men and the chronology of the planets were synchronized. Such references can be validated by many people and the self-correcting devices and criteria of science. Then there were the subjective levels in which the individuals involved possessed non-rational beliefs and feelings about time. Rational concepts were rearranged in a non-logical manner. These were systems of feeling non-rationally organized. Ideas were syncretistically arranged.

The symbols of non-logical or subjective time, on the other hand, are laden with affect. These non-logical feeling systems are not necessarily individual; more often they are social. The vast world of feelings and the images which express them are passed on from generation to generation and change as experience affects them. The subjective, non-logical (social) time of Yankee City can compress the objective time of half-centuries into nothingness and extend a mere ten years into what, measured by objective time, would be a century.

The symbols of time (and of space and all other meanings) are not only signs of constructs and logical thinking, but are available and used by the non-logical feeling systems of a people and their culture. Moreover, they are subject to the needs and demands of a still deeper level of being and understanding. The non-logical meanings of our mental life are products of the species group in interaction with its environments; meanings accumulate in, and are reordered by, the organisms that compose the species. The limitations of the species, and the actual extension of its capabilities into experience and environment (accepting or not accepting available stimuli), provide the limits of knowing. For time, and indeed all knowing, cannot go beyond the nature of species being. The turtle, the chimpanzee, the firefly, and the angleworm, as species, by their own nature and being have their inherent limitations and extensions of understanding. So it is with man. That which makes the human species different from all others makes its knowledge different.

The logical objective categories of time and space, the nonlogical affective systems, and the species sensations constitute three levels of understanding. Each refers to worlds of reality. They refer to the physical objective world beyond man, to the ongoing organismic world of the species, and to what the individual experiences when he experiences himself. In terms of time, physical time is the sequence of events (which may or may not have the form it is believed to have) that occurs in the world beyond man. Social time is beyond the self; it is a sequence of happenings, with or without form, which take place in the world of social relations. Self time is a sequence of events, with or without form, having to do with what it is I am and do.

We thus have three broad categories referring to the several realities: objective time and space references to physical, social, and self phenomena; non-logical systems of feeling, which refer to the same three; and species sensations, which order experience about the objective world, beyond other organisms as they are socially related to each other, and the self as a being apart. . . .

33.

HISTORY AS FICTION

Bill Kinser and Neil Kleinman

We approach Germany—often a vague and diffuse entity even for Germans themselves—as though it had a continuous consciousness. Our intention is not to personalize Germany and its history, nor to invent a German *Zeitgeist*—an invisible and amorphous spirit that loosely justifies all. We believe that societies produce parallel and interconnected systems of expression and statement which reflect a total social complex of meaning and value.

With varying degrees of enthusiasm, societies try to articulate the logic of these interconnections through their use of myth and historical interpretation. Yet these explanations come from *within* a society; therefore, they are part of the total

Bill Kinser and Neil Kleinman, *The Dream That Was No More a Dream: The Search for Aesthetic Reality in Germany, 1890–1945* (New York: Harper & Row, 1969), pp. 5–9, 12–23. Copyright © 1969 by Neil Kleinman. Reprinted by permission of Harper & Row.

complex of meaning, not above or outside it. Hence such explanations by a society of itself add but another level to the total complex of meaning, without being able to take in the significance of what they have added, for they cannot study their own reflections. The way in which a society explains itself—the style and purpose of its history—is, therefore, as important as the specific content of its history.

Some societies are particularly interested in explaining themselves to themselves and in producing a social system and history that will validate these explanations. Germany is a classic example of one of these societies. For that reason, we treat the German consciousness as though it belonged to an artist, one who has deliberately constructed a pattern of historical meaning and events so that the beginning must imply the end. Throughout this book, we discuss why this was true for Germany and what this means.

We have said that the structures within a society reflect and present the values and meaning of the entire system, that is, each component part of a society has a homologous relationship to every other one as well as to the whole. Another way of saying this is that each social feature, or level—for example, the political institutions developed to carry the society forward, the pattern of social life, the very buildings erected to house social and political activity, the style and shape of social myths and the configurations of historical action—each one of these carries the stamp of the total social enterprise.

. . . What the aesthetic and structuralist approaches suggest is that we may refine the various levels of society—levels that on the surface appear quite different and unconnected—and after extracting the essential pattern of each, we should find comparative logics and meanings. We have tried to make comparisons of this kind throughout the book. We examined, simultaneously, certain patterns in German history (for example, Bismarck's wars of consolidation, the World War I Schlieffen plan and Hitler's blitzkrieg) and certain patterns in popular art (e.g., the use of the feudal myth); after studying each we compared them to see if they were translatable into each other and, therefore, shared a commonality of perception and meaning.

We discovered not only that a translation between German history and art was possible but that the Nazis had deliberately intensified the feedback between the two. This feedback was, it turned out, the basis for their propaganda; it allowed them to aestheticize reality and historicize myth. But we also found that this impulse to aestheticize reality was itself a basic element in the meaning of German history, even before the emergence of Hitlerian propaganda.

Maurois offers a hint as to what this aesthetic impulse may mean when he says that we need narrative fictions "because our real life is passed in an incoherent universe. We long for a world subject to the laws of the spirit, an ordered world. . . . From the novel we seek a universe which will help us, wherein we can seek emotions without exposing ourselves to the consequences of authentic emotions. . . ." This, too, was the purpose of the aesthetic in Germany. It became clear to us that the Germans needed an aesthetic reality because they felt they lived in a totally incoherent universe, a universe in which they were uncertain about their national identity and, thus, uncertain about their individual public identities. In short, they felt vulnerable. This vulnerability is expressed in German history (the mixture of fascination with and fear of a second front woven into the battle plans mentioned above) and was also expressed in popular art (the continual images of a feudal kingdom). What linked the history and the art was this common expression of vulnerability—what we have called "the myth of the feudal kingdom under siege." And what was characteristic of this expression in all its permutations and elaborations was—as Maurois says—an attempt to "seek emotions without exposing [oneself] to the consequences of authentic emotions. . . ." In this, one finds the essential meaning and nature of German propaganda.

We have said that, to find out whether one level of German society could be translated into another, it is necessary to refine the levels of German society. This is a process of reduction and simplification that attempts to condense the variety and diversity of the social mixture until the nonessentials have been left behind, leaving only the fundamental elements in their purest form. The task, then, is to discover the equation that will link them together. Since this process of reduction, simplification and condensation is also the method of German propaganda (a method which became the content of Hitler's Aryan doctrine), and since the purpose of the totalitarian system was equally to translate one level of society into another (in this case to make individuals interchangeable), it seems important from the beginning to understand what this process entails.

We may call the equation that links social or cultural elements together a cultural metaphor, for it functions in the same way a literary metaphor does: one starts with the perception of dissimilarity and then attempts to discover a yoke which will creatively bond these dissimilarities together. In such a definition of metaphor, we stay within the limits set by Aristotle's observation that metaphor is "the perception of the similarity of dissimilars." [1] We must also remember that a metaphor is not necessarily static; it is susceptible to permutations. But no matter how much the surface of a metaphor seems to change, its basic elements remain constant. What is more, the relationship among its elements remains fixed. (Thus one may write: $A + B = C$ or $A = C - B$ or $B = C - A$ or even $C = A + B$.) Each formulation has a different emphasis, suggests a different priority, but the values remain the same. Hence, although the specific point of balance or outer configuration of a metaphor may change, the basic distance and tension of the elements cannot change. Applied to a study of culture, this means that an important clue to the meaning of a culture is to be found not only in the basic metaphor—its basic elements—but also in the shift in balance and in emphasis between the elements of that metaphor.

This clue suggests an interesting problem. The elements a society is attempting to balance turn out to be surprisingly limited in number. A satisfactory balance does not seem impossible to develop, the permutations are many but not infinite; yet the balance between these elements is never quite achieved—except perhaps in primitive societies. First one side of the equation and then the other has too much weight, too disproportionate an emphasis. We begin to notice that the elements that are so precariously balanced are often the culture's most bothersome "dissimilars," its most crucial concerns. A perpetual imbalance built into a cultural metaphor raises an important question: Is the imbalance itself critical to the meaning and purpose of the metaphor? (The nature of Germany's metaphor seems to indicate that the answer is yes, although Germany's effort to construct a viable cultural metaphor was motivated by the conscious wish to do away with this imbalance.)

The implications of this question can at least be partially answered by returning to Aristotle's definition of metaphor. His view assumes that the fact of dissimilarity always remains even after the metaphor has been made, for it is only in the marriage of dissimilars and the resulting tension caused by this marriage that the making of metaphor has value. Therefore, if the metaphor were totally successful in achieving a permanent unity, thus absolutely destroying the ability to perceive disparity, it would also destroy its reason for being. With this reading, Aristotle's definition becomes a description of the nature and structure of thought, especially post-Aristotelian thought: the mind does not wish to create a finished unity, although it appears to be striving after it; it reaches instead for perceptions that counterfeit unity. The very virtue of cultural metaphors lies in their ability to counterfeit unity while at the same time being able to take advantage of the dynamism of built-in imbalance.

When we pick up German history in 1890 with the removal of Bismarck from power, we soon perceive that under Bismarck the German metaphor had become frozen and therefore useless. It is in the peculiar nature of cultural metaphors like Germany's—informed as it was by the vision of vulnerability—that successful stabilization of dissimilars threatens their societies more than imbalance. A culture's reason for being is imperiled. The problem with Bismarck's solution was that he had too completely managed to control the dissimilarities; he provided a unity so total that it seemed to be counterfeit. It lacked luster; it had lost its inherent tension. Hence Bismarck's unity seemed merely spurious and empty.

Germany under Wilhelm II moved back toward the logic of vulnerability and imbalance. And because it did, it could also renew its search for unity. As we shall see, Germany's concept of unity affected both the style of its history and the facts of its historical existence. The attempt to make unity led to Germany's manifestly artificial and theatrical political style. And paradoxically, the concern for unity brought Germany to the disunity and dislocations of World War I. It appears that Germany could afford unity—and then lushly and extravagantly—only when the dynamics of imbalance were in motion; that is to say, when unity did not threaten stability. (We do not discuss Hitler here—although obviously he would fit in quite nicely—because we will consider his experiments with the unity of artificial forms in some detail later in the book. But we should say in passing that Hitler and Goebbels as well as the Nazi propaganda machine were the first to recognize that propaganda must provide order and instability at the same time, if it was to be successful.)

Thus far, we have simply tried to sketch out the general manner in which the aesthetic method approaches a social system. But it may be worthwhile to stand back for a moment in order to collect any of the assumptions and implications of our method that may remain hidden. First, we assume that reality (or, quite loosely, the flux of events in the past and present) is to be perceived and understood in the way we understand any art form. Thus we look for its symmetries and asymmetries, its leitmotivs or archetypes, its world view or vision and its metaphors and their variations.

But how do we begin to find these patterns? We start with a set of ground rules: we may exclude one detail in favor of another, since there could be no meaning if we were surrounded by an array of details, each of which had equal claim upon our attention. Hence we begin to select. We try to recognize those details that have similarities or that are in some way identical, and then we try to organize them. We sift out the "relevant" details from the "irrelevant" and subordinate one fact to another. Finally we put together a structure in which the parts do not contradict the whole, in which the logic is consistent, in which the obscure has been given meaning because it is informed by order. All this time we have worked with the belief that if we could remain objective and consistent and honest about what we saw, we would discover a truth inherent in the details that we have been sorting through. Have we discovered truth? Perhaps, but certainly a truth. Still we must wonder, did we discover this truth or did we create it? If the man at work is an artist, one says he has created a truth—but with artists, one does not quibble over words. On the other hand, if he is a historian we insist that he has made a discovery—or else he must be a charlatan.

We must stick with this mock argument because it takes us very near a serious question that has been hovering behind our discussion. "What is a novel? Very simply, a narrative of fictitious happenings." If we accept the historian as a creator, an artist, it seems that we shall have to say that history too is "a narrative of fictitious happenings" and that reality is also fictitious.

There is, however, another route through this maze, the one taken by Henry James. When faced with this question in the course of discussing the art of fiction, he said "the novel is history." He then went on to say that the view that holds the novel is "making believe," or is composed of fictitious happenings, is a view which "implies the novelist is less occupied in looking for the truth (the truth, of course I mean, that he assumes, the premises that we must grant him, whatever they may be) than the historian. . . . To represent and illustrate the past, the actions of men, is the task of either writer. . . ." [2] Henry James solves the problem, then, by making art a vehicle for truth, a truth no less true than that of the historian. Reality—at least what we can know of it—appears safe; it is not to be relegated to the realm of fictitious happenings.

Nevertheless upon reconsidering James's statement—"the truth, of course I mean, that [the artist] assumes, the premises that we must grant him, whatever they may be . . ."—we find that we are back where we started, with the question of objectivity; but we now find that our concept of reality has been drastically altered. If we *must* grant the artist his premises, *whatever* they may be, we have given to the artist, and the historian, an immense power over reality. Henry James, not surprisingly, knew this. In a letter to H. G. Wells, he writes: "It is art that *makes* life, makes interest, makes importance, for our consideration and application of these things, and I know of no substitute whatever for the force and beauty of its process. . . ." [3] And by "art" James means "form." Form has force *and* beauty! With that, we find the realm of aesthetics considerably enlarged to include not only history but also all systems of meaning, all constructs that depend upon order for their existence and value—hence even political ones, or for that matter logical ones.

Perhaps we go too far. But we do so intentionally. For, as we started by saying, we treat the German consciousness as belonging to a deliberate artist. We have, in part, already explained what we mean by this: that Germany *can* be analyzed in the way one analyzes a work of art. What we shall try to show in the course of this book is a more intriguing dimension to this problem—one that we have indicated was true in the case of Nazi propaganda: that the German consciousness treated its own reality—developed and lived its history—as though it were a work of art. It was a culture committed to its aesthetic imagination. And through this commitment, it extended and exaggerated the principles of the aesthetic beyond their original, self-contained universe: they became political statements, serving to prescribe as well as to describe. By Hitler's time aesthetic principles had become precepts like the following: life *is* form (or order); force *is* beauty; and force *is* meaning.

Obviously the effect of the aesthetic perception upon the perceiver is to reorient the perceiver's relationship to reality. Reality takes on a sensuous richness, for it, too, is now a work of art; all around him shines with new clarity. Still he is an observer, detached much in the way of a visitor in a museum. A logical (but not necessary) next step is for the aesthetic imagination to turn upon itself—upon the observer, thus making him into a work of art. But even when the observer sees himself a participant, he still retains his air of detachment. (This double perspective is not unlike that created for the audiences of modern dramas or reserved for characters within these dramas.)

To be both participant and observer—engaged and detached at the same time—changes the shape of reality. Reality is transformed into a drama in which the actors are permitted a heightened awareness of their own value and identity. In such consciously perceived drama, everything is pregnant with significance, full of connections and implications; every event becomes "a moment of truth" and every decision, an act of definition.

Pushed too far, the ability (or desire) to perceive reality aesthetically—as was the case in Germany—can be disastrous. It can lead to a distortion of the real, producing the grotesque and the surreal. It leads to the "reality" of propaganda where truth and identity become subject to the "force and beauty" of form; a kind of visual hypnosis results. But despite these dangers, the ability to perceive reality aesthetically is still essential to our ability to understand the meaning of reality and, in turn, to understand history. We must be able to stop the process and flux of reality—freeze it, stand back from it and ourselves—if we are to see the long-term implications of present decisions and events as well as to make some sense of the past.

Nevertheless, whatever the necessities (and virtues) of aesthetic imagination, there are obvious risks in using a methodology based upon aesthetic principles. The reader cannot help but be aware of the fact that our critical theory reinforces the very applications of aesthetic perception we intend to examine and to criticize. Such an overlapping of method and subject may seem a curious (or worse, futile) exercise. Yet such an exercise can, perhaps, be instructive, if only to make apparent the limits and implications of the critical language we are speaking.

To the degree that an aesthetic system reflects its own limits, it has parted company with the aesthetic system that makes possible propaganda and social manipulation. For as we shall see, propaganda deliberately tries to silence the internal, verbal and discursive dialogue we carry on with ourselves. We lose much without this discursive dialogue; we become victims in dramas we act in but cannot understand. If we can create a reflexive aesthetic, we are freed from the totalitarian threat that the aesthetic implies. We are, at once, aware of the methods by which form produces meaning and, at the same time, reminded that certain forms create and, thus, structure reality for us. . . .

Myth and Symbol: History Fulfills Itself

The mythic, like any statement, organizes meaning by highlighting and shaping details and by arranging them into a declarative plot. A myth explains the past, the present and the future, and its narrative shape establishes its historical reliability—or at least that is its purpose. But declarative or narrative form does not make every myth a truth, any more than it makes any other kind of statement true. In some cases, the mythic may be pure distortion, an invention whose purpose is to falsify the meaning of the past. Nevertheless some myths are fair interpretations of the past and recognitions of basic patterns (archetypal patterns) that appeared and will reappear when specific circumstances are present. There is a problem, then, in distinguishing a mythic invention from the legitimate recognition of an archetypal pattern. This difficulty is most particularly apparent in the case of Germany as it attempted to retain in some form its feudal identity.

Bismarck's model of Germany, for instance, was in some measure a solution to a real historical problem, a problem that Germany had faced in its feudal form and one that had been central in persuading the feudal kingdoms that a unified Germany was in their best interests. Before its unification, Germany had indeed been the victim of countless invading armies; therefore it had a long memory of encirclement, siege and vulnerability. In quite reasonable response to this memory, Bismarck had constructed his centripetal, corporate system, erected his protective tariff walls and developed his subtle isolationist diplomacy. His wish had been to create a walled fortress which would be able to withstand siege if attack could not be avoided, and which would be able to satisfy its internal needs while the siege lasted. He envisioned a Germany that was self-contained and self-sufficient.

When the confusions of German society weakened Bismarck's system, Wilhelm's response to the memory of former invasions was simply to reverse the centripetal direction of the German state. This produced an expansionist, centrifugal state that still retained the old grammar of vulnerability, encirclement and siege. But now, in place of preventive diplomacy and a self-contained economy, Wilhelm and his ministers lowered tariff walls, planning to replace them with the walls of empire. The new colonies were to extend the enclosure, so as to include within it a new source of raw materials and a new market for finished goods. And instead of preventive diplomacy, Wilhelm and his ministers talked of preventive wars as the solution to the threat of invasion.

In comparing these two political models, we can see that the dissimilarities belie their fundamental unity. Germany was, after all, vulnerable. It was surrounded by powerful and established nations who had been tempted by the ease with which German fragments could be scooped up, and Germany's history of invasions showed that this temptation was often indulged. While both of these models tried to offer political and economic solutions to this long-standing German problem, the solutions they offered—rather ironically—only perpetuated and sometimes accelerated the crisis of vulnerability. Bismarck's unification of Germany and his establishment of an empire—whatever his intentions—pushed Germany right into the circle of the powerful and now suspicious neighbors it had been trying to avoid: France, Russia and Austria-Hungary. Wilhelm's expansionist policies inexorably led to the confrontations of the First World War. One might add—to continue this progression of self-induced vulnerabilities—that Hitler's strategies produced not the thousand-year Reich but the very sort of disaster he (and Germany) had tried to escape.

Germany's long-term history suggested an archetype, the recurring image of which the Germans were quick to recognize. The perpetual German dread, the glance over the shoulder at the enemy who may be about to attack, has its most distinctive formulation in Wagner's *Ring* cycle, in which the infamous "stab in the back" is administered to heroic Siegfried by a dwarfish and clearly alien Hagen. The theme is picked up by Hitler in *Mein Kampf* in his explanation of the German defeat of 1918, where once again, it seems, "the warring German Siegfried received a stealthy stab in the back." [4] This fear was written into the strategies of both the First World War Schlieffen plan and the Second World War blitzkrieg: in each, the central aim was to neutralize the western front with sufficient dispatch so that Germany could turn to protect its exposed rear. The hysteria of an enemy at its back, thus, lead to the fantasy of "three-week" fronts. When Germany raced west, it did so with a distracted, and distracting, foreboding of an enemy in the east.

In Germany, one discovers that a set of historical facts has developed into a mythic declaration with a prophetic power. The logic of such a process is simple and circular: Events and situations require explanation. Explanations—universalized, generalized and given imaginative flesh—become myths. Myths shape perception. Perceptions produce policies. Policies cause events and situations. And (to begin again at the beginning) events and situations require explanation. How *can* one separate the beginning of the circle from the end, the mythic invention from the archetypal situation, or the fabrication from the candid recognition of a geopolitical fact? They share a self-perpetuating cycle. The first feeds the last, and the last vindicates—and reinstates—the first. This cycle is what Freud meant by "the self-fulfilling prophecy"—the manufactured statement that creates historical circumstances, thereby validating itself.

For Germany, the original, historical vulnerability of the divided states called for a larger, more protective nation-state. But once established for this reason, it continually returned to situations that would justify its existence by reconfirming its vulnerability. Solutions seem to demand the old problems, else what is the value of the solution? Hence, Germany's need to confirm its national meaning made vulnerability an essential part of its continuing myth, for it was the original pattern of vulnerability that informed Germany's concept of "nationhood." To subtract vulnerability from the equation would have demanded an entirely new definition of the term "nation." Of course, this process of national confirmation through weakness cut across the major purpose of the myth's rhetoric, which was to give to the nation a vision of heroism, energy and success. On one hand, the myth presented the role of hero; on the other, it required the condition of victim. Some way had to be found to join these contradictions.

It was necessary to produce minds or perceivers who would not perceive the contradictions. And to do this, it was necessary for Germany to break with the present, to make impossible a reading of the present that exposed the realities hidden there. Germany had to dwell in the past if it was to escape the meaning of the present; yet even this past had to be treated in a special way, or else it might signal truths Germany could not afford to hear. The past that Germany entered could have no present, because the present reminds one of the events of the past that have made this particular present what it is. (We have seen that this was Wilhelm's problem in his position of real political figure.) A recognition of the relationship between past and present would have made clear to Germany the logic of its myth; and it was precisely this logic that Germany did not wish to understand: that to be a hero it had first to be vulnerable; that to fulfill its myth and desires it had first to be degraded and betrayed by them.

A number of attempts were made to portray the German myth. Each did in a way manage to enunciate its unique integrity without exposing the implications of its larger logic. And although each was only partial, each deepened the meaning and fascination Germany had for its slowly crystallizing mythic statement. Conservative social critics like Julius Langbehn and Moeller van den Bruck, for example, looked to the past for meaning, but they made the mistake of trying to use that past to explain the details of the present and, thus, returned to the present even as they tried to escape it. They catalogued evidence which seemed to them to prophesy the imminent collapse of Germany. Yet in direct contradiction to their sense of Germany's inevitable doom, they were able to prophesy that salvation and glory were somehow immanent in the facts of Germany's present. Fritz Stern in speaking of their work remarks, "It was as if their own Jeremiads on the real evils of the present so frightened them that they were forced to project a future or a regeneration beyond all historical possibility." [5]

Richard Wagner provided Germany a mythic reality of another sort, a reality that totally excluded the present. Through the elaborations of his operatic plots as well as through the experience of seeing them performed in the hermetic and florid environment of Beyruth, Wagner gave his audiences an opportunity to escape from present time in an artificial cycle of fixed history. He was the artist of Germany's dream. Yet despite this total Wagnerian environment, his audience did finally have to leave the theater. His theatrical reality could only be suggestive, a moment free from history and outside the struggle and confusion. The proscenium was still there. Beyond Beyruth was still the historical Germany.

Hitler's contribution to the process we have been considering was to take Beyruth's aesthetic drama and make it into an explicit, national drama. He is different from Bismarck and Wilhelm II in that the content of their myths was always just below the surface—an implicit symbolic drama. Hitler treated the myths openly, as if they were self-evident truths. And he is different from writers like Langbehn, Moeller and Wagner in that he would satisfactorily (or persuasively) translate aesthetic roles into the public reality.

In Hitler's favor was the fact that when he emerged, Germany was in a state of extreme and real crisis. Its defeat in the First World War, the resulting breakdown of the social structure and the economic collapse had wiped away virtually all possibility of perpetuating earlier social roles. The unsatisfactory identities that had been maintained by tradition and habit were destroyed with the destruction of the social and economic order. Poverty and chaos are in that way great levelers; few identities or roles remained which could pull individuals back into a historical past. At the same time, the prophesied doom had come. By the time Hitler came to power, the German search for unambivalent social roles had become an absolute necessity. The historical present and the mythic past had for a moment converged (one might think that Germany, in fact, had unconsciously made them converge).

Hitler believed in the power of the aesthetic but took the aesthetic one step further than Langbehn, Moeller or Wagner; he believed reality could be treated like any theatrical form—susceptible to fabrication and manipulation. And he not only believed in the ability to fabricate but in the power of fabrications to be real. ("The Greatness of a lie always contains an element of being believed." [6]) Thus he was able to stage ceremonies, know the details of their construction, and yet still be pleased and surprised by the organized ovations and cued adulations. He was not caught in a self-awareness that forced him to see that his reality was his own fabrication. He had become a propagandist of self—one who could create a dramatic role and identify without remembering how it had been done—and it was this model he presented to the Germans and to Germany.

Mein Kampf was his experiment with himself. In it he created a biographical, or past, self. At the same time *Mein Kampf* projected a living self—the Hitler who lived concurrently with the audience that read the biography. The function of this living self was to fulfill the prophetic voice of the biography; in turn, the function of the biography was to establish the authenticity of this living Hitler. Hitler's experiment was to merge the historical tense and the present tense in order to move beyond the historic into the mythic.

The relationship of the *Mein Kampf* Hitler to the living Hitler is similar to the relationship of the Old Testament Messiah to the New Testament Christ; one vindicates the other. Like other "religious" scripture, *Mein Kampf* is an attempt to merge documentable history with undocumentable myth, an attempt which makes myth documentable and present history mythic. When the documentation becomes—as it did in the case of Hitler—the underpinning of myth, the net effect is that reality can become a self-contained event. It is no longer related to, or changed by, the passing of time. And it is this timelessness, an escape into the mythic, that Hitler gave to Germany.

He made programmatic the various versions of the feudal myth that had existed before him and constructed the drama with a simplicity that made obvious and self-evident the roles to be played. Every defeat, every failure, was a justification and a vindication. The history of defeat was redeemed, by itself becoming a myth that was being fulfilled in each moment of the present. The feudal kingdom was encircled and under siege, would, in fact, always be under siege. This continuous threat of a potentially tragic end hidden in every moment made every role significant and every defeat promising.

With Hitler's success at fabricating and projecting a myth, Germany concluded the undertaking begun by Wilhelm II. On one level, Germany had settled finally on the content of its social drama; it now had a clearly visualizable set of roles and diagram of actions. But equally important is the style this drama took. It was increasingly characterized by high melodrama and accentuated theatrics, especially apparent during the Hitlerian period, when the German myth was articulated through a series of mass-rally performances.

Germany's theatrical style grew directly out of its confusions and its search for identity. Such theatricality is, in fact, one of the chief symptoms of a society undergoing an identity crisis. This is natural enough, for societies in attempting to define themselves become extremely self-conscious. Their dialogue is cluttered with discussions of "national purpose" and "national heritage and tradition"; they scrutinize their "culture," consider whether they have one and what it might be. While to some degree salutary, such public soul-searching can be debilitating because it intensifies the very crisis being explored. Social self-consciousness imposes a proscenium on the society as well as the citizens. And in the case of the individual citizen, he feels as if he were "on stage," plagued by a numbing sensation that he is only an "actor," but uneasy because he has a role still to discover.

Societies have deliberately taken advantage of this need for roles, especially in times of crisis, when the weakness of identities is most obvious. They construct new social identities not only to stabilize the individuals within their community but also to limit the number of roles available. This limitation is most important to societies in stress, since it makes social regulation and control easier. They are helped in this control by the citizens themselves. Once an individual has found an acceptable role, the general confusion and his private ambivalence tempt him to be no more than the role requires. For this reason, even though a national scenario may be coercive and repressive (as it ultimately was in Germany), it appeals to individuals because it guarantees coherence and form. In this cycle, we witness a self-regulating system, one in which the weakness of social and political identity brings on a crisis and the crisis manufactures new identities, albeit simplified ones. Generally, in fact, it is this extreme simplification of the social drama that we associate with totalitarian socieities: they are unitary and one-dimensional dramas in which everyone is asked, and most agree, to play the same part.

While it is true that such simplified social dramas can be caused and maintained by an intensified self-consciousness, it does not, of course, necessarily follow that all societies betraying self-consciousness are (or will become) totalitarian. The question at issue is how the society meets its self-consciousness and its need for drama. Nontotalitarian societies treat what we can call "theatrical uneasiness" as a symptom of cultural neurosis; they use it as a means to diagnose, locate and correct the neurosis and, thus, themselves. Totalitarian societies are encouraged—perhaps encourage themselves because their crisis is so paralyzing—to make a social virtue of the theatricality of self consciousness; they program it into the system in such a way that the neurosis is institutionalized. What started as the symptom is now taken for the cure.

Germany is a good example of a society in which theatricality was institutionalized. We have already seen a portion of this process unfold in the theory of men like Langbehn, Moeller, Wagner and Hitler. The view of reality behind that theory together with that contained in the heightened sense of social drama we have just considered merged in Germany in a common proscenium—an aesthetic frame for reality that was imposed upon the normal political rhythms. The effect of a dramatic proscenium is to isolate men and institutions, then freeze them into rigid shapes, and finally to separate them from their normal backdrops. Individuals become artifacts, purposeful constructs that can be coaxed, controlled, manipulated and dismantled—treated in the same way raw material is treated by a craftsman.

In such an arena, a curious thing happens to the forms of reality: they become palpable. One sees them in three dimensions with rich and vivid substance. And as a result, one's sense of "meaning" and "truth" is altered. Truth, now based upon a version of optical experience, becomes equivalent to visual symmetry; and the mark of reality is an object's starkness. No longer following its normal continuum in reality, the object is "framed." Its viewer suddenly is aware of it as form, a self-contained dramatic event, and feels as though he is "seeing" it for the first time. The time within the frame is similar to that of theater. As with theater, the presentation is in present time—the ongoing time of the audience's normal world—but the performance engages the audience in a fixed pattern of time that can be played over and over again. This explains why the aesthetic is so perfectly suited to the institutionalization of a mythic past.

We have said that the imposition of aesthetic space upon social reality springs from a cultural self-consciousness, caused by the insufficiency of public and private roles. This is true, but such self-consciousness itself is rarely brought to a verbal or discursive level; frequently it remains submerged exactly because the process that brought these symptoms on is one which the society cannot afford to face. There is, after all, a difference, and a crucial difference, between being victimized by self-consciousness and being able to liberate oneself from it by understanding what it implies. However, even when the existence and oppressiveness of self-consciousness cannot be admitted, it (and the crisis that produced it) is expressed in a crypto-language—a symbolic code—that releases and works out the conflict without having to recognize its presence.

The symbolic is a drama in its own right, but not one its participants are conscious of being involved in; hence it is not the mythic statement a society articulates to explain itself. In fact, the symbolic drama determines social behavior without being the explicit or historically apparent cause for such behavior. If this is so, a symbolic reading of history requires a somewhat different relationship to historical facts and causes than is normal. For example, when individuals commit themselves to certain political acts or groups with a reasoned sense of what their commitment entails, one usually starts by assuming that their rationality has tried to take into account the political and social consequences of their decisions—they knew what they wanted and were acting to achieve it. Yet often a set of conscious decisions of this sort produce circumstances that are at odds with the original political intent. One may say at this point that the reason of the individuals acting was insufficient to understand the political realities. But when this happens consistently with an individual or a nation, one may choose to find instead another drama at work beneath the explicit surface, a drama which has nothing to do with "political realities." Thus, as we have tried to show, Wilhelm's actions mean one thing on a political level but imply an entirely different set of meanings beneath the literal surface. Wilhelm did not let the treaty with Russia lapse *in order to* make Germany vulnerable again; at least consciously, his intent was the exact opposite. For him the act made simple political sense. With the distance of historical vision, one can see that the act made no political sense but a great deal of symbolic sense.

We must stop here for definition. One cannot undertake a discussion of *the symbolic* without making certain distinctions, since the term, unfortunately, is muddied, having accumulated at least two meanings. The first denotes the visible agent that serves to reflect a hidden system of values, and the second stands for the hidden system of value itself. Thus the term *symbolic* expresses two quite different, although connected, levels of apprehension.

To make plain what these two meanings entail, suppose we imagine that reality can be simplified into a three-dimensional diagram, whose surface we can call our literal reality. Being on this surface, we can only guess as to the texture and composition of the internal material. But this substructure is important, for it not only supports but also molds the contours of the surface. So although we cannot get in immediate touch with this core, we still wish to find a way to get at least an indirect view of it. The literal reality is not useless; it does offer some help in determining what we wish to know. It is studded (at least we may imagine this is so) with jewel-like excrescences, bubbles that clarify the surface. And like prisms, they permit us to glimpse beneath the surface. What is confusing here is that the term *symbolic* can be applied equally well either to these prismatic agents or to the substructure. In the first case, a portion of literal reality (the prisms are, after all, on the surface) is designed as *the symbolic*. In the second case, *the symbolic* is only what can be seen indirectly.

By calling these prisms *symbols,* we are stressing their function to refer to the nonexplicit, their character as agents—that is, we stress their ability to "symbolize" meaning or, to use French structuralist vocabulary, to be "signifiers." In this sense, the Nazi swastika is symbolic; it is an explicit object that clearly represents a set of values. In the same way, the German Michael—the feudal knight figure in German art—is symbolic; it was for Germans a conscious representation of the myth they had adopted. According to this definition, a symbol reverberates with obvious significance. In fact, it is this ability to be so obvious in its prismatic function that makes it symbolic.

When we call the substructure symbolic, we are stressing what is referred to: what is implicit rather than explicit or, again to use structuralist vocabulary, what is being signified.'' The difference between these two meanings is the difference between stating that the figure of the knight Michael symbolizes Germany's conscious use of the feudal myth and stating that this figure with its peculiarly German configuration *signifies* a part of a cultural drama—that part in which Germany, unconsciously attempting to divest itself of history, tried to give itself a childlike identity.

It is perhaps already evident that in this book the primary meaning of symbolic is the latter one—the unconscious cultural drama. Thus Germany's symbolic drama is not its explicit statement of the feudal myth, although the explicit may run parallel in form with the symbolic. Instead, the symbolic is the underlying structure of attitudes and desires signified by the particularly German implementation of the myth.

Symbolic drama of this type permits little or no detachment. One participates in it by being within the act, the word or the gesture—in short, by being *within* the drama. Consequently, it operates at the level of pure presence, pure act, pure word. And by not allowing consciousness, it is able to exist prior to the awareness of structure, even prior to its actual embodiment in structure. The identity it provides is the identity that *adheres* to the participant as he fulfills the *inherent* intention of his language or action. On this view, the symbolic is a rather silent force which nevertheless has a singular power to affect *who* one is.

The symbolic is a gentle and subliminal persuader. Its nature seems to place it in a direct conflict with the hard-edged awareness of the aesthetic. But this need not be the case; the aesthetic may, in fact, be but one more extension of the symbolic drama. We can return to an earlier discussion of the aesthetic to make this point clear. It has been observed that the aesthetic effectively sealed Germany off from the consequences of its history. If we are correct in contending that a part of the content of Germany's symbolic drama was the creation of a child-like identity free from the restrictions of guilt, time and experience, the aesthetic in satisfying this impulse also satisfies the symbolic. The same relationship between the symbolic and the aesthetic can be found in the aesthetic's ability to make neurotic self-consciousness into an acceptable private and public style. When serving to make the neurotic acceptable, the aesthetic serves the primary function of the symbolic, which is to create an integrated set of identities. To put it perhaps too baldly, one may read back through the aesthetic—even an aesthetic which denies permanent identities by projecting a world of make-believe—and find on the other side the shapes of symbolic dramas and their meaning.

In a review of the propaganda of Hitler (and here one must include Goebbels), one can see how this subtle interplay between aesthetic and symbolic fitted the requirements of the Nazi totalitarian state. By first aestheticizing the symbolic drama (making the buried pattern of German culture explicit), Hitler produced perceivable forms which he had control over. He could tailor them to his needs. When he later made the proscenium inherent in the aesthetic almost invisible by making consciousness (or reflective thought) a crime against the state, he returned these forms to their subliminal condition—but now they had his stamp upon them. Because he was able to control the proscenium, he was also able to produce roles that settled the confusion over identity but destroyed the possibility of autonomous, private identities. In this way he substituted for self-conscious identities one-dimensional roles.

How did Hitler manage to collapse the proscenium and yet maintain control over the material in it? Goebbels' edict forbidding art criticism is a classic example of the principles of Nazi propaganda in operation: "The reporting of art will take the place of . . . art criticism. . . . The critic is to be superseded by the art editor. The reporting of art should not be concerned with values, but should confine itself to description. Such reporting should give the public a chance to make its own judgments, should stimulate it to form an opinion about artistic achievements through its own attitudes and feelings." [7] The effect and purpose of this edict *was not* (one must say this categorically even before discussion) to "stimulate" the formation of opinions; its purpose was the opposite, to stifle judgments. Neither was its purpose to liberate the audience from the tyranny of the critic. When it is dangerous to be a professional critic, it is equally dangerous to be a critical member of the audience. For both the critic and the audience, reportage became a general condition.

The principle underlying Goebbels' edict was to denerve consciousness by neutralizing the act of seeing. The act of seeing was to become a stony gaze instead of remaining a way of perceiving—and conceiving. This meant that visual information was to pass through the eye in the form of sensory data, but it was no longer to be mediated by the mind. The eye (and the mind's eye) were to be transformed into simple glass windows, incapable of refraction. The net effect of this was to make the mind itself incapable of reflection. Seeing had, under Goebbels' edict, been changed into a pure act—an act no longer conscious of itself.

This condition stimulates not opinions but passive voyeurism; it creates not evaluators but passive observers. Under the kind of pressure suggested by Goebbels' edict, the intellect, no longer inclined to perform its analytical function, disappeared. And when it went, so went the capacity to absorb visual information while being aware that one is absorbing it. And so also went all the uniqueness of the mind that makes autonomous identity possible. The Germans were within the drama, unaware that there was a drama—neither able to assess it nor able to reject it. It simply was.

The Nonverbal and the Symbolic:
We Are What We Observe and
We Do What We See

Symbolic dramas are expressed in a number of ways. We have already considered some of them: the pattern of "real" historical events, the mythic statement that is formulated to explain these events, and the "style" and form of a culture. One more social expression of the symbolic—the one that ties together these others—is the nonverbal; it is the means by which a culture projects the invisible drama onto a literal stage and does so without making the drama explicit.

Clothing, buildings, gestures and oral inflections—all examples of nonverbal material—are a part of a grammar of meaning. But unlike verbal grammars, nonverbal meaning is transmitted through form, not through content. Because of this, the nonverbal is neither discursive nor logical; it is presentational. Put more impressionistically, the communication of nonverbal meaning occurs as an exchange of portraits or performances. Hence, nonverbal meaning is not communicated, as we often assume meaning must be, through the accumulation and logical connection of sequences of ideas. The operating principle at work here is: "We are what we do." This disavowal of the discursive and the logical makes the nonverbal appear far too limited to be taken seriously as an effective language system. But despite this, it can be (and is) a very powerful means of persuasion and coercion.

Since the nonverbal has no tangible argument, one cannot argue with it: there is nothing to disprove. And because its meaning cannot be paraphrased, it is difficult to destroy; one either employs it or one does not. It must be taken whole, complete and intact. For these reasons, the medium of the nonverbal is an effective way for a culture to train its young and to transmit its symbolic meanings. It provides a kind of cultural mirror; as one stands before it, one duplicates what one sees. These acts of duplication are both acts of communication and assertions of community; one not only exchanges information but also indicates that one wishes (or needs) to belong.

This process of duplication requires participation that is visible and concrete. But although its literalness links it with aesthetic reality, certain distinctions must be made. The aesthetic is above all a drama with a form that is clearly a statement. And participation in the aesthetic is something the actor is, on some level, aware of. The nonverbal, on the other hand, depends upon participation but does not make one conscious of oneself in the midst of acting nor aware of the symbolic values one's nonverbal language expresses. This is a difficult distinction to make; because the nonverbal is concrete, we often assume it is explicit—that it is what its form says it is. That this is not the case becomes clear when one recognizes that nonverbal forms change their values when we become aware of them, when we are conscious of using them.

What confuses matters even more is that dramas which are apparently aesthetic may offer both explicit and nonverbal forms of participation. Thus, one may enact a drama, wear a specific and labeling costume and strike a pose, knowing all the time what these forms are supposed to mean, yet be involved *within* another drama of participation whose forms and values remain invisible. To show how this is so, let us demonstrate this point by using a literary example, *Oedipus Rex,* a play whose very structure and meaning depends upon the tension between these two types of participation. The character Oedipus Rex knows he is in a drama of judgement and purgation as king and of self-discovery as an individual, but he cannot see that this very drama is the process by which he becomes culpable. This latter drama is one no one *within* the play can be successfully articulate about; only the *total* presentation of Oedipus' actions and statements can express it. Hence the incredible irony and suspense of *Oedipus Rex,* no matter how many times it is seen or read. To return to the context of German culture: the German soldier going to battle as a knight to defend the kingdom could not recognize that this role belied its "adult" character— that his nonverbal forms of participation happened to assert childhood rather than adulthood.

It should now be obvious that the nonverbal shares much with the symbolic in their common reliance upon mute and unself-conscious forms to transmit meaning and reproduce social values. And the fact that the nonverbal is tangible, in the way the symbolic is not, makes it a valuable aid in exposing the meanings and values that remain invisible and silent. . . .

Here one must examine individual figures and objects in order to see how they are presented. One must view clothing as if it were costume, architecture as if it were solely designed as backdrop and objects (guns, planes, horses, etc.) as if they were only props. It was necessary to consider the bearing and gestures of men. And it was also useful to guess at the kind of material houses and buildings were made of, or what it was to seem they were made of, and to see how they were put together, to notice their proportions, and so forth.

On the level of technical execution, the perspective or point of view of the pictures was studied. For instance in taking photographs, did the photographer use a low eye level or a high one, and to what effect? Also examined were the use of lighting and shadows; the use of space, the distance between the foreground and the background; and the effect of cropping—what was included, what had been excluded and why.

Finally we looked to see if an artist relied upon visual clichés that have a wider currency than those which are purely German. On one hand, there were artists who blended into their work visual patterns and textures from classical Western art. An example is the German photographer who used as the composing axis of his photograph the pastoral style of Millet's French Romanticism. In the foreground of his picture is a peasant in the pose of Millet's sower; in the background, a factory is placed against the horizon as in a Romantic painter's gothic conception of a distant, looming castle. What is distinctive in this picture is that, despite its Romantic ancestry, nature is not threatened by industrialization. A castle takes shape out of the smoke of the factory, and the farmer seems no less safe sowing in front of these new walls than he was in the older, agrarian, feudal world. The picture recognizes the power of this new force; in fact, the factory appears to engender itself out of the shrouds of smoke it produces. Nevertheless, the agrarian life remains untouched; it is an image of continued tranquillity. The general effect of the photograph is to include both the farmer and the industrial reality in the creative, yet polarized harmony of the German version of the Romantic myth.

On the other hand, there were artists who restricted themselves to distinctly German images when more common and universal visual clichés were available. The presentation of the mother figure, for example, tended to be bold, drawn with harsh lines and often out of proportion to the rest of the picture in a way that made the children by comparison seen dwarfed, diminished and isolated—this instead of the more traditional soft and balanced composition unifying mother and child.

After one had determined what each specific frame showed, it was then necessary to compare one series of images with another in order to see what forms, shapes and techniques they had in common. Here it became possible to fix the larger context, or drama, that gave the individual frames meaning. It was apparent, for instance, that Bismarck, Wilhelm II, Hindenburg, Hitler and popular drawings of the knight shared many of the same gestures, positions and often even the same facial expressions and lines about the mouth. Image after image had forms reminiscent of the feudal romance: buildings that looked like castles; houses that looked like peasant cottages; turbine factories that looked like fortresses; field whorehouses that looked like medieval icon wagons; and processions of flags and fields of tents that recalled chivalric lists. In the figure that represented the knight, one found that the eye level was often low, requiring the viewer to look up into the picture and, thus, up at the knight. The clothing of an individual acting the role of knight, even when it was relatively contemporary, was drawn or photographed to look stiff, shiny and inflexible as if it were armor; in some cases, when the material worn was soft, the posture and bearing of the figure was itself stiff and bent, as if the soldier were encased in armor.

Art and Propaganda: Making a Reality

By the time one has finished looking through the visual material of Germany, especially that of Hitlerian Germany, it is difficult not to be struck by its documentary clarity. One sees its pronounced visual texture and the planes of shadows that indicate three-dimensional space. In the perception of this documentary sheen, we are faced, once again, with the aesthetic sensibility at work on the surface of reality.

One remembers here the elaborate expense of energy, imagination and technological skill that was invested by the Germans in the documentation of their national experience—an expense that became more elaborate as Germany moved toward a totalitarian state. In one way their immense amount of visual documentary material simply suggests what we have contended earlier: that the Germans could never quite trust their national reality until it had been reaffirmed by an image they could visualize. But their use of the documentary style also reveals the clear understanding the Germans—in particular Hitler and Goebbels—had of the close connection between propaganda and visual matter. At the same time, their use of the documentary reflects the important contribution Germany made to the aesthetic principles of modern propaganda.

By being able to superimpose, for instance, the documentary style upon the visual displays of Nazi public celebrations, Hitler and Goebbels had at their disposal the authority of the documentary's objective and impersonal voice—a voice that ostensibly is so detached and impersonal that it is voiceless. Thus pseudo events like the Nuremberg Party Convention of 1934, presented in Leni Riefenstahl's film *Triumph of the Will,* although in themselves staged propaganda dramas, were made over into real historical events. Generally speaking, they were "real" because they were given the weight and substance that documentary style is able to provide.

But the process of constructing the credibility of a documentary can be a subtle one. *Triumph of the Will* is a good case in point. The Nazis called the convention with an eye to constructing an event that would have the permanence of history even as it was unfolding for the first time. To envision such an event requires an imagination which is able to picture the event *in advance* as if it were already history—that is, to see it as if it had already been documented. As Kracauer observes, "the Convention was planned not only as a spectacular mass meeting, but also as spectacular film propaganda.'' [8] For this reason it is difficult to locate the ''true'' event. How does one determine the true historical event when all the layers and perceptions of the event—including the production of the film—compose the event? For that matter, what does it mean to talk of ''documentary credibility'' in such a case? The completed film is as much a ''fact'' in the event as were those who participated. Perhaps the film is even more important than the participants, since its aesthetic requirements determined what the participants would do. One might say that it was, in fact, only with the completion and exhibition of the film that the event finally came into existence.

Triumph of the Will is an elaborate lamination consisting of surfaces upon surfaces—facts upon facts, events upon events—with each surface refracting the meaning of the surfaces beneath it. To begin at any one level is something of an arbitrary act, since each level is defined by the levels above and below it. However, for the moment, let us disregard the film as film in order to reconstruct what the camera itself saw. When we witness the ''event'' in place of the camera, we discover that we are looking at little but a series of aesthetic forms composed of the members of the Nazi party who were in attendance. They have been arranged and ordered so that we cannot help but be conscious of the artificiality of their stance. In addition if we had been in Nuremberg at the time of the convention, we would have witnessed carefully orchestrated choral recitatives, elaborately choreographed parades—one lasted for five hours without a break in the precision—and, finally, the obviously staged illumination of lights. What we would have seen is one human tableau after another.

Of course, it is always clear to the viewer—when he sees this event by watching the film—that all these effects have been arranged with the camera in mind. And this awareness explains, perhaps, the uneasiness felt by contemporary audiences when they viewed this film. As Kracauer contends: ''The deep feeling of uneasiness *Triumph of the Will* aroused in unbiased minds originates in the fact that before our eyes palpable life becomes an apparition—a fact the more disquieting as this transformation affected the vital existence of people. . . . This film represents an inextricable mixture of a show simulating reality and of German reality maneuvered into a show. . . .'' [9] But we miss the point and strategy of this film if we stop with this, assuming that the Nazi propagandists did not wish the German audience to recognize this very same thing: that the film (and the original staging, for that matter) was exactly this—''a show simulating reality and . . . German reality maneuvered into a show.''

To achieve this recognition, the film first presents its audience with a transparently artificial overlay of aesthetic forms which organized the human participants. There could be no doubt for the audience that what it was viewing were actors functioning within a role, rather than independent and autonomous human beings. Thus although the German audience might have started watching this film thinking it was going to see the ''reality'' of fellow Germans at a party convention, the effect of this layer of the film was to displace the expectations of ''reality,'' persuading the audience that what it was seeing was in some way unreal.

To make an audience aware of the unreal when it views ''reality,'' or what normally passes for its reality, is the true cutting edge of the propagandist's skill. He has understood the first tenet of the modern sensibility—and of modern art. (The "modern," for our purposes, is not simply the contemporary; it is continuous with the sensibility projected by writers like Machiavelli and Castiglione—those who wrote that peculiarly modern genre of tracts, the "how-to" books: "How to Be a Prince"; "How to Be a Courtier.") As we have seen, Henry James expressed this modern sensibility most succinctly: "It is art that *makes* life, makes interest, makes importance. . . ." What links the propagandist's art to that of James is their common understanding that without the form of art there can be no reality, or to say it another way, there can be no perception of a reality.

The awareness of "unreality" engendered by the German propagandists is an awareness that springs from a conciousness of forms. It is an awareness that fortifies the belief in a reality which exists only when it can be examined as form. This is to subscribe to a reality that is all composition, all structure. But this kind of awareness, rather than diminishing the sense of reality, reasserts it all the more.

On this point: A. J. Liebling, an American journalist, remarked once in a dispatch sent from the German front that a battle never seemed more "real" than when it evoked the memory of some John Wayne movie he had seen. This sensation is similar to what the tourist feels when he visits the Grand Canyon and finds that the scene is ready-made for his camera. As often as not, faced with such a prospect, he will write home on a picture postcard: "How picturesque it all is." By that he means two things: how like a picture *and* how real. Both meanings are true. The scene is real; and his camera—a device we use to authenticate—will document its reality. And of course, the scene is also ready-made; after all, it does appear on the obverse side of his postcard.

This tourist finds himself in a position parallel to the one Liebling found himself in, although the tourist may not be as aware of its restrictions and liabilities as was Liebling. He is a camera, a camera programed to take pictures of scenes he has been taught to recognize. And it will be impossible for him to recognize, appreciate or photograph any others. They simply do not exist since they cannot be perceived. (Taking this perceptual dilemma into account, Oscar Wilde quite correctly, albeit sardonically, observed that "the first duty of life is to be as artificial as possible." A writer like Henry James—and here one might add Flaubert—and propagandists like Riefenstahl can be said to hold a view that extends without distorting the logic of Wilde's epigram: the first duty of the artist is to make life as artificial as possible in order to make its reality, or *a* reality, more apparent.)

The effect of establishing a sense of the unreal in the audience of *Triumph of the Will* was to saturate that audience with forms, so that it could not escape the feeling that if there were no forms there could be no reality and no meaning. José Ortega y Gasset describes a similar effect when he writes: "The beauty of a painting does not consist in the fact, which is of no importance so far as the painting is concerned, that it causes us pleasure, but on the contrary we begin to think it a beautiful painting when we become conscious of the gently persistent demand it is making on us to feel pleasure." [10] This "gently persistent demand" is the power of the form upon us, and its power to make us feel or see is what draws our attention and validates its "reality." The beauty of art, or any form, is our recognition of this power. Our awe—and in some cases our fear—springs from its mastery over our feelings; our delight and fascination, from its ability to make us see.

It is this power of forms to which Riefenstahl pays tribute (and it explains both her title and technique) in *Triumph of the Will*. The German will, and identity, has finally emerged triumphant, ready to translate itself; it is now ready to master political reality. But this was only possible after Germany had discovered its form, its way of becoming visualizable. Hitler and the Nazi aesthetic provided this form; it is this discovery and its implementation which Riefenstahl "documents."

Her film, as it praises and renders the forms of the Nazi imagination, is also an encomium to propaganda. Again we find that the film delivers its praise on several levels. Within the film, Goebbels reminds his audience (both that of the convention and that of the film) of the virtues and successes of Nazi propaganda, thus praising the propaganda successes of the very spectacle he is participating in. Goebbels sees propaganda as a deep and unifying victory for the German people: it is not to him a devious or shabby political tool of the state that one must hide from the people. It is to be embraced. Riefenstahl, in re-presenting the aesthetic form of the convention within the aesthetic form of the film, celebrates not only the successes of the German will, Goebbels' propaganda and the party convention but also the success of her own film as propaganda. This is, itself, an *exemplum* of the will triumphant.

As our discussion of *Triumph of the Will* shows, to be caught up in an awareness of forms is to become increasingly engrossed in the details that make up these forms. Here a film like *Triumph* betrays its connection to the aesthetic traditions of surrealism and Dada art. Detail after detail accumulates; reality made unreal is supersaturated and intensified documentary realism. All of these—realism, surrealism and the documentary—depend upon the ability to reinforce a pattern of thought (one that post-Cartesian man is particularly susceptible to) which holds that whatever one sees clearly and distinctly must be true and, therefore, must also be real. When this inclination to accept a universe of details as real is merged with art that deliberately manufactures artifice, reality and pseudo reality become equivalent. An imitation Grand Canyon will do as well as the real thing—whatever the "real" thing, at this point, can be said to be. (Disneyland draws as many tourists sending postcards home as does the Grand Canyon; and what is more important, postcards from each probably say the same thing—how picturesque!) The result of this—be it through Riefenstahl's form or Disney's—is that one is no longer able to apprehend or perceive the existence of the fluid process we sometimes call reality, since it has no form and thus has no way of making itself visible.

A film like *Triumph of the Will* and what it photographs is the culmination of a long search for a coherent form and a coherent German identity. One way to understand Germany's history and its fascination with borders, frames and boundaries is to see this search as a series of aesthetic operations in which limits (that is, forms) were continually being drawn. The object of all this "drawing" was to exclude that which was not German and, thereby, create the perfect outline of the "true German." The theory at work here is that if one can exclude a sufficient amount of the non-German, one will ultimately come upon a definition which will say what it is to be German. But as can be seen, this process starts with negative space and negative definitions: the exclusion of what one is *not,* or senses one is not, rather than a positive set of definitions of what one is.

As the first step in this process of exclusion, Germany under Bismarck drew its feudal boundaries around one nation. Once this had been reasonably successful, Germany started to draw circles, such as Bismarck's Kulturkampf, within the German community itself in order to drain off the un-German characteristics. Each of these stages had a limited success, but *the* German was still not defined. The positive definition seemed always just beyond the present set of distinctions; and since, as we have argued, the Germans could not be satisfied by a negative series of definitions, they continued to pursue the course of boundary-making until they could hear the click of absolute certainty and absolute meaning. When Bismarck's centripetal system of consolidation proved unsatisfactory, Wilhelm's solution was to expand the circle into a new imperialism: the vision of a pan-Germany. Hitler's solution was to fuse the two systems; he tried both expansionism and concentration—the imperialism of his Aryan Germany and the concentration of his concentration camps. While it lasted, this double helix provided a satisfactory conclusion to the German search for identity through the search for form, a search that moves *between* a perception of what one is not and what one is.

NOTES

[1] *Poetics* XXII.

[2] "Art of Fiction," *The Portable Henry James,* ed. Morton Zabel (New York: Viking Press, 1965), pp. 394–95. Reprinted by permission of Charles Scribner's Sons.

[3] *Ibid.,* p. 489; James's italics.

[4] Adolph Hitler, *Mein Kampf,* trans. John Chamberlain *et al.* (New York: Reynal & Hitchcock, 1939), p. 912, reprinted by permission of Harcourt, Brace & World; cf. Peter Viereck, *Meta-Politics: The Roots of the Nazi Mind* (New York: Putnam's, 1965), p. 139.

[5] *The Politics of Cultural Despair* (Berkeley, Cal.:. University of California Press, 1961), p. 269. Reprinted by permission of The Regents of the University of California.

[6] Compare Arthur Koestler's short essay on this sentence, entitled "The Great Crank," in *The Yogi and the Commissar and Other Essays* (New York: Macmillan, 1967).

[7] Quoted in George L. Mosse, ed., *Nazi Culture* (New York: Grosset & Dunlap, 1966), pp. 162–63.

[8] Siegfried Kracauer, *From Caligari to Hitler* (Princeton, N.J.: Princeton University Press, 1947), p. 301.

[9] *Caligari,* p. 303.

[10] *The Modern Theme,* trans. James Cleugh (New York: Harper & Row, 1961), p. 45. Reprinted by permission of Revista de Occidente, S.A., Madrid.

34.

THE PRESENT STATE OF THE DOCUMENTARY

James Arnold

Despite the authentic claims of film as an art, the fundamental power of the medium, as Siegfried Kracauer and André Bazin recognized, is its ability to take you there, some place where you might not ordinarily go, or even want to go, to witness something that "really happened." This kind of trip has always been a basic aim of the documentary filmmaker, and developments in moviemaking technology have deepened the possibilities to a degree that is both exquisite and alarming. With only slight losses in ultimate quality, cameras and sound equipment have become portable (one man or woman can carry them anywhere), virtually foolproof (a well-coordinated layman can learn their intricacies creditably in a few hours), and unobtrusive (subjects, already conditioned to a camera-filled world, hardly notice them).

Filmmakers now have the physical capacity to observe and record every aspect of human life under the most difficult and confining conditions, with little fear of disturbing the "truth" of reality by the presence of their crew, lights, ponderous equipment, etc. (There may always be reasonable doubt about the camera-consciousness of subjects, especially if they are professionals used to being "on"; e.g., how really candid were the sequences on CBS's "60 Minutes" of Nixon and Humphrey in their hotelrooms watching themselves win the nominations?) At the same time, a permissive society has slowly broadened the legal and moral limits of documentary subject matter; the relaxation of old codes and taboos has had its impact on nonfiction as well as fiction films. Blessed with this double push toward freedom, most documentarists have been busy probing their new limits, lugging their new portable gear into previously unexplored territories. Their style (capturing reality without prejudging or altering its shape) is called *cinéma-vérité* and now dominates the whole field of the documentary; their subject matter has tended to be somewhat more bizarre and a great deal more personal.

This development has its sobering aspects. After all, the dream of the documentarist, who would watch and record through his lens all that is meaningful and significant in human life, is not so vastly different from the dream of the Peeping Tom. The difference is in the definition of what is meaningful and significant. The power to get and then show "almost anything" on film carries with it heavy responsibility, and a surprising amount of time at gatherings of film professionals (such as the annual Robert Flaherty seminars) is devoted to ethical questions. The impulses of conscience are strong, but so are the impulses of reporter, explorer, and showman which bring a man into the documentary profession in the first place.

Freedom in documentary also has its practical limits. There is a major built-in

---

Reprinted by permission from *Films 1968*, The United States Catholic Conference Film and Broadcasting Office.

inhibition in the nature of the market, which is chiefly distribution through televi-sion, schools, and libraries. Even the most liberal of these outlets (and National Ed-ucational Television and its Public Broadcast Laboratory have undoubtedly spurred the most adventuresome documentaries) maintain restrictions on content and even on style. The only alternative market is in theaters, where documentaries have never had great success without some special mass appeal (the sex and sadism of the *Mondo*-type films, the names of Dylan and Baez to carry a *vérité* film like *Don't Look Back*). The avant-garde documentarists, anxious for more freedom, are look-ing increasingly to theatrical distribution, a fact that is likely to push them toward more sensational subjects. An instructive example is the case of Allan King's *War-rendale*. Originally intended for Canadian television, it was never shown, perhaps partly because of its four-letter words, but chiefly because of its severe *vérité* style, which never allows a clear explanation of what is going on. Now it is being shown in theaters, where its honesty and lack of sensationalism will be a commercial hand-icap. (The history of *One Step Away,* rejected by NET-PBL as "too strong," is sim-ilar.) So the documentarist has freedom to "do" but considerably less freedom to "sell," and the latter is often crucial in raising money for his project in the initial stages.

On top of all this there is a continuing intramural struggle between more tradi-tional filmmakers (chiefly those working for and in the news departments of the networks), who want to absorb *vérité* techniques into the structure of the standard objective film report, and the new generation, who want to abandon "old-fashioned" and "restrictive" preconceptions and do all the fresh, exciting, and unpredictable things that *vérité* allows them to do. In McLuhanesque terms, the conflict is between those who see the documentary as a "hot" or structured package, with verbal interpretation of the visual realities, and those who see the documentary as "cool," unstructured, ambiguous, an image of reality that emo-tionally involves the viewer and forces him to his own subjective conclusions.

The argument has several roots. One is perhaps philosophical: does the filmmaker simply record reality, and let the structure of that reality control his edit-ing and selection of shots? Or is he an interpretive expert or artist, who imposes his own reactions and vision, and shapes his film to produce a specific emotional or in-tellectual effect? Another root is simply the ancient dispute between the journalist, who hopes to remain detached from the event and somehow explain it, and the filmmaker showman, who is more interested in shaking up his audience and making it undergo an emotional experience.

. . . In the old documentaries, the filmmaker discovered things and told you about them, much as the traditional artist does; in the new documentary, as in the new art, the viewer is presented with complexity and makes his own discoveries. The difference was amusingly exemplified at the 1968 Flaherty seminar, with the screening of young Jim McBride's *David Holzman's Diary*. This fictional feature which combines *vérité* with the styles of Warhol and Godard, purports to be a per-sonal documentary in which the filmmaker hero describes and films a whole week in his hectic life. When the film is over, the closing credits reveal it is fiction. The Flaherty audience of experts had been fooled and was now outraged. The insights they believed they had been discovering in "cool" fashion for themselves in Holzman's real life had actually been discovered by director McBride, who then served it up to them in a traditional "hot" fiction film.

Regardless of differences in approach, documentarists tend to measure achievement by their success in getting "new" or "impossible" footage. The films that excited them most in 1968 broke new ground because of both *vérité* equipment and their daring entry into previously uncovered subjects. The amazing thing about *Warrendale* is that King was able to get inside a small cottage and film intimate moments of affection and violence without noticeably falsifying them, an effect made possible only by months of rapport-building, hanging about and finally becoming "invisible" to children and staff. In *Titicut,* the triumph was mainly in getting all those incredible unstaged shots of unhumanity in a mental hospital. In Robin Spry's *Flowers on a One-way Street,* it was capturing on film the tragicomedy of a big city government (Toronto) hung up on its own procedural red tape, a matter (for Spry) largely of patience and good luck. In Lewis Freedman's *Interview With Ingmar Bergman,* only the rare footage of an English-language interview with the enigmatic Swede saved what was otherwise a muffed opportunity for enlightenment, and in Brian Moser's *End of a Revolution* there were the fascinating shots of Guevara and Debray in Bolivia, the hard-nosed comments by the Green Beret sergeant, and the unforgettable glimpse of the U.S. Ambassador playing croquet amid the intrigue.

By its nature *vérité* involves shattering some taboos, e.g., the vulgar language incidental to *Warrendale, Titicut,* and *Don't Look Back,* the nudity in *Titicut,* the drug use and lovemaking in *One Step Away.* But documentarists now also feel free, like many novelists, to detail the lives of marginal groups and social outcasts whose activities may be shocking and offensive to the general public. This may be done responsibly or exploitatively.

Long-range, however, the most mischievous documentary steps were via *vérité* into the private lives of ordinary people: the dehumanizing patient-objects of *Titicut,* the shallow men of the Duluth Lions Club in Arthur Barron's *Great American Novel,* the comical middle-class "soldiers" of the Pope's army in Canada's prizewinning *Avec tambours et trompettes,* the Wallace-admiring family in Elizabeth Farmer's *Hear Us, O Lord.* In these and many other similar films, one has the uncomfortable feeling that people, once persuaded to sign a legal release, are used as a source of sophisticated entertainment. In Lord Snowden's *Don't Count the Candles* real old people are used to demonstrate the misery of old age in a youth-oriented world. In *Birth and Death* we are obviously voyeurs at sacred private moments, and in *One Step Away* we are in a private bedroom watching a real husband make love to a real "other woman" while his wife looks on.

Some, perhaps all, of these films have social relevance and an aspect of legitimate public interest, but the line between useful knowledge and mere curiosity is inevitably fuzzy. Filmmakers fret over such problems, but usually avoid solving them. Thus Shirley Clarke confessed being "monstrous" to Jason in order to have him bare his soul on film, and worried about the film's effect on his life. But the resulting footage is truly harrowing and unique, and Miss Clarke could not resist either distributing it or touring the college circuit with it in person. Documentarists are disturbed also by older ethical problems, such as whether a camerman first photographs a "victim" or gives him first-aid and spoils the picture. At the Flaherty seminar, some were highly critical of Silverstein (*What Harvest for the Reaper?*) for simply following with his camera while a crew chief recruited black laborers he intended to exploit.

There have also been interesting experiments in cross-breeding documentary and fiction. Already mentioned is *David Holzman's Diary,* in which an utterly convincing *vérité* and "home movie" style, as well as large numbers of "real" people, are used to tell a fictional story. *The Great American Novel* was a unique attempt to gain modern documentation for the insights of two old novels ("Babbitt," "The Grapes of Wrath"), and John Ford's *Four Days to Omaha* (NBC "Experiment in Television") unsuccessfully tried to blend fiction with interviews of real Englishmen recalling the days before the Normandy invasion. Still another approach is that of French journalist Danielle Hunebelle, who uses real people to act out makebelieve situations. Her *Negroes Next Door* has whites in St. Louis improvising their impulsive reactions to the hypothesis that a black family is moving into their neighborhood. Some documentarists are also not above prodding reality a bit: e.g., in *No Vietnamese Ever Called Me Nigger,* David Loeb Weiss used an aggressive and pretty blonde interviewer in Harlem deliberately to arouse hostile responses to on-the-street questions about whether blacks were being fairly treated by the draft.

If these were the problems at the frontiers of documentary-making at the end of 1968, there are also brief observations necessary to describe the state of the genre in its more controversial forms back "in the mainstream":

1. Perhaps never has there been so much impressive (and largely unappreciated) work in the areas of wildlife and nature study which are always popular and seldom controversial: e.g., the brilliant ABC-Wolper Cousteau series, *Search in the Deep,* and the CBS-Wolper "National Geographic" series, especially Jeffrey Myrow's beautiful film on the national parks.

2. The film approach to the problems of race and cities was too often simply a collection of interviews with experts and endless confrontations and panel discussions. There was too little pictorial documentation. The best films on this subject were probably the *vérité Hear Us, O Lord* (NET-PBL), with its insight into backlash; William Greaves's more conventional but enlightening *Still a Brother* (NET), an examination of the black middle class; some of the expert compilation films in CBS' "Of Black America" summer series; and *Color Me Black,* Richard McCutchen's study (for NET) of student unrest at middle-class Howard University.

3. The responsible but dreary network series on urban problems were, with few exceptions, outdone in film expertise by several poetic explorations of cities in terms of their music and culture: e.g., Ed Spiegel's *Music of Chicago* for NBC's "Telephone Hour" series, which went *vérité* and was altogether a milestone in the history of musical documentary; *West Pole,* Ralph Gleason's survey of the new adult Pop culture in San Francisco; and Marc Brugnoni's sensitive *New York Night.* Urban renewal, perhaps the dreariest of city subjects, received fresh treatment in Manfred Kirchheimer's wordless yet profound *Claws,* the ultimate in "cool" docu-

mentaries which unfortunately has been shown so far only at the Flaherty seminar.

4. Religion has received little distinguished attention from documentarists, but in 1968 there were Stuart Schulberg's *New American Catholic* and its memorable use of the four-way split screen to record varying reactions to progressive movements in the Church, and Palmer Williams's hard-hitting but wordy *Business of Religion* (CBS). Best films in this category were probably Peter Adair's *Holy Ghost People,* a *vérité* study of Appalachian snake-handlers, and the highly praised, highly visual *Beggar at the Gates,* WBZ-TV examination of the problems of modern churches in turmoil.

5. Memorable compilation films included Jack Kaufman's three-hour version (for ABC-Wolper) of William L. Shirer's *Rise and Fall of the Third Reich,* the showing on NET of Paul Rotha's 1961 *Life of Adolf Hitler,* Harry Chapin's intelligent and cinema history-oriented boxing film, *The Legendary Champions,* and [*Point of Order*], Emile de Antonio's kinescope record of the traumatic Army-McCarthy hearings of 1954.

6. The special ability of film, aided by the close-up and most recently by *vérité,* to capture and reveal a personality, encourages an annual rush of portrait documentaries. The most interesting during 1968 were Thomas Teichman's pure *vérité* study of jazz bassist-composer Charles Mingus, Warren Forma's inspiring and highly visual sketch of Gordon Parks, and Dick Fontaine's extraordinary profile (for NET) of the complexity of Norman Mailer.

7. The most novel and courageous sports documentary of the year was John Sharnik's little-heralded *The Football Scholars* (CBS), which forthrightly detailed colleges' exploitation of high-school football stars.

8. If there were a prize for controversy, it would have to go to the opposing film reports on the violence surrounding the Democratic Convention in Chicago, *What Trees Do They Plant?* and *The Seasons Change.* These films, using the same events to come to opposite conclusions, amply demonstrate that "film truth" is a slippery thing. There was also CBS' *Hunger in America,* a brave network effort which may have made mistakes (picturing an infant victim of premature birth as dying of malnutrition) but achieved the kind of reformist impact dear to the hearts of social documentarists of all ages and philosophies.

9. Despite all the footage on Vietnam, there were only two outstanding war documentaries, Eugene Jones's *A Face of War* and Peter Watkins's *Culloden.* Watkins' bloody reconstruction (shown on NET) devastated the British "victory" and Bonnie Prince Charles Stuart with the ruthless hindsight of 200 years. It also showed that the documentary of "reconstructed history" is far from dead. Unfortunately, *A Face of War* did not receive the attention it deserved. A review of the film follows.

35.

TRASH, ART, AND THE MOVIES

Pauline Kael

Like those cynical heroes who were idealists before they discovered that the world was more rotten than they had been led to expect, we're just about all of us displaced persons, "a long way from home." When we feel defeated, when we imagine we could now perhaps settle for home and what it represents, that home no longer exists. But there are movie houses. In whatever city we find ourselves we can duck into a theatre and see on the screen our familiars—our old "ideals" aging as we are and no longer looking so ideal. Where could we better stoke the fires of our masochism than at rotten movies in gaudy seedy picture palaces in cities that run together, movies and anonymity a common denominator. Movies—a tawdry corrupt art for a tawdry corrupt world—fit the way we feel. The world doesn't work the way the schoolbooks said it did and we are different from what our parents and teachers expected us to be. Movies are our cheap and easy expression, the sullen art of displaced persons. Because we feel low we sink in the boredom, relax in the irresponsibility, and maybe grin for a minute when the gunman lines up three men and kills them with a single bullet, which is no more "real" to us than the nursery-school story of the brave little tailor.

We don't have to be told those are photographs of actors impersonating characters. We know, and we often know much more about both the actors and the characters they're impersonating and about how and why the movie has been made than is consistent with theatrical illusion. Hitchcock teased us by killing off the one marquee-name star early in "Psycho," a gambit which startled us not just because of the suddenness of the murder or how it was committed but because it broke a box-office convention and so it was a joke played on what audiences have learned to expect. He broke the rules of the movie game and our response demonstrated how aware we are of commercial considerations. When movies are bad (and in the bad parts of good movies) our awareness of the mechanics and our cynicism about the aims and values is peculiarly alienating. The audience talks right back to the phony "outspoken" condescending "The Detective"; there are groans of dejection at "The Legend of Lylah Clare," with, now and then, a desperate little titter. How well we all know that cheap depression that settles on us when our hopes and expectations are disappointed *again*. Alienation is the most common state of the knowledgeable movie audience, and though it has the peculiar rewards of low connoisseurship, a miser's delight in small favors, we long to be surprised out of it—not to suspension of disbelief nor to a Brechtian kind of alienation, but to pleasure, something a man can call good without self-disgust.

A good movie can take you out of your dull funk and the hopelessness that so

---

Excerpted from *Going Steady*, Little Brown and Company, 1970.

often goes with slipping into a theatre; a good movie can make you feel alive again, in contact, not just lost in another city. Good movies make you care, make you believe in possibilities again. If somewhere in the Hollywood-entertainment world someone has managed to break through with something that speaks to you, then it isn't *all* corruption. The movie doesn't have to be great; it can be stupid and empty and you can still have the joy of a good performance, or the joy in just a good line. An actor's scowl, a small subversive gesture, a dirty remark that someone tosses off with a mock-innocent face, and the world makes a little bit of sense. Sitting there alone or painfully alone because those with you do not react as you do, you know there must be others perhaps in this very theatre or in this city, surely in other theatres in other cities, now, in the past or future, who react as you do. And because movies are the most total and encompassing art form we have, these reactions can seem the most personal and, maybe the most important, imaginable. The romance of movies is not just in those stories and those people on the screen but in the adolescent dream of meeting others who feel as you do about what you've seen. You do meet them, of course, and you know each other at once because you talk less about good movies than about what you love in bad movies.

Let's clear away a few misconceptions. Movies make hash of the schoolmarm's approach of how well the artist fulfilled his intentions. Whatever the original intention of the writers and director, it is usually supplanted, as the production gets under way, by the intention to make money—and the industry judges the film by how well it fulfills that intention. But if you could see the "artist's intentions" you'd probably wish you couldn't anyway. Nothing is so deathly to enjoyment as the relentless march of a movie to fulfill its obvious purpose. This is, indeed, almost a defining characteristic of the hack director, as distinguished from an artist.

The intention to make money is generally all too obvious. One of the excruciating comedies of our time is attending the new classes in cinema at the high schools where the students may quite shrewdly and accurately interpret the plot developments in a mediocre movie in terms of manipulation for a desired response while the teacher tries to explain everything in terms of the creative artist working out his theme—as if the conditions under which a movie is made and the market for which it is designed were irrelevant, as if the latest product from Warners or Universal should be analyzed like a lyric poem.

. . . The craftsmanship that Hollywood has always used as a selling point not only doesn't have much to do with art—the expressive use of techniques—it probably doesn't have very much to do with actual box-office appeal, either. A dull movie like Sidney Furie's "The Naked Runner" is technically competent. The appalling "Half a Sixpence" is technically astonishing. Though the large popular audience has generally been respectful of expenditure (so much so that a critic who wasn't impressed by the money and effort that went into a "Dr. Zhivago" might be sharply reprimanded by readers), people who like "The President's Analyst" or "The Producers" or "The Odd Couple" don't seem to be bothered by their technical ineptitude and visual ugliness. And on the other hand, the expensive slick techniques of ornately empty movies like "A Dandy in Aspic" can actually work against one's enjoyment, because such extravagance and waste are morally ugly. If one compares movies one likes to movies one doesn't like, craftsmanship of the big-studio variety is hardly a decisive factor. And if one compares a movie one likes by a competent director such as John Sturges or Franklin Schaffner or John Frankenheimer to a movie one doesn't much like by the same director, his technique is probably not the decisive factor. After directing "The Manchurian Candidate" Frankenheimer directed another political thriller, "Seven Days in May," which, considered just as a piece of direction, was considerably more confident. While seeing it, one could take pleasure in Frankenheimer's smooth showmanship. But the material (Rod Serling out of Fletcher Knebel and Charles W. Bailey II) was like a straight (i.e., square) version of "The Manchurian Candidate." I have to chase around the corridors of memory to summon up images from "Seven Days in May"; despite the brilliant technique, all that is clear to mind is the touchingly, desperately anxious face of Ava Gardner—how when she smiled you couldn't be sure if you were seeing dimples or tics. But "The Manchurian Candidate," despite Frankenheimer's uneven, often barely adequate, staging, is still vivid because of the script. It took off from a political double entendre that everybody had been thinking of ("Why, if Joe McCarthy were working for the Communists, he couldn't be doing them more good!") and carried it to startling absurdity, and the extravagances and conceits and conversational non sequiturs (by George Axelrod out of Richard Condon) were ambivalent and funny in a way that was trashy yet liberating.

Technique is hardly worth talking about unless it's used for something worth doing: that's why most of the theorizing about the new art of television commercials is such nonsense. The effects are impersonal—dexterous, sometimes clever, but empty of art. It's because of their emptiness that commercials call so much attention to their camera angles and quick cutting—which is why people get impressed by "the art" of it. Movies are now often made in terms of what television viewers have learned to settle for. Despite a great deal that is spoken and written about young people responding visually, the influence of TV is to make movies visually less imaginative and complex. Television is a very noisy medium and viewers listen, while getting used to a poor quality of visual reproduction, to the absence of visual detail, to visual obviousness and overemphasis on simple compositions, and to atrociously simplified and distorted color systems. The shifting camera styles, the movement, and the fast cutting of a film like "Finian's Rainbow"—one of the better big productions—are like the "visuals" of TV commercials, a disguise for static material, expressive of nothing so much as the need to keep you from getting bored and leaving. Men are now beginning their careers as directors by working on commercials—which, if one cares to speculate on it, may be almost a one-sentence résumé of the future of American motion pictures.

I don't mean to suggest that there is not such a thing as movie technique or that craftsmanship doesn't contribute to the pleasures of movies, but simply that most audiences, if they enjoy the acting and the "story" or the theme or the funny lines, don't notice or care about how well or how badly the movie is made, and because they don't care, a hit makes a director a "genius" and everybody talks about his brilliant technique (i.e., the technique of grabbing an audience). . . .

When we are children, though there are categories of films we don't like— documentaries generally (they're too much like education) and, of course, movies especially designed for children—by the time we can go on our own we have learned to avoid them. Children are often put down by adults when the children say they enjoyed a particular movie; adults who are short on empathy are quick to point out aspects of the plot or theme that the child didn't understand, and it's easy to humiliate a child in this way. But it is one of the glories of eclectic arts like opera and movies that they include so many possible kinds and combinations of pleasure. One may be enthralled by Leontyne Price in "La Forza del Destino" even if one hasn't boned up on the libretto, or entranced by "The Magic Flute" even if one has boned up on the libretto, and a movie may be enjoyed for many reasons that have little to do with the story or the subtleties (if any) of theme or character. Unlike "pure" arts which are often defined in terms of what only they can do, movies are open and unlimited. Probably everything that can be done in movies can be done some other way, but—and this is what's so miraculous and so expedient about them—they can do almost anything any other art can do (alone or in combination) and they can take on some of the functions of exploration, of journalism, of anthropology, of almost any branch of knowledge as well. We go to the movies for the variety of what they can provide, and for their marvellous ability to give us easily and inexpensively (and usually painlessly) what we can get from other arts also. They are a wonderfully *convenient* art.

. . . We generally become interested in movies because we *enjoy* them and what we enjoy them for has little to do with what we think of as art. The movies we respond to, even in childhood, don't have the same values as the official culture supported at school and in the middle-class home. At the movies we get low life and high life, while David Susskind and the moralistic reviewers chastise us for not patronizing what they think we should, "realistic" movies that would be good for us—like "A Raisin in the Sun," where we could learn the lesson that a Negro family can be as dreary as a white family. Movie audiences will take a lot of garbage, but it's pretty hard to make us queue up for pedagogy. At the movies we want a different kind of truth, something that surprises us and registers with us as funny or accurate or maybe amazing, maybe even amazingly beautiful. We get little things even in mediocre and terrible movies—José Ferrer sipping his booze through a straw in "Enter Laughing," Scott Wilson's hard scary all-American-boy-you-can't-reach face cutting through the pretensions of "In Cold Blood" with all its fancy bleak cinematography. We got, and still have embedded in memory, Tony Randall's surprising depth of feeling in "The Seven Faces of Dr. Lao," Keenan Wynn and Moyna Macgill in the lunch-counter sequence of "The Clock," John W. Bubbles on the dance floor in "Cabin in the Sky," the inflection Gene Kelly gave to the line, "I'm a rising young man" in "DuBarry Was a Lady," Tony Curtis saying "avidly" in "Sweet Smell of Success." Though the director may have been responsible for releasing it, it's the human material we react to most and remember longest. The art of the performers stays fresh for us, their beauty as beautiful as ever. There are so many kinds of things we get—the hangover sequence wittily designed for the CinemaScope screen in "The Tender Trap," the atmosphere of the newspaper offices in "The Luck of Ginger Coffey," the automat gone mad in "Easy Living." Do we need to lie and shift things to false terms—like those who have to say Sophia Loren is a great actress as if her *acting* had made her a star? Wouldn't we rather watch her than better actresses because she's so incredibly charming and because she's probably the greatest model the world has ever known? There are great moments—Angela Lansbury singing "Little Yellow Bird" in "Dorian Gray." (I don't think I've ever had a friend who didn't also treasure that girl and that song.) And there are absurdly right little moments—in "Saratoga Trunk" when Curt Bois says to Ingrid Bergman, "You're very beautiful," and she says, "Yes, isn't it lucky?" And those things have closer relationships to art than what the schoolteachers told us was true and beautiful. Not that the works we studied in school weren't often great (as we discovered *later*) but that what the teachers told us to admire them for (and if current texts are any indication, are still telling students to admire them for) was generally so false and prettified and moralistic that what might have been moments of pleasure in them, and what might have been cleansing in them, and subversive, too, had been coated over.

Because of the photographic nature of the medium and the cheap admission prices, movies took their impetus not from the desiccated imitation European high culture, but from the peep show, the Wild West show, the music hall, the comic strip—from what was coarse and common. The early Chaplin two-reelers still look surprisingly lewd, with bathroom jokes and drunkenness and hatred of work and proprieties. And the Western shoot-'em-ups certainly weren't the schoolteachers' notions of art—which in my school days, ran more to didactic poetry and "perfectly proportioned" statues and which over the years have progressed through nice stories to "good taste" and "excellence"—which may be more poisonous than homilies and dainty figurines because then you had a clearer idea of what you were up against and it was easier to fight. And this, of course, is what we were running away from when we went to the movies. All week we longed for Saturday afternoon and sanctuary—the anonymity and impersonality of sitting in a theatre, just enjoying ourselves, not having to be responsible, not having to be "good." Maybe you just want to look at people on the screen and know they're not looking back at you, that they're not going to turn on you and criticize you.

Perhaps the single most intense pleasure of moviegoing is this non-aesthetic one of escaping from the responsibilities of having the proper responses required of us in our official (school) culture. And yet this is probably the best and most common basis for developing an aesthetic sense because responsibility to pay attention and to appreciate is anti-art, it makes us too anxious for pleasure, too bored for response. Far from supervision and official culture, in the darkness at the movies where nothing is asked of us and we are left alone, the liberation from duty and constraint allows us to develop our own aesthetic responses. Unsupervised enjoyment is probably not the only kind there is but it may feel like the only kind. Irresponsibility is part of the pleasure of all art; it is the part the schools cannot recognize. . . . It's the feeling of freedom from respectability we have always enjoyed at the movies that is carried to an extreme by American International Pictures and the Clint Eastwood Italian Westerns; they are stripped of cultural values. We may want more from movies than this negative virtue but we know the feeling from childhood moviegoing when we loved the gamblers and pimps and the cons' suggestions of muttered ob-

scenities as the guards walked by. The appeal of movies was in the details of crime
and high living and wicked cities and in the language of toughs and urchins; it was
in the dirty smile of the city girl who lured the hero away from Janet Gaynor. What
draws us to movies in the first place, the opening into other, forbidden or surprising,
kinds of experience, and the vitality and corruption and irreverence of that experience are so direct and immediate and have so little connection with what we have
been taught is art that many people feel more secure, feel that their tastes are becoming more cultivated when they begin to *appreciate* foreign films. One foundation
executive told me that he was quite upset that his teen-agers had chosen to go to
"Bonnie and Clyde" rather than with him to "Closely Watched Trains." He took it
as a sign of lack of maturity. I think his kids made an honest choice, and not only
because "Bonnie and Clyde" is the better movie, but because it is closer to us, it
has some of the qualities of direct involvement that make us care about movies. But
it's understandable that it's easier for us, as Americans, to see *art* in foreign films
than in our own, because of how we, as Americans, think of art. Art is still what
teachers and ladies and foundations believe in, it's civilized and refined, cultivated
and serious, cultural, beautiful, European, Oriental: it's what America isn't, and it's
especially what American movies are not. Still, if those kids had chosen "Wild in
the Streets" over "Closely Watched Trains" I would think that was a sound and
honest choice, too, even though "Wild in the Streets" is in most ways a terrible picture. It connects with their lives in an immediate even if a grossly frivolous way,
and if we don't go to movies for excitement, if, even as children, we accept the cultural standards of refined adults, if we have so little drive that we accept "good
taste," then we will probably never really begin to care about movies at all. We will
become like those people who "may go to American movies sometimes to relax"
but when they want "a little more" from a movie, are delighted by how colorful
and artistic Franco Zeffirelli's "The Taming of the Shrew" is, just as a couple of
decades ago they were impressed by "The Red Shoes," made by Powell and Press-
burger, the Zeffirellis of their day. Or, if they like the cozy feeling of uplift to be
had from mildly whimsical movies about timid people, there's generally a "Hot
Millions" or something musty and faintly boring from Eastern Europe—one of
those movies set in World War II but so remote from our ways of thinking that it
seems to be set in World War I. Afterward, the moviegoer can feel as decent and
virtuous as if he'd spent an evening visiting a deaf old friend of the family. It's a
way of taking movies back into the approved culture of the schoolroom—into
gentility—and the voices of schoolteachers and reviewers rise up to ask why
America can't make such movies.

Movie art is not the opposite of what we have always enjoyed in movies, it is not
be be found in a return to that official high culture, it is what we have always found
good in movies only more so. It's the subversive gesture carried further, the
moments of excitement sustained longer and extended into new meanings. At best,
the movie is totally informed by the kind of pleasure we have been taking from bits
and pieces of movies. But we are so used to reaching out to the few good bits in a
movie that we don't need formal perfection to be dazzled. There are so many arts

and crafts that go into movies and there are so many things that can go wrong that they're not an art for purists. We want to experience that elation we feel when a movie (or even a performer in a movie) goes farther than we had expected and makes the leap successfully. Even a film like Godard's "Les Carabiniers," hell to watch for the first hour, is exciting to think about after because its one good sequence, the long picture-postcard sequence near the end, is so incredible and so brilliantly prolonged. The picture has been crawling and stumbling along and then it climbs a high wire and walks it and keeps walking it until we're almost dizzy from admiration. The tight rope is rarely stretched so high in movies, but there must be a sense of tension somewhere in the movie, if only in a bit player's face, not just mechanical suspense, or the movie is just more hours down the drain. It's the rare movie we really *go* with, the movie that keeps us tense and attentive. We learn to dread Hollywood "realism" and all that it implies. When, in the dark, we concentrate our attention, we are driven frantic by events on the level or ordinary life that pass at the rhythm of ordinary life. That's the self-conscious striving for integrity of humorless, untalented people. When we go to a play we expect a heightened, stylized language; the dull realism of the streets is unendurably boring, though we may escape from the play to the nearest bar to listen to the same language with relief. Better life than art imitating life.

If we go back and think over the movies we've enjoyed—even the ones we knew were terrible movies while we enjoyed them—what we enjoyed in them, the little part that was good, had, in some rudimentary way, some freshness, some hint of style, some trace of beauty, some audacity, some craziness. It's there in the interplay between Burt Lancaster and Ossie Davis, or, in "Wild in the Streets," in Diane Varsi rattling her tambourine, in Hal Holbrook's faint twitch when he smells trouble, in a few of Robert Thom's lines; and they have some relation to art though they don't look like what we've been taught is "quality." They have the joy of playfulness. In a mediocre or rotten movie, the good things may give the impression that they come out of nowhere; the better the movie, the more they seem to belong to the world of the movie. Without this kind of playfulness and the pleasure we take from it, art isn't art at all, it's something punishing, as it so often is in school where even artists' little *jokes* become leaden from explanation.

In American movies what is most often mistaken for artistic quality is box-office success, especially if it's combined with a genuflection to importance; then you have "a movie the industry can be proud of" like "To Kill a Mockingbird" or such Academy Award winners as "West Side Story," "My Fair Lady," or "A Man for All Seasons." Fred Zinnemann made a fine modern variant of a Western, "The Sundowners," and hardly anybody saw it until it got on television; but "A Man for All Seasons" had the look of prestige and the press felt honored to praise it. I'm not sure most movie reviewers consider what they honestly enjoy as being central to criticism. Some at least appear to think that that would be relying too much on their own tastes, being too personal instead of being "objective"—relying on the ready-made terms of cultural respectability and on consensus judgment (which, to a rather shocking degree, can be arranged by publicists creating a climate of importance around a movie). Just as movie directors, as they age, hunger for what was meant by respectability in their youth, and aspire to prestigious cultural properties, so, too, the movie press longs to be elevated in terms of the cultural values of their old high schools. And so they, along with the industry, applaud ghastly "tour-de-force" performances, movies based on "distinguished" stage successes or prize-winning novels, or movies that are "worthwhile," that make a "contribution"—"serious" messagy movies. This often involves praise of bad movies, of dull movies, or even the praise in good movies of what was worst in them.

This last mechanism can be seen in the honors bestowed on "In the Heat of the Night." The best thing in the movie is that high comic moment when Poitier says, "I'm a police officer," because it's a reversal of audience expectations and we laugh in delighted relief that the movie is not going to be another self-righteous, self-congratulatory exercise in the gloomy old Stanley Kramer tradition. At that point the audience sparks to life. The movie is fun largely because of the amusing central idea of a black Sherlock Holmes in a Tom and Jerry cartoon of reversals. Poitier's color is used for comedy instead of for that extra dimension of irony and pathos that made movies like "To Sir, with Love" unbearably sentimental. He doesn't really play the super sleuth very well: he's much too straight even when spouting the kind of higher scientific nonsense about right-handedness and left-handedness that would have kept Basil Rathbone in an ecstasy of clipped diction, blinking eyes and raised eyebrows. Like Bogart in "Beat the Devil" Poitier doesn't seem to be in on the joke. But Rod Steiger compensated with a comic performance that was even funnier for being so unexpected—not only from Steiger's career which had been going in other directions, but after the apparently serious opening of the film. The movie was, however, praised by the press as if it had been exactly the kind of picture that the audience was so relieved to discover it wasn't going to be (except in its routine melodramatic sequences full of fake courage and the climaxes such as Poitier slapping a rich white Southerner or being attacked by white thugs; except that is, in its worst parts). When I saw it, the audience, both black and white, enjoyed the joke of the fast-witted, hyper-educated black detective explaining matters to the backward, blundering Southern-chief-of-police slob. This racial joke is far more open and inoffensive than the usual "irony" of Poitier being so good and so black. For once it's *funny* (instead of embarrassing) that he's so superior to everybody. . . . The audience enjoyed the movie for the vitality of its surprising playfulness, while the industry congratulated itself because the film was "hard-hitting"—that is to say, it flirted with seriousness and spouted warm, worthwhile ideas.

Those who can accept "In the Heat of the Night" as the socially conscious movie that the industry pointed to with pride can probably also go along with the way the press attacked Jewison's subsequent film, "The Thomas Crown Affair," as trash and a failure. One could even play the same game that was played on "In the Heat of the Night" and convert the "Crown" trifle into a sub-fascist exercise because, of course, Crown, the superman, who turns to crime out of boredom, is the crooked son of "The Fountainhead," out of Raffles. But that's taking glossy summer-evening fantasies much too seriously: we haven't had a junior executive's fantasy-life movie for a long time and to attack this return of the worldly gentlemen-thieves genre of Ronald Colman and William Powell *politically* is to fail to have a sense of humor about the little romantic-adolescent fascist lurking in most of us. Part of the fun of movies is that they allow us to see how silly many of our fantasies are and how widely they're shared. A light romantic entertainment like "The Thomas Crown Affair," trash undisguised, is the kind of chic crappy movie which (one would have thought) nobody could be fooled into thinking was art. Seeing it is like lying in the sun flicking through fashion magazines and, as we used to say, feeling rich and beautiful beyond your wildest dreams.

But it isn't easy to come to terms with what one enjoys in films, and if an older generation was persuaded to *dismiss* trash, now a younger generation, with the press and the schools in hot pursuit, has begun to talk about trash as if it were really very serious art. College newspapers and the new press all across the country are full of a hilarious new form of scholasticism, with students using their education to cook up impressive reasons for enjoying very simple, traditional dishes. . . .

It's appalling to read solemn academic studies of Hitchcock or von Sternberg by people who seem to have lost sight of the primary reason for seeing films like "Notorious" or "Morocco"—which is that they were not intended solemnly, that they were playful and inventive and faintly (often deliberately) absurd. And what's good in them, what relates them to art, is that playfulness and absence of solemnity. There is talk now about von Sternberg's technique—his use of light and décor and detail—and he is, of course, a kitsch master in these areas, a master of studied artfulness and pretty excess. Unfortunately, some students take this technique as proof that his films are works of art, once again, I think, falsifying what they really respond to—the satisfying romantic glamour of his very pretty trash. "Morocco" is great trash, and movies are so rarely great art, that if we cannot appreciate great *trash,* we have very little reason to be interested in them. The kitsch of an earlier era—even the best kitsch—does not become art, though it may become camp. Von Sternberg's movies became camp even while he was still making them, because as the romantic feeling went out of his trash—when he became so enamored of his own pretty effects that he turned his human material into blank, affectless pieces of décor—his absurd trashy style was all there was. We are now told in respectable museum publications that in 1932 a movie like "Shanghai Express" "was completely misunderstood as a mindless adventure" when indeed it was completely *understood* as a mindless adventure. And enjoyed as a mindless adventure. It's a peculiar form of movie madness crossed with academicism, this lowbrowism masquerading as highbrowism, eating a candy bar and cleaning an "allegorical problem of human faith" out of your teeth. If we always wanted works of complexity and depth we wouldn't be going to movies about glamorous thieves and seductive women who sing in cheap cafés, and if we loved "Shanghai Express" it wasn't for its mind but for the glorious sinfulness of Dietrich informing Clive Brook that, "It took more than one man to change my name to Shanghai Lily" and for the villainous Oriental chieftain (Warner Oland!) delivering the classic howler, "The white woman stays with me."

If we don't deny the pleasures to be had from certain kinds of trash and accept "The Thomas Crown Affair" as a pretty fair example of entertaining trash, then we may ask if a piece of trash like this has any relationship to art. And I think it does. Steve McQueen gives probably his most glamorous, fashionable performance yet, but even enjoying him as much as I do, I wouldn't call his performance art. It's artful, though, which is exactly what is required in this kind of vehicle. If he had been luckier, if the script had provided what it so embarrassingly lacks, the kind of sophisticated dialogue—the sexy shoptalk—that such writers as Jules Furthman and William Faulkner provided for Bogart, and if the director Norman Jewison had Lubitsch's lightness of touch, McQueen might be acclaimed as a suave, "polished" artist. Even in this flawed setting, there's a selfawareness in his performance that makes his elegance funny. And Haskell Wexler, the cinematographer, lets go with a whole bag of tricks, flooding the screen with his delight in beauty, shooting all over the place, and sending up the material. And Pablo Ferro's games with the split screen at the beginning are such conscious, clever games designed to draw us in to watch intently what is of no great interest. What gives this trash a lift, what makes it entertaining is clearly that some of those involved, knowing of course that they were working on a silly shallow script and a movie that wasn't about anything of consequence, used the chance to have a good time with it. If the director, Norman Jewison, could have built a movie instead of putting together a patchwork of sequences, "Crown" might have had a chance to be considered a movie in the class and genre of Lubitsch's "Trouble in Paradise." It doesn't come near that because to transform this kind of kitsch, to make art of it, one needs that unifying grace, that formality and charm that a Lubitsch could sometimes provide. Still, even in this movie we get a few grace notes in McQueen's playfulness, and from Wexler and Ferro. Working on trash, feeling free to play, can loosen up the actors and craftsmen just as seeing trash can liberate the spectator. And as we don't get this playful quality of art much in movies except in trash, we might as well relax and enjoy it freely for what it is. I don't trust anyone who doesn't admit having at some time in his life enjoyed trashy American movies; I don't trust *any* of the tastes of people who were born with such good taste that they didn't need to find their way through trash.

. . . Does trash corrupt? A nutty Puritanism still flourishes in the arts, not just in the schoolteachers' approach of wanting art to be "worthwhile," but in the higher reaches of the academic life with those ideologues who denounce us for enjoying trash as if this enjoyment took us away from the really disturbing, angry new art of our time and somehow destroyed us. If we had to *justify* our trivial silly pleasures, we'd have a hard time. How could we possibly *justify* the fun of getting to know some people in movie after movie, like Joan Blondell, the brassy blonde with the heart of gold, or waiting for the virtuous, tiny, tiny-featured heroine to say her line so we could hear the riposte of her tough, wisecracking girlfriend (Iris Adrian was my favorite). Or, when the picture got too monotonous, there would be the song interlude, introduced "atmospherically" when the cops and crooks were both in the same never-neverland nightclub and everything stopped while a girl sang. Sometimes it would be the most charming thing in the movie, like Dolores Del Rio singing "You Make Me That Way" in "International Settlement"; sometimes it would drip with maudlin meaning, like "Oh Give Me Time for Tenderness'' in ''Dark Victory'' with the dying Bette Davis singing along with the chanteuse. The pleasures of this kind of trash are not intellectually defensible. But why should pleasure need justification? Can one demonstrate that trash desensitizes us, that it prevents people from enjoying something better, that it limits our range of aesthetic response? Nobody I know of has provided such a demonstration. Do even Disney movies or Doris Day movies do us lasting harm? I've never known a person I thought had been harmed by them, though it does seem to me that they affect the tone of a culture, that perhaps—and I don't mean to be facetious—they may poison us collectively though they don't injure us individually. There are women who want to see a world in which everything is pretty and cheerful and in which romance triumphs (''Barefoot in the Park,'' ''Any Wednesday,''); families who want movies to be an innocuous inspiration, a good example for the children (''The Sound of Music,'' ''The Singing Nun''); couples who want the kind of folksy blue humor (''A Guide for the Married Man'') that they still go to Broadway shows for. These people are the reason slick, stale, rotting pictures make money; they're the reason so few pictures are any good. And in that way, this terrible conformist culture does affect us all. It certainly cramps and limits opportunities for artists. But that isn't what generally gets attacked as trash, anyway. I've avoided using the term ''harmless trash'' for movies like ''The Thomas Crown Affair,'' because that would put me on the side of the angels—against ''harmful trash,'' and I don't honestly know what that is. It's common for the press to call cheaply made, violent action movies ''brutalizing'' but that tells us less about any actual demonstrable effects than about the finicky tastes of the reviewers—who are often highly appreciative of violence in more expensive and ''artistic'' settings such as ''Petulia.'' It's almost a class prejudice, this assumption that crudely made movies, movies without the look of art, are bad for people.

If there's a little art in good trash and sometimes even in poor trash, there may be more trash than is generally recognized in some of the most acclaimed ''art'' movies. Such movies as ''Petulia'' and ''2001'' may be no more than trash in the latest, up-to-the-minute guises, using ''artistic techniques'' to give trash the look of art. The serious art look may be the latest fashion in *expensive* trash. All that ''art'' may be what prevents pictures like these from being *enjoyable* trash; they're not honestly crummy, they're very fancy and they take their crummy ideas seriously.

. . . Part of the fun of movies is in seeing ''what everybody's talking about,'' and if people are flocking to a movie, or if the press can con us into thinking that they are, then ironically, there is a sense in which we want to see it, even if we suspect we won't enjoy it, because we want to know what's going on. Even if it's the worst inflated pompous trash that is the most talked about (and it usually is) and even if that talk is manufactured, we want to see the movies because so many people fall for whatever is talked about that they make the advertisers' lies true. Movies absorb material from the culture and the other arts so fast that some films that have been widely *sold* become culturally and sociologically important whether they are good movies or not. Movies like ''Morgan!'' or ''Georgy Girl'' or ''The Graduate''—aesthetically trivial movies which, however, because of the ways some people react to them, enter into the national bloodstream—become cultural and psychological equivalents of watching a political convention—to observe what's going on. And though this has little to do with the art of movies, it has a great deal to do with the appeal of movies.

An analyst tells me that when his patients are not talking about their personal hangups and their immediate problems they talk about the situations and characters in movies like "The Graduate" or "Belle de Jour" and they talk about them with as much personal involvement as about their immediate problems. I have elsewhere suggested that this way of reacting to movies as psychodrama used to be considered a pre-literate way of reacting but that now those considered "post-literate" are reacting like pre-literates. The high school and college students identifying with Georgy Girl or Dustin Hoffman's Benjamin are not that different from the stenographer who used to live and breathe with the Joan Crawford-working girl and worry about whether that rich boy would really make her happy—and considered her pictures "great." They don't see the movie as a movie but as part of the soap opera of their lives. The fan magazines used to encourage this kind of identification; now the *advanced* mass media encourage it, and those who want to sell to youth use the language of "just let it flow over you." The person who responds this way does not respond more freely but less freely and less fully than the person who is aware of what is well done and what badly done in a movie, who can accept some things in it and reject others, who uses all his senses in reacting, not just his emotional vulnerabilities.

Still, we care about what other people care about—sometimes because we want to know how far we've gotten from common responses—and if a movie is important to other people we're interested in it because of what it means to them, even if it doesn't mean much to us. The small triumph of "The Graduate" was to have domesticated alienation and the difficulty of communication, by making what Benjamin is alienated from a middle-class comic strip and making it absurdly evident that he has nothing to communicate—which is just what makes him an acceptable hero for the large movie audience. If he said anything or had any ideas, the audience would probably hate him. "The Graduate" isn't a *bad* movie, it's entertaining, though in a fairly slick way (the audience is just about programmed for laughs). What's surprising is that so many people take it so seriously. What's funny about the movie are the laughs on that dumb sincere boy who wants to talk about art in bed when the woman just wants to fornicate. But then the movie begins to pander to youthful narcissism, glorifying his innocence, and making the predatory (and now crazy) woman the villainess. Commercially this works: the inarticulate dull boy becomes a romantic hero for the audience to project into with all those squishy and now conventional feelings of look, his parents don't communicate with him; look, he wants truth not sham, and so on. But the movie betrays itself and its own expertise, sells out its comic moments that click along with the rhythm of a hit Broadway show, to make the oldest movie pitch of them all—asking the audience to identify with the simpleton who is the latest version of the misunderstood teen-ager and the pure-in-heart boy next door. It's almost painful to tell kids who have gone to see "The Graduate" eight times that once was enough for you because you've already seen it eighty times with Charles Ray and Robert Harron and Richard Barthelmess and Richard Cromwell and Charles Farrell. How could you convince them that a movie that sells innocence is a very commercial piece of work when they're so clearly in the market to buy innocence? When "The Graduate" shifts to the tender awakenings of love, it's just the latest version of "David and Lisa." "The Graduate" only wants to succeed and that's fundamentally what's the matter with it. There is a pause for a laugh after the mention of "Berkeley" that is an unmistakable sign of hunger for success; this kind of movie-making shifts values, shifts focus, shifts emphasis, shifts everything for a surefire response. Mike Nichols' "gift" is that he lets the audience direct him; this is demagoguery in the arts.

Even the cross-generation fornication is standard for the genre. It goes back to Pauline Frederick in "Smouldering Fires," and Clara Bow was at it with mama Alice Joyce's boyfriend in "Our Dancing Mothers," and in the Forties it was "Mildred Pierce." Even the terms are not different: in these movies the seducing adults are customarily sophisticated, worldly, and corrupt, the kids basically innocent, though not so humorless and blank as Benjamin. In its basic attitudes "The Graduate" is corny American; it takes us back to before "The Game of Love" with Edwige Feuillère as the sympathetic older woman and "A Cold Wind in August" with the sympathetic Lola Albright performance.

What's interesting about the success of "The Graduate" is sociological: the revelation of how emotionally accessible modern youth is to the same old manipulation. The recurrence of certain themes in movies suggests that each generation wants romance restated in slightly new terms, and of course it's one of the pleasures of movies as a popular art that they can answer this need. And yet, and yet—one doesn't expect an *educated* generation to be so soft on itself, much softer than the factory workers of the past who didn't go back over and over to the same movies, mooning away in fixation on themselves and thinking this fixation meant movies had suddenly become an art, and *their* art.

When you're young the odds are very good that you'll find something to enjoy in almost any movie. But as you grow more experienced, the odds change. I saw a picture a few years ago that was the sixth version of material that wasn't much to start with. Unless you're feebleminded, the odds get worse and worse. We don't go on reading the same kind of manufactured novels—pulp Westerns or detective thrillers, say—all of our lives, and we don't want to go on and on looking at movies about cute heists by comically assorted gangs. The problem with a popular art form is that those who want something more are in a hopeless minority compared with the millions who are always seeing it for the first time, or for the reassurance and gratification of seeing the conventions fulfilled again. Probably a large part of the older audience gives up movies for this reason—simply that they've seen it before. And probably this is why so many of the best movie critics quit. They're wrong when they blame it on the movies going bad; it's the odds becoming so bad, and they can no longer bear the many tedious movies for the few good moments and the tiny shocks of recognition. Some become too tired, too frozen in fatigue, to respond to what *is* new. Others who *do* stay awake may become too demanding for the young who are seeing it all for the first hundred times. The critical task is necessarily comparative, and younger people do not truly know what is new. And despite all the chatter about the media and how smart the young are, they're incredibly naíve about mass culture—perhaps *more* naíve than earlier generations (though I don't know why). Maybe watching all that television hasn't done so much for them as they seem to think; and when I read a young intellectual's appreciation of "Rachel, Rachel" and come to "the mother's passion for chocolate bars is a superb symbol for the second coming of childhood" I know the writer is still in his first childhood, and I wonder if he's going to come out of it.

One's moviegoing tastes and habits change—I still like in movies what I always liked but now, for example, I really want documentaries. After all the years of stale stupid acted-out stories, with less and less for me in them, I am desperate to know something, desperate for facts, for information, for faces of nonactors and for knowledge of how people live—for revelations, not for the little bits of show-business detail worked up for us by show-business minds who got them from the same movies we're tired of.

But the big change is in our *habits*. If we make any kind of decent, useful life for ourselves we have less need to run from it to those diminishing pleasures of the movies. When we go to the movies we want something good, something sustained, we don't want to settle for just a bit of something, because we have other things to do. If life at home is more interesting, why go to the movies? And the theatres frequented by true moviegoers—those perennial displaced persons in each city, the loners and the losers—depress us. Listening to them—and they are often more audible than the sound track—as they cheer the cons and jeer the cops, we may still share their disaffection, but it's not enough to keep us interested in cops and robbers. A little nosethumbing isn't enough. If we've grown up at the movies we know that good work is continuous not with the academic, respectable tradition but with the glimpses of something good in trash, but we want the subversive gesture carried to the domain of discovery. Trash has given us an appetite for art.

A Concluding Remark:

Existence,

Communications,

and the Dramaturgical

Perspective

T HE INTRODUCTORY ESSAY that opened this collection attempted to acquaint the
reader with the range and "sense" of the dramatic vision of human life. These
concluding remarks will attempt to state some of the implications of the perspective
variously presented in this reader. The effort is to suggest the link of contemporary
strands of thought with the image of man presented in this book.

We stated in the opening essay that the dramaturgical perspective constituted at
base an "image" of human life, identifiable from other reconstructions of human
activity. Here we want to stress the philosophical and sociological context within
which it may be usefully integrated. As it stands now, the dramaturgical perspective
as "image" constitutes a description of human activity; if it is to achieve the status
of explanation, it must be placed in an intellectual framework that specifies its assumptions. It is our suggestion that the image in question may most usefully be
linked with two other modern strands of thought: existentialism and communications theory. Such an integration would most clearly delineate the dramaturgical perspective as an "ontology," a systemic assumption of being and acting.

From existentialism the social inquirer may derive an ontological position within
which dramatic action is possible. Existential philosophers tend to see the world as
problematic, as without essential meaning, as "absurd." For the existentialist, one

cannot answer the Big Questions about the meaning of the universe or our existence in it; one can only describe what it means to be a human being. The universe is capricious, and personal existence is burdened by the "anguish" of the impression that the world is without meaning. Man is thrown into a formless world out of which he creates meaning, but the meaning he creates is ultimately arbitrary, because the world itself has no meaning. Men are characterized by "ontological insecurity," a condition of fundamental estrangement from a world they never made, and also from each other. We are all "strangers." From this condition there is no exit. Men are existentially constrained to deal with estrangement, with the knowledge of death and limits, the necessity of choice, and the fact of mental and physical singularity and loneliness. Attempts to avoid the real conditions of our existence, to slip into a "safe" line of action or thought, is called "bad faith."

These ideas may seem remote from communications theory, but reflection shows the confluence. For the communications theorist, the central fact of human life is the communication of symbols between social actors. As in existentialism, meaning is something attributed to, rather than inherent in, the world. Communications with others gives us knowledge of the boundaries of our existence and structures our thoughts and actions, especially in relation to other people. The boundaries of communications are the boundaries of our existence; whatever exists for us exists in some communicable form, since meaning derives from communication. The self, for example, develops through communication, and becomes that meaningful structure that filters our relations with the external world. Roles are communicated lines of action (husband, teacher, etc.) which may be enacted in either "good faith" or "bad faith," depending on one's conception in the situation.

The thrust of contemporary communications theory and of segments of social and political theory has been to recognize the complexity of human relatedness. Symbolic interactionists speak of society as a "negotiated order," an episodic, even absurd communications net of the negotiation of meaning in a particular context (e.g., a hospital), but which is constantly being altered or even abolished by changes in the definition of the situation. Reality is "socially constructed," a definitional process that is never fixed or irreducible, but rather "transactional" and arbitrary. Social existence, then, is problematic, constructed eventually without meaning in an immanent sense. The world envisioned by the communications theorists, many contemporary social scientists and the existential philosophers is in large measure, therefore, convergent.

We feel that the dramaturgical perspective may usefully be discussed in this philosophical and sociological context. The image of the world the writers in this book conjure for us is an existential world of men coping, building meaning in the face of meaninglessness, inserting themselves into the world, attempting to build relationships—both interpersonal and social—that overcome their fundamental estrangement. Men communicate meaning, and since such meanings are symbolic, they are capable of being expressed by a kind of behavior apparently peculiar to human beings: dramatic. If this were not an existential world, if men were not estranged, if conflict did not occur, if meaning were not problematic, if situations did not have to be defined, if choices did not have to be made, then drama, either staged or real, would not be possible. But given the existential character of the human world, then the ontological roots of the dramaturgical perspective are understandable. The human drama is a drama of communication, where men dramatize to one another the whole miasma of existential problems. It is no accident that Sartre and Camus wrote plays and novels as well as philosophical treatises, nor that social inquirers have turned to the dramatic image for the study of human action.

Hence, at base, existentialists and communications theorists are interested in the boundaries of the human condition, what men are limited by and what they are capable of. The dramatist is concerned with the same thing. Tragedy, for example, describes situations in which a "flaw" (*hubris*) moves the action to an inevitable end which the actors nonetheless choose. The existential point is clear: life is ultimately beyond our personal control, and all that we may do is cope with absurdity, against the ultimate rule of *fortuna*. The dramatic in human life may well have this ontological root: men dramatize their behavior to present meaning to others (and themselves) in such a way as to "insert" that meaning into an otherwise meaningless world. The Christian praying, the Nazi saluting, the political candidate speaking, the homosexual promenading all are acting in reference to a dramatically conceived meaning. Even the "phony" acting in bad faith attributes a private meaning to his actions (the make-out artist attaches no meaning to his women, but does to their conquest.) But as the dramatist understands, the injection of meaning into the world, the construction of the complex fabric of human interaction, creates the condition for human action and for that species of human relations we term drama.

The germ of dramatic action, then, appears to emerge from the fact that man's destiny is not determined like the rest of nature's is; he can stand apart from the struggle, can understand the play, and perhaps even change the conduct of the action, if not control the ending. He can engage in dramas of war or peace. (On the basis of the evidence, it seems clear which has been therefore the most dramatic!) He can construct societies with healthy or pathological "scripts," he can attribute religious or natural ends to the world that define his dramatic role in it. Man's destiny, as the existentialists understand, is to be condemned to be free, to choose, to act; we must, as Wittgenstein saw, run against "the walls of our cage" in seeking the meaning of the cage and our place in the cage. The writers collected in this book have dealt variously with the dramatic dimensions of the occupant of that cage, the social actor who struts and frets his hour upon the stage, and then is heard no more.

CONTRIBUTORS'
BIOGRAPHICAL NOTES

JAMES ARNOLD was a member of the faculty of Marquette University, when his article "The Present State of the Documentary" appeared in *Films 1968*.

ERNEST BECKER was a professor in the department of political science, sociology and anthropology at Simon Fraser University in Vancouver, when he authored *The Birth and Death of Meaning*. One of his most recent works is *The Denial of Death, 1973*. Becker died in 1974.

BERNARD BECKERMAN was professor and chairman of the department of theatre arts at Columbia University when he published *Dynamics of Drama*. He is the author of several articles and reviews and recipient of the 7th Annual Award of the American Shakespeare Festival Theatre and Academy, 1962.

PETER BERGER came to the United States in 1946 from his native Austria. He became a professor in the department of sociology at Rutgers University in 1970. He has written numerous books and articles as well as his *Invitation to Sociology*.

ERIC BERNE was noted for his extensive experience in psychiatry. He received national attention for works such as *Games People Play* and *What Do You Say After You Say Hello?* He passed away in July, 1970.

DANIEL J. BOORSTIN has been a professor of American history at the University of Chicago. A noted author, his works include: *The Image: What Happened to the American Dream* and *American Primer*. He was named Librarian of Congress in 1975.

NORMAN O. BROWN is a Wilson Professor of Classics at the University of Rochester and is an author of several books including *Love's Body*.

KENNETH BURKE has had extensive experience as an author, teacher, poet, literary critic, and translator. His many works include: *The Rhetoric of Religion* and *Language as Symbolic Action.*

HUGH DUNCAN was the author of *Communication and Social Order, Symbols in Society,* and many other works. He was a professor of sociology and english at Southern Illinois University, Carbondale until his untimely death in 1971.

MURRAY EDELMAN is the George Herbert Mead Professor of political science at the University of Wisconsin. In addition to *The Symbolic Uses of Politics* he recently published *Politics as Symbolic Action.*

HAROLD GARFINKEL is a professor of sociology at the University of California at Los Angeles. He is the author of "Conditions of a Successful Degradation Ceremony" and *Studies in Ethnomethodology.*

BARNEY G. GLASER is the co-author of *Awareness of Dying.*

ERVING GOFFMAN has published extensively including: "On Face Work," *The Presentation of Self in Everyday Life, Asylums,* and *Relations in Public.* He is a professor of anthropology and sociology at the University of Pennsylvania.

GEORGE N. GORDON is an author of over 14 books including: *The Languages of Communication, Persuasion: The Theory and Practice of Manipulative Communication,* and most recently *Communications and Media: Constructing a Cross-discipline.* He is chairman of the communications department at Hofstra University.

JOSEPH R. GUSFIELD is a professor of sociology at the University of California, San Diego. His many works include *Symbolic Crusade: Status Politics and the American Temperance Movement.*

ROBERT W. HAWKES is a professor in the School of Public Communication, Boston University. He is the co-author of "The Fiddle Factor: Social Binding Functions of Distractions."

DONALD HORTON was an assistant professor at the University of Chicago when he co-authored "Mass Communication and Parasocial Interaction: Observations on Intimacy at a Distance."

PAULINE KAEL is a free-lance writer and film critic who is currently a regular contributor to *New Yorker* magazine. She is a noted film historian and authored the following books: *Going Steady, Kiss Kiss Bang Bang,* and *Deeper into Movies.*

BILL KINSER is a co-author of *The Dream That Was No More a Dream: The Search for Aesthetic Reality in Germany.*

ORRIN KLAPP is an accomplished author. In addition to *Symbolic Leaders: Public Dramas and Public Men,* he has written *Collective Search for Identity* and *Models of Social Order.* He is a professor of sociology at Western Ontario University.

NEIL KLEINMAN is co-author of *The Dream That Was No More a Dream: The Search for Aesthetic Reality in Germany.*

WALTER LIPPMANN was a renowned editorial writer, magazine contributor, author, and Pulitzer Prize recipient. The author of *Public Opinion* died in 1974.

STANFORD M. LYMAN is a professor of sociology at New School of Social Research. He has written numerous articles and books including *A Sociology of the Absurd* and *The Revolt of the Students*.

RICHARD MERELMAN is a professor of political science at the University of Wisconsin. He has authored many works including: "The Dramaturgy of Politics."

SHELDON L. MESSINGER is the Dean of the School of Criminology at the University of California at Berkeley. He has written several works including: *The State of the University* and "Life as Theater: Some Notes on the Dramaturgic Approach to Social Reality."

MAURICE A. NATANSON is a professor of philosophy at Conwell College, University of California at Santa Cruz. In addition to "Man as Actor" he recently published a two volume work entitled: *Phenomenology and Social Science.*

DAN D. NIMMO is a professor of political science at the University of Tennessee. He is the author of numerous books and articles. His most recent book is *Candidates and Their Images.*

HAROLD SAMPSON is co-author of "Life as Theater: Some Notes on the Dramaturgic Approach to Social Reality" and is Director of Research Psychiatry, Department of Psychiatry, Mount Zion Hospital, San Francisco, California.

MARVIN B. SCOTT is a professor of sociology at Hunter College and coauthor of *A Sociology of The Absurd.*

EDWARD SHILS has served as chairman and professor for the department of industry at the Wharton School, University of Pennsylvania. He is currently conducting research at the Netherlands Institute for Advanced Studies in Humanistic and Social Science. He is co-author of "The Meaning of the Coronation."

GEORG SIMMEL was a renowned German sociologist who authored many works

including: "The Dramatic Actor and Reality." He died in 1918.

ROBERT R. SMITH is professor of communication and chairman of the division of broadcasting and film in the School of Public Communication at Boston University. He is the co-author of "The Fiddle Factor: Social Binding Functions of Distractions."

WILLIAM STEPHENSON is the author of many works which have influenced theory and research in psychology, communication, and the social sciences. In recent years he has held the position of Distinguished Professor of Advertising Research and professor of psychology at the University of Missouri where he currently is Professor Emeritus. Two of his most notable works are: *The Study of Behavior* and *The Play Theory of Mass Communications.*

ANSELM STRAUSS is a professor of sociology at the University of California at San Francisco. He is co-author of *Awareness of Dying* and *Discovery of Grounded Theory.*

VICTOR THOMPSON is a professor of political science at the University of Florida and author of *Modern Organizations.*

WILLIAM LLOYD WARNER is the author of *The Living and the Dead.*

R. RICHARD WOHL was a professor of social science at the University of Chicago and co-author of "Mass Communication and Parasocial Interaction: Observations on Intimacy at a Distance."

MICHAEL YOUNG is co-author of "The Meaning of the Coronation." He is a professor at the Institute of Communication Studies, Bethnell Green England.

INDEX